Biographies and Jesus

What Does It Mean for the Gospels to be Biographies?

Craig S. Keener
Edward T. Wright
Editors

EMETH PRESS
www.emethpress.com

Biographies and Jesus: What Does It Mean for the Gospels to be Biographies?

Copyright © 2016 Edward T. Wright, Craig S. Keener
Printed in the United States of America on acid-free paper

All rights reserved. No part of this book may be reproduced, or stored in a retrieval system or transmitted in any form or by any means, electronic, mechanical, photocopying, recording, scanning or otherwise, except as permitted by the 1976 United States Copyright Act, or with the prior written permission of Emeth Press. Requests for permission should be
addressed to: Emeth Press, P. O. Box 23961, Lexington, KY 40523-3961. http://www.emethpress.com.

Library of Congress Cataloging-in-Publication Data

Names: Keener, Craig S., 1960- editor.
Title: Biographies and Jesus : what does it mean for the gospels to be
　biographies? / Craig S. Keener and Edward T. Wright, editors.
Description: Lexington : Emeth Press, 2016. | Includes bibliographical
　references and index.
Identifiers: LCCN 2016043276 | ISBN 9781609471064 (alk. paper)
Subjects: LCSH: Bible. Gospels--Criticism, interpretation, etc. | Biography.
　| Jesus Christ--Biography--History and criticism.
Classification: LCC BS511.3 .B624 2016 | DDC 226/.066--dc23
LC record available at https://lccn.loc.gov/2016043276

Front Cover Photo is Public Domain

"A growing scholarly consensus holds the gospels to be ancient bioi, but what does this say about the reliability of the Jesus traditions that they contain? In this meticulously argued book, Keener and his colleagues demonstrate that biographers were deeply attached to their historical sources, especially when their subject belonged to the recent past. The implications of these findings demand careful consideration by scholars of the Gospels and the Historical Jesus alike."

—Professor Helen K Bond
Professor of Christian Origins, Director of the Centre for Christian Origins
School of Divinity, New College, University of Edinburgh

Craig Keener and his colleagues have addressed the most important questions relating to the New Testament Gospels: In what sense are these Gospels historical writings? In what sense are they biographies? Through careful comparative study of the relevant ancient sources, with which many contemporary interpreters are not sufficiently acquainted, Keener and company convincingly demonstrate that the Gospels represent competently written, reliable biographical information about Jesus of Nazareth. *Biographies and Jesus* is a great book that will go a long way toward setting the record straight.

—*Craig A. Evans, John Bisagno Distinguished Professor of Christian Origins, Houston Baptist University*

"I am delighted to commend this collection of essays about the implications of the biographical genre of the gospels. Craig Keener and his colleagues and students have produced a fascinating mixture of studies of various ancient writers and biographies, looking particularly at their use of sources and the implications both for their historical reliability and that of the gospels. Where these essays build upon my initial research into this field, I am honoured by their subsequent attention, but the consequences go much further and wider than I had hoped or imagined. The results of this work must not only be taken into account in future research into the gospels' use of sources and historical reliability, but they will also provide further avenues for profitable future research. This collection deserves a wide circulation – and I look forward to the debates it will inevitably engender!"

—Richard Burridge, Dean of King's College London and Professor of Biblical Interpretation

Craig Keener is recognized for his voluminous and well-researched books. In seminary during the sixties and seventies, we were told no one can or will ever publish a biography of Jesus, because we have insufficient sources and they are all extremely biased. Then I discovered that Joseph was hailed as "the Son of God" in *Joseph and Aseneth*, and that the Gospels are not to be compared to modern biographies. We also now have hundreds of compositions from Jesus' time that were either unknown to previous scholars or were misinterpreted by them. The Gospels are ancient biographies and thus highlight claims of uniqueness about the subject. Keener's collection is to be praised. It is also ideal for classes.

—James H. Charlesworth
Director and Editor, Princeton Dead Sea Scrolls Project
George L. Collord Professor of New Testament Language and Literature
Princeton Theological Seminary

Keener, Wright, Walton et al. have moved the needle forward in advancing our knowledge of the Jesus of the Gospels. What role did ancient biography play in

recounting events that were alleged to have taken place in real time and space? Does the *bios* model solve more problems in adjudicating what is more reliable in historical recounting than other genres such as *historia* or philosophic dialogues, etc.? If so, how do these 'lives' affect our sensitivities in perceiving Jesus as both a human being and one whose relation to God is judged by the emerging church catholic to be unprecedented? New piercings of this Christological mystery abound in *Biographies and Jesus: What Does It Mean for the Gospels to be Biographies?*
—David P. Moessner A. A. Bradford Chair of Religion Texas Christian University

*To Melinda,
Thank you for your continual
love, support, and sacrifice.
This work does not get done without it.*

-ETW

*To my students,
past and present.
Thank you for your hard
work and dedication.*

-CSK

Table of Contents

Chapter 1. Ancient Biography and the Gospels: Introduction 1
    Craig S. Keener

Chapter 2. What are the Gospels? Richard Burridge's Impact on Scholarly Understanding of the Genre of the Gospels 47
    Steve Walton

Chapter 3. Charting the (Un)charted: Gospels as Ancient Biographies and Their (Un)explored Implications 59
    Youngju Kwon

Chapter 4. Source Valuation in Greek and Roman Biography: From Xenophon to Suetonius 77
    Chris Alfred

Chapter 5. Cornelius Nepos's *Themistocles:* A Targeted Comparison with the Histories of Herodotus and Thucydides with Implications for the Historical Reliability of the Gospels 103
    Timothy J. Christian

Chapter 6. Otho: A Targeted Comparison of Suetonius's Biography and Tacitus's History, with implications for the Gospels' Historical Reliability 143
    Craig S. Keener

Chapter 7. Galba: A Comparison of Suetonius's and Plutarch's Biographies and Tacitus's *Histories* with Implications for the Historical Reliability of the Gospels 173
    Benson Goh

Chapter 8. Source Criticism of Accounts of Alexander's Life with Implications for the Gospels' Historical Reliability 201
    Soo Kwang Lee

Chapter 9. A Targeted Comparison of Plutarch's, Xenophon's, and Nepos's Biographies of Agesilaus, with Implications for the Historical Reliability of the Synoptics 217
Fasil Woldemariam

Chapter 10. An Initial Exploration of the Historical Reliability of Ancient Biographies 235
Edward T. Wright

Chapter 11. A Comparison of Josephus' Life and Jewish War: An Attempt at Establishing the Acceptable Outer Limits of Biographies' Historical Reliability 261
John Jordan Henderson

Chapter 12. A Redaction-Critical Study on Philo's *On the Life of Moses*, Book One... 277
Esteban Hidalgo

Chapter 13. Comparing First and Second Maccabees: Do Their Differences Make Them Unreliable? 301
Adrian Reynolds

Chapter 14. The Importance of the "How" and "Why" in Ancient Biographies 319
Holly J. Carey

Chapter 15. Viewing the Gospels as Ancient Biographies Resolves Many Perceived Contradictions   323
Michael R. Licona

Appendix. Before Biographies: Memory and Oral Tradition.......... 329
Craig S. Keener

Bibliography 355

Index of Modern Authors 403

Subject Index 411

Scripture Index 413

Extrabiblical Ancient Sources Index 419

Acknowledgments

Special thanks to Dr. Larry Wood and Emeth Press for publishing this manuscript and providing counsel during editing, Also, a sincere thanks to Dr. Shawn Craigmiles for his outstanding commitment to helping us with the typesetting. We are also incredibly grateful to all the contributors and their willingness to endure several rounds of edits.

Special permission is granted for the following essays:

Steve Walton's essay, "What are the Gospels? Richard Burridge's Impact on Scholarly Understanding of the Genre of the Gospels," was originally published by SAGE Publications in Currents in Biblical Research 14 (1, 2015).

John Jordan Henderson's essay, "A Comparison of Josephus' Life and Jewish War: An Attempt at Establishing the Acceptable Outer Limits of Biographies' Historical Reliability" is an adaptation of his original article published by Sheffield Phoenix Press in the Journal of Greco-Roman Christianity and Judaism 10 (2014).

Craig Keener's essay, "Otho: A Targeted Comparison of Suetonius's Biography and Tacitus's History, with implications for the Gospels' Historical Reliability," was originally published by Eisenbrauns in the Bulletin for Biblical Research 21 (2011).

Craig Keener's appendix, "Before Biographies: Memory and Oral Tradition," was originally published in *Orality and Theological Training in the 21st Century,* ed. W. Jay Moon (DOPS: Nicholasville, KY, 2016).

Chapter 1

Ancient Biography and the Gospels: Introduction

Craig S. Keener
Asbury Theological Seminary

Originally this book's planned title was "Intersections in Ancient Genre: What can Gospels studies learn from ancient biography?" It may be somewhat more descriptive than our livelier current title, but it sounds as if it promises more treatment of the Gospels than the focus of this volume allows. Perhaps the most descriptive title would be: "How historical were ancient biographies in the modern sense of historical? A primer for those with interest in the New Testament." But whereas such a title would have been welcome in the nineteenth century, it is a bit cumbersome for twenty-first century readers.

This volume includes groundbreaking research from a team of motivated, (mostly) young, and internationally diverse scholars.[1] In a discipline with as narrow a literary canon as New Testament studies, it is unfortunately common to rehash overworked debates and to rearrange widely known data, as Martin Hengel once complained in his Society for New Testament Studies presidential address.[2] The contributors to this volume, however, have united to seek to break new ground and share our research so that we and others may build on it.

This work is meant to break new ground, but our interest at this initial level is more in quick dissemination than in massive circulation. This is because *Ancient Biography and the Gospels* is seeking to spearhead an approach that remains in progress. We have sampled some ancient biographies, but not the entire corpus; we have asked some questions of our sources, but not all possible ones. Most of the essays focus on major specimens of the genre rather than exploring its margins or more mixed-genre works.

Each of us also approaches these texts with our own lenses that are most easily readjusted through dialogue with our academic peers working on these projects. Regarding the accuracy of the Gospels, contributors in this volume hold a range of views (mostly from moderate to conservative), views that surface at various points. Such perspectives can affect what we hope to find (whether variations

---

[1] Nations of origin represented in this work include Ethiopia, Singapore, South Korea, the United Kingdom, the United States, and Zimbabwe; continents include Africa, Asia, Europe, and North America (with Puerto Rico also belonging to Latin America).

[2] Hengel, "Aufgaben"; published with slight revisions in English as Hengel, "Tasks." Cf. similar comments in Hengel and Schwemer, *Damascus and Antioch*, 6-7, 15.

among accounts to help explain differences among the Gospels or signs of biographies' reliability to support expectations of accuracy among the Gospels)—though hopefully we are all ready to be chastened by the evidence we find.

Ultimately, because biographers differed among themselves in such respects, identifying biographic genre does not allow us to impose a uniform genre-based grid on all ancient biographies or Gospels.[3] The basic genre does, however, suggest a range of the sort of continuity in substance and flexibility in some kinds of detail that we might expect. Scholars and students who work on the Gospels often chart differences and especially patterns of differences. One unsurprising conclusion in the study of ancient biography is that such differences are not unusual in ancient biography. The Gospels may reflect a more popular level of writing than most extant biographies by members of the elite, but (in favor of more substantial information in them) they are also closer in time to their subject than are most ancient biographies.

A final reason for publishing first at this initial level is that, with several significant exceptions, most of the contributors (and my coeditor) are doctoral students at Asbury Theological Seminary, where I teach.[4] Most of their work reflects research for papers for my doctoral historical Jesus, Matthew or Acts seminars. Several are developing their research much more fully for dissertations. Nevertheless, this work is meant to lay foundations for further work. Once the book is published, all of us can make use of the others' work, citing them appropriately, in our further developments of this research. As readers, you too are invited to build on this exciting fresh area of research in Gospels studies.

This Book's Purpose

Biographies flourished in the early empire; many of the most prominent extant samples stem from a few decades after the Gospels, but others, such as the works of Cornelius Nepos, predate the first century CE.[5] Many works about Nero stem

---

[3] Mixed genres also exist, though the Gospels appear to fit well within the range of expectations for ancient biography even if some Gospels include elements of other genres (e.g., if Luke's Gospel also functions as a historical monograph as does its sequel, as some argue). Genres may be adapted, but genre is necessarily about expectations, so exploring the contours of the biographic genre helps us consider what to expect.

[4] The professors, who each represent different institutions, are Holly Carey (Point), myself (Asbury), Michael Licona (Houston Baptist), and Steve Walton (St. Mary's University and Cambridge).

[5] Nepos (ca. 110-ca. 27 BCE) is the earliest biographer in Latin whose work survives today, others having been lost; see Pryzwansky, "Nepos." Note also many philosophic biographies, many now preserved only in fragments, from previous centuries (Hägg, *Biography*, 187); biographic interest appears among Peripatetics in the fourth century BCE (Laistner, *Historians*, 18). For Greek works showing biographic interest from the fifth century BCE onward, see (although including forms other than what we in this work designate as biographies), Hägg, *Biography*, 10-98, passim (note esp. Xenophon's memoirs on Socrates, 23-30; on Agesilaus, 41-51; Aristoxenus, 69-77; memoirs of Antigonus, 89-93); cf.

from before Josephus writes in the 90s, thus from roughly the period of the Synoptic Gospels.[6] Because Jesus was, among other things, a teacher or sage, philosophers' *bioi*, honoring philosophic schools' founders and recounting their teachings, provide the closest available biographic analogy for the Gospels.[7] Though many extant examples of sage biographies postdate the period of the Gospels, fragments reveal that this form of biography began flourishing long before the Gospels.[8] Indeed, disciples had published memoirs about their sages (or about others) centuries before this time.[9]

A majority of scholars today regard the Gospels as ancient biography.[10] Thus

---

also biographies from the period of the Republic, esp. Nepos's Latin *Atticus* (Hägg, *Biography*, 188-97) and Nicolaus's Greek *Augustus* (197-204). For first-century BCE forms of autobiographic writing, see Laistner, *Historians*, 35-37; autobiographic writing in some form appears as early as ancient Egypt (Simpson, *Literature*, 401-27).

[6] Josephus *Ant.* 20.154, although Josephus denounces many of these contemporary accounts (a genre he labels as *historia*) as biased and containing falsehoods, partly because they were too *close* to the events to write impartially (a criticism he would not be consistent enough to apply to his *Life*). Nero died in 68, so these "many" (*polloi*, cf. Luke 1:1) writers, obviously varying in perspective and in some reports they included, composed their works mostly within two decades after Nero's death.

[7] See e.g., Culpepper, *John*, 64-66; so also some of Josephus' biographies (see Van Veldhuizen, "Moses," 215-24). For cultural memory's interest in origins and founders, cf. Galinsky, "Introduction," 23 (following Jan Assman).

[8] Hägg, *Biography*, 187: "Of the lost late Hellenistic authors, most wrote varieties of philosophical biography," fragments of which surface later in Diogenes Laertius and Pythagorean lives; cf. also fragments of lives from the early empire (Hägg, *Biography*, 283).

[9] Cf. Polybius 12.25e.1; Kennedy, "Source Criticism," 129-37; Laistner, *Historians*, 33-37. Some later examples of this form may borrow the gospel form (see Dillon and Hershbell, "Introduction," 25, who also suggest that John's Gospel may well have been available); but Peripatetics displayed special interest in philosophers' biography as early as the fourth century BCE (Laistner, *Historians*, 18). "Lives" of divine men might provide the closest content, but these appear especially in the third century; they may depend on the Gospels, and the reverse cannot be true chronologically.

[10] See Talbert, *What is a Gospel?*, passim; Kennedy, "Source Criticism," 128-34; Aune, *Literary Environment*, 46-76; Stanton, *Preaching*, 117-36; Robbins, *Teacher*, 10; Burridge, *Gospels?* (1992), 109-239; idem, "About People," 121-22; idem, "Biography"; idem, "Biography, Ancient"; idem, "Genre"; Cross, "Genres," 402-4; Frickenschmidt, *Evangelium* (exploring 142 examples and their most common characteristic elements, including character-revealing words and deeds and death); Plümacher, *Geschichte*, 13-14; Zuntz, "Heide"; Keener, *Matthew*, 16-24; idem, *John*, 11-37; Ytterbrink, *Biography*; Crossan, "Necessary," 27. Kee, *Origins*, 144-47, argues that Luke combined Mark with Greco-Roman biography; but Mark was itself already biography. Note also the response in Burridge, "Review," to the otherwise generally helpful work of Hägg, *Biography*. Hägg, *Biography*, 163, finds the one-year focus of Mark unusual in biography (though paralleling Plato's *Phaedo* as even more distinctive), but biographies often focused on public careers and Burridge, "Review," 476-77, notes the frequency of disproportionate attention to highlighted periods in other biographies (cf. Hägg's own comments in e.g., 208, 293).

Graham Stanton of Cambridge regards as "surprisingly inaccurate" earlier decades' skepticism about the Gospels being biographies.[11] Indeed, Richard Burridge's argument[12] has proven so compelling that one reviewer claims that it ought to end any further dissent about the matter.[13] To claim that the Synoptics (and even John) are biographies is not to limit the distinctiveness of the character they portray (sometimes the basis for denial), but to contend that biography is the most obvious category for an ancient audience approaching a prose volume about a single historical individual.

Biography is the only kind of work about a real, individual historical figure other than a historical novel—virtually[14] none of which were about *recent* historical persons. A biography was understood as a basically factual narrative about a real individual. Biography thus offers the closest available analogy for how audiences would initially approach the narrative first-century Gospels. This does not mean that the Evangelists in composing Gospels added nothing distinctive to the traditional, wider genre; there is little doubt, in fact, that they did.[15] But because uninitiated readers would initially approach the first Gospels with the expectations they had for ancient biography, this broader genre category remains relevant for helping us to better understand the Gospels.[16]

Surprisingly few scholars, however, have worked to develop the implications of this general consensus for the question of how we approach the Gospels for historical information about Jesus.[17] In fact at least a few scholars, such as one of my doctoral professors, have suggested that ancient biographies were fictitious and therefore the Gospels should be approached accordingly. (When I cautiously challenged his assumption, since I had already read some ancient biographies, the professor humbly acknowledged that he lacked firsthand knowledge about the subject, and had simply read that view somewhere.)

The scholars and doctoral students in this volume explore this question, seeking to establish the expected range of reliability typically found in ancient biographies. (More research remains to be done in terms of implications for the Gospels' literary and rhetorical methods as well, although that is not the focus of the present project.)

---

[11] Stanton, *New People*, 63-64; idem, *Truth?*, 137, reversing his own earlier skepticism in idem, *Gospels*, 19.

[12] See especially Burridge, *Gospels* (1992).

[13] Talbert, "Review," 715; cf. also Stanton, *New People*, 64.

[14] I know of no exceptions in antiquity to this pattern, yet I recognize that almost every rule of genre has at least a few exceptions. If there are such exceptions here, however, they are extremely rare in comparison to the usual pattern.

[15] See helpfully e.g., Pennington, *Reading the Gospels Wisely*, 25-35; somewhat differently, Freyne, "Imagination," 10.

[16] Ehrman, *Introduction*, 64-65, rightly notes that their shared, distinctive subgenre does not diminish the larger biographic genre in which a reader would naturally place them.

[17] Indeed, several noted historical Jesus scholars display fairly little awareness of Gospel scholars' research, even while mining the Gospels selectively for information supporting their a priori hypotheses.

The overlap between the genres of ancient biography and ancient historiography is substantial.[18] (George Kennedy, in fact, classifies biography "as a subdivision of history.")[19] Thus Philip Stadter regards the boundaries between these two genres as quite "fluid";[20] certainly boundaries between imperial biography and history weakened by the late first century,[21] because emperors were central to the historical action. Andrew Pitts, following David Balch and others, notes that there is no "hard and fast distinction between history and biography."[22] Although biographies could serve a wide range of literary functions,[23] ancient biographers intended their works to be more historical than novelistic.[24] Thus later biographers often simply repeat what earlier biographers said.[25]

Genre does not answer all historical questions or eliminate the value of the more common historical-critical criteria. It does, however, rightly adjust our default expectations; in view of our research we should thus expect historical intention and significant use of prior information in biographies, whereas we do not ordinarily expect such concerns in, for example, ancient novels. With regard to biographies of recent characters, a default expectation that much of the information is accurate is usually likelier than are a priori skeptical assumptions. In an argument, one making a case bears the burden of proof, whether for or against

---

[18] E.g., Bravo, "Antiquarianism," 516. Although especially biographies, the Gospels also include historiographic elements (Byrskog, *Story as History*, 45, noting esp. Cancik, "Gattung"), a point now sometimes noted even for the Fourth Gospel (esp. Bauckham, *Testimony*, 19-21, 93-112; idem, "Historiographical Characteristics").

[19] Kennedy, "Source Criticism," 136. For one recent examination of the level of historical content in biographies of recent characters, see Keener, "Otho."

[20] Stadter, "Biography and History," 528; see also Burridge, *Gospels?* (1992), 63-67.

[21] Hose, "Historiography: Rome." Roman biographers, in view here, preferred to report all significant public acts, whereas Greek biography (more directly relevant to the Gospels, written in Greek) had traditionally limited itself more to key actions that revealed character (Hägg, *Biography*, 192, 234).

[22] Pitts, "Source Citation," 377-78.

[23] Burridge, *Gospels?* (1992), 149-52, 185-88. For the divergence see further Barr and Wentling, "Biography and Genre," 81-88, although I would not regard all their examples as biographies. Ps.-Callisthenes (treated below under novels) does not belong to the mainstream of this genre; Kennedy, "Source Criticism," 139, more accurately cites Plutarch and Suetonius (both from close to the Gospels' period) as the prime examples of biography.

[24] For substantial overlap between the biography and history (as well as other) genres in antiquity, see Burridge, *Gospels?* (1992), 63-67. While biographers might "tweak" their sources and select the most useful, we should not downplay their mimetic function too much (cf. the comparison with artistic representation in Kaesser, "Tweaking"). Satirical elements appear in autobiographies of satirists (Keane, "Satiric Memories").

[25] E.g., Dion. Hal. *Lysias* 1.

authenticity;[26] but the Evangelists' use of the biographic genre itself offers an argument that somewhat shifts that burden by significantly increasing the likelihood, other factors being equal, of any given reported event's authenticity.[27]

The character of ancient biography also helps explain the flexibility that we find when we compare different Gospel accounts. Biographers depended on historical information but addressed audiences with expectations very different than those of most readers of modern biographies. That does not mean that the modern genre is unrelated to the ancient genre from which it evolved.[28] Nevertheless, the conventions of ancient biography, like the oral sources that transmitted much of the information that biographers used,[29] permitted considerable flexibility in how biographers recounted their information. Some Evangelists and some biographers exploited this literary freedom more than did others.

Understanding the range of treatments in the ancient biographic genre helps us understand better both the information content behind the Gospels and the rhetorical and literary flexibility the gospel traditions and authors exercised.

Biographies and Literary Flexibility

When we speak of ancient biography's historical character, we should be careful to distinguish ancient historiography (what is meant here) from its modern descendant. In what follows, I will comment on flexibility in the Gospels and ancient biography, the importance of taking into account various authors' perspectives (*Tendenz*), the commitment of ancient biographers and historians to providing morally useful examples, their frequent political and apologetic agendas, their occasional theological lessons, and their usual commitment to providing engaging narratives.

Flexibility in the Gospels and Ancient Biography

What was the usual relationship of ancient biographies to other genres, such as historiography, novels, and epideictic speeches? As elaborated below, ancient readers expected the genre of biography in their day to rest on prior information; in that sense, it was a historical genre. This recognition does not, however, mean that we can approach it in a mathematically or scientifically rigid sort of manner; ancient historiography was not ordinarily rigid, either. That is, both historians and biographers varied among themselves in historiographic quality, and even the

---

[26] See esp. Winter, "Burden of Proof."

[27] Here scholars will normally distinguish events from details, because these could be preserved differently in terms of memories; see this book's appendix regarding oral tradition. This observation also takes into account that the Gospels reflect less than a century of tradition as opposed to works written centuries after their subjects.

[28] For similarities and differences, see recently Hägg, *Biography*.

[29] See here Allison, *Constructing*, 29, on the observation of anthropologists that, "Tradents are always introducing changes."

most careful writers were expected to tell a good story and were permitted some liberties in doing so.[30] Given the emphasis of this book, it is important to establish this observation at the beginning.

That ancient biographers could exercise at least some flexibility will not surprise any attentive reader of the Gospels who has taken time to compare parallel accounts. For some particularly conspicuous examples, did Jesus speak regularly of the kingdom of God, as in Mark and Luke, or of the kingdom of heaven, as usually in Matthew? Did the centurion cry out, "Truly, this was God's son!" (Mark 15:39), or (what Mark's version would necessarily entail), "Certainly, this man was righteous/innocent!" (Luke 23:47)?

Although some modern readers find these differences troubling, such differences rarely bothered ancient audiences. Indeed, writing in the early second century, Papias offers the following report about Mark's Gospel: "Mark, having become Peter's interpreter, wrote down accurately everything he [Mark] remembered, though not in order, of the things either said or done by Christ. For he [Mark] neither heard the Lord nor followed him, but afterward, as I said, followed Peter, who adapted his teachings as needed but had no intention of giving an ordered account of the Lord's sayings. Consequently Mark did nothing wrong in writing down some things as he remembered them, for he made it his one concern not to omit anything that he heard or to make any false statement in them."[31] Moreover, we find the same sorts of features when we compare other ancient biographies; such features belonged to the flexibility inherent in the ancient biographic genre.

Certainly paraphrase was a conventional rhetorical exercise,[32] but flexibility extended much further than this. In various biographies, various factors can account for the flexibility.

Historians often could be careless about details; most did not care about minor variations.[33] Thus, for example, two ancient historians report that a son died, and another reports the death as that of a daughter; historians normally did not care much about minutiae irrelevant to their point.[34] Likewise, in his separate works,

---

[30] See also here Sanders, *Paul*, 98, recognizing that ancient historians distinguished truth from fiction but also composed in ways to make their stories flow well.

[31] Papias frg. 3.15 (Holmes). Many interpreters think that Papias prefers the Johannine chronological sequence to Mark's here, but *taxis* might refer instead to rhetorical arrangement, in which Mark's plot was deemed deficient (see Moessner, "Voice"). Likewise, he reports that Peter's listeners "begged Mark (whose gospel is extant), since he was Peter's follower, to leave behind a written record of the teaching given to them verbally, and did not quit until they had persuaded the man" (frg. 21.1, Holmes).

[32] See e.g., Theon *Progymn.* 1.93-171 (Butts); Hermog. *Method in Forceful Speaking* 24.440; Libanius *Anecdote* 1.4; 2.3; *Maxim* 1.2-5; 2.3; 3.2; cf. Fronto *Eloq.* 3.5; Hock, "Paul and Education," 202-3. Phaedrus feels free to adapt Aesop for aesthetic reasons, meanwhile seeking to keep to the *spirit* of Aesop (Phaed. 2, *prol.* 8). Rhetorical presentation of events also sought to stir emotion; see e.g., Quintilian *Inst.* 4.2.113.

[33] As Allison, *Constructing*, 454, notes, the majority of variations in Synoptic tradition are minor.

[34] Massey, "Disagreement," 54-55

Josephus has Antipas banished to different distant locations.[35] More than likely, simple lapse of memory (sometimes based on how sources were envisioned) is often responsible for the variation, and the matters were too minor to warrant revision or concern. Still, some historians complained when some of their peers went too far; Plutarch complains that some writers added details missing elsewhere, for example composing a proper tragic finale for Alexander's life (Plut. *Alex.* 70.3).[36]

How much flexibility was permitted in ancient biographies? That depended on individual biographers and on the sources available to them; variation was ordinarily much greater about figures of the distant past, for whom existing competing traditions were more often available. By contrast, comparison of biographies of a figure such as Otho, composed half a century after the events described, reveals substantial overlap similar to what we witness in a synopsis of the Gospels.

Perspectives in Ancient Biography and Historiography[37]

Like other sources covering the same events, the various Gospels reflect different perspectives and approaches.[38] Ancient writers, no less than modern ones, betray different perspectives and agendas.[39] Ancient historians themselves recognized that they investigated their subjects according to interpretive grids;[40] for example, Polybius noted that one must have some understanding of the nature of events to be "able to pose the right questions" rather than simply rambling random thoughts.[41] Historians recognized that they were supposed to remain impartial,[42] but even today this objective is usually easier said than done.

Even today, different biographers frequently offer divergent perspectives on their subjects in their selective narrations.[43] Dunn points to the varying estimates

---

[35] Josephus *Ant.* 18.252 (probably more accurate); *War* 2.183.

[36] His own romantic description of Darius' death (Plut. *Alex.* 43.2) is missing in Arrian (*Alex.* 3.21-23), but was evidently not his own invention (the LCL note, 7:352 n. 1, cites Quint. Curt. 5.13, 28; Diod. 17.73).

[37] See more fully here Keener, *Acts*, 1:148-65, from which much of this material is extracted and adapted.

[38] This observation is hardly limited to skeptical scholars; a careful and informed Christian apologist will also concede this point at the outset. See e.g., Wallace, *Christianity*, 74-77, 80-81; an experienced cold-case detective, Wallace regards such differences not as problematic but rather as characteristic even of different eyewitnesses to the same scene, and is accustomed to evaluating the differences when interviewing witnesses.

[39] For Jewish apologetic historiography, see Sterling, *Historiography*; in Josephus's autobiography, see also Stern, "Life of Josephus."

[40] Byrskog, *Story as History*, 186-90. The historian's own participation was thus valuable (Byrskog, *Story as History*, 188).

[41] Byrskog, *Story as History*, 187.

[42] Even during the Roman Republic; see Laistner, *Historians*, 33-35.

[43] Postmodern historians rightly note that while historians may correctly include facts, their selection and framing of material reflects particular perspectives. For one discussion of the strengths and weaknesses of postmodern historiography, favoring critical realism in approaching the Gospels, see Licona, *Resurrection*, 71-89. But already Caird distinguished

of Winston Churchill and Margaret Thatcher today as examples.[44] Biographers exercised even greater editorial and compositional freedom in earlier eras.[45] No historian can escape subjective bias; but a perspective concerning events does not make the information about the events bad history.[46]

Moreover, biographers, like historians (but unlike most novelists), typically sought to communicate moral, political, or even theological lessons.

Moral Lessons in Ancient Biography and Historiography

Like historians, biographers frequently sought to teach moral lessons from their stories;[47] one early biographer claimed, in fact, that biographers focused on the virtues of their subject more than historians could.[48] Biographic information was meant to be used to instruct learners in virtue through the process of imitation.[49] Some ancient biographers emphasize moral lessons in their stories more than others; some writers, like Plutarch, vary in their moralizing even from one biography to the next.[50]

In this way biography resembled historiography more generally. Unlike most novelists, historians often sought to communicate moral lessons through their historical accounts.[51] As Edwin Judge observes, "The ancient historians ... took it

---

between events' actuality and their significance, noting that "no historical statement is purely referential" (Caird, *Language*, 201-2). In general, scholars have been more ready to accept T. P. Wiseman's skepticism about the early Republic than A. J. Woodman's skepticism toward "authors of contemporary or near-contemporary history" (Damon, "Rhetoric," 439), but at times Woodman himself recognizes that likelihood increases with proximity; see e.g., Woodman, *Rhetoric*, 204.

[44] Dunn, *Acts*, xvi. Laistner, *Historians*, 95, points to how it took perhaps a century for British and U.S. historians to be "fair to both sides" regarding "the American Revolution." For varied applications of Francis Asbury (some quite one-sided), see Wigger, *Saint*, 405-18.

[45] Suiting biographic standards of their era, the biography of Wilberforce by his sons selects information that would present their father in the best light (Tomkins, *Wilberforce*, 15-16), and rewords matters to suit their own high-church preferences (16); nevertheless, it often depends on records (16) and recollections heard from their father and his friends (16-17).

[46] Judge, "Sources," 280-81, even challenges the disengaged, depersonalizing preference of much modern (as opposed to ancient) historiography as unrealistic.

[47] Burridge, *Gospels?* (1992), 150; Hägg, *Biography*, 274; cf. Dihle, "Biography," 367-74. One could learn from past teachers by proxy, as "disciples" of their recorded teachings (Robbins, *Teacher*, 110-11).

[48] Corn. Nep. 16 [Pelopidas], 1.1.

[49] Proclus *Poet*. Essay 5, K58.6-14, on encomia. Cf. Kurz, "Models," 182-83, on biography and narrative models for imitation.

[50] Burridge, *Gospels* (1992), 68-69. Beneker, *Statesman*, finds connections between figures' personal self-mastery in Plutarch and their public success.

[51] E.g., Polybius sometimes digresses in asides to give lessons related to the events narrated (1.35.1-10). Cf. e.g., Chaplin, "Conversations"; McInerney, "Arrian and Romance"; Galinsky, "Introduction," 4, 21; Gowing, "Memory," 43-48, esp. 46-47 (on Livy

for granted that remembering the good and evil deeds of others was morally instructive."[52] Or as Jörg Rüpke emphasizes, "exemplarity is by no means necessarily opposed to history"; it simply finds lessons in the past with values considered consistent with "continuing normativity."[53]

The moral agenda constituted a paramount one for historians; one taught history not simply to memorize the past but to draw lessons from it.[54] Thus some felt that historians should choose a noble subject, so their work would contribute to good moral character as well as providing information (e.g., Dion. Hal. *Ant. rom.* 1.2.1). No less a careful ancient historian than Polybius begins his multivolume history by observing its utilitarian value: people "have no more ready corrective of conduct than knowledge of the past" (Polyb. 1.1.1, LCL). As Fornara points out, Polybius "treasured history as a sound inferential basis for present and future political activity"; his "rationalistic bias" did not obscure for him history's "hortatory value."[55]

Likewise, Tacitus, one of our most reliable historical sources for the early empire, emphasizes that the study of history promotes virtue (*Agr.* 1); without claiming to have invented events, he notes that he freely omitted material not of value to history's primary, moral objective (*Ann.* 3.65). Tacitus himself felt no constraint to avoid editorial statements at times (e.g., *Ann.* 4.33); often lamenting the decline of traditional Roman values, he was (like his contemporaries) "a moralist, who regards it as his duty to hold vice up to scorn and to praise virtue."[56] Lucian, a stickler for historical accuracy, as we have noted, allows for history's edifying value, i.e., moral lessons (although not mere entertainment), provided they flow from truth (e.g., *Hist.* 59).

Valerius Maximus was not the most careful collector of historical anecdotes, but his perspective on the utility of historical examples is representative: It is helpful to know history "so that a backward look...may yield some profit to modern

pref. 9-10 and *Agr.* 46.3-4). Note Kelhoffer, "Maccabees at Prayer," on application-driven differences between 1 and 2 Maccabees.

[52] Judge, *First Christians*, 249; see also 250-51.

[53] Rüpke, "Knowledge," 94.

[54] On the hortatory value of history in Roman historians, see Fornara, *Nature of History*, 115-16; for history providing models for living, see fully the thorough work of Lang, *Kunst*, 7-13, 97-167 (esp. note problem-solving strategies in Sallust and Tacitus, 108-37). For moralizing elements in ancient historiography, Marguerat, *Histoire*, 28-29 cites examples from Dionysius, Livy, Sallust and Plutarch. See e.g., Livy's use of the legendary Romulus as an example (Stem, "Lessons").

[55] Fornara, *Nature of History*, 113, noting (115-16) that Romans emphasized this even more.

[56] Moore, "Introduction," xiii; cf. similarly Hadas, "Introduction," xvii-xix (noting the popular model of Livy); Laistner, *Historians*, 113-14 (citing *Ann.* 2.65.1; 4.33.2), 123, 131-39 (criticizing his tendentiousness); Williams, "Germanicus" (addressing Tacitus' perspective in one work). In other cases, the ways he reports the accounts reveal his opinions as well as explicit asides would have (e.g., *Ann.* 5.1-2; 14.39).

manners" (Val. Max. 2.pref.; LCL).[57] The intellectual orator Maximus of Tyre opines that history preserves the memories of humanity and so "guards its virtues" (Max. Tyre 22.5, trans. Trapp). Historians frequently included even moralizing narrative asides to interpret history's meaning more directly for their readers, to illustrate the fulfillment of prophetic utterances, or to provide the author's perspective.[58] Jewish historiography was certainly no less interpretive.[59]

Dionysius of Halicarnassus lists three purposes for writing history: first, that the courageous will gain "immortal glory" that outlives them; second, that their descendants will recognize their own roots and seek to emulate their virtue; and finally, that he might show proper goodwill and gratitude toward those who provided him training and information.[60]

Historians' moral illustrations, social commentary in speeches, and political interests often reveal their distinctive philosophic and theological perspectives.[61]

Political and Apologetic Agendas

Historians often wrote to inculcate "good citizenship,"[62] hence usually displayed, in varying measures, national or ethnic biases. Polybius, for example, exhibits a pro-Roman *Tendenz* (e.g., 36.9.1-17).[63] Livy claimed that history teaches a nation's greatness and what one may imitate (Livy 1, *pref.* 10); naturally he had

---

[57] On Valerius's moralistic aims, see further Rüpke, "Knowledge," 89, though noting (93-94) that the objective of exemplarity does not inherently conflict with interest in genuine historical information.

[58] E.g., Polyb. 1.35.1-10; Diod. Sic. 31.10.2; Dion. Hal. *Ant. rom.* 7.65.2; Vell. Paterc. 2.75.2; Dio Cass. 1.5.4; Arrian *Alex.* 4.10.8; Corn. Nep. 16 (Pelopidas), 3.1; Tac. *Ann.* 16.15; characterizing asides throughout Velleius Paterculus (e.g., 2.41.1-2; 2.66.3-5; 2.72.1-2; 2.91.2-3; 2.98.2-3). For narrative asides in histories and biographies, see Sheeley, *Asides*, 56-93; for Herodotus' judgments (e.g., 1.34; 2.123.3; 4.205; 9.120), see Dewald, "Construction," 95; for Xenophon, ibid., 98; for Tacitus' (Laistner, *Historians*, 139, unhappily); for "parenthesis" as a rhetorical technique, see Rowe, "Style," 147; Black, "Oration at Olivet," 87, citing Quint. *Inst.* 9.3.23; Anderson, *Glossary*, 89-90).

[59] See e.g., von Dobbeler, "Geschichte"; van der Kooij, "Death of Josiah"; Reinmuth, "Zwischen Investitur und Testament"; Bergren, "Nehemiah"; Borgen, "Reviewing and Rewriting."

[60] Dion. Hal. *Ant. rom.* 1.6.3-5; cf. Diod. Sic. 15.1.1; 37.4.1.

[61] For example, some Socratic ideas appear in Xenophon's Cyrus (e.g., *Cyr.* 3.1.17; Xenophon's other work reveals his admiration of Socrates), though the *Cyropedia* is not a true historical work or biographic work in the later sense (Cic. *Quint. fratr.* 1.1.8.23 argues that Xenophon's *Cyropaedia* was intended to teach proper government, not primarily to report historical truth). Cf. causation by Fortune or deities in Tacitus in Tac. *Ann.* 3.18; Hadas, "Introduction," xvi; Fortune in Polybius in Walbank, "Fortune."

[62] Penner, "Discourse," 73-77. Hägg, *Biography*, 273, finds greater political interest in historiography and greater ethical interest in biography, but in practice these categories overlapped.

[63] Cf. Momigliano, *Historiography*, 71-73. Many suggest that he also shares his peers' lack of affection for Aetolians (Laistner, *Historians*, 6, 95; for discussion and nuancing, see Champion, "Aetolia," esp. 357-62). For Polybius's appreciation for history's political value, see Fornara, *Nature of History*, 113.

especially the greatness of Rome, his subject, in view. One also thinks of Josephus' apologetic attempt to whitewash his people from excess complicity in the revolt while simultaneously appealing to the dignity of his Roman readership.[64]

Yet writers often tried to evaluate character impartially.[65] Thus despite Thucydides's biases as a participant in the Peloponnesian War, he proves surprisingly impartial.[66]

Biographers also wrote at times for apologetic and polemical purposes.[67] Historians, and particularly minority historians, also composed apologetic historiography.[68] This particular concern that sometimes appears in biography and historiography is surely relevant to the Gospels, which flourished in a particular, sectarian subculture.

Theological Interests in Ancient Biography and Historiography

Most ancient historians also sought to interpret the divine will in some patterns in history.[69] Thus some deity helped the Greeks escape, Xenophon decides (Xen. *Anab.* 5.2.24). Elsewhere historians often emphasize deities punishing violations of temples, for example.[70]

---

[64] Often noted, e.g., Mason, *Josephus and New Testament*, 60-71, 77-81; cf. ibid., 196-98; Crossan, *Jesus*, 93; for Josephus' pro-Flavian propaganda, see Saulnier, "Josèphe" (though for Josephus being less closely tied with Vespasian than some suggest, cf. Hollander, *Josephus*, on which see also the assessment in Darko, "Review"). Partisan agendas were not limited to politics, also appearing among schools of thought; cf. e.g., Eshleman, "Sophists," on biographies of sophists.

[65] See e.g., Herodotus 2.4, 32, 50, 58, 77, 82 (and remarks in Meister, "Herodotus," 268); Dion. Hal. *Ant. rom.* Bk. 3; 9.39.1-6; Livy 21.1.3; Vell. Paterc. 2.18.1; cf. Marincola, "Speeches," 119.

[66] Cf. Wade-Gery, "Thucydides," 1519, adding that "Perhaps no good historian is impartial." Dion. Hal. *Pomp.* 3 accuses Thucydides of focusing on Athens' failings, but, importantly here, not of inventing them.

[67] Burridge, *Gospels?* (1992), 151, 180; for apologetic autobiography, cf. e.g., Jos. *Life* 336-67; 2 Cor 11:8-33; Gal 1:11-24; discussion in Lyons, *Autobiography*. As noted earlier, autobiographic writing in some form appears as early as ancient Egypt (Simpson, *Literature*, 401-27), though honor conventions created some problems for it in Republican Rome (see Riggsby, "Memoir"). For autobiography as a type of biography, often with apologetic or propagandistic purposes, see Stadter, "Biography," 530.

[68] Sterling, *Historiography*, 103-310; see also idem, "Appropriation," 234-38; Wandrey, "Literature: Jewish-Hellenistic," 696; cf. Meiser, "Gattung."

[69] Cf. Seneca the Elder *Historical Fragments* 1, who divided Rome's history into ages corresponding to human maturation. Contrary to the claims of some modern interpretations of ancient historiography, some ancient historians did think in terms of cause and effect, though not all of these were divine (e.g., Polyb. 2.56.13; 3.6.1—3.7.3; 3.31.11-13; 3.32.2).

[70] E.g., Polybius 31.9.1-4; 32.15.14; Diod. Sic. 14.63.1; 14.69.4; 14.76.3; 16.58.6; 27.4.3; Corn. Nep. 17 (Agesilaus), 4.8; Val. Max. 1.1.18-21; 1.1. ext. 3 (posthumously); 1.1. ext. 5; Livy 42.28.12; Pliny *N.H.* 33.24.83; Appian *Hist. rom.* 3.12.1-2; Babr. 78; Phaedrus 4.11.1-13; Lucian *Z. Rants* 24, 32; Paus. 3.23.5; 9.33.6; 9.39.12; Quint. *Decl.* 323 intro; Athen. *Deipn.* 12.523ab; cf. Cicero *Verr.* 2.5.72.184-89; 2 Macc 3:25-26; Jos. *Ant.* 12.358-59.

Oracles and omens were said to reveal Rome's divine destiny.[71] Despite Herodotus' occasional rationalism, he reports dreams, omens, and other signs of divine activity, his ideal audience's consensus on the reality of which he seems to assume.[72]

Hellenistic historians saw providence in history, so that Diodorus could describe "historians as 'ministers of divine providence' who arrange their accounts in the light of their understanding of providence in human events."[73] Dionysius of Halicarnassus includes among history's lessons the virtue of piety toward the gods (Dion. Hal. *Ant. rom.* 8.56.1). Josephus is often explicit about providence in human affairs, sometimes using it to justify reporting apparently supernatural phenomena (*Ant.* 17.353; cf. 17.350-52).

Pleasure in Reading Ancient Historiography

Whereas novels were intended primarily for entertainment,[74] historians believed that they could entertain without abandoning historical truth.[75] (It was novels that borrowed elements from history and other earlier genres, rather than the reverse.)[76]

Thus Maximus of Tyre, while believing that philosophic lectures are the most entertaining pastime at banquets, also finds history pleasurable (Max. Tyre 22.5). Likewise, the author of 2 Maccabees notes that he employed many possible sources, but that his document was also written in such a way as to be enjoyed and easily remembered (2:24-25). Tacitus apologizes that the period he covers offers less intriguing stories than histories of earlier Rome.[77] Readers found various forms of pleasure in histories, whether the pleasure of knowledge or that of being able to pity others' misfortunes.[78]

---

[71] E.g., the interpretation of a head found beneath Rome (Dion. Hal. *Ant. rom.* 4.59.2; 4.61.2; Plut. *Cam.* 31.4; Dio Cass. frg. in Zonaras 7.11). Perhaps they inadvertently dug into part of an old burial site (an archaeologically plausible surmise, though our literary sources claim a freshly severed head), but their interpretation became the dominant cultural memory.

[72] Meister, "Herodotus," 269.

[73] Squires, "Plan," 38, citing Diod. Sic. 1.1.3.

[74] With e.g., Talbert, *What is a Gospel?*, 17. The Gospels' audiences probably needed encouragement much more than entertainment (Witherington, *Acts*, 378).

[75] Dio Cass. 1.1.1-2; Fornara, *Nature of History*, 120-33; Palmer, "Monograph," 3, 29, citing e.g., Cic. *Fam.* 5.12.5; Polyb. 1.4.11; 3.31.13; Aune, *Literary Environment*, 80; Aune, *Dictionary*, 285; cf. also Dion. Hal. *Demosth.* 47; Plümacher, "Fiktion und Wunder"; Krasser, "Reading," 554 (though including Ps.-Callisth. *Alex.* too readily in the history category). For biographies, see Burridge, *Gospels?* (1992), 149-51. One can write essentially factual accounts in the entertaining style of fiction current in one's day (see examples in Sterling, *Sisters*, 78; Hunt, *History and Legacy*, 208, 239).

[76] Aune, *Dictionary*, 321.

[77] Tac. *Ann.* 4.32-33.

[78] Fornara, *Nature of History*, 120-33, esp. 121, 133-34, citing Cic. *Fam.* 5.12.4. Cf. Gorg. *Hel.* 9 on suffering in others' failures through poetry.

Ancient Biography and History

Despite the flexibility in ancient biography noted above, the *substance* of events in biographies about recent characters was expected to be, and probably usually was, reliable information. Sometimes scholars have counted against this expectation Plutarch's distinction between biography and historiography (*Alex.* 1.1), but this is not what Plutarch claimed. In context, "the continuation 'for it is not Histories that I am writing, but Lives', is in the first place an excuse for summarizing or omitting historically important facts in the cases of Alexander and Caesar (in reality, mostly the former), to focus instead on character-revealing incidents. It is not a matter of Plutarch drawing a sharp line between history and biography (as it is often supposed to mean when quoted in isolation) or stating what is generally suitable or admissible for each of these literary genres."[79]

Naturally, for Christians the Gospels are more than simply historical information about an ancient historical figure. But even from a purely secular historiographic perspective, we should expect the Gospels, as accounts of a recent historical figure, to be full of significant information about Jesus.

The biographies most relevant for comparison with the Gospels are biographies of figures from the recent past (a generation or two, as in the case of the Gospels). If one asks why the Evangelists whose work we know did not write even earlier, it may be that no one yet deemed it necessary. Although contemporaries often wrote history and biography, some writers considered some events almost *too* recent for such treatment.[80] They also could criticize those who wrote too soon after events because emotions were still too fresh.[81] Nevertheless, some may have written accounts about Jesus much earlier than our best guesses for the dates of our extant Gospels; clearly many sources circulated that have not survived (Luke 1:1).

When a biography of a recent figure by Suetonius or Plutarch offers information that is not corroborated elsewhere, we do not for that reason dismiss its claims (although we may question them if we have specific reason to do so). We can corroborate these writers' accounts frequently enough from parallel sources

---

[79] Hägg, *Biography*, 269. Likewise, his biographic emphasis on "signs of the soul" (*Alex.* 1.3) refers in context to the character's "sayings and jokes" (Hägg, *Biography*, 271). The contrast is not about genuine events but of one's literary focus; "Both historiography and biography may have a didactic purpose, but while historians convey political lessons, the biographer professes to teach ethics" (Hägg, *Biography*, 273).

[80] See Velleius Paterculus 2.126.1; cf. 2.92.5. Political exigencies could also affect those writing current history; see e.g., Pliny *Ep.* 5.8.12-13 (considering earlier times more praiseworthy); Tac. *Ann.* 4.33; Brown, *Historians*, 125; Hose, "Cassius Dio," 462-63. But contrast Nepos on Atticus or Tacitus on Agricola; likewise, as noted in Hägg, *Biography*, 349, Philostratus later reports directly on some of his contemporaries (in *Vit. soph.*).

[81] Thus see, e.g., the criticism of works from Nero's time in Josephus *Ant.* 20.154. Biographies of living persons may prove too encomiastic, though they also provide invaluable information once we take into account their perspectives (Laistner, *Historians*, 34-35).

to recognize that they are not simply wildly inventing stories.[82] The biographers themselves could not know which accounts would survive two millennia and allow us to check them, so it is logical to generally expect the same degree of accuracy or imprecision in their unique accounts as in their parallel ones, insofar as these accounts reflect the same general character.[83]

This pattern offers a sort of default expectation in the Gospels as well: although multiple attestation is helpful, we need not approach even unique accounts (such as, for example, distinctly Lukan parables) with dismissive skepticism. Accounts in a writer who elsewhere normally depends on material the substance of which we can verify are themselves a form of evidence.

Limiting Bias[84]

Scholars have noted the encomiastic element in biography;[85] but just as Polybius warns against inappropriate praise or blame in historiography,[86] it seems appropriate to explore the typical limits of this in biographies, which often sought to balance praise and blame in what the biographer considered measures appropriate to the actual figure.[87] Even the oft-criticized Cornelius Nepos usually balances these features in his biographies.[88] Biographers could report unflattering accounts of individuals they generally respected.[89] Rhetorical conventions appeared in ancient biography, though more so in rhetorical biographers like Isocrates than others.[90]

---

[82] Thus, e.g., "Plutarch may indeed invent, reconstruct, and manipulate for literary reasons, to make his narrative effective or his characters convincing, but he is not inclined to make up stories of his own or to sacrifice what he himself believes to be the truth in matters of historical importance" (Hägg, *Biography*, 254, following Plutarch scholar Pelling, *Plutarch*, 143-70, 301-38).

[83] Origen recognized some adjustments of precision in the Gospels; see Origen *Comm. Jo.* 10.2, 4 (with the qualification in *Princ.* 4.3.4; both in Allison, *Constructing*, 445-46).

[84] In this section I am adapting Keener, *Acts*, 1:54-59, which in turn adapts and builds on Keener, *John*, 12-13, 15-16.

[85] Shuler, *Genre*; cf. Penner, *Praise*, 135; deeds in ancient encomia in Malina and Neyrey, *Portraits*, 28-33.

[86] Polybius 3.4.1; 8.8.3-6; 12.7.1; 10.21.8; cf. Hägg, *Biography*, 96-97. See also e.g., Dio Cass. 1.1.1-2; Pliny *Ep.* 5.8.9-11; Lucian *Hist.* 8-9, 39-40; comments about Suetonius in Rolfe, "Introduction," xix. Rhetorical interest did not eradicate the goal of historical truth; see Byrskog, *Story as History*, 213; Rothschild, *Rhetoric of History*, 88-91; Nicolai, "Place of History," 21.

[87] Polybius notes that the appropriate place to praise or blame people's character was only while recounting their behavior (10.26.9). Part of the point of history-writing, no less than biography, was honoring those who merit it, thus motivating meritorious acts (Pliny *Ep.* 5.8.1-2).

[88] Hägg, *Biography*, 189.

[89] E.g., Philost. *Vit. soph.* 2.21.603 (of his own teacher, 2.21.602); the biographer Eunapius *Lives* 461 (of Iamblichus, whom Eunapius considered supernatural, 459-61).

[90] See Burridge, "Biography." But biographies were rarely as partisan as forensic speech, where a primary object was legal victory (e.g., Dion. Hal. *Lysias* 8).

As Aune notes, "while biography tended to emphasize encomium, or the one-sided praise of the subject, it was still firmly rooted in historical fact rather than literary fiction."[91] Ancient historians such as Tacitus thus felt free to draw on biographies as well as annals and memoirs.[92]

Nor were biographies generally uncritical glorifications of their subjects, though partisanship was rife.[93] Honoring subjects could but need not produce distortion of what one did report.[94] Most biographers critiqued even their heroes' shortcomings,[95] and most biographies mixed some measure of praise and blame.[96] One could tell a less than flattering story even about one's own teacher, though apt to report especially favorable matters about him.[97] One could also criticize some activities of other figures one regarded highly.[98] Of course some teachers were regarded as exceptional, hence meriting unmixed praise; Xenophon has only good to report about Socrates (*Mem.* 4.8.11), and it is hardly likely that the Gospel writers would find flaws in one they worshiped (cf. later Iambl. *V.P.* passim). But normally disciples respected their teachers enough to preserve and transmit their teachers' views accurately, even when they disagreed with them, rather than to distort their teachers' views to fit their own.[99] We should not then expect the respect Jesus' disciples had for their teacher to lead them to fabricate his teachings.

Even in biographies, most writers felt free to record negative as well as positive features of their protagonists, when appropriate.[100] Thus, for example, while Suetonius' *Vespasian* is mostly adulatory (a striking contrast to his biographies of Caligula, Nero or Domitian), he reports his *pecuniae cupiditas*, love of money.[101]

---

[91] Aune, "Biography," 125. On its epideictic character, see e.g., Penner, *Praise*, 135; this was also true of Jewish apologetic historiography (Penner, *Praise*, 229-35).

[92] Hadas, "Introduction," xviii. Cicero already regarded history as arranging annals so as to teach public morals (Galinsky, "Introduction," 4, citing Cicero *De or.* 2.52).

[93] Ancients did, however, permit biography more freedom to be one-sided in praise than academic history; cf. Polyb. 10.21.8.

[94] Fornara, *Nature of History*, 64-65.

[95] E.g., Arrian *Alex.* 4.7.4; 4.8.1-4.9.6. For his moral purposes, Plutarch may employ stock character traits from comedy to critique his protagonists; see Xenophontos, "Comedy."

[96] E.g., Plut. *Cim.* 2.4-5; Corn. Nep. 11 (Iphicrates), 3.2; Suet. *Dom.* 3.2. For Plutarch, see Lavery, "*Lucullus.*"

[97] Philost. *Vit. soph.* 2.21.602-3. One might be thought biased when writing about close friends (Philost. *Vit. soph.* 2.33.628), but Tacitus wrote well of his father-in-law because he genuinely believed his virtues (Tac. *Agr.*). One pupil reportedly did omit *some* of his teacher's sayings, but because they were rhetorically inappropriate (Philost. *Vit. soph.* 2.29.621).

[98] Eunapius *Lives* 461 (on Iamblichus, who is supernatural in 459); Plut. *M. Cato* 5.1, 5; 12.4; for writers' style, Dion. Hal. *Thuc.* 1. One could also disagree with the dominant view of one's school (e.g., Sen. *Ep. Lucil.* 117.6).

[99] See e.g., Sen. *Ep. Lucil.* 108.17, 20, 22; 110.14, 20; Mus. Ruf. 1, 36.6-7.

[100] E.g., Arrian *Alex.* 4.7.4; 4.8.1-4.9.6; Plut. *Cim.* 2.4-5; Corn. Nep. 11 (Iphicrates), 3.2; much more fully, see Keener, *John*, 16 (cf. idem, *Matthew*, 51 n. 157).

[101] Likewise, Suet. *Jul.* 52 (like much of the work) is full of scandal about Julius, but 53 praises him. After recounting his noble deeds (e.g., *Jul.* 73—75), Suetonius concludes

He reports Nero's good deeds first "to separate them from his shameful and criminal deeds, of which I shall proceed now to give an account."[102] The character of Suetonius' differing treatment of different persons also indicates that he did not view his task as indiscriminate praise, but as of assigning praise and blame on what he viewed as the preponderance of positive and negative actions—that is, based on an interpretation of, rather than free creation of, information. Plutarch, too, knows how to criticize even his favorite figures at times.[103]

Ancients were well aware that their affection or respect for a person could bias their judgments, but they also recognized that such affection could be based on sound evaluations (Pliny *Ep.* 3.3.5). This is likely the case in Tacitus' encomiastic biography of his father-in-law Agricola;[104] certainly bias would influence presentation while praising an emperor's virtues, even if one avoided telling any untruths (e.g., Pliny *Ep.* 6.27.1-2).[105] Naturally one would omit negative perspectives if one genuinely viewed the protagonist favorably (mostly the case in Tacitus' *Agricola*) or even as divinely authoritative (the Gospels; later, Iamblichus *V.P.*). These emphases and omissions are normally cases of perspective, however, rather than of deliberate distortion. Historians themselves recognized the need for selectivity;[106] while this sometimes reflects what we would call bias,[107] it can also reflect their need to focus on the narratives' primary concerns.[108]

---

that his negative actions "so turn the scale, that it is thought that he abused his power and was justly slain" (76.1, LCL 1:99).

[102] Suet. *Nero* 19.3 (LCL 2:115).

[103] See e.g., Hägg, *Biography*, 260, 265, on Plutarch's *Cicero*.

[104] On the *Agricola*, see e.g., Hägg, *Biography*, 204-14, esp. 213 (following esp. Martin, "Tacitus on Agricola," 12; Hanson, "Agricola"): without distorting his historical core, Tacitus employs stock epideictic stereotypes to expand the account; archaeology confirms many of Tacitus's reports.

[105] The pre-Christian biography of Atticus by Nepos is also the biography of a friend whom the author knew personally (Hägg, *Biography*, 189-90).

[106] Historians themselves sometimes deemed selectivity a major distinction between "history" and "chronicles" (Whittaker, "Introduction," li-lii, citing Lucian *Hist.* 4-6, 27). Good historians should not focus on points they considered minor (Dion. Hal. *Thuc.* 13).

[107] Some accuse of bias, based on omissions, Xenophon (Brownson, "Introduction to *Anabasis*," ix-x; Brown, *Historians*, 95-97, though regarding Xenophon as otherwise mostly evenhanded, 93-94), Arrian (Baynham, "Quintus Curtius," 428), and Tacitus (Laistner, *Historians*, 132). For omissions, see e.g., Jos. *Life* 339; *Ag. Ap.* 1.60-66; Dio Cass. 1.1.1-2; for apologetic reasons, Josephus omits the golden calf (*Ant.* 3.79-99).

[108] Tacitus frankly admits that he does not treat all Senate business, but only that of moral value for his audience (Tac. *Ann.* 3.65). Polybius complains that some writers focus too much of their narrative on irrelevant matters (Polyb. 15.36.10); he insists that he must omit some matters about Roman customs (Polyb. 6.11.4-6), pleading with his critics that they should evaluate writers by what they recount, and assume that omissions are due to ignorance only when what they recount is found to contain errors (6.11.7-8). Historians did not regard it as a criticism when someone else testified to the accuracy of what they reported but offered to supply additional information (Jos. *Life* 365-67); sometimes hints of information suggest that a historian who omitted it did not lack the information itself (Whittaker, "Introduction," xlviii-lii, on Herodian).

Lucian writes that good biographers avoid flattery that falsifies events (*Hist.* 12) and criticizes historians who praise their own leaders while slandering the other side as engaging merely in panegyric (*Hist.* 7). Tacitus declares that history should cater to leaders neither by flattering nor by attacking them (*Hist.* 1.1).

Expectations of Accuracy

Historians claimed for themselves the objective of accuracy. Polybius argues that the goal of history is purely truth (34.4.2).[109] In the early empire, Tacitus warned against comparing his sober history with implausible rumors and fictions (*Ann.* 4.11). Likewise, even the most rhetorically lavish historians recognized that historical inquiry required not merely rhetorical skill but research,[110] and those thought guilty of inadequate research or firsthand acquaintance with their reports were likely to be doubted (Arrian *Ind.* 7.1). Dionysius of Halicarnassus warns that history involves truth rather than legends, and that one should pursue facts, "neither adding to nor subtracting from" them.[111] Herodian criticizes earlier historians for preferring rhetorical style to truth (1.1.1-2) and emphasizes that he never depended on unconfirmed information (1.1.3).[112]

Nor were historians themselves alone in this demand for correct information in historiography.[113] The satirist Lucian insists on accuracy in historiography (*Hist.* passim); only bad historians invent data (e.g., *Hist.* 24-25). Aristotle noted that the difference between "history" and "poetry" was not their literary style, for one could put Herodotus into verse if one wished; but that the former recounts what actually happened whereas the latter recounts what might happen.[114] Lucian opines that truth "is the one thing peculiar to history"; one writing history must ignore all other concerns (*Hist.* 40).[115]

In the imperial period the perspectives of Pliny the Younger, a public figure who never found leisure to write history yet valued it,[116] are informative. Ideal

---

[109] Saïd, "Myth," 85, notes Polybius' refusal to recount myth (see e.g., Polyb. 2.16.13-15; 4.40.2; 9.2.1; 12.24.5), though he reports critically some local legends connected with myth (4.43.6) and accepts some historical basis behind legends (34.2.4, 9-11). For further discussion of Polybius's high ideal standards, see Keener, *Acts*, 1:124-26.

[110] Dion. Hal. *Ant. rom.* 1.1.2-4; 1.4.2.

[111] Dion. Hal. *Thuc.* 8 (LCL 1:478-79); this is an ideal, not the writer's exceptionless practice.

[112] Herodian did not achieve this ideal (on his chronology, cf. e.g., Whittaker, "Introduction," xxxix-xl), but that it was in fact the ideal.

[113] Thucydides (a careful historian by our standards) remained a primary model (see Marincola, "Speeches," 123-27; Croke, "Historiography," 567-68; for rhetorical reasons, cf. Kennedy, "Source Criticism," 145-46).

[114] Arist. *Poet.* 9.2, 1451b; thus poetry is more philosophical, conveying general truths, whereas history conveys specific facts (9.3, 1451b). Cf. Pliny *Ep.* 9.33.1; Lucian *Hist.* 8. For history recounted in epic poetic form, as in Ennius' *Annales*, see Cic. *Leg.* 1.2.5 (Galinsky, "Introduction," 5).

[115] Trans. K. Kilburn, LCL 6:55.

[116] As is clear, for example, in his correspondence with Suetonius and especially Tacitus.

subjects for history offered original and interesting material, he opined, but only provided that the material was based on genuine facts (Pliny *Ep.* 8.4.1).[117] Historians used rhetorical principles, but in contrast to some other genres, history's *primary* goal was truth and accuracy rather than rhetorical display (Pliny *Ep.* 7.17.3), and accuracy was praiseworthy (Pliny *Ep.* 5.5.3; 5.8.5).[118] Historians would insist that their duty was to present facts accurately, though acknowledging that some individuals who were discussed in their histories viewed the facts (and the political perspectives informing their presentation) quite differently (Pliny *Ep.* 9.19.5).

A still later orator noted that poets have greater license to use myth and other such language, writing about the gods; historians and other writers of prose, however, must keep to their sources, writing about people.[119]

Expectations of Some Research[120]

For the Greeks the very term often used for research or investigation, ἱστορία (*historia*), left "no doubt possible about what was early considered the defining characteristic of the genre... the interrogation of witnesses and other informed parties" before weaving their responses into a cohesive narrative.[121] Herodotus initiated this emphasis on research (Hdt 1.1), traveling widely; Thucydides, who cross-examined his sources, assumed this approach as the standard (1.22.2; 5.26).[122] Diodorus Siculus claims to have visited the sites of his history in Asia and Europe, complaining that even some of the best historians err when they do not visit the sites in question (1.4.1).[123] Appian (*Hist. rom.* pref. 12) claims to have checked out his reports by traveling to Carthage, Spain, Sicily, Macedonia, and elsewhere. Likewise, the later historian Herodian insisted that he accepted nothing

---

[117] For the emphasis on facts in ancient historiography, see also Byrskog, *Story as History*, 179-84.

[118] Even rhetorical historians writing essays on earlier historians' rhetoric might emphasize the importance of truth-telling (Dion. Hal. *Thuc.* 55).

[119] Menander Rhetor 1.1.333.31—1.1.334.5.

[120] Adapted from Keener, *Acts*, 1:183-85.

[121] Fornara, *Nature of History*, 47. See also Aune, *Literary Environment*, 81-82, noting the interviewing of eyewitness (Polyb. 4.2.2); other sources, when traveling to the scenes in question (Hdt 2.52; Polyb. 3.48.12; 4.38.11; 10.11.4); and reading accounts of eyewitnesses (Polyb. 28.4.8; 38.4.8). The practice weighs more than the terminology; Schepens, "History," 39-40, notes this concept of *historia* (see also 47), but on 41-42 notes modern disagreements about it.

[122] Fornara, *Nature of History*, 47-48; Schepens, "History," 47-48. Thucydides notes that he procured (and investigated) reports of speeches from others who heard them (1.22.1-2), and sometimes had to evaluate conflicting claims of eyewitnesses (1.22.2-3).

[123] He also claims to have consulted records (1.4.4-5). While granting Diodorus' travels to some locations, Oldfather, "Introduction," xiii, doubts that Diodorus visited either Mesopotamia or Athens (though his argument regarding Athens is from silence).

secondhand without tracking down all the facts (1.1.3). Although most of Philostratus' sophistic subjects were long deceased, he interviewed some who lived, even on multiple occasions (*Vit. soph.* 2.23.606).[124]

Polybius avers that investigation is "the *most* important part" of writing history (12.4c.3).[125] His proposed method for conducting investigation, given the limitations of space and time, was to interview people, critically evaluate reports, and accept the most reliable sources (12.4c.4-5).[126] He severely criticizes Timaeus for neglecting travel to the locations about which he writes (12.25e.1), complaining that written sources alone are not sufficient (12.25e.7) or even the most critical part of historical study (12.25i.2). While interviews were impossible when dealing with the distant past,[127] writers preferred them when living witnesses remained available.[128] Greek historians often traveled to the locations of events and consulted those considered reliable oral sources.[129] Condemning writers who sought to make guesses sound plausible, Polybius noted that in his research he had also come across documentary evidence.[130] Probability is one helpful test, but visiting a location and interviewing witnesses there is much better (Polyb. 12.9.2).[131]

Greek historians had their weaknesses, but primary research was one of their strengths.[132] In practice, not all historians in this period traveled.[133] Romans focused on Roman history, most of which was available locally through armies and legates sending word back to the senate. Thus Roman historians sometimes

---

[124] On other occasions his research came up empty, but he incidentally confirms that he had done some (*Vit. soph.* 2.5.576).

[125] LCL 4:316-17. Polybius' emphasis on investigation appears throughout 12.4c.1-5.

[126] It was possible, however, to visit places, consult witnesses, and still prove mistaken (Polyb. 12.4d.1-2, on Timaeus). Like a historian researching recent events, a prosecutor preparing a case would do research, such as tracking down eyewitnesses (e.g., Lysias *Or.* 23.2-8, §§166-67).

[127] Even here, ancients sometimes found local oral sources that purported to have survived over the centuries (e.g., Paus. 1.23.2). Scholars today often question the local oral information from a much earlier period, however (Pretzler, "Pausanias and Tradition").

[128] E.g., Philost. *Vit. soph.* 2.23.606 (who unsuccessfully tried to evaluate conflicting reports this way in 2.5.576), in contrast to his lack of interviews for earlier information.

[129] Aune, *Literary Environment*, 81, citing Hdt 2.52; Polyb. 3.48.12; 4.38.11; 10.11.4; for travel research, see also Diod. Sic. 1.4.1 (though he certainly did not visit Nineveh).

[130] Polyb. 3.33.17-18 (citing here a bronze tablet of Hannibal).

[131] Also Plut. *Demosth.* 2.1-2.

[132] Meister, "Historiography: Greece," 421. For the preference for oral sources, see also the discussion in Aune, *Literary Environment*, 81.

[133] Consulting distant records would be even more difficult (cf. Ben Zeev, "Capitol"), though this is different from consulting people orally when one traveled to a region.

simply collected information without field research;[134] they nevertheless expected accuracy in their writing.[135]

Historical Reports used Sources

Although many (and for the first case, all) of the sources for the Gospels were surely oral, the ancient penchant for using sources offers another reminder that writers on historical subjects did not simply fabricate their stories. In contrast to the limited resources we have today for reconstructing history in the early empire, enterprising biographers and historians of that era normally had a plethora of available sources, often both written and oral, from which to draw. Thus the limited extant first-century sources available today should not be used to judge what sources ancient writers typically had available.[136]

Historians and biographers frequently had multiple sources available,[137] and modern historians sometimes try to reconstruct what these were.[138] Although for reasons of style, historians did not acknowledge all their sources,[139] historians often felt constrained to indicate some of them,[140] especially if they depended on written sources and wrote for upper class readers who might have access to these various works. One could establish one's point better by naming various earlier sources supporting it (Suet. *Jul.* 9.3). A historical writer who does not include everything that has been written might need to explain that he had in fact read almost everything but did not judge it all suitable for inclusion (Dio Cass. 1.1.1-2).

That ancient historians, biographers and anthologists depended on earlier sources is not in question; both biblical[141] and Greco-Roman traditions[142] frequently cite them. They often cite varying accounts, even when preferring one

---

[134] Fornara, *Nature of History*, 56. Second-century sources (Aul. Gel. 11.17; 13.20.1; Fronto *Ep. M. Caes.* 4.5) might suggest that in libraries slaves brought books to the scholars, rather than scholars having to search for the works themselves (Houston, "Library"). Apart from Athens (Aul. Gel. 7.17.1-2), Rome, (later) Ephesus, and (earlier) Alexandria (e.g., Aul. Gel. 7.17.3), however, the majority of libraries were private ones (Aune, *Dictionary*, 273-75). By its nature, historical writing about earlier (rather than more recent) events necessarily depended on earlier historians (Pliny *Ep.* 5.8.12).

[135] Fornara, *Nature of History*, 61, citing Suet. *Caesar* 56.

[136] This section is borrowed and adapted from Keener, *Acts*, 1:170-73.

[137] For Livy, despite him following esp. Polybius, see Évrard, "Polybe."

[138] E.g., Martin, "Tacitus," 1470; Rondholz, "Crossing"; Muntz, "Sources"; Muntz, "Diodorus Siculus."

[139] Laistner, *Historians*, 51, 86.

[140] Dion. Hal. *Ant. rom.* 1.1.1; see Keener, *John*, 22-23; for historians ideally using sources, see also Marguerat, *Histoire*, 30.

[141] E.g., Num 21:14; Josh 10:13; 2 Sam 1:18; 1 Kgs 14:19, 29; 15:7, 23, 31; 1 Chron 27:24; 29:29; 2 Chron 16:11; 20:34; 24:27; 2 Macc. 2:24-25.

[142] E.g., Dion. Hal. *Ant. rom.* 1.6.1; Arrian *Alex.* 6.2.4; Plut. *Alex.* 30.7; 31.2-3; 38.4; and further below. Cf. Cook, "Plutarch's Use," for a suggested stylistic source indicator in Plutarch; for Plutarch's range of sources, see Rhodes, "Documents," 65-66.

above another.[143] Arrian prefers above other sources his two earliest ones, which often agree, and he chooses between them when they diverge;[144] when sources diverge too much he frankly complains that the exact truth is unrecoverable.[145] Likewise Philostratus notes a point where his sources diverge, and his research provided no definitive resolution of which was most accurate;[146] his concern in wanting to resolve this question was thus historical accuracy. At one point Plutarch names five sources for a "majority" position and nine for a minority one,[148] plus an extant letter attributed to the person about whom he writes; but then adds that the minor divergence does not affect our view of his hero's character (the main point for him; *Alex.* 46.1-2).[149]

The Gospels do not identify specific sources for the gospel tradition, but merely surveying a synopsis of the Gospels shows that this lack of explicit identification cannot mean that they lacked sources. The Gospel writers' reticence to name sources might follow some Jewish conventions on this point; in some such works we can identify the sources only because they are extant.[150] The more popular audience anticipated might be a more important factor, since popular works of various genres were less likely to cite sources, even when they clearly depended on them. Earlier exaggerated contrasts between elite and popular literature aside,[151] the Gospels do not reflect an elite audience (though Luke's audience appears socially higher than the others').

---

[143] E.g., Dion. Hal. *Ant. rom.* 1.87.4; 3.35.1-4; 8.79.1; Livy 9.44.6; 23.19.17; 25.17.1-6; Appian *Hist. rom.* 11.9.56; 12.1.1; Plut. *Alex.* 31.3; 38.4; *Demosth.* 5.5; 29.4-30.4; *Themist.* 25.1-2; 27.1; 32.3-4; Apollod. *Bib.* 1.4.3; 1.5.2; 1.9.15, 19; 2.3.1; 2.5.11; Ovid *Fasti* 6.1-2, 97-100; Philost. *Vit. soph.* 2.4.570; Paus. 2.5.5; 2.26.3-7; Arrian *Alex.* 4.9.2-3; 4.14.1-4; 5.3.1; 5.14.4; 7.14.2; 7.27.1-3; Hdn 7.9.4; 7.9.9; Corn. Nep. 7 (Alcibiades), 11.1; 9 (Conon), 5.4; *p. Sot.* 9:13, §2; see further Livy LCL 12:320 n. 2.

[144] Arrian *Alex.* 1, *pref.* 1-2.

[145] Arrian *Alex.* 3.3.6.

[146] Philost. *Vit. soph.* 2.5.576.

[148] I.e., thereby implying for the majority position far more than the five sources he has named. On the multiplicity of first-generation Alexander accounts, now lost, see Zambrini, "Historians."

[149] Valerius Maximus, a more popular and less careful writer than some others, rarely cites his sources (and often confuses his data), but he mentions them occasionally when they diverge (e.g., 5.7.ext. 1; 6.8.3). Occasionally historians also found ways to harmonize traditions (Diod. Sic. 4.4.1-5). Sometimes they probably have smoothed out contradictions in their sources in their own rewriting; Damon, "Source to *sermo*," suggests this approach with respect to Livy 34.54.4-8 and Tacitus *Ann.* Bks. 1, 14.

[150] E.g., 1 Esdras blends Chronicles, Ezra, and Nehemiah with some midrash (if the latter designation is not too anachronistic). Josephus does not state most of his extrabiblical sources (Nicolas of Damascus being an important exception); even Livy can mention that there are many while citing only one (Livy 42.11.1).

[151] Schmidt, "Die Stellung der Evangelien"; Kümmel, *Introduction*, 37; see discussion in Keener, *Matthew*, 17. "High" literature influenced "low" literature, creating an overlap of style (Burridge, *Gospels?* (1992), 11, 153; Aune, *Literary Environment*, 12, 63; Downing, "A Bas Les Aristos").

Their failure to mention sources might also be partly because sources have not yet diverged widely regarding these events of a recent generation. Although writers often cited eyewitnesses when this might add authority to their claims, recent eyewitness or oral sources did not always require documentation.[152] Moreover, ancient historians most often mentioned their sources only when they conflicted or the author disagreed or was unsure about their reliability[153] or about which sources were best.[154]

Such conflicts arose more often when treating events of the more remote past than when treating the present, making citation of present sources rarer. Thus Polybius feels compelled to explicitly explain why he himself depends on Aratus rather than the often contradictory accounts of his contemporary Phylarchus (2.56.1-2), whom he contends "makes many random and careless statements" (2.56.3). A historian might also more generally refer readers interested in more detail to "other historians" (e.g., Vell. Paterc. 2.48.5), not unlike Luke's oblique reference to other authors in Luke 1:1.

Because most ancient material is no longer extant, we need not presume fabrication when an ancient writer includes material missing from earlier now-surviving sources. Even aside from our inability to check all extant writers' sources, a writer providing information missing in some earlier historians sometimes was drawing from sources unavailable to those other historians, whether the sources were written, oral, or both.[155] Moreover, even writers who preserved their sources redacted them, even in the case of sacred cultural texts[156] and philosophic works.[157] Less persuasively, yet worthy of consideration, some scholars argue that such changes were more common at the written than the oral level,[158] perhaps because the former reflected literary urban culture and the latter more traditional society.

---

[152] Cf. e.g., Tacitus, who naturally does not need to cite many sources on his father-in-law *Agricola*.

[153] See Hemer, *Acts in History*, 65; cf. Laistner, *Historians*, 120, 127. Livy cites many sources (Laistner, *Historians*, 84), and cites a major source, Quadrigarius, especially where his account varies from Livy's (Forsythe, "Quadrigarius," 391), hence may follow him at other times without citing him. See e.g., Val. Max. 5.7.ext. 1; 6.8.3; Tac. *Ann*. 2.73, 88; 4.57; 13.20.

[154] E.g., Philost. *Vit. soph*. 2.4.570; note examples above.

[155] E.g., Dion. Hal. *Ant. rom*. 1.6.1, 3; sometimes earlier oral traditions probably also surface later in rabbinic literature (see e.g., Keener, *John*, 189-90). Oral and written traditions sometimes overlapped (Jeremias, "Pap. Egerton," 1:95). The vast majority of ancient histories (on which extant ancient historians could have also depended) have since perished (cf. Laistner, *Historians*, 5-6; Brown, *Historians*, 107).

[156] E.g., Cic. *Nat. d*. 3.16.42 (concerning Hom. *Od*. 11.600ff; see especially Cicero [trans. Rackham], LCL 19:324-25, n. a); Diog. Laert. 1.48 (Solon into Hom. *Il*. 2.557).

[157] Possibly Hierocles in Stobaeus; Malherbe, *Exhortation*, 85. Jewish scribes, however, rarely practiced redaction criticism on Scripture (despite an occasional fourth-century Palestinian Amora; cf. *Lev. Rab*. 6:6; 15:2).

[158] Gundry, "Genre," 102; Witherington, *Christology*, 22; contrast the older approach of Dibelius, *Tradition*, 3.

Both when historical writers cited sources explicitly and when they did not, the ideal required making use of them. Polybius complains that Timaeus failed to make appropriate use of earlier historians' works, though living in Athens provided him access to them (12.25d.1);[159] this complaint reinforces the picture that many sources were available and that good historians expected other good historians to consult them when possible.[160]

We should not underestimate the research sources available to ancient writers, especially if (as in Luke 1:1) they sometimes mention the existence of such works.[161] Clearly an abundance of contemporary sources existed then that are no longer extant (cf. the many contemporary histories of Nero noted in Jos. *Ant.* 20.154); for example, Pliny, explaining that he could not survey everything (*N.H.* pref. 18), notes that he surveyed about two thousand volumes (though using especially a hundred), and supplemented them with other data (*N.H.* pref. 17). Few of his sources remain extant, but we can appreciate Pliny's preservation of much of the content. Tacitus omits reporting most of Seneca's dying words, recorded by the latter's secretaries, simply because in Tacitus' day they remained too well-known to merit repetition in his work (*Ann.* 15.63).[162]

Critical Use of Historical Sources[163]

Nor were historians necessarily uncritical with their sources. Accuracy of one's sources, unimportant in some genres, was known to be a concern of historians (Pliny *Ep.* 9.33.1). Thus, for example, Plutarch disputes a claim of Herodotus (Hdt 9.85) based on the numbers and an extant inscription (*Arist.* 19.5-6). Elsewhere he tries to distinguish more accurate from less accurate sources based on reason (Plut. *Them.* 25.1-2),[164] or questions a later source including information missing in an allegedly primary source (Plut. *Alex.* 20.4-5).

---

[159] For comment on this passage, see also Byrskog, *Story as History*, 117. For Polybius' use of documents, see Rhodes, "Documents," 64-65.

[160] For Polybius, real history requires a study of documents, though this must take a third place after visiting the locations in question and reviewing their historical context (12.25e.1, 25i.2).

[161] Luke may, however, imply his personal knowledge superior to investigation, namely, his thorough acquaintance with the matters because of his long-term involvement with the Jesus movement (see discussion of Luke's and other historians' use of *parakoloutheô* in Moessner, "Poetics"; "Prologues").

[162] For Tacitus using sources (and using them fairly critically), see Laistner, *Historians*, 121; for historians' use of documents (legal documents, inscriptions and the like), see Rhodes, "Documents" (though they did not always cite them; Laistner, *Historians*, 51).

[163] Borrowed from Keener, *Acts*, 1:122-24.

[164] Cf. also Philost. *Vit. soph.* 1.21.516.

Dionysius of Halicarnassus,¹⁶⁵ himself a rhetorician, critiques Thucydides' failure to achieve the expected standard of historical accuracy; "art," the rhetorician opines, "does not excuse history from such exaggeration."¹⁶⁶ Yet Thucydides himself, today usually respected as among the most accurate of ancient historians,¹⁶⁷ was hardly oblivious to the need for critical evaluation. Thucydides (1.3.2-3) recognizes that Greeks were not called "Hellenes" before the Trojan War, since Homer, writing long after that war, does not yet use the term.¹⁶⁸ He refused to dismiss Mycenae's past splendor based on limited remains in his day, noting that cities of his own day might hold power without impressive physical structures (Thucyd. 1.10.1-2).¹⁶⁹

Based on historical plausibility, the Jewish historian Josephus similarly argues against various claims (*Ant.* 19.68, 106-7). When a distinction between accurate and inaccurate sources proved impossible, writers often simply presented several different current opinions on what had happened.¹⁷⁰

Sometimes writers employed a criterion of coherency with other evidence,¹⁷¹ such as known customs of a report's day;¹⁷² other historical context¹⁷³ (including chronological data);¹⁷⁴ coherence with documentary sources;¹⁷⁵ consistency of reported behavior with a person's other known behavior (something like form critics' criterion of coherence);¹⁷⁶ or even material remains.¹⁷⁷ Following the probability argument standard in the law courts,¹⁷⁸ Dionysius of Halicarnassus

---

¹⁶⁵ He could regard as inauthentic speeches that reflected conditions unrelated to the alleged author's time (here, "before his prime")—e.g., Dion. Hal. *Din.* 11. He used stylistic criteria to evaluate authenticity, when other factors were not compelling (*Lysias* 11; cf. *Demosth.* 57).

¹⁶⁶ Dion. Hal. *Thuc.* 19 (LCL 1:512f); see Thucyd. 1.1.1-2; 1.21.2; 1.23.1-2.

¹⁶⁷ See e.g., Wade-Gery, "Thucydides," though cf. Brown, *Historians*, 49. In antiquity, see e.g., Dion. Hal. *Thuc.* 34; Jos. *Ag. Ap.* 1.18; Dio Chrys. *Or.* 18.10.

¹⁶⁸ Cf. similar evaluation of ancient contexts in Thucyd. 1.3.3; Vell. Paterc. 1.3.2-3; also Theopompus in Rhodes, "Documents," 62.

¹⁶⁹ Rulers also favored property claims that could appeal to ancient inscriptions and poetry (Tac. *Ann.* 4.43).

¹⁷⁰ E.g., Diog. Laert. 1.23: "But according to others"; 6.1.13; 8.2.67-72; Vell. Paterc. 2.4.6; 2.27.5; 2.48.4; Plut. *Lyc.* 1.1; Tac. *Ann.* 2.67; 3.16, 18; 4.10; 14.51 (though happy to report negative views of Nero), 58-59; 15.38, 54; 16.3, 6 (though expressing his view); Philost. *Vit. soph.* 1.21.516; 2.5.576; *p. Sot.* 9:13, §2.

¹⁷¹ Polyb. 3.32.4.

¹⁷² Dion. Hal. *Ant. rom.* 9.22.1-5.

¹⁷³ Polyb. 3.20.1-5; 3.32.5. Polybius insisted on providing the longest-range historical context possible, both early (3.6.1—3.7.3, e.g., 3.6.10) and subsequent (9.2.5).

¹⁷⁴ Plut. *Themist.* 27.1, though admitting uncertainty. Thucydides sought to take into account the relative dates of his sources (1.3.2-3); cf. Tac. *Dial.* 16.

¹⁷⁵ Polyb. 3.33.18; Plut. *Alex.* 46.2; *Demosth.* 5.5; Philost. *Vit. soph.* 2.1.562-63.

¹⁷⁶ Arrian *Alex.* 7.14.4-6; Dio Cass. 62.11.3-4; cf. Athen. *Deipn.* 5.215-16, 219ab. The same criterion could apply, however, in fictitious composition or historical reconstruction based on plausibility (cf. Arist. *Poet.* 15.4-5, 1454a; Theon *Progymn.* 1.46-52; 2.79-81; 8.2-3).

¹⁷⁷ As noted above, Thucyd. 1.10.1-2, evaluating the *Iliad*.

¹⁷⁸ See sources and discussion in Keener, *Acts*, 4:3503-4.

challenges an event recounted in earlier histories because of intrinsic improbabilities in their accounts.[179] Arrian often evaluates various reports by comparing them; he notes that one story too prominent to ignore is not reported by any of the eyewitness writers, hence is likely unreliable.[180]

Even Herodotus' methodology of reporting a range of sources without evaluating their accuracy[181] did not thereby assume or pronounce judgment in their favor, provided the audience would be duly warned to, or would understand that they were obligated to, make their own decisions. Sometimes they simply repeated apparently incredible information and warned readers to use discretion.[182] Thus Lucian advises that the historian should report a myth found in one's source without committing oneself to it; "make it known for your audience to make of it what they will—you run no risk and lean to neither side."[183]

Preference for Sources closer to the events[184]

One aspect of ancient historians' caution was concern for earlier sources. Ancient as well as modern historians valued firsthand sources most highly (all other factors being equal), and after that those closest in date to the events reported.[185] Ancient historians, like their modern successors, generally preferred writers closer in time to the events reported rather than later sources.[186] Ancient biographers were especially happy, when reporting fairly recent events, to include oral tradition from eyewitnesses.[187] The second best source after the author being an eyewitness was the author's use of eyewitnesses;[188] eyewitnesses who participated in

---

[179] Dion. Hal. *Ant. rom.* 4.6.1. Cf. also Tac. *Ann.* 15.53; 16.6; Paus. 9.31.7; Plut. *Isis* 8, *Mor.* 353F; and Theon's reasons for thinking the account of Medea murdering her children implausible (*Progymn.* 5.487-501; cf. 3.241-76, 4.112-16, 126-34).

[180] Arrian *Alex.* 6.28.2. Hearsay without eyewitness testimony is much less credible (Arrian *Ind.* 15.7). Arrian does exhibit pro-Alexander bias (Bosworth, "Pursuit," 447; Baynham, "Quintus Curtius," 428), though it can be overstated (Bosworth, "Pursuit," 452-53).

[181] See Meister, "Herodotus," 268, on Hdt 7.152.

[182] E.g., Livy 4.29.5-6; 23.47.8; cf. (more skeptically) Lucian *Hist.* 60.

[183] *Hist.* 60 (trans. K. Kilburn, LCL 6:71).

[184] Adapted from Keener, *Acts*, 1:127-31.

[185] E.g., Tac. *Ann.* 15.73 (citing sources of the time described). Historical distance multiplies the possibility of gratuitous errors (as in 4 Macc 4:15). Of course, modern historians also prefer reports closer in time to the events recounted (e.g., Robeck, *Mission*, 293-94, 296).

[186] E.g., Livy 7.6.6; 25.11.20; Plut. *Mal. Hdt.* 20, *Mor.* 859B.

[187] E.g., Xen. *Apol.* 2; *Ages.* 3.1; Dion. Hal. *Thuc.* 7; Corn. Nep. 23 (Hannibal), 13.3; 25 (Atticus), 13.7; 17.1; Plut. *Demosth.* 11.1; *Otho* 14.1; Suetonius *Otho* 10.1; *Vesp.* 1.4; Arrian *Alex.* 1, pref. 2-3; 6.11.8. Aune, *Literary Environment*, 81, cites for this practice also in Hdt 2.99; Polyb. 12.27.1-6; 20.12.8; Lucian *Hist.* 47 (and Polybius' somewhat self-serving view that participants made the best historians—3.4.13; 12.25g.1; 12.28.1-5); cf. Alexander, *Preface*, 34. Historians today are apt to trust eyewitness knowledge even in otherwise questionable ancient historians (e.g., Brown, *Historians*, 142, 146; in more recent history, see e.g., Wigger, *Saint*, 363).

[188] Jervell, "Future," 118.

events were considered ideal.[189] Josephus concurs with Gentile historians in preferring this practice.[190] Of course, whether due to bias[191] or memory lapse,[192] even eyewitnesses did not always agree on details, requiring some weighing of individual testimony.[193] (Among logical principles deemed useful then as today, witnesses were considered most dependable shortly after the events they purported to attest.)[194]

Because oral traditions were most reliable in the generation they recounted, Greek historians liked to travel to compile oral sources in the generation of the current events they reported. Thus "the historians of each generation establish the record of their own time" most effectively.[195] Nevertheless, sources that were committed to writing often held a special authority;[196] even an eyewitness might even cite another eyewitness source written before his own work had been committed to writing.[197] Writers often recognized that whereas oral tradition could be modified over time, written sources were fixed.[198]

Josephus emphasizes that he wrote his autobiography while witnesses remained alive who could verify or falsify his claims (*Ant.* 20.266), and complains that Justus, one of his rivals, waited twenty years to publish, till after the eyewitnesses were dead (Jos. *Life* 359-60).[199] Josephus contends that Justus should be

---

[189] Byrskog, *Story as History*, 153-57.

[190] See Jos. *Life* 357; *Ag. Ap.* 1.45-49, 56; *War* 1.2-3.

[191] Byrskog, *Story as History*, 176-79, notes that ancient historians were aware that eyewitnesses could be biased, and tried to take this into account (sometimes through the grid of their own biases).

[192] Cf. more recently e.g., divergent versions of the same event in 1980 (differing in details while communicating the basic substance) evaluated in Jackson, *Quest*, 72-74.

[193] Thucyd. 1.22.3. For gist generally being reliable in memory even where details are not, see Bauckham, *Eyewitnesses*, 333-34 (citing psychological memory studies). Historians themselves often quoted their sources from memory, hence could get correct the gist while being confused on some details (Marincola, "Introduction," 2).

[194] In a forensic setting, see e.g., Lysias *Or.* 20.22, §160.

[195] Fornara, *Nature of History*, 48. For accuracy in certain kinds of ancient Mediterranean oral traditioning over the span of one or two generations, see Keener, *Matthew*, 27-30; idem, *John*, 54-65; idem, *Historical Jesus*, 139-61; but for failure to learn accurately from purported travels, see Strabo 2.5.10; Hengel, "Geography," 31.

[196] Eunapius *Lives* 460. Suetonius depends more heavily on older written records than interviews of more recent persons (Rolfe, "Introduction," xviii). The Greek method preferred interviews, but even Romans could write about contemporary figures (e.g., Pliny *Ep.* 9.19.5); even some Greek writers like Ephorus and Timaeus critically emphasized written sources, though Polybius appreciated the former and attacked the latter (Schepens, "History," 50-51).

[197] Xen. *Hell.* 3.1.2; those who attribute the Gospel of Matthew to one of the Twelve yet accept its dependence on Mark (like R. Gundry; see his *Matthew*, 609-22) could adduce that case as a further example.

[198] Eunapius *Lives* 453; for anthropological observations consistent with this practice, see Lord, *Singer*, 138.

[199] Criticizing someone should best be done while they remain alive or, if they have died, only shortly afterward (Pliny *Ep.* 9.1.3-4).

less believable than himself, given that Josephus's work was known to the eyewitnesses and never contradicted by them (Jos. *Life* 361-66).[200]

Josephus condemns Greek historians willing to write about events where they were neither present nor dependent on those with firsthand knowledge (Jos. *Ag. Ap.* 1.45). Some, he complained, wrote about the war without having been there, which was inadequate research for appropriate histories (1.46).[201] By contrast, Josephus says, he was present (1.47) and he alone understood the Jewish refugees and wrote the information down (1.49); his accusers did not *know* the Jewish side of the story (1.56). Justus was not present when the events he describes took place in Galilee, and those who could have supplied Justus with such information perished in the siege of Jerusalem (Jos. *Life* 357).[202]

I have frequently noted above that the Gospels treat events that, by the standards of ancient biography and historiography, were fairly recent. The distinction I have made between writers concerning events within living memory and those concerning much earlier information is one that was not lost on ancient historiography. Ancient historians were less accurate when they wrote about people of the distant past than when they wrote about recent events,[203] and they were themselves aware of this difference.[204] Many ancient writers pointed out the obscurity of reports from centuries earlier, expecting a much higher standard of accuracy when handling reports closer to their own period.[205]

---

[200] This also suggests that if Josephus embellished his story with some details, the eyewitnesses accepted that embellishment as relatively minor, fitting acceptable historical canons. Undoubtedly the portrayal was also not to their detriment; Josephus was careful to praise surviving political figures like Agrippa and any member of the Flavian dynasty.

[201] Naturally, Josephus would be happy to enforce a criterion that excluded his competitors but not himself. Yet Josephus hardly invented this criterion, useful as it proved in his case (for his *War* and *Life* more than his *Antiquities*).

[202] Josephus is not above depicting a scene, such as the suicide of the Sicarii at Masada (see discussions in e.g., Ladouceur, "Masada"; Ladouceur, "Josephus"; Cohen, "Masada"; Cohen, "What Happened?"; Luz, "Masada"; Bauernfeind and Michel, "Beiden Eleazarreden"; Bünker, "Disposition der Eleazarreden"), where he lacks potential eyewitnesses (unless we think of the two women who survived), though if challenged he might have protested that this represented a special scene rather than a consistent pattern.

[203] See e.g., Mosley, "Reporting," 26.

[204] E.g., Diod. Sic. 1.6.2. See further Kennedy, "Source Criticism," 139 on the mythical character of "early history," citing Quint. *Inst.* 2.4.18-19 and Livy's repeated qualifications in his first ten books.

[205] E.g., Thucyd. 1.21.1; Livy 6.1.2-3; 7.6.6; Diod. Sic. 1.6.2; 1.9.2; 4.1.1; 4.8.3-5; Dion. Hal. *Ant. rom.* 1.12.3; *Thuc.* 5; Paus. 9.31.7; Jos. *Ag. Ap.* 1.15, 24-25, 58; cf. Bowersock, *Fiction as History*, 1-2. Some also considered the earlier period qualitatively different because of divine activities (Hesiod *W.D.* 158-60, 165; Arrian *Alex.* 5.1.2); by contrast, others mistrusted its reports precisely because of such unusual events (Thucyd. 1.23.3).

Introduction 29

Most ancient historians recognized that the earliest period was shrouded in myth,[206] even if they sometimes found the myths' basic outline acceptable.[207] They were also aware that propaganda helped create legend (Arrian *Alex*. 4.28.1-2). When writing about characters of the distant past, then, historians would have to sort through legendary as well as actual historical data,[208] and might well have difficulty ascertaining which was which.[209] Sometimes they sought to "demythologize" their reports.[210] When depending on historically remote sources, historians sometimes thus had to settle for historical verisimilitude, rather than high probability concerning the events that ancient historians reported.[211]

Ancient Biography's Distinction from Historiography and Modern Biography

Biographies were meant to be historical, but they differed from the genre of multivolume histories. First-century historiography often focused on notable individuals,[212] but biography focused on a single character whereas history included a broader range of characters and events.[213] History thus contained many biographic elements, but normally lacked the focus on a single person and displayed less emphasis on characterization.[214] Nevertheless, characterization does appear in histories,[215] and even a single biographer such as Plutarch could hold both static

---

[206] Dion. Hal. *Thuc*. 5-7; cf. Plut. *Thes*. 1.3; Keener, *John*, 20. At least the early period was regarded as unusual (Thucyd. 1.23.3).

[207] E.g., Thucyd. 1.21.1 (complaining in 1.21.2 that people make ancient events greater than they were); again, see Keener, *John*, 20.

[208] They often tried to distinguish between accurate and inaccurate sources, when a consensus view was available (cf. Livy 1.1.1). Interestingly, archaeology occasionally and incidentally confirms even some information behind etiological explanations once deemed mythical; see e.g., Egelhaaf-Gaiser, "Sites," 212.

[209] Historians might recognize exaggerations in an account, while averring that genuine historical tradition stood behind it (Livy 3.8.10), or might regard an account as too implausible altogether (Aul. Gel. 10.12.8-10). Some sources, like the *Life of Aesop*, may simply string together all available popular traditions into a narrative; these traditions had grown over six centuries (see Drury, *Design*, 28-29).

[210] See e.g., Thucyd. 1.21.1-2; Dion. Hal. *Ant. rom*. 1.39.1; 1.41.1 (cf. Dion. Hal. *Ant. rom*. 1.84.4); Dion. Hal. *Thuc*. 6; Plut. *Thes*. 1.3; Arrian *Alex*. 2.16.6; Philost. *Vit. soph*. 2.1.554. See also examples in Saïd, "Myth," 81-88.

[211] See Dio Cass. 62.11.3-4; Aune, *Literary Environment*, 83; Fornara, *Nature of History*, 134-36.

[212] Fornara, *Nature of History*, 34-36, 116.

[213] Lucian *Hist*. 7; also Witherington, *Sage*, 339, citing Plut. *Alex*. 1.1-2.

[214] See Fornara, *Nature of History*, 185. For characterization in biography, see e.g., Hägg, *Biography*, 5-6, 11-15, 23, 27-30, 45, 89.

[215] Pitcher, "Characterization," esp. 103-4, 106, 117, though sometimes indirectly (105, 107-10), through actions and words (110-12; speeches in Marincola, "Speeches," 119) or other characters' observations (Pitcher, "Characterization," 107-8). Likewise, character development does appear in history (e.g., Pitcher, "Characterization," 115-17; see also e.g., Vell. Paterc. 2.18.5; 2.25.3; 2.28.2; Tac. *Ann*. 4.54; 6.51; cf. Hadas, "Introduction," xiv-xv). See now esp. Ash, Mossman, and Titchener, *Fame*.

and developmental approaches to character simultaneously.[216] Biographies were less exhaustive, focusing more on the models of character they provided (Plut. *Alex.* 1.1-3).[217] Histories also elaborated speeches in a way that biographies did not.[218]

Although ancient biographies influenced their modern namesakes,[219] they also differed from them. For example, they often began in their subject's adulthood[220] and were not constrained by chronological sequence.[221] Topical arrangements were not uncommon; Suetonius, for example, is often noted for this.[222] (Matthew is arranged topically; Luke follows Mark's sequence more closely.[223] But Jewish interpreters sometimes even doubted whether the biblical story of Moses was fully chronological.)[224] Historians, by contrast, while not able to reproduce sequence at all points, laid a greater emphasis on chronology. That Luke usually follows Mark's sequence (except at rare, key points like his programmatic reworking of the Nazareth synagogue scene) might suggest that Luke views his biography of Jesus as part of his larger project of writing a history.

---

[216] See Duff, "Models," though attributing one to his philosophic and the other to his biographic approach.

[217] For character traits in biographies, see e.g., Corn. Nep. 4 (Pausanias), 1.1; Feldman, "Jehoram." Sometimes biographers wrote for more leisurely, less technical audiences; see e.g., Corn. Nep. 16 (Pelopidas), 1.1.

[218] See Keener, *Acts*, 1:271-304. Hägg, *Biography*, 209, notes that Tacitus's inclusion of speeches in the *Agricola* resembles historiography.

[219] Despite differences, ancient biography influenced modern forms (see e.g., Mossman, "Plutarch and Biography"). For classical influence more generally on English literature, see esp. Copeland, *History*.

[220] E.g., many political biographies (such as Plut. *Caes.* 1.1-4); the *Life of Aesop* (Drury, *Design*, 29); or Mark or (after his prologue) John.

[221] See e.g., Thorburn, "Tiberius." Cf. e.g., the accidental repetition in Plut. *Alex.* 37.4; 56.1. This contrasts with the more chronological practice of historians (e.g., Thucyd. 2.1.1; 5.26.1), although even most historians tended to follow events to their conclusion and not simply strict chronology (Dion. Hal. *Thuc.* 9; *Pomp.* 3) and some offered topical digressions (Velleius Paterculus 1.14.1; 2.38.1—2.40.1; esp. 2.59.1); the writer of 4 Macc is aware that the mother's speech should occur at a certain point in his narrative, and says so (4 Macc 12:7; cf. 2 Macc 7), but chooses to recount it later. Ancients themselves recognized that recollections were often random (Sen. *Controv.* 1.pref.4).

[222] Cf. topical arrangement of anecdotes earlier in Valerius Maximus (Rüpke, "Knowledge," 89, 93). Topical arrangement suited episodic narratives about a person (Hemer, *Acts in History*, 74); topical forms were much more common (Aune, *Literary Environment*, 31-34, 63-64; Stanton, *Preaching*, 119-21). Even sayings could be arranged topically (e.g., Epictetus *Enchir.*) Writers could expand or abridge accounts freely (2 Macc 2:24-25; Theon *Progymn.* 3.224-40; 4.37-42, 80-82; see further further Sanders, *Tendencies*, 19, 46-189, 272; Stein, "'Criteria,'" 238-40).

[223] Augustine did not expect the Gospels to be fully chronological (*Harmony of the Gospels* 21.51); for Mark, see possibly Papias frg. 3.15 (Holmes) in Euseb. *H.E.* 3.39, though Papias might have rhetorical arrangement in view (Moessner, "Voice").

[224] See 4Q158; Wise, "Introduction to 4Q158."

Jewish Biographies

Although extant first-century Gospels reflect abundant Judean/Galilean material, they cannot be compared as easily with non-hellenistic ancient Jewish biographies—since such biographies are quite scarce.[225] That later rabbis lacked interest in composing biographies is well-known.[226] Closer and more accessible to Gospel readers would be the stories of Ruth, Judith, Jonah, Esther, Daniel and Tobit in the Greek Bible. Nevertheless, events rather than the public lives of leading characters dominate.[227] Except for Daniel, these works also are unified narratives, missing the apparent compilations of prior anecdotes that appear in most ancient biographies, including the Gospels.

This is not to deny that the Gospel writers drew on such models (with which they were likelier familiar than with individual Greek biographies); they may have even viewed some of these as biographies of a sort.[228] The most conventionally Jewish of the Gospels, namely Matthew and John, may have also incorporated some midrashic techniques at least to a minor degree.[229] Surely the OT and the experience of Jesus offer the primary theological backdrop for the Gospels,[230] but this does not negate their use of a contemporary genre where the life or public life of an individual dominates a cohesive narrative.

Nevertheless, Diaspora Jewish audiences in the first century—our closest available analogy for most of the circles that first received the Gospels—expected some biographic conventions inherited from the Greek world even in their own stories. And if this is so, one should not expect fewer biographic conventions from biographic works for Diaspora Christian audiences (with mixed Jewish and Gentile memberships) in the same period.

Scholars often argue that biographic treatments in Josephus's Jewish history, where he retains but adapts stories in ways more intelligible and amenable to a

---

[225] See much fuller discussion in Keener, *John*, 25-29.

[226] With e.g., Neusner, *Legend*, 8; idem, "Idea of History." Neusner, *Talmudic Biography*, is skeptical even of the attributed sayings.

[227] Stanton, *Preaching*, 126; Aune, *Literary Environment*, 37. Jewish haggadic expansions of Pentateuchal characters (on which cf. e.g., Fisk, "Bible"; Harrington, "Bible") are not close (cf. Keener, *Acts*, 1:146); they sometimes resemble mythography because they treat the distant past (see Keener, *Acts*, 1:145). The suggestion that ancient Near Eastern models provided the later Greek emphasis on individual characters (cf. Dihle, "Biography," 366-67) is overstated.

[228] Some do see OT and rabbinic biographic material as primary background for the Gospels; see e.g., Baum, "Biographien." For focus on OT background, Hägg, *Biography*, 155n28, cites Hartman, "Reflections"; Reiser, *Sprache*, 102-5 (distinctively regarding Jeremiah as a chief model, pp. 17-20).

[229] These may appear to a small extent already in the OT; e.g., compare 2 Kgs 9:27 with 2 Chron 22:9, discussed in Keener, *Spirit Hermeneutics*, 196-97.

[230] At least some of the Gospel writers apparently saw themselves as continuing the earlier biblical salvation history; see Smith, "Gospels."

Hellenistic audience,[231] reflect Greek literary, often biographic, conventions.[232] Other Hellenistic Jewish historians probably used these conventions as well.[233] *Lives of the Prophets* resembles Greek lives of poets,[234] drawing on a history of legendary developments.

Philo's essays on biblical personalities, probably somewhat widely known in Diaspora Judaism,[235] are more philosophic yet also reflect some Greek biographic influence.[236] Much more work needs to be done on Philonic biography and the Gospels, perhaps particularly the Fourth Gospel. Although Philo is from a relevant period, however, analogies with the Gospels are somewhat limited by his philosophic penchant for allegorizing Pentateuchal narratives.[237]

Of perhaps greatest interest is Philo's *Life of Moses*, which includes fewer allegorical features than many of his other works.[238] Philo presents Moses as a philosopher-king and corrects outsiders' misunderstanding of Moses as divine.[239] Later in this book, Esteban Hidalgo charts some of Philo's use of and departure from the biblical narrative that provides Philo's most important (although not exclusive) source in his account (see further discussion below).

Some of these features are more relevant for studying the Gospels than are others. Synopses of the Synoptic Gospels suggest, at least where we can test Matthew's and Luke's adaptations of Mark, that they may treat their sources more conservatively than Philo treats the biblical life of Moses (i.e., more like Suetonius than like Philo). Nevertheless, the mixture of retaining substance while employing

---

[231] See e.g., Begg, "Elisha's Deeds"; idem, "Jotham"; idem, "Rape of Tamar"; and other sample sources in the bibliography.

[232] See e.g., Van Veldhuizen, "Moses," 215-24; Höffken, "Hiskija"; Feldman, "*Aqedah*"; idem, "Jacob"; idem, "Jehu"; idem, "Joshua"; idem, "Samson"; idem, "Saul"; idem, "Solomon"; Begg, "Zedekiah"; the multiple articles by Feldman and Begg sampled in Keener, *John*, 2:1262, 1298-99; idem, *Acts*, 4:3807-8, 3866-67. Some particular adaptations are debated (e.g., Roncace, "Portraits"; Feldman, "Roncace's Portraits"; Roncace, "Samson").

[233] Cf. Rajak, "Justus of Tiberias," 92; Cohen, *Maccabees*, 194; cf. in general Attridge, "Historiography," 326; cf. Eisman, "Dio and Josephus."

[234] See Aune, *Literary Environment*, 41-42.

[235] Philo was selected as the chief representative of Jews to the emperor (Josephus *Ant.* 18.259).

[236] Canevet, "Remarques sur l'utilisation." Philo adjusts figures to suit his idealizations of virtue (cf. Petit, "Traversée exemplaire"). For similarities between Philonic biography and Plutarch, see Niehoff, "Philo."

[237] His focus on characters of the distant past also probably allows him more freedoms than most biographers about more recent figures.

[238] Burridge, *Gospels?* (2004), 128 (though noting on 129 the possibility of some features of a philosophic treatise as well as biography). It is modeled on Xenophon's *Agesilaus* (Burridge, "Review," 477). On biography and philosophy in Philo, cf. Termini, "Part." For comparison of this work with a Gospel, deeming both "encomiastic biography," see Shuler, "Moses."

[239] Feldman, *Portrayal*; cf. Scott, "Divine Man" (agreeing with Carl Holladay).

flexibility to reframe a message persists. The addition of full speeches, as in Josephus's hellenistic Jewish historiography,[240] clearly exceeds what appears in the Synoptic tradition, but might warrant more comparisons with Johannine discourses.[241]

Josephus and Philo wrote for more elite and very different sorts of audiences than any of our first Gospels; we may learn relevant points from their adaptations, while recognizing that the Gospel writers, especially Mark, probably wrote from their own monotheistic, biblical matrix with less self-conscious appeal than Philo or Josephus to audiences different from themselves.

Person-centered Works That Are Not Biographies

Novels, most of which were romances, are rarely confused with biographies, but the margins of the genre do contain exceptions.[242] Although we know of *no* historical novels about *recent* historical figures, a minority of ancient novels did exist about figures of the distant past.[243] These likely include Xenophon's *Cyropedia*, Ps.-Callisthenes's *Alexander* romance, and Philostratus's *Life of Apollonius*.[244] Probably these are better classified as ancient historical novels, a form of the wider ancient romance novel (though Xenophon's would have been a forerunner of the genre). That is also how the later apocryphal gospels are often classified.

In contrast to the Gospels, none of the above-named historical novels derive from the early imperial period, and all were composed long after living memory of their subjects (i.e., long after anyone who knew the eyewitnesses had died). Moreover, scenes in these novels tend to be fleshed out with far more copious details than is possible in many biographies' (including the Synoptics') anecdotes and often barer focus on events.

Xenophon wrote his *Cyropedia* centuries before the era of the Gospels. Cyrus died in 530 BCE, a century before Xenophon's birth (for the interval, one might compare the mid-second century Gospel of Thomas, written probably well over a

---

[240] On Josephus and speeches, see sources in Keener, *Acts*, 1:301-4. Some Judean haggadic works also supplied interpretive speeches (cf. Endres, *Interpretation*, 198-99).

[241] See Bauckham, "Historiographical Characteristics." For Johannine discourse, see also particularly helpfully Parsenios, "Rhetoric."

[242] One may also note Polybius's distinction between treating an individual encomiastically or (with greater rhetorical attention to moral lessons) historically; cf. Farrington, "Action."

[243] The fictionalizing (or epicizing) of historic events such as we find in Lucan *C.W.* (see e.g., Chiu, "Importance") is largely limited to poetry (cf. Fantuzzi, "Historical epic").

[244] Interestingly, the size of these works also distinguishes them from virtually all ancient extant ancient biographies (note the offhanded observations in Hägg, *Biography*, 7, 320-21, though Hägg classes them loosely as biographic; but cf. 197-98 for Nicolaus's *Augustus*, undoubtedly longer than usual), though the size also differs from typical ancient novels. For two fictitious eyewitness accounts of the Trojan War, naturally written centuries after the legendary war, see Merkle, "True Story," 183-84; Schmeling, "Spectrum," 23.

century after Jesus's crucifixion). This alone would not prevent his work from being biography or depending on substantial information (since later works, such as Arrian's treatment of Alexander, often depended on significantly earlier sources), but ancient readers also recognized that this work was meant to teach politics, not to recount Cyrus's actual life[245] (although a work could easily do both). Its "constant deviations from known history" suggest that in this particular work "Xenophon simply did not set out to write history," but simply to depict various ideals.[246]

Although Philostratus's *Apollonius* includes some characteristics of biography, it defies many biographic conventions, including in length and structure.[247] Many scholars think that Philostratus' main "source" for Apollonius' life, Damis, is a fiction of either Philostratus[248] or an earlier pseudepigrapher.[249] In any case, Philostratus' own portrait suits a second- or third-century setting (i.e., his own) much better than a first-century setting (i.e., Apollonius's); a number of his accounts of Apollonius even resemble reports from Christian gospels,[250] though especially of the "apocryphal" variety.[251] Christian stories at least were among the serious influences on his storytelling approach (offering literary fodder for miracle stories). The parts of the story most apt to be confirmed by Apollonius' letters[252] exhibit the least parallels with the Gospels.[253]

Whereas Philostratus did have some prior information about Apollonius, Ps.-Callisthenes was more interested in his own creative depiction of Alexander. Though some basic information about Alexander was widely known, this author is not writing biography. One leading expert opines that "the historical nucleus is small and unusable";[254] another rightly distinguishes this "popular fiction" from Alexander histories.[255] Pseudo-Callisthenes wrote somewhere between 460 and

---

[245] Cic. *Quint. fratr.* 1.1.8.23. For the verdict of a modern commentator, see Hägg, *Biography*, 51-52.

[246] Hägg, *Biography*, 65, following also Stadter, "Narrative," 467, and calling it a "utopian biography" (I would prefer "utopian novel," but Xenophon predates the later narrative categories).

[247] Hägg, *Biography*, 321, though his exceptionally broad definition of biography includes it.

[248] Jones, "Apollonius' Passage"; Klauck, *Context*, 170; Hägg, *Biography*, 325, 331-32 (citing Bowie, "Apollonius," 1663-64; idem, "Philostratus," 189; Gyselinck and Demoen, "Author," 99-101).

[249] Though cf. Conybeare, "Introduction," vii.

[250] See Keener, *Miracles*, 1:53-56, esp. 55; and sources cited there.

[251] Klauck, *Context*, 170. Admittedly, stories of Jesus as miracle-worker are limited in extant apocryphal gospels (Achtemeier, *Miracle Tradition*, 177-78; cf. Remus, *Healer*, 92-95); but miracle stories are abundant in apocryphal acts (Achtemeier, *Miracle Tradition*, 179-88; cf. Remus, *Healer*, 102-3).

[252] Regardless of their authenticity (it may be doubtful), they predate Philostratus' story. The letters focus on Greek cities where Apollonius probably actually traveled (not Ethiopians, Indians, etc., where Philostratus' most fanciful tales transpire).

[253] See further Keener, *Acts*, 1:330-33.

[254] Bosworth, "Pseudo-Callisthenes." On historical information dramatically transformed for narrative purposes, see Hägg, *Biography*, 126-27.

[255] Zambrini, "Historians," 211; cf. Hägg, *Biography*, 4.

760 years after Alexander's death—i.e., likely over half a millennium later, centuries after *living* memory of Alexander and his associates had perished.[256]

Later audiences may well have viewed the Life of Aesop as a biography, but it represents a much longer period of oral tradition than is under consideration with the Gospels or even most biographies from the early Empire.[257] More analogous, then, are biographies written closer to time of the figure they describe.

Some have gone so far as to compare apocryphal Gospels as closer analogies for the Gospels.[258] This comparison, however, is anachronistic, since apocryphal Gospels are a later and dependent genre, and should no more be read into first-century Gospels than we should conform first-century Gospels to the theology of Origen, Tertullian, or Cyprian from that later period. The majority of scholars recognize these later Gospels as novels, not biographies,[259] and there is in them (as opposed to Matthew, Mark, Luke and John) little indication of Judean or Galilean elements or other signs of earlier tradition.

Mere use of historical characters is a far cry from historical research and sources (such as the use, on the majority view, by Matthew and Luke of Mark and Q in their Gospels). Indeed, *most* novels focus on fictitious characters,[260] and

---

[256] Hägg, *Biography*, 99, on the Alexander romance and Life of Aesop, suggests "some six hundred years or more for the stories to grow, coalesce, and diversify" before early codifications. Hägg, *Biography*, 100, deems both as "largely fictitious" and notes they are usually deemed romances.

[257] Wojciechowski, "Tradition," 101-2, even considers it "a Hellenistic novel with satirical elements." Hägg, *Biography*, 99, suggests its present form dates to over 600 years after Aesop and notes (p. 100) that most scholars today deem it a romance (cf. 310 for its "novelistic plot").

[258] Thus, for example, one knowledgeable scholar seriously proposes that while comparing the Gospels to biographies I should have taken "into account ancient works like the *Protevangelium of James* and other apocryphal Gospels that closely resemble the canonical Gospels in genre but obviously did invent material wholesale" (Powell, *Figure*, 260, summarizing the suggestion of Levine, "Christian Faith," 103). I know of no mainstream historical Jesus scholars (such as E. P. Sanders, John Meier or Gerd Theissen) who appeal to such documents, whereas a biographic genre for the first-century Gospels is currently and historically the dominant position in Gospels scholarship.

[259] See Aune, *Dictionary*, 199-204; Bauckham and Porter, "Apocryphal Gospels"; Charlesworth and Evans, "Agrapha." Cf. also apocryphal acts as novels, Aune, *Literary Environment*, 151-52; Lalleman, "Apocryphal Acts," 67; Rebenich, "Historical Prose," 307-8; Bauckham, "Acts of Paul"; Keylock, "Distinctness," 210; Krasser, "Reading," 554; Hofmann, "Novels: Christian," 846-48; Perkins, "World." The gnostic gospels reflect a different, mostly non-narrative genre, probably with knowledge of the earlier Gospels (Tuckett, *Nag Hammadi*, 149, 155, 158-59); even Thomas may be largely derivative (see Tuckett, "Thomas"; idem, "Gospel of Thomas"; idem, "Sources," 130; Heyer, *Jesus Matters*, 102-5; Charlesworth and Evans, "Agrapha," 496-503; cf. possibly Perrin, "Overlooked Evidence"; idem, *Thomas and Tatian*; but contrast DeConick, *Recovering*). Canonical sources (Paul, Q and Mark) are our earliest extant sources (Allison, *Jesus of Nazareth*, 17).

[260] Porter, "We Passages," 550, shows that most ancient novels were not historical novels (possibly excepting Xenophon's *Cyropedia* and Ps-Callisthenes' *Alexander Romance*, neither of which became standard generic models).

when using genuine characters they reveal little knowledge about events in the genuine characters' lives.²⁶¹ Typically novels portray historical figures anachronistically, often placing them in the wrong periods.²⁶²

This procedure contrasts starkly with historical works, which used real characters and events but sometimes embellished their sources (to varying degrees) with educated guesses about what was probable (and with a view to what was edifying and entertaining).²⁶³ None of this denies the value of comparing the Gospels with ancient novels to identify literary devices,²⁶⁴ but merely suggests that identifying literary techniques does not necessarily indicate a work's genre or the degree of historical information available in it.²⁶⁵ Characterization, for example, appears also in ancient biographies and histories.²⁶⁶

Summary of Chapters

Here I briefly introduce the following chapters, as well as comment on some additional issues germane to some of the chapters.

The first section following this introduction further introduces the question of the Gospels as biographies. In an article originally published in *Currents in Biblical Research*, Professor Steve Walton of St. Mary's University, Twickenham, and Tyndale House, Cambridge, summarizes the monumental impact of Richard Burridge's biographic paradigm on Gospels studies. Burridge's contribution is foundational for our project, since this volume seeks to develop Burridge's insights further in terms of their implications for historical research.

---

²⁶¹ Greek and Roman novels typically reflect the milieu of their ideal readers; see Wiersma, "Novel." Droge, "Anonymously," 515, correctly (if understatedly) notes that "the romances do not purport to be a historical record of facts in quite the same way as Luke-Acts does."

²⁶² See examples in Morgan, "Fiction," 554; cf. also Tob 1:2-4; Jdt 1:1, 7.

²⁶³ Penner, *Praise*, 138, suggests that many texts belong in the intermediate category of "historical novels"; while this is partly a matter of definition, the category shrinks considerably so long as one recognizes a degree of fictionalization in some history, as opposed to novelists who took a free or (in the rare cases of "historical novels") a mostly free hand.

²⁶⁴ The present work's focus is on the degree of a work's correspondence to prior information and thus the likelihood of recovering information we would deem historical (in modern terms), but this is not meant to dismiss the value of literary comparisons with other sorts of narrative works. That I have worked through and profited from a range of such sources will be evident to anyone perusing the ancient sources indexes of my Matthew, John and (especially) Acts commentaries.

²⁶⁵ Cf. e.g., Rothschild, *Rhetoric of History*; Johnson, *Acts*, 5-7; also the borrowing of style from Roman epics in Roman historiography (Rebenich, "Historical Prose," 312). Some find novelistic techniques even in LXX expansions (e.g., Boyd-Taylor, "Adventure").

²⁶⁶ See now esp. Ash, Mossman, and Titchener, *Fame*. Direct, individualistic characterization is of course more common in modern biography (Burridge, "Review," 478).

In chapter 2, Youngju Kwon, who is writing his dissertation on literary techniques in ancient biographies and the Gospels, offers a further introduction to interpreting the Gospels as biographies and to some of the literary techniques that this observation invites. Rhetorical handbooks suggest that such techniques flourished in other genres as well; given the limitations of human memory, it is not surprising that one could move anecdotes into new contexts.[267]

The second and longest section of the book explores the question of historical information and literary flexibility in ancient biography by contributing detailed comparisons of ancient sources. In one of the most detailed and innovative contributions, Chris Alfred in chapter 3 surveys the use of sources in a wide range of ancient biographers. Historians usually had multiple sources.[268] Where ancient historians and biographers do not cite sources, modern scholars debate about what sources they may have used, including many that are now fragmentary or no longer extant.[269] Often, however, these writers state their sources, and it is to these undebated sources that Alfred turns.

Alfred's survey of source citations in ancient biographies indicates that most biographers, especially in the era of the early empire (more so than in earlier eras), evaluated their sources critically. Even more important and more conspicuous is these biographers' regular appeal to sources where they felt that citations were needed. Their approach demonstrates that they understood their genre as one that drew morals from historical examples, not a more novelistic genre that simply invented events.

Timothy Christian, in chapter 4, focuses his attention on Cornelius Nepos, a key example of a biographer from well before the period of the Gospels. He selects Nepos's *Themistocles* because this work on occasion cites sources that are extant, sources with which this biography may therefore be compared at other points. Christian illustrates how Nepos often closely follows earlier historical sources even where he does not explicitly note that he is doing so. Although many historians today consider Nepos careless, it is clear at least that he seeks to communicate historical information rather than freely inventing events, and that he often may follow a source even when he does not explicitly identify one.

Christian's conclusions fit some recent work on Nepos. Of the minority of surviving biographies by Nepos, "some are openly laudatory, a few vituperative, the rest more historically balanced."[270] Nepos does make historical errors in his biographies, but these are most evident in the sources most distant from his sphere of cultural and historical knowledge. Tomas Hägg observes that Nepos "has been singularly unlucky regarding what happened to survive of his main work: among the famous men he chose to depict, the non-Roman military commanders were no doubt the figures farthest from his competence." He lacks the context "necessary to assess and recreate their historical particularity," and he was less "versed in

---

[267] See e.g., Theon *Progymn.* 4.73-79; cf. 5.388-441.
[268] See Évrard, "Polybe."
[269] For debates in historiography, see e.g., Muntz, "Sources"; idem, "Diodorus Siculus"; in ancient biography, Buszard, "Parallel."
[270] Hägg, *Biography*, 189. The verb tenses in Corn. Nep. 25 (Atticus), chapters 13—18, might suggest that these chapters are revisions for Nepos's 2d edition.

Greek culture, or fluent in Greek."[271] By contrast, his work on Atticus is strong,[272] fitting our expectations for a subject closer to the author's own period.[273]

In chapters five and six, Craig Keener and Bensoh Goh compare various biographic sources regarding Otho and Galba, respectively. The purpose of these essays is to evaluate the historical character of biographies about then-recent characters (from the preceding half century or so) in the era of the Gospels. In both cases, synoptic comparisons among such works reveal that the key biographers viewed their role as adapters of historical information rather than as free inventors of stories. (Keener's work is slightly adapted from his earlier essay in *Bulletin for Biblical Research*.) Nevertheless, even some works written much longer after their protagonists' decease can continue much reliable information, as the next essay illustrates.

Soo-Kwang Lee's essay on biographies of Arrian notes that most scholars regard Arrian as our most reliable source concerning Alexander, even though Arrian writes centuries after Alexander's death and at many points must decide among radically inconsistent reports. This is partly because Arrian depends on some sources from the period of those who knew Alexander. By comparison, the Gospels also stem from the period of those who knew Jesus, and are much more consistent on key points such as the manner of Jesus's death. By the standards of ancient biography and historiography, then, the Gospels should be respected as valuable sources.

Fasil Woldemariam's essay on biographies of Agesilaus further illustrates how works even centuries after a figure's death could include abundant information drawn from earlier sources contemporary with a figure. Xenophon's treatment of Agesilaus reflects eyewitness and contemporary information, although, as Alfred has observed, Xenophon was also tendentious in his approach to his subject. Although the principles of biography in play by the early empire were not all established already in Xenophon's time (and tendentiousness did not die with him in any case), the question here is not so much the reliability of Xenophon's treatment of Agesilaus as the use that later biographers made of him. Nepos and Plutarch have a commitment to information, not simply to telling a lively story.

Edward Wright compares four biographers' accounts of their subjects' deaths with other surviving data from antiquity, seeking to evaluate the degree of accuracy or freedom with which they worked. In some cases the paucity of evidence may suggest the reluctance of the biographers in question to invent details to which they lacked access. Wright also urges appropriate caution, however, given the limited evidence available in the cases considered.

The third section explores some specifically Jewish sources. How much flexibility could biographers exercise? John Jordan Henderson's essay, previously published in the *Journal of Greco-Roman Christianity and Judaism*, examines Josephus's apologetic autobiography in light of parallel (and sometimes contrasting) information in Josephus's historiographic corpus. In this case, the differences belong to the same author writing in two genres, suggesting some flexibility

---

[271] Hägg, *Biography*, 196.
[272] Hägg, *Biography*, 197.
[273] In this case, he knew Atticus personally; see Hägg, *Biography*, 189-90.

(or sometimes carelessness or tendentiousness) in how Josephus tells the same story. For various reasons, Josephus took considerable latitude. That Josephus does not feel a need to qualify or defend such differences might suggest that he expected his Diaspora audience to appreciate a measure of flexibility in the biographic genre, certainly more than readers of modern biographies anticipate.[274]

Thus while biography was firmly rooted in historical information, it also potentially allowed great freedom in details (at least in apologetic autobiography such as that of Josephus, but probably more widely). This observation, too, is relevant for the genre expectations we should bring to the Gospels. Both the similarities among the Gospels and their differences match the sorts of similarities and differences found when we compare ancient biographers of then-recent figures.

Although Philo is influenced by elite hellenistic philosophy far more than are any of our Gospels, he offers a specifically Jewish biography that is not (unlike Josephus's *Life*) an autobiography. Numerous other works also address features of Philo's *Life of Moses*.[275] Like the Gospels, Philo certainly shapes his material to communicate his message, for example, presenting Moses as a philosopher-king[276] or contrasting Moses and Balaam.[277] He selects and omits elements according to what suits his purposes.[278] Not unlike traditional Jewish haggadic expansions, though here not to the same degree, Philo enhances his image of Moses by elaborations.[279] Consciously or not, he might also read his own background

---

[274] Josephus published his history when some witnesses were alive (*Life* 359) and presented his work to some of them (362); King Agrippa thoroughly attested to his content (364-367). In his *Life* he defends himself against the charges of Justus (336-367), implying that his (Josephus's account) is the more reliable on details regarding Josephus, including in the *Life* itself. In other respects, the divergence between Josephus and Justus may resemble multiple versions of a story today where personal disputes are involved.

[275] E.g., Goodenough, "Exposition"; Robbins, *Study*; Granata, "Introduzione"; Feldman, *Portrayal*; for cosmological theology here, see Steyn, "Elemente"; for mediation in this work, see Parker, "Swiftly runs the word." On other particulars, see e.g., McKnight, "Lion Proselytes"; Riaud, "Réflexions"; Berchmann, "Arcana Mundi." Damgaard, *Recasting Moses*, places this life in the larger framework of accounts of Moses from the LXX to later Christian works; on patristic use of this work, see e.g., Geljon, *Exegesis*; cf. Malherbe and Ferguson, *Gregory of Nyssa*.

[276] Fitting Greek expectations; Feldman, "Birth"; idem, *Portrayal*; earlier, Meeks, *Prophet-King*, 115; for Moses as philosopher-sage, see Clifford, "Moses"; as prophet, Meeks, *Prophet-King*, 125-29; as prophet-king, Meeks, *Prophet-King*, 107-17.

[277] Remus, "Thaumaturges" (emphasizing the distinguishing of Moses from magic). Balaam is contrasted with Moses not only in Philo (Feldman, "Balaam," on *Mos.* 1.263-99) but in some later Jewish sources; see e.g., *Sipre Deut.* 357.18.1-2; *b. B.B.* 15b; *Exod. Rab.* 32:3; *Num. Rab.* 14:20; *Eccl. Rab.* 2:15, §2; see further discussion in Bowman, "Prophets," 108-14.

[278] See e.g., Feldman, "Calf"; idem, "Philo's Interpretation of Joshua."

[279] See e.g., Begg, "Moves"; cf. expansion in Begg, "Rephidim Episode"; expansion in Philo but more omissions in Josephus, in Begg, "Retelling." For additional details about, e.g., the thornbush, see Jos. *Ant.* 2.266; Philo *Mos.* 1.65-66. On regular haggadic and other early Jewish elaboration, see sources and discussion in Keener, *John*, 1:27-28; idem, *Acts*,

into Moses's life.²⁸⁰ Philo sometimes downplays other characters in order to highlight Moses's role more fully.²⁸¹ Some of Philo's adaptations of biblical narrative, however, such as his education,²⁸² may also adapt prior traditions.²⁸³ Thus scholars find both distinctive features and overlap with other early Jewish retellings.²⁸⁴

When it appeared that this book would include a major lacuna by its lack of treatment of Philo's *Life of Moses*, doctoral student Esteban Hidalgo graciously and competently stepped in to supply comments on the first of Philo's two books on this subject.²⁸⁵ Although space constraints in this book limited the amount of his research that Hidalgo could include, he helpfully charts some of Philo's use of and departure from the biblical narrative that provides Philo's most important source in his account. Those familiar with ancient rhetoric will recognize many patterns that Hidalgo highlights, such as Philo's frequent paraphrase of his material, occasional elaboration, and composition of speeches. The Gospels address a much less elite audience, as perhaps seen in Matthew's and Luke's occasional use of verbatim material, but Philo's Diaspora Jewish biography may nevertheless provide insights for Matthew's and Luke's rearrangement of sayings and shorter discourses into speeches and perhaps especially for John's longer discourses.

Adrian Reynolds offers a study on a different Jewish historical work²⁸⁶ that is believed to have taken considerable latitude, and shows major points of agreement with another extant source, supporting the pattern found elsewhere. Second Maccabees is not a biography, but given the limited availability of ancient Jewish biographies in Greek from the relevant period, this study offers a valuable comparison for our other materials. Although we must allow for some hyperbole in Maccabean literature,²⁸⁷ external evidence confirms some of the claims in 2 Maccabees.²⁸⁸

1:145. Milikowsky, "Midrash," suggests that the rabbis themselves recognized that midrashic additions were homiletic, distinct from historical reconstructions.

²⁸⁰ Cf. Bloch, "Alexandria."

²⁸¹ See e.g., Feldman, "Philo's Interpretation of Joshua"; idem, "General" (on the same Num 31 chapter as Feldman, "General," cf. Begg, "Retelling"). On Moses as a military leader, see also Canevet, "Remarques sur l'utilisation"; Feldman, "Spies"; as a wise political leader (vs. the rabble), cf. Feldman, "Korah." Moses is never king in Josephus (Meeks, *Prophet-King*, 134-36; not surprising given his apologetic), but is a commander (Meeks, *Prophet-King*, 133-34).

²⁸² Cf. Feldman, "Birth"; Philo *Mos.* 1.20-23; Jos. *Ant.* 2.232-37. For Philo and Greek education, see Piccione, "Παιδεία."

²⁸³ Cf. e.g., Ezekiel's *Exagoge* as a source in Lanfranchi, "Reminiscences."

²⁸⁴ E.g., Begg, "Marah Incident"; idem, "Retelling." Josephus may have known this work of Philo; see Robertson, "Account," ch. 2.

²⁸⁵ Although he acknowledges his use of Feldman's detailed work, Hidalgo first charted the material in *Life of Moses* 1 inductively, yielding a plethora of valuable data.

²⁸⁶ Penner, *Praise*, 136-37, notes that while everyone acknowledges 1 Macc as history, the measure of history and fiction in 2 Macc is debated. (By contrast, 3 Macc is universally agreed to be a novel; see e.g., Johnson, "Fictions"; Hacham, "Polemic.")

²⁸⁷ See Hilbert, "185,000 Slain."

²⁸⁸ Gera, "Olympiodoros"; cf. Jones, "Inscription"; Shanks, "Inscription."

The remaining two essays in the book, found in Section 4, focus more directly on the Gospels yet also more concise, offering merely samples of the sorts of explorations that consideration of the Gospels' biographic genre invites. Both, like Walton's opening essay, are by published scholars.

Holly Carey helpfully turns us to questions of meaning: how did ancient biographers and other writers of biographic information adjust their sources to augment the praise of their positive protagonists, and what implications might this have for the study of the Gospels? Professor Carey rightly notes that ancient biographers had their favorites and presented the best side of their most heroic protagonists.

One may note that this observation seems particularly relevant to Jewish biographies such as Philo's *Life of Moses*. Indeed, more traditional Judean haggadic materials[289] carry this tendency even further, whitewashing their heroes, although this was probably not originally understood historically.[290] Writers used amplification to answer questions posed by a narrative;[291] to heighten the praise of God or the protagonist[292] (sometimes by fanciful midrash);[293] or to improve the story.[294] Sometimes they added names,[295] sometimes arrived at midrashically or for symbolic value.[296] One could emphasize a theme already present in one's source by reiterating it where it appeared and occasionally adding it elsewhere.[297]

---

[289] Haggadic adaptation appears in both midrash and folk literature (Wright, "Midrash," 129).

[290] As noted, even the rabbis themselves probably recognized that midrashic additions were homiletic, distinct from historical reconstructions (Milikowsky, "Midrash"), though one generation's traditions may have filled another's historical curiosity. Haggadic elaboration resembles techniques in Greek mythography more than historiography; see e.g., the elaboration of sacred stories in Maclean and Aitken, *Heroikos*, li-lii.

[291] E.g., Demetrius the Chronographer (third century BCE), *frg.* 5 (Euseb. *P.E.* 9.29.16); *Jub.* 4:1, 9; 12:14; 13:11; 27:1, 4-5 (Esau and Jacob, vs. Isaac and Jacob); *p. Ket.* 12:4, §8 (fanciful midrash).

[292] 2 Macc 2:1-8 (expanding Jeremiah's mission); *Jub.* 29:14-20 (rhetorically contrasts Jacob's respect for his parents with Esau's disrespect); *Test. Job* 9-15 (see OTP 1:832); *Test. Jos.* 3:1; cf. Josephus' expansion of Philistine casualties (*Ant.* 6.203; cf. 1 Sam 18:27, though the LXX reduced them). Cf. Jael in *L.A.B.* 31 (Burnette-Bletsch, "Jael").

[293] *Pesiq. Rab Kah.* 4:3 ("the rabbis" on Solomon); *Gen. Rab.* 43:3; *Ex. Rab.* 10:4; *Pesiq. Rab.* 49:5; cf. Artapanus on Pharaoh's behavior toward Moses in light of 1 Sam 18:17, 21-25 (Euseb. *P.E.* 9.27.7). Genre conventions also could dictate amplifications; Joseph and Asenath, a Hellenistic romance, incorporates features ideal in such romances.

[294] *Jub.* 11:14-15, 13:18, 22; possibly 4Q160, fr. 3-5, 7; *Tg. Ps.-Jon.* on Gen. 50:26; *Ps.-Jon.* on Ex. 13:19.

[295] *Jub.* 11:14-15; *Liv. Pr.* 19 (Joad) (§30 in Schermann's Greek text); *Jos. Ant.* 8.231; *L.A.B.* 40:1 (in *L.A.B.* in general, cf. Bauckham, "Liber antiquitatum," 67; in Jewish sources more generally, Pilch, "Naming"); cf. Plut. *Alex.* 20.4-5 (questioning Chares' report).

[296] See Rook, "Names," on patriarchal wives in Jubilees. (Names are sometimes, however, the elements of tradition most resistant to change; cf. e.g., the observation of Bernal, *Athena*, 2:337.)

[297] As *L.A.B.* does in its polemic against idolatry (Murphy, "Idolatry").

Similarly, negative incidents could be toned down,[298] omitted,[299] or justified[300] in the character's favor.

The genres of history and biography did not require such treatment.[301] Neither ancient epics nor ancient biographers were averse to reporting flawed heroes;[302] biographers often did include unpleasant reports about even mostly positive characters.[303] Nevertheless, biographers and historians had their own biases and naturally focused more on positive traits of characters whom they perceived as positive figures. Thus, for example, Plutarch omitted or minimized Caesar's affairs.[304] Ancient biographies commonly provided descriptions of their heroes,[305] especially when they were physically magnificent.[306] (Still, ancient writers often did

---

[298] *L.A.B.* 12:2-3 (Aaron's sin with the golden calf). *T. Job* 39:12-13 (OTP)/39:9-10 (Kraft) and 40:3/4 seems concerned to soften God letting Job's children die for his test.

[299] *Jub.* 13:17-18 (conflict between Lot's and Abram's servants), 14:21-16:22 (omitting Sarah's problems with Hagar, though they surface in 17:4-14), 29:13 (omits Jacob's fear); *T. Zeb.* 1:5-7 (Zebulon did not act against Joseph). In *Jubilees* (e.g., Abram passing off his sister as his wife), see Wintermute, "Introduction," 35-36; in Josephus, cf. Aune, *Literary Environment*, 108; in Greco-Roman literature, see Shuler, *Genre*, 50 (following Cic. *Part. or.* 22).

[300] CD 4.20—5.3 (David's polygamy, behavior that the Qumran community otherwise disapproved; also 11QT 56.18); *Jub.* 19:15-16 (Rebekah, in light of current morality); 27:6-7 (how Jacob could leave his father); 28:6-7 (Jacob's sororal polygyny); 30:2-17 (Simeon and Levi), 41 (Judah and Tamar both made more innocent, especially Judah); 1Qap Gen^{ar} 20.10-11 (Sarah rather than Abraham proposes the pretense that she is his sister); *Jos. Asen.* 23 (Levi and Simeon); *T. Jud.* 8-12 (whitewashing Judah, and to a lesser extent Tamar, though Judah confesses it as a lesser sin; cf. the improvement of both in *Tg. Neof.* 1 on Gen 38:25; *Tg. Ps.-Jon.* on Gen. 38:25-26); *T. Iss.* 3:1 (cf. Gen 49:15); *Tg. Ps.-Jon.* on Gen. 49:28 (all twelve patriarchs were equally righteous).

[301] This is not to enter into debate about the extent of midrash in Matthew (see Goulder, *Midrash*, 32-34; Gundry, *Matthew*, 628-29; Soares Prabhu, *Quotations*, 159-60; Payne, "Midrash"; Cunningham and Bock, "Midrash"; Blomberg, *Historical Reliability*, 43-53; Keener, *Matthew*, 21-23, 81-83, 660). Most Jewish works in Greek (especially those from outside Judea) followed Greek models to varying degrees. Cohen suggests that 2 Maccabees and Josephus follow hellenistic historiographic models more than they do earlier Israelite historiography (*Maccabees*, 194). Nevertheless, Matthew is steeped in the OT; see Luz, *Matthew*, 44-45. Rabbis may have recognized most midrashic additions as homiletic, distinct from historical reconstructions; see

[302] The plot of the *Iliad* turns partly on the heroically magnified pride of Achilles and Agamemnon; the character of Odysseus in the sequel is flawed in different respects.

[303] E.g., Arrian *Alex.* 4.7.4; 4.8.1-4.9.6; Plut. *Cimon* 2.4-5; Corn. Nep. 11 (Iphicrates), 3.2; Philost. *Vit. soph.* 2.21.602-3.

[304] See Beneker, "Chaste Caesar." Cf. the function of royal spinmeisters in Philost. *Hrk.* 31.5 and presumably behind 1—2 Samuel (in the context of ancient Near Eastern royal apologies, see Long, "Samuel," 270); probably also the apologetic for Socrates in Xenophon and Plato. Josephus' autobiography is widely recognized as apologetic (with e.g., Lamour, "Organisation").

[305] E.g., Suet. *Jul.* 45.1; *Tib.* 68.1-2; *Nero* 51; Tac. *Agr.* 44.

[306] E.g., 1 Sam 9:2; Plut. *Alex.* 60.6. I do find considerably more comment in fiction than in biographies and histories, however (e.g., Philost. *Hrk.* 10.1-4, esp. 10.3; 26.4, 13; 29.2; 33.39-40; 48.1; 49.3).

not hesitate to present weaknesses in their heroes' appearances, whether in epics' statements about Odysseus or historical memories of Socrates' snub nose.)[307]

Again, Jewish thinkers who engaged the wider Greco-Roman world as minority voices often apologetically played down incidents in their history that could appear embarrassing.[308] Already, for primarily Judahite consumption, the Chronicler omitted David's sin (contrast 2 Sam 11:1-27; 12:9-10; 1 Kgs 15:5).[309] In the first century, Josephus combines both forty-day fasts of Moses into one so he can skip the golden calf episode (*Ant.* 3.79-99, especially 95-99).[310] Philo omits Aaron's role in the episode (later rabbis also excluded his guilt) and may focus on Israel imitating an Egyptian bull deity.[311] Philo and Pseudo-Philo omit the command to destroy Canaan's nations, and Josephus explains it in a manner intelligible to Romans.[312]

Since the Evangelists regard Jesus as God's Son, their uniformly (or, on some approaches, their almost uniformly) positive depiction of Jesus is not surprising—although, as Professor Carey notes, elements that would strike outsiders as negative, such as Jesus's crucifixion, are not minimized. Perhaps of particular interest is that the leading apostolic witnesses, though ultimately viewed as a "foundation" for the church (Eph 2:20; Rev 21:14), never achieve a heroic status in the Gospels. In fact, in Mark, the Gospel most closely associated in early church tradition with Peter (Papias frg. 3.15), Jesus appears as the only true hero, for whom Peter and other disciples provide something of a narrative foil.

The volume proper concludes with relevant insights from a scholar who has already made significant contributions regarding the Gospels as ancient biographies. Drawing on recent research in classics, Michael R. Licona identifies literary techniques in Plutarch's biographies and their relevance to the Gospels. Although biographers based their work on historical information, they also adjusted

---

[307] For Socrates' nose, see e.g., Max. Tyre 1.9; cf. also Aesop's physical deformities in *Life of Aesop* 1. Some criticisms of Odysseus's appearance admittedly derived from his enemies (Philost. *Hrk.* 34.5).

[308] E.g., Josephus may play down negative elements of the biblical picture of Israelites during the exodus (Cheon, "Plagues"); the horror of the raped concubine (Feldman, "Concubine"); and problematic elements in Gen 18:22-33 and Gen 22 (Niehoff, "Josephus' Narrative Technique.").

[309] Also Solomon's; cf. e.g., Williamson, *Chronicles*, 236.

[310] See also H. St. J. Thackeray in LCL 4:362-63 n. *c*: "this is the most glaring exception" to Josephus's promise "to omit nothing" (*Ant.* 1.17). *War* 4.3 refers to the later calf idol of Jeroboam. This presumably reflects Josephus' apologetic for a Gentile audience (though Feldman, "Levites," suggests that Josephus' preference of priests over Levites also helps explain the omission).

[311] So Feldman, "Calf," on *Mos.* 2.161-73 (esp. 2.165, 169), though Feldman may overplay this point. Those who wrote for Israel, however, found the narrative much more useful; Ps.-Philo in *L.A.B.* 12:1-10 elaborates the narrative, highlighting Israel's unfaithfulness, though Fisk, "Scripture," notes that Ps.-Philo uses biblical citations to provide the interpretive context (Gen 11:6 in *LAB* 12:3; Gen 12:7 in *LAB* 12:4). For later rabbis' diverse treatment of the story, see comment in Keener, *Acts*, 2:1407-8.

[312] Feldman, "Command"; for Philo, see also Berthelot, "Conquest."

how they presented that information based on various moral, pragmatic and literary concerns, some of which Licona highlights here. (Others have also noticed such features; thus, for example, in the final quarter of his *Cicero* Plutarch takes for granted his readers' knowledge of the civil war and Caesar's assassination and addresses these details only when Cicero has a role.)[313] Licona has authored a more complete book on this subject for Oxford University Press.

Biographies cannot be more reliable than their sources, however, and this remains true even when, as in the case of the Gospels, the subject belongs to fairly recent history. Because this prehistory of biographic information does not belong to the subject of biography per se, discussion of it in this volume belongs to a closing appendix (also by Keener) concerning memory and oral tradition.

Popular writers who compare the Gospels primarily to mythography, however, are far from the mark.[314] Granted, over the course of a century legendary elements, poetic flourishes and deliberate propaganda sometimes entered historical biographers' arsenal of sources undetected, as is likely the case of the supernatural figure at Caesar's crossing of the Rubicon[315] or infancy narratives about famous figures.[316] But in Greco-Roman antiquity I know of *no* cases of full-scale mythography about figures within two generations of their time, even in political propaganda. Even were an exception to turn up, it would be historically quite idiosyncratic. Popular writers today who treat the Gospels as mythography act in a manner that is historically irresponsible; it is such writers, not those who treat the Gospels as biographies of Jesus, who ignore genuine historical analogies.

Closing Words

Inevitably, presuppositions and objectives inform one's comparisons; one could thus emphasize, for example, more differences in biographies of Otho or Galba than we have, or emphasize more common features in different works by Josephus than we have. But the essential twofold thesis remains clear: biographies of recent figures are intended to recount historical information (normally for edifying purposes); and biographers could exercise a degree of flexibility in how they recounted that information.

That is, ancient audiences did not expect biographers to invent events, but they did allow them to flesh out scenes and discourse for the purpose of what they considered narrative verisimilitude. To note this flexibility is not to claim a priori that a given biography or a Gospel exploited this flexibility, but it should prevent undue surprise (or, for some, scandal) in cases where we discover it.

---

[313] Hägg, *Biography*, 261.

[314] As with novels, I refer here to distinctive elements of the genre, not to widespread narrative techniques or to wider definitions of "myth."

[315] Cf. discussion in Beneker, "Crossing."

[316] Cf. e.g., Suet. *Augustus* 94.4; Aulus Gellius 6.1.2-4; Philostratus *Vit. Apoll.* 1.4-5; Menander Rhetor 2.1-2, 371.5-6; Hermogenes *Progymn.* 7.15; Shuler, *Genre*, 94; Klauck, *Context*, 300; Keener, *Matthew*, xxix, 84-85.

Traditional skeptical and fundamentalist approaches to the Gospels have generally made the same mistake: judging the Gospels by standards foreign to their genre. This book is an attempt to provide reasons for a sounder, mediating approach.

Chapter 2

What are the Gospels? Richard Burridge's Impact on Scholarly Understanding of the Genre of the Gospels[1]

Steve Walton
St Mary's University, Twickenham & Tyndale House, Cambridge

Introduction

It was 22 May 1995, and I was sitting in a room being interviewed for the post of Tutor in New Testament at St John's College, Nottingham. Facing me was what, with hindsight, was an intimidating panel: being asked what you mean by 'hermeneutics' by John Goldingay with Anthony Thiselton—who is 'Mr Hermeneutics'—in the room could certainly be considered intimidating! There was a moment in the interview when I was asked which recent scholarly New Testament book I had read and appreciated, and I responded, a little hesitantly, to say that Richard Burridge's *What are the Gospels?* (Burridge 1992; revised ed.: Burridge 2004) was the most stimulating and helpful thing I had read recently. The hesitation was because there, on the panel, was Richard Burridge himself, and he had the grace to chuckle, I recall, when I mentioned his book.

Reading that book was one of those relatively rare moments when I found my view changed, and wondered afterwards why I ever held the other view. What was it that made Burridge's work on the four canonical Gospels (hereafter 'the Gospels') so remarkable? It was not that no-one had ever proposed the idea that the Gospels shared characteristics with Graeco-Roman 'lives'. This had been the standard view in the nineteenth century and, not long before Burridge's work, Talbert and Shuler had argued for it,[2] although their arguments had not carried the day because of significant errors or weaknesses.[3]

---

[1] This article was originally published in *CBR* 14 (1, 2015); see Walton, "Impact."
[2] Talbert, *What is a Gospel?*; Shuler, *Genre*.
[3] Burridge, *Gospels?* (2004), 83-86; also Aune, "Problem," 9-60.

This study is significant because it is not given to many to turn round a scholarly consensus in their lifetime, and it is given to even fewer to do that with their PhD work. Yet this is what Burridge's study of Gospel genre did: scholarship largely adopted his view that the Gospels are a form of Graeco-Roman biography. As Burridge himself is wont to remark, he has spent his scholarly career stating the 'bleeding obvious' (to echo the British comedians Peter Cooke and Dudley Moore): the Gospels are books about Jesus! To reflect on his contribution and impact, we shall consider the setting in scholarship into which Burridge made his contribution, the key arguments which he used to make his case, and the impact over subsequent years of his results.

Setting the Scene in Twentieth-century Gospel Studies

The dominant view of the Gospels' genre in twentieth-century Gospel scholarship came from Germany, and it was that the Gospels were *sui generis*—they did not fit any previously-known genre of literature. This consensus grew in reaction to the nineteenth-century 'lives of Jesus', which took the Gospels as biographies and combined them to produce a 'biography' of Jesus.[4] Karl Ludwig Schmidt and Rudolf Bultmann represent key figures in this reaction, as Burridge notes.[5] Central to their response is the distinction between *Hochliteratur* and *Kleinliteratur*—roughly, literary writing and popular or folk-writing. They identify the Gospels as folk writing because they see them as closer to stories concerning people such as Dr Faustus and St Francis, rather than Graeco-Roman biographies. In particular, they see the Gospels as oral traditions about Jesus strung together—hence their original anonymity. This shows, they claim, that the evangelists had no pretensions to write *Hochliteratur*. Bultmann regards the Gospels as stemming from worship of Jesus, and thus as being significantly different from biographies, which present an individual for admiration or imitation. Indeed, the Gospels lack the desiderata of a modern biography: the origins, childhood, education, psychological development, and personality of Jesus are notable by their absence or thin coverage.[6] The evangelists, on this view, are not seeking to write biography, but aiming to unite the exalted Christ with stories of the earthly Jesus.[7] Thus Gospels are 'an original creation of Christianity,'[8] a comment Bultmann makes about Mark, but extensible to all four Gospels.[9]

To give some examples of standard New Testament and Gospels books which adopt this approach, consider these:
From C.F.D. Moule in 1962:

---

[4] Renan, *Vie de Jésus*; ET: Renan, *Life of Jesus*.
[5] Burridge, *Gospels?* (2004), 8-12; for Schmidt's and Bultmann's original works see Schmidt, "Die Stellung der Evangelien"; ET: Schmidt, *The Place of the Gospels*; Bultmann, *Die Geschichte*; ET: Bultmann, *History*.
[6] Bultmann, *History*, 372.
[7] Ibid.
[8] Ibid., 74.
[9] Ibid., 347-48.

...two new genres of literature offered by the New Testament. First, the 'Gospel'. Imagine (if possible) that an otherwise educated person of our own day, with absolutely no knowledge of Christianity or its literature, were suddenly presented with St Mark's Gospel. What would he make of it? He would quickly recognize that it was quite unlike any other genre of writing known to him. It is concerned with Jesus of Nazareth, yet there is no description of his personal appearance, practically no attempt to date the action, only the barest indications of its place. It starts with no family history or background, it presents little ordered sequence of events. It springs straight into what it describes as good news, *euangelion*, and points to the coming of John as the fulfilment of a certain passage in the Old Testament. From this jumping-off point it goes on, through a series of brief, loosely linked paragraphs describing the activity or (more rarely) the sayings, of Jesus, to a proportionately very long account of his arrest, trial, and execution; and at the point where the tomb is found empty it seems to end abruptly—for the few verses which follow are patently from a later hand and constitute a summary of the traditions about the sequel.

This is certainly not biography, real or fictional. Yet neither is it an ethical or moralistic writing. It has no real parallels before it. *It is the first extant specimen of a new genre: it is what we have learnt to call 'a Gospel'*, although the term *euangelion* is used by Mark himself not for his book but for its contents.[10]

From Ralph Martin in 1975, although note his caveat:

It is doubtful that the term "biography" really fits the case when we ask about the scope of the Christian Gospels. Certainly, *if we give a modern connotation to the term*, it becomes inappropriate for several reasons.[11]

Martin goes on to cite the absence of Jesus' predecessors, culture, and environment, and the lack of interest in the mental and psychological development of Jesus.

From Hans Conzelmann and Andreas Lindemann, writing in 1985:

There are no parallels to the NT literary type "Gospel." A comparison with certain literary types of antiquity, such as the biography and the historical monograph, demonstrates this. The substantial difference to the classical biography, such as that of Plutarch or Suetonius, is made clear especially in the Gospel of Mark: The person of the author cannot be recognized and the action of the "hero," namely of Jesus of Nazareth, is not presented biographically. Apparently the issue is not at all a continuous description of the life of Jesus or a presentation of his character; instead, the primary focal point is the work of Jesus as the revealer sent by God, as seen in his deeds, teaching, and passion. Events are of interest only from this vantage point...There is not even a trace of a development of the self-consciousness and character of Jesus.[12]

---

[10] Moule, *Birth*, 4-5; (italics mine).
[11] Martin, *New Testament*, 1:16; (italics mine).
[12] Conzelmann and Lindemann, *Interpreting*, 26-27.

From Graham Stanton in 1989, in a widely-used textbook:

> The more widely accepted view is that the form of the gospels is unique and that Mark had no literary models at all…It was frequently claimed that the early church was so taken up with its proclamation of the Risen Christ that it was not interested at all in the past of Jesus. On this view the gospels stemmed from the proclamation of the early church and not in any sense be seen as 'memoirs' or 'records'…The gospels must be read against the backdrop, not of modern biographical writing, but of their own times. When this is done, the gospels do not emerge as fully-fledged biographies of Jesus, but it then becomes clear that the evangelists are concerned with the *story* as well as the *significance* of Jesus…We can be almost certain that Mark did not intend to write a biography of Jesus in the Graeco-Roman tradition…[the gospels] can only be linked with the Graeco-Roman biographical tradition only with very considerable qualifications.[13]

It is notable that Stanton takes this view, given that in his ground-breaking doctoral thesis, published as *Jesus of Nazareth in New Testament Preaching*, he argues carefully and cogently that the earliest Christians have an interest in the past of Jesus and sought to preserve memories of his past in the Gospels.[14] Not only that, he argues that a comparison with the Graeco-Roman biographical tradition is helpful to illuminate the Gospels.[15] At this point and for some years later, however, Stanton is unwilling to take the step of placing the Gospels in the genre of ancient biography, for he writes of '[t]he wholly justifiable insistence that the gospels are not biographies.'[16] Burridge acknowledges that Stanton's work critiquing the Bultmannian consensus prepared the ground for his own argument (which persuaded Stanton to reverse his opinion on Gospel genre).[17]

Finally, from Larry Hurtado, writing in the widely-used *Dictionary of Jesus and the Gospels* in 1992, which sums up the 'state of the art' of Gospel studies at the time[18]:

> The Gospels are not fully explainable, however, simply in terms of the Greco-Roman literary setting or by linking them with literary genres of that era. The impetus for the Gospels derives from the religious complexion and needs of early Christianity; and their contents, presuppositions, major themes and literary texture are all heavily influenced by their immediate religious setting as well. In very general terms, the Gospels can be likened to other examples of Greco-Roman popular biography, but they also form a distinctive group within that broad body of ancient writings.[19]

---

[13] Stanton, *Gospels*, 15-20.
[14] Stanton, *Jesus*.
[15] Ibid., 117-36.
[16] Ibid., 135.
[17] Burridge, "Gospel," 6-9, 12-13, 16.
[18] It is noteworthy that Burridge himself wrote the article 'Gospel: Genre' in the 2013 edition of this dictionary; see Burridge, 'Gospel: Genre.'
[19] Hurtado, "Gospel (genre)," 282.

The implication of this view is that the Gospels should be studied to identify the authentic sayings of Jesus, and to understand the process of transmission of the stories about Jesus, a process that was assumed to be long. The form-critical approach instantiated in this approach was followed by the development of redaction criticism, which taught scholars to reconstruct the *Sitz im Leben* of the evangelists, and 'mirror read' the Gospels for the situation of the church(es) to which each was addressed, the Gospel communities, as we might say. Thus both form and redaction criticism treated the Gospels as windows into the earliest churches, rather than windows on Jesus—and they considered this choice as a clear either/or. However, redaction criticism's rediscovery of the author in the third quarter of the twentieth century began to raise questions of authorial intention (even with all its attendant difficulties), which itself led to reopening the question of Gospel genre. Following the failed attempts of Talbert and Shuler to argue for Graeco-Roman biography, Burridge entered the field.

Burridge's Contribution

Burridge came into this discussion with a training in Classics which included awareness of discussions of genre in such circles. He came to his doctoral work with the sense that the then-consensus view was correct, and expected to show that the Gospels are not Graeco-Roman 'lives' (Greek *bioi*; Latin *vitae*).[20] His doctoral work under Maurice Casey made pioneering use of (then) new computer technology to engage with the texts of Graeco-Roman 'lives' and the Gospels—extraordinarily, these days you could probably do it on a mobile phone!—as well as painstaking study of some of the texts by hand, including the Gospels. His work is interdisciplinary, crossing the boundaries of Classics, genre criticism, and New Testament studies, using all three disciplines to inform his approach.

Burridge identifies four significant markers of Graeco-Roman 'lives' which, in combination, allow him to recognise this genre with confidence.[21]

First, *opening features*: there is usually a title and an opening formula which identify the book's focus on the subject of the biography.

Secondly, the *subject* of the biography is the subject of the lion's share of the main verbs in the book, and is given the lion's share of the space, placing the subject in the spotlight (cf. Plutarch, *Alex.* 1.1). This is where Burridge's groundbreaking computer analysis fits, allowing him to get a good 'feel' for the focus of the verbs by considering nominative nouns and pronouns, which tend to be verb subjects. Studying verbs 'by hand' then allows him to fine tune his analysis by noting verbs without explicit subjects which are nevertheless performed by the book's subject.

Thirdly, *external features* including the structure of the book, its style, etc., which enhance the focus on the subject.

---

[20] Burridge, *Gospels?* (2004), 101.
[21] Ibid., 105-23, esp. 107.

Fourthly, *internal features* such as the settings, the topics and content included, the values and attitudes espoused or promoted by the work, and the author's intention and purpose (whether stated explicitly or not).

When Burridge studies a selection of Greek and Latin 'lives' and compares the four Gospels one by one with this pattern, he finds each of these features to be present in a comparable form in each Gospel. This strongly suggests that an ancient reader hearing Mark and the others read aloud (the normal means of 'reading' in the ancient world, e.g. Acts 8.30)[22] would recognise them as *bioi*—'lives'—of Jesus. This does not mean that we should think of them like *modern* biographies, of course—comparing the Gospels with today's biographies was the error which Bultmann and his generation made—but it does mean that the evangelists have chosen a vehicle which would be recognisable to a wide readership around the Mediterranean basin. That seems intrinsically likely, for to use a literary form which was *sui generis* to communicate a new worldview, belief system and lifestyle focused on Jesus would be to place a double barrier to communication.

Burridge here identifies a key point which moves the debate forward, and which implies that *the focus of the Gospels is Jesus*, the subject of the 'life'. This might sound blindingly obvious—and some, such as Tuckett and Petersen, regard this claim as trite or trivial[23]—but for much of the last hundred years the heart of Gospels scholarship has been in examining the communities supposed to be behind the Gospels, the process of transmission of individual stories, and so on, rather than their true subject, Jesus himself. Burridge followed this study up with his own attempt to read the Gospels for their Christology in his excellent, less technical *Four Gospels, One Jesus?*, a book that has been valued by generations of students.

The Impact of Burridge's Work

Burridge's work was rapidly seen as highly significant, not to say game-changing, in understanding the genre of the Gospels, and his conclusions were widely accepted. This sea change in scholarship is Burridge's major contribution to the scholarly world; he was not alone in contributing to this argument—Graham Stanton is another. As we noted, Stanton's doctoral work argued that the earliest believers did regard preserving memories of Jesus and his teaching as important,[24] and Burridge's work built on this by offering a rigorous case that the Gospels were intended as books telling the story of Jesus, rather than being a 'coded' version of early church history. It is noteworthy that Stanton wrote a commendation of the first edition of Burridge's *Four Gospels, One Jesus?*, describing it as a book which would enable '[n]ovices and old-hands alike [to] read the gospels with new

---

[22] See Walton, "Rhetorical Criticism," 8n52.
[23] Tuckett, "Review"; Petersen, "Can One Speak," 146.
[24] Stanton, *Jesus*.

eyes.' Thus by 1995, only three years after the publication of Burridge's book, Stanton wrote:

> Ancient biographers often wrote with several different intentions, including apologetic and polemic. Some wrote in order to uphold (or to challenge) a system of beliefs or values personified in the subject of the biography. So too with the evangelists, whose accounts of the life and teaching of Jesus were 'foundation documents' for the newly emergent Christian communities.
>
> *The Gospels, then, can be seen as a special kind or sub-set of ancient biographical writing*...They tell the story of the career of Jesus in order to persuade the reader of its significance.[25]

In their discussion of genre in the New Testament, Brook Pearson and Stanley Porter state in 2002: 'the overwhelming trend has been towards seeing the Gospel genre as some kind of biography.'[26] They cite Burridge as the key scholar who had moved debate in this direction.[27]

Bart Ehrman's widely-used introduction to the New Testament states in 1997: 'Scholars have come to reject the view that [the Gospels] are totally unlike anything else...some of these investigations have suggested that the Gospels are best seen as a kind of Greco-Roman (as opposed to modern) biography.'[28] Burridge's influence is clear, for Ehrman cites W*hat are the Gospels?* as '[a] thorough study that emphatically argues that the Gospels are best understood as a kind of ancient biography.'[29]

It is also worth noting that some subsequent work, while not necessarily being directly dependent on Burridge's work, was done in a context and atmosphere in the scholarly guild which was more open to such discussions. In particular, the collaboration of Richard Bauckham and others (including Burridge himself)[30] in arguing that the Gospels were written with a wide audience in mind, rather than the narrow communities envisaged in redaction criticism.[31] In the key essay in that book, Bauckham cites Burridge's work in support of his argument: 'it seems very unlikely that anyone would expect a *bios* to address the very specific circumstances of a small community of people...its relevance would be pitched in relatively broad terms for any competent reader.'[32]

Bauckham draws a further implication from the written nature of the Gospels, which is that it seems strange for a member of a community (an evangelist) to *write down* a 'coded' message for his own community's situation, rather than address the situation orally. Indeed, by contrast with a letter, which would probably

---

[25] Stanton, *Truth?*, 138-39; (italics mine).
[26] Pearson and Porter, "Genres," 138.
[27] Ibid., 141-42.
[28] Ehrman, *New Testament*, 52.
[29] Ibid., 55.
[30] Burridge, "About People."
[31] Bauckham, *Gospels*.
[32] Bauckham, "For Whom," 28.

stop circulating with its first, named recipients, a 'life' would be highly likely to circulate *and be intended to circulate* more widely.[33]

Whence Scholarship?

Let us turn to consider one area where Burridge's work might be expected to make an impact, commentaries on the Gospels, and one area where there is unexploited capital to be gained.

Gospel Commentaries since *What are the Gospels?*

Given the wide acceptance of Burridge's conclusions, it is worth considering commentaries on the Gospels since 1999, on the basis that a seven-year interval should give sufficient time for Burridge's conclusions to permeate scholarship sufficiently to affect the commentaries—for good quality commentaries generally take a long time in the making.

There is some discussion of Gospel genre in the introductions to some (but not all) commentaries, and this shows that the issue is now on the agenda of Gospel commentators. Examples, among about twenty samples considered, are the work of Craig Keener on Matthew and John,[34] the work of Andrew Lincoln on John,[35] and the work of both R.T. France and Robert Stein on Mark.[36] All four scholars substantially accept Burridge's case.

In his Matthew commentary, Keener summarises and accepts Burridge's conclusion that the Gospels are 'lives', and spends the largest part of his introduction to the Matthew's themes on Christology.[37]

On John, Lincoln sketches the range of the genre *bios*, from ancient history writing to encomium, and draws important implications from the differences between this genre and ancient historiography, notably that a *bios* would be likely to build on core events 'with substantial correspondence to what happened in the past' by adding 'varying amounts of embellishment' to present the story.[38] Lincoln's fine commentary carries through Burridge's hermeneutical programme, of focusing attention on the portrait of Jesus in John, well.

Keener, in his John commentary, discusses Gospel genre and strongly sides with Burridge's view.[39] In a careful discussion of Graeco-Roman biography and history, Keener rejects the false dichotomy of historical or theological and argues rather that John should be seen as 'both historical *and* literary/theological', while

---

[33] Ibid., 29.
[34] Keener, *Matthew*, 16-24; idem, *John*, 1.3-34.
[35] Lincoln, *Saint John*, 14-17.
[36] France, *Mark*, 4-11; Stein, *Mark*, 19-21.
[37] Keener, *Matthew*, 53-68.
[38] Lincoln, *Saint John*, 17.
[39] Keener, *John*, 1.11-12.

recognising that John is the most literary/theological of the four Gospels.[40] Keener's two-volume study of John holds its focus commendably on Jesus.

France on Mark also accepts Burridge's case, and notes how it turned around the consensus of a previous generation.[41] Stein, similarly, states that Mark is a form of Graeco-Roman biography, citing Burridge in support.[42] France goes on to recognise that Mark writes to tell the story of Jesus in order to summon people to follow him as disciples, and identifies three distinctives in Mark's 'life of Jesus' compared to other Graeco-Roman 'lives': first, the subject matter of Mark is one who was more than a great man, but one who is even now alive and worthy of worship, although rejected and humiliated while on earth; secondly, the material of Mark bears the signs of being used in Christian proclamation; and thirdly, it is written not for private use, but for reading in communities which were not composed only of the highly educated. France's commentary is a fine example of reading Mark christologically.

We should also note that James Edwards' valuable narrative-critical commentary on Mark focuses attention strongly on Jesus throughout, and his introduction strongly highlights the portrait of Jesus in Mark,[43] although he does not engage explicitly with questions of genre (and, surprisingly, Burridge does not appear in his index).

That is not to say that Burridge's work has entirely carried the day among the commentators. Joel Marcus offers an interesting half-way house position, in placing Mark within 'the Markan community', whose composition he appears to know rather well,[44] and yet in accepting, too, that it shares many features of hellenistic biography.[45] Marcus places himself clearly in the camp influenced by Schmidt and Bultmann, however, for he regards the continuing presence of Jesus in the church as marking the Second Gospel as an incomplete *bios*.

Adela Yarboro Collins, in her commentary on Mark, appears to give with one hand and then take back with the other, when she concedes that Burridge makes a good case for the likeness of Mark to Graeco-Roman *bioi*, but argues that Burridge should have considered other models, especially in the Old Testament.[46] Collins herself prefers to think of Mark as a new genre, eschatological historical monograph. Burridge has to a degree responded to this criticism in his essay 'Gospel Genre, Christological Controversy and the Absence of Rabbinic Biography: Some Implications of the Biographical Hypothesis', appended to the second edition of *What are the Gospels?*.[47]

Ulrich Luz, in his commentary on Matthew, considers that treating Matthew as a Graeco-Roman 'life' would be foreign to what he takes to be a predominantly

---

[40] Ibid., 17; (his italics).
[41] France, *Mark*, 4-6.
[42] Stein, *Mark*, 19-21.
[43] Edwards, *Mark*, 12-15.
[44] Marcus, *Mark*, 1.25-39.
[45] Ibid., 1.64-69.
[46] Collins, *Mark*, 27-29.
[47] Burridge, *Gospels?* (2004), 322-40.

Jewish audience. He considers that Matthew modelled his work on Mark, and wrote it as a 'foundation story', much like some Old Testament books (e.g. Chronicles).[48]

The debate is clearly far from over. Indeed, some commentary writing appears to go on just as before, with little recognition that genre must affect exegesis. It may be that such commentators have read Burridge and rejected his view, but if so they show no sign of engaging with his work. This appears to be the case with François Bovon's commentary on Luke.[49] Disappointingly, although David Turner mentions genre (including citing Burridge) in his commentary on Matthew, he focuses mainly on the historical value of Matthew in his discussion of genre, suggesting that he sees the generic question as not greatly relevant to the interpretation of Matthew.[50] There is still room for good commentating (perhaps particularly on Luke) which takes the biographical nature of the Gospels seriously, and which works out the agenda set by Burridge's research at every level of the exegesis of the text.

Unexploited Capital: Fine-tuning the Genre Description

Burridge himself recognises that the Graeco-Roman *bios* is a broad genre, ranging over books which are rather different in style and contents, and others repeat this point.[51] So a key question is whether we can get a more fine-grained description of the genre of the Gospels, perhaps by more detailed comparison with specific types of *bios*. Burridge hints at this in writing:

> since many *bioi* were used by philosophical groups or schools for teaching about their beliefs and founder, as well as for attack and defence in debate with other groups, and some of their generic features are also found in the gospels, we can begin interpreting them with the expectation that we will find didactic, apologetic and polemical purposes and material here also.[52]

One valuable suggestion comes from Scot McKnight, who accepts Burridge's 'now established conclusions' concerning Gospel genre,[53] and seeks to fine-tune them by comparing Matthew with the content of Paul's gospel message. McKnight sketches four key claims based on studying both the key Pauline texts (notably 1 Cor. 15) and other 'gospel' passages (especially in Acts)[54]: (i) the gospel narrates and declares the whole life of Jesus, from incarnation through exaltation and onto consummation; (ii) the gospel treats the Jesus story as fulfilling Israel's story—it necessarily involves a hermeneutic of Israel's story; (iii) a key feature of the Christian gospel's instantiation of Israel's story is that Jesus is the

---

[48] Luz, *Matthew*, 13-15, esp. 15.
[49] Bovon, *Luke*, 1.5-6.
[50] Turner, *Matthew*, 5-6.
[51] e.g. Alexander, "Review," 75-76.
[52] Burridge, *Gospels?* (2004), 248.
[53] McKnight, "Matthew," 61.
[54] Ibid., 61-67.

Davidic Messiah of Israel; (iv) the gospel story saves, frees and gives victory to those who receive it. Thus, turning to Matthew, McKnight argues that as a *bios*, Matthew is '*a gospelling bios about Jesus, who is Messiah and Lord and Saviour,*'[55] and he goes on to argue that Matthew fulfils each of the four distinctives of 'gospel.'[56] This is helpful and suggestive, and may open doors into further work—many will hear resonances with some of N.T. Wright's work on the Gospels (notably Wright 2012—he mentions McKnight's work, but not this essay).[57]

Building on McKnight's work, there is an as-yet-unfulfilled agenda for potential PhD students to pursue. Can we develop a more fine-grained description of the Gospels in dialogue with a range of ancient *bioi* and thus deepen our understanding of the Gospels' testimony to Jesus yet further? It is a considerable tribute to Richard Burridge's work that we are now ready and able to engage with such a question.

---

[55] Ibid., 67; (his italics).
[56] Ibid., 69-74.
[57] Wright, *How God*.

Chapter 3

Charting the (Un)charted: Gospels as Ancient Biographies and Their (Un)explored Implications[1]

Youngju Kwon
Asbury Theological Seminary

Introduction

Authors typically use genres that they expect their readers to recognize. An author will carefully choose a specific genre because he or she believes that this genre is the best way for conveying the intended message. As readers engage the work they pick up on various features that alert them to the intended genre. Thus Richard A. Burridge observes, "Genre forms a kind of contract or agreement ... between an author and a reader, by which the author sets out to write according to a whole set of expectations and conventions and we agree to read or to interpret the work using the same conventions, giving us an initial idea of what we might expect to find."[2] Determining the Gospels' genre and understanding the conventions of that genre are therefore essential to properly interpreting their message.

In the last few decades, scholars have debated this issue and proposed several possible genres for the Gospels from fiction to history. Because the majority of scholars currently view the Gospels as ancient biographies since Burridge's *magnum opus*,[3] I will not reiterate those arguments here. Instead, I will build my argument on the assumption that the Gospels are ancient biographies and focus more on the implications of this determination.

---

[1] I would like to express my gratitude to my *Doktorvater* Craig S. Keener who has been developing the significance of considering the Gospels as ancient biographies and has guided me in developing this topic for my dissertation as well as this project. I am also grateful for Dr. David R. Bauer who kindly read and gave helpful comments on the early draft of this essay. I also thank Dr. Michael Licona for sharing his sources with me.

[2] Burridge, "About People," 114.

[3] Burridge, *Gospels?* (1992; 2nd ed. 2004); see also Burridge, *Four Gospels*, 5–8. For foundational works before Burridge that had argued for this position of Gospel genre, see Talbert, *What Is a Gospel?*; Aune, *Literary Environment*, 46–76; idem, "Greco-Roman Biography," 107–26; Shuler, *Genre*; Stanton, *Jesus*, 117–26; idem, *New People*, 62–4. It is interesting to note that Stanton's position on this issue has changed primarily due to Burridge's work. Although his earlier work in 1974 demonstrated the remarkable similarities between the Gospels and ancient biographies, Stanton was not ready to label the Gospels as ancient biographies per se. In his 1990 work he admits that his conclusion was too

Despite this primary concern, I will revisit two proposed genres for the Gospels—folk literature and *sui generis*—to demonstrate the inadequacy of some twentieth-century alternatives to the biographic genre. After the critical appraisal of these positions, I will map out some charted and uncharted areas in which the implications of the Gospels' genre as ancient biography have been both explored and as yet unexplored.

Selected Scholarship on Gospel Genre

Other than the genre of ancient biography, scholars have suggested a number of other possibilities for the Gospels: aretalogy,[4] history,[5] novel or fiction,[6] midrash,[7] drama,[8] folk literature,[9] and *sui generis* (or unique genre).[10] Each position has its own merits and limitations, and the major arguments for each position have been well presented elsewhere.[11] As mentioned earlier, only the last two genre proposals listed above will receive attention here. Although these two positions share many assumptions and arguments, we will handle them separately in order to bring out some of their more nuanced points.

Folk Literature

Karl Ludwig Schmidt proposed and defended the view that the Gospels are folk literature. According to Schmidt, the Gospels are *Kleinliteratur* (or low literature/folk literature) in which disjointed stories and episodes are loosely connected with no chronological order. On the other hand, biographies, which he considers to be *Hochliteratur* (or high literature), are concerned with the orderly presentation of the life of a hero. Schmidt's remarks are worth quoting at length:

---

cautious then and he can "now accept that the Gospels are a type of Graeco-Roman biography" (64). For other works after Burridge, still adding fresh perspectives, see Frickenschmidt, *Evangelium*; Ytterbrink, *The Third Gospel*; Fitzgerald, "The Ancient Lives," 209–21; Stanton, *Gospels*, 14–8; Dunn, *Jesus Remembered*, 184–86; Hengel, "Eye-Witness Memory," 72; Keener, *Matthew*, 16–24; idem, *Historical Jesus*, 73–84; idem, *John*, 11–34; idem, "Assumptions," 30–39; idem, "Biographies of a Sage," 59–61.

[4] Hadas and Smith, *Heroes and Gods*; Smith, "Prolegomena," 174–99.

[5] Balch, "The Genre of Luke-Acts," 5–19; Collins, *The Beginning of the Gospel*, 1–38.

[6] Helms, *Gospel Fictions*; Tolbert, *Sowing the Gospel*, 59–70.

[7] Goulder, *Midrash*.

[8] Bilezikian, *The Liberated Gospel*; Smith, "A Divine Tragedy," 209–31; England, "Mark as Drama."

[9] Schmidt, "Die Stellung der Evangelien," 50–134; For the English translation, see Schmidt, *The Place of the Gospels*.

[10] Bultmann, *History*; Stuhlmacher, "The Genre(s) of the Gospels," 484–94.

[11] For the general discussion and evaluation of the different positions of gospel genre, see Eddy and Boyd, *The Jesus Legend*, 309–50; Aune, *Literary Environment*, 23–32; Blomberg, *Historical Reliability*, 298–303; Epp and MacRae, *Modern Interpreters*, 253–58; Keener, *Historical Jesus*, 74–84.

The earliest outline (*Aufriss*) of the story of Jesus is that of the Gospel of Mark. The inconsistencies in the traditions it contains show us what the earliest Jesus tradition looked like: there was no continuous narrative, but an abundance of individual stories, which for the most part are arranged topically . . . Luke is also a part of the process, though he is the only evangelist who additionally has literary aspirations . . . The church took Matthew as its favorite gospel, the gospel, that is to say, which even more than Mark sought to offer a topical arrangement of the individual stories and which discarded a good deal of the framework material that was superfluous . . . *In general there is no life of Jesus in the sense of a developing narrative of his life, no chronological outline (*Aufriss*) of the story of Jesus*; there are only individual stories, pericopes set within a framework (*Rahmenwerk*).[12]

Although Schmidt's position (i.e., "continuous narrative" being the core feature of biographies) may be generally true of *modern* biographies, a number of both New Testament scholars and classicists have rightly emphasized that the lack of chronological presentation and the topical arrangement of biographical material are quite common in *ancient* biographies, just like what we find in the Gospels.[13]

Another factor that inclines Schmidt to refuse to identify the Gospels as ancient biographies is that, in Schmidt's view, ancient biographies are full of literary intentions and techniques, whereas the Gospels are largely void of these. Thus Schmidt says:

Do the Gospels hark back to biography at all? . . . A glance at various handbooks and technical introductions shows just how difficult this can be. A full-fledged biography employs the techniques of narrative art to describe the life of a person, including both inward and outward development. To that end, questions about the order of the material (sequences of content and chronology), pragmatics, psychology, characterization, and portraiture are of decisive importance. The Gospels are almost entirely devoid of such things.[14]

Building on Ernst Bernheim's massive work,[15] Schmidt declares that the survey of "various handbooks and technical introductions" refutes the view that the Gospels are ancient biographies. There are problems with Schdmidt's appraisal, however. For example, his reliance on the programmatic statements in handbooks and introductions might not reflect the actual practices of ancient biographers. Many classicists, based on the close reading of actual texts, have strongly warned

---

[12] Schmidt, *Der Rahmen*, 317. The quotation is from Riches, "Introduction," xii–xiii (emphasis added).

[13] Votaw, "Contemporary Biographies," 55; Stanton, *Jesus*, 119–21; Kennedy, "Source Criticism," 141; Aune, *Literary Environment*, 31–2; Görgemanns, "Biography: Greek," 2:649; Keener, *Historical Jesus*, 82; Burridge, "Biography," 379; Stadter, "Biography and History," 529.

[14] Schmidt, *The Place of the Gospels*, 32.

[15] Bernheim, *Lehrbuch*.

against the rigid application of the general principles found in handbooks and introductions.[16] In particular, they argue that the mechanical and sweeping application of general principles found in handbooks to similar generic works may distort the result; therefore, a more nuanced approach should be adopted, considering the specific context and purpose of a given work. The programmatic statements in handbooks and introductions can sometimes be helpful in understanding an ancient work in question, but there is always the possibility that an actual practice may deviate from its theory. Thus, after studying Plutarch's several biographies, Christopher Pelling, a renowned voice on Plutarch's works, concludes, "A writer's programmatic statements can sometimes be a poor guide to his work, and some Lives fit Plutarch's theory better than others. Any account of the Lives must bring out their *versatility*."[17] As a consequence, Schmidt's methodology is questionable for identifying the proper genre of the Gospels.

Furthermore, Schmidt's judgment of the core elements of biographies is also unconvincing. According to Schmidt, biographies need to contain the descriptions about a hero's "inward and outward development" such as "[chronological] order of the material, pragmatics, psychology, characterization, and portraiture."[18] But one should ask whether these elements are equally important in ancient biographies, though they are essential in modern counterparts. Some scholars suggest that personality development is foreign to ancients because the conception of personality in the ancient world is more static than developmental.[19] In addition, although modern biographies often contain an author's description of a hero's psychology and physical appearance, these are "far from being universal feature[s] of ancient biographical writing," though they are not completely absent.[20] It should also be noted that ancient biographers prefer to portray the character of a hero in more *indirect* ways. In other words, rather than an author directly describing a hero's character, the words and deeds of the subject often speak for themselves. Many scholars point out that this indirect characterization is widely employed by ancient biographers.[21]

Ultimately, Schmidt searches the Gospels with an aim to identify modern biographical conventions and incorrectly concludes that because the Gospels lack such qualities they should not be labeled as biographies. Indeed, the elements of

---

[16] Hack, "Literary Forms," 1–65; Wardman, "Plutarch's Methods," 254–61; Georgiadou, "Lives of the Caesars," 349–51; Beneker, "Nepos' Method," 109–21.

[17] Pelling, "Plutarch's Adaptation," 139 (emphasis original).

[18] A similar line of argument can be found in Bultmann, *History*, 372: "There is no historical-biographical interest in the Gospels, and that is why they have nothing to say about Jesus's human personality, his appearance and character, his origin, education and development; quite apart from the fact that they do not command the cultivated techniques of composition necessary for grand literature, nor let the personalities of their authors appear."

[19] Aune, *Literary Environment*, 28; for an extended discussion of this issue, see Russell, "Reading Plutarch's Lives," 144–7.

[20] Stanton, *Jesus*, 124.

[21] Ibid., 125; Burridge, *Gospels?* (2004), 117; Duff, *Plutarch's Lives*, 13–4; for the methods of characterization in ancient historical writings, see Pitcher, "Characterization," 102–17.

folk literature that Schmidt thought would prove that the Gospels are not biographies—the topical arrangement of biographical material, the Gospels' lack of interest in personality development, and the paucity of authors' direct statements about a hero's appearance and psychology—are common features in ancient biography, and so might serve as counterevidence against his thesis.

Sui Generis or Unique Genre

Rudolf Bultmann shares many of Schmidt's assumptions. Like Schmidt, Bultmann argues that the Gospels display the features of popular writings that "lack scientific character and a developed technique of composition, interest in chronology, factual connections and psychological motivations."[22] Due to the lack of literary intentions, Bultmann similarly claims that the Gospels are not biographies.[23] He also asserts, along with Schmidt, that the absence of biographical characterization in the Gospels precludes making a substantial generic link between the Gospels and biography.[24] However, Bultmann goes one step further by arguing that the Gospels are *sui generis*, i.e., that they reflect a unique genre that cannot be explained in comparative literary terms. Schmidt's work also hints at the uniqueness of the Gospels' genre,[25] but it is Bultmann who makes this claim more explicit.

Bultmann's ingenuity comes from his belief that the gospel genre should be understood first and foremost in the context of the Christian faith, not in the history of literature. For this reason, he concedes that the Gospels share some characteristics of folk literature, but then refuses to identify them as folk literature per se.[26] According to Bultmann, not only Schmidt's enterprise (i.e., the endeavor to find the parallels of the Gospels in the folk literature) but also any attempts to define the Gospels in literary terms are eventually doomed to failure. The Gospels,

---

[22] Bultmann, *History*, 372–73.

[23] Bultmann, "The Gospels (Form)," 87: "They [Gospels] cannot be included in the category of biographies . . . In no sense do they belong to the category of major literature, characterized by a skillful technique of composition, the display of the personality of the author, and aesthetic or scientific concerns."

[24] Ibid.

[25] Schmidt, *The Place of the Gospels*, 25, 27. Schmidt first lays out the two possibilities of finding the parallels of the Gospels in the history of literature: "by means of analogy (the Gospels originate *like* writings of another similar genre)" and "by means of genealogy (the Gospels originate *from* writings of another similar genre)" (25; emphasis original). Then he argues that the only viable option is the former, namely, by means of analogy. In other words, although one can find some parallels of the Gospels in another similar literary form (by means of analogy), he or she should not seek the origin of the Gospels from that specific literary form (by means of genealogy). Thus he argues, "*The Gospels do not belong to any specific strand in the history of literature*, and despite their borrowings from 'the world,' neither do their non-canonical offshoots, since *the earlier Gospels always remained their prototype*" (27; emphasis mine).

[26] Ibid., 87–8; Bultmann, *History*, 372.

Bultmann argues, are intelligible only from the perspective that they are essentially the kerygma of Christ, not a kind of literature. A collection of his terse, but powerful, statements is sufficient to make the point:[27]

> There had been no such thing as a gospel in the previous history of literature.[28]

> The question whether there are other *analogies to the gospels* in the history of literature leads us to a clearer view of their distinctive nature.[29]

> They [Gospels] grow up from the *cult of Christ*, and their unity is provided by the Christ myth. They are the cult *legends* of Christian worship . . . Thus they are a unique phenomenon in the history of literature.[30]

> The gospel tradition did not arise within a literary movement, but had its origin in the preaching of Jesus in the life of the community of his followers.[31]

> Their [Gospels'] own specific characteristic, a creation of Mark, can be understood only from the *character of the Christian kerygma*.[32]

> The kerygma of Christ is cultic legend and the *Gospels are expanded cult legends*.[33]

> They [Gospels] have grown out of Christian worship and remain tied to it . . . The formation of our Gospels . . . is comprehensible only because there is a kerygma which proclaims a man who lived in the flesh as the Lord.[34]

> It is hardly possible to speak of the Gospels as a literary genus; the Gospel belongs to the history of dogma and worship.[35]

It is true that the Gospels have unique content. Thus some scholars partially agree with the view that the Gospels may be classified as *sui generis*.[36] However, from a literary point of view, the claim that the Gospels are so unique that one cannot speak of their genre at all is unconvincing. Thus Burridge says, "It is hard to imagine how anyone could invent something which is a literary novelty or unique kind of writing. Even supposing it were possible, no one else would be able to

---

[27] In the following series of quotations, all italics are original.
[28] Bultmann, "The Gospels (Form)," 87.
[29] Ibid.
[30] Ibid., 88–9.
[31] Ibid., 90.
[32] Bultmann, *History*, 370.
[33] Ibid., 371.
[34] Ibid., 373.
[35] Ibid., 374.
[36] Eddy and Boyd, *The Jesus Legend*, 320: "If David Hellholm is correct that genre involves aspects of content, form, and function—and we believe that he is—then it seems undeniable that there is sui generis dimension to the Gospel genre. At the very least, it is hard to deny that the specific *content* of the Gospels is, in an important sense, unique" (emphasis original).

make sense of the work, with no analogy to guide their interpretation."[37] In short, Bultmann's position can no longer be held.

In sum, Bultmann's conclusion that the Gospels find no parallel in any genre and Schmidt's evaluation of the Gospels by modern biographical standards and subsequent determination are imprecise and untenable. In what follows, *pace* Bultmann and Schmidt, we will speak of the Gospels as if they belong to a genre and discuss the implications of them being ancient biographies.

Charting the Charted: Gospels as Ancient Biographies and Their Explored Implications

Although the first edition of Burridge's work drastically impacted the scholarly view on the genre of the Gospels by forcefully arguing that they are indeed ancient biographies, it did not sufficiently address the *implications* of such a designation. As a way of filling this lacuna, in the second edition Burridge adds an additional chapter,[38] in which he mentions four possible areas of implications of his study: literary, sociological, historical, and theological.[39] The following four sections will look at how these areas have been explored in previous scholarship.

Literary or Generic Implications

One of the profound contributions of Burridge's work to Gospel studies is that it emphasized the importance of identifying a genre for scholarly interpretation. For writers and readers, different genres must be written with different conventions and read with different expectations.[40] If we write or read a newspaper as though it were poetry, it would be unproductive, if not meaningless. Richard Bauckham's essay in *Gospels for All Christians* is one example that takes the genre of the Gospels seriously and pursues its implications for gospel audiences.[41] According to Bauckham, a mistake in identifying a work's genre is a major obstacle to identifying its intended audience. In other words, many scholars have treated the Gospels almost as if they were one of Paul's letters that was written for a specific community.[42] However, Bauckham argues that the genre of the Gospels as ancient biographies seems to necessitate the conclusion that they were intended for a wider audience, not necessarily limited to specific audiences such as

---

[37] Burridge, *Gospels?* (2004), 12.
[38] Burridge, *Gospels?* (2004), 252–307.
[39] Ibid., 258–61.
[40] Ibid., 33–4.
[41] Bauckham, "For Whom," 9–48.
[42] Ibid., 26–7.

the Matthean or Johannine communities.[43] A similar line of argument is also presented in Burridge's essay in the same volume, providing many more concrete examples of ancient biographies being written for general audiences.[44]

Another important implication of Burridge's study is that more precision is needed regarding genre analysis. Several faulty assumptions concerning the genre of the Gospels arise when genre analysis is performed with limited knowledge. For instance, as noted earlier, Bultmann's position that the Gospels are *sui generis* cannot be accepted from a literary point of view because every work must belong to a certain genre; if not, the communication between writers and readers is muted. The oft-quoted statement of Wellek and Warren still has resounding echoes: "The totally familiar and repetitive pattern is boring; the totally novel form will be unintelligible—is indeed unthinkable."[45]

Precision in genre analysis may also clarify some of the confused attempts to identify the Gospels' genre. Burridge's discussions on two topics are extremely helpful here: (1) the different levels between genre and mode, and (2) the flexibility of genre. With regard to genre and mode, Burridge argues, "Many possible genres proposed for the Gospels are actually modal relationships: thus the dramatic, tragic or tragicomic elements (mode) do not make the Gospels into drama or tragedy (genre)."[46] Similarly, the presence of apocalyptic elements does not mean that the Gospel of Mark should be identified as an apocalypse.[47] For this reason, any attempts to classify the Gospels based on the higher level of mode such as "styles or motifs" are not precise and thus cannot be justified.[48] Regarding the flexibility of genre, Burridge argues that genres are in constant flux and the boundaries between the neighboring genres are often hard to draw; but there is still "family resemblance" by which it is possible to judge whether a given work is to be included in or excluded from an ideal genre.[49] If we apply this principle to various proposed genres, some misconceptions can be corrected. To give an example, Adela Yarbro Collins suggested that the Gospel of Mark is to be viewed as a historical monograph.[50] Her position is certainly understandable because history, among other genres, is the closest neighboring genre to biography and thus one can expect that the Gospels as biographies would contain some historical elements or features.[51] However, the primary difficulty in Collins's position is

---

[43] Ibid., 27–8.

[44] Burridge, "About People," 113–45.

[45] Wellek and Warren, *Theory of Literature*, 245.

[46] Burridge, *Gospels?* (2004), 239-40.

[47] Contra Perrin, "Historical Criticism," 365–6.

[48] Thus Downing's suggestion that the search for recurring motifs is more productive than the study of genre (Downing, "Contemporary Analogies," 51–65) cannot be substantiated.

[49] Burridge, *Gospels?* (2004), 40–1.

[50] Collins, *The Beginning of the Gospel*, 1–38; more briefly, see Collins, "Genre and the Gospels," 239–46.

[51] For helpful discussions on the general relationship between biography and history, see Aune, *Literary Environment*, 29–31; Stadter, "Biography and History," 528–9; Adams, *The Genre of Acts*, 114.

Mark's extended focus on one person or subject, which is the quintessential feature of ancient biography.

Sociological Implications

Is it possible that the evangelists read or heard Greco-Roman biographies and then chose to narrate the story of Jesus in a similar fashion according to the conventions of that genre? To put it differently, would the evangelists have had sufficient exposure to Greco-Roman literature so that they would have been able to emulate the style and features of other ancient biographies? To this question, Burridge replies with a yes. His comments are worth repeating here at length:

> The penetration of literary ideas through ancient society was widespread ... the concepts and nature of *bioi* were taught indirectly at primary level, followed by direct teaching of genres and other aspects of rhetoric and composition at secondary level. Such schools were all over Asia Minor and Syria, and were set up in Palestine, especially in Greek areas like the Decapolis, as part of the process of Hellenization ... [Further,] literary and cultural awareness was mediated down the social scale from the higher educated classes through public debates, the Cynic philosopher on the corner and the crowded marketplace, the theatre, courts and assembly, as well as the after-dinner entertainment, which the lower classes attended as servants and slaves, if not as guests; he concludes, 'there is no sign of a culture-gap between the highly literate aristocracy and the masses.'[52]

In addition, F. Gerald Downing argues that Quintilian also indicated that it is certainly possible for uneducated people to have access to high literature: "Writers like Quintilian are sure you must be able to adjust your material to a diverse audience; you must be able to appeal to the listening crowd as much as to the highborn judges or assessors; you must be able to write imaginary speeches in the style of ordinary people; you must be able to interrogate rustics (*Institutes* 3.8)."[53]

Although the Gospels are not elite literature, they were hardly written by illiterate peasants; illiterate persons do not write works as substantial as the Gospels.

Thus, the social context that form critics imagined (i.e., that the gap between high literature and low literature makes it impossible to claim that the Gospels are written in biographical genre) is more assumed than argued. Given the remarks by Burridge and Downing regarding the socio-literary situation in antiquity (mainly the fact that biography was a common feature across a wide spectrum of ancient Mediterranean society),[54] it makes far more sense for the evangelists to write a biography of Jesus than to create and deploy a unique genre.

---

[52] Burridge, *Gospels?* (2004), 244–5.
[53] Downing, "Contemporary Analogies," 55–6.
[54] For the general discussion about a more flexible continuum between low literature and high literature, see Burridge, *Gospels?* (2004), 149; Keener, *Matthew*, 17; Downing, "A Bas Les Aristos," 212–30.

Historical Implications

Given that many scholars have devoted their research to evaluating the historical reliability of the Gospels,[55] it is surprising that Burridge does not explore this issue very much in his book. In the first edition he does not explicitly mention the historical implications of his study, though they may be implied from other discussions. Burridge's study on the flexibility of genre may give some hint at his position on this issue. When he deals with the genre flexibility of ancient biography, he states that "*bios* as a spectrum or band of literature [is] positioned between history at one extreme and encomium at the other."[56] In other words, biographies can be either rigidly historical or highly encomiastic, or anywhere in between. In the second edition Burridge adds some explicit statements on this issue, but they take up only one paragraph and the points made are not much different from the ones implied in the first edition.[57] Burridge's position has certain merits because it reminds us that when examining historical reliability it is essential that we take into consideration the particulars of each biography. Despite this not being his primary focus, we all would have benefited greatly had he explored the general range of expected historical reliability in ancient biographies.

One scholar who has done research in this area is Craig S. Keener.[58] Along with other scholars,[59] Keener emphasizes that biographies are essentially historical works and biographers shared a similar concern with historians in providing factual accounts about their subject(s). Keener notes, "Lucian writes that good biographers avoid flattery that falsifies events and only bad historians invent data."[60] This could imply that much of what was expected of ancient historians can be arguably applied to ancient biographers. For instance, the most proficient ancient historians were committed to rigorous research before their writing. This often involved participation in the events, wide travel, interrogation of eyewitnesses, and critical analysis of available sources—the elements that modern historians also value. It is possible that biographers used the same methods to pursue and obtain truth. Unlike an often-held assumption that ancients had lower standards of truth and history, Keener argues that ancients were in fact very conscious of the issue of truthfulness.[61] This sometimes led even non-historians to comment on this issue: "Pliny, a rhetorician, felt that history's *primary* goal, in contrast to

---

[55] I have found the following two works particularly helpful; Blomberg, *Historical Reliability* and Eddy and Boyd, *The Jesus Legend*.

[56] Burridge, *Gospels?* (1992), 65.

[57] Burridge, *Gospels?* (2004), 259–60.

[58] Keener, *Historical Jesus*, 73–161; idem, *Matthew*, 16–36; idem, "Luke-Acts," 600-623; idem, *John*, 11–34; idem, "Otho," 331-56; idem, "Assumptions," 30–39; idem, "Biographies of a Sage," 59–61. The following discussion in the next two paragraphs draws from these works, unless otherwise indicated.

[59] Talbert, *What Is a Gospel?*, 17; Kennedy, "Source Criticism," 136; Aune, "Greco-Roman Biography," 125.

[60] Keener, *Historical Jesus*, 111.

[61] Byrskog's work addresses this issue, with a particular attention to autopsy or eyewitness. Byrskog, *Story as History*.

that of some other genres, was truth and accuracy rather than rhetorical display."[62] Keener has provided numerous pieces of evidence from ancient texts in order to demonstrate that ancient biographers had historical intention and that their writings included substantial historical information.

On the other hand, Keener also deals with the rhetorical dimension of historical writings. According to him, "Where necessary, [ancient] historians had the generic freedom to fill in a missing detail to make sense of their sources, to flesh out a speech or even a scene."[63] In addition, as noted earlier, ancient biographers' topical arrangement of available sources for their purposes was a common practice. The contradictions and discrepancies that may result from these rhetorical practices have often caused many to deny the historical reliability of the Gospels. However, Keener maintains that one should respect *ancient* biographical conventions and expectations when interpreting the Gospels. To judge ancient texts with modern standards is unfair because it is asking them to implement conventions that were simply unavailable to them. These kinds of rhetorical practices might be performed because "ancient writers emphasized a cohesive narrative more than simple recitation of facts."[64] However, in Keener's view, there were limits to rhetorical embellishment because ancient historians were not supposed to invent or fabricate events.

Theological Implications

In the previous section we explored some of the potential influence of ancient historiography on the related genre of biography. Here it is important to see the proper distinction between the two genres. Let us consider the nuanced words of Charles H. Talbert on this issue:

> Our comparison of biography and history must treat contents, form, and function. In its contents history usually tends to focus on the distinguished and significant acts of great men in the political and social spheres. Biography is concerned with the study of character or the essence of the individual . . . In antiquity, history was concerned with a man's place in the process of political and social events. Biography was interested in the individual's character, his involvement in a historical process being important only insofar as it reveals his essence. In form and function history and biography are also different. In form, though both are prose narration, history attempts to give a detailed account in terms of causes and effects of events, whereas biography presents a highly selective, often anecdotal, account of an individual's life with events chosen to illumine his character . . . To summarize: ancient biography is prose narration about a person's life, presenting supposedly historical facts which are selected to reveal the character or essence of the individual.[65]

One point that Talbert particularly emphasizes here is that biographers were intent on portraying the essence of a person's life. They intended to give a singularly

---

[62] Keener, *Historical Jesus*, 97 (emphasis original).
[63] Ibid., 110.
[64] Ibid.
[65] Talbert, *What Is a Gospel?*, 16–17.

focused account that would best illuminate the subject's character. History may contain biographical elements, but it lacks an extended focus on a single individual.[66] This generic feature of biography (i.e., the sustained attention on a singular hero) is theologically important because it implies that the christological interpretation of the Gospels should take precedence over other interpretive options. As Burridge puts it: "If genre is the key to a work's interpretation, and the genre of the Gospels is *bios*, then the key to their interpretation must be the person of their subject, Jesus of Nazareth."[67]

This observation reminds us of what the central focus of Gospel studies should be. In Gospel studies, much ink has been spilled on issues such as identifying forms, sources, evangelists' redactions, community profiles, and so forth. Despite the validity of these studies and the numerous ways they enrich our understanding of the Gospels, it must be stressed that the Gospel genre itself tells us that the ultimate concern of our study should be asking what this text tells us about Jesus of Nazareth—the hero in the Gospels. As Burridge points out, "The Gospels are nothing less than Christology in narrative form, the story of Jesus."[68]

Furthermore, the need to focus on the christological implications of the Gospels becomes even more apparent when one can see how distinctive they are in relation to other Jewish literature. It is astounding that despite numerous anecdotal episodes in rabbinic literature, there is not a single freestanding biography of any rabbi, as many scholars note.[69] The absence of rabbinic biography is due to the fact that the stories of different rabbis are ultimately written to highlight the centrality of the Torah, not of the rabbis themselves.[70] Burridge even suggests:

> The literary shift from unconnected anecdotes about Jesus, which resemble rabbinic material, to composing them together in the genre of an ancient [Greco-Roman] biography is making an enormous Christological claim. Rabbinic biography is not possible, because no rabbi is unique and each is only important as he represents the Torah, which holds the central place. To write a biography is to replace the Torah by putting a human person in the centre of the stage. The literary genre makes a major theological shift which becomes an explicit Christological claim—that Jesus of Nazareth is Torah embodied.[71]

---

[66] Keener, *Historical Jesus*, 80.

[67] Burridge, *Gospels?* (2004), 248.

[68] Burridge, "Absence of Rabbinic Biography," 141.

[69] Burridge, "Reading the Gospels," 39–42; Burridge made this important observation, depending on other scholars such as Alexander, "Rabbinic Biography," 40-42, Neusner, *Talmudic Biography*, 1–3; idem, *The Incarnation of God*, 213, Goshen-Gottstein, "Hillel and Jesus," 34–35.

[70] Neusner, *Why No Gospels*, 52–3: "Sage-stories turn out not to tell about sages at all; they are stories about the Torah personified. Sage-stories cannot yield a gospel because they are not about sages anyhow. They are about the Torah . . . The gospel does just the opposite, with its focus on the uniqueness of the hero." Similarly, Alexander, "Rabbinic Biography," 41: "The centre of Rabbinic Judaism was Torah; the centre of Christianity was the person of Jesus, and the existence of the Gospels is, in itself, a testimony to this fact."

[71] Burridge, "Reading the Gospels," 42.

It would seem then that the decision by the evangelists to compose their Gospels in the form of ancient Greco-Roman biography was more intentional than not. This allowed them to adopt a form that had as its sole purpose to highlight the life and character of a single individual. Naturally, because of this built-in focus, exploring the Christology communicated in each gospel is of utmost importance.

Charting the Uncharted: Compositional Techniques of Ancient Biographers and Their Implications for the Same yet Different Gospel Accounts

After surveying the charted areas for the implications of the gospel genre, there is still one uncharted territory that has been rarely explored by New Testament scholars: the compositional techniques of ancient biographers and their implications for the distinctive character of gospel accounts—"the same yet different."[72] Again and again, we see that the evangelists narrate the same story of Jesus with different wording and various details. Of course, there have been numerous proposals that attempt to explain *the same yet different gospel accounts* (SDGA), many of which may offer valuable partial explanations: source criticism, redaction criticism, performance criticism, media criticism, memory studies, and orality studies, to name a few. However, since the view that the Gospels are ancient biographies now receives wide support, it is surprising that New Testament scholars have rarely considered the implications of the Gospels' genre for explaining SDGA.

A full treatment of this issue will appear in my dissertation with detailed analysis of compositional techniques of various ancient biographers. However, in this paper, I will offer a truncated version by primarily focusing on the compositional techniques of Plutarch. Unfortunately, space constraints will not permit us to determine how these same techniques are used in the Gospels. My assumption is that, if other ancient biographers commonly make use of these techniques, then it is more than likely that the evangelists (also ancient biographers) do too. I hope to prove this assumption in a more extensive treatment of the topic in my dissertation. What follows are my preliminary efforts in explicating this area of research.

Paraphrase Is a Rule; Verbatim Citation Is an Exception

Ancient writers are generally expected to paraphrase available sources rather than copy them verbatim.[73] Dionysius of Halicarnassus succinctly expresses this

---

[72] To my knowledge, one exception would be Michael R. Licona, who has conducted serious research on this issue. See Licona, "Contradictions"; idem, "Using Plutarch's Biographies"; idem, *Why Differences*. The phrase "same yet different" comes from Dunn, *Oral Gospel*, 5.

[73] Aune, *Literary Environment*, 82–3; Downing, "Contemporary Analogies," 60; Niehoff, "Josephus' Narrative Technique," 31–45; Gregory, "Literary Dependence," 96; Pitts, "Source Citation," 358–9; Stadter, "Compositional Technique," 670.

tendency in his treatise on literary composition: "The science of composition . . . is to judge whether any modification is required in the material used—I mean subtraction, addition or alteration—and to carry out such changes with a proper view to their future purpose" (Dionysius of Halicarnassus, *Comp.* 6 [Cary, LCL]).[74] The major Jewish writers who have Diaspora audiences in mind also follow this common practice of paraphrasing available sources.[75] Ancient writers would adapt their sources for several reasons, including composition based on memory,[76] lack of concern about verbatim accuracy,[77] and having different aims and concerns.[78]

Because paraphrasing was a common practice in antiquity, not an exceptional one, the variations and discrepancies in the Gospels should not cause us to quickly abandon the hope that they recount historical information.[79] Instead, the more appropriate way of responding to different kinds of variations found in the Gospels is to ask whether the variation in question is within the usually allowable limits of ancient compositional techniques. The following ancient compositional techniques are proposed as boundaries in which the variations of the gospel accounts can fall. We will use Dionysius of Halicarnassus's three types of modifications in ancient literary composition as the framework for our discussion: subtraction, addition, and alteration.

Subtraction

There are a variety of ways an author can utilize "subtraction" to articulate his or her intended message. When an author feels it unnecessary to delineate a series of separate events in narrating the overall story, he or she sometimes conflates similar items into one, which gives an impression that they all happened simultaneously.[80] In *Caesar* 7.7, Plutarch knew that the three senatorial debates on the Catilinarians were held separately (*Cic.* 19.1–4, 20.4–21.5; *Crass.* 13.3), but then

---

[74] The quotation is from Derrenbacker, *Ancient Compositional Practices*, 44.

[75] Keener, *Historical Jesus*, 105–6; McGing, "Philo's Adaptation," 122–3.

[76] Pelling, "Plutarch's Method," 92: "A writer would not normally refer back to that reading to verify individual references, and would instead rely on his memory, or on the briefest of notes"; cf. Small, *Wax Tablets*, 192: "Studies of natural memory have demonstrated that we are incredibly good at remembering gist and just as incredibly bad at remembering verbatim."

[77] Small, *Wax Tablets*, 219–20.

[78] Pelling, "Plutarch's Method," 77: "Caesar's assassination is naturally treated most lavishly in *Brutus* and in *Caesar*. *Cicero* had mentioned these events briefly; *Antony* has a little material on the murder, then rather more on the immediate sequel. *Cicero* adds little to this analysis. Its account is brief and shows no signs of great background knowledge; but brevity is only to be expected, for Cicero's role was so small."

[79] Downing, "Redaction Criticism," 33. Thus Downing claims, "It is not the divergences among the synoptists (or even between them and John) in parallel contexts that are remarkable: it is the extraordinary extent of verbal similarities."

[80] Pelling, "Plutarch's Adaptation," 127.

blended two debates into one because "he was, after all, concerned with Caesar's role."[81]

The subtraction of elements in a story is sometimes expressed in such a way that the chronology of the actual events is compressed.[82] Thus in *Cato Minor* 51, Plutarch made a close link between "Cato's proposal to surrender Caesar to the Germans" and "the context of the outbreak of the civil war," despite the time lapse of five years between them; by way of this thematic link, Plutarch nicely explained "Cato's further attacks on Caesar."[83]

An author sometimes reduces a story by removing some elements that are not desirable. Philo, while recomposing the biblical narrative in Exodus 17:1–7, removes several elements such as "the complaints of the people [and] any talk of stoning" that may give an "unflattering image of the Israelites."[84] In light of these kinds of subtraction employed by ancient writers, many missing details or minor contradictions in the Gospels may be more understandable.

Addition

Ancient writers often add circumstantial details in order to produce a coherent narrative or to highlight some points that may illuminate the character of a hero. When adding circumstantial details the majority of ancient writers do not fabricate events that are unlikely to have happened, but flesh out the scenes either by using other available sources or based on "what must have been the case."[85]

D. A. Russell's important article includes illustrative examples of this.[86] In his article, Russell investigates Plutarch's adaptation of his main source (Dionysius of Halicarnassus's *Roman Antiquities*) in writing the *Marcius Coriolanus*. Russell argues that the ways Plutarch adapted his main source reveal the author's compositional techniques. One of the recurring compositional techniques, Russell claims, is the expansion or elaboration of the material based on what it "must have been like."[87] To give one example among many,[88] in *Marcius Coriolanus* 2.2, Plutarch narrates an episode of rivals' ill-intentioned claim that Marcius's success is not due to his courage or skill but simply because of his physical excellence. It is interesting to note that there is no trace of this episode in Dionysius. In other words, according to Russell, this episode must be a "speculative embellishment . . . based on the story of Marcius's untiring exploits at Corioli and against Antium." Such a judgment seems to be correct because the two motifs in this episode ("freedom of fatigue" and "the jealous rivals") come up again in the later episodes of the

---

[81] Ibid.
[82] Ibid., 127–8.
[83] Ibid., 128.
[84] McGing, "Philo's Adaptation," 124.
[85] Keener, "Otho," 349; the phrase is from Stadter, "Introduction," xxiv.
[86] Russell, "Coriolanus," 21–28.
[87] Ibid., 23.
[88] Ibid. To avoid unnecessary footnotes, I notify that the subsequent discussion and quotations in this paragraph are from this page.

same work (*Cor.* 9,9, 10.7–8, 13.6). Russell's theory that the elaboration of material is a common practice is applicable not only to the *Marcius Coriolanus* but also to other *Lives* of Plutarch as well.[89]

One minor point needs to be considered before concluding this section. Russell's comments on Plutarch's tendency to expand materials are worth noting: "The most important cause of Plutarch's deviations from Dionysius is of course the difference between the demands of *bioi* and those of *historia*. Thus the scanty hints about Marcius's youth and upbringing had to be expanded . . . Nowhere is Plutarch's technique of expansion more in evidence than in the account of his hero's youth."[90] This statement invites us to explore the possibility that Matthew and Luke felt the freedom to add extended accounts of Jesus's early life due to the conventions of ancient biography. Given that ancient biographers commonly use the accounts of a hero's birth and youth as a means of revealing his or her character,[91] it is a reasonable inference that Matthew and Luke, the more literary-conscious evangelists, decided to add the accounts of Jesus' early life in their writings. The fact that the most literary-conscious among the evangelists (Luke) offered the most elaborated accounts of Jesus's birth and youth might strengthen this possibility.

Alteration

The compositional technique of alteration involves some radical rearrangements of source material, and may be regarded as unacceptable from the modern perspective. Ancient writers often alter the chronological order of events, or transfer one's words or actions to another person in order to make the narrative more coherent.[92]

Pelling's observations are illuminating here. In *Cato Minor* 30.9–10, Plutarch highlights Cato's rejection of any marriage relationship with Pompey. Here the marriage connection with Pompey is described as the one "which began the train of events which led to war." Plutarch's emphasis on Cato's denial of such a relationship becomes obvious when Plutarch portrays the events of 59 BCE. In this portrayal, Plutarch rearranges the order of original events by placing "Pompey's betrothal to Julia at the beginning of the account" (*Cat. Min.* 31.6), which actually happened later (*Caes.* 14.7; *Pomp.* 47.10; Cicero, *Att.* ii 17.1). The compositional technique of chronological alteration is often used by Plutarch to bring out points that he wants to make about the hero in question. The recognition of this compositional technique may explain many of the gospel passages that have similar contents but are placed in different chronological contexts. One may immediately

---

[89] Pelling made the same point after reviewing six later Lives of Plutarch. Pelling, "Plutarch's Adaptation," 129–31.

[90] Russell, "Coriolanus," 22–3.

[91] Ibid., 23; Titchener, "Cornelius Nepos," 88; Pelling, "Childhood and Personality."

[92] Pelling, "Plutarch's Adaptation," 128–9. Again, to avoid unnecessary footnotes, all the discussions (including citations) in the following two paragraphs come from these pages, unless otherwise indicated.

think of the "cleansing of the temple" episode, which in John occurs at the beginning of Jesus's ministry whereas in the Synoptics it occurs at the end.[93]

Pelling says that "the transfer of an item from one character to another" is "an extreme form of a technique," though it is "often visible." For instance, "At *Ant.* 5.10 Antony and Cassius are given the speech to Caesar's troops before the crossing of the Rubicon; at *Caes.* 31.3 Plutarch says that Caesar incited the troops himself... At *Pomp.* 58.6 Marcellus is given a proposal which Plutarch knows to be Scipio's, and a remark (Caesar as *lēstēs*) which he elsewhere gives to Lentulus (*Caes.* 30.4, 6)." Since the transfer of one's sayings or actions to another person is an extreme form of ancient compositional techniques, it would be helpful to mention such an example from the Gospels. In Mark 10:35–37, James and John came to Jesus and ask a favor that they may sit on his right and left sides in his glory. But in the parallel passage in Matthew 20:20–21, it was their mother, not James and John, who approached Jesus and made the same request.[94] It is quite possible that Matthew felt that he had the freedom to make this alteration because it was within the conventions of the genre.

Conclusion

The question of "so what?" has driven this study. If the Gospels are ancient biographies, why is such a designation important? This essay is ultimately about the implications of labeling the Gospels ancient biographies. Our study identified several areas where these implications have been more explored and one area that has been rarely investigated.

As to the former (i.e., the charted areas), we have seen: the task itself of determining the Gospels' genre is *literarily* important because it affects our interpretation of the Gospels on various levels; the evangelists' choice of this specific genre has a *sociological* implication in that the Gospels are intended to reach a wider audience; it also has a *historical* implication in that ancient biographies are concerned with sharing truths rather than fabricating events (as are the Gospels); finally, it is *theologically* important because it requires our primary focus in interpretation be on Jesus, the hero of the Gospels.

In regards to the latter (i.e., one uncharted area), because the Gospels are best understood as ancient biographies in respect to their genre, extensive research is needed in order to comprehend the conventions the evangelists were working with. What I have shown in this final section are a few of the ancient compositional techniques that ancient biographers (and likely the evangelists) were most familiar with and also utilized.[95] Understanding these techniques helps to explain some of

---

[93] Pointed out in Licona, "Differences".

[94] Ibid.

[95] Stadter, "Introduction," xxiv, summarized these compositional techniques of ancient biographers: "In adapting the historical material, Plutarch took several steps to focus attention on his protagonist. Thus he may abridge his source by simplifying it, either conflating

the features we find in the Gospels, primarily the variances in wording and different arrangements of their parallel material.

---

several similar incidents into one (e.g. meetings of the senate), by chronological compression (making two items seem to follow closely which in fact were separated by a period of time), or reorganizing events in non-chronological order, especially to bring out causal or logical connections. Occasionally he may even transfer an item from one character to another, whether consciously or not ... On the other hand, he will expand inadequate material, not by free invention but by a visualization of what must have been the case, what antecedents would naturally precede an action, or what context seems to be implied by a historical notice."

Chapter 4

Source Valuation in Greek and Roman Biography: From Xenophon to Suetonius

Chris Alfred
Asbury Theological Seminary

Critics more readily locate areas of bias in the works they criticize than in our own evaluations. For this reason, it is helpful to find controls on our evaluative methods. Ancient historians and biographers, like modern ones, were in no way immune to bias. Nevertheless, most of them in the Roman period usually strove to evaluate their sources critically to obtain the most accurate information. When they deemed particular accounts more reliable than others, they normally did so not simply based on personal likes or dislikes of the writers in question.

This essay will seek to evaluate how fairly various ancient biographers attempted to evaluate their own sources. To do so, I construct and apply an evaluative method for source citation in Greek and Roman biographies from their inception to Suetonius.

Introduction

In an effort to examine source valuation in ancient biography all instances of source citations—named or unnamed—are listed. Beside each reference is a number representing the author's perceived evaluation of each source. The numbers used imply the following: (1) the author appeals to the source as authoritative without qualification; (2) he appeals to the source as authoritative insofar as it supports his thesis; (3) he views the source as more authoritative than it is unauthoritative; (4) the source's reliability on the subject cannot be confirmed; (5) he views the source as more unauthoritative than it is authoritative; (6) the source is considered unauthoritative, but is used persuasively to strengthen the biographer's thesis; and (7) the author appeals to the source as unauthoritative without qualification. The numerical designations will ultimately show that biographers regularly used sources and normally tried to evaluate them even if they were sometimes biased.

This approach of grading source valuation in ancient biographies seeks to examine the writer's bias or impartiality in his approach to the sources he uses. It serves to more appropriately interpret the intent of the author in certain passages that may be commonly misunderstood. In an endnote concerning Plutarch's *Theseus*, a twentieth-century classicist wrote, "This *Life* is a remarkable demonstration of Plutarch's inability or unwillingness to decide between conflicting sources, his arbitrary approval of some, his acceptance of majority opinions, and his general reliance on 'probability'."[1]

By contrast, the majority of the objections raised here can be explained by the following: ancient writers often approach un-confirmable source material with a neutral attitude (as demonstrated by the grade of 4). The writer often uses this approach regarding: a) legendary/mythic material; b) events behind closed doors; or c) (generally) inconsequential details on which multiple sources disagree. In the cases in which Plutarch chooses not to decide between divergent accounts, it is because they are legendary accounts, thus being un-confirmable.[2] As Plutarch himself writes, "[I]t is not astonishing that history, when dealing with events of such great antiquity, should wander in uncertainty."[3] Moreover, the tendency in Plutarch, Suetonius, and other biographers writing a century or more after the events, to assess the probability of conflicting accounts should not be considered a weakness, but a strength—for this practice involves a measure of critical attention to detail that strengthens the narrative.

Before proceeding to individual selections of source valuation in ancient biography, one caveat must be noted. The use of named sources—and even the use of unnamed sources—is not the ultimate indicator of whether a work is rooted in strong source material. Named source material is more often cited in accounts which occurred in the past.[4] Nevertheless, the focus here is on each biographer's handling of source material insofar as it reveals the presence or absence of bias within his account.

Source Valuation in Greco-Roman Biography

The first biographer to be examined is Xenophon, a very early contributor to the genre. Duane Reed Stuart points to Xenophon's *Memorabilia* and *Agesilaus*, and to the *Evagoras* of Isocrates, as "the earliest extant prose treatises devoted exclusively to the transmission of historical lives and personalities."[5] After survey-

---

[1] Gossage, "Plutarch," 76 n63.

[2] See the chart for Plutarch and the corresponding notes below.

[3] Plutarch, *Thes.*, 27.3 (LCL 1:63, trans., Perrin). From a modern perspective, to be sure, Plutarch may be credulous for crediting *any* history in accounts of the mythical Theseus or Romulus, for example. But this involves the nature of his material, not a completely uncritical attitude toward it.

[4] Examples of more recent biographies in the present study include most notably Nicolaus of Damascus' *Life of Augustus* and Tacitus' *Agricola*, with parallels also in the biographies of *Galba* and *Otho* in Plutarch and Suetonius. Part of the process in determining which biographies to analyze in this paper was to include examples of individuals from the distant past (Plutarch's *Lives of Theseus and Romulus*), from 400-200 years past, as well as from the recent past. While biographies containing more sources will provide more data to be analyzed in this study, such information also illumines aspects of biographies of figures from the recent past. With respect to naming their sources, biographies of figures from the recent past are naturally more comparable to the Gospels.

[5] Stuart, *Epochs*, 31.

ing Xenophon's relevant works, the focus will shift to biography in the Roman era.

Source Valuation in Xenophon's *Agesilaus*

Source	Reference (Grade from 1-7)
Spithridates the Persian	3.2-3 (2)
Entire city-state of Lacedaemon	4.5 (2)
Xenophon	11.9 (2)
Absence of a report	5.6 (2)

The earliest extant Greek biographies fit within the type known as encomiastic biography. These works are particularly constructed to honor the subject and the author is straightforward with his readers about this intent. Xenophon illustrates this in the *Agesilaus* when he writes, "Now I am not going to say that his forces were far inferior in numbers and in quality, and that nevertheless he accepted battle. That statement, I think, would but show a want of common sense in Agesilaus and my own folly in praising a leader who wantonly jeopardized interests of vital moment."[6] Almost from the very beginning, then, he informs the audience about his ultimate purpose to praise the Spartan king.

Xenophon combines this encomiastic interest with his particular style of argumentation which consists of proposing thesis statements, then offering proofs as evidence.[7] When Xenophon cites sources in the *Agesilaus*, he always does so within the context of proofs for his individual arguments, thus achieving a grade of 2 for each instance of citation. In general, the grades 2 and 6 are the ones indicative of an author's use of sources for the benefit of his own argument. Xenophon even goes so far as to read significance into the absence of a report in *Ages*. 5.6. In other parts of the work he seems overly aware of implications one might draw from the narrative he provides.[8]

These persuasive tactics Xenophon uses in the *Agesilaus*—and also in the *Memorabilia*—signal the early date of their composition (4th century BCE). As the genre developed further during the Roman period, biographers' approach to sources became much more objective, even within the context of encomiastic

---

[6] *Ages*. 2.7 (LCL, trans. Marchant and Bowersock). Cf. 4:7: "If I speak this falsely against the knowledge of the Greek world, I am in no way praising my hero, but I am censuring myself" (trans. Marchant and Bowersock). Cf. also Isoc. *Evag*. 8: "I am fully aware that what I am proposing to do is difficult—to eulogize in prose the virtues of a man" (LCL: trans. Norlin); also *Evag*. 48-49. The similarity in purpose, and the chronological proximity between Xenophon's work and Isocrates' *Evagoras* spawned a healthy debate near the end of the twentieth century about whether Xenophon was dependent upon Isocrates. For this conversation, see Stuart, *Epochs*, 80-81.

[7] For example, *Ages*. 3.1: *nun de tēn en tē psychē aytou aretēn peirasomai dēloun* ("But now I will try to make apparent the excellence in his soul"); also 4.1; 5.1; 6.1; 7.1; 8.1; 9.1; 11.1.

[8] Cf. 2.21; 2.7.

biography.⁹ Nevertheless, it is worthwhile to examine source valuation in biography's early stages, and in a more complex composition of Xenophon: his *Memorabilia* of Socrates.

Source Valuation in Xenophon's *Memorabilia*

Source	Reference (Grade from 1-7)
Polycrates	1.1.1 (5); 1.2.9 (5); 1.2.49 (5); 1.2.51 (5); 1.2.56 (5); 1.2.58 (5); 1.2.64 (5)
Xenophon	1.2.31 (2); 1.2.53 (1); 1.4.2 (2); 1.4.19 (2); 1.7.5 (2); 2.1.1 (1); 2.4.1 (1); 2.5.1 (1); 2.6.1 (2); 2.9.1 (2); 2.10.1 (2); 4.3.2 (2); 4.5.2 (2); 4.7.1 (2); 4.8.11 (1)
Hermogenes	4.8.4 (2)
Unattributed	1.1.10 (2); 1.2.30 (2); 1.2.58 (5); 1.4.1 (5)

Xenophon is likewise forthright about his apologetic purposes for the *Memorabilia*.¹⁰ In keeping with this purpose, the source chart for this work reveals the author's non-objective use of sources, and a closer evaluation of these cases confirms this observation to an even greater degree. Before continuing, an important methodological consideration must be noted. When any biographer's source valuation is analyzed, attention must be paid to the way the author treats individual sources. For example, if the author uses a source three times, with all instances achieving a grade of 7, this constitutes a non-objective use of sources. On the other hand, if a source is used continuously with a grade of 1, one must examine what is driving the author's decision.¹¹

In Xenophon's case, his consistent negative interaction with Polycrates here immediately suggests bias. This is of course no great revelation, however, since he most often calls Polycrates, "*ho katēgoros*" ("the accuser"), and the *Memorabilia* is widely recognized as a response to Polycrates' indictment of the philosopher. On the other hand, Xenophon takes a slightly different approach to Polycrates in 1.2.53, when he acknowledges certain statements of Socrates which he heard firsthand, even though they seem to confirm Polycrates' view. Nonetheless, Xenophon eventually contextualizes these statements in 1.2.55, thus reaching a solution suitable for a more palatable characterization of Socrates' teach-

---

⁹ For comparison, see the comments below on Tacitus' *Agricola*, which keeps the early traditions of proclaiming outright his encomiastic interests, but uses sources in a much more objective manner than his earlier, Greek counterparts.

¹⁰ Cf. *Mem.* 1.3.1.

¹¹ In some cases, the biographer may simply be relying on an account with a strong reputation, such as the work of Thucydides, in which case the biographer's concurrence with the source indicates interest in historical accuracy and objectivity. Thus the numbers alone cannot paint the entire picture.

ing. Moreover, the only other sources with which Xenophon disagrees (1.2.58; 1.4.1) come also from disparaging reports against Socrates. It is clear, then, that Xenophon is unapologetically using his source material to portray Socrates in a manner counter to certain contemporary portraits of him.

Furthermore, when these nine instances of grade-5 source interaction are removed, one finds that Xenophon claims to use a source in eighteen other places in the *Memorabilia*. Of these, thirteen are treated with a degree of 2, demonstrating Xenophon's high level of interest in propelling his own conception of Socrates over against other accounts. The majority of these grade-2 instances operate in conjunction with a thesis statement Xenophon offers concerning Socrates.[12] The following chart tracks each thesis statement in the *Memorabilia*, followed by the range of material it governs, and any source(s) provided in its support.

Thesis Statement	Range Governed by Thesis	Source(s)
1.3.1	1.3.1-4	N/A
1.3.5	1.3.5-15	N/A
1.4.1	1.4.1-19	Self: 1.4.2[13] (2); Self: 1.4.19 (2)
1.5.1	1.5.1—1.6.15	N/A[14]
1.7.1	1.7.1-5	Self: 1.7.5 (2)
2.1.1	2.1.1-34	Self: 2.1.1 (1)
2.6.1	2.6.1-39	Self: 2.6.1 (2)
2.7.1	2.7.1—2.10.6	Self: 2.9.1 (2); Self: 2.10.1 (2)
3.1.1	3.1.1—3.7.9	N/A
3.10.1	3.10.1—3.11.18	N/A
4.1.1	4.1.1-5	N/A
4.2.1	4.2.1-40	N/A
4.3.1	4.3.1-17	Self: 4.3.2[15] (2)
4.4.1	4.4.1-25	N/A
4.5.1	4.5.1-12	Self: 4.5.2[16] (2)
4.6.1	4.6.1-14	N/A
4.7.1	4.7.1-10	Self: 4.7.1 (2)

---

[12] Cf. Stuart, *Epochs*, 73-74, who speaks of Xenophon's "conscientious effort to dress his language to suit the occasion." It may be noted, however, that while this is certainly evident in places, Xenophon chooses to nuance his perspectives on some issues when they do not seriously threaten the argument (cf. "somewhat as follows" in *Cyr.* 2.2.5, contra his insistence on exact wording in *Mem.* 1.5.6; 1.6.14). Nevertheless, Xenophon seems to rely uncomfortably heavily upon source citation in arguing his own opinions on individuals, a practice corrected during the Roman era of biography.

[13] This source material constitutes the entire narrative from 1.4.1-18.

[14] However, Xenophon reaffirms the veracity of Socrates' speech in 1.5 by stating, "*Toiauta de legōn*"("such were his words") (1.5.6).

[15] This source material constitutes the narrative from 4.3.2-17.

[16] This material continues through 4.5.11.

| 4.8.1 | 4.8.1-10 | Hermogenes: 4.8.4 (2) |

As this chart suggests, Xenophon cites no sources during Book 3, which pertains more to Socrates' philosophy than his values, which were specifically under attack.[17] Moreover, Xenophon utilizes the majority of sources not directed at Polycrates as proofs within his argument, suggesting an altogether different purpose for his source citation than is present in later biography. Thus, he generally implements sources strategically, whereas later authors use them for historical purposes. To these authors we will now turn.

Source Valuation in Cornelius Nepos' *On Great Generals*

Source	Reference (Grade from 1-7)
Thucydides	*Them.* 1.1 (1); 9.1 (3); 10:4 (3) *Alc.* 11.1, twice (1)
Plato	*Alc.* 2.2 (1)
Theopompus	*Alc.* 11.1, twice (3; 1); *Iph.* 3.2 (1)
Timaeus	*Alc.* 11.1, twice (3; 1)
Dinon	*Con.* 5.4 (3);
Atticus	*Han.* 11.1 (4)
Polybius	*Han.* 11.1 (4)
Sulpicius Blitho	*Han.* 11.1 (4)
All biographers of Alcibiades	*Alc.* 1.1 (1)
Unattributed	*Them.*, 9.1 (5); 10.4 (5); *Lys.* 4.1-3 (1); *Alc.* 11.1 (7/5); *Con.* 5.4 (5); *Han.* 8.2, twice (4; 4)

Nepos' work on *Generals* contains only one instance of grade-7, outright rejection of a source without qualification (*Alc.* 11.1). In this case, the biographer notes many ("*plerisque*") who have defamed Alcibiades' reputation. Although he adds no more about this, he has made clear his reasoning that he prefers instead the works of other writers such as Thucydides, Theopompus, and Timaeus on this point, hence the nuanced grade of 7/5. The grades assigned for the three historians in this passage are 1, 3, 3, respectively, since Nepos points out that Theopompus is somewhat later than Thucydides and that Theopompus and Timaeus, who are generally "strongly inclined to abuse," somehow ("*quo modo*") agree with Thucydides here.

Two additional observations must be made about this passage before proceeding. First, despite using such strong language against Theopompus here, the

---

[17] Nevertheless, this extended material demonstrates that Xenophon's overall purpose in the *Memorabilia* is to provide a general picture of Socrates (cf. 4.8.11), transcending the purpose of his use of sources, which only appears in contested portions of his argument.

biographer nonetheless cites him unequivocally in *Iphicrates* 3.2. It may hardly be said that his citation in either case is the result of bias against Theopompus.

Secondly, Nepos appeals to Thucydides as the most authoritative source in all his work. John C. Rolfe's statement that Nepos makes little use of other historical sources is incongruous with the biographer's close interaction with Thucydides' writings, as Francis Titchener contends.[18] Titchener examines these direct appeals to Thucydides, as well as Nepos' engagement in some source criticism of Thucydides' work, showing the biographer's interaction with historical accounts. Moreover, it is best to view Nepos' evaluation of Thucydides on its own terms—namely, that he does so in the interest of historical accuracy—rather than to assume bias in his universal preference of the historiographer's accounts.[19] Therefore, Nepos' positive view of Thucydides stems from reasoned consideration of all factors involved in these accounts.

Two other instances of grade-5 source valuation exist in this work of Nepos. In the first case, the author prefers Thucydides over unattributed accounts about the location of a burial site.[20] In the final example, *Con.* 5.4, the author softly handles the testimony of some (*"nonnulli"*) in favor of Dinon's rendering of Conon's escape before death. In this case, still, the biographer notes where Dinon is unsure and stops short of an unequivocal agreement with this version. Notwithstanding, he lauds Dinon's credibility regarding Persian affairs.[21]

In other places in the *Generals*, Nepos decides not to speculate on unconfirmable events. In *Alc.* 10.4, he avoids speculating on Themistocles' death. Likewise, the biographer makes reference to two different accounts of the death of Mago in *Han.* 8.2 without taking a formal position. Finally, shortly thereafter in 11.1, Nepos considers three divergent sources on the issue of which consuls were in power when Hannibal died, choosing not to affirm any of them.

This highlights a fairly common trend in the *Generals*: that Nepos is often conservative in his approach to historical events even if it does not promote his own estimation of the event or person being studied.[22] In *Alc.* 7.3, the writer mentions his own conviction regarding why something occurred without supplying a source. It is noticeable, then, that he feels no need to defend his authority on the material presented, nor does he sense a challenge from his audience to defend his view of the events.[23] As may thus be observed in the chart above,

---

[18] Titchener, "Cornelius Nepos," 85-99, 88-90; *pace* Rolfe, *Nepos*, 39.

[19] In *Them.* 9.1, for example, this preference is based upon chronological proximity to the event in question. Nepos himself states, "I am aware that many have written that Themistocles passed over into Asia during the reign of Xerxes, but I prefer to believe Thucydides, because among the writers who have left a history of those times he was most nearly contemporary with Themistocles, besides being a native of the same city" (trans., Rolfe). Thucydides' highly revered status as a reliable historian no doubt has factored into Nepos' valuation.

[20] *Them.* 10.4.

[21] *Con.* 5.4. Rolfe translates that Nepos views Dinon as "an historian in whose account of Persian affairs we have the most confidence" (trans., Rolfe).

[22] Cf. the lack of source material provided for some of Nepos' favorite subjects: *Thras.* 1.1-5; *Ep.* 10.1-4; and cf. also *Tim.* 4.5-6 and *Dat.* 6.8.

[23] For more on this, see the "Discussion" section below.

Generals is marked by a usage of source material which holds the highest respect for the events in question.

Source Valuation in Nicolaus of Damascus' *Life of Augustus*

Source	Reference (Grade from 1-7)
Augustus' friends	36 (1)
Unattributed	30 (5); 59 (4); 66 (4); 74 (4); 96 (1)

Nicolaus of Damascus' *Life of Augustus* in its present form contains many lacunae, but sufficient portions of this work exist for at least a preliminary discussion of this biographer's evaluation of sources. He overtly cites few sources, but a reading of the work in its present form confirms the strength of its source material.[24] Jane Bellemore states, "We are faced with the uncertainty of how far Nicolaus altered his primary and subsidiary sources to produce the type of encomiastic work which we now possess."[25] While this is the case, it is possible to examine his overall approach to these subsidiary sources.

Bellemore contends that Nicolaus was almost certainly using Augustus' autobiography as a source. While it is not the ultimate goal of my essay to confirm or deny this claim, Bellemore does make some important points that are somewhat confirmed by his use of sources. In Section 30, Nicolaus dismisses a common opinion from many about Augustus' nepotism. In the other instance in which Nicolaus cites a source without unqualified acceptance, the biographer notes an alternative account of the actions of Antony (74).

Section 36 contains an anecdote from Augustus' friends, also in favor of Augustus. Nicolaus accepts this account (grade of 1), demonstrating Augustus' prudence as a young man. In contrast, other unattributed sources—in sections 59 and 66, which are used (grade of 4)—supply details about the conspiracy against Caesar. Nicolaus' familiarity with Augustus' account and lack of familiarity with those of others supports Bellemore's claim that Nicolaus was using the autobiography. Bellemore further notes that, in the days in which Nicolaus composed his *Life*, there would have been pressure upon him not to deviate from Augustus' official autobiography,[26] which adds to the pro-Augustinian flavor of Nicolaus' work.[27]

Nicolaus' work is not preoccupied with his own judgment of Augustus, and some bias in his work may be due to its presence in the sources Nicolaus uses.[28] Although the approach of source valuation is not greatly helpful for interpreting Nicolaus' work, it nonetheless speaks to some of its source-critical issues. Fur-

---

[24] Cf. Bellemore, *Nicolaus*, xxiv-xxvi.

[25] Bellemore, *Nicolaus*, xxvi.

[26] Bellemore, *Nicolaus*, xxiv.

[27] Although imposed by political exigencies, the pressure to depict reigning emperors or dynasties positively constitutes a particular form of bias.

[28] This statement must also be qualified by the fact that the length at which Nicolaus wrote suggests his own affection for the emperor.

thermore, the *Augustus* serves as an example that Greco-Roman biographies written within a generation of the events did not always cite numerous sources.

Source Valuation in Tacitus' *Agricola*

Source	Reference (Grade from 1-7)
Agricola	4 (1)
Livy	10 (5)
Fabius Rusticus	10 (5)
Unattributed	22 (1); 29 (1); 40 (4); 43, twice (4; 1)

The chart for the *Agricola* appears to reflect less highly on Tacitus' use of sources than some other biographers, but this is deceptive in two ways. First, what may seem to be a dearth of source material is explained, as with Nicolaus' *Augustus*, by the fact that Tacitus wrote Agricola's biography within a generation after his subject's death. Biographies on figures contemporary with the biographer relied on eyewitness material and other sources which may or may not receive overt citation. Additionally, Tacitus' status as a family member gave him unique access to his subject, not to mention a motivation for bias, as will be discussed soon.

The second deceptive feature of the chart is the fact that Tacitus disagrees with the only two sources he names, apart from his personal correspondence with Agricola. This is, however, a debate over a very small issue—the shape formed by the geographical boundaries of Rome in *Agr.* 10 —which many may not even consider sources for Agricola's *bios* at all. Even still, he handles his disagreement with these sources gingerly, with no hint of the animosity of a scorned family member.

Nevertheless, Tacitus is honest about his encomiastic purpose.[29] Again, his knowledge of the subject is vast due to his standing as Agricola's son-in-law. The closeness of his contact with his subject is far more valuable than potential biases involved when he recapitulates events. This depth of knowledge causes his accounts, such as the battle scene in section 37, to be exciting and invigorating. Moreover, he resists the temptation to allow his proximity to Agricola to make him the omniscient source on the general's life. For example, in section 40, Tacitus explains that he cannot verify a particular account involving Agricola. Tacitus also claims to hold no relevant information regarding the cause of Agricola's death, and he refuses to speculate where other accounts have. In neither case does Tacitus feel the need to exaggerate his knowledge or plunge into narrative territory with which he is unfamiliar.

Tacitus' use of sources, then, is for the purposes of additional historical detail, and he implements them in an honest way. His refusal to speculate on unconfirmable events further shows his intentional aim to be historically objective

---

[29] For this reason, the *Agricola* has been considered an "encomium" as opposed to biography, but the genre preferred by the present study is "encomiastic biography."

despite his encomiastic interests. With this biography surveyed, it is fitting to move ahead to the next: a representative sample of Plutarch's *Parallel Lives*.

Source Valuation in Plutarch's *Theseus* and *Romulus*

Source	Reference (Grade from 1-7)
Aristotle	*Thes.* 3.2 (1); 16.2 (4); 25.2 (3)
Euripides the tragedian	*Thes.* 3.2 (4); 15.2 (1); 29.4-5 (5)
Archilochus	*Thes.* 5.3 (1/2)
Philochorus	*Thes.* 16.1 (5); 19.2 (1); 26.1 (5); 29.4 (4/5)[30]; 35.2 (1);
Pherecydes	*Thes.* 19.1 (1); 26.1 (3)
Demon	*Thes.* 19.2 (4); 23.3 (1)
Hellanicus	*Thes.* 17.3 (4); 25.5 (1); 26.1 (3)
Simonides	*Thes.* 17.5 (4); 26.1 (3); 27.2 (5)
Herias the Megarian	*Thes.* 20.2 (1); 32.5 (4)
Paeon the Amathusian	*Thes.* 20.3-4 (4)
Dicaearchus	*Thes.* 21.2 (1); 32.4 (1)
Homer	*Thes.* 25.2 (3); 34.1 (4)
Andron of Halicarnassus	*Thes.* 25.5 (1)
Herodorus	*Thes.* 26.1 (3); 30.4 (5)
Bion	*Thes.* 26.2 (1)
Menecrates	*Thes.* 26.2-3 (4)
Cleidemus	*Thes.* 27.3-4 (4)
Author of the Theseid	*Thes.* 28.1 (5/7)
Pindar	*Thes.* 28.2 (1)
Aeschylus	*Thes.* 29.5 (1)
Ister	*Thes.* 34.2 (7)
Diodorus the Topographer	*Thes.* 36.3 (4)
Promathion	*Rom.* 2.6 (5)
Diocles of Peparethus	*Rom.* 3.1 (3); 8.7 (3)
Fabius Pictor	*Rom.* 3.1 (3); 8.7 (3); 14.1 (1)
Herodorus Ponticus	*Rom.* 9.5 (1/4)
Varro	*Rom.* 12.3-4 (1)
Valerias Antias	*Rom.* 14.6 (3)
Juba	*Rom.* 14.6 (3); 15.3 (4); 17.5 (1)[31]
Sextius Sulla	*Rom.* 15.2 (4)
Dionysius of Halicarnassus	*Rom.* 16.8 (5)

---

[30] Plutarch probably disagrees with Philochorus here because of discrepancies between Philochorus' account and tradition about Heracles.

[31] Here Plutarch is quoting Juba's citation of Sulpicius Galba.

Simylus	*Rom.* 17.5 (7)
Butas	*Rom.* 21.6 (1)
Caius Acilius	*Rom.* 21.7 (1)
Prevalent tradition (*ho polys logos*)	*Thes.* 10.1 (4)
Some of the Naxians	*Thes.* 20.5 (4)
General consensus	*Thes.* 15.1 (1); 31.1 (4); *Rom.* 12.1 (1); 15.3 (4); 21.2 (1); 26.1 (3); 16.8 (3)
Other writers	*Thes.* 10.2-3 (4); 19.1 (1)[32]; 29.4 (2); 30.5 (3); 31.1 (5); 32.2 (1); 23.3 (4); 25.3 (5)
Unattributed	*Thes.* 10.1 (4); 11.2 (4); 11.2 (4); 12.2 (4); 16.3 (4); 18.2 (4); 20.1, three (4; 4; 4); 20.2 (4); 21.2 (4/1); 22.1 (4); 22.3 (4); 23.1 (4); 23.2 (4); 25.4, twice (4; 4); 26.1 (5); 27.4 (4); 27.6 (4); 34.1, twice (4; 4); 29.1, twice (1; 1); 29.2 (1); 32.1 (1); 32.5 (4); 33.2 (1); 34.2 (4); 36.1 (1); 36.3 (4); *Rom.* 1.1 (5); 1.2 (5); 2.1, four times (5; 5; 5; 3); 2.2 (4); 2.3, twice (4; 4); 4.2 (4); 4.3 (5); 5.3 (1); 5.4 (4); 9.3 (4); 12.1 (1); 13.2, thrice (5; 5; 5); 13.3 (3); 14.1-2 (7); 14.4 (4); 14.6 (5); 14.7 (4); 15.5 (1); 12.1 (5); 20.4 (1); 20.6 (1); 22.1, twice (4; 4); 22.4 (1); 23.3 (4); 27.5 (4); 27.6 (4); 28.1 (1); 29.3 (4); 29.6-7 (5); 29.7 (1)

Concerning Plutarch's historical method, A. J. Gossage writes, "In any case, the variety of his sources and his apparent intellectual honesty in reporting what writers before him had written make it probable that he himself had read many, if not most, of the sources that he quotes, and that his biographies were fresh and original in their composition rather than copies or recollections of earlier biographies on the same subject."[33] There is little that has been examined in the course of this study that contradicts Gossage's assertion. Perhaps no other topic serves as a clearer introduction to Plutarch's (judicious) approach to history than his response when sources disagree concerning mythic material. In the majority of these instances, Plutarch considers each of the sources as being unconfirmable (grade of 4).[34] In a few other passages, the biographer prefers a particular

---

[32] Here he cites "many historians and poets."

[33] Gossage, "Plutarch," 52.

[34] *Thes.* 25.4, concerning the person in whose honor Theseus instituted the Isthmian Games; *Thes.* 34.1, regarding an account of Theseus' mother; *Rom.* 9.5, concerning the vultures seen by Romulus and/or Remus; *Rom.* 10.1, when he discusses who killed Remus; also *Rom.* 21.2, on the identity of Carmenta; *Rom.* 22.1, on who instituted the consecration of fire; and *Rom.* 27.5-6, as he discusses diverging theories of the disappearance of Scipio's body.

version over another.[35]

As further evidence of Plutarch's judiciousness concerning his sources, one may examine the numerous instances cited above in which Plutarch treats his sources with either a grade of 3 or 5, representing that his intellectual judgment was not typically clouded by a view of confirmable events as having "*a priori* likelihood*,*" as Gossage suggests.[36] The source valuation charts for this sample of Plutarch indicate that this is not at all present in these works.[37] Plutarch demonstrates a measurable degree of fastidiousness in evaluating various accounts with knowledge of cultural information and certain realia.[38]

The individual cases to which Gossage refers concerning Plutarch's acceptance of majority opinions are not cited by Gossage, but likely involve 19.1, in which Plutarch supplements the majority opinion with the additional assent of Pherecydes, as well as 15.1, in which Plutarch does not mention the positions of others—even briefly. But the case is very different in other occurrences in *Theseus*. Furthermore, the presentation of mythic material in ancient sources and in Plutarch must be borne in mind.[39] When the author prefers an account concerning mythological events, it does not always follow that he considers these events 100% fact.[40] On the other hand, in the vast majority of cases in which Plutarch disagrees with an account, he does this on the basis of reason, as Gossage describes when he mentions Plutarch's affinity at times for probability, or by supplying other evidence for his disagreement. Although my essay examines only a handful of his *Lives*, no evidence raised by this particular method of source valuation for these selections disputes Stuart's consideration that Plutarch's *Lives* is the "high-water mark of ancient biographical aptitude".[41]

Nevertheless, the four instances of Plutarch's outright rejection of source material (grade of 7) require further discussion. In *Thes.* 34.2, the author cites Ister's rendering of unattributed source material concerning Aethra, concluding

---

[35] In *Thes.* 29.4, Plutarch probably disagrees with Philochorus because of discrepancies between Philochorus and accounts of Heracles. He prefers Pherecydes and others over Philochorus in *Thes.* 26.1. In *Thes.* 29.4-5 (5), Euripides is disproven by an account of Aeschylus.

[36] Gossage, "Plutarch," 64. For example, Plutarch applies reasoning to rule out an account from Simonides in *Thes.* 27.2: the army probably did not cross over ice.

[37] In the future, all of Plutarch's *Lives* will be analyzed by this method.

[38] Plutarch makes reference to a location and sacrificial rites of a modern cult to confirm details in an account, in *Thes.* 27.5. Similarly, he notes cleansing practices in *Rom.* 12.1 in order to reject an unattributed source. Plutarch notes contemporary practices in his confirmation of an account in *Rom.* 13.3, as well. Finally, in *Rom.* 20.2, the biographer disagrees with another unattributed source because he appeals to the names of the subjects involved. Concerning realia, Plutarch mentions statues which depict Romulus as being on foot when dismissing a report from Dionysius of Halicarnassus in *Rom.* 16.8.

[39] See the comments in the introductory section of this paper.

[40] For instance, Plutarch's hesitancy with many of the normative accounts is evident in *Thes.* 29.1, when he makes positive mention of other stories "which were neither honorable in their beginnings nor fortunate in their endings," but which "have not been dramatised" (Perrin, *Plutarch*, 1:67).

[41] Stuart, *Epochs*, 64.

that the account itself is "very doubtful" ("*pollēn alogian*"). Plutarch's special mention that he is citing a person who himself received this version from other, unattributed sources naturally convey a level of uncertainty about the source's legitimacy. Another consideration may also be in play, namely the distinction in genre between history and biography.[42] Perhaps if Plutarch were writing historiography proper, he might have chosen to discuss each and every instance in full. However, his dismissal of Ister's story here is not an indication of poor or insufficient writing, since too many discussions of external material may distract from the author's main purpose: a portrayal of Theseus.

This consideration also factors into Plutarch's dismissal of an unattributed report in *Rom.* 14.1-2, when he gives the story of Romulus' attempts to start war against the Sabines. It is likely that the biographer's reasoning to reject this account as "not truthful" (*ouk eikos*) is based upon the person of Romulus as revealed by the most authoritative accounts he has received about him. In both *Thes.* 34.2 and *Rom.* 14.1-2, the historical gap of centuries between the legendary material and Plutarch's account has placed the author in a situation where he is required to make such judgments based upon what he knows about the subject from the sources he trusts most.

Evidence of this is found in Plutarch's third grade-7 passage: the rejection of the author of the Theseid's account of the Amazons in *Thes.* 28.1 as "*periphanōs eoike mythō kai plasmati*" ("seen all around as fiction and fable"). This, in fact, is a veiled statement of Plutarch's reasoning for omitting the account, as is noticed by its grade of 5/7. In the account cited, he sees little reliable source material and numerous indications of a tall tale.

Finally, Plutarch exercises less prudence than is probably warranted when he calls Simylus "absurd" in *Rom.* 17.5, without giving a full explanation for his rejection of the account. This *ad hominem* does not further the biographer's narrative and distracts from the character of Romulus. This may be compared, however, with Plutarch's high view of Butas' historical writings expressed only chapters later: that Butas, "wrote fabulous explanations of Roman customs in elegiac verse."[43] As with his estimation of Simylus, this ascription interrupts the author's ongoing discussion of historical detail.

Source Valuation in Plutarch's *Alcibiades* and *Coriolanus*

Source	Reference (Grade from 1-7)
Antisthenes	*Alc.* 1.2 (1)
Plato	*Alc.* 1.2 (1)

---

[42] Cf. Momigliano, *Development*, 15. Momigliano further states that readers' expectations also influenced the writing process of biographies (idem., 56-57). Furthermore, he writes that Plutarch's biographies employ a much higher level of historiographic method as compared with other biographies of his time. Thus, it may be concluded that the depth of source material and interaction in Plutarch is already well beyond what may have been required of him by the genre, and to ask him to do more seems unsuitable for the genre.

[43] *Rom.* 21.6 (trans., Perrin).

Aristophanes	*Alc.* 1.4 (1)
Archippus	*Alc.* 1.4 (1)
Antiphon	*Alc.* 3.1 (5)
Thucydides	*Alc.* 6.2 (1); 11.1 (1); 13.3 (1); 20.4 (1/5)
Theophrastus	*Alc.* 10.3 (3)
Euripides	*Alc.* 11.1 (7)
Eupolis	*Alc.* 13.2 (1)
Pheax	*Alc.* 13.2 (1)
Plato (comic poet)	*Alc.* 13.5 (1)
Phrynichus (comic poet)	*Alc.* 20.4 (1)
Hellanicus	*Alc.* 21.1 (4)
Duris the Samian	*Alc.* 32.2-3 (5)
Theopompus	*Alc.* 32.5 (3/2)
Ephorus	*Alc.* 32.5 (3/2)
Xenophon	*Alc.* 32.5 (3/2)
Ctisias son of Callaeschrus	*Alc.* 33.1 (1)
Dionysius of Halicarnassus	*Alc. and Cor.* 2.2 (1)
Public Record (*eisangelia*)	*Alc.* 22.3 (1)
General consensus	*Alc.* 29.2 (1); *Cor.* 37.3 (1)
Unattributed	*Alc.* 1.1 (1); 1.2 (1); 1.4 (1); 10.1 (1); 12.2 (1); 16.2 (1); 17.4, twice (3; 4); 23.3 (1); 23.4, twice (1; 1); 26.6 (1); 39.2 (4); 39.4 (1); 39.5 (4); *Cor.* 3.4 (1); 14.4 (1); 20.4 (1); 24.1 (1); 26.2 (1); 38.1 (1)

Plutarch's interaction with sources in *Alcibiades* is rather straightforward. He rarely uses the same named source in more than one place, with Thucydides constituting the lone exception. The majority of sources cited receive a grade of either 1 or 4. In *Alc.* 33.1, Plutarch cites Ctisias son of Callaeschrus for something Ctisias himself accomplished. Another interesting example of a grade-1 is his critique of Thucydides' omission of the names of individuals in the account, to which Plutarch assumes Thucydides had access.[44] Although the biographer concurs with his source's version of the story, it appears as though Plutarch is almost chastising Thucydides for this oversight. This passage stands as one of the only three cases of Plutarch's qualified disagreement with a source (grade of 5) in *Alcibiades*.

In the second example, 3.1, he considers bias on a source's part to be reason for rejecting the statement. This is noteworthy, because, upon looking at the chart above, it may appear that Plutarch is not discerning enough with regard to his sources in *Alcibiades*, which is simply not the case. One may note also the

---

[44] *Alc.* 20.4.

four instances of grades of 4, in which the author intentionally chooses not to overstep the bounds of his historical knowledge.[45]

His strong use of sources in *Alcibiades* is also observed in cases when he disagrees with them. In one place, he notices bias in a source's material.[46] Most notable, however, is his handling of Duris the Samian's material in 32.2-3. Here Plutarch uses an argument from silence in the accounts of more reputable historical writers, and also appeals to the logic of the narrative as inconsistent with Duris' claims. Additionally, Plutarch subtly doubts the authenticity of Duris' claim of descent from Alcibiades, possibly noting it as a reason for potential bias in Duris' account. The other writers named here—Theopompus, Ephorus, and Xenophon—all receive a grade of 3 or possibly 2. It is on logical grounds, however, that Plutarch doubts Duris' claim and prefers Theopompus, Ephorus, and Xenophon instead. By today's standards, Plutarch's handling of Duris' statements would hardly be considered biased.

The only instance in *Alcibiades* of Plutarch's outright rejection of source material is his treatment of Euripides in comparison with Thucydides on the very minor detail of racing chariots at the Olympic Games in 11.1. This is a highly inconsequential matter in the story, and it also seems to follow the same reasoning listed above regarding general practice in the genre of biography. Plutarch does, however, take time to address Thucydides' rendering in more detail.

As may be noted in the chart above, Plutarch's source material for the *Coriolanus* is especially shallow. This serves as a wonderful test case for the biographer's actions when he has difficulty finding source material. Since the *Parallel Lives* were to mirror one another in length as closely as possible, Plutarch's two choices were to either reduce the *Alcibiades* to mirror the *Coriolanus*, or to lengthen the latter to match the former. The biographer decides the second option of course, but instead of lengthening the story of Coriolanus upon improper foundation, he chooses to discuss social and cultural issues which are secondary—or even tertiary—to the narrative. Plutarch often cites sources for certain of these details, although these sources receive no grade since they do not pertain at all to the life of the subject.[47]

---

[45] In *Alc.* 21.1, he places distance between himself and mythical material by writing that Hellanicus included Andocides the orator as a direct descendant of Odysseus. In this case, one may consider that Plutarch's notation of his direct source is proof of his hermeneutical distance from his anecdote. In other words, if Plutarch had not cited his source, it would give the illusion that Plutarch gives assent to knowing the family tree of a legendary figure. Moreover, in 17.4, he expresses uncertainty about the internal motivations of an astrologer. In 39.4, he presents an unconfirmable report of a dream Alcibiades had before his death. Finally, in 39.5, he presents the statements of others who attribute the deeds of Pharnabazus to Alcibiades.

[46] Antiphon, in *Alc.* 3.1.

[47] The citations in the *Coriolanus* which are not historical include an unattributed source (1.2); Cato the Elder (8.3); Plato (15.4); Homer (32.4-6); Heacleitus (38.4); and, in *Alc. And Cor.*, Dion (2.3) and Antipater (3.2). Plutarch relies more heavily upon material regarding social issues as in *Cor.* 1.2, 8.3, and 11.2-5. With the use of this material, Plutarch is "stacking the deck" with interesting material since he lacks the amount of heavy material at his disposal in the *Alcibiades*.

The sources Plutarch does use are all cited with a grade of 1, perhaps reflecting a paucity of material with which he may interact about the subject's life. (2) When Plutarch does return to the topic of Coriolanus, however, he uses these sources—mostly unattributed ones—in most places. In one notable instance, a third-person, unattributed source is credited with material stretching across two larger chapters.[48]

Source Valuation in Plutarch's *Galba*

Source	Reference (Grade from 1-7)
General consensus	3.1 (1)
Unattributed	3.2 (1); 3.3 (1); 4.2 (1); 4.4 (1); 14.4 (5); 19.4 (1); 19.5, thrice (1; 4; 4); 25.1 (1); 25.3 (1); 27.2-4, thrice (4; 4; 4)

Plutarch's almost equal use of authoritative (grade of 1) and unconfirmable (grade of 4) sources in the *Galba*, as well as the *Otho*, confirms that he holds demonstrable command over what may be definitively stated about this Caesar, and what may not. Part of this is explained by the fact that these events occurred during Plutarch's lifetime, thus giving him an even stronger sense of what may be stated unequivocally.[49] He notes the words of Icelaus in 7.2—and it is even possible that he is citing Icelaus as a source here—but the grammar is unclear. Plutarch may also give some firsthand knowledge when he provides reasons why the people were furious with government in 8.1, facts which are further bolstered by the relatively short gap of time between the event and Plutarch's writing.

Plutarch rejects an unattributed source in 14.4 in favor of another version. In 19.4-5, Plutarch makes four citations, with three of them in 19.5. His first citation in 19.5 is positive and builds upon his affirmative citation in 19.4, while it is followed by two unconfirmable sources which are presented as possible reasons for these events. Likewise, the biographer treats the details of Galba's death as unconfirmable in 27.2-4, with several unattributed sources cited in that place as well.

Source Valuation in Plutarch's *Otho*

Source	Reference (Grade from 1-7)
Cluvius Rufus	3.2 (1)
Secundus the rhetorician	9.3 (3)
Most participants in a battle	14.1 (1)

---

[48] *Cor.* 24.1—25.3.

[49] Gossage concurs that it would have been much easier for Plutarch to confirm events which occurred in his lifetime (Gossage, "Plutarch," 63).

Self as eyewitness	18.1 (1)
Unattributed	6.5 (4); 9.1 (4); 9.3 (5)

Source valuation in the *Otho* is quite similar to that in the *Galba*, for obvious reasons. His firsthand information, however, seems to be even stronger than the previous biography. He cites most of the participants in a battle when describing the event in 14.1, and he appeals to the consul and historian Cluvius Rufus in 3.2. Plutarch provides his own eyewitness testimony in 18.1, as one who has visited Otho's burial site.

On the basis of such solid firsthand materials and Plutarch's own knowledge of the events in question, he gives added distance between his biography of *Otho* and his unattributed sources. In one case, Plutarch prefers the rendering of Secundus the rhetorician to an unattributed version on the basis of common sense and rationalization. This is perhaps a fitting note on which to close the discussion of Plutarch the biographer, seeing as reason and firm source material define his work.

Source Valuation in Suetonius' *Lives of the Caesars*

Source	Reference (Grade from 1-7; *Denotes firsthand citation of a letter)
Tanusaias Geminus	*Jul.* 9.2, twice (1; 4)
Marcus Bibulus	*Jul.* 9.2 (1); 10.1 (1)
Gaius Curio	*Jul.* 9.2 (1); 9.4 (4); 49.1 (4); 52.3 (1)
Cicero	*Jul.* 9.2 (1); 30.5 (1); 42.3 (1); 49.3-4 (1); 55.1, twice (1; 1); 56.2 (1); *Aug.* 3.2 (1)
Marcus Actorius Naso	*Jul.* 9.3 (1)
Gnaeus Pompus	*Jul.* 30.2 (5)
Asinius Pollio	*Jul.* 30.4 (1); 55.4 (1); 56.4 (4)
Licinius Calvinus	*Jul.* 49.1 (4)
Dolabella	*Jul.* 49.1 (4)
Marcus Brutus	*Jul.* 49.2 (1)
Gaius Memmius	*Jul.* 49.2 (1)
Gaius Oppius	*Jul.* 52.2 (6)
Marcius Cato	*Jul.* 53.1 (1)
Augustus	*Jul.* 55.4, twice (3; 4); 71.2* (1); 71.3* (2); 71.4* (1); 74.1 (1); 76.1* (1); 76.2*, twice (1; 1); 86.2 (2); 86.3 (2); 86.4 (2); 21.4-6* (1); *Claud.* 4.1-4* (1); *Claud.* 4.5* (1); *Claud.* 4.6* (1)
Hirtius	*Jul.* 56.3 (1)
Titius Ampius	*Jul.* 77.1 (1)
Cornelius Balbus	*Jul.* 81.2 (2)
Quintus Tubero	*Jul.* 83.1 (1)

Cassius of Parma	*Aug.* 4.2 (1)[50]
Ennius	*Aug.* 7.2 (2)
Marc Antony	*Aug.* 10.4 (1); 63.2 (1); 69.2* (4)
Aquilius Niger	*Aug.* 11.1 (1)
Cremetius Cordus	*Aug.* 35.2 (1)
Valerius Messala	*Aug.* 74.1 (1)
Cornelius Nepos	*Aug.* 77.1 (1/2)
Julius Marathus	*Aug.* 79.2 (6); 94.3 (1)
Asclepias of Mendes	*Aug.* 94.4-8 (4)
Tiberias	*Tib.* 61.1 (7)
Seneca	*Tib.* 78.2 (4)
Gnaeus Lentulus Gaetulicus	*Cal.* 8.1 (5)
Pliny the Elder	*Cal.* 8.1 (3)
Valerius Catullus	*Cal.* 36.1 (2)
Claudius	*Claud.* 21.2 (1)
Licinius Crassus	*Ner.* 2.2 (1)
Suetonius Laetus	*Oth.* 10.1, twice (1; 1)
Quintus Elogius	*Vit.* 1.2-3 (4)
Domitian	*Dom.* 11.3 (1)[51]; 18.2 (1)
Common knowledge/belief	*Jul.* 1.3 (1); 49.1 (1); *Aug.* 70.4 (4); *Tib.* 21.2 (5); *Claud.* 44.2 (1); *Tit.* 8.1 (1)
General consensus	*Aug.* 72.1 (1); *Cal.* 3.1 (1); *Claud.* 1.4 (1); *Gal.* 4.1 (1); 20.1 (3); *Ner.* 18.2 (1); *Ves.* 1.1 (1); 16.2 (1); 25.1 (1)
Songs of charioteers	*Jul.* 49.4 (1)
Realia	*Aug.* 7.1 (3); 70.2 (5); *Cal.* 8.3 (1)
Reputable authorities	*Tib.* 61.6 (1); *Claud.* 33.4 (1)
Secondhand report	*Cal.* 19.3 (1); *Claud.* 15.3 (1); *Ner.* 19.1[52] (1); *Tit.* 3.2 (1); *Dom.* 19.1 (1)
Public records	*Cal.* 23.2 (1)
Notebooks of Caligula	*Cal.* 49.3 (1)
Unattributed Material	*Jul.* 29.1 (1); 30.3 (3); 33.1 (5); 45.3 (1); 46.1 (4); 47.1 (1); 48.1 (1); 55.2 (1); 56.1 (4); 78.1, twice (4; 4); 83.1, twice (1; 1); 86.1 (4); 86.2, twice (4; 5); *Aug.* 80.1 (1); 90.1 (1)[53]; 94.8 (4); *Tib.* 5.1, thrice (5; 5; 3); 52.3, twice (3; 3); 67.2 (3); 78.2, thrice (4;

---

[50] John C. Rolfe notes that Suetonius misreads Cassius due to terminology which was foreign to him (Rolfe, *Suetonius*, 1:155 n9).

[51] This particular citation does not follow the traditional rules of speeches or declarations in Greco-Roman historical writing, since Suetonius precedes Domitian's speech with a note confirming that Domitian spoke the exact words he has recorded.

[52] Here Suetonius cites presumed eyewitnesses whom he views as very reputable.

[53] The contents of this material carry through ch. 96.

	4; 4); *Cal.* 1.2 (1); 2.1 (1); 4.1 (1); 5.1 (1); 12.2 (1); 19.3, twice (5; 5); 25.1 (4); 32.1 (2); 50.2 (4); *Claud.* 1.4, twice (4; 4); 32.1 (1); 44.2, twice (4; 3); 44.3, twice (4; 4); *Ner.* 1.1, twice (3; 1); 1.2 (3); 7.1 (1); 13.2 (3); 21.3 (1); 23.3 (4); 37.2 (2); 53.1 (1); 54.1 (4); *Gal.* 3.1, four times (4; 4; 4; 4); 3.2 (1); 15.1 (1); 18.3 (1); 20.1 (5); 22.1, twice (4; 4); *Oth.* 2.1 (1); 3.2 (1); 6.2 (1); 7.2 (1); 12.1 (1); 12.1, twice (1; 1); *Vit.* 1.1, twice (5; 5); 2.1 (4); 7.1 (5); 14.5 (1); *Ves.* 1.2, twice (4; 4); 1.4 (5); 4.3 (1); 16.2 (2); 16.3, twice (5; 3); 25.1 (1); *Tit.* 2.1, twice (1; 1); 9.2 (2); *Dom.* 1.1 (1); 14.2 (1); 22.1 (2); 23.2 (4)

The final biographer evaluated here is Suetonius, whose *Lives of the Caesars* is likewise supported by a dense quantity of named and unnamed sources. The chart above shows in Suetonius a broad range of evaluations that he applies to his sources. Of the 37 named sources he cites four are the emperor being studied, while Suetonius compiled information regarding another—Caligula—from the Caesar's personal notebooks. Judging from the use of his imperial sources, it is clear that Suetonius views Augustus quite favorably. On the contrary, his singular rejection of a claim in Tiberius' autobiography does not indicate, nor does it stem from, a harsh view of the Caesar.[54] In this particular instance, Suetonius addresses a historical inaccuracy in the interest of historical transparency.

This view of history can be easily observed in the varied way he treats his named sources. Although Suetonius later calls Curio, "the most reckless of the tribunes," he authoritatively cites him as an eyewitness in *Jul.* 9.2.[55] Moreover, the majority of the other eyewitness accounts Suetonius includes are presented favorably, unless a contradiction arises with other testimony.[56] In such cases, the

---

[54] *Tib.* 61.7. This may be contrasted with Suetonius' general agreement with the contents of Augustus' letters. On the other hand, the biographer uses Tiberius' speeches as unqualified fact in favor of a contested account in *Tib.* 67.3-4, evidence that his rejection of the claim in Tiberius' autobiography is more likely due to comparative analysis against with other evidence and facts than anti-Tiberian bias.

[55] In *Jul.* 52.3, Suetonius even appeals to Curio's account as authoritative proof for the portrayal of Julius Caesar. There is significant reason to conclude that his use of Curio's authority here is influenced by Curio's status as an eyewitness who worked alongside Julius. The tribune's general standing in Suetonius' eyes does not prevent him from being credited with certain valuable statements for the *Life of Julius* in the biographer's eyes, as one may notice in the chart above.

[56] Cf. above, for example, his citations of Curio, Brutus, Gaius Memmius, Titius Ampius, Marcius Cato, Quintus Tubero, and Cornelius Balbus. Noting the latter's unseemly reputation, Barry Baldwin writes, "There are those who would find the notion of Cornelius Balbus as a reliable source for anything frankly hilarious" (Baldwin, *Suetonius*, 111-12).

biographer works quite smoothly to rectify the issues at hand. In some places, Suetonius uses reasoning to determine between differing accounts.[57] In *Ves.* 16.3, for example, Suetonius makes his determination based on what he knows of Vespasian's personal traits. In *Cal.* 19.3, Suetonius uses testimony his grandfather received from courtiers to Caligula to dispute two common renderings of an account. Particularly when the account refers to the Caesar's private death or early life, Suetonius presents the options as he is aware of them, but chooses not to take a firm position.[58] Finally, in a widely attested account which had differing versions, the biographer prefers the one with a more general following.[59]

Suetonius, as a proficient accountant of history, stacks source citations with varying valuation grades at important sections of the narrative, particularly in some places in the *Julius*.[60] Moreover, as Suetonius begins the *Vitellius*, he dismisses two particular versions of his early life on account of their being either flatterers or detractors of the Caesar.[61] In other cases as well, Suetonius alerts the audience of his own opinions without conflating them with what he knows to be documented fact.[62]

Perhaps the most complex analysis of Suetonius' source valuation pertains to his descriptive sections of Julius and Augustus in their respective biographies. Suetonius gives assent to unattributed rumors about Julius' dress (*Jul.* 45.3), but in the very next section (*Jul.* 46.1) decides not to take a position on a statement from many ("*multi*") concerning Julius' luxury. Moreover, Suetonius demonstrates later in this very same context that he is working from firsthand accounts (49.1). Here he cites three individuals—Licinius Calvinus, Dolabella, and Curio—all of whose indictments of Julius Suetonius documents without affirming their validity. Suetonius then affirmatively cites the testimony of Gaius Memmius, another noted associate of Julius (49.2). Even if some of the specific material Suetonius relates in such passages as *Jul.* 45.3, 47.1, or 48.1 (as noted in the chart above), does not stem from the same sources cited in 49.1, he demonstrates the ability to funnel his information through the firsthand accounts at his disposal. In the *Julius*, his (numerous) firsthand accounts often come from those who themselves fell victim to Julius' shortcomings.[63] Thus, if an anti-Julius slant

---

[57] *Jul.* 30.3; *Ves.* 16.3. Cf. also *Cal.* 8.1-4; *Vit.* 7.1.

[58] *Jul.* 78.1; *Tib.* 78.2; *Claud.* 1.4; 44.2; 44.3; *Gal.* 3.1; *Vit.* 1.2—2.1; *Ves.* 1.2.

[59] *Gal.* 20.1.

[60] E.g., *Jul.* 9.2-4; 49.1-4, which both contain a mixture of neutral (4-grade) valuations along with grades of 1, to ensure that he does not transcend his boundaries as an accountant of history.

[61] *Vit.* 1.1. Similarly, in *Jul.* 33.1, the biographer disagrees with a popular understanding of an event and explains how the particular misinformation came to be. In this instance, there is little at stake for him in the argument he makes.

[62] For reference, contrast his approach to his own, unsupported opinion in *Cal.* 51.1 with the testimony of the ex-consul in *Tib.* 61.6.

[63] This is not necessarily the case, however, with Gaius Oppius, whom Suetonius references in 52.2. It is an interesting citation since it blurs the line between strict source material and an offhand reference, but Suetonius uses Oppius' book to confirm a point concerning Julius' general untrustworthiness in his relations with women and in fatherly responsibility. Since Suetonius here firmly disagrees with Oppius, Julius' only friend

does surface at certain times in the work, it appears as a result of surveying first-hand accounts and after consulting a large number of other sources.

His portrait of Augustus, on the other hand, is less objective. Suetonius' admiration of the emperor is evident, for instance, in the way the biographer uses the testimony of Augustus' aide Julius Marathus in *Aug.* 79.2. The biographer's record is clear that Augustus was short in stature, yet he includes the testimony of Marathus—with which he clearly disagrees—to further develop the dignified portrait of the Caesar he presents elsewhere.[64] On the other hand, one must wonder again to what degree his high view of Augustus elsewhere is informed by his exceptional source material.[65] Throughout the *Augustus* in particular, Suetonius makes extensive use of the letters of Augustus, almost all of which are cited as unqualified fact. The sources he uses in this account are in fact so strong that Suetonius does not even appeal to general, unattributed material until the eightieth chapter! It is quite possible, then, that Suetonius holds such high regard for Augustus in part because of these sources' quality.[66] With the Caesar's personal letters, his biographer had unique access into the life of his subject and was free to make his own decisions on the emperor's character, for good or for ill.[67]

Moreover, less significant issues arise in Suetonius' implementation of sources. His repugnance at the violence of Nero is noticeable when he introduc-

---

cited by Suetonius, it is clear where the biographer's sympathies lie. But Suetonius' reference does not even make clear that he even had direct access to Oppius' book, and the use of numerous other testimony from eyewitnesses shows that Suetonius is more likely allowing his sources to dictate his allegiances, than his allegiances dictating his valuation of sources.

[64] In other words, Suetonius says in effect, "Augustus was short, but some—such as Julius Marathus—have provided a more dignified account of his stature, which you may adopt if you will."

[65] After all, Augustus is cited twice in the *Julius*, and in one instance, he affirmatively cites the later emperor, but only after qualifying Augustus' statements with the help of Suetonius' own considerations (*Jul.* 55.4). In the other citation in the same passage, he does not take a position on Augustus' statement. Notably, this constitutes the only instance outside the *Augustus* in which Suetonius cites Augustus without noting that the material is from his letters. Therefore, it stands to reason that it may not be quite so much Augustus' testimony alone which he reveres—although the biographer no doubt makes it clear that he views the Caesar favorably—but rather the strength of the source which he has acquired. This proposal has evidence elsewhere: when Suetonius makes particular mention of his unique access to a single source, he always cites it affirmatively without qualification (cf. a direct report from many eyewitnesses in *Dom.* 19.1; the notebooks of Caligula in *Cal.* 49.3; personal interaction with many eyewitnesses in *Tit.* 3.2; the report from Suetonius' grandfather in *Cal.* 19.3. In contrast, Suetonius makes mention of letters Julius sent to the Senate which were extant at the time of his writing in *Jul.* 56.6, but he does not cite from them. In light of Suetonius' practice of directly citing the letters of Augustus, it does not seem that the biographer had access to these letters.

[66] The rate of preservation for sources with a high view of the emperor was much higher than negative ones.

[67] Suetonius is also quite impressed with the nature and quality of Augustus' writing ability. He includes a rather lengthy section (*Aug.* 87—88) in which he praises the vocabulary, penmanship, and writing style of Caesar Augustus.

es unattributed source in *Ner.* 37.2. Nero begins this report with the phrase, "*Creditur eitam...*" ("It is *even* believed..."), thus successfully implementing this source material into his larger discussion of Nero's violence. Suetonius uses this same construction again in *Tit.* 9.2, this time to speak more positively of his subject. In each of these situations, Suetonius supplements his descriptions of the Caesar's character with this source material, but the sheer number of grade-4 evaluations in Suetonius—including those found within the *Lives* of *Julius, Augustus, Nero, Domitian,* and *Titus*—are equally informative of the way the biographer handles unconfirmable reports, even when he admires or loathes the emperor.

Suetonius consistently supports his *Lives* with strong evidence. That he does not refer to a source does not entail that the account has not met a general burden of proof that he requires. In one instance in the *Vespasian*, Suetonius rejects an account because he searched carefully for supporting evidence and found none.[68] In addition, although he does not cite a source from *Ves.* 21—23, Suetonius gives several accounts that are highly specific, which seem to come from a source who knew the Caesar personally. Some of his unattributed evidence also comes from eyewitness accounts. In *Aug.* 35.2, the biographer has received inside information from senatorial meetings under Augustus' rule from Cremetius Cordus.[69] As noted above, the direct use of firsthand accounts from individuals in the narrative bespeaks his general pursuit of rigid historicity.

It may be observed that certain Caesars' *Lives* contain fewer citations than others. For example, the *Galba* and the *Otho*, as in Plutarch, have fewer strong sources than others, but this is explained by their brief tenures as Caesar and the seeming lack of information elsewhere concerning their respective reigns.[70] When firsthand accounts are not available, as in these cases, he makes use of the common tradition related to these emperors, choosing not to confirm certain, unknowable facts.[71]

Moreover, Suetonius' sources for the *Caligula* are not as strong as those in his earlier *Lives*. As such, he has to rely more heavily upon unattributed sources. Later, however, he introduces certain material which is too strong to dispute, such as the Caesar's personal notebooks.[72] It is quite reasonable that this disparity in the first part of his work is due in part to the general practice of Greco-Roman biography to focus much more heavily on one's public life than private

---

[68] *Ves.* 1.4.

[69] Suetonius also makes mention of letters Julius sent to the Senate which were extant at the time of his writing (*Jul.* 56.6). In light of Suetonius' practice of directly citing the letters of Augustus, it does not seem that the biographer had access to these letters.

[70] Cf. the relative lack of sources in Plutarch's *Lives* of *Galba* and *Otho* in comparison with his other *Lives* as well. Just as in Suetonius' case, this is most likely explained by external factors rather than the capability of either biographer.

[71] Cf. *Gal.* 3.1; 22.1.

[72] *Cal.* 49.3. Suetonius also states that he had access to the personal notebooks of Nero in forming his *Life* of the emperor (*Ner.* 52.1).

details.⁷³ When sources differ with one another in *Caligula*, however, Suetonius uses the same critical reasoning he utilizes in previous biographies to authenticate accounts as is evidenced, for example, by his appeal to proof noted by Pliny the Elder concerning Caligula's birthplace.⁷⁴ Further demonstrating his critical engagement with source material, Suetonius critiques even the account he prefers, noting that Pliny was wrong in his chronology of the event.

Suetonius also uses realia in his assessment of history. In *Aug.* 7.1, he appeals to an inscription on a bronze statue which contains the surname Augustus had as a child. Since this fact had been questioned, the biographer uses the inscription as conclusive evidence in its favor. Reference is also made to proscriptions on another statue as well as a vase in *Aug.* 70.2. Not only does he dispute the content of these proscriptions, he refers to them as slander in 71.1. In *Cal.* 8.3, Suetonius cites an inscription on an altar to further solidify, on the basis of confirmable evidence, his preference for Pliny the Elder's position on Caligula's birthplace. Somewhat related, too, is his use of a cultural point of reference as authoritative in a certain place in the *Julius*.⁷⁵ In all these instances, Suetonius employs a variety of resources to evaluate existing accounts and discover new sources for events which occurred before his time.

Discussion

The early roots of biography lie in encomiastic biography, noted especially in Isocrates' *Evagoras* and Xenophon's *Agesilaus* and *Memorabilia*. In his works studied here, Xenophon uses several verifiable sources, such as Hermogenes in *Mem.* 4.8.4-10 and even himself.⁷⁶ Because of the general strength of this type of eyewitness testimony, such testimony must not be disregarded outright. Nevertheless, Xenophon's explicit exploitation of much of his source material to support his own opinions significantly weakens our expectation for his accounts' objectivity.

Notwithstanding this, Xenophon's influence on the genre during the Roman period appears negligible in this regard. For instance, even though Thrasybulus is Nepos' favorite (cf. *Thras.* 1.1-5), the biographer supplies no account for his early life. If Nepos were to have felt an urge toward persuasive embellishment, certainly it would have manifested when portraying a subject for whom he has professed such pleasant thoughts. Similarly, when Nepos praises Timotheus' wisdom and prudence in the encomiastic section after Timotheus' death, he of-

---

⁷³ It is a general rule across the biographies treated here that the early portions of biographies which treat the figure's early life are generally supported by hearsay and oral reports.

⁷⁴ *Cal.* 8.1. This evidence counters a conflicting claim from Gnaeus Lentulus Gaetulicus.

⁷⁵ *Jul.* 49.1. Here Suetonius cites the songs of charioteers which had continued during subsequent battles in remembrance of the historical account.

⁷⁶ E.g., *Mem.* 1.2.31; 1.2.53; 1.4.2; 1.4.19; 1.7.5; 2.1.1; 2.4.1; 2.5.1; 2.6.1; 2.9.1; 2.10.1; 4.3.2; 4.4.5; 4.5.2

fers a proof but without any source citation. Since the author chooses not to include even something so small as unattributed citations to bolster an argument he proposes, it may be argued that Nepos' use of sources elsewhere in the *Generals*—attributed and unattributed—meet specific criteria that transcend simply confirming the author's personal opinions or making him appear more credible.[77]

Suetonius also resists these urges. In *Cal.* 51.1, Suetonius proposes his own theory and recounts historical events, but offers no external sources or data which give further credence to it. The biographer's decision here demonstrates that he is less interested in defending his own positions than presenting the concrete facts as best he knew them. His proposal was no doubt important to him, yet he treats it as a grade-4, unconfirmable event. In this case, his preference instead is to provide his audience with an accurate historical understanding rather than force them into blind acceptance of his own position.

One final example of Nepos' self-restraint particularly contrasts with Xenophon's use of himself as an eyewitness. In Nepos' *Latin Historians*, the biographer cites himself as an eyewitness to the funeral of Atticus' mother (*Att.* 17.1). Nepos does not parade the information for the sake of establishing a point about Atticus, but instead reports the event conclusively. Similarly, when Suetonius makes an effort to highlight a firsthand account of an ex-consul in *Tib.* 61.6, he does this on the subject of a dinner party involving Tiberius' call for the death of Paconius, an account for which Suetonius appears to hold no apologetic or ulterior purpose.[78] This careful approach among Roman biographers is mirrored also in the *bioi* of the Greek Plutarch, who rarely holds grade-2 or grade-6 valuations of his sources.[79] Thus, there exist in Greco-Roman *bioi* no obvious parallels to the less honest presentation of source material found in early Greek biography.

Few overt biases are revealed by this study of source valuation in the Greco-Roman biographies examined here. While Tacitus' bias in favor of Agricola is

---

[77] In another case, Nepos expresses great respect for Datames and admits that few sources exist for his life when he writes, "I now pass to the bravest and ablest of all the barbarians ... (T)he greater number of his exploits are less familiar and ... his successes were due, not to the greatness of his forces, but to his strategy, in which he excelled all the men of his day" (*Tim.* 4.5-6; Rolfe, *Nepos*, 143-45; cf. Datames, 6.8). See also *Ep.* 10.1-4.

[78] His record of this event also has implications for the overall reliability of this *Life*, since it suggests that there may be other, contemporaneous sources for Atticus with whom he has interacted and is simply not informing the reader, as is also found in Nicolaus' *Augustus*.

[79] Out of the 212 total sources cited in these works of Plutarch, no grade-6 valuations are present, and only one citation may constitute grade-2 valuation. In *Thes.* 5.3, the biographer quotes Archilochus as confirmation of his account. While ultimately Plutarch's version is indeed bolstered by this quotation, Plutarch's use of it in context functions more as grade-1 valuation since the biographer places special focus upon the historical events themselves and little concentration upon their implications. His persistent carefulness with his own biases and intrinsic concentration upon historicity, then, place these works of Plutarch on equal footing with the judiciousness of his Roman contemporaries.

undoubtedly the most well-known of the subjects evaluated here, his use of sources does not reveal persuasive tricks. The sources with which he disagrees are not on the basis of historical accounts of Agricola's life, which shows that he was not actively attempting to discounts rumors or proposed events that defame his beloved father-in-law. Any perceived bias regarding his use of sources must be acknowledged by an argument from silence—that Tacitus omitted or tweaked the narrative—but which is not found in the account itself.

The most evident bias revealed by this study is Suetonius' favorable view of Augustus, which owes much to the biographer's access to the Caesar's personal materials. Yet Suetonius' account is written over a century after the events took place. The biographer's internal motivation for this may hardly be related to a dark, ulterior motive guiding Suetonius' retelling these events. Moreover, his disdain for emperors such as Nero, Caligula, and Domitian is often supported by strong source material employed without any obviously dishonest tricks of persuasion.

Unattributed sources are used in these biographies in a variety of ways. Greco-Roman biographers used them for historical purposes. In most cases, the formulations *legetai* ("it is said"), *phasi* ("they say"), or other signifiers of unattributed sources are used to treat legends (concerning figures who lived long ago, as in Plutarch's *Theseus and Romulus*) or rumors (concerning figures who lived even in the recent past, such as many Caesars portrayed by Suetonius). These constructions most often place a distance between the writer and the material being presented, also subtly suggesting that he does not have as close an interaction with the source at hand.[80] Some biographies of less broadly attested figures, such as many of the *Generals* of Cornelius Nepos and Plutarch's work on *Coriolanus*, rely more heavily upon unattributed sources because of the general lack of information on the subject.

Conclusion

Although admittedly this is merely one measure for bias within writings of antiquity, the present study concludes that Greco-Roman biographers held a high view of history. Less reliably attested events are regularly proposed with proper distance, as may be observed in the high volume of grade-4 evaluations. Reason and probability are regularly consulted concerning events in the distant past. Even when an author's motivation for giving an account may be questioned, the example of Tacitus' *Agricola* reveals an author much more forthright and judicious in his presentation of sources than were the authors of some earlier Greek works. Questions of bias aside, these biographers depended on sources rather than freely inventing reports of events. In conclusion, the biographers' handling of sources in the Greco-Roman era has much to tell us, not only about contem-

---

[80] This is most clearly seen in Nicolaus of Damascus' *Augustus*, since he is relying upon uncited source material and only makes such an attribution to fill gaps in his account.

porary biographies, but about our own preconceived notions as we approach ancient texts.

Chapter 5

Cornelius Nepos's *Themistocles*: A Targeted Comparison with the Histories of Herodotus and Thucydides with Implications for the Historical Reliability of the Gospels

Timothy J. Christian
Asbury Theological Seminary

Introduction

With his landmark publication in 1992 *What Are the Gospels? A Comparison with Graeco-Roman Biography*, Richard A. Burridge cut a new and influential path for Gospels and historical Jesus scholarship by classifying the Gospels as the genre of ancient biographies (*bioi*).[1] Since then, a number of Greco-Roman *bioi* have been utilized by scholars for the study of the Gospels and the historical Jesus.

However, the time of writing for many of those *bioi* dates to after the compositions of the Gospels and most after the first century CE (Tacitus, Plutarch, Suetonius, Lucian, Philostratus, etc.). While this observation does not weaken Burridge's case (he also examined *bioi* written before the NT), it could entice some scholars to disregard the comparison by arguing that the Greco-Roman genre of *bioi* arose only after the composition of the Gospels.

This genre, however, existed long before the Gospels. In fact, the earliest extant Roman *bioi* come from Cornelius Nepos, a prolific writer and biographer who lived ca. 99-24 BCE.[2] His extant works consist of twenty three short *bioi* on great generals of foreign (mainly Greek) nations (Miltiades, Themistocles, Aristides, Pausanias, Cimon, Lysander, Alcibiades, Thrasybulus, Conon, Dion, Iphicrates, Chabrias, Timotheus, Datames, Epaminondas, Pelopidas, Agesilaus, Eumenes, Phocian, Timoleon, on kings, Hamilcar, and Hannibal), two surviving short *bioi* from a lost work on Roman historians (Cato and Atticus), and other fragments from the same work (a letter of Cornelia the mother of Gracchi and

---

[1] Burridge, *Gospels?* (2004), 76-77.
[2] Rolfe, *Nepos*, vii; Burridge, *Gospels?* (2004), 128. Some estimate his birth as early as 110 BCE. See Pryzwansky, "Nepos," 97; and Rolfe et al., "Nepos," *OCD* 380.

the eulogy of Cicero).³ The *bioi* on the great foreign generals (*De Excellentibus Ducibus Exterarum Gentium*) were published somewhere between 35-34 BCE with a second edition not long after in 27 BCE.⁴

This chapter will focus upon one of Nepos's *bioi*, namely, the *bios* of Themistocles, by comparing it with Herodotus' and Thucydides' histories in order to discover the relationship between ancient *bioi* and history. In other words, it will seek to answer the question, "Were ancient *bioi* based upon historical data?" As such, I will demonstrate that Cornelius Nepos, although often regarded by classicists as historically unreliable, is quite historically attentive to his historical sources in his *bios* of Themistocles. Overall, this will provide a piece of evidence for the substantially historical nature of ancient Greco-Roman *bioi* broadly and the Gospels in particular. That is, we have good reason to believe that such works were normally based upon historical data and were not fictitious novels.

Cornelius Nepos and Classical Scholarship

Within the past 50 years, classical scholarship experienced a revolution not only regarding the genre of ancient biographies generally, but also regarding Cornelius Nepos specifically. Focus has often shifted from questions of value for historical reconstruction to questions of rhetorical presentation. Both approaches can be valuable for different objectives.

In 2009, Molly M. Pryzwansky laid out this revolution regarding Nepos scholarship in her article "Cornelius Nepos: Key Issues and Critical Approaches" by first setting forth the traditional view of Nepos from Edna Jenkinson's 1967 work in *Latin Biography* edited by T. A. Dorey.⁵ This traditional view highly denigrated the historical value and accuracy of Nepos's *bioi* as Jenkinson espoused it to be "happy hunting-ground for those in quest of historical errors."⁶ Even J. C. Rolfe, the translator of the Loeb edition of Nepos, says, "the deviations of Nepos from the historical sources are too numerous to mention in detail."⁷ Some even go so far to claim that Nepos did not research before composing his *bioi* and used no sources. According to Jenkinson, the only worth that Nepos possesses is found in the fact that by chance he is the earliest extant Roman biographer.⁸

In the 1970s-1980s, classicists began to reassess this negative assessment of Nepos within the broader trend of understanding ancient *bioi* as their own distinct genre apart from other Greco-Roman literary genres. This new approach emphasized that the features of ancient *bioi* were more focused upon morals,

---

[3] Nepos also wrote in other genres of literature, namely, love poems, *chronica*, *exempla*, and even treatises on geography; see Rolfe, *Nepos*, viii-ix.
[4] Rolfe, *Nepos*, xi. Burridge, *Gospels?* (2004), 128
[5] Pryzwansky, "Nepos," 97-100.
[6] Pryzwansky, "Nepos," 98 citing Jenkinson, "Nepos," 10.
[7] Rolfe, *Nepos*, 36.
[8] Pryzwansky, "Nepos," 98.

encomium, and rhetoric than they were on history. Joseph Geiger then applied this approach to the *bioi* of Cornelius Nepos.⁹ This approach, then, stressed "Nepos' context and significance over his style and historical precision."¹⁰

In recent scholarship on Nepos, Pryzwansky describes the focus now to be upon "Nepos' influence on other authors, use of sources and rhetorical devices, moral convictions, biographical technique and calls for cultural relativism."¹¹ As such, she notes that the emphasis is still not upon Nepos's style and historicity, but his context and significance, which she also adopts.¹²

Some classicists, however, have swum against the current established by Jenkinson and others to show that Nepos does in fact (1) use sources and (2) possess some historical reliability. Frances Titchener demonstrates that "there is no compelling reason to conclude that Nepos failed to consult directly the authorities appropriate to his subject matter and use them for the historical framework of his writing."¹³ Likewise, Larry Jason Musnick has provided a historical commentary on Nepos's *Themistocles*.¹⁴ Although he admits that Nepos is historically flawed at times, Musnick still acknowledges that Nepos provides a historical perspective and interacts heavily with his sources (mainly Thucydides, Herodotus, and Ephorus).

Throughout *De Excellentibus Ducibus Exterarum Gentium,* Nepos cites his sources often from multiple ancient authors. The most cited source is Thucydides' *History of the Peloponnesian War* (see *Them.* 1.4; 9.1-2; 10.4-5; *Paus.* 2.2; *Alc.* 11.1). Others include Plato (*Alc.* 2.2), Theopompous (*Alc.* 11.1-6), Timaeus (*Alc.* 11.1-6), Dinon (*Con.* 5.4), Homer (*Dat.* 2.2), Xenophon (*Ag.* 1.1), Atticus (*Han.* 13.1), Polybius (*Han.* 13.1), Sulpicius Blitho (*Han.* 13.1), Silenus (*Han.* 13.3), and Sosylus of Lacedaemon (*Han.* 13.3); while sometimes Nepos cites only in a general way (*Them.* 9.1 "many have written"; 10.4 "many different accounts are given by numerous writers"; *Lys.* 2.1 "it is enough to cite a single instance"; *Alc.* 1.1 "all who have written his biography"; 2.3 "I would give an account of these if…"; *Epam.* 4.6 "I might cite a great many instances"; *Pel.* 1.1 "historians"; *Ag.* 1.1 "all other historians"; *Han.* 8.2 "two accounts"; *Han.* 13.3 "many writers";) or cites from the person's own writings (*Alc.* 4.6 "as he himself used to declare"; *Han.* 13.2 "several books of his"; and *Cat.* 3.3 "he left seven books [of history]"). It is noteworthy too that in some *bioi*, Nepos cites no explicit sources, namely, in *Miltiades, Aristides, Cimon, Thrasybulus, Dion, Iphicrates, Chabrias, Timotheus, Eumenes, Phocion, Timoleon, On Kings, Hamilcar, Atticus,* and the fragments.

---

⁹ Joseph Geiger is the major authority during this period; see Geiger, *Cornelius Nepos.* He was the pioneer on Nepos.
¹⁰ Pryzwansky, "Nepos," 103.
¹¹ Pryzwansky, "Nepos," 103.
¹² Pryzwansky, "Nepos," 104-5.
¹³ Titchener, "Cornelius Nepos," 90.
¹⁴ See Musnick, "Historical Commentary."

Comparison Chart on Themistocles

The following comparison chart parallels the accounts of Themistocles' life from Herodotus' *Histories* (column 1), Thucydides' *History of the Peloponnesian War* (column 2), and Cornelius Nepos's *Themistocles* (column 3). The three accounts are in chronological order of composition from left to right.[15] A fourth column consists of pertinent notes on Nepos's use of his sources. The sequence follows Nepos's *Themistocles* verse by verse, chapters 1 through 10. I have inserted general topic headings into the chart for ease in distinguishing each of the major sections and topics discussed concerning Themistocles. The general headings are as follows:

I. The Early Life of Themistocles (*Them.* 1.1-4)
II. The Early Career of Themistocles (*Them.* 2.1-6)
III. Themistocles Interprets the Oracle at Delphi (*Them.* 2.6-3.1)
IV. The Battle of Artemisium (*Them.* 3.2-4)
V. The Battle of Salamis (*Them.* 4.1-5.1)
VI. Themistocles Commits Treason (*Them.* 5.1-3)
VII. Themistocles in Sparta and Rebuilding the Walls of Athens (*Them.* 6.1-7.6)
VIII. The Exile and Flight of Themistocles (*Them.* 8.1-7)
IX. Themistocles in Persia (*Them.* 9.1-10.3)
X. The Death and Burial of Themistocles (*Them.* 10.3-5)

Furthermore, the contents within the chart are my own summaries of the texts in Herodotus, Thucydides, and Nepos.[16] Also, an *italicized* summary statement indicates that Nepos has explicitly cited his source. Furthermore, the dates displayed at the head of each column are rough estimations for the date of composition for each of these works, not the dates of the authors' life and death.

HERODOTUS (ca. 450-420 B.C.E.)	THUCYDIDES (ca. 431-404 B.C.E.)	CORNELIUS NEPOS (ca. 35-34 B.C.E.)	NOTES
I. The Early Life of Themistocles			
Themistocles was the son of Neocles (*Hist.* 7.143; 7.173; 8.110).		Themistocles was the son of Neocles, an Athenian (*Them.* 1.1).	Nepos is dependent upon Herodotus. This may also be common knowledge.
		Themistocles performed such great merits that none were better	Nepos is dependent upon another source besides

---

[15] The format will roughly follow Craig S. Keener's recent article entitled, Keener, "Otho," 331-356.

[16] The only exception to this is with Themistocles' letter to Artaxerxes. There I quote the Loeb translations for these texts. Each summary statement has the relevant verse reference(s) if one wanted to view them for their exact content.

Cornelius Nepos's Themistocles: A Targeted Comparison 107

			than him; he was without equal (1.1).	Herodotus and Thucydides. Perhaps the source is Ephorus.
			Neocles was of high birth (1.2).	u.s.
			His mother was Acarnanian yet a citizen (1.2).	u.s.
			As a youth, Themistocles lived a reckless and lawless life (1.2).	u.s.
			Themistocles, thus, was disinherited by Neocles (1.2).	u.s.
			These circumstances aroused Themistocles' ambition instead of breaking his spirit (1.3).	u.s.
			Thereafter, Themistocles devoted all of his time to public life, gaining friends and distinction (1.3).	u.s.
Themistocles had come into prominence (7.143).			Themistocles became an involved public speaker in civil law suits, for the public assembly, and for commerce (1.3).	Nepos provides more details than Herodotus. Perhaps he has another source.
			Themistocles had a gift to see people's needs and to express his views clearly (1.3).	This may be a logical inference from Thucydides (v.i.) or from a different source. The former is more likely.
		Themistocles was a natural sage and deserved high admiration. By natural intuition and wisdom, he	*Nepos cites Thucydides and says that Themistocles possessed intelligence for*	Nepos summarizes and condenses Thucydides here.

	could accurately judge present situations and forecast the distant future. He was also able to explain with clarity matters about which he had little knowledge of with little time. He was especially keen at forecasting the future. To summarize, because of his natural wisdom and intuition and his little need for preparation, Themistocles was one of the ablest men of Greece to hit the nail on the proverbial head (*Thuc.* 1.138.3).	present and future matters; this made him famous (1.4).	
II. The Early Career of Themistocles			
Themistocles was the Athenian commander at Thermopylae (7.173).		Themistocles' public career began when he was chosen as the Athenian commander for the war against Corcyra (2.1).	Both Nepos and Herodotus state that Themistocles was Athens' commander. The difference lies in that Nepos is emphasizing the inception of Themistocles' career whereas Herodotus is not.
		Themistocles inspired the Athenians with great courage (2.1).	This is a logical inference.
Themistocles persuaded the Athenians to use the money from the mines of	Themistocles persuaded the Athenians to build a fleet for the wars against	Themistocles persuaded the Athenians to use the money from the mines to build 100	There are slight differences here with the numbers and countries.

Laurium to build a fleet of 200 war ships; this was intended for war with Aegina, but used to fight Persia (7.144).	Aegina and Persia; these ships were used at the battle of Salamis (1.14.3). Themistocles was the first to suggest that the Athenians should apply themselves to the sea (1.93.4).	warships to fight the war against Corcyra; these were also later used in the war against Persia (2.2-4).	Concerning the former, numbers were often different among ancient writers. It is also only a difference between 200 and 100. Later on in 2.8, Nepos actually accounts for an extra 100 ships, thus making his total 200. Concerning the latter, Herodotus and Thucydides say Aegina and Persia, whereas Nepos has Corcyra and Persia. This is probably due to Nepos's focus on Corcyra. Overall, Nepos and Thucydides depend on Herodotus here, though they shape him for their own purposes in their own words. The core content is the same in all three: Themistocles persuaded the Athenians to build ships.
		Themistocles defeated the Corcyreans and rid the sea of pirates with his navy; as such, Themistocles made Athens rich and highly skilled in naval warfare (2.3).	This may be from another source. It could also be encomium of Themistocles which was common in ancient biographies. It is

			quite hyperbolic and perhaps unhistorical.
Themistocles' fleet was ready and available during Greece's time of need against Persia (7.144).		Themistocles' navy provided safety for all of Greece during the Persian invasion (2.4).	Nepos depends on Herodotus here.
By the time the Persian forces entered Greece, these were their numbers: 1,207 ships + 3,000 penteconters = 517,610 fighting marines; with 1,700,000 infantry and 80,000 cavalry; and 20,000 more camel and chariot corps; the total of Asian forces was 2,317,610. Adding to that the troops they collected during war [2,641,610], the grand total of fighting men was 5,283,220 (7.184-186).		Xerxes warred against all of Europe with 1,200 navy ships, 2,000 transports, 7,000 foot soldiers, and 400,000 horses (2.5).	This is a major divergence from Herodotus. As already noted, numbers were commonly different among ancient authors and often exaggerated. Nepos actually has much less fanatical numbers here than Herodotus. He shrinks Herodotus' 1.7 million infantry to a mere 7,000 which is a much more likely number. He does assert 5 times the amount of Xerxes' cavalry, but that is not as fanatical as 1.7 million. Nepos really provides much more historical numbers here than Herodotus.
Xerxes' war target was Athens, though broadly all of Greece (7.138).		Because of the battle of Marathon, Athens was the focus of Greek attack by Xerxes (2.6).	Nepos depends on Herodotus here.

Cornelius Nepos's Themistocles: A Targeted Comparison   111

III. Themistocles Interprets the Oracle at Delphi			
After news of Xerxes' Athenian intent (see 7.138-139), the Athenians sent envoys to inquire at Delphi (7.140).		After news of Xerxes' Athenian intent, the Athenians inquired at Delphi (2.6).	Nepos depends on Herodotus here.
The first oracle from Aristonice the Priestess was foreboding. They inquired a second time and part of it said that the wooden wall would not fall but help them and that "Divine Salamis" would bring death (7.140-141).		The oracle from the Pythia declared that they must defend themselves with wooden walls (2.7).	Nepos depends on Herodotus here and condenses this material.
Two mutually exclusive interpretations arose: either that the Acropolis would escape destruction or that "wooden wall" meant ships. Those preferring the latter were disturbed however about "Divine Salamis" bringing death and thought it meant their death (7.142).		No one understood the Delphi oracle (2.7).	Nepos depends on Herodotus here and highly condense this material.
Themistocles interpreted the Delphi oracle: wooden walls did indeed mean ships and "Divine Salamis" meant that the Athenians would bring death, the		Themistocles interpreted the Delphi oracle: what Apollo meant by wooden wall was to fight primarily with their ships and navy (2.7-8).	Nepos depends on Herodotus here and condenses this material.

death of their enemies (7.143).			
The Athenians preferred Themistocles' interpretation over the professional interpreters (7.143).		The Athenians accepted Themistocles' interpretation and built 100 triremes in addition to their fleet (2.8).	Nepos depends on Herodotus here and adds 100 more ships. This makes the total ships 200 (see note on *Them.* 2.2-4 and *Hist.* 7.144 above).
After the battle of Artemisium, the Athenians sent their women and children and all their household members out of Attica to Troezen, Aegina, and/or Salamis (8.40-41).	After the Persian war, the Athenians retrieved their wives and children from the places outside of Athens where they had put them for protection (1.89.3).	The Athenians moved all their property out of Athens into Salamis and/or Troezene (2.8).	Nepos and Thucydides depend on Herodotus. While Thucydides condenses and lacks details of location, Nepos again omits Aegina.
The Athenians thus abandoned Attica (7.143). The Persians entered an abandoned Athens except for a few temple stewards and the poor who had barricaded themselves inside the temple [their interpretation of wooden walls] (8.51).		The Athenians thus abandoned their city, but left the priests and elderly there to continue the sacred rites (2.8).	Nepos depends on Herodotus here.
The Greeks decided to hold the pass at Thermopylae and also send the navy to Artemisium (7.175).		Many of the other Greek cities disagreed with Themistocles' plan and preferred to fight on land (3.1).	Herodotus does not report a conflict. Nepos interprets this to mean that they should fight only with their navy. Nepos also wants to elevate the

Cornelius Nepos's Themistocles: A Targeted Comparison 113

			words and decisions of Themistocles (encomium).
The battle at Thermopylae was led by Leonidas the Spartan general against the Persians (7.213-234).		As such, Leonidas was sent with handpicked men to reinforce the troops at Thermopylae battling on land against the Persian barbarians (3.1).	Nepos depends on Herodotus here.
Many of the Greeks abandoned their post before the battle of Thermopylae as defeat was certain. The remaining Greeks [Spartans, Thebans, and Thespians] were utterly defeated at Thermopylae (7.223-234).	The Spartan army was destroyed at the battle of Thermopylae because the Persians surrounded them front and back (4.36.3).	All the Greeks perished in the pass at Thermopylae by the Persians (3.1).	Both Nepos and Thucydides depend on and summarize Herodotus in their own words.
IV. The Battle of Artemisium			
At Artemisium, the total number of warships was 271, of which 147 were Athenian [127 manned by Plataeans] (8.1-2). The total number of the Greek warships was 378 (8.48).	Themistocles was the commander of 400 warships, 2/3 of which were Athenian (1.74.1). The Plataeans fought in the battle of Artemisium with Sparta (3.54.4).	The Greek fleet numbered about 300 warships and 200 were from Athens [2/3 of 300] (3.2).	All three have different numbers here, though they are all quite similar within the range of 300-400 with roughly 2/3 being Athenian. Nepos omits the detail about the Plataeans and rounds up Herodotus' numbers.
Themistocles was bribed by the Euboeans to remain at Euboea until it could be evacuated. Themistocles then bribed the			Nepos omits this detail of Themistocles' bribe. This is probably due to Nepos's encomium bias, though he is

Greek commanders Eurybiades and Adeimantus to remain at Euboea with part of the money and kept some himself (8.4-6).			honest elsewhere concerning Themistocles' downfalls.
The first navy battle was at Artemisium (8.6).		The Greek fleet first battled the Persian fleet at Artemisium, between Euboea and the mainland (3.2).	Nepos depends on Herodotus and adds a detail concerning the location.
Eurybiades was the Greek navy commander at Artemisium (8.2).		Themistocles chose this narrow location so that they would not be surrounded and outnumbered (3.2).	Nepos does not specify Eurybiades as the commander, but places his biographical emphasis upon Themistocles as a key leader.
There were heavy losses on both sides, though more so on the Persians. But the fleets were evenly matched (8.15-17).		The naval battle at Artemisium was indecisive (3.3).	Nepos succinctly summarizes Herodotus here.
		The Greeks feared being surrounded at Artemisium had the Persians rounded Euboea (3.3).	This is probably an inference.
The Greeks retreated from Artemisium to Salamis and Themistocles proposed a plan of retreat and defeat of the finest Persian units (8.18-21).		The Greeks, then, retreated from Artemisium to Salamis, opposite Athens (3.4).	Nepos summarizes Herodotus here.
Along the way, Themistocles			Nepos omits these details.

inscribed pleas to the Ionians and Carians to leave the Persians and join the Greeks (8.22).			
V. The Battle of Salamis			
The Persians slaughtered those left in Athens, left no survivors, and burned everything on the Acropolis (8.52-53).		Xerxes massacred the priests of Athens and burned the city (4.1).	Nepos summarizes Herodotus here.
When news of the Acropolis' burning reached the fleet, some immediately left to defend the Isthmus, but some stayed (8.56).		When the fleet saw Athens flaming, fear struck them and they proceeded to withdraw and flee elsewhere (4.2).	Nepos depends on Herodotus here, though he is vague and lacks details.
Mnesiphilus, an Athenians, tells Themistocles that he should object to the decision to flee to the Isthmus, for it will be the ruin of Greece (8.57).			Herodotus had a bias against Themistocles and this is one prime example as he does not want to give him full credit.[18] This then is unhistorical. Nepos rightly omits this bias either because he views it as unhistorical or for his own encomiastic purpose.
Themistocles convinced		Themistocles alone objected and urged	Nepos depends on Herodotus

---

[18] Musnick points out that, "Herodotus is strongly biased against Themistocles, while Nepos defends Themistocles and commends him for his actions" ("Historical Commentary," 9). Clearly Musnick believes that Nepos not only used Herodotus, but evaluated him and thus shaped his *bios* to fit his moral purpose to elevate Themistocles. On the whole, Musnick also comments that Nepos, "followed Thucydides' overall [positive] attitude toward Themistocles" ("Historical Commentary," 9).

Eurybiades and the whole Greek navy and commanders (except Adeimantus) to stay and fight at Salamis, and not flee to the Isthmus. At one point during the discussion, Adeimantus had persuaded Euryibiades, but he ultimately changed his mind and sided with Themistocles (8.57-63). After the official decision was made to stay and fight at Salamis, the men [particularly those from the Peloponnesus] became hostile and divided, thinking it was useless to defend a captured city (8.74).		that they should remain united and fight at Salamis, for if they split apart, then they would be no match for Persia. He reassured Eurybiades, the chief commander and king of the Lacedaemonians, that this was true, but he was not convinced (4.2-3).	here. However, Nepos does not mention that Eurybiades and the Spartans at one point agreed with Themistocles. Rather, Nepos states the ultimate conclusion that they did not want to stay and fight.
Aware of this, Themistocles sent Sicinnus his slave to the Persian commanders to get them to surround Salamis [a trick] and the Persians did so (8.75-76).		Themistocles sent his most faithful slave by night to Xerxes to tell him that the Greeks were planning to disband [a trick]. Themistocles urged him to destroy them at once before they dispersed, so that it would save Xerxes time and effort (4.3-4).	Nepos depends on Herodotus here. He also omits the name of the slave (Sicinnus). This may be evidence that Nepos is using and recalling Herodotus from memory.
Themistocles was responsible	Themistocles was responsible for	Themistocles' plan was to force the	Both Nepos and Thucydides

for getting the Persian fleet to surround the Greeks at Salamis which forced them to fight (8.75-76, 80).	battle in the straight (1.74.1).	Greeks to fight a decisive naval battle against their will (4.5).	depend on and summarize Herodotus here, though Thucydides is much briefer.
The Persians believed the report from Sicinnus and surrounded them quietly in the night and attacked in the morning (8.76).		Xerxes believed Themistocles and attacked them the next day (4.5).	Nepos depends on Herodotus here.
Aristides reported to the Greeks that the Persians had surrounded them at Salamis; most did not believe him until the Tenians confirmed the report (8.78-82).			Nepos omits this detail.
Themistocles gave a speech at dawn to rally the troops (8.83).			Nepos omits this detail.
The battle of Salamis happened in the bay (8.83-98).	The battle of Salamis was in the straight which is what saved Greece (1.74.1).	The battle of Salamis was in a very narrow part of the sea (4.5).	Both Nepos and Thucydides depend on and summarize Herodotus here.
A few of the Ionians listened to Themistocles' appeal and fought for them, but most did not (8.85).			Nepos omits this detail because he omitted the previous detail concerning this.
The Persians lost rank, had no plan, and thus were in hopeless confusion, while the Greeks fought together		The place was too narrow for Xerxes to maneuver his large fleet (4.5).	Nepos depends on and summarizes Herodotus here.

in unity (8.86, 91).			
During the battle, Polycritus ironically reproached Themistocles about Aegina's loyalty to Greece (8.92).			Nepos again omits a detail about Aegina.
		Xerxes' fleet was defeated at Salamis because of Themistocles' strategy more than the power of the Greeks (4.5).	Herodotus does not attribute the victory to Themistocles because of his bias against him, yet Nepos emphasizes this because of his encomiastic bias.
Xerxes still had enough troops to overpower the Greeks even though he lost at Salamis, but was too afraid to stay and fight (8.97-107).		Xerxes still had enough troops to overpower the Greeks even though he lost at Salamis (5.1).	Nepos depends on Herodotus here.
VI. Themistocles Commits Treason			
		Themistocles baffled Xerxes a second time (5.1).	This is an inference and part of Nepos's narrative.
When the Greeks discovered that the Persians had retreated, Themistocles suggested that they pursue them and destroy the bridges at the Hellespont, thus cutting off Xerxes from returning to Asia (8.108).			Nepos omits this detail.
Eurybiades disagreed and the			Nepos omits this detail.

majority supported him (8.108).			
Themistocles addressed the Athenians and urged to them to take Eurybiades' advice; he spoke this publically to have a basis with the Persians in case he later got into trouble with the Athenians (8.109).			Nepos omits this detail. According to Herodotus, Themistocles ultimately submits and agrees not to pursue the Persians.
Themistocles secretly sent Xerxes a message by Sicinnus telling him that he stopped the Greeks from pursuing his navy and destroying the bridges at the Hellespont, though they wanted to, and that he was now safe to return to Asia. This of course was a lie because the Greeks did not want to do either of these things, and Themistocles was the one to suggest that they pursue Xerxes (8.108-110). Immediately after his defeat at Salamis, Xerxes feared that the Greeks would break the bridges at the Hellespont	In his letter to Artaxerxes, Themistocles reminded him that he helped his father [Xerxes] by warning him to retreat and informing him of the Greeks' failure to destroy the bridges. Themistocles however falsely claimed responsibility for it (1.137.4).	Themistocles informed Xerxes of the Greek plan to destroy the bridge over the Hellespont, thus cutting off Xerxes' return to Asia and Xerxes believed him (5.1-2).	Both Nepos and Thucydides depend on Herodotus here, though they both omit that Xerxes himself already suspected all this. Nepos does not specify the originator of this plan or include the disagreement. Furthermore, Nepos does not make explicit that Themistocles was lying as Herodotus and Thucydides do, though Nepos does say that he baffled Xerxes through this.

and cut him off in Europe. He made secret plans to escape Greece quickly (8.97).			
Xerxes left Greece a few days after the battle at Salamis (8.113). In retreat, Xerxes reached the Hellespont in 45 days (8.115). It took the Persian army 3 months to march from the Hellespont to Attica and 1 month to cross the straight (8.51).	The Persians withdrew most of their army out of Greece immediately after their defeat at the battle of Salamis because they knew that they were no match for the Greeks (1.73.5).	Xerxes believed Themistocles again and thus left Greece in 30 days by the same route which originally took 6 months (5.2).	Nepos again has different numbers from Herodotus, and Thucydides does not mention any numbers. Nepos focuses on Xerxes leaving Greece in 30 days, whereas Herodotus emphasizes the 45 days to the Hellespont. But the Hellespont was not considered to be in Greece, but generally Europe. A harmony is possible here between the two divergent numbers. However, even if one does not accept the harmony, the numbers are relatively close. This could also be another piece of evidence that Nepos was recalling the details of Herodotus from memory.
After his defeat at Salamis, Xerxes sent news of his defeat to Persia immediately		Xerxes was convinced that Themistocles saved him, not so much that Greece had conquered him	Herodotus portrays Xerxes as accepting his defeat, whereas Nepos shapes this to praise

(8.98).		(5.2).	Themistocles once more. His encomiastic purposes thus shapes this detail.
The Athenians esteemed Themistocles so clever and successful that they believed and followed him in everything (8.110).		Because Themistocles was so clever, Greece remained free and Asia submitted to Europe (5.3).	Nepos depends on Herodotus while he adds an inference and draws his own conclusion.
		Themistocles' triumph at Salamis was as victorious as that of Marathon (5.3).	Nepos's conclusion.
		At Salamis, a small number of ships defeated the largest known fleet ever (5.3).	Nepos's conclusion.
After the battle of Salamis, Themistocles demanded money from the Andrians (8.111).			Nepos omits Themistocles' greed, probably because of his encomiastic purpose.
Themistocles was always greedy for money (8.112).			u.s.
Themistocles demanded money from the other islanders – particularly Carystus and Paros (8.112).			u.s.
After the war, Themistocles was voted second by the Greek commanders for the prize of valor, while everyone else put themselves as			Nepos omits this detail.

first (8.123-24).			
The Spartans awarded Themistocles with a wreath of olive [the prize of valor] similar to the one they gave to Eurybiades their king, and was the only person to receive an honored escort out of Sparta (8.124).			u.s.
Upon his return to Athens, Themistocles was jealously and continually reviled by Timodemus of Aphidna (8.125).			u.s.
VII. Themistocles in Sparta and Rebuilding the Walls of Athens			
		Themistocles showed greatness not only in war, but also during peace (6.1).	This is part of Nepos's narrative.
	When archon, Themistocles persuaded the Athenians to complete the walls of Peiraeus, which had three natural harbors, was an exceptional site to develop seafarers, and would be advantageous for Athens (1.93.3). The walls were very thick, the width of two wagons, and the	Themistocles advised that the Athenians build and fortify Piraeus, a triple port, to harbor their fleet. It equaled Athens in grandeur, but exceeded it in efficacy (6.1).	Nepos depends on Thucydides and summarizes him in his own words.

Cornelius Nepos's Themistocles: A Targeted Comparison 123

	stones inside were large square stones bound by iron clamps and lead, but only half the desired height. Themistocles hoped that it could be manned by very few ineffective men, so that the rest could focus on the sea (1.93.5-6).		
	Themistocles focused on the navy and thought Peiraeus was more helpful than Athens, and he frequently directed the Athenians to flee to Peiraeus and the fleet if ever hard pressed on land (1.93.7).		Nepos omits this detail.
	After the war, the Athenians rebuilt their city and its walls (1.89.3).	Themistocles also rebuilt the walls of Athens, risking his own life to do so (6.2).	Nepos depends on Thucydides here, and his focus is upon Themistocles himself which is expected for a biography.
	Only small portions of the encircling wall and only a few houses remained; mostly everything was ruined (1.89.3).		Nepos omits this detail.
	The Spartans did not want any Greek city besides Sparta to have walls and used the excuse that enemies	The Spartans did not want any Greek city outside the Peloponnesus to have walls and their reason was that it could fall	Nepos depends on Thucydides here.

		could use it as a base and that the Peloponnesus was large enough to house all of Greece during war (1.90.1-2).	into the hand of enemies (6.2).	
			Thus, the Spartans interfered with the rebuilding of Athens' walls (6.3).	This is a logical inference and part of Nepos's narrative.
		The real reason was because of the size of the Athenian navy and the courage they showed during the war with Persia; the Spartans hid this real purpose from the Athenians (1.90.1).	The real reason was because they produced two major victories [Marathon and Salamis] and they would have to contend with them for hegemony in Greece; the Spartans hid this motive from the Athenians (6.3-4).	Nepos depends on Thucydides here.
			The Spartans wanted the Athenians to be as weak as possible (6.4).	This is a logical inference.
		The Spartans went on an embassy to Athens and requested that the Athenians cease rebuilding their walls and help them raze the walls of all the other Greek cities outside the Peloponnesus (1.90.1-2).	The Spartans sent envoys to Athens to stop the rebuilding of the walls (6.4).	Nepos depends on and summarizes Thucydides here.
		Through Themistocles' advice, Athens suggested sending ambassadors to Sparta in order to discuss the matters (1.90.3).	The Athenians stopped the work whenever the envoys were watching, and themselves sent envoys to Sparta to discuss it (6.4-5).	Nepos depends on Thucydides here.

		Themistocles went alone immediately to Sparta after giving a plan and instructions (1.90.3-4).	Themistocles led the envoy and went alone at first to Sparta (6.5).	Nepos depends on Thucydides here.
		Themistocles proposed that the rest of the ambassadors not arrive until the walls were high enough for defense (1.90.3)	Themistocles ordered the envoy not to come to Sparta until the walls were defendable (6.5).	Nepos depends on Thucydides here.
		Themistocles ordered all in Athens – men, women, and children – to rebuild the walls and use any material available (1.90.3). The Athenians rebuilt their wall in haste and the structure shows its hasty construction; the lower portion has all sorts of stones, some unhewn, and many columns came from grave monuments and stones for other uses; even the circuit wall was extended in every direction (1.93.1-2).	Themistocles ordered every able-bodied person in Athens to work on the rebuilding of the walls. This is the reason for shrines and tombs being part of the walls of Athens (6.5).	Nepos depends on and summarizes Thucydides here.
		Themistocles entered Sparta but refused to see the magistrates, and thus kept putting it off and making excuses such that	Themistocles entered Sparta but refused to see the magistrates to buy time by pretending that he was waiting for the rest of the	Nepos depends on and summarizes Thucydides here.

	he was waiting for the rest of his colleagues who were late due to urgent business. He expected them soon and wondered why they were taking so long (1.90.5).	envoy (7.1).	
Themistocles was highly honored and praised by the Spartans, that after the war they crowned him with a wreath of olive [the prize of valor] similar to the one they crowned their king Eurybiades with (8.124).	The Spartans were content with Themistocles' excuses because of their friendship with him (1.91.1). The Spartans honored Themistocles above any stranger who ever visited Sparta (1.74.1).	The Spartans protested and thought Themistocles was lying (7.2).	This is a major divergence from Thucydides and to a lesser part Herodotus. Nepos may (1) be unaware of the Spartans' love for Themistocles, (2) disagree with Thucydides and Herodotus here, (3) have a different source here, (4) be depending on a faulty memory of Thucydides' detail here, or (5) be drawing a logical inference. It is also possible that Nepos does this because ultimately the Spartans indict Themistocles for treason in *Thuc.* 1.135.2 and *Them.* 8.2-3.
	The Athenian ambassadors arrived and announced to the Spartans that the walls were being rebuilt already with some height (1.91.1).	The Athenian envoy arrived and informed Themistocles that the walls were mostly complete (7.2).	Nepos depends on Thucydides here.

	Habronichus and Aristides – Themistocles' colleagues – informed him that the walls were high enough (1.91.3).		
	The Spartans were confused and did not believe them due to their trust in Themistocles' original report (1.91.1).		Nepos does not share this view. See not above on *Them*. 7.2.
	Themistocles suggested that the Spartans send their own trustworthy men to Athens to bring back a true report (1.91.2).	Themistocles addressed the Spartans and convinced them to send high officials to see for themselves that the building stopped (7.2).	Nepos depends on Thucydides here.
	Themistocles was afraid that the Spartans would refuse his release when they would hear about the completion of the walls (1.91.3).	Themistocles offered himself freely as a hostage (7.2).	Thucydides emphasizes Themistocles' fear. Perhaps Nepos omitted this for encomiastic purposes. Regardless, he offers himself in both.
	The Spartans sent men as Themistocles suggested (1.91.3).	The Spartans sent their three highest officials to Athens (7.3).	Nepos depends on Thucydides here, though he adds the specific number of three. Perhaps this is from another source or mirrors the three Athenian officials named in Thucydides below.
	Themistocles	Themistocles sent	Nepos depends

	secretly sent a message to the Athenians to detain these Spartans covertly and not release them until he, Habronichus, and Aristides returned safely to Athens (1.91.3).	his envoy back with the Spartan officials and ordered them not to allow them to return to Sparta until he himself had been sent back to Athens (7.3).	on Thucydides here but omits the details of their names.
	After the Athenians detained the Spartan envoys, Themistocles frankly declared to the Spartans that the walls of Athens were rebuilt and now able to protect its citizens. This was for Athens' own interest and the general interest of Greece (1.91.4).	When he estimated the Spartan official's arrival at Athens, Themistocles addressed the Spartan magistrates and senate confessing with frankness that the Athenians had rebuilt the walls of Athens for protection against enemies and the welfare of Greece because Athens was an outpost against enemies and had defeated Xerxes twice (7.4-5).	Nepos depends on Thucydides here.
	Themistocles reminded them that the Athenians alone decided for themselves to abandon their city, and did not need the approval of Sparta (1.91.5).		Nepos omits this detail.
	Themistocles told the Spartans that the rebuilding of the Athenian walls was for the advantage of Athens and the body of Greek allies (1.91.6).	Themistocles told the Spartan magistrates and senate that they were wrong and unjust in their decision about the walls of Athens and did not have	Nepos depends on Thucydides here though he summarizes the content in his own words.

		the best interests of Greece in mind (7.6).	
	Themistocles justified Athens' disregard for Sparta's insistence by explaining that without walls, they would be inferior to Sparta and not an equal among the Greek alliance (1.91.7).		Nepos omits this detail.
	Themistocles concluded that the alliance should either do away with walled cities altogether, or consider the Athenians justified in their actions (1.91.7).		Nepos omits this detail.
	The Spartans did not resent the Athenians openly, but were secretly vexed (1.92.1).		Nepos omits this detail.
	The Spartans claimed that their real intention was only to offer a suggestion, not to stop the work, because they were friends due to their zeal against the Persians (1.92.1).		Nepos omits this detail.
	The envoys on both sides returned home without formal complaints against each other (1.92.1).	Themistocles demands that the Spartans release him, lest their three highest officials never return (7.6).	Nepos ends this narrative abruptly without clarifying whether or not they released him, just with his demand of release. Thucydides makes explicit

			that all returned safely.
	This is how the Athenians rebuilt their walls and other fortifications immediately after the retreat of the Persians (1.93.8).		Nepos omits this as it is Thucydides' end to his narrative on this subject. So then, Nepos and Thucydides end this narrative in different ways.
VIII. The Exile and Flight of Themistocles			
		The Athenian citizens did not trust Themistocles (8.1).	This is a logical inference and part of Nepos's narrative.
	Themistocles was ostracized from Athens (1.135.3).	The Athenians banished Themistocles from Athens by the "shard-vote" (8.1).	Nepos depends upon Thucydides here and makes explicit how he was banished. This is either an inference or from another source.
	Afterwards, Themistocles lived in Argos and frequently visited other places on the Peloponnesus (1.135.3).	Themistocles went to Argos (8.1).	Nepos depends on and summarizes Thucydides here.
		Themistocles was held in high honor in Argos because of his many accomplishments (8.2).	This is either a logical inference or from another source.
	The Spartans sent envoys to Athens to accuse Themistocles of conspiring in the treasonous plot with Pausanias and demanded he be punished as a traitor (1.135.2).	The Spartans sent envoys to Athens to accuse Themistocles of high treason, conspiring with Xerxes to enslave Greece. He was guilty without a hearing (8.2-3).	Nepos depends on Thucydides here. See note above on *Them.* 7.2.

	The Athenians and Spartans began pursuing Themistocles (1.135.3).		Nepos omits this detail.
	Themistocles fled the Peloponnesus to Corcyra because he was their benefactor (1.136.1).	Themistocles fled Argos to Corcyra (8.3).	Nepos specifies that Themistocles was in Argos which is on the Peloponnesus. He depends on Thucydides here.
	The Corcyreans feared that Sparta and Athens would declare war against them because of Themistocles, so they sent him with protection to the other side of Greece while being pursued by Athens and Sparta; and circumstances forced Themistocles to take refuge with Admetus, king of the Molossians who was not his friend (1.136.1-2).	Themistocles feared that Sparta and Athens would declare war against Corcyra because of him, so he fled to Admetus, king of the Molossians, his ally and friend (8.3).	Thucydides says that Admetus was not Themistocles' friend, yet Nepos does. Rolfe points out a textual variant in Nepos where scribes have inserted non ("not") to agree with Thucydides here.[19] This is a major divergence from Thucydides. However, within Nepos's narrative, ultimately Admetus helps Themistocles. Perhaps for the sake of his readers, Nepos clarifies that in the end Admetus was Themistocles' ally.
	Themistocles arrived when Admetus was not home (1.136.3).	Themistocles arrived when Admetus was not home (8.4).	Nepos depends on Thucydides here.

---

[19] Rolfe, *Nepos*, 36.

		Themistocles petitioned Admetus' wife who then instructed him to take their child [son – see 1.137.1] and sit in the hearth (1.136.3).	To ensure his own protection, Themistocles took Admetus' daughter as hostage into the household shrine (8.4).	Nepos omits Admetus' wife from Thucydides and has Admetus' daughter, whereas Thucydides says that he takes his son. Perhaps this is from another source, or he is recalling this from memory and thus confuses his wife for his daughter. The gist is still intact with different details.
		Admetus arrived, and Themistocles revealed his identity and gave many reasons why he should spare his life and not hand him over to the Spartans and Athenians (1.136.4).	Admetus arrived, and Themistocles would not come out until Admetus gave him protection (8.4).	Nepos depends on and summarizes Thucydides here.
		Admetus raised Themistocles up while he was still holding onto his son, the highest form of supplication (1.137.1).		Nepos omits this detail.
		Admetus did not hand Themistocles over to Sparta and Athens when they came and demanded his arrest (1.137.1).	Admetus did not hand Themistocles over to Sparta and Athens when they came to arrest him (8.5).	Nepos depends on Thucydides here.
			Admetus advised Themistocles to leave Greece in	Nepos adds an inference.

Cornelius Nepos's Themistocles: A Targeted Comparison   133

		order to ensure his safety (8.5).	
	Admetus sent Themistocles to Pydna, the capital of Alexander of Macedonia on the Aegean Sea, with an escort (1.137.1).	Admetus sent Themistocles to Pydna with an escort (8.5).	Nepos depends on Thucydides here.
	Themistocles anonymously boarded a merchant ship headed for Ionia (1.137.2).	Themistocles anonymously boarded a ship leaving from Pydna to leave Greece (8.6).	Nepos depends on and summarizes Thucydides here.
	A storm drove the ship toward Naxos where the Athenian fleet was blockading the island (1.137.2).	A violent storm drove the ship toward Naxos where Athens was warring at that time (8.6).	Nepos depends on Thucydides here.
	Themistocles was afraid and thus revealed his identity to the captain and his reason for flight, and he promised recompense to him if he saved him (1.137.2).	Themistocles revealed his identity to the captain so that he would be saved from the Athenians and promised recompense (8.6).	Nepos depends on Thucydides here.
	The captain did as Themistocles had pleaded, road out the storm for a day and night just outside the Athenian fleet, and he did not allow any on the ship to leave as Themistocles had requested (1.137.2).	The captain took pity on Themistocles and anchored the ship away from Naxos and did not allow anyone to leave the ship (8.7).	Nepos depends on Thucydides here.
	The ship landed at Ephesus and Themistocles payed the captain with a large gift	The captain landed the ship at Ephesus and Themistocles payed the captain for saving his life	Nepos depends on Thucydides here.

	of money (1.137.3).	(8.7).	
	Themistocles was able to pay the captain because his friends from Athens and Argos quickly sent him his funds that were deposited there (1.137.3).		Nepos omits this detail.
IX. Themistocles in Persia			
		Nepos cites Thucydides as his source for when Themistocles entered Asia and sent a letter to King Artaxerxes, not Xerxes as other sources espoused (9.1).	Nepos's citation of Thucydides begins this narrative section.
		Nepos says that Thucydides is a reliable source because he was the closest contemporary to Themistocles compared to the other sources and was also a native of Athens too (9.1).	u.s.
	Themistocles went inland from Ephesus with a Persian who lived on the coast (1.137.3).		Nepos omits this detail.
	Themistocles sent a letter to Artaxerxes (1.137.4).	*Themistocles sent a letter to Artaxerxes (9.2-4).*	Nepos depends on Thucydides here.
	4 "I, Themistocles, am come to you, who of all Hellenes did your house most harm so long as your father assailed me and I	*2 "I, Themistocles, have come to you, the man of all the Greeks who brought the most ills upon your house, so long as it was*	Nepos does not provide a verbatim translation into Latin, but rather puts it in his own words while preserving the

	was constrained to defend myself, but still greater good by far when, his retreat being in progress, I was in security and he in dire peril. And there is a kindness due to me (here he related the timely warning to retreat given at Salamis, and the failure of the Hellenic fleet to destroy the bridges at that time, which he falsely claimed to have been due to his own efforts), and now I am here, having it in my power to do you great good, being pursued by the Hellenes on account of my friendship to you; and my desire is to wait a year and then in person explain to you that for which I am come."	necessary for me to war against your father and defend my native land. 3 But I also did him many more favours, so soon as I began to find myself in safety and he was in danger. For when he wished to return to Asia after having fought the battle at Salamis, I informed him by letter of the enemy's plot to destroy the bridge which he had made over the Hellespont and to cut off his retreat; and it was that message which saved him from danger. 4 But now I have sought refuge with you, hounded as I am by all Greece, seeking your friendship; if I obtain it, you will have in me as good a friend as I was a courageous foeman of Xerxes. But with regard to the matters about which I wish to confer with you, I ask you to allow me a year's delay and let me come to you at the end of that time."	content from Thucydides. Perhaps this is further evidence that Nepos is writing from memory of his sources.
	Artaxerxes marveled at Themistocles and granted his desires (1.138.1).	Artaxerxes granted Themistocles' request (10.1).	Nepos depends on Thucydides here.

	Themistocles spent a year acquainting himself with the Persian language and customs (1.138.1).	Themistocles spent a year in Ephesus studying the literature and language of the Persians (10.1).	Nepos depends on Thucydides here.
	Themistocles went to Artaxerxes after the year and influenced him more than any other Greek had ever done. This was due to his reputation, his promise to subjugate Greece, and his wisdom (1.138.2).	Themistocles became more well versed and orally astute in the Persian literature and language than any other Persian natives (10.1).	Nepos depends on Thucydides here, though Thucydides emphasizes Themistocles' influence on Artaxerxes and Nepos on hyperbolic encomium of Themistocles.
	Themistocles promised Artaxerxes repeatedly that he would make Greece subject to him (1.138.2).	Themistocles promised Artaxerxes that he would subjugate Greece under his advice (10.2).	Nepos depends on Thucydides here.
		Artaxerxes gave Themistocles many gifts (10.2).	This is a logical inference and points to the narrative that follows below.
	Artaxerxes made Themistocles the governor of Magnesia in Asia (1.138.5).	Themistocles returned to Asia and resided in Magnesia (10.2).	Nepos depends on Thucydides here.
	Artaxerxes gave Themistocles the cities of Magnesia for bread, Lampsacus for wine [the best wine country], and Myus for meat (1.138.5).	Artaxerxes gave Themistocles the cities of Magnesia for bread, Lampsacus for wine, and Myus for all other food (10.3).	Nepos depends on Thucydides here.
	Magnesia had an annual revenue of 500 talents (1.138.5).	Magnesia had an annual revenue of 500 talents (10.3).	Nepos depends on Thucydides here.

	X. The Death and Burial of Themistocles		
	A monument was made for Themistocles in the *agora* of Magnesia (1.138.5).	Two memorials survived for Themistocles: a tomb near Magnesia and a statue in the forum of Magnesia (10.3).	Nepos depends on Thucydides here, but adds a second memorial. This may be from another source.
	There were different accounts of Themistocles' death (1.138.4).	Nepos comments that there were many accounts of Themistocles' death (10.4).	Nepos depends on Thucydides here.
		Nepos cites his preference for Thucydides as the best source (10.4).	Nepos cites Thucydides here and acknowledges that he had access to other sources on Themistocles' death.
	Themistocles died a natural death by an illness (1.138.4).	*Thucydides says that Themistocles died a natural death at Magnesia* (10.4).	Nepos depends on Thucydides here.
	Others claimed that Themistocles committed suicide by poisoning himself because he failed to fulfill his promise to subjugate Greece for Artaxerxes (1.138.4).	*Thucydides notes other conflicting accounts that Themistocles poisoned himself because he failed to keep his promise to Artaxerxes to subjugate Greece* (10.4).	Nepos depends on Thucydides here.
	Themistocles' family claimed that his bones were secretly buried in Attica by his command even though it was unlawful to do this for a banished traitor (1.138.6).	*Thucydides says that Themistocles' friends secretly buried him in Attica even though it was unlawful to do so for a traitor* (10.5).	Nepos depends on Thucydides here and abruptly ends his biography.
	Themistocles [along with Pausanias] was the most distinguished		Thucydides ends his narrative on Themistocles [and Pausanias] in this way.

| | Greek of his time (1.138.6). | | |

Synthesis

At this juncture, it is necessary to summarize and synthesize the results and implications of the above comparison chart on Themistocles.

Sources

Nepos cites 3 explicit sources within his *bios* of Themistocles. First, he cites *Thuc.* 1.138.3 in *Them.* 1.4 concerning Themistocles' natural ability and intelligence to understand present and future events: "Furthermore, he was no less active in carrying out his plans than he had been in devising them, because, as Thucydides expresses it, he judged present events with great exactness and divined the future with remarkable skill." Second, he cites *Thuc.* 1.137.4 in *Them.* 9.1 as his source for Themistocles' letter to Artaxerxes during his exile and flight:

> I am aware that many have written that Themistocles passed over into Asia during the reign of Xerxes, but I prefer to believe Thucydides, because among the writers who have left a history of those times he was most nearly contemporary with Themistocles, besides being a native of the same city. Now he says that it was to Artaxerxes that Themistocles came, and that he sent a letter to the king in the following words.

Third, Nepos cites *Thuc.* 1.138.4-6 as his source for the death and burial of Themistocles in *Them.* 10.4-5:

> Of his death many different accounts are given by numerous writers, but once more I prefer to accept the testimony of Thucydides. That historian says that Themistocles died a natural death at Magnesia, admitting, however, that there was a report that he had poisoned himself, because he despaired of being able to keep his promises to the king with regard to the subjugation of Greece. Thucydides has also stated that Themistocles' bones were buried in Attica by his friends secretly, since his interment there was contrary to law, because he had been found guilty of treason.

Besides these explicit citations, Nepos also relies heavily upon Thucydides and Herodotus elsewhere throughout his *bios* of Themistocles, even though he does not cite them. First, in *Them.* 1 (I. The Early Life of Themistocles), Nepos primarily uses a source other than Herodotus and Thucydides, which is perhaps Ephorus, as Geiger and Musnick suggest.[20] However, this material overlaps with

---

[20] Geiger, *Nepos*, 56. Musnick, "Historical Commentary," ii and 7.

Herodotus twice, and contains one of Nepos's explicit citations of Thucydides in *Them.* 1.4 which actually condenses Thucydides' material.

Second, in *Them.* 2-6 (II. The Early Career of Themistocles; III. Themistocles Interprets the Oracle at Delphi; IV. The Battle of Artemisium; V. The Battle of Salamis; VI. Themistocles Commits Treason), Nepos solely uses Herodotus as his source although Thucydides also occasionally overlaps with Herodotus here. On the whole, Nepos tends to follow closely and depend upon Herodotus, preserving his content and giving the gist of his material. Furthermore, Nepos tends to condense and summarize Herodotus in his own words which includes omitting many details from his work. With regard to Herodotus' numbers, Nepos keeps some and changes others. This could possibly be evidence that Nepos used Herodotus from memory. In addition, Nepos often draws logical inferences from Herodotus' material, and always ignores his bias against Themistocles. This observation suggests that Nepos was critically engaging Herodotus and thus sometimes he might actually be more historically accurate than Herodotus. Lastly, Nepos shaped Herodotus for his own encomiastic purposes which resulted in omitting some character flaws of Themistocles in Herodotus (greed and bribes) while also adding some praise.

Third, in *Them.* 7-10 (VII. Themistocles in Sparta and Rebuilding the Walls of Athens; VIII. The Exile and Flight of Themistocles; IX. Themistocles in Persia; X. The Death and Burial of Themistocles), Nepos exclusively uses Thucydides as his source though some very brief overlap occurs also in Herodotus. On the whole, Nepos tends to follow closely and depend upon Thucydides. In most instances, he summarizes and condenses the material in Thucydides, which often results in omissions of many extra details. Nepos also draws many logical inferences which often move his narrative along. Furthermore, he puts Thucydides' content in his own words, especially the letter to Artaxerxes which may be evidence that he used Thucydides from memory at certain points. Infrequently Nepos adds to Thucydides. Lastly, Nepos cites Thucydides twice in this section and prefers him over the many other sources and accounts which were available to him on Themistocles.

Overall then, Nepos uses three main sources for his biographical material (Ephorus? [*Them.* 1], Herodotus [*Them.* 2-6], and Thucydides [*Them.* 7-10]) and yet only explicitly cites Thucydides three times (*Them.* 1.4; 9.1; 10.4-5).

Conflict with Sources

Throughout his *bios* of *Themistocles*, Nepos diverges from Herodotus and Thucydides on six occasions (*Them.* 2.5; 3.2; 5.2; 7.2; 8.3, 4), three times from each. With regard to his conflict with Herodotus, first, Nepos has smaller numbers for Xerxes' forces than does Herodotus, 1.7 million soldiers (*Hist.* 7.184-186) versus Nepos's mere 7,000 (*Them.* 2.5). As John Marincola suggests, these numbers from Herodotus are "wildly fantastic" and unhistorical.[21] Nepos's smaller number then is probably more historically reliable than Herodotus here,

---

[21] Herodotus, *Histories* (trans. John Marincola), 671.

though some of his other numbers are larger. Second, Nepos also has different numbers for the size of the Greek navy (*Them.* 3.2). As noted above, however, Nepos here rounds up Herodotus' numbers and was possibly relying upon his memory for these. Third, Nepos again has different numbers than Herodotus for the amount of days it to Xerxes to retreat. These numbers are very close (45 to 30) and have different nuances in each author which accounts for this discrepancy. So then, Nepos's major divergences from Herodotus regard numbers which commonly fluctuated in antiquity, and yet Nepos tends to be more historical and still sticks fairly close to Herodotus.

With regard to his conflict with Thucydides, first, Nepos asserts that the Spartans thought Themistocles was lying about the delay of the Athenian ambassadors (*Them.* 7.2). Thucydides, however, says that they were content because they thought so highly of him (*Thuc.* 1.91.1). As noted in the charts, this divergence was due most likely to Nepos's emphasis on the ultimate perspective as the Spartans ultimately indicted Themistocles causing his flight to Persia. Given his incline toward the ultimate, this is more so a logical inference than a purposeful divergence. Second, Nepos states that Admetus was Themistocles' friend and ally, whereas Thucydides says the opposite (*Them.* 8.3). Again, the ultimate perspective trumps here too, because ultimately Admetus did help and aid Themistocles in fleeing from his pursuers. From the perspective of his audience, Admetus is an ally. Lastly, Nepos misremembers the details concerning Themistocles' petition with Admetus' child. Nepos says it was his daughter, though Thucydides his son. As noted above, this is probably an instance where Nepos was using Thucydides from memory and assimilated Admetus' wife (from Thucydides) into the child, thus claiming that Themistocles held his daughter. So then, Nepos's major divergences from Thucydides are due to his ultimate perspective and his faulty memory of the source.

While there are many other differences in the comparison chart above, they are minor points of detail and style. Hopefully, these "major" divergences discussed above have been shown to be minor as well.

Conclusion

On the whole, Nepos relies heavily upon his sources from Herodotus and Thucydides. Throughout each of the major sections, the overall storyline and points are the same in Nepos as in Herodotus and Thucydides: the Athenians upset the Persian fleet at Salamis, Themistocles cleverly brought about the rebuilding of the walls of Athens while in Sparta, Themistocles fled for Ephesus once the Athenians and Spartans pursued him for treason, and so forth. By and large, then, Cornelius Nepos's *Themistocles* suggests a strong reliance upon and agreement with the available historical data on the details of Themistocles' life.

In conclusion, then, Nepos depends heavily upon Greek works of historiography as his main sources on Themistocles. He moralizes him for his own purposes and context; but this does not take away the historical value or substantial reliability of Nepos. Moreover, those places in Nepos's biography that do betray historical carelessness do not negate the larger picture of Nepos using and accurately relaying the relevant historical information contained within Herodotus' *Histories* and Thucydides' *History of the Peloponnesian War*.

The research question above, "Were ancient *bioi* based upon historical data?", can be answered, at least in the case of Nepos's *Themistocles*, definitively *yes*. So then, if Nepos, though notorious for being historically inept and writing over 400 years removed from the time of Themistocles, provides historically reliable information in his *bios*, would it not follow then that other ancient biographies, particularly the few extant ones that, like the Gospels, were written within a generation or two of their events, likely provide historically reliable information, and perhaps to an even greater degree? This study suggests that the answer to this question is also *yes*.

For Further Study

As stated earlier in this chapter, Cornelius Nepos cites his sources on many occasions throughout all his *bioi*. The most notable places besides his *bios* of Themistocles are his *bioi* of Alcibiades, Agesilaus, and Hannibal. For example, with regard to Alcibiades, Nepos states in *Alc.* 1.1 that many have written a *bios* of Alcibiades. In *Alc.* 2.2, he cites Plato and later in *Alc.* 11.1-2 he cites Thucydides, Theopompous, and Timaeus as his sources, the latter two also being his sources for *Alc.* 1 and 2. Furthermore, concerning Agesilaus, Nepos cites "all other historians" as his sources in *Ag.* 1.1, and explicitly cites Xenophon. Concerning Hannibal, Nepos provides two divergent accounts of Mago's death in *Han.* 8.2, but more importantly he later cites many sources concerning the death of Hannibal himself in *Han.* 13.1, namely, Atticus' *Annals*, Polybius, and Sulpicius Blitho. Apparently, he also used Hannibal's own letters and several of his authored books as sources (*Han.* 13.2), and "many writers" (*Han.* 13.3), namely, Silenus and Sosylus of Lacedaemon. These are but a few examples of Nepos's citation of sources, many of which are historical in nature. Nepos, therefore, needs to be further studied and evaluated by classicists and New Testament scholars alike for the purpose of discovering the historical quality of his *bioi*, comparing his *bioi* with his cited sources as this chapter has exhibited above.

Chapter 6

Otho: A Targeted Comparison of Suetonius's Biography and Tacitus's History, with implications for the Gospels' Historical Reliability[1]

Craig S. Keener
Asbury Theological Seminary

Viewing the Gospels as biographies invites discussion of whether this view of their genre leads us to expect substantial historical information in them. Elsewhere I have argued as if it does,[2] but here I offer some of the supporting evidence with which I previously simply assumed most Gospels scholars should have been familiar. Here I examine Suetonius's Otho as a case study. I originally chose Suetonius's Otho as a test case because of its manageable size, but it appears to fit the evidence now emerging from the other studies also published in this book.

Accounts in Suetonius, Plutarch and the historian Tacitus correspond with one another in ways similar to how the Synoptics correspond.[3] This is significant because Suetonius and Plutarch are the key extant examples of biographers from the early Empire.[4] This brief comparison of elements in Suetonius's biography of a recent figure with his contemporaries' treatment of the same figure illustrates that biographers drew on and, like historians, adapted a repository of historical information available to them.[5] (I start with Suetonius rather than Plutarch here simply because Plutarch's parallel information appears in two biographies.)

---

[1] This chapter adapts my 2011 *BBR* article, Keener, "Otho."
[2] Keener, *Historical Jesus*, 73-84, esp. 79-81 (cf. also 85-94, on the historiographic character of Luke-Acts, and 95-125, on the character of ancient historical writing); cf. also my *Matthew*, 16-36, esp. 16-24; idem, *John*, 3-80, esp. 11-17.
[3] For my own argument concerning the Gospels' relation to their sources, see *Historical Jesus*, 126-61.
[4] Kennedy, "Source Criticism," 139.
[5] On average, modern readers will invest greater confidence in more concise historical works that summarize information rather than those that indulge rhetorical elaboration, such as Tacitus (Woodman, *Rhetoric*, 204, preferring Velleius Paterculus to Tacitus on this point). Yet the lavish praise of Tiberius in Velleius Paterculus (passim, e.g., 2.94.2-3; 2.129.1—2.130.5), as opposed to later authors, is presumably not unrelated to Tiberius reigning at the time of writing (e.g., 2.94.3). Tacitus remains a highly respected source (see e.g., Laistner, *Historians*, 132-34; Hadas, "Introduction," xviii; Mosley, "Reporting," 20-22), and this chapter's comparison of Tacitus with other extant sources suggests that he followed the story line of his sources for recent history, or, if Tacitus is the source for

Why the Question Matters

That biographers drew on preexisting sources is important for Gospels studies because, as we have noted, a growing majority of scholars today recognize that ancient audiences would have heard the extant first-century Gospels as a form of ancient biography. Establishing that biographers drew on historical sources thus has implications for placing the Gospel writers' handling of preexisting information in a larger context of their genre. That is, an ancient audience would have *expected* the features of both reliance on prior material and adaptation that we find in critical study of the Gospels today.

Observing biographers' dependence on sources is important for another reason. While the trend to recognize the Gospels as biography seems to be a growing consensus, some scholars deny that this assignment of genre implies much about the Gospels' dependence on historical tradition.[6] These scholars cite a range of ancient "lives" to argue that the line between ancient biographies and novels was sometimes thin.[7] Some of these comparisons stretch the definition of "biography" too far.[8] More importantly, legendary and fictitious "lives" generally involve characters of the remote or distant rather than the recent past; their historical deficiencies tell us more about the sources available to the biographer in these cases than anything about the genre itself.[9]

What about biographies involving recent persons? Only a fairly small number of such biographies besides the Gospels remain extant, but the ones that do remain extant normally preserve substantial reliable information. That is, biographers normally intended to use historical information, and that information was more reliable during a period when eyewitnesses or those who knew them remained

---

Suetonius and Plutarch (despite their omission of his added speeches), that these biographers from Tacitus's era believed him to be accurate. They depend on information, not the free composition that was possible in the case of novels.

[6] See e.g., Crossan, "Necessary," 27.

[7] See e.g., *Life of Aesop* in Wills, "Aesop Tradition," 225. More problematically, some include in the biographic genre not merely legendary works but largely novelistic ones like Xenophon's *Cyropedia*, Philostratus' *Life of Apollonius*, and Ps.-Callisthenes' *Alexander Romance*.

[8] Thus while Pervo, *Acts*, 15, designates Ps.-Callisthenes as a "history," Zambrini, "Historians," 211, rightly distinguishes this "popular fiction" (a historical novel) from Alexander histories. As noted above, Kennedy, "Source Criticism," 139, more accurately cites Plutarch and Suetonius (both from close to the Gospels' period) as the prime examples of biography. Classification can be to some extent a matter of semantics, but most ancient narratives do diverge into fundamental categories in terms of historical content.

[9] Thus, for example, where legendary elements appear in Suetonius they ordinarily reflect his sources, appearing particularly in his depictions of characters who lived some 150 years earlier; see Hägg, *Biography*, 218.

alive. Ancients themselves often recognized that legendary and speculative elements increased with chronological distance from eyewitness material, especially after the living memory of eyewitnesses had passed.[10]

Objectives and Methods

As noted in this book's introduction, classicists often designate biography as a genre related to or even a subtype of history.[11] Despite their often greater encomiastic character, the biographic genre "was still firmly rooted in historical fact rather than literary fiction."[12]

To explore the question beyond general impressions, however, it is necessary to examine more concretely a biography about a then-recent historical figure to demonstrate that numerous elements match elements about that figure in a historical work of comparable date. These matching elements suggest that ancient biographers and historians did draw heavily on prior material. The examination of Suetonius does not oblige us to generalize that all biographers would share his method, but it does at least establish that, where testable in the chosen sample, biography reworks rather than creates information about events. That the same features appear in his older contemporary Plutarch's biography of the same person reinforces the likelihood that our sample is representative.

The observation that biographers depended heavily on source material is important in a climate in which many scholars increasingly emphasize the rhetorical side of ancient historiography as over against its historical value; on the basis of that emphasis, some knowledgeable scholars write as if the line between history and fiction is fairly thin.[13] While these scholars' emphasis on ancient historians' rhetorical strategies and overarching perspectives is legitimate, historians did not employ them to the exclusion of historical information.[14] Although they exercised freedom to select, adapt and often embellish their material, ancient writers made explicit claims to the effect that their material itself should be factual.[15] Comparing our sources below should demonstrate that the biographers and historians in

---

[10] See e.g., Thucydides 1.21.1; Livy 6.1.2-3; 7.6.6; 25.11.20; Diodorus Siculus 1.6.2; 1.9.2; 4.1.1; 4.8.3-5; Dionysius of Halicarnassus *Ant. rom.* 1.12.3; *Thuc.* 5; Pausanias 9.31.7; Josephus *Ag. Ap.* 1.15, 24-25, 58; further Kennedy, "Source Criticism," 139.

[11] Bravo, "Antiquarianism," 516; Kennedy, "Source Criticism," 136; Stadter, "Biography," 528; Hose, "Historiography: Rome," 6:422-426); Burridge, *Gospels?* (1992), 63-67; Pitts, "Source Citation," 377-78.

[12] Aune, "Greco-Roman Biography," 125.

[13] Counting the rhetorical side against historical value, see e.g., Penner, "Discourse," 72-73; idem, *Praise*, 175. For the thin line between history and fiction, see Penner, *Praise*, 6.

[14] For the right balance, see Rothschild, *Rhetoric of History*, passim; Tucker, *Knowledge*, 254-62; Dewald, "Construction," 90-91, 101; Porciani, "Enigma," 333.

[15] E.g., Aristotle *Poet.* 9.2-3, 1451b; Dionysius of Halicarnassus *Ant. rom.* 1.1.2-4; 1.4.2; *Thuc.* 8; Pliny *Ep.* 7.17.3; 8.4.1; 9.33.1; Tacitus *Ann.* 4.11; Lucian *Hist.* 12, 24-25;

question reworked substantial preexisting information, rather than composed freely the way that novelists did.

Although we have biographies earlier than the Gospels (such as the collection by Cornelius Nepos and fragments of earlier Greek philosophic biographies), finding extant biographies written so soon after the events narrated narrows the sources available for comparison. Most scholars date Mark to within roughly forty years (about a generation) after Jesus' crucifixion; biographies of comparable date after their subjects would include works such as Tacitus's *Agricola*, fragments of Nicolaus's *Augustus*, and Josephus' autobiography (his *Life*). In the latter case, we can compare Josephus' *Life* with events narrated in the *War* or the later part of the *Antiquities*, showing how the same author treats the same period in both biography and history.[16] Because Josephus might have greater *personal* apologetic incentive than the average biographer would have, and because someone might complain that we would expect the same author to have access to the same accounts, I have preferred to explore a different example here.

Here I have chosen instead to compare a biography of Suetonius with historical writing of Tacitus and a biography of Plutarch, concerning a figure who lived roughly forty to fifty years before they wrote.[17] The briefly reigning emperor Otho lived c. 32-69, with most of the relevant events assigned to his final decade. Writing about him a generation later, Suetonius lived c. 70-130 CE, composing his imperial biographies before 121 CE. Tacitus lived c. 56 to at least 118 CE, and may have composed the *Histories* c. 109-110 CE.[18] Plutarch was born before 50 CE and died after 120; he seems to have become most prolific in the last two decades of his life.[19]

I have chosen the particular figure of Otho simply because Suetonius's biography of him provides more concise material for comparison, though Galba or Vitellius would have worked as well. Suetonius treats Otho in twelve chapters of about twenty-eight paragraphs. That Suetonius, Tacitus and Plutarch, though contemporaries and all members of the elite, do not share all the same perspectives on every historical figure also strengthens the value of their independent attestation of some elements of historical information.

As stated above, my thesis is that biographers, unlike pure novelists, constructed their portraits largely from the raw materials of available tradition. Nevertheless, biographers had some freedom in how they constructed their portraits

---

Josephus *Ag. Ap.* 1.26. Pliny the Younger knew both Suetonius and Tacitus and even tried to stage a guest appearance in the latter's history (*Ep.* 7.33).

[16] There are significant variations but also substantial shared information; see Henderson, "*Life* and *War*."

[17] As Pliny, a contemporary of Suetonius and Tacitus, wrote, the days of Nero seemed near history, even though none of the consuls from that period, normally older men, remained alive (*Ep.* 3.7.11).

[18] Bradley, "Suetonius," 1451; Martin, "Tacitus," 1469.

[19] Russell, "Plutarch," 1200. Chronologically, it is possible that Plutarch could have written before Tacitus and Suetonius, but he is not likely their (esp. Tacitus's) direct source; many other writers no longer extant flourished in antiquity (as noted further in the book introduction).

from this raw material, so I will also offer a few comparisons on the extent to which they employed that freedom. Here my observations must be more limited because of the limited nature of the evidence; my focus therefore remains on establishing the basic principle that biographers mostly edited and adapted historical information rather than inventing new stories.

Admittedly, the freedom that biographers exercised in adapting their material varied from one biographer to another. (Biblical scholars might similarly infer as much by comparing our extant first-century Gospels: most scholars believe that John, for example, exercised more freedom than Mark.) The more sensitive a historian to a rhetorically elite audience, for example, the greater the incentive to compose speeches conforming to the expectations of those audiences.[20] (Including speeches was a recognized practice of the elite historical genre.)[21] Though their shared biographic form invites comparison, that the Gospels (especially Mark) address more popular audiences (where popular storytelling techniques may matter more than elite rhetoric), and a more distinctively Jewish subculture, could limit how far we should press some elements of an analogy with Suetonius or Plutarch. Since we lack surviving biographies on a "popular" level for recent characters, however, it is unfair to argue from silence about what the differences might be. Allowing that some differences may exist, our extant biographies from the early empire provide the closest analogies for the Gospels and must be used accordingly.

An important limitation for reconstructing how much freedom Suetonius himself exercised inheres in the severely limited nature of extant evidence. It is precarious to make negative arguments from omissions in either source, since these would constitute arguments from silence. Suetonius's biography of Otho is very brief (we have estimated the equivalent of twenty-eight paragraphs), for which reason it could not accommodate all the details found in Tacitus or Plutarch (if we include Plutarch's *Galba* as well as his *Otho*). This work especially lacks much information about Otho's conflict with Vitellius (whether for textual reasons or reasons of Suetonius's interest).

For recent figures for whom information abounded, different writers would naturally select different information, except where one was copying from another or both copied the same common source (for the variety of information possibly available for the Gospels, cf. the claim in John 21:25). Given the nature of our sources, it is usually not possible to demonstrate concretely whether the writer has additional material no longer extant. Nevertheless, probability plainly favors writers' dependence on sources more often than only where we can confirm them directly. If the writer draws on genuine preexisting information where we can check him, it is reasonable to infer that, writing for an era where readers could have checked him on many other issues, the writer would have drawn on preexisting

---

[20] Josephus is notorious for this practice; for discussion of both Josephus' accuracy and his freer adaptation, see the sources cited in Keener, *Historical Jesus*, 105-8, 114, 118.

[21] See Diodorus Siculus 20.1.2; 20.2.1; Dionysius of Halicarnassus *Dem.* 41; Hadas, "Introduction," xvi-xvii; Kennedy, *Classical Rhetoric*, 110; Talbert, *Mediterranean Milieu*, 211. Nevertheless, they often reworked the information in earlier historians' speeches, where they were available; see comments below.

information in many more cases than where the information happens to remain extant today. Extant correspondences with other surviving sources, therefore, are undoubtedly merely a sample of correspondences that the works had with their real sources.

While it is thus possible to explore the degree of Suetonius's literary freedom to some extent, our answers in matter of detail will often remain as tentative as they are in studies of the Gospels themselves. While I include some comments on this subject below, my focus remains on the simpler matter of noting positive correspondences between Suetonius's biography and Tacitus's history. This focus facilitates my primary objective, namely, showing that biographers, like historians, worked from preexisting material. The line between biography and novel was normally not so thin as some have suggested.

I should offer one further caveat: I will not elaborate my comparison with the similarities and differences among the Synoptic Gospels by comparing parallel passages in them. Comparing the Synoptics is a basic exercise that I and most Gospels professors assign to our students, and I take for granted that most readers have made such comparisons and contrasts themselves. My interest here is to show that the textual phenomena with which we are already familiar in the Gospels (parallels and variation) fall within the range of textual phenomena expected in analogous works of the era, hence should not be deemed idiosyncratic or (for those with theological concerns) problematic so long as we do not read the Gospels with anachronistic expectations.

Listing Parallels and Some Differences

The parallels among authors exhibit the same sorts of variations one finds in the gospel tradition (although in keeping with elite practices there is less verbatim material).[22] To discuss each of the following parallels and differences in the way commentators discuss variations in the Gospels would prove prohibitively long; that length would also prove superfluous at many points in view of my primary objective. After the following chart, I will discuss some specific examples, but first I must list parallel information. Some may question the need for such a long chart, but to establish (rather than to merely assert) the dependence of Suetonius on information I must provide the information on which my conclusions are based. The most concise and visually effective way to note areas of overlap among Suetonius, Tacitus and Plutarch here is to simply list them.[23]

I have omitted most details found in one work that are not paralleled in the other (in view of my comment above about the very limited evidential value of

---

[22] See Aune, *Literary Environment*, 125; for discussions of ancient views of plagiarism, see Seneca the Elder *Controv.* 1.pref.19; *Suas.* 2.19; 3.7; McGill, "Seneca on Plagiarizing," 337-46. Rewording an account increases the danger of changing its meaning (see observations on differences in our sources below).

[23] Illustrating the range in ancient biography, Plutarch is far more moralistic than Suetonius in these accounts, yet, like Suetonius, preserves substantial information. For Plutarch's emphasis on ethics in his parallel lives, see e.g., Hägg, *Biography*, 239-81.

arguments from omissions, which constitute arguments from silence). The abundance of common information, however, should lay to rest any idea that a biographer like Suetonius was engaging primarily in free composition without regard for information.

Suetonius *Otho*	Tacitus *Histories*	Plutarch's *Galba, Otho*
Otho's parentage and ancestry (Suetonius *Otho* 1.1-3)	Otho's parentage and ancestry (*Hist.* 2.50)	Otho had honorable lineage (Plutarch *Galba* 19.2)
Otho's birth (Suetonius *Otho* 2.1)	-	-
Otho's wasteful, dissolute youth (Suetonius *Otho* 2.1)	Otho's wasteful, dissolute youth (*Hist.* 1.13)	Otho's luxury-corrupted youth (Plutarch *Galba* 19.2)
Otho used an affair with an imperial freedwoman to gain access to Nero's court (Suetonius *Otho* 2.2)	-	-
Otho gained friendship with Nero through their shared vices (Suetonius *Otho* 2.2)	Otho gained friendship with Nero through their shared vices (*Hist.* 1.13; cf. *Ann.* 13.12, 45)	Their shared vices endeared Otho to Nero (Plutarch *Galba* 19.3)
Nero took Poppaea Sabina from her husband and entrusted her in marriage to Otho (Suetonius *Otho* 3.1)[24]	Nero entrusted his own mistress, Poppaea Sabina, to Otho for the present (*Hist.* 1.13); in *Ann.* 13.45, Otho seduced her from her first husband (his friendship with Nero enhancing his influence) and only afterward (*Ann.* 13.46) did she begin an affair with Nero[25]	Otho seduced Poppaea from her husband with promises of Nero's favor, obtaining her as his wife (Plutarch *Galba* 19.4)
Nero himself was already having affairs	Nero himself was already having affairs	Poppaea played on the rivalry between

---

[24] *Otho* 3.1 initially presents the marriage as a sham, but this reflects Suetonius's moral perspective rather than a legal one, as becomes clear in 3.2 (as well as in Tacitus *Ann.* 13.45).

[25] Given Tacitus's cynical style, the instance in *Hist.* 1.13 might imply only that she was going to be Nero's mistress and that his power aided Otho's objective of securing her; or the perspective may simply differ from that of the source followed in *Histories*, Suetonius and Plutarch.

with Poppaea Sabina, and Otho's rivalry (Suetonius *Otho* 3.1-2) led to his removal as general to Lusitania (3.2)	with Poppaea Sabina, and Otho's rivalry led to his removal as general to Lusitania (1.13; cf. *Ann.* 13.46)	Otho and Nero, but wanted Nero only as a lover (Plutarch *Galba* 19.4-5); Nero thus wanted Otho dead (19.5), but Seneca arranged for him to be spared and sent to Lusitania (20.1)
Otho governed Lusitania well for ten years (Suetonius *Otho* 3.2)	Not in *Histories*, but cf. *Ann.* 13.46: Otho governed Lusitania nobly, in contrast to the behavior of his youth	Otho governed Lusitania well (Plutarch *Galba* 20.1)
Once Galba revolted, Otho supported him (Suetonius *Otho* 4.1)	Otho was Galba's chief supporter (*Hist.* 1.13)	Otho was the first governor to support Galba (Plutarch *Galba* 20.2)
An astrologer named Seleucus promised Otho that he would survive Nero and become emperor (Suetonius *Otho* 4.1; cf. 6.1)	An astrologer named Ptolemy predicted that Otho would survive Nero and become emperor (*Hist.* 1.22)	An astrologer named Ptolemy predicted that Otho would survive Nero and become emperor (Plutarch *Galba* 23.4)
Galba thus pursued his ambition by flattering nobles and obligating his soldiers (Suetonius *Otho* 4.2), and later bribing soldiers to share his plot (5.2)	Most of the soldiers favored Otho (*Hist.* 1.13); he had long curried their favor (1.23), including with bribes (1.24-25)	Otho helped and curried favor with the soldiers (Plutarch *Galba* 20.3-4), and they favored especially Otho for Galba's successor (Plutarch *Galba* 21.2). Otho's friends had been corrupting the soldiers for him even before the conspiracy, but in the midst of the conspiracy corrupted them further with money and promises (Plutarch *Galba* 24.1).

Otho eagerly hoped to be adopted by Galba; Galba adopted Piso instead, incurring Otho's resentment (Suetonius *Otho* 5.1)	Otho eagerly hoped to be adopted by Galba (*Hist.* 1.13); Galba adopted Piso instead (1.14-15), incurring Otho's anger toward Galba and envy toward Piso (1.21)	Galba failed to adopt Otho because of the latter's fiscal irresponsibility (Plutarch *Galba* 21.1-2); for the adoption of Piso, see Plutarch *Galba* 23.1; for Otho's anger toward both Galba and Piso, see Plutarch *Galba* 23.4
Thus Otho realized that only by seizing the empire could he hope to pay his debts (Suetonius *Otho* 5.1); he extorted a million sesterces from an imperial slave to finance his goal (5.2)	Once he realized that war might turn against Galba, Otho considered switching sides (*Hist.* 1.14); one consideration for betraying Galba was Otho's massive debts (1.21)	Plutarch reports that Otho had debts of five million sesterces (Plutarch *Galba* 21.2); Galba, by contrast, was independently wealthy (*Galba* 3.1; 29.1)
Galba's adoption speech is mentioned (though not recounted) in Suetonius *Galba* 18.3[26]	Galba's adoption speech (*Hist.* 1.15-16)	Galba's adoption speech is mentioned (though not recounted) in Plutarch *Galba* 23.2
A delay of several days (Suetonius *Otho* 6.1)	Five days (*Hist.* 1.29) before the assassination: January 10 (1.18) to the fifteenth (1.27)	Galba was assassinated on January 15, on the sixth day after the adoption (Plutarch *Galba* 24.1)
Otho was with Galba at a sacrifice and heard the diviner's predictions (Suetonius *Otho* 6.2)[27]	Otho was with Galba at a sacrifice in the temple of Apollo when the seer Umbricius declared unfavorable omens (*Hist.* 1.27)	Othp was present at the sacrifice when the divining priest Umbricius declared unfavorable omens (Plutarch *Galba* 24.2; 25.4)
A freedman announcing that the architects	His freedman Onomastus announcing that his	His freedman Onomastus arrived at

---

[26] Naturally there could not but have been a speech on this occasion, whether or not Tacitus freely composed his version.

[27] Suetonius has already indicated that a diviner's predictions involved assassins seeking Galba's life (Suetonius *Galba* 19.1).

had arrived served as Otho's prearranged excuse to leave Galba, to inspect a house for sale (Suetonius *Otho* 6.2); Suetonius also offers an alternative report (ibid.)	architect and contractors awaited him served as Otho's prearranged excuse to leave Galba, to examine properties he was buying (*Hist.* 1.27)	this point with the prearranged excuse, namely that the builders had come and were waiting at the old house he had bought, where he wanted to negotiate down the price (Plutarch *Galba* 24.3-4)[28]
Otho's coconspirators awaited at the golden mile marker in the Forum right by the temple of Saturn (*aede Saturni*, Suetonius *Otho* 6.2)	Otho's coconspirators (23 members of the bodyguard) awaited at the golden mile marker right by the temple of Saturn (*aedem Saturni*, *Hist.* 1.27)	Otho was first hailed (Plutarch *Galba* 25.1) at this golden column in the Forum where the roads of Italy met (24.4)
Otho exited a palace door (Suetonius *Otho* 6.2)[29]	Otho walked through the palace to leave (*Hist.* 1.27)	Otho walked through the house of Tiberius on his way to the forum (Plutarch *Galba* 24.4)
Soldiers took Otho on their shoulder, hailing him as emperor, and others who met them joined in (Suetonius *Otho* 6.3)	Otho feared because initially just 23 members of the bodyguard hailed him as emperor; they drew other support and acquiescence more slowly and often reluctantly (*Hist.* 1.27-28)	Otho feared because initially only 23 hailed him initially as emperor (Plutarch *Galba* 25.1), but others quickly joined and hailed him (25.2)
-	Martialis, tribune in charge of the camp that day, was not part of the conspiracy but fearing death, fell in with Otho's conspiracy (*Hist.* 1.28)[30]	Martialis, tribune in charge of the camp that day, was not part of the conspiracy but fearing death, fell in with Otho's conspiracy (Plutarch *Galba* 25.3)

---

[28] Even before this scene, Plutarch agrees that Otho's freedman was named Onomastus and that he was involved in Otho's conspiracy (Plutarch *Galba* 24.1).

[29] If they were at the Temple of Apollo rather than in the palace for a sacrifice (Tacitus *Hist.* 1.27), Suetonius has condensed something or depends on a source that has done so.

[30] He was later wounded in Otho's service (*Hist.* 1.82).

	Piso's speech (*Hist.* 1.29-30)	-
Otho dispatched agents to kill Galba and Piso (Suetonius *Otho* 6.3)	The conflict is depicted in much greater detail (*Hist.* 1.31-49); the soldiers in the camp favored Otho, who welcomed them (1.36); Galba (1.41) and Piso (1.43) were killed[31]	Plutarch is more detailed here than Suetonius, but less than Tacitus (Plutarch *Galba* 26.1—27.6), and also recounts the assassinations of Galba and Piso
-	Atilius Vergilio, the standard-bearer for the cohort with Galba, cast his portrait on the ground (*Hist.* 1.41)	Plutarch *Galba* 26.4 reports that Atilius Vergilio cast down an "image" (LCL too readily translates "statue") of Galba
-	Galba had assigned the centurion Sempronius Densus to guard Piso, and Densus defended him bravely (*Hist.* 1.43)	The centurion Sempronius Densus bravely defended Galba himself (Plutarch *Galba* 26.5)[32]
-	Sulpicius Florus and Statius Murcus dragged Piso (who was wounded) outside the temple of Vesta and killed him at the entrance (*Hist.* 1.43)	Murcus killed the wounded Piso at the temple of Vesta (Plutarch *Galba* 27.4)
Otho promised the soldiers that he would have only whatever they left for him (Suetonius *Otho* 6.3)	Otho's speech to the soldiers (*Hist.* 1.37-38), including promises of money (1.37); out of traditional control, the soldiers ruled themselves (1.46)	Otho's agents had been giving soldiers money and promises (Plutarch *Galba* 24.1)
Otho told the Senate that the people had forced this role on him (Suetonius *Otho* 7.1)	Once Otho prevailed, the Senate switched allegiance to him (*Hist.*	The Senate immediately convened and switched allegiance

---

[31] Tacitus *Hist.* 1.41 offers varying versions of Galba's last words (Plutarch *Galba* 27.1 choosing only the most positive of these), but Tacitus rightly observes that the assassins, who alone could have lived to report his words, would not have cared to report them.

[32] Here Plutarch clearly diverges from Tacitus. If Plutarch is working from memory, the confusion is understandable, though one might have hoped that Plutarch would have been more careful about one he so valorizes.

	1.45) and honored him (1.47)	to Otho (Plutarch *Galba* 28.1)
Otho honored Nero's memory, setting up again his statues, and did not refuse acclaim as his successor (Suetonius *Otho* 7.1)	Otho honored Nero's memory, allowing people to set up statues of Nero, and did not refuse acclaim as his successor (*Hist.* 1.78)	Otho honored Nero's memory, allowing people to set up statues of Nero, and did not refuse acclaim as his successor (Plutarch *Otho* 3.1; cf. 3.2)
Galba had depended on Titus Vinius and Icelus Marcianius (Suetonius *Galba* 14.2; 22; cf. *Nero* 49.4; *Vitellius* 7.1)	Titus Vinius ran (corruptly) Galba's affairs (*Hist.* 1.6), and Otho's agents killed him (*Hist.* 1.42; cf. 1.48); Otho had Marcianus Icelus executed (1.46)	Galba had depended on Icelus (Plutarch *Galba* 20.4) and especially Vinius (e.g., *Galba* 4.4; 17.1-2; 20.3; 21.1-2; 25.4; 26.1; 27.4; 29.4)
-	Tacitus allows that Vinius' protest that his execution was against Otho's orders may have simply been trying to prolong his life, but suspects that he was part of the conspiracy (*Hist.* 1.42)	Plutarch opines that Vinius' protest that his execution was against Otho's orders identifies him as part of the conspiracy (Plutarch *Galba* 27.4; but contrast 25.4)
Galba was influenced by Laco as well as Vinius and Icelus Marcianus (Suetonius *Galba* 14.2); he was Galba's praetorian prefect (*Galba* 14.2), but proud and incompetent (*Galba* 14.2)	Galba had relied on Laco as well as Vinius (*Hist.* 1.6, 14); he was Galba's praetorian prefect (*Hist.* 1.26), loyal but proud, corrupt and incompetent (*Hist.* 1.6, 26); after being banished to an island, he was assassinated (*Hist.* 1.46)	Galba appointed Laco the praetorian prefect (Plutarch *Galba* 13.1); Laco remained loyal to him (Plutarch *Galba* 26.1) but was corrupt (Plutarch *Galba* 29.4) and was killed by Otho's followers[33]
-	Otho spared consul-elect Marius Celsus, despite his fidelity to Galba (*Hist.* 1.45, 71), and Celsus became one	Otho spared Marius Celsus, despite his fidelity to Galba (Plutarch *Otho* 1.1), and Celsus became

---

[33] Apparently quickly, but Plutarch is summarizing (*Galba* 27.5).

	of his generals (Tacitus *Hist.* 1.71, 87)	one of his generals (Plutarch *Otho* 5.3)
-	To the people's pleasure, Otho ordered Tigellinus' death; at Sinuessa (the famous baths there), Tigellinus cut his own throat with a razor (*Hist.* 1.72)	To the people's pleasure, Otho ordered Tigellinus' death (Plutarch *Otho* 2.1-3);[34] at his estate at Sinuessa, Tigellinus cut his own throat with a razor (Plutarch *Otho* 2.3)
(Galba disliked Dolabella; Suetonius *Galba* 12.2)	Otho banished Dolabella to Aquinum, without harm (*Hist.* 1.88)	Otho banished Dolabella to Aquinum, without harm (Plutarch *Otho* 5.1)
A dream of Galba's avenging shade tormented Otho (Suetonius *Otho* 7.2)	Galba's death disturbed the imagination of Otho's mind (*Hist.* 1.44; "gloomy visions," LCL)	-
Vitellius planned to revolt (Suetonius *Otho* 8.1)	Vitellius planned to revolt (*Hist.* 1.50-70)	Plutarch elaborates on how disaffected soldiers in Germany sought Vitellius (Plutarch *Galba* 22.5-6) and he agreed (22.7—23.1; *Otho* 4.1)
Otho offered Vitellius a share in the empire and a marriage union between the families (Suetonius *Otho* 8.1)	Otho offered Vitellius money and favor if he would accept peace, and Vitellius made the same offers to Otho (*Hist.* 1.74)	Otho offered Vitellius great wealth and a city of his own (Plutarch *Otho* 4.2)
-	After offers failed, Otho and Vitellius each reproached the other—both speaking truth (*Hist.* 1.74)	After offers failed, Otho and Vitellius each reproached the other—both speaking truth (Plutarch *Otho* 4.3)
-	Otho treated Vitellius' brother Lucius Vitellius	Otho treated Vitellius' brother Lucius

---

[34] According to Plutarch *Galba* 17.4-5, Vinius had previously prevented this popular decision.

	graciously as a friend (*Hist.* 1.88)	Vitellius graciously as a friend (Plutarch *Otho* 5.2)
When some weapons were being moved near dusk, a mob of soldiers, suspecting treachery, hurried to the palace, demanding the death of the senators in honor of Otho (Suetonius *Otho* 8.1-2, emphasizing Otho's lack of solid control over the revolution)[35]	When the seventeenth cohort was being brought from Ostia to Rome, Crispinus was moving some weapons in the camp near dusk, to equip this cohort. The soldiers, however, suspected the senators' slaves of opposing Otho (*Hist.* 1.80), and Otho tried to disperse them to protect the senate (1.81)	When Crispinus at night was having some weapons loaded in the camp because of his errand to bring back the seventeenth legion from Ostia, some soldiers claimed that the senate was arming itself against Otho (Plutarch *Otho* 3.3). They wanted to kill the senators dining with Otho (Plutarch *Otho* 3.4); Otho dismissed his guests (3.6)
The soldiers burst into Otho's banquet hall (wounding and killing some who tried to stop them), demanding to see Otho before they were quieted (Suetonius *Otho* 8.2)[36]	The soldiers burst into Otho's banquet hall, (wounding some who tried to stop them), demanding to see Otho, who had to stand on the couch to quiet them (*Hist.* 1.82)	The soldiers burst into Otho's banquet hall, forcing their way past the guards, and Otho had to quiet them, standing on his couch (Plutarch *Otho* 3.6-7)
-	Otho's speech to the army, demanding that a few be punished for the army's actions (*Hist.* 1.83-84)	Otho demanded that a few be punished for the army's actions (Plutarch *Otho*

---

[35] Details among the accounts vary, as noted in Rolfe's LCL note in Suetonius (LCL 2:238-39 n. *d*): "The same story is told by Tacitus (*Hist.* 1.80) and Plutarch (*Otho*, 3), but the three accounts seem to vary. According to Suetonius the arms were sent from the praetorian camp to Ostia, to fit out the (seventeenth) cohort, and the riot started in the praetorian camp; the account of Tacitus seems to imply that it was the soldiers from Ostia (joined by the praetorians) that burst into Otho's dining room … The arms in question would seem to be a part of those belonging to the cohort." Suetonius might suppose that the arms were being sent to the cohort in Ostia before bringing them to Rome. Laistner, *Historians*, 129, notes that Suetonius's information makes Tacitus's account intelligible. (Earlier Gospels studies emphasized such interlocking, "undesigned coincidences" in the Gospels.)

[36] Some think that Suetonius's brevity here is because something is missing in the text.

		3.8, while not offering a full speech)
Flavius Sabinus holds an important role in Rome (Suetonius *Vitellius* 15.2-3; *Vesp.* 1.3; *Dom.* 1.2)	Otho left Rome in charge of his brother Salvius Titianus (*Hist.* 1.90);[37] yet Otho quickly brought Titianus (*Hist.* 2.23) to help with the war (*Hist.* 2.33). The soldiers requested and received Vespasian's brother Flavius Sabinus as Rome's prefect (*Hist.* 1.46), which he remained for a time (2.55, 63; 3.64)[38]	Otho left Rome in charge of Vespasian's brother Flavius Sabinus (Plutarch *Otho* 5.2); yet Plutarch also knows that Titianus held significant rank on Otho's side (Plutarch *Otho* 8.1; 13.3) and that he was Otho's brother (*Otho* 7.4)
Rather than going to the front himself, Otho retired to Brixellum (Suetonius *Otho* 9.1)	Rather than going to the front himself, Otho retired to Brixellum (*Hist.* 2.33; cf. 2.39); this disheartened the soldiers (2.33)	Rather than going to the front himself, Otho retired to Brixellum (Plutarch *Otho* 5.3; 10.1); this disheartened his soldiers (*Otho* 10.1)
Otho won the first three battles (in the Alps; near Placentia; and at Castor's place), though these were not decisive (Suetonius *Otho* 9.2)	The war started well for Otho (*Hist.* 2.11-12, 14, 25-28, and mostly 2.15); this included battles at Placentia (*Hist.* 2.17-23) and Castor's place (*Hist.* 2.24)	The war started well for Otho (Plutarch *Otho* 6—7), including his soldiers holding Placentia (Plutarch *Otho* 6.1—7.1)
-	Proculus became a praetorian prefect (*Hist.* 1.46, 82, 87; 2.33) and Otho depended *especially* on him (*Hist.* 1.87)[39]	Plutarch notes that Proculus was Otho's praetorian prefect (Plutarch *Otho* 7.4), and that he held far more power than Titianus (Plutarch

---

[37] He had earlier been consul (*Ann.* 12.52), but was now connected to Otho's reign (*Hist.* 1.75) and was consul with Otho (*Hist.* 1.77). Like Proculus, Titianus was less than competent (2.39-40).

[38] He appears also in this prominent role in *Hist.* 2.99; 3.59, 65, 69-70, 73-75. He should not be confused with T. Flavius Sabinus, consul suffect for two months in 69 CE (Tac. *Hist.* 1.77; 2.36, 51).

[39] Otho's dependence on the advice of his praetorian prefect Proculus spells his doom in *Hist.* 2.33.

Suetonius	Tacitus	Plutarch
		Otho 7.4), Celsus and Paulinus (Plutarch *Otho* 7.5)[40]
-	Suetonius Paulinus was one of Otho's generals (Tacitus *Hist.* 1.87, 90; 2.25-26, 32; cf. *Ann.* 14.31-39)	Suetonius Paulinus was one of Otho's generals (Plutarch *Otho* 5.3; 7.3-5; 8.2-3; 13.1)
-	Marius Celsus was one of Otho's generals (Tacitus *Hist.* 1.71, 87; 2.60)	Celsus was one of Otho's generals (Plutarch *Otho* 5.3; 13.4-5)
-	Fabius Valens was one of Vitellius' generals against Otho (e.g., *Hist.* 1.74; 2.24, 27-31, 55)	Fabius Valens was one of Vitellius' generals against Otho (e.g., Plutarch *Galba* 22.6; *Otho* 5.1; 6.4; 11.4)
-	Caecina was one of Vitellius' generals (e.g., *Hist.* 1.90; 2.21-27)	Caecina was one of Vitellius' generals (e.g., Plutarch *Otho* 5.1; 6.3, 5; 7.1; 10.3; 13.5-6)
Most advised Otho to prolong the war, but he insisted on deciding it quickly (Suetonius *Otho* 9.1)	The best advisers (Paulinus—*Hist.* 2.32; Celsus and Gallus—2.33) urged Otho to prolong the war (*Hist.* 2.32—33; cf. 2.37), but following the inexperienced advice of Titianus and Proculus, he insisted on fighting quickly (2.33)[41]	The general Paulinus urged Otho to delay battle (Plutarch *Otho* 8.2-3), and Celsus agreed (8.4), but Proculus and Titianus urged him to fight quickly (Plutarch *Otho* 8.1); Otho chose to fight quickly (Plutarch *Otho* 8.4—9.3)
-	The Vitellians began building a bridge at the Po, which the Othonians were trying to set ablaze (*Hist.* 2.34); Otho's gladiators, trying to reach an island in the river, were beaten	The Vitellians began building a bridge at the Po, which the Othonians were trying to set ablaze (Plutarch *Otho* 10.2), to the

---

[40] He appears as a general also in Plutarch *Otho* 13.1.
[41] Unlike the biographers, Tacitus provides Paulinus a full speech (*Hist.* 2.32).

	by Vitellius' Germans (*Hist.* 2.35)	Othonians' disadvantage (10.2-3); Vitellius' Germans beat Otho's gladiators at an island in the river (10.3)
The Vitellians prevailed near Betriacum (Suetonius *Otho* 9.2)	The Vitellians prevailed (*Hist.* 2.42-45) near Bedriacum (2.44-45; cf. 2.50, 57)[42]	Otho's army's camp settled near Betriacum (Plutarch *Otho* 8.1; 9.1), where the Vitellians won (Plutarch *Otho* 13.5; *Vitellius* 10.1; 15.2)
The Vitellians prevailed especially because the Vitellians attacked when Otho's soldiers were expecting terms of peace (Suetonius *Otho* 9.2)	Otho's army wrongly thought that the Vitellians had deserted, and were unprepared for the Vitellian onslaught (*Hist.* 2.42); Vitellius granted terms to the vanquished, though delay caused confusion (2.45)	A rumor claimed that the Vitellians were surrendering, so the Othonian vanguard greeted Vitellius' men in a friendly way as fellow-soldiers, but the Vitellians responded with hostility, making other Othonians suspect their own vanguard of treachery (Plutarch *Otho* 12.1)
His soldiers were not ready to give up the war (Suetonius *Otho* 9.3), and initially refused to believe the report that they had experienced a defeat (10.1)	His soldiers were not ready to give up the war (*Hist.* 2.46)	The soldiers with him pledged their continuing loyalty (Plutarch *Otho* 15.1-3)
Otho wanted to spare his followers further suffering on his behalf (Suetonius *Otho* 9.3; 10.1; cf. 10.2—11.1)	Otho wanted to spare his followers further suffering on his behalf (*Hist.* 2.47)	Otho wanted to spare his followers further suffering on his behalf (Plutarch *Otho* 15.3-6)

---

[42] Both spellings (Bedriacum and Betriacum) appear in Salmon and Potter, "Bedriacum."

Otho's final instructions, summarized (Suetonius *Otho* 10.2)	Otho's final speeches and instructions (*Hist.* 2.47-48)	Otho's final speech and instructions (Plutarch *Otho* 15.3—17.2)
Otho gave final instructions for the safety of several people whom he addressed, including his nephew (Suetonius *Otho* 10.2)	Otho consoled his nephew Salvius Cocceianus, noting that Otho had spared Vitellius' family hence mercy should be expected, and warning him to remember neither too much nor too little that Otho had been his uncle (*Hist.* 2.48)	Otho consoled his nephew Cocceianus, noting that Otho had spared Vitellius' family hence mercy should be expected, and warning him to remember neither too much nor too little that Otho had been his uncle (Plutarch *Otho* 16.2)
Otho destroyed any letters that could incriminate his friends to Vitellius (Suetonius *Otho* 10.2)	Otho destroyed any letters that could incriminate his friends to Vitellius (*Hist.* 2.48)	-
He distributed money to his servants (Suetonius *Otho* 11.1)	He distributed money, though frugally (*Hist.* 2.48)	He distributed money to his servants, but carefully rather than lavishly (Plutarch *Otho* 17.1)
Those beginning to leave the camp were being detained as deserters, but Otho prohibited harming them, and met with friends until late (Suetonius *Otho* 11.1)	He urged his friends to depart and provided means (*Hist.* 2.48); the soldiers tried to prevent those departing, requiring his harsh intervention, and he met with those departing until late (*Hist.* 2.49)	Otho persuaded his friends, especially those of rank, to depart (Plutarch *Otho* 16.1-2), and provided means for their departure (17.2); the soldiers threatened to kill them unless they remained, forcing Otho to intervene harshly (16.3)
At a late hour Otho quenched his thirst with cold water (*gelidae aquae*, Suetonius *Otho* 11.2)	Near evening Otho quenched his thirst with cold water (*gelidae aquae*, *Hist.* 2.49)	That evening, Otho quenched his thirst with some water (Plutarch *Otho* 17.1)

Otho chose the sharper of two daggers to place under his pillow (Suetonius *Otho* 11.2)	Otho chose the sharper of two daggers to place under his head (*Hist.* 2.49)	Otho chose the sharper of two daggers to place under his head (Plutarch *Otho* 17.1)
Otho then slept soundly one more night (Suetonius *Otho* 11.2)	Otho then spent a quiet night, reportedly even sleeping some (*Hist.* 2.49)	Otho then slept so deeply for the rest of the night that his attendants heard his breathing (Plutarch *Otho* 17.1)
At dawn he stabbed himself to death (Suetonius *Otho* 11.2)	At dawn he fell on his weapon (*Hist.* 2.49)	Just before dawn Otho fell on his sword (Plutarch *Otho* 17.3)
People rushed in when he groaned, as he was dying from a single wound (Suetonius *Otho* 11.2)	People rushed in when he groaned, as he was dying from a single wound (*Hist.* 2.49)	Hearing his groan the servants hurried in (Plutarch *Otho* 17.3, leaving the implication that the single blow was sufficient to end his life)
He was quickly buried at his request (Suetonius *Otho* 11.2)	He was quickly buried at his request, to prevent disfigurement by his enemies (*Hist.* 2.49)	Plutarch implies that he was buried quickly (Plutarch *Otho* 17.3-4)
Many soldiers killed themselves in mourning by his bier (Suetonius *Otho* 12.2)	Some soldiers killed themselves in mourning by his bier (*Hist.* 2.49)	Some soldiers killed themselves at his funeral pyre (Plutarch *Otho* 17.4)
He died in his thirty-eighth year (Suetonius *Otho* 11.2)[43]	He died in his thirty-seventh year (*Hist.* 2.49)	He lived 37 years (Plutarch *Otho* 18.2)

---

[43] Differences between Suetonius and the others here could reflect differences between inclusive and exclusive means of reckoning years. On inclusive reckoning, see Koester, *Introduction*, 2:102.

Samples of Differences

One could add some other comparisons, but this list should be sufficient for our purposes. Before summarizing positive comparisons, I shall note some sample areas of difference and some possible reasons for them. These differences are important in helping to establish a potential range of accepted variation among contemporary biographies, so that we do not evaluate variations in the Gospels anachronistically.[44]

For example, the sequence of information in our sources sometimes differs, sometimes in a manner that affects how we understand the events: for example, did Otho urge quick engagement before (Suetonius *Otho* 9.1-2) or after (Tacitus *Hist.* 2.11-33) his initial victories? In the former case, events seemed to initially vindicate his choice; in the latter, his victories spurred on false hopes that his rashness quickly dashed. Since both writers consider his choice rash in retrospect (cf. *Otho* 8.3—9.1), one might think that Tacitus rearranged the events to reinforce this point; but given his enormous detail and sequencing of the material, and the fact that Suetonius merely summarizes various points here, it appears far more likely that Tacitus preserves the original sequence.[45]

Some differences in sequence probably reflect lack of knowledge or concern for sequence rather than deliberate changes. Sometimes, however, events may have happened more than once, so that different sources may occasionally involve different occasions. Thus Plutarch recounts that Otho was not only in Brixillum earlier (*Otho* 5.3), but that he returned to it (*Otho* 10.1) after visiting the camp at Bedricum (*Otho* 8.1).

Sometimes details appear garbled through Suetonius condensing the story (Suetonius *Otho* 6.2; 8.2-3). While these paragraphs appear to us to include inadequate information for full understanding, we should keep in mind that sometimes Suetonius's elite readers already knew the basic stories to which he was alluding. Thus for example Tacitus similarly claims to omit reporting most of Seneca's dying words, recorded by the latter's secretaries, because in his day they remained too well-known to bear repeating (*Ann.* 15.63).

Our sources contradict each other in designating the name of the astrologer who spurred on Otho's ambitions. Suetonius designates him as Seleucus (*Otho* 4.1), whereas Tacitus and Plutarch designate him Ptolemy (Tacitus *Hist.* 1.22; Plutarch *Galba* 23.4). In this case one might conjecture that Suetonius, working from memory, failed to look at his source here, having simply remembered the name as the same of one of Alexander's successors (Seleucus and Ptolemy were both among Alexander's successors). Much more likely (or perhaps partly for the

---

[44] Differences in ancient historical reports are not uncommon; see e.g., divergent approaches to crossing Rubicon in sources in Beneker, "Crossing"; cf. Rondholz, "Crossing." Still, even in recounting Nero's death, where Suetonius may take a particularly free hand, the parallels in Dio Cassius 63.27.3—63.29.2 might suggest a common source, perhaps even Nero's secretary (Hägg, *Biography*, 226-27).

[45] Biography was typically less concerned with chronology than history was (e.g., Görgemanns, "Biography: Greek"; Stanton, *Preaching*, 119-21); for history as sequential, see e.g., Pliny *Ep.* 1.1.1.

same reason), he apparently confused Ptolemy with Vespasian's court astrologer (Tacitus *Hist.* 2.78). In any case, typical biographers sometimes confused some details.

Likewise, Plutarch contradicts Tacitus in having the centurion Sempronius Densus bravely defend Galba himself (Plutarch *Galba* 26.5), whereas Tacitus has him defending Galba's adoptive son Piso (*Hist.* 1.43). This difference likely reflects an oversight of Plutarch's, the sort of detail that writers could easily confuse even in the first generation unless they had substantial feedback from audiences familiar with their stories.[46] We should note, however, the significant overlap in facts and the essential story in both of these accounts, despite the confusion of secondary details.

In some cases differences may amount to a matter of semantics, such as who was left in charge of Rome. Tacitus claims that Otho left his brother Titianus in charge of Rome (*Hist.* 1.90); but while Titianus undoubtedly wielded great influence, it is clear even from Tacitus that Titianus did not remain in Rome (*Hist.* 2.33), whereas other sources seem clear that Flavius Sabinus did (Suetonius *Vitellius* 15.2-3; *Vesp.* 1.3; *Dom.* 1.2). One might therefore incline to favor Plutarch's view that Otho left Flavius Sabinus in charge in Rome (Plutarch *Otho* 5.2), whatever Titianus' official designation may have been. Tacitus himself observes that Flavius Sabinus was Rome's prefect (*Hist.* 1.46).

Only Suetonius reports the dream in *Otho* 7.2, though the wording included in Tacitus *Hist.* 1.44 could possibly imply that he knows of it. Dreams are an interest of Suetonius, who also recounts a terrifying and ominous dream to Galba shortly before his own death (*Galba* 18.2).[47] Yet Tacitus also could include predictive dreams among his lists of omens (note the favorable one in *Ann.* 2.14) and divine signs (*Hist.* 4.83). Like other omens, they are common in historical works,[48] though we cannot be certain at what point they entered the historical traditions that report them. Generals often depended on dreams before battles and in other situations, probably both in reality and in their post-battle propaganda as well as in later embellishments about them.[49] None of this is surprising, since people do often dream and ancient readers usually believed that dreams portended the future.[50]

---

[46] Feedback did occur in various genres during oral recitation; see e.g., Suetonius *Vergil* 33; see also Winterbottom, "*Recitatio,*" 1296 (citing Pliny *Ep.* 5.12.1-2).

[47] Elsewhere, Augustus took dreams seriously (*Aug.* 91); Vespasian dreamed positively before becoming emperor (*Vesp.* 5.5).

[48] See e.g., Meister, "Herodotus," 269.

[49] E.g., Alexander (Quintus Curtius 4.2.17; Plutarch *Alex.* 24.3; 41.3-4; 49.3; Arrian *Alex.* 2.18.1; Ps.-Callisth. *Alex.* 1.35; cf. Hermog. *Issues* 33); P. Scipio (Polybius 10.4.5—10.5.5); Hannibal (Valerius Maximus 1.7. ext. 1; Silius Italicus 3.168-71); Sulla (Plutarch *Sull.* 9.4; 28.6); Pompey (Plutarch *Caes.* 42.1); Caesar (Valerius Maximus 1.7.1); and others (Valerius Maximus 1.7.3).

[50] E.g., Valerius Maximus 1.7.1-8; 1.7. ext. 1-10; Velleius Paterculus 2.70.1; Plutarch *Caes.* 42.1; 69.5; *Cic.* 44.2; *Sulla* 37.2. Note e.g., Calpurnia's dream for her husband Julius Caesar (Valerius Maximus 1.7.2; Velleius Paterculus 2.57.2; Suetonius *Jul.* 81; Plutarch *Caes.* 63.5; 64.3; cf. 68.2).

Even where the accounts clearly depict the same events, they vary on matters of detail, for example, the soldiers who came close to killing senators after some weapons were moved. In this case, comparing all three of our sources allows us to better reconstruct the larger context that makes sense of some details, though minor conflicts remain. In the absence of sufficient information, ancient historians sometimes did elaborate details or speeches to flesh out scenes for the sake of a cohesive narrative,[51] and ancient readers were aware of this practice. (Josephus does not mind anyone noticing his rhetorical adaptations of biblical narratives in much of the *Antiquities*,[52] though his story line mostly follows the biblical text.)

Nevertheless, differences need not all be explained in these terms. For example, multiple sources may have diverged on some such details by this point, or (very likely) some writers or their sources misconstrued some of their information. It is also possible (as I have learned by experimenting with more recent recollections of witnesses that can be tested) that more genuine information usually remains in the accounts than we are tempted to suspect, but we lack the additional information that would reconcile more of the details in these accounts.[53]

We thus have variation in detail, while the substance of the account most relevant to the larger story remains. If we treat the Gospels as ancient biographies, therefore, we can trust that they report substantial historical information about Jesus. At the same time, the variations among the gospel accounts appear well within the range of acceptable variation in ancient biographies from roughly the same period.

---

[51] E.g., Tacitus develops dramatic scenes and dialogues (see Hadas, "Introduction," xx-xxi), and infuses scenes with pathos where the events narrated invite this approach (e.g., Tacitus *Ann.* 3.1; 4.62-63; 5.9; 16.30-32). Various writers report private conversations in direct discourse (Josephus *Ant.* 19.78-83; cf. Acts 25:14-22; Tacitus *Ann.* 12.65).

[52] Including speech composition, e.g., *Ant.* 1.46; 4.25-34, 134-38; cf. his adaptation of speeches in 1 Maccabees (Gafni, "Josephus and Maccabees," esp. 126-27). While archaeology confirms much of Josephus' narrative about Masada, most count Eleazar's speech there implausible (Cohen, "What Happened?").

[53] See e.g., Eddy and Boyd, *The Jesus Legend*, 424. I compared various sources regarding my wife's account of the civil war that she endured as a refugee (before writing Keener and Keener, *Impossible Love*), as well as compared some earlier miracle reports from different eyewitnesses while working on Keener, *Miracles*. For examples from my former project: my journal for events of April 23, 2001, seemed to contradict my wife's journal for the same time; her journal of April 19, 2001, however, reconciled the contradiction. We discovered that a French translation variant explained the differences between my wife's journal and (three years later) her oral account regarding a detail of June 14, 1997. Different accounts also included additional details that others omitted without expressly contradicting each other (e.g., phone interview with Emmanuel Moussounga, Feb. 20, 2010; my wife's journal from March 13, 1999; note Keener and Keener, *Impossible Love*, 236). Only a minority of the divergences remained after careful examination.

Differences Due to Genre

Although first-century historiography often focused on notable individuals,[54] biography, unlike multivolume historical works more generally, addressed a single chief character.[55] History thus contained many biographic elements, but normally lacked the focus on a single person and displayed less emphasis on characterization.[56]

Some differences (especially regarding omissions in one source) among our selected sources involve distinctions between the interests of biographic and historical genres. The rules of ancient elite historiography required not merely brief summaries of speech points or statements about the historian's inferences, but direct speech to fill out cohesive narratives. It is thus no surprise that Tacitus includes set speeches that Suetonius lacks (see e.g., *Hist.* 1.15-16, 29-30).[57] Even when Suetonius is aware of Otho offering instructions, he is far less interested in fleshing them out for his readers (*Otho* 6.3 vs. *Hist.* 1.37-38; *Otho* 10.2 vs. *Hist.* 2.47-48). Indeed, we have good reason to think that Tacitus took liberties here that Suetonius did not; Tacitus and Plutarch (another biographer) offer different versions of Otho's final speech (despite agreements in narrative).[58] On other occasions we may infer that speeches must have been offered, but again, providing speeches for readers remains Tacitus's interest (*Hist.* 1.83-84), not that of Suetonius.[59]

Of course, historians often would simply adapt speeches in their sources when these were available, continuing to depend on prior tradition.[60] Sometimes Tacitus probably does so in this section.[61] Nevertheless, Tacitus's works include many speeches for which we cannot expect exact words to have been preserved (e.g., *Ann.* 2.71-72, 76, 77; 6.48; 11.7; 12.48; 13.21; 16.22), including private conversations (*Ann.* 4.7, 52, 54, 68-69; 12.65). Indirect speech also appears at events

---

[54] Fornara, *Nature of History*, 34-36, 116.
[55] Lucian *Hist.* 7; also Witherington, *Sage*, 339, citing Plutarch *Alex.* 1.1-2.
[56] See Fornara, *Nature of History*, 185. Fleshing out character traits also appears in drama (e.g., tragedians expanding on Homeric characters) or practice orations (e.g., Dio Chrysostom *Or.* 61, on Chryseïs). Nevertheless, characterization does appear in histories; see Pitcher, "Characterization"; Ash, Mossman, and Titchener, *Fame*; and discussion in this book's introduction.
[57] Plutarch, however, is not unwilling to provide a few speeches in this section, e.g., Plutarch *Galba* 22.4-5; *Otho* 15.3-6.
[58] Talbert, *Mediterranean Milieu*, 211, cites Plutarch *Otho* 15 and Tacitus *Hist.* 2.47.
[59] This is not to deny that biographers could also create conversations or imagine characters' motives; see correctly Hägg, *Biography*, 3. Suetonius, in fact, displayed special interest in emperors' private lives (Hägg, *Biography*, 5).
[60] See Fornara, *Nature of History*, 160-61; Gempf, "Speaking," 283-84; Forsythe, "Quadrigarius," 396; Marincola, "Speeches," 129.
[61] Tacitus elaborates speeches where Suetonius and Plutarch omit them (*Hist.* 1.29-30) or merely mention them (*Hist.* 1.15-16 with Suetonius *Galba* 18.3; Plutarch *Galba* 23.2), but sometimes includes material that also appears in their summary (Tacitus *Hist.* 1.83-84 with Plutarch *Otho* 3.8; Tacitus *Hist.* 2.47-48 with Suetonius *Otho* 10.2; Plutarch *Otho* 15.3—17.2; cf. Tacitus *Hist.* 1.37-38 with Suetonius *Otho* 6.3).

where we cannot be certain that scribes would have kept records (e.g., *Ann.* 12.2; 14.53-54, 55-56; 15.51).

Speeches do not represent the only area of difference based on genre. Tacitus specifies more names of collaborators in the plot against Galba (*Hist.* 1.24-25), perhaps again reflecting the difference in genre expectations. Tacitus (and Plutarch) name generals; Suetonius summarizes the war and simplifies by omitting the names of generals even where he includes their role (e.g., those advising Otho, Suetonius *Otho* 9.1). Writing a simpler, one-volume biography of Otho rather than a more technical multivolume history, Plutarch also condenses, omitting some names, though less than does Suetonius (e.g., Plutarch *Galba* 27.4; Tacitus *Hist.* 1.43).

Tacitus recounts some of Otho's background only at the end of his life; information about one's early life is more often characteristic of biographies than histories (and even there, where it appears, often constitutes only a small portion of the work).[62] By contrast, Tacitus elaborates in much greater detail aspects of Otho's plot (e.g., *Hist.* 1.24-26). Tacitus also describes the military operations in far more detail (*Hist.* 2.11-45); these were directly relevant to his interests and his form of historiography.

Sometimes Suetonius may forgo details about other figures in the *Otho* because he says more about these figures elsewhere in his larger work. Thus Tacitus elaborates Galba's demise in far more detail than Suetonius does in his *Otho*; but Suetonius had a separate biography for Galba (though he treats the matter briefly there as well; *Galba* 19—20). The same reason accounts for Tacitus's greater elaboration of Vitellius' revolt than found in Suetonius's *Otho* (a separate biography in the series for Vitellius), and for his extensive treatment of Vespasian (*Hist.* 2.1-7) that Suetonius reserves for that biography. Because Plutarch wished to avoid duplication, much of his information about Otho appears only in his *Galba*.

Points of Contact

While there are a few points at which the writers conflict and many points on which one is silent (not all of the latter are included in my list), the points of contact listed above are too numerous to entertain the possibility of random coincidence. Contrary to what some scholars have argued, the line between novelistic composition based on imagination and biographic or historical composition that constructs narratives with heavy reliance on preexisting information is not very thin. Even if the line appears thin in some kinds of sources, it is not at all thin in our sample biography concerning a recent figure.

---

[62] E.g., Josephus summarizes the first thirty years of his life in *Life* 1-16 (around 4 percent of the *Life*, despite Josephus's direct knowledge of the events). Others simply began with the subject's adulthood (e.g., Plutarch *Caesar* 1.1-4; *Life of Aesop* in Drury, *Design*, 29).

Which elements one counts makes the exact count subjective, but speaking roughly, in Suetonius's brief biography, I found thirty-one points with close correspondence to Tacitus and eighteen additional points of significant correspondence. I found thirty points of close contact between Suetonius and Plutarch, with eighteen further points of significant correspondence; besides these, I found twenty-eight further points of close correspondence between Plutarch and Tacitus.

Keep in mind again that Suetonius's biography of Otho is brief, the equivalent of roughly only twenty-eight paragraphs, with a total of less than two thousand words. This biography is less than one-fifth the length of Mark's Gospel, so if we extrapolated to suggest a comparable amount of information in Mark, we would be thinking of perhaps 250 points of correspondence with external reality. Moreover, these are only the points in Suetonius's *Otho* that may be confirmed externally. In Suetonius's own day, when much more information remained extant and some eyewitnesses could be consulted, the figure was undoubtedly much higher.

One would not expect anything like this level of correspondence in a novel of comparable length, even in the rarer historical novels where some correspondences are possible. The genre difference between such biographies and novels should, then, be plainly evident. At least two of our three sources, and probably all three of them, are closely bound to their own sources. Such an observation need not surprise us; ancient historians and biographers do sometimes name their sources.[63] They were particularly apt to identify their sources when alternate stories came to circulate over time.[64] What our comparison of some sample sources indicates is just how closely bound to their sources they could be. This appears particularly evident for Otho's final hours; as in the gospel passion narratives, the chief character's end was a matter of interest inviting detailed comment.

Use of Sources

Suetonius, then, follows sources. Some of the material regarding Otho's conspiracy and death corresponds so closely as to require the supposition of some common source or sources. If Suetonius drew on Tacitus, so that their works were not independent,[65] this dependence would still illustrate our primary point about Suetonius the biographer: he developed sources rather than engaging in purely

---

[63] For historians: e.g., Dionysius of Halicarnassus *Ant. rom.* 1.1.1; 1.6.1; Josephus *Ant.* 1.94, 159; 1 Kgs 14:19, 29; 15:7, 23, 31; for biographers: Arrian *Alex.* 6.2.4; Plutarch *Alex.* 30.7; 31.2-3; 38.4.

[64] For historians: Dionysius of Halicarnassus *Ant. rom.* 1.87.4; 3.35.1-4; 8.79.1; Livy 9.44.6; 23.19.17; 25.17.1-6; Valerius Maximus 5.7.ext. 1; 6.8.3; Herodian 7.9.4; 7.9.9; Appian *Hist. rom.* 11.9.56; 12.1.1; for biographers: Cornelius Nepos 7 (Alcibiades), 11.1; 9 (Conon), 5.4; Arrian *Alex.* 1, *pref.* 1-2; 4.9.2-3; 4.14.1-4; 5.3.1; 5.14.4; 7.14.2; 7.27.1-3; Plutarch *Alex.* 31.3; 38.4; 46.1-2; *Dem.* 5.5; 29.4-30.4; *Them.* 25.1-2; 27.1; 32.3-4; Philostratus *Vit. soph.* 2.4.570; 2.5.576.

[65] Dependence is more easily demonstrated in some cases than in others. Some argue, for example, that Arrian drew on Plutarch (Buszard, "Parallel"); others demur. Hägg, *Biography*, 240-41, suggests that Suetonius and Plutarch, who organize their works quite differently, may have even invented imperial biographies independently.

free composition. (Chronology makes less likely that Tacitus drew on Suetonius. Had he done so, however, the historian would have been accepting Suetonius's biographies as a legitimate historical source.)[66] Such dependence would also not oblige us to suppose that this was the only source available to him. Nevertheless, that they agree so closely, even in sequence, only at particular points, might suggest that Suetonius drew not on Tacitus here but on a source or sources that Tacitus used.[67]

One source that they sometimes shared might be the no-longer-extant work of Fabius Rusticus (cf. Tacitus *Ann.* 13.20.2; 14.2; 15.61).[68] The case of Fabius Rusticus indicates that even some of those writing within a generation of events (such as Mark) might conceivably depend on even earlier sources written by those who lived during the events in question and knew some of the participants. (Observe for example the many contemporary histories of Nero noted already in Josephus *Ant.* 20.154, though Josephus did not like the ones with whose perspectives he disagreed.)[69] Tacitus elsewhere cites "historians of that era" (*Ann.* 5.9) as sources for events a century before his time.[70]

Tacitus knows of various earlier historians, sometimes naming them only when they themselves become subjects of history (e.g., Tacitus *Ann.* 4.34; his books survived, 4.35), and often mentioning both the verdict of "the majority" of historians from the earlier era noted and dissenters from that consensus (e.g., *Ann.* 4.57).[71] Tacitus normally follows annals and earlier histories, but also consulted personal memoirs from perhaps half a century earlier (*Ann.* 4.53).

The biographers likewise reveal some of their sources. Plutarch consulted witnesses, including an officer who described to him what he saw while Plutarch was touring the site with him (Plutarch *Otho* 14.1).[72] Suetonius apparently made some

---

[66] Because Tacitus would have known contemporary expectations for ancient biographies far better than we could, his verdict would likewise reinforce our point about the historical texture of ancient biography (in view of ancient historians' interest in history, revealed both in the above correspondences and in explicit statements; cf. Keener, *Historical Jesus*, 96-105). Similarly, Matthew and Luke, who knew much more about Mark than we do, regarded Mark as a reliable source for their biographies.

[67] Many Gospels scholars analogously infer the existence of Q based on differences between Matthew and Luke that suggest neither's knowledge of the other's full work (especially the infancy narratives and Judas's death).

[68] Cf. Martin, "Tacitus," 1470.

[69] Josephus published the *Antiquities* perhaps 27 years after Nero's death.

[70] Historians could also refer readers more generally to "other historians" (Velleius Paterculus 2.48.5); cf. Luke 1:1. Earlier, Polybius readily critiqued historians who failed to consult earlier historians (12.25d.1); later, Dio Cassius had to defend his omission of some material by explaining that he had in fact read almost everything but did not judge it all suitable for inclusion (1.1.1-2).

[71] Tacitus recounts the views of the majority and most reliable historians, but then mentions another view (*Ann.* 4.10), which he goes on to refute logically (4.11) despite its utility for his perspective.

[72] In this case Plutarch confesses that he does not know why the scene was as his witness described it (bodies gathered and piled up at a temple; *Otho* 14.2). Plutarch also visited Otho's tomb at Brixillum (Plutarch *Otho* 18.1). For Plutarch's range of sources, see

local inquiries for his work as well (Suetonius *Vesp.* 1.4), and sometimes could establish his point by naming various earlier sources supporting it (Suetonius *Jul.* 9.3). Suetonius's sources more generally include notes that he took from official "libraries and archives," and while he proved less critically discerning about his various sources than Plutarch,[73] modern historians appreciate "his hesitation to impose his own judgments" on his material.[74]

One of Suetonius's sources is clear: his own father Suetonius Laetus was a tribune serving under Otho, and shared with him information about Otho's character and actions (*Otho* 10.1).[75] When considering major public events, a generation is, after all, not a very long time, for it remains within living memory of eyewitnesses and participants who would naturally be consulted. This is true, in any case, of biographies, which worked from preexisting material; novels, which usually did not, rarely if ever were composed about historical figures a mere generation earlier.

That writers used sources does not prove that the sources are always correct.[76] Even eyewitnesses have biases, and gossip and speculation was surely rife in the setting that Suetonius depicts.[77] Nevertheless, that Suetonius, writing within about half a century, depends on earlier sources (some from those who experienced some of the events described) reinforces our suspicion that biographers writing within the first generation or two often had considerable historical information on which to depend.

This analogy cannot prove that an early gospel writer, say Mark, would have depended on earlier written eyewitness sources, but it confronts the historical prejudice of those who a priori suppose it unlikely. In Mark's case, oral tradition may be likelier than written sources, though we need not rule out the possibility of written sources as well (cf. Luke 1:1). Since biographers appealed to eyewitness sources where possible, there is no intrinsic historical reason to rule out the possibility that Mark depended on Peter, as later tradition suggests. What is more

---

Rhodes, "Documents," 65-66; Hägg, *Biography* 256-58, 264; for his creative use of them, see Badian, "Skill."

[73] One of the standard criticisms of Suetonius, though criticism focused on what he omitted more than on errors of fact (Hägg, *Biography*, 230). Others comment on Plutarch's interest in sources and evaluation of explanations (Hägg, *Biography*, 243, noting esp. Badian, "Skill"), though Plutarch is far more creative in form (Hägg, *Biography*, 281) and far more given to moralizing comments than is Suetonius.

[74] Kennedy, "Source Criticism," 141. Kennedy notes (141) that the Gospels rely on simpler tradition, but nevertheless deems useful this comparison with hard data.

[75] Not to be confused with Suetonius Paulinus, a prominent general of the time.

[76] Still, accuracy of sources, unimportant in some genres, was known to be a concern of historians (Pliny *Ep.* 9.33.1).

[77] Ancients themselves noted the effectiveness of rumor, e.g., rumors of conspiracy (Tacitus *Ann.* 14.58); of catastrophic losses in Germany (Tacitus *Hist.* 4.12); of mass exile (Tacitus *Ann.* 4.46); rumors exaggerating enemy numbers (Tacitus *Ann.* 4.23); a false rumor of a leader's death (*Hist.* 4.34) or survival (Josephus *Ant.* 19.134; Tacitus *Ann.* 2.82-83) or that the enemy had fled (Tacitus *Hist.* 2.42); or even deliberately false rumors (disinformation; *Hist.* 4.38, 54; *Ann.* 4.24). Conflicting reports also emerged this way (e.g., Tacitus *Hist.* 1.51). Of course, even rumor was not always wrong (Tacitus *Agr.* 9).

clear from the analogy is that Mark very probably would have depended on earlier information of some sort.

Certainly writers like Matthew and Luke (on the most common reconstruction of the Gospels' relationship) depended heavily on their sources, and they treat Mark as a valid biographic source of reliable information rather than as a work of fiction. Matthew and Luke wrote at a time when the identity and qualifications of Mark were likely known. Whatever the exact actual sequence of the Gospels' publication, if they are biographies, they expect their audiences to assume that they depend on information. If the Synoptics date to within forty to sixty years of the events on which they focus, as most scholars believe, a historian should be able to expect that a high degree of the information they recount is likely accurate.

Conclusion

While the degree of adaptation in Suetonius is debatable, his heavy dependence on source material is not. In a work of perhaps twenty-eight paragraphs, we found nearly fifty correspondences with each of the other two works (a history and another biography) with which we compared it. Suetonius's understanding of biography involved not free composition but dependence on prior information; where we can test him, this biographer mostly edited and adapted historical information rather than inventing new stories. Given its chronological proximity to eyewitness sources, a large amount of Suetonius's information about events (if not always the participants' motives) is likely correct.

These features of Suetonian biography also confirm our expectations based on the Gospels: Matthew and Luke plainly depend on prior information. According to a majority of scholars, these consist of at least Mark and probably "Q," as well as other possible information; on this or any other configuration of Synoptic sources, they do employ prior reports. On the majority view, Matthew and Luke presumably made use of Mark for their biographic projects because they believed that Mark likewise conveyed accurate information, whether from earlier published sources (cf. Luke 1:1) or oral information from eyewitnesses (as Papias suggests; cf. Luke 1:2). Fictional accounts were not typically interested in prior information, nor written about recent historical figures.

Because Mark wrote his biography within a generation of Jesus (closer to his time, in fact, than Suetonius is in relation to Otho), we may expect that he also depends on substantial preexisting information, whatever his (or Suetonius') literary adaptations for their respective sorts of audiences. If his approach is anything like that of Suetonius, he probably narrates prior information in every pericope of his work. In any case, Matthew and Luke, who probably wrote biographies within two decades of Mark, considered him a reliable source and were in a much better position to know circumstances surrounding his work than we are.

Ancient biographers, including the Gospels, sought to make their points on the basis of historical information available to them. As David Aune puts it, "while the Evangelists clearly had an important theological agenda, the very fact that they chose to adapt Greco-Roman biographical conventions to tell the story of Jesus indicates that they were centrally concerned to communicate what they thought really happened."[78]

---

[78] Aune, "Biography: Greek," 125; cf. ibid., 64-65; Witherington, *Sage*, 339. Shuler, *Genre*, regards his subject (Matthew's Gospel) as primarily encomium, or laudatory, biography; but such a *specific* genre probably did not exist (Burridge, *Gospels?* (1992), 88), since encomiastic elements were common in many biographies, including Suetonius (who apportions both praise and blame).

Chapter 7

Galba: A Comparison of Suetonius's and Plutarch's Biographies and Tacitus's *Histories* with Implications for the Historical Reliability of the Gospels

Benson Goh
Asbury Theological Seminary

Introduction

Scholars have long debated the genre of the Gospels. Their suggestions range from identifying them as "unique," to labeling them as folk literature, memoirs, drama, and even novels.[1] For example, various scholars have identified the Gospel of Mark as a Greek drama,[2] a novel-like piece of popular literature,[3] and a historical monograph.[4] Despite these varied suggestions, a majority of scholars today treat Mark as an ancient biography.[5] This is due, in part, to Richard A. Burridge's definitive work comparing the Gospels with Graeco-Roman biographies, particularly his detailed and extensive analysis of the similarities in their opening features, subjects, external features, and internal features. The evidence he provides in *What are the Gospels?* to support his claim regarding the genre of the Gospels is more than sufficient to place the burden of proof on those who claim otherwise.

This increasing agreement among scholars that the Gospels belong to the genre of ancient biography highlights the necessity of comparing the Gospels with other extant ancient biographies. Such comparative analysis is extremely important for evaluating the degree of historical reliability the Gospels' first audiences would expect from them. This issue is a major concern for many biblical scholars. Are the narrative accounts in the Gospels fabricated or can we say that they have a substantial degree of historical accuracy? Craig S. Keener attempts to address the issue by looking at how other ancient biographies edited and

---

[1] Keener, *Historical Jesus*, 74-78.
[2] Beavis, *Mark's Audience*, 31-35; Hooker, *Gospel*, 18-19.
[3] Tolbert, *Sowing the Gospel*, 48-79. This idea is briefly introduced in Beavis, *Mark's Audience*, 35-37.
[4] Collins, *The Beginning of the Gospel*, 1-38.
[5] Keener, *Historical Jesus*, 78-84; Witherington, *Gospel of Mark*, 3-11; Bryan, *Preface to Mark*, 23-25; Marcus, *Mark*, 1:65-67.

adapted historical information.⁶ By observing the numerous points of contact in the details about Otho's life as found in Suetonius' *The Lives of the Caesars*, Tacitus' *The Histories*, and Plutarch's *Lives*, Keener confirms that the biographers, Plutarch and Suetonius, "sought to make their points on the basis of historical information available to them."⁷ He also notes that in a similar fashion to the way Suetonius and Plutarch made use of Tacitus, Matthew and Luke make use of Mark.

Following an approach similar to Keener's examination of Otho biographies, this chapter provides a comparative study on the biographical and historical accounts of the life of the emperor Galba. I will be using Suetonius' *Galba*, Tacitus' *Histories*, and Plutarch's *Galba*, three writers who were contemporaries of one another during the early second century.⁸ My aim is to determine the degree to which these ancient biographers depended on or adapted historical information in producing their biographies (that historians generally use for genuine historical information).

This approach has direct implications for the historical reliability and genre⁹ of the Gospels.¹⁰ I have presented a chart in Table 1 that displays the comparisons among these three authors' works in such a way that similarities and differences can be easily observed and compared. The accounts of Suetonius and Plutarch are placed on the left and right of Tacitus' *Histories* respectively for easier comparison of both biographies with the work of historiography. Following the table, the parallels between the biographers, and also between each of the biographers with Tacitus, are noted and evaluated. Likewise, their marked differences are also discussed.

---

⁶ Keener, "Otho," 332.

⁷ Ibid., 336, 355.

⁸ Mellor, *Roman Historians*, 133; Keener, *Introduction*, 129-130. Keener highlights the value of choosing these three writers in view of their contemporaneousness. He writes: "Ancient historians, like their modern successors, generally preferred writers closer in time to the events reported rather than later sources ... We depend heavily on writers of the early empire, such as Tacitus and Suetonius, who report relatively recent events (of the past century to century and a half, with accuracy increasing further later in that period); despite their biases, they provide an invaluable source for understanding the early empire."

⁹ Pennington, *Reading the Gospels Wisely*, 19. Pennington recently uses the term "family resemblance" to refer to identifiable characteristics shared by different literary works that set them apart as a genre. Borrowing this idea, the repeated reliance on historical information by ancient biographies, as argued in Keener's work on Otho, could be considered as one important "family trait" that characterizes the genre of ancient biographies.

¹⁰ Keener writes (*Introduction*, 59): "Among Greek and Roman biographies, numerous examples exist from a few decades after the Gospels (e.g., those of Plutarch, Tacitus, and Suetonius and Josephus's autobiography), and others ... much earlier. Other works related to biography appear even earlier, but the more historically oriented works, such as the biographies from roughly the Gospels' era, may provide the most fruitful comparisons regarding genre."

Table 1. Comparison of Suetonius' *Galba*, Tacitus' *Histories*, and Plutarch's *Galba*[11]

Suetonius' *Galba*	Tacitus' *Histories*	Plutarch's *Galba*
Galba's parentage and illustrious ancestry (2.1-3.4)		
Galba's family was an old and powerful one of noble origin (2.1)	Galba's family was one of ancient nobility (1.49)[12]	Galba had connection with the noble house of the Servii (3.1)
Galba was the great-grandson of Quintus Catulus Capitolinus (2.1)		Galba prided himself on his relationship to Catulus, the foremost man in his time in virtue and reputation (3.1)
Galba's name was noted as Servius Galba (4.1)		Galba's name was noted as Sulpicius Galba (3.1)
Signs, omens, and dreams foretold of Galba's rise to be emperor (4.2-3)		
Galba was related to the house of the Caesars and showed marked respect to Livia Augusta (2.1; 5.2)		Galba was somehow related to Livia, wife of Augustus Caesar (3.1)
Galba was shown favor during Livia Augusta's lifetime (5.2) After governing the province of Aquitania for a year, he became consul for six months in 33AD (6.1)		Because of Livia's insistence, Galba was made consul in 33AD (3.1)
Galba almost became a rich man by Livia	Galba possessed great wealth (1.49)	Galba was the richest private person to be

---

[11] Parallels among their accounts can be readily observed across each row. Where there is only one entry in that row it signals that the content is unique to that biography or history.

[12] A number of Tacitus' similarities with Suetonius and Plutarch here were actually written at the end of his account of Galba, not in his introduction.

Suetonius' *Galba*	Tacitus' *Histories*	Plutarch's *Galba*
Augusta's last will. He had the largest bequest among her legatees but did not get anything in the end (5.2)		enthroned (3.1)
Galba was persistent in keeping an old custom of Rome (4.4)		
	Galba was frugal with his own property and stingy with the state's. He was not greedy for another's property (1.49)	Galba had a simple and contented way of living. He had a sparing hand with which he dealt out money, always avoiding excess (3.2)
Galba insisted on strict discipline within his troops (stopped furlough requests; got veterans and recruits into condition with hard work) and observed justice even in trifling matters (7.2; 6.3)	The soldiers were grumbling over toilsome marches, lack of supplies, and hard discipline (1.23) Galba was ruined by his old-fashioned strictness and excessive severity (1.18); Galba ruled Hither Spain with uprightness (1.49)	
Galba was governor of Upper Germany (6.2); He was also proconsul of Africa for 2 years (7.1); He was recognized by the triumphal regalia and three priesthoods. He was chosen as a member of the Fifteen, brotherhood of Titius, priests of Augustus (8.1)	Galba enjoyed a reputation for his military service in the German provinces. He governed Africa with moderation (1.49)	Galba commanded with distinction an army in Germany and was proconsul of Africa in 45AD, winning praises as few had done (3.2)
Galba was offered Hispania Tarraconensis in 60AD, in which he governed for 8	Galba ruled Hither Spain as an old man with uprightness (1.49)	Galba was sent out by Nero as governor of Spain in 61AD (3.3), until the revolt against

Galba: A Comparison 177

Suetonius' *Galba*	Tacitus' *Histories*	Plutarch's *Galba*
years (8.1; 9.1)		Nero happened in the eighth year of his governorship (4.2)
Auspices and omens encouraged Galba about becoming emperor (8.2)		
	Galba's approach to Rome was slow (1.6)	
Galba received letters from Vindex, calling him to be the liberator and leader of mankind (9.2)		Galba received letters from Vindex, inviting him to assume the imperial power and to head the revolt against Nero (4.2-3)
Galba proclaimed a holiday and pretended to attend the manumitting of slaves when in fact he mounted the tribunal, being hailed as emperor by the people, though he declared he was their governor, representing the senate and people of Rome, and urged all men to join the revolution in every way (10.1-3)		Galba issued an edict appointing a day on which he would grant individual manumissions to all. Then he was seen upon the tribunal being hailed as emperor. But he chose his title to be General of the Roman Senate and People (5.1-2)
More signs and omens of victory for Galba reported (10.4)		
When some messengers reported that Nero was dead and that everyone had sworn allegiance to him, Galba immediately took the title of Caesar and marched to Rome in a general's cloak with a dagger hanging from		Icelus, a Roman freedman, reported and confirmed that Nero was dead. Titus Vinius came from the camp and reported in detail the decrees of the senate (7.1-3)

Suetonius' *Galba*	Tacitus' *Histories*	Plutarch's *Galba*
his neck in front of his chest (11.1)		
Nymphidius Sabinus was prefect of the praetorian guard (11.1)	Nymphidius Sabinus, the prefect of the praetorians, had promised the soldiers a large sum of donative in Galba's name (1.5)	Nymphidius Sabinus, with Tigellinus, persuaded soldiers to proclaim Galba as emperor by promising them large sums of money[13] that were impossible to be raised (2.2)
	Nymphidius was killed	Nymphidius was killed by the praetorian guards
	because he wanted to secure the empire for himself (1.5)	because of his evil deeds (14.3)
Galba overthrew those who plotted against him: Nymphidius Sabinus, prefect of the praetorian guard; Clodius Macer, governor in Africa; and Fonteius Capito, governor in Germany (11.1)	Galba ordered the execution of Clodius Macer in Africa by Trebonius Garutianus, and of Fonteius Capito in Germany by Cornelius Aquinus and Fabius Valens (1.7)	Galba executed Macer by the hands of Trebonius, and Fonteius in Germany by Valens (15.2)
Galba has a double reputation for cruelty and avarice (12.1)		
	Many commented unfavorably about Galba's age and greed (1.5)	

---

[13] Specifically, 7,500 drachmas for the court or praetorian guards, and 1,250 drachmas for those in service outside of Rome (Plutarch, *Galba* 2.2).

Galba: A Comparison 179

Suetonius' *Galba*	Tacitus' *Histories*	Plutarch's *Galba*
Galba demoted some marines, whom Nero had made regular soldiers back to being rowers, when they obstinately demanded an eagle and standards. When they refused, he not only dispersed them by a cavalry charge but also decimated them (12.2)	Galba's entrance into Rome was ill-omened because many thousands of unarmed soldiers, possibly consisting of a Spanish legion, which Nero enrolled to be an additional force in the city to crush the attempt of Vindex, were massacred (1.6)	Galba was approaching the city when he was met with a disorderly and tumultuous crowd of seamen whom Nero formed into a legion and labeled them soldiers. They demanded standards for their legion and regular quarters as their rights as soldiers. When he postponed their requests, they were incensed and some threatened him with swords. Then he ordered his horsemen to charge upon them and all were killed (15.3-4)
Galba presented flute player Canus only five denarii from his own purse with his own hand when the latter pleased him greatly (12.3)		After Canus had played on the flute, Galba took a few gold pieces from his purse and gave them to Canus, commenting that the gift was his own, not from the public money. Galba also praised him loudly (16.1)
Galba's popularity and prestige were greater when he won, than while he ruled the empire. Galba was hated for his acts during his reign, which were opposite to the characteristics he displayed before (14.1)	Galba was becoming unpopular, regardless of his deeds (1.7)	
	Under Galba, there were the same evils in the	After initial assurances of a different mode of

Suetonius' *Galba*	Tacitus' *Histories*	Plutarch's *Galba*
	new court as in the old (Nero's) (1.7)	government from Nero, Galba took on a style that was similar to Nero's (15.2)
	Fate, signs and oracles predestined Vespasian and his sons for power (1.10)	
Titus Vinius was one of Galba's generals in Spain (14.2)	Titus Vinius was Galba's colleague during his second consulship (in Spain) (1.11)	
	Galba, old and feeble, infirm and confiding, was being taken advantage of by men like Titus Vinius to increase their power and fortune (1.12)	Galba's old age and feebleness was taken advantage of by Vinius to amount his own fortune (16.4)
Galba was wholly under the control of three men, who were known as his tutors: Titus Vinius, one of his generals in Spain and a man of unbounded covetousness; Cornelius Laco, prefect of the Guard; and Icelus, his own freedman. He trusted them and gave himself over to them as their tool, becoming exacting and stingy, extravagant and reckless (14.2)	Three men held the actual power of the Principate: Titus Vinius the consul, Cornelius Laco the praetorian prefect, and Icelus, Galba's freedman (1.13)	Galba was easily and badly persuaded and advised by Titus Vinius to abandon his own good course, to make use of Nero's riches and not to shrink from "a regal wealth of outlay" (11.2; 12.3)
	Galba had to bear the burden of the hatred felt for the crimes of Titus Vinius and of men's scorn for the lethargy of Cornelius Laco (1.6)	Galba suffered injustice when Vinius administered affairs badly and prevented wise measures of Galba himself (17.1)

Suetonius' *Galba*	Tacitus' *Histories*	Plutarch's *Galba*
Icelus received the honor of the gold ring and the surname of Marcianus, yet already aspired to be of the equestrian order (14.2)	Icelus was presented with the ring of a knight, and people called him Marcianus, an equestrian name (1.13)	Icelus was allowed to wear the gold ring and received the name Marcianus, becoming the chief influence among the freedmen (7.3)
Galba condemned to death distinguished men without trial due to trivial matters (14.3)	Galba put to death Cingonius Varro and Petronius Turpilianus without trial and undefended, leading many to think they were innocent (1.6)	Galba ordered Petronius Turpilianus to take his own life without a chance to defend himself (15.2)
Galba revoked all the grants of Nero, allowing only a tenth part to be retained. With the help of 50 Roman knights, he exacted repayment and stipulated that if actors and athletes had sold anything previously given to them, the item must be taken away from the buyer in case the former people already spent the money (15.1)	A large sum of 22 hundred million sesterces was squandered by Nero. It was voted that a tenth of the gifts Nero made to individuals should be kept. 30 knights were appointed to collect the money. But these people had hardly any left after wasting them extravagantly (1.20)	Galba ordered the gifts Nero had made to people of the theatre and palaestra should be demanded back strictly. When only a small amount was recovered, he ordered a search to exact from them, giving him a bad name (16.2-3)
Galba was unfairly favorable to his friends and freedmen, allowing them to bestow taxes and freedom from taxation or to sell anything (15.2)	Galba's freedmen were extremely powerful, his slaves clutched greedily after sudden gains with impatience. Everything was for sale (1.6)	

Suetonius' *Galba*	Tacitus' *Histories*	Plutarch's *Galba*
Galba not only saved the lives of Halotus and Tigellinus, but he honored Halotus with a very important stewardship, and issued an edict rebuking the people who wanted Tigellinus dead, though they were the most hated officials of Nero and the people called for their punishment (15.2).	Under Galba, and by the influence of Titus Vinius, who claimed that Tigellinus saved his daughter, Tigellinus was protected (1.72)	Galba initially planned to kill Helius, Polycleitus, Petinus and Patrobius. The people demanded justice on Tigellinus as well. But under Vinius' bad influence, Tigellinus was spared. Ironically, Tigellinus offered sacrifices and had a great feast upon being freed (17.2-5)
Galba was detested most by the soldiers, who were promised unusually large gifts for swearing allegiance to Galba in his presence. Instead of keeping the promise, Galba declared that it was his habit to levy soldiers, not to buy them (16.1)	The city soldiers were promised a "donative" in Galba's name but this was not given to them. Galba said that "he was wont to select, not buy, his soldiers." (1.5)	Galba was increasingly disliked and hated by the soldiers (18.3-4); The soldiers thought that they would at least receive part of the promised largess that Nero had given them formerly. Galba replied that it was his custom to enroll soldiers, not to buy them (18.1-2)
Galba was most hated by the army in Upper Germany because they were defrauded of the reward due them for fighting against the Gauls and Vindex (16.2)		Galba was finally killed because the soldiers did not get what was promised to them by Nymphibius and Tigellinus (2.3)
Otho was the first to espouse Galba's cause (*Otho* 4.1)	Otho was the first to join Galba's party during the revolt (1.13)	Otho was the first of the provincial governors to go over to Galba's revolt (20.2)
	Otho was the most brilliant of Galba's immediate supporters (1.13)	Otho aided Galba a lot and proved inferior to none as a man of affairs (20.2)

Suetonius' *Galba*	Tacitus' *Histories*	Plutarch's *Galba*
	Vinius favoured Marcus Otho as Galba's successor. People had been gossiping that Otho would be Vinius' son-in-law (1.13)	Vinius recommended Otho to be Galba's successor. In return, Otho would marry Vinius' daughter when he has been adopted by Galba (21.1)
	Galba thought of the state in choosing his successor and did not want to leave it to Otho, who was unrestrained and extravagant (1.13)	Galba placed the public good of Rome before his private interest in his choice of successor, and was not going to leave his private fortune to Otho, who was unrestrained and extravagant and immersed in great debts (21.2)
	Galba received word of the disloyal movement in Germany and being uncertain about Vitellius, he became distressed about the violence and wary of the soldiers (1.14)	Galba learned of the revolution in Germany that Vitellius was proclaimed emperor, and he no longer deferred his adoption plan (23.1)
Galba chose Piso Frugi Licinianus from the midst of the throng at one of his morning receptions. Galba favored him highly and named him in his will as heir (17.1)[14]	Galba adopted Licinianus Piso as his son at a kind of imperial comitia and made him heir to the throne (1.14, 18)	Galba suddenly sent for Piso, instead of Dolabella and Otho, both of whom he did not approve and in the camp declared him Caesar and heir to the throne, (23.1-2)
Galba addressed the soldiers at Piso's adoption (18.3)	Galba's speech at Piso's adoption given in detail (1.15-16)	Galba read his address to the soldiers at Piso's adoption (23.2)
The adoption took place in the praetorian camp before the soldiers who were as-	The adoption was declared in the praetorian camp first in honor of the soldiers (1.17, 18).	Galba went down to the camp to declare Piso as Caesar (23.2)

---

[14] This slight variation in the three accounts will be discussed subsequently.

Suetonius' *Galba*	Tacitus' *Histories*	Plutarch's *Galba*
sembled there (17.1)		
At the adoption of Piso, Galba made no mention of the largest to the soldiers (17.1)	Galba said no flattering words and made no mention of a gift to the soldiers (1.18)	At the adoption, Galba did not give the largest to the soldiers (23.2)
	People reported that Piso gave no sign of anxiety or exaltation at the adoption (1.17)	Piso was observed to be without great emotion when he was adopted by Galba (23.3)
	There was a gloomy silence among the soldiers whose loyalty could have been won by the slightest generosity from Galba (1.18)	The soldiers were secretly disloyal and sullen, since not even then was their largess given to them (23.2)
A series of incidents and dreams were treated as signs of the end of Galba's reign (18.1-3)		
	The day of adoption began with heavy rain, thunder, lightning and unusual threats but Galba would not be deterred, instead he despised them as mere chance (1.18)	Great signs from heaven accompanied Galba when he went to the camp. When he had finished his address, there were many peals of thunder and lightning, much darkness and rain came, signaling that the adoption was inauspicious and not approved by the heavenly powers (23.2)
	Four days past after the adoption, during which frequent reports of revolt in Germany arrived daily (1.19)	
	Otho placed his freedman Onomastus in charge of the crime he	Onomastus went around corrupting the soldiers with money

Galba: A Comparison   185

Suetonius' *Galba*	Tacitus' *Histories*	Plutarch's *Galba*
	planned (1.25)	and fair promises (24.1)
When Galba was offering sacrifice, (*Otho* 6.2) he was repeatedly warned by a soothsayer on the morning he was killed to look out for danger and that assassins were nearby (19.1)	Galba, when sacrificing in front of the temple of Apollo, was warned by seer Umbricius that the omens were unfavorable, that a plot was imminent, and the enemy was in his house (1.27)	At dawn, when Galba was sacrificing in the Palatium, Umbricius declared clearly and at length that there were signs of a great commotion and that peril mixed with treachery hung over the emperor's head (24.2)
Otho heard the predictions of the soothsayer (*Otho* 6.2)	When Otho heard Umbricius' declaration, he interpreted it as favorable to himself and auguring well for his purposes (1.27)	Otho noted what Umbricius had said but he stood in confusion and with a mixed countenance of fear (24.3)
A freedman came to announce that the architects had come, which was the signal agreed on, and going off as if to inspect a house which was for sale, Otho rushed from the Palace by a back door (*Otho* 6.2)	Onomastus came to announce to Otho that his architect and contractors were ready for him. This was the sign that the soldiers were gathered and the conspiracy was ripe (1.27)	Onomastus came and told Otho that his builders were waiting for him at his house. This was the token that Otho should meet the soldiers (24.4)
	Julius Martialis the tribune was the officer of the day in the camp (1.28)	Martialis the military tribune was in charge of the watch at the time (25.3)
Learning that Otho had control of the praetorian camp, Galba decided to hold his position by getting together a guard of legionaries (19.1)	Under the advice of Titus Vinius, Galba decided to stay in the palace instead of acting immediately to squash the revolt. But later he favored the more specious advice and went out (1.32-34)	Vinius would not allow when Galba wanted to go forth (26.1)
	Piso was first sent to the praetorian (1.33) Piso's	Piso went out and held a conference with the

Suetonius' *Galba*	Tacitus' *Histories*	Plutarch's *Galba*
	speech to the soldiers given in detail (1.29-30)	guards (25.5)
Galba was fooled by a soldier who claimed that he had killed Otho. He was lured out by false reports that the rebels had been overthrown (19.2)	Then Julius Atticus announced that he had killed Otho. At this, Galba was lured out of the palace, seated and raised on a chair (1.33-35)	Rumor spread that Otho was killed in the camp. Julius Atticus announced to Galba that he had killed his enemy. Galba then went out being carried in a litter (26.1-2)
		Many who were ignorant of what was happening soon joined in under persuasion (25.3)
	Otho's speech to rally the soldiers (1.37-38)	
Galba was killed by horsemen riding through the streets towards him, butchering him (19.2)	There was a great surging mob when Galba's litter went out. The people were anticipating what was to come. Roman soldiers rushed on, trampled down senators, and burst into the forum at full gallop (1.40)	There was much confusion surrounding Galba. Then horsemen and men-at-arms charged through the basilica of Paulus. A javelin was thrown at him but missed (26.3-4)
None of those present tried to lend aid to Galba (20.1)[15]	A centurion Sempronius Densus, whom Galba had assigned, defended Piso and allowed him to escape. He was wounded in the process (1.43)	A centurion Sempronius Densus defended Galba for a long time before falling with a wound in the groin (26.5)
Galba offered them his neck without resistance to strike him. Others said that he tried to win them by claiming he was for them and promising	Many reported that Galba voluntarily offered his throat, asking them to kill him for the interests of the state. Some others said that Galba appealed to what	Galba merely presented his neck to the soldiers and told them to kill him if that was better for the Roman people (27.1)

---

[15] This is a point of contradiction among the three writers.

Suetonius' *Galba*	Tacitus' *Histories*	Plutarch's *Galba*
them largess (20.1)	crime he had committed and begged for a few days to pay the donative (1.41)	
Galba was killed beside the Lake of Curtius (20.2)	Galba was thrown from his chair near the Lacus Curtius and rolled on the ground (1.40)	
	Galba's legs and arms were mutilated, and cruel savagery wounds were inflicted on his body even after his head was cut off (1.41)	After being wounded in his legs and arms, Galba was killed (27.2)
	Three names were offered as Galba's assassin: some say Terentius, some say Laecanius, mostly say Camurius who pierced his throat with a thrust of the sword (1.41)	Most writers stated Galba was killed by Camurius, others by Terentius, others by Lecanius, still others by Fabius Fabulus (27.2)
A company of German soldiers whom Galba had shown kindness and great indulgence came to his aid but they were too late (20.1)	A German detachment hesitated to join the revolt for a long time. They were those whom Galba had taken great pains to care for when they became sick from their long voyage from Alexandria (1.31)	

Suetonius' *Galba*	Tacitus' *Histories*	Plutarch's *Galba*
A common soldier who was returning from grain distribution cut off Galba's head and gave it to Otho, who had it set on a lance and paraded about the camp with jeers. It was bought by a freedman of Patrobius Neronianus and thrown aside in the place where his patron had been executed by Galba's order (20.2)	Galba's head had been fixed to a pole and maltreated and found before the tomb of Petrobius (1.49)	Fabius Fabulus, said to be the one who cut off Galba's head, impaled it on his spear and ran with it, whirling about and brandishing the spear for all to see (27.3); Galba's head was bestowed upon the servants of Patrobius, and cast into a place called Sessorium, where those under condemnation of the emperors were put to death (28.3)
Galba's head was bought by Patrobius Neronianus for 100 pieces of gold (20.2)	The assassins kept the heads of their victims for profit (1.47)	Vinius and Laco's head were cut off and brought to Otho with demand for largess (27.4) Vinius' head was sold to his daughter for 2500 drachmas (28.2)
Galba's steward, Argivus, placed Galba's head in the tomb with the rest of his body in his private gardens on Aurelian Road (20.2)	Galba's steward and former slave, Argius, gave Galba's body a humble burial in Galba's private garden (1.49)	A freedman, Argivus, buried Galba's body, which was first taken by Prisus Helvidus (28.3)
	Piso fled into the temple of Vesta and a public slave hid him in his chamber. But Sulpicius Florus and Statius Murcus dragged him out and killed him at the door of the temple (1.43)	Piso had been wounded and tried to escape. Murcus ran him down and killed him at the temple of Vesta (27.4)
	Those who had committed the murders, those who were present, and	Many who had no part in the murder smeared their hands and swords

Galba: A Comparison 189

Suetonius' *Galba*	Tacitus' *Histories*	Plutarch's *Galba*
	those who boasted of their share in the killings, whether true or false, exhibited their bloody hands (1.44)	with blood and showed them to Otho with petitions for largess (27.5)
	Vitellius found more than 120 petitions made demanding rewards for their participation in the killing in the revolt. He hunted for them and killed them, following the traditional custom of emperors to secure his own protection (1.44)	Vitellius discovered 120 petitions demanding for largess for taking part in the murder that day. He sought them out and put them to death (27.5)
	The soldiers demanded to punish Marius Celsus, consul elect and Galba's faithful friend, but Otho ordered to arrest him to suffer severe punishment (1.45)	Many denounced and wanted the death of Marius Celsus for persuading the soldiers to defend Galba, but Otho said he must first be questioned, kept him under guard and handed him over to those whom he trusted (27.6)
Galba's physical features, eating habits, inclination to unnatural desires for men, and age were recounted (21.1-23.1)	Galba's lineage, wealth, lack of virtue, complacent and indolent towards his friends, military and political career recounted (1.49)[16]	Galba's lineage, wealth, reputation, worthiness to be emperor, age, and failure in the hands of his insatiate favorites were recounted (29.1-4)
Galba died at 73 years old, in the 7th month of his reign (23.1)	Galba lived 73 years (1.49)	Galba was in his 73rd year of age (7.1)

---

[16] A number of details here have been listed as similarities with Suetonius and Plutarch's introductions.

Parallels

My first observation from this comparative study is the high frequency of agreement between the two biographies written by Suetonius and Plutarch. Of Suetonius' roughly 35 paragraphs equaling about 3,000 words and Plutarch's roughly 39 paragraphs of about 6,500 words, I found that there are about 98 points of contact, 63 of which bear very close resemblance to each other by using nearly identical wording. This equates to an average of about 2.5-2.8 points of similarity for each paragraph between the two biographies.

Such high instances of similarity between two biographers who authored and published their biographies at about the same time after the death of their subject is best explained as a result of the authors referring to the same sources or sources that contained similar information. It is unlikely that these biographies and the episodes they contain are the unique inventions of either writer. Probably these biographers surveyed the various sources available to them concerning the life of Galba, taking into account each source's degree of reliability, and both may have come to the conclusion that the source now shared by the two was the most trustworthy. This would be a more reasonable explanation for the similarities that exist between Suetonius and Plutarch's biography of Galba than the suspicion of free invention or fabrication.

Furthermore, I also found that there are about 76 points of contact between Suetonius and Tacitus, with 53 of them (approximately 70%) being very similar; and 131 between Plutarch and Tacitus, with 80 of them (approximately 61%) being significant. Tacitus' *Histories* is considered to be a fairly reliable account of the history of the Roman Empire[17] so for a biographical work to agree closely with it helps to establish that biography's concern for historical reliability as well. This further strengthens our proposal that Suetonius and Plutarch used substantially historically reliable data in their writings.

It is interesting to note that Plutarch agrees 55 times more with Tacitus than Suetonius does. One possible explanation could be that Plutarch shared a common source of information with Tacitus that Suetonius did not possess. Another possibility could be that because Plutarch's *Galba* is a significantly longer piece of work than Suetonius' this allows more opportunities for parallels. It is also possible that the higher number of similarities between Plutarch and Tacitus than Suetonius and Tacitus is due to the fact that Plutarch has higher historical aims than does Suetonius.

Regarding Suetonius, D.W.P. Burgersdijk and J.A. van Waarden write:

> Suetonius, unlike Plutarch, makes a distinction between descriptive and narrative elements, which determines the structure of his *vitae*. In a somewhat simplified way one could say, that his biographies start with the [*genos*] ('origin') of the emperor and his life up to the moment when he starts his reign. This section is narrative and progresses chronologically. After this follows the description of his

---

[17] Keener writes (*Introduction*, 167): "The Roman historian Tacitus ... recorded much of the history of first-century Rome, often using imperial annals; he is widely regarded as one of the most reliable sources for the history of this period."

conduct in public and in private. The *vita* is rounded off with an account of the end of his life. In this sequence of narrative and descriptive sections the depiction of the behavioral aspects forms the centre of gravity.[18]

Because Suetonius' interest in portraying the character of Galba takes center stage, this could have led him to organize his materials in such a way as to help him develop Galba's personality and ethical behavior more than to give a chronological account of his life like a purely historical record.[19] This does not mean Suetonius' writings or sources are not historically based; it could mean, however, that his material were structured to suit his aim of producing a biography that focused more on his subject's character.

The distinctiveness of these two biographers has been recognized earlier by Catherine Edwards who, in her introduction to her own translation of Suetonius' *Lives of the Caesars*, suggests that "Suetonius' work is much more emphatically 'not-history' than that of Plutarch," and that "Plutarch's mode of organization is essentially chronological in contrast to Suetonius' thematic approach."[20] (Chronology characterized history proper in a way that it frequently did not characterize biographies.) Philip A. Stadter, in his introduction to Robin Waterfield's translation of eight Roman lives also attests that for Plutarch, "historical narratives provide the base for his biographies."[21] He even elaborates the steps that Plutarch could have taken to adapt historical material.[22] Keener also posits that "Plutarch plainly believes that it is historical data he is using to make his moral points, and his record frequently parallels other historical sources."[23]

Despite Plutarch betraying a larger number of similarities to Tacitus' *Histories* than does Suetonius, all three works nevertheless share a large amount of similar material. While these many similarities may not by themselves completely prove that the biographers used historical information, they should allay suggestions that their authors invented the content and point to the more likely

---

[18] Burgersdijk and van Waarden, *Emperors and Historiography*, 88.

[19] Keener writes (*Introduction*, 57): "Ancient biographies differed from their typical modern namesakes. For example, they often began with their subject's adulthood and were not constrained by chronological sequence."

[20] Edwards, "Introduction," xiv.

[21] Stadter, "Introduction," xxiii.

[22] Stadter writes ("Introduction," xxiv): "In adapting the historical material, Plutarch took several steps to focus attention on his protagonist. Thus he may abridge his source by simplifying it, either conflating several similar incidents into one (e.g. meetings of the senate), by chronological compression (making two items seem to follow closely which in fact were separated by a period of time), or reorganizing events in non-chronological order, especially to bring out causal or logical connections. Occasionally he may even transfer an item from one character to another, whether consciously or not. More commonly, he may attribute to his protagonist an action which might be generally ascribed to a group (the senate, the city) in his source, personalizing an impersonal action. On the other hand, he will expand inadequate material, not by free invention but by a visualization of what must have been the case, what antecedents would naturally precede an action, or what context seems to be implied by a historical notice."

[23] Keener, *Introduction*, 168.

scenario that the authors consulted and employed reliable historical sources. Similar to Suetonius's and Plutarch's biographies of Galba, the Gospels also bear close resemblance with one another, especially among Matthew, Mark and Luke. They could very likely have adopted similar methodology when it came to referring to, depending on and including reliable historical data in their biographies of Jesus. Let us now examine the content of our ancient biographies to see what they tell us about the historicity of the sources being used.

Contents

The previous section highlighted a number of similarities between two biographical works which pointed to their fidelity to their sources. While valuable, it is also necessary to evaluate, as much as possible, the sources themselves. Primarily, if at all possible, it is important to determine whether the source was written or oral and whether it stems from an eyewitness account or from a secondhand report.[24] Identifying sources would not only further dispel the notion of free invention by these ancient biographers, but if it was found that the biographer was using a reliable source, like an eyewitness account, then it would also give us the confidence that such biographies had a considerable amount of historically reliable information.

Tacitus began Book I of his accounts of the Roman rulers in *The Histories* by saying that he wrote so that "we may understand not only the incidents and the issues of events, ... but also their reasons and causes" (Tacitus, *Hist.* 1.4 [Moore, LCL]). This surely determined the way he wrote about each emperor, and certainly of Galba, because he did not give his readers any background information on Galba prior to his involvement in overthrowing Nero.[26] Instead, he introduces Galba in the heat of military mutiny and the troubles that were happening in the revolt in Rome (*Hist.* 1.5), leaving much of Galba's background to

---

[24] Keener writes (*Introduction*, 127-28): "Ancient historians were especially happy, when reporting recent events, to include oral tradition from eyewitnesses. The second best source after the author himself being an eyewitness was the author's use of others as eyewitnesses; eyewitnesses who participated in events were considered ideal ... Because oral traditions were most reliable in the generation they recounted, Greek historians liked to travel to compile oral sources from the generation of the current events they reported... Nevertheless, sources committed to writing often held a special authority; even an eyewitness might cite another eyewitness source written before his own work had been committed to writing. Writers often recognized that whereas oral tradition could be modified over time, written sources were fixed."

[26] An interesting idea regarding what Tacitus chose to include or exclude material is given by Griffin. Basing on Tacitus' *Annals* 3.65.1, where Tacitus "explains that he will not record individual opinions given in the senate, unless they show outstanding virtue or the reverse," Griffin judges that "the true usefulness of history, in the view of Greek and Roman historians, does not consist in supplying a complete archive." See Griffin, "Tacitus," 174-75.

appear only in *Hist.* 1.49 after Galba's death as a kind of epilogue. Keener also observed this trend with regards to the emperor Otho's background.[27]

Suetonius, however, gives extensive information about Galba's background, in particular his parentage and ancestry (Suetonius, *Galba* 2.1-3.4); his belief in signs, omens and dreams (4.1-3); his studies and marital fidelity (5.1); how he began his career (5.2-6.1); the way he commanded his soldiers (6.2-8.2); and the circumstances that led to his involvement in the revolt against Nero (9.1-2). This information found in Suetonius is also contained in Plutarch's *Lives*, though in much lesser detail (Plutarch, *Galba* 3.1-4.4).[28] This observation concurs with Keener's statement that "information about one's early life is more often characteristic of biographies than histories,"[29] and demonstrates that Suetonius and Plutarch could have obtained this information about Galba from sources that Tacitus might not have had or chose not to include.

The additional information about Galba, which both Suetonius and Plutarch have included, certainly appears to be historical in nature. The information includes important people associated with Galba (like his grandparents and parents, the emperor's wife Livia Augusta, his colleagues and associates in various posts) and prominent positions of governance (like consulship and governorship) that could easily have been checked by his readership. Considering that the two biographers would have published their works about 50-60 years after Galba's death,[30] this background information on Galba would have been open to the scrutiny of other witnesses who would have been able to testify to their reliability, or lack there of.[31] This historical information of Galba was crucial to Suetonius's and Plutarch's biographies as it serves to develop Galba's character.[32] In

---

[27] Keener, "Otho," 351.

[28] Regarding Plutarch's choice of information and how it compares with historical works, Burgersdijk and van Waarden remark that (*Emperors and Historiography*, 87), "Plutarch selects the facts he wants to present on the basis of the contribution they can make to the revelation of character and the moral lessons they can teach. The selection of facts in which this results would be seen as trivial and insignificant in a work of history."

[29] Keener, "Otho," 351.

[30] Keener affirms that Suetonius could have composed his imperial biographies before 121 A.D., and that Plutarch could have completed his writing around 120 A.D. ("Otho," 335). Given that Galba lived from 3 B.C. (Suetonius, *Galba* 4.1) to 69 A.D., it is reasonable to estimate that their works were published about 50-60 years after 69 A.D., and likely withstood the correction of those who would have witnessed the events of 69 A.D., or knew of Galba's background from reliable sources such that they could attest to Suetonius and Plutarch's historical material.

[31] Keener ("Otho," 333) also writes that "biographers normally intended to use historical information, and that information was more reliable during a period when eyewitnesses or those who knew them remained alive. Ancients themselves often recognized that legendary and speculative elements increased with chronological distance from eyewitness material, especially after the living memory of eyewitnesses had passed."

[32] As Keener points out ("Otho," 350): "Although first-century historiography often focused on notable individuals, biography, unlike multivolume historical works more generally, addressed a single chief character. History thus contained many biographic elements but normally lacked the focus on a single person and displayed less emphasis on characterization."

doing so, they were honest about Galba's strengths and weaknesses, his achievements as well as failures, his triumphs and defeats.[33] Thus, we can conclude that ancient biographers were concerned to use historically accurate data in developing the character of their subjects.

Keener notes that ancient biographers often reveal their sources.[34] Let us consider where Suetonius might have obtained the detailed information about Galba's parentage, ancestry and reception of dreams and signs. At *Galba* 3.1, Suetonius was able to recount three possible explanations about how Galba's surname was derived: at 4.2, there is a story of the "foaling of a mule as a sign that highest dignity has come upon the Galba family" and fulfillment of this "omen;" and 4.3 contains a vivid description of Galba's dream of Fortune when he "just became a man." Such information with such specific detail might have been written or spoken by someone close to Galba himself. Suetonius states that Galba's grandfather had "published a voluminous and painstaking history" (3.3). Although it is not known what exactly was contained in this history, it is possible that it included some details about his own family and that Suetonius knew of and used it in his biography. If so, barring blatant fabrications, this would have been a reliable source that Suetonius could have made use of.

Gavin Townend postulates "that Suetonius undertook the composition of the *Caesares* at some time during his tenure of office on the Palatine" and that he would "have had access to the archives" and "worked extensively in the imperial secretariat and could compare documents of all sorts."[35] This would make it likely that Suetonius had access to Galba's parentage record left by his prestigious family. Assuming that the archives and records available to him were for the most part reliable and that he used them, his biography would have had a considerable amount of historically accurate information. Jones notes that there are some questions as to whether Suetonius was already dismissed from his office before completing his writing of the *Caesars* and that he might not have had access to the imperial archives for the "less detailed lives."[36] Though we cannot be certain whether Suetonius was still in office when he completed the *Caesars*, it is very likely that he, as Jones also points out, made "occasional use of the archival material."[37]

Having a number of sources available may give a biographer an advantage, but it is how he utilizes his sources and whether or not he does it responsibly that determines the quality of his work. In this regard, Suetonius might have fallen short. Jones says that Suetonius's use of archives was conducted "in a way that today seems fairly casual and haphazard."[38] Townend says that Suetonius, "unlike orthodox historians, ... did not mind quoting in full, Greek and all."[39]

---

[33] Keener writes (*Introduction*, 112): "In biographies, most writers felt free to record negative as well as positive features of their protagonists when appropriate."
[34] Keener, "Otho," 353.
[35] Townend, "Date of Composition," 285-93.
[36] Jones, *Suetonius*, xii.
[37] Ibid.
[38] Ibid.
[39] Townend, "Date of Composition," 286.

Keener also notes that "Suetonius's sources more generally include notes that he took from official 'libraries and archives,'" though he "proved less critically discerning about his various sources than Plutarch."[40] He further elaborates that "Suetonius's biographies of the twelve Caesars provide critical information to modern historians of antiquity; they may be less reliable than Tacitus, but where Suetonius errs, it is by depending too uncritically on his sources, not by fabricating material."[41] Regardless of Suetonius' writing style, his ability to access imperial records, at least before his dismissal from office is sufficient to conclude that he had historically reliable sources available for his biographical works.

In other parts of Suetonius' *Galba* it is not explicitly clear who or what his sources were, but it is more likely than not that Suetonius relied on sources for the information he provides, some of which were closed-door situations. For example, we cannot immediately tell how Suetonius came to know:

- 5.2: that Livia Augusta had bestowed one million sesterces to Galba, and that the sum was reduced to five hundred thousand by Tiberius, and that Galba eventually did not receive any of it;
- 9.2: the "insider" news that Galba had intercepted Nero's agents about plans to kill him, and the omens and dreams not reported by Tacitus and Plutarch;
- 10.5: about the discovery of a plot to assassinate Galba;
- 11.1: that Galba was "panic-stricken and came near taking his own life in the belief that all was lost";
- 12.3: the "tale" that Galba "groaned aloud when an unusually elegant dinner was set before him," that he handed his steward a dish of beans in return for his industry and carefulness in presenting his expense account, and that he gave only five denarii to Canus for greatly pleasing him;
- 15.1-2: Galba's intention to limit offices open to senators and knights to two years and to give only to those who did not want them and decline them;
- 18.1-3: the details of a runaway ox, earthquake, Fortune's displeasure over pearl necklace, and other incidents not found in Tacitus and Plutarch;
- 19.1: that Galba decided to put on a linen cuirass;
- 22.1: the unidentified "they" who knew of Galba's unnatural relationship with Icelus;
- 23.1: the senate's vote to set up a statue for Galba which was annulled by Vespasian.

Some might not stop to consider the sources behind these portions of Suetonius' biography. However, because of Suetonius's consistent use of sources throughout the rest of his biography, it is highly likely that he is dependent upon sources for the information presented above. This is a much more likely scenario than the proposal that he simply fabricated these details.

---

[40] Keener, "Otho," 353; Keener, *Introduction*, 173.

[41] Keener, *Introduction*, 168. Despite this, Keener further notes that (*Introduction*, 173) "modern historians appreciate 'his hesitation to impose his own judgments' on his material. Suetonius apparently made some local inquiries for his work (*Vesp.* 1.4), and sometimes could establish his point by naming various earlier sources supporting it (*Jul.* 9.3)."

Furthermore, Suetonius at times alludes to information that he assumed his readers would have already known.[42] For example, at 2.1 and 17.1, he gave the full names Quintus Catulus Capitolinus, Piso Frugi Lisinianus and Marcus Salvius Otho without clarification as to who they were, except that Catulus was the great grandfather of Galba. Perhaps Catulus was already a well-known name whom Suetonius's readers were familiar with, but he had certainly expected them to know who Piso and Otho were and did not bother to say anything more about them. To me, these instances demonstrate Suetonius's dependence on common and reliable information known and available to all, information thus not necessary for him to reproduce in his work. Moreover, these characters do not contribute to his development of Galba's character in a big way, compared to Titus Vinius, Cornelius Laco, and Icelus Marcianus who had a direct influence on the kind of emperor that Galba turned out to be.

Plutarch also shows dependence on prior information, some of it possibly common knowledge. For example in *Lives* 3.2, he wrote "we are told also" and in 4.2 and 8.4, "it is said."

Finally, we need to consider the abundance of material related to omens, signs, predictions, and dreams in Suetonius' *Galba*. His first paragraph describes the omen that symbolized the success of the house of the Caesars which, together with other signs from the sky, foretold of its end in Nero's reign. At three points in his introduction of Galba's background (*Galba* 4.2-3; 8.2; 10.4), he included various tales that were believed to be omens along with Galba's dream of Fortune (which foretold of Galba's attainment of greatness). Then, interestingly, his next mention of the supernatural is not until 18.1-3 when he describes a series of incidents and dreams that were treated as signs of the end of Galba's reign. These observations form a literary inclusio around Galba's brief rule. Tacitus and Plutarch, on the other hand, point out only the observed natural phenomena on the day of Galba's adoption of Piso as inauspicious, in *Histories* 1.18 and *Galba* 23.2 respectively.

Keener notes that Suetonius had an interest in dreams and that Tacitus, in other works, also included dreams, omens, and divine signs.[43] He further notes that omens, signs, and dreams are common in historical works and that it was a common belief that they "portended the future."[44] He supports this based on the presence of such content in many other works of classical literature.[45]

By contrast, Miriam T. Griffin, in agreement with another earlier scholar, regards Tacitus' references to fate and the gods as nothing more than his writing

---

[42] Keener writes (*Introduction*, 177): "If a writer alluded to well-known works that the hearers might recognize, the thought was not plagiarism but literary sophistication; if he could assume his audience's knowledge, he did not need to state the source of his quotes."
[43] Keener, "Otho," 348.
[44] Ibid., 348-49.
[45] Ibid., 348-49, n.30 and n.31.

style.[46] Ronald Mellor also lists omens and portents as part of the historian's devices, which enabled him to dramatize his writing.[47]

Griffin's and Mellor's proposals might be applicable for some other historical writers but probably not for all ancient biographers. Dreams, omens, and signs certainly add drama to history-telling but to suggest that they are nothing more than a device minimizes their importance in the account. That we treat dreams and omens differently from the historians' other reports might say more about our modern assumptions about history-writing than about their ancient ones. How can the plethora of such material in numerous classical works be treated as mere dramatization or writing style?[48] Future scholars can test the proposed practice by observing whether historians and biographers repeated portents from their sources or introduced entirely new ones. Because we lack most of their sources, however, the comparisons will prove most effective in cases where we know that the writer generally follows a given, extant source.

The above observations in this section suggest that the Gospels, at least Matthew and Luke, would have made use of sources as did most other ancient biographers, and that these were sources that they felt were trustworthy enough to be used in biographies. Luke makes this approach explicit in his preface when he writes, "many have undertaken to compile an account of the things accomplished among us, just as they were handed down to us by those who from the beginning were eyewitnesses and servants of the word … so that you may know the exact truth about the things you have been taught" (NASB). He clearly mentions the existence of numerous accounts, the presence of eyewitnesses, and the fact that common information was "handed down," in the context of sources for his own account of Jesus' life. Having considered at length how the contents of the biographies reveal the sources that the biographers used, we now need to consider the differences among them.

Differences

In this final section I will address the differences between the Plutarch's and Suetonius' biographies specifically with an eye towards determining how their differences impact the general reliability of each document.

First, Suetonius seems more interested to develop Galba's character than do Tacitus and Plutarch. This also appears from the fact that a majority of Suetonius' content relates directly to Galba or contributes to Suetonius' ongoing description of the effects of Galba's rule, which reflects back on Galba's character. Plutarch, on the other hand, does not provide as detailed of a description of Gal-

---

[46] Griffin, "Tacitus," 174.
[47] Mellor, *Roman Historians*, 106.
[48] Though it is difficult to authenticate ancient writers' references to omens, signs, and dreams in their writings, it seems implausible to me that these writers would invent them on such a frequent basis.

ba as Suetonius, and seems to devote space and content to other characters, even though his biography is on Galba.[49]

For example, Suetonius has more to say about Galba's relationship with Livia Augusta in *Galba* 2 and 5 than Plutarch's ambiguous use of the phrase "somehow related" in *Galba* 3. Suetonius also goes to more length to describe how Galba trained and disciplined his soldiers, and the specific awards and recognitions he received as a result of his command of the army in Germany and as proconsul in Africa. Plutarch does not mention how Galba commanded the troops, and only reports that he did it with distinction and won praises that few had done (3.2). There is no doubt that Suetonius' readers receive a better impression of who Galba was and why he was chosen to be emperor despite his old age. These details also help to paint the contrast between Galba before and after his enthronement, especially the extent to which he allowed himself to be manipulated and used by his three vice advisors. Plutarch contains more descriptions and activities of Piso and Otho than does Suetonius, which might have better served his (Plutarch's) purpose. Differences in their purposes for writing thus led them to emphasize different aspects of Galba's life.[50]

In addition to these two general observations, some of Keener's observations and conclusions regarding Otho are relevant to our current study. For example, Keener has noted that some differences in sequence or details among our sources are due to a lack of or an assumption of knowledge on the part of the biographers and not deliberate changes.[51] Thus, Suetonius (*Galba* 17.1) and Plutarch (*Galba* 23.2) describe Galba's adoption of Piso in a public setting, while Tacitus (at *Hist.* 1.14) reports that he held a kind of imperial comitia, a form of private election, with four other key leaders in order to decide whether or not to adopt Piso. This is followed by his adoption speech in 1.15-16, and then a description of the adoption scene before the soldiers in 1.18. It thus might seem uncertain as to exactly when and how the adoption took place. But neither Suetonius nor Plutarch necessarily make a mistake or change the detail here, because it was not uncommon for upper-class Romans to make decisions by convening an advisory group first before announcing it to the public.[52] It is thus likely that Suetonius and Plutarch have assumed their readers have this prior knowledge and so do not mention it in their writings.

---

[49] Keener writes (*Introduction*, 57): "First-century historiography often focused on notable individuals, but biography focused on a single character whereas history included a broad range of characters and events. History thus contained many biographic elements but normally lacked the focus on a single person and consequently displayed somewhat less emphasis on characterization ... Biographies were less exhaustive, focusing more on the models of character they provided (Plutarch, *Alex.* 1.1-3)."

[50] Keener states (*Introduction*, 58): "Like historians, biographers frequently sought to teach moral lessons from their stories ... Biographers also wrote at times for apologetic and polemic purposes. Some ancient biographers emphasize moral lessons in their stories more than others, and some writers, such as Plutarch, vary in their moralizing even from one biography to the next."

[51] Keener, "Otho," 338.

[52] Levene, "Speeches," 216.

Another apparent difference between Plutarch and Tacitus is with regard to the location where Galba sacrificed on the day of his assassination. Tacitus reports that it was in the temple of Apollos while Plutarch locates it in the Palatium. This no longer is an issue when one realizes that the temple of Apollos where Tacitus situated the event was built on the Palatium. This demonstrates different viewpoints by Plutarch and Tacitus rather than fabrication or invention.

Another difference among them concerns the question of whether anyone came to Galba's help when he was being attacked. Suetonius claims that no one who was present tried to help him (*Galba* 20.1). Plutarch reports that the centurion Sempronius Densus defended him for a long time before falling with a wound in the groin (*Galba* 26.5). Tacitus instead names this same centurion as the one defending Piso, as Galba had assigned him, and who became wounded in the process (*Hist.* 1.43). It seems almost impossible to reach a verdict without the availability of additional data. Keener has noted this variation too and proposes that this could have likely resulted from biographers becoming forgetful or confused with details instead of a result of invention or fabrication.[53]

Variations are to be expected in multiple works on the same subject. As we have discussed, differences in the authors' purposes would affect what they would emphasize in their writings. If they had referred to different sources, then these variations would also show up in their works. In the absence of modern tools like voice recorders, still and motion cameras etc., memory is all that people in antiquity had to rely on to recall the past. Over time, some people's memories become blurry or garbled. This would certainly affect what they recounted orally or wrote to their audiences. Authors and their sources were subjected to such human frailties, resulting in some variations in their accounts. In our examples above, we see that some variations could be the results of different viewpoints of the writers themselves. The point I hope to stress through this section is that differences with other biographies or history usually do not critically or seriously undermine the overall truthfulness of a biography.[54] In that regard, biographers and historians ought not to be accused of free-invention or fabrication because of such variations.

---

[53] Keener, "Otho," 348.

[54] Audience is another factor that could cause variations. This has not been explored in this study but Keener writes about Luke's editing and adaptation of his Gospel with his Diaspora audience in mind (*Introduction*, 180-81): "Certainly Luke, like other Greco-Roman writers, feels free to vary details, since he does so even when retelling the same event in his finished narrative work, yet in such cases he preserves the basic core of the account. In the Gospel he preserves the basic substance of his sources where we can compare them ... Luke also edits to adapt details of the tradition for his Diaspora audience ... Luke's practice on this point fits what we expect for rhetorical adaptation of narratives (outlined, e.g. in Aelius Theon's *Progymnasmata*)." Perhaps we could consider using a "relationship of complementation" to describe these differences, as Massey very recently did for the Gospels ("Disagreement," 51-80). After examining sixteen Greco-Roman authors using more than forty separate texts, Massey concludes that many apparent contradictions in the Gospels "must not be viewed as a case of outright contradiction, but rather, may suggest a relationship of complementation" ("Disagreement," 78).

Conclusion

This comparative study of Suetonius' and Plutarch's biographical and Tacitus' historical accounts of Galba's life has demonstrated that ancient biographies contained a substantial degree of historically reliable information. The close degrees of resemblance between the two biographies, and between them and Tacitus' *Histories*, establishes that they were not likely to have invented the stories in their works but that they made use of generally historically reliable sources. Though Suetonius' ability to access the imperial records and archives was not a norm for other biographers, his commitment to and dependence on historically accurate data gathered from reliable sources could be a likely standard for ancient biographers.

The differences among these accounts might appear to weaken the argument for their reliability, but, as my examples above have shown, these variances could be caused by differences in biographers' purposes, sources, memories and degrees of specificity. Moreover, it is important to note that the majority of the variations do not critically diminish the overall reliability of the biographers' works.

In this paper, I have demonstrated that ancient biographers depended considerably on historically reliable information in producing their works. My findings enable us to draw reasonable implications to affirm that our Gospels, being first century *bioi*,[55] composed within roughly the same time frame as these other biographies, would also bear substantial degrees of historical content. To the degree that our present study permits us to attest to the historical reliability of these ancient biographies about Galba, they also help to corroborate the historical reliability of the Gospels about Jesus. While more work needs to be done regarding the historical reliability of the Gospels, this study provides another example of how "ancient readers could expect substantial historical information in biographies from the first two generations after the person they describe."[56]

---

[55] Keener writes: "From a Hellenistic-Roman perspective, the Gospels (as accounts of a sage) seem most comparable in subject to philosophers' *bioi* (lives), which honored founders of philosophic schools and reported their teachings." See Keener, *Introduction*, 59.

[56] Keener, "Otho," 332.

Chapter 8

Source Criticism of Accounts of Alexander's Life with Implications for the Gospels' Historical Reliability[1]

Soo Kwang Lee
Asbury Theological Seminary

Historical Jesus researchers, who often complain about the lack of or complexity of sources posed by the four canonical Gospels, might be grateful for the sources they have available when considering surviving sources concerning Alexander the Great. Despite the debate on whether Alexander's achievements can be seen as positive, there is no doubt that Alexander is regarded as one of the most influential figures in Greco-Roman history, especially when one considers his conquests of over two million square miles; his victories in every battle (especially over the Persian Empire); and his role in producing the Hellenistic Age.[2]

Nevertheless, the study of Alexander is both challenging and frustrating because not only archeological, inscriptional and numismatic evidence tells little about Alexander,[3] but also no contemporary accounts of his life have survived. What remains of them can be found in much later writers in quoted or paraphrased forms.[4] There is a gap of about three centuries between the death of

---

[1] This paper is based on Craig S. Keener's argument that the Gospels are ancient biographies, and that ancient biographers and historians depended heavily on preexisting historical sources rather than inventing events freely (see Keener, "Otho," 331-56).

[2] The dominant view of Alexander before the late 1950s was positive, arguing that his achievement was a civilizing force for the entire Near East (Droysen, *Geschichte*, 4) or was an attempt "to reconcile the world to bring together as one people all humanity" (Tarn, *Alexander*, 444-48). However, Ernst Badian first began to criticize the majority view. Later J. M. O'Brien, Ian Worthington, E. A. Fredricksmeyer, and K. R. Thomas continued to evaluate Alexander negatively, such as depicting him as a chronic alcoholic or a person who suffered from paranoia or an Oedipal complex. Nevertheless, no scholar denies that his impact was immense; for negative views, see Badian, "Alexander," 425-44; Fredricksmeyer, "Alexander," 300-15; O'Brien, *Alexander*; Worthington, "How 'Great'?", 39-55; Thomas, "Psychoanalytic," 859-901.

[3] Worthington, *Alexander*, 1.

[4] Felix Jacoby provides in his monumental book, *Die Fragmente der griechischen Historiker* (*FGrH*), two hundred pages of fragments of lost Alexander historians (Jacoby, *Die Fragmente*, 618-828); for example, Alexander's army engineer Aristobulus of Cassandria (*FGrH* 139), Alexander's historian Callisthenes of Olynthus (*FGrH* 124), Alexander's chamberlain or head of protocol Chares of Mytilene (*FGrH* 125), Cleitarchus of Alexandria (*FGrH* 137), Alexander's general Nearchus of Crete (*FGrH* 133), Alexan-

Alexander in 323 BCE and the first continuous account of Alexander by Diodorus Siculus, which would be the earliest surviving work composed, perhaps in the latter part of the first century BCE.[5] It is surprising that whereas no one questions that Alexander actually conquered and reigned, despite the relative lateness of the sources, many doubt Jesus' miracles and resurrection, despite sources much closer to the time of the events.

Granted, Alexander's activity was more widely known and its political effects more immediate, but we depend on far later sources for details about his life. Mark's Gospel was written within roughly forty years after Jesus' death,[6] and many of the reports are supported by multiple attestation and coherence. In addition, many biblical scholars today recognize that the Gospels are also ancient biographies that depend on preexisting information.[7]

My thesis, then, is that if some parts of the biographies or histories about Alexander are trustworthy due to their dependence on earlier sources or shared tradition, how much more reliable should we expect the canonical Gospels to be. Works by Diodorus Siculus, Quintus Curtius Rufus, Arrian, Justin, and Plutarch provide the content for comparison for this project.

Date of Composition: Five Extant Accounts of Alexander

There are five accounts of Alexander that have survived: two histories by Diodorus Siculus and Justin, and three biographies by Quintus Curtius Rufus, Arrian, and Plutarch. First, the earliest extant work was written by the Greek historian Diodorus between 80 and 20 BCE, as I mentioned above. The accounts about Alexander can be found in the seventeenth book of his *Bibliotheca historica,* a universal history treating mythical times down to the period of Julius Caesar.[8] The second is Curtius' ten books, *The History of Alexander the Great of Macedon,* which was almost certainly composed in the first century CE (de-

---

der's chief navigator Onesicritus of Astypalaea (*FGrH* 134), and Alexander's front-line commander Ptolemy, son of Lagus (*FGrH* 138).

[5] Bosworth, *Arrian to Alexander,* 1-15.

[6] Most scholars generally agree that Mark was written in the mid-to-late 60s or as late as 75, based on the mention of Temple destruction in 13:1-2, the "abomination of desolation," and the "flight to the mountains" in 13:14 (Brown, *Introduction,* 163-64; Marcus, *Mark 1-8,* 37-39).

[7] Keener, *Historical Jesus,* 73-84; Keener, "Otho," 331. Here, Keener notes a majority of biblical scholars who categorize the Gospels as ancient biographies, such as Charles H. Talbert, George A. Kennedy, Philip L. Shuler, David E. Aune, Richard A. Burridge, Dirk Frickenschmidt, and Maria Ytterbrink.

[8] Diodorus' forty books of world history consist of three parts. The first deals with mythical history of people (Greek and non-Greek) to the destruction of Troy by describing geographically. The second covers the Trojan War to Alexander's death (323 BCE). The third covers history to 54 BCE.

spite a range of proposed dates from 29 BCE to 226 CE).[9] It is the only extant work written in Latin for the life of Alexander, although in an incomplete form (the first two books are wholly lost).[10] Third, Plutarch wrote a biography of Alexander in his *Parallel Lives* early in the second century CE. We can estimate Plutarch's composition date based on the fact that he lived from ca. 46 CE - 120 CE.[11] The fourth work is Arrian's *Anabasis*, which contains the most detailed narratives of the four major battles in which Alexander conquered the armies of Darius and the Indian king Porus.[12] Although the exact date of composition is debatable, a commonly held view is that Arrian might have written it before 125 CE or after 140 CE, based on the fact that he was Archon at Athens in 147 CE and died around 180 CE.[13] The last surviving work is found in two books of Justin's epitome of Pompeius Trogus. It is believed that Pompeius Trogus may have composed a Latin universal history, which is now lost, in the first century BCE under Augustus, and that Justin epitomized this history probably in the third or fourth century CE.[14]

Although the exact date of composition for all of these works is debatable, it is certain that a roughly three hundred-year gap exists between the death of Alexander (323 BCE) and the earliest extant work about our subject. Indeed, the most reliable work, Arrian's *Anabasis*, to which most modern historians give priority for its accounts about Alexander,[15] was composed four centuries after Alexander's death. This gap is significant for biblical scholars who reconstruct the historical Jesus, given that the gap between Jesus' death and the date of the latest canonical Gospel is probably less than seven decades. This considerably shorter gap could suggest that the Gospels' sources would be more intact or undistorted than those about Alexander.

Scholars may well respond that later accounts about Alexander are reliable due to their citation of earlier (contemporary) sources (or sometimes due to their common tradition supported by multiple attestation). But if so, it is no less plausible that the Gospels also depend on very early sources going back to eyewitnesses, as Luke may even suggest (Luke 1:1-2).[16] So, in the next section, I will

---

[9] Baynham, *Alexander,* 201-19.

[10] Also, there are long gaps between the end of Book V and the beginning of Book VI, and between Book X (1.45) and Book X (2.1).

[11] Hendricks, "Comparison," 2.

[12] Arrian later composed a shorter work, the *Indica*, which gives a day-by-day account of Nearchus' coastal voyage (*Ind.* 18-42) in the Southern Ocean in 325-324 BCE with the natural decriptions of India. Arrian sees the *Indica* to be crucial portion of Alexander's accounts (*Ind.* 43.14).

[13] Hendricks, "Comparison," 2-3.

[14] Bosworth, *Arrian to Alexander*, 1.

[15] Bosworth notes that "Arrian's work is the most complete and sober, and it provides explicit information about the sources used" (Bosworth, *Arrian to Alexander*, 13-14); see also Romm, *Alexander*, xix-xxi; I will discuss source criticism of Alexander's accounts in the next section.

[16] The canonical Gospels show a remarkable similarity in several ways: 1) obvious agreement in the wording of the parallel accounts, 2) the common order of individual

examine the primary sources, which these writers of Alexander's accounts quoted or paraphrased in their histories and biographies.

Source Criticism: Primary Sources of Accounts of Alexander

Ancient biographers and historians often reveal the sources that they used.[17] Although they usually have their own political or moral agendas,[18] historians in the period of the early empire not only valued historicity, but also preserved substantial historical information.[19] This is also the same for the case of the accounts about Alexander, despite the fact that the sources are no longer available to us. Indeed, quite a number of contemporary or near-contemporary historians wrote about Alexander.[20]

Contemporary works about Alexander begin with Anaximenes' historical work on Alexander in his lifetime.[21] Callisthenes of Olynthus, who has been called the first official historian of Alexander and joined the expedition from the beginning in Asia until his death in 327 BCE, also wrote the *Deeds of Alexander* (*FGrH* 124). Callisthenes' work is believed to be the only history exactly contemporaneous with the events down to 330 BCE.[22] However, despite its influence on the early tradition of Alexandrian history, his work is almost completely lost.[23] Later generations rejected it by blaming Callisthenes for corrupting Alexander's character by making a god of him.[24]

---

pericopes, 3) the same parenthetical sources, and 4) Luke's explicit reference (1:1-4) to other sources; see Stein, *Synoptic Gospels*, 29-47.

[17] Keener, *Historical Jesus*, 128-29 (citing Dion. Hal., *Ant. rom.* 1.6.1; Livy 9.44.6; 23.19.17; Appian, *Hist. rom.* 11.9.56; etc); Keener also notes here that writers usually mentioned their sources when they were unsure about their reliability.

[18] Keener, *Historical Jesus*, 118-21 (citing Polybius 1.1.1). Here, Keener points out that even Polybius, a careful ancient historian, emphasizes the utilitarian value of history.

[19] Pliny, *Nat.* pref. 17, 22, "we have collected in 36 volumes 20,000 noteworthy facts obtained from one hundred authors that we have explored."

[20] See my footnote 4; Jacoby, *FGrH*, 618-828. Editor's note: As opposed to Arrian or Plutarch, some of these earlier sources come from a period with less-defined genre categories for biography and historiography than are found in the late republic and early empire.

[21] *FGrH* 72 F 15-17, 29.

[22] Bosworth, *Arrian to Alexander*, 1-15

[23] No more than a dozen references could be attributed to his *Deeds of Alexander*, and the majority of them are in Strabo's observations on Asia Minor (Strabo 11.11.4; 13.1.13; 13.1.27; 13.4.6-8; 14.1.7; 14.3.9; 14.4.1; 17.1.43).

[24] Polybius criticizes Callisthenes for his exaggeration of Persian numbers and his eulogistic bias towards Alexander in surveying the battle of Issus (Polybius 12.17.1-22.7). Also, Strabo regards Callisthenes' account as historical flattery (Strabo 17.1.43). Here, Strabo says that the story of two ravens, which guide Alexander to the oasis for the consultation of the oracle, is a form of flattery. This kind of flattery culminates in the priest's comment that Alexander was son of Zeus. See also Pearson, *Lost Histories*, 4-5, 22-49;

Next, Onesicritus of Astypalaea and Nearchus of Crete apparently wrote their reports of his voyage in the early period of the Successors.[25] While Nearchus' account, his voyage from South India to Susa, underlies the second half of Arrian's work (*Indica* 18-42), Onesicritus' narrative focuses on flattering Alexander by praising him in terms of Cynic ideals.[26] Then, Ptolemy, a Macedonian officer in Alexander's army, composed his work some time before Ptolemy's death in 283 BCE, and Aristobulus of Cassandreia, an army engineer, wrote his history of the reign after the battle of Ipsus (301 BCE).[27] The most important factor here is that Ptolemy, Nearchus, and Aristobulus were all eyewitnesses and major actors in the events that they depicted. This is one of the reasons why Arrian's work, which heavily relies on work of Ptolemy and Aristobulus, is considered the most reliable extant source for Alexander's life.

The next notable source is the work of Cleitarchus of Alexandria, which was also written during the first generation after Alexander's death.[28] Cleitarchus may have been the most widely read and cited among all the Alexander historians in the Roman period (in the first two centuries of the empire).[29] Despite his popularity, his remaining work consists of only 36 fragments, which Felix Jacoby sees as authentic (*FGrH* 137).[30] Due to his preoccupation with rhetoric, he was considered to be an orator rather than a historian. For example, Cicero (*De Legibus* 1.2),[31] Quintilian (*The Orator's Education* 10.1.74-75)[32] and Strabo (11.5.4)[33] doubted the historicity of his work. Many modern scholars also see his

---

here, Pearson points out that "Callisthenes' guilt was held to be so much greater since he was supposed to be a philosopher, a relative and protégé of Aristotle" (5).

[25] Onesicritus was a steersman of Alexander's ship on the voyage to the Indus (Arrian, *Indica* 18.9), and Nearchus was his superior officer. Nearchus was an officer who served first under Alexander and afterwards under Antigonus (Arrian, *Indica* 20). Onesicritus seemed to hold the post of chief steersman under Nearchus' command on the voyage from the mouth of Indus to the Persian Gulf (Plutarch, *Alexander* 66; Arrian, *Anabasis* 6.2.3).

[26] Pearson, *Lost Histories*, 83-98 (citing Strabo 15.1.8; 15.1.13)

[27] Bosworth, *Arrian to Alexander*, 1-15.

[28] Pearson, *Lost Histories*, 212-42.

[29] Pearson, *Lost Histories*, 213.

[30] The most extensive fragments can be found in Aelian of Praeneste (Claudius Aelianus), who cited Cleitarchus' depictions of the animal curiosities in India (*FGrH* 137F 18-19, 21).

[31] "His friend Sisenna has easily surpassed all our other historians up to the present time ... Yet he has never been considered an orator of your rank, and in his historical writing he has an almost childish purpose in view, for it seems that Clitarchus is absolutely the only Greek author whom he has read, and that his sole desire is to imitate him ... he would still be considerably below the highest standards" (Cicero, *Leg.* 1.2 [Keyes, LCL]).

[32] "Among the crowd of later historians ... Philistus deserves to be singled out; he imitated Thucydides, but was much feebler than his model ... Cleitarchus' talents are respected, his veracity is impugned" (Quintilian, *The Orator's Education* 10.1.74-75, [Russell, LCL]).

[33] "Alexander associated in Hyrcania and had intercourse for the sake of offspring; for this assertion is not generally accepted. Indeed, of the numerous historians, those who

works as sensationalism or imaginative fiction,[34] although this perspective is debated.[35] Nevertheless, his work plays a crucial role in the source criticism of Alexander's account because Cleitarchus seems to be the key source for a common tradition that Curtius, Diodorus, and Justin share (for the common tradition, see table comparing these authors' works below).

Last, some contemporary or near-contemporary works had existed for a certain period of time as informal documents: the treatises on the death of Alexander by Ephippus of Olynthus (*FGrH* 126) and documentary (or pseudo-documentary) works, such as the Stages (*stathmoi*) of the Royal surveyors (*FGrH* 119-23) and the *Royal Diaries* (*Ephemerides, FGrH* 117).

All these primary sources can be found in our five extant accounts of Alexander in citations that are normally short, indirect, and indistinctive. First, Arrian clearly notes in the preface of his *Anabasis* of Alexander that he depended heavily on two authors among the many different sources of Alexander: Ptolemy and Aristobulus (*Anabasis* proem 1). Here, Arrian regards the accounts of Ptolemy and Aristobulus as the most reliable primary sources, because they not only accompanied Alexander on his expedition, but they also wrote the accounts after Alexander's death when there was no compulsion or incentive to add anything otherwise.[36] Moreover, Arrian cites these two sources critically. For example, Arrian agrees with Ptolemy's account of Porus' son's action before the battle of Hydaspes, while he rejects Aristobulus' account by giving a reasonable explanation (*Anabasis* 5.14.3-6).[37] In addition, Arrian uses other sources: Eratosthenes (*Anabasis* 5.5.1-6.8), Megasthenes (*Anabasis* 5.5.1; 5.6.2; *Indica* 5.3; 17.6),

---

care most for the truth do not make the assertion, ... Cleitarchus says that Thalestria set out from the Caspian Gates and Thermodon and visited Alexander; but the distance from the Caspian country to Thermodon is more than six thousand stadia" (Strabo, *Geogr.* 11.5.4 [Jones, LCL]).

[34] For more details, see Hammond, *Three Historians*, 25-27; Tarn, *Alexander*, 54-55.

[35] Bosworth refuses to conclude that everything Cleitarchus composed was fictional and sensational because the verbatim quotations that survive are only five lines, which can hardly be representative (Bosworth, *Arrian to Alexander*, 1-5).

[36] "In fact other writers have given a variety of accounts of Alexander ... but in my view Ptolemy and Aristobulus are more trustworthy in their narrative, since Aristobulus took part in king Alexander's expedition, and Ptolemy not only did the same, but as he himself was a king, mendacity would have been more dishonorable for him than for anyone else; again, both wrote when Alexander was dead and neither was under any constraint or hope of gain to make him set down anything but what actually happened" (Arrian, *Anab.* proem 2 [Brunt, LCL]).

[37] "Aristobulus says that Porus' son arrived with sixty chariots before Alexander made his last crossing from the small island ... But Ptolemy son of Lagus, with whom I too agree, gives a different account. He too states that Porus sent his son, but not with only sixty chariots ... If these were sent for reconnaissance, they were too many, as well as too cumbrous for withdrawal, but if the aim was to keep the enemy who had not yet crossed from doing so and to attack those who had already landed, they were altogether unequal to the task" (Arrian, *Anab.* 5.14.3-6, [Brunt, LCL]); so Arrian's text is often read "as though it were practically the same as Ptolemy" (Bosworth, *Arrian to Alexander*, 14), even though Arrian could access detailed documentary from Aristobulus, such as in Darius' battle order at Gaugamela (*Anabasis*, 3.11.3-7).

Nearchus (*Indica* 18-42), and the *Royal Ephemerides* (Royal Journals or Diaries; *Anabasis* 7.26). From Book 5, Arrian not only includes Nearchus' narratives, which are later at the base of the second half of his work, but also the geographical work of Eratosthenes. The *Royal Ephemerides*, an archival record, is quoted for the days leading up to death of Alexander. For these reasons, Arrian's work is considered as "the most complete and the most sober account of Alexander's reign"[38] with considerable literary skill.

Second, unlike Arrian, Plutarch is eclectic in using sources. He mentions twenty-four earlier writers as his sources in the *Life of Alexander*.[39] Except for following the common tradition of Diodorus and Curtius, Plutarch often uses distinctive sources, such as Chares, Callisthenes, and Onesicritus. Plutarch notes in the preface of his biography of Alexander that he will select certain parts of the events in order to reveal a person's character, not major battles or sieges of cities (*Alexander* 1).[40]

Third, the key source of the other writers, Diodorus, Curtius, and Justin, is Cleitarchus. Indeed, since Diodorus, Curtius, and Justin share some features in common by narrating the same information and by supplementing each other, many scholars think that they worked from the same source, and call them the "vulgate tradition."[41] The crucial passage for the vulgate tradition is described by Curtius (9.8.15).[42] Here, Curtius mentions Cleitarchus as his source for the number of Indians killed during Alexander's campaign, and Diodorus gives the

---

[38] Bosworth, *Arrian to Alexander*, 13; see also Hammond, *Three Historians*, 3-5.

[39] J. R. Hamilton summarizes the earlier writers Plutarch quotes in his *Life of Alexander* (Hamilton, *Plutarch, Alexander,* 49): Aristobulus (15.2; 16.15; 18.4; 21.9; 46.2; 75.6), Chares (20.9; 24.14; 46.2; 54.4; 55.9; 70.2), Onesicritus (8.2; 15.2; 46.1; 60.6; 61.1; 65.2), Callisthenes (27.4; 33.1; 33.10), Eratosthenes (3.3; 31.5), Duris (15.2; 46.2), Royal Journal (23.4; 76.1), Antigenes, Anticleides, Aristoxenus (4.4), Cleitarchus, Dinon (36.4), Hegesias (3.6), Hecataeus of Eretria, Heracleides (26.3), Hermippus (54.1), Ister, Philip of Chalcis, Philip of Theangela, Philon, Polycleitus, Ptolemy, Sotion (61.3), and Theophrastus (4.5).

[40] "In case I do not tell of all the famous actions of these men, nor even speak exhaustively at all in each particular case, but in epitome for the most part, not to complain. For it is not Histories that I am writing, but Lives; and in the most illustrious deeds there is not always a manifestation of virtue or vice, nay, a slight thing like a phrase or a jest often makes a greater revelation of character than battles where thousands fall, or the greatest armaments, or sieges of cities ... so I must be permitted to devote myself rather to the signs of the soul in men, and by means of these to portray the life of each, leaving to others the description of their great contests" (Plutarch, *Alexander* 1 [Perrin, LCL]).

[41] For the history of interpretation of the "vulgate tradition," see Hammond, *Three Historians of Alexander*, 1-11; here, Hammond notes that E. Schwartz and F. Jacoby first label three works as the "Cleitarchan Vulgate," because one of their common source was from Cleitarchus. However, W. W. Tarn and J. E. Atkinson oppose to their claim by arguing that three works also frequently differ from one another, despite their similarity.

[42] "Cleitarchus states that 80,000 Indi were killed in that region, and many captives sold at auction" (Quintus Curtius, *History of Alexander* 9.8.15 [Rolfe, LCL]).

same information on the same event (17.102.5-7).[43] Indeed, the sources of Curtius are clearer than those of Diodorus, since Curtius explicitly reveals his sources: Cleitarchus and Timagenes (9.5.21).[44] Although Diodorus does not clearly reveal his source for Alexander's accounts, and mentions ambiguous terms, such as "they say" or "it is said" (17.4.8; 65.5; 73.4; 85.2; 92.1; 110.7; 115.5; 118.1), it seems likely that he composed his work from the same tradition as Curtius. William N. Hendricks III in his dissertation shows the close relationship between Didorus and Curtius on their sources by examining the events, such as "the siege of Celaenae through the battle of Issus," "the siege of Tyre," "the capture of Gaza and the conquest of Egypt," and "the battle near Gaugemela through the death of Bessus."[45] Moreover, the only author Diodorus cites is Cleitarchus, although he is not mentioned in the Alexander accounts (17.1-18.6), but in the earlier part of his book as his source for as his authority for the walls of Babylon (2.7.3).[46]

Overall, it is certain that ancient historians and biographers who wrote about Alexander depended on preexisting historical information about him. This is supported by their mention of earlier authors, even though they usually tend to name their authorities especially when the veracity of information is questionable. Although it is also probable that their sources might be biased or include speculation or editing by later writers, it is unlikely that they freely composed their works like pure novelists would.[47]

Nevertheless, the two main source-critical problems regarding Alexander's accounts are: (1) all the extant accounts of Alexander date from three centuries or more after Alexander's death, and (2) all their primary sources are now lost (apart from a few short citations or paraphrases). Worse, a more than two hundred-year gap between the extant works about Alexander and their primary sources further decreases our assurance about the historical accuracy of their works.

With respect to some portions of the Gospels, it is likely that a gap of only two decades exists between their composition and the composition of the sources that originally contained the material. For example, Mark's Gospel, which a majority of scholars take to be the main source of Matthew and Luke,

---

[43] "Next he ravaged the kingdom of Sambus. He enslaved the population of most of the cities and, after destroying the cities, killed more than eighty thousand of the natives" (Diodorus Siculus, *Library of History* 17.102.5-7 [Welles, LCL]).

[44] "Cleitarchus and Timagenes are our authorities for the statement that Ptolemy, who was later king, was present at this battle, but he himself, who certainly was not inclined to depreciate his own glory, has written that he was not there, since he had been sent on an expedition" (Quintus Curtius. *History of Alexander* 9.5.21 [Rolfe, LCL]).

[45] Hendricks, "Comparison," 11-77.

[46] "Taking the Euphrates river into the centre she threw about the city a wall with great towers set at frequent intervals...as Ctesias of Cnidus says, but according to the account of Cleitarchus and certain of those who at a later time crossed into Asia with Alexander, three hundred and sixty-five stades" (Diodorus Siculus, *Library of History* 2.7.3 [Oldfather, LCL]).

[47] Keener also supports this argument by giving an example of Suetonius' biography and Tacitus' history on Otho (Keener, "Otho," 331-56).

has been well preserved, unlike earlier sources about Alexander. The table below shows how soon the canonical Gospels were composed after Jesus' death in comparison to the existing accounts of Alexander's life. The table assumes the two-source hypothesis.[49]
- Each row indicates a generation (around forty years)
- A: Anaximenes, Ar: Aristobulus, C: Callisthenes, Cl: Cleitarchus, N: Nearchus, O: Onesicritus, and P: Ptolemy
- Dotted line: not surviving contemporary (or near-contemporary) work

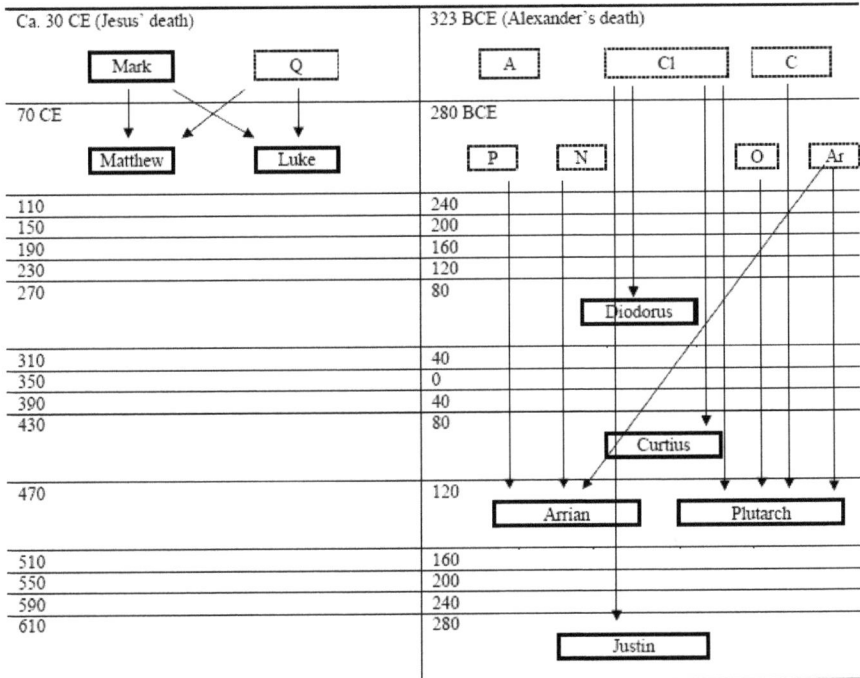

Further, the Gospels' accounts show a close correspondence among them in depicting Jesus' character and important events, while the works of Alexander reveal a noticeable discrepancy in some cases. For example, there is a discrepancy on how Alexander died ('poison' or 'natural cause') among the writers, while all the writers of the Gospels agree on the manner of Jesus' death (execution on a cross). In addition, Arrian, Plutarch, and Diodorus praise Alexander for his achievement, while Curtius and Justin focus on Alexander's darker side. Arrian portrays Alexander as "zealous for honor" and "insatiable of glory alone" (*Anabasis* 7.28.2). Plutarch praises Alexander's "virtue and fame" (5.5-6). Diodorus also thinks highly of Alexander's courage and intelligence by reporting his "achievement that surpassed those of all kings from the beginning of time" (17.1.3). In contrast, Curtius depicts Alexander as immoderate in his use of au-

---

[49] Stein, *Synoptic Gospels*, 49-123.

thority (3.12.18-20), and Justin portrays him as apt to anger and drunkenness (9.8.14-15) and not to love (9.8.17). By contrast, despite differences in perspective, characterization and details, all the writers of the Gospels portray Jesus as the Son of God and the Savior of the world. Next, I will examine the case of Alexander's last days to show the differences from one another, greater than differences in the depiction of Jesus' death among the Gospels.

Alexander's Death and Jesus' Death

The nature of Alexander's death still remains a matter of some speculation since there are two divergent views on how Alexander died. Some claim that a fever and the inability to speak both came on gradually and eventually this led to Alexander's death. Arrian (7.25.1-26.3) and Plutarch (76-77.3) report this account by abbreviating and paraphrasing the passage in the *Royal Ephemerides* (Diaries or Journals), allegedly kept in Alexander's court.

Arrian (7.25.1-26.3)[50]	Plutarch (76-77.3)[51]
25. The *royal journals* have this account. He drank and made merry with *Medius* ... again drank till late in the night ... after bathing ate a little and slept just where he was, as he was already in a *fever*. However, he was carried out on a couch *to perform the sacrifices custom prescribed for each day*...was carried again to the canopied bed and *remained in a high fever the whole night*. Next day he bathed, and after bathing sacrificed and explained to *Nearchus* and the other officers all about the voyage, and how it was to be conducted in two days' time ... and after bathing *was now very ill*. Yet next day ... summoned the most important officers and gave them further instructions for the voyage ... *He was now extremely ill* and was carried from the garden to the palace. When the officers came in, he	76. Moreover, in the *court "Journals"* there are recorded the following particulars regarding his sickness. On the eighteenth of the month Daesius, he slept in the bathing-room because he had a *fever*. On the following day, after his bath, he removed into his bedchamber, and *spent the day at dice with Medius*. Then, when it was late, he took a bath, *performed his sacrifices to the gods*, ate a little, and *had a fever through the night* ... and lying in the bathing-room, he devoted himself to *Nearchus*, listening to his story of his voyage and of the great sea ... during the night he was in a grievous plight, and all the following day *his fever was very high*. So he had his bed removed and lay by the side of the great bath, where he conversed with his officers about the vacant posts in the army ... On the twen-

---

[50] Arrian, *Anab.* (Brunt, LCL). Items are in italics to highlight the parallels.
[51] Plutarch, *Alex.* (Perrin, LCL).

knew them, *but said no more; he was speechless. He was in high fever that night and day, and also the next night and day.*

26. All this is written in the *royal journals*, which add that his soldiers longed to see him, some simply to see him still alive ... They say that *he was already speechless* when the army filed past ... *The royal journals* say that *Pithon*, Attalus, Demophon and Peucestas, with Cleomenes, Menidas and *Seleucus*, slept in the temple of Sarapis enquiring of the god whether it would be more desirable and better for Alexander to be brought into the temple of the god ... and that it would be better for him to stay where he was, and that, shortly after the Companions announced this, *Alexander died*; so it was in fact this that was now 'better' *Aristobulus and Ptolemy have recorded no more than this.* Some have also recorded that his Companions asked him to whom he was leaving his kingdom, and he replied, 'To the best man'; others that he added that he saw that there would be a great funeral contest over him.

27. *I am aware, of course, that there are many other versions recorded of Alexander's death*; for instance, that *Antipater sent him a drug, of which he died*, and *that it was made up for Antipater by Aristotle*, as he had already come to fear Alexander on account of Callisthenes' death, and brought by Cassander, Antipater's son.

ty-fourth *his fever was violent* and he had to be carried forth to perform his sacrifices ... He was carried to the palace on the other side of the river on the twenty-fifth, and got a little sleep, *but his fever did not abate*. And when his commanders came to his bedside, *he was speechless*...therefore the Macedonians made up their minds that he was dead, and came with loud shouts to the doors of the palace ... During this day, too, *Python* and *Seleucus* were sent to the temple of Serapis to enquire whether they should bring Alexander thither; and the god gave answer that they should leave him where he was. And on the twenty-eighth, towards evening, *he died*.

77. Most of this account is word for word as written in the "*Journals*." And as for suspicions of poisoning, no one had any immediately ... But those who affirm that Aristotle counselled *Antipater* to do the deed, and that it was entirely through his agency that the poison was provided, mention one Hagnothemis as their authority, who professed to have heard the story from Antigonus the king; and the poison was water, icy cold, from a certain cliff in *Nonacris* ... *Most writers, however, think that the story of the poisoning is altogether a fabrication.*

Many similarities between the two accounts probably suggest that each writer depended on the same passage in the *Royal Ephemerides*. Both report that Alexander only spoke about military and naval plans without mentioning the succession, and then was speechless with a gradual fever before he died. Granted, Arrian and Plutarch also knew another account of Alexander's death, namely that Antipater conspired to kill Alexander by poison. However, Arrian confirms his narrative by adding at the end of this account that his source (the *Royal Ephemerides*) is not different from that of Aristobulus and Ptolemy ("Aristobulus and Ptolemy have recorded no more than this"). Also, Plutarch supports his view by citing Aristobulus' report that Alexander died due to a raging fever (75.6). Further, he comments that the story of poisoning is a fabrication (77.3).

By contrast, Diodorus (17.117.3-4), Curtius (10.5.1-6) and Justin (12.15) report that the reason for Alexander's death was poison by Antipater. They all record the conversation between Alexander and his companions about the succession, and describe Alexander's giving his signet-ring to Perdiccas. This indicates that the accounts of Arrian and Plutarch are "totally incompatible with those of Diodorus, Curtius, and Justin," as N. G. L. Hammond points out.[52]

Diodorus (17.117.3-118.2)[53]	Curtius (10.5.2-6; 10.14-17)[54]	Justin (12.14-15)[55]
No one was able to do anything helpful and Alexander continued in great discomfort and acute suffering. When he, at length, despaired of life, *he took off his ring and handed it to Perdiccas*. His Friends asked: "To whom do you leave the kingdom?" and he replied: "To the strongest." They say that *Antipater*, who had been left by Alexander as viceroy in Europe, was at variance with the king's mother Olympias ... so by the hand of his own son, who was the king's winepourer, *he adminis-*	When the king saw them he said: "*After I am gone will you find a king worthy of such men?*" ... And having dismissed the common throng, as if he had discharged every debt to life—*he drew his ring from his finger and handed it to Perdiccas* ... When they asked to whom he left his kingdom, he replied, *to him who was the best man*, but that he already foresaw that because of that contest great funeral games were in preparation for him ... These were the king's last words, and shortly afterwards he died ...	The instigator of the conspiracy was *Antipater*. He could see that his closest friends had been put to death by Alexander ... he suborned his own son, Cassander, who, along with his brother Philip and Iollas, used to wait upon the king. He gave Cassander a poison, the virulence of which was such that it could be transported only in a horse's hoof ... After three days Alexander felt that his death was certain and he declared that he could recognize the fate that had overtaken the house of his

---

[52] Hammond, *Three Historians*, 4-11.

[53] Diodorus Siculus, *Library of History* (Welles, LCL). As with the table above, the italicized portions are meant to highlight those portions that are similar to one another.

[54] Quintus Curtius, *History of Alexander* (Rolfe, LCL).

[55] Justin, *Epitome* (Yardley).

tered poison to the king. After Alexander's death, *Antipater* held the supreme authority in Europe and then *his son Cassander* took over the kingdom, *so that many historians did not dare write about the drug.*	Many believed that he had been slain by *poison*; that *a son of Antipater among his attendants, Iollas by name, had administered it by his father's command* ... Now it is a fact that the power of the poison ... This was brought by Cassander and delivered to his brother Iollas, and by him was put in the last draught given to the king.	forefathers, for most of the Aeacids were dead by their thirtieth year ... When his friends saw that he was sinking, they asked him whom he appointed as heir to his throne, to which he replied 'the most deserving man.' ... On the sixth day Alexander's voice failed. He removed his ring and handed it to *Perdiccas*, a gesture which quelled the growing dissension amongst his friends. For even though *Perdiccas* had not been verbally designated heir by Alexander, it seemed that he was the chosen one in the king's judgment.

Many scholars support the reports of Diodorus, Curtius, and Justin by arguing that the *Royal Ephemerides*, which Arrian and Plutarch cites, were a forgery made in antiquity. Lionel Pearson, Alan E. Samuel, J. R. Hamilton, A. B. Bosworth, and Lane Fox argue that the *Royal Ephemerides* might be composed after Alexander's death in order to stop the rumors that Alexander was poisoned.[56] Only a few scholars, such as N. G. L. Hammond, claim that the *Royal Ephemerides* were genuine, given that this work is in agreement with the accounts of Aristobulus and Ptolemy.[57] Although it is still debatable whether the *Royal Ephemerides* is authentic due to the total loss of all contemporary sources, it seems clear that "Alexander had failed to designate or prepare a successor or make any arrangements for a transfer of executive power," as James Romm notes.[58]

By contrast, all canonical Gospels provide the same essential core depiction about Jesus' death. Despite some variations regarding which other details they include and emphasize, they all agree on Jesus' crucifixion. Even noncanonical

---

[56] Pearson, *Lost Histories*, 194-95; Samuel, "Royal Journals," 1-2; Hamilton, *Plutarch*, 210; Bosworth, "Death," 117-23; Fox, *Alexander*, 464-65.

[57] Hammond, *Three Historians*, 5-11.

[58] Romm, *Alexander*, 170.

writings of the first or second century CE report Jesus' death. First, Josephus' work (*Ant.* 18.63-64; the so-called "testimony of Flavius Josephus") portrays Jesus' execution on the cross.[59] The Roman historian Tacitus (ca. 56 – ca. 118) in his *Annals* also reports that Christ was executed by Pontius Pilate during the reign of Tiberius when depicting of Nero's use of the Christians in Rome as scapegoats (15.44).[60] In addition, the satirist Lucian of Samosata (ca. 115 – ca. 200) wrote in his *The Passing of Peregrinus* about Jesus' crucifixion, mocking the Christians who worship the crucified sophist.[61] By the principle of multiple attestation, the confluence of such testimonies suggests that the Gospels' testimonies about Jesus' death cohere better than do those of Alexander's biographers or historians. There is no basis for questioning Jesus' death on the cross by Pontius Pilatus. Indeed, several significant events in the Gospels, such as Jesus' crucifixion and resurrection, his cleansing the temple, and his feeding of the five thousand, are reported by all the Gospel writers (Matthew, Mark, Luke, and John), whatever the variation in details reported.

Conclusion

Critically appraising the sources of Alexander's accounts reveals that a number of traditions about him circulated before the histories or biographies of Alexander that now survive were written. Careful examination of the content shows that the authors normally selected the events from the abundant preexisting material based on their standards or agendas. When the preexisting sources contradict one another, such as regarding Alexander's death, the writers often name their sources to strengthen their view or to avoid responsibility.

Similarly, writers of Jesus biographies presumably drew on existing sources as well. Instead of sources centuries earlier, however, they were able to draw on sources within a few decades of their time, when much would be known of the witnesses and any other early sources. But unlike Alexander historians of their time, the writers of the Gospels could gather and check oral information about

---

[59] "About this time there lived Jesus ... When Pilate, upon hearing him accused by men of the highest standing amongst us, had condemned him to be crucified" (Josephus, *Ant.* 18.63-64 [Feldman, LCL]).

[60] "Therefore, to scotch the rumour, Nero substituted as culprits, and punished with the utmost refinements of cruelty, a class of men, loathed for their vices, whom the crowd styled Christians. Christus, the founder of the name, had undergone the death penalty in the reign of Tiberius, by sentence of the procurator Pontius Pilatus, and the pernicious superstition was checked for a moment, only to break out once more, not merely in Judaea, the home of the disease, but in the capital itself." (Tacitus, *Ann.* 15.44 [Jackson, LCL]).

[61] "It was then that he learned the wondrous lore of the Christians, by associating with their priests and scribes in Palestine ... they revered him as a god, made use of him as a lawgiver, and set him down as a protector, next after that other, to be sure, whom they still worship, the man who was crucified in Palestine because he introduced this new cult into the world" (Lucian, *The Passing of Peregrinus*, 11 [Harmon, LCL]).

Jesus,[63] selecting and editing the accounts based on their theological agendas in the form of ancient biographies. It is therefore not surprising that the Gospels show a closer correspondence among themselves regarding key aspects of Jesus' character and events of his public life than do accounts about Alexander.

By the standards of skepticism often employed in studying the Gospels, we know quite little about Alexander's activity beyond the bare details preserved by coins and inscriptions. Conversely, by the standards of research used to study Alexander and many other ancient figures, the first-century biographies of Jesus are remarkably informative treasures.

---

[63] Even in the Diaspora, churches were well-networked, not the sort of isolated communities that some historical Jesus scholars have imagined; see Keener, *Historical Jesus*, 127, noting Christians' travel (1 Cor 16:10, 12, 17; Phil 2:30; 4:18), relocation (Rom 16:3, 5), and "greetings to other churches (Rom 16:21-33; 1 Cor 16:19; Phil 4:22; Col 4:10-15)."

Chapter 9

A Targeted Comparison of Plutarch's, Xenophon's, and Nepos's Biographies of Agesilaus, with Implications for the Historical Reliability of the Synoptics

Fasil Woldemariam
Asbury Theological Seminary

In his article, "Otho: A Targeted Comparison of Suetonius's Biography and Tacitus's History, with Implications for the Gospel's Historical Reliability," Keener rightly argues that ancient biographies written at a time closer to the person's death exhibit "substantial historical information" that are not freely invented, but, instead, they "depended heavily on preexisting historical information." He supports his claim by comparing Suetonius's biography of Otho with both the story of Otho in Tacitus's Histories and the biography of Otho by Plutarch.[1]

My work here aims to supplement Keener's by demonstrating that when a biography of an ancient figure depends on an eyewitness, subsequent biographies of the same person are likely to include substantial historical information even when written centuries later. I will use evidence found in the biographies of Agesilaus (ca. 444-360 BC) by Xenophon (ca. 430-354 BC), Cornelius Nepos (ca. 100-24 BC) and Plutarch (ca. AD 46-120) to support my claim.[2]

This chapter is comprised of three major sections. In the first, I work to show how ancient biographers were intentional in providing their readers with historically reliable information when they composed their biographies. This is accomplished by showing a) that biographers prefer eyewitness testimony when it is accessible to them, which they consider to be the most reliable, and when they use other types of sources, whether oral traditions or other literary sources, it is based on their assessment that these sources are historically reliable; and b) by showing that thematic unity points to historical reliability despite occasional discrepancies. In the second, I will take some samples from the biographies that exhibit apparent discrepancies and show that those discrepancies could be resolved when the right approach to the biographies is applied. Finally, I will conclude with the results of the study and its implications for the study of the Synoptics.

---

[1] Keener, "Otho," 331-56.
[2] In our case, the eyewitness to Agesilaus's life was Xenophon and the two biographies written centuries later were those by Nepos and Plutarch.

The intended consequence of this study is to show that ancient biographers, which I consider "Matthew," "Mark," "Luke," and "John" to be, were concerned with providing historically accurate information to their readers and that they were careful in both their selection of sources and adaptation of those sources to fit their needs.

Historical Intention

Xenophon wrote the biography of Agesilaus after having been an eyewitness to various parts of Agesilaus's life. However, he had a concern that his biography might not be embraced as an accurate historical description of the life of Agesilaus, presumably because of his close friendship to Agesilaus.[5] After all, Agesilaus was his hero (Xenophon, *Ages.* 3.1; 5.7; 6.1[Bowersock, LCL]).[6] This concern led him to make the following remark:[7] "Such, then, is the record of my hero's deeds, so far as they were done before a crowd of witnesses. Actions like these need no proofs; the mere mention of them is enough and they command belief immediately" (Xenophon, *Ages.* 3.1).

In this remark Xenophon claims that his record of the deeds of Agesilaus, his encomiastic biography, is historically reliable because Agesilaus's deeds mentioned in his book could be verified by a "crowd of witnesses." Thus he denies the novelistic or fictitious nature of his work. He refers to the eyewitnesses because if anything was incorrect, the witnesses would have objected; they could testify otherwise. This remark also reflects the expectations of the readers of ancient biographies: that is, they expected historically accurate information. Moreover, Xenophon explains why he does not include, perhaps lists of names, who could prove his biography as, for example, Plutarch did. That is not because biographies should not be supported by evidences or proofs, but because the witnesses are too many to mention, including some of the people mentioned in the biography as well. For him, historically reliable information must be presented, not only because it was the expectation of readers, but, because writing otherwise neither brings glory to Agesilaus nor to himself: "If I speak this falsely against the knowledge of the Greek world, I am in no way praising my hero; but I am censuring myself" (Xenophon, *Ages.* 5.7).

Xenophon's approach is, if at all typical, suggestive for the study of the Gospels. Since the Gospels are also biographies of Jesus, we might expect that their writers intended and their audiences expected historically reliable information.[8]

Plutarch was also very concerned about conveying historically reliable information. In his *Lycurgus*, he acknowledges that different accounts of the life

---

[5] Nepos describes Xenophon as Agesilaus's intimate friend (Nepos, *Ages.* 1.1).

[6] Unless otherwise indicated, all citations taken from Xenophon are translated by Bowersock.

[7] This remark implies that there might have been reports of the deeds of people which did not correspond to reality.

[8] For a detailed discussion on the biographical nature of the gospels see Burridge, *Gospels?* (2004).

of Lycurgus were presented by historians, he nevertheless says that he shall try "to follow those authors who are least contradicted, or who have the most notable witnesses for what they have written about the man" (Plutarch, *Lyc.* 1 [Perrin, LCL]).[9] In other words, he would choose his sources based on the principle that favors eyewitness testimony over second-hand testimony. This principle is also clearly reflected in his biography of Agesilaus. He depends on eyewitness testimony and those closer to the events than others. His eyewitness and contemporary witnesses include: Lacedaemonian records, Theopompus (378-320 BC), and Xenophon.[10] The other sources he used were probably written 30-100 years later by the following authors: Dicaearchus (326-296 BC)[11], Duris (ca. 340 – ca. 260 BC), Erasistratus the son of Phaeax (315-240 BC), and Hieronymus the philosopher (364-260 BC). Plutarch's choice of these authors' sources was due to their proximity to the events surrounding the life of Agesilaus. His dependence on eyewitnesses more so than others indicates that he wanted to write a biography that was more historically reliable than not.[13] After all, why would someone use such a carefully selected and diversified number of sources if he did not intend to convey genuine information about his subject? Moreover, the fact that Xenophon is referenced more in the biography than others suggest that Plutarch uses this eyewitness as a foundational source.

Another example that shows Plutarch's preference for eyewitness testimony is seen in his use of Xenophon's *Hellenica*, where he tells of Lysander's response to the mistreatment he received at the hand of Agesilaus. See the table below, noting the portions in italics.

(Xenophon, *Hell.* 3 [Brownson, LCL])	Plutarch, *Ages.* 8
But being distressed at his disgrace, he went to Agesilaus and said: "*Agesilaus*, it seems that *you*, at least, understand how to humiliate *your friends*." "*Yes*, by Zeus, I do," said he, "at any rate *those who wish to* appear greater *than I*; but as for those who exalt me, if I should prove not to know how to honour them in return, I should be ashamed." And *Lysander said*: "*Well, perhaps* it is indeed true that you are acting more	Lysander, then, deeply pained, said to him: "I see, *Agesilaus*, that *thou* knowest very well how to humble *thy friends.*' "*Yes* indeed," said the king, "*those who wish to* be more powerful *than I* am." Then *Lysander said*: "*Well, perhaps* these words of thine are fairer than my deeds. Give *me*, however, some post and place where I shall be of service *to thee*,

---

[9] Unless otherwise indicated, all citations taken from Plutarch are translated by Perrin.
[10] For the approximate date of the sources see Appendix at the end of this chapter.
[11] Plutarch uses him as a source elsewhere because he considers his testimony reliable; see Plutarch, *Thes.* 21.1; 32.3.
[13] Xenophon was mentioned (8X), Timotheus (1X), Theopompus (4X), Lycurgus (4X), Homer (1X), Hieronymus the philosopher (1X), Erasistratus (1X), Duris (1X), Dicaearchus (1X), Cleon of Halicarnassus (1X).

properly than I acted. Therefore grant *me* this favour at least: in order that I may not be shamed by having no influence with you, and may not be in your way, send me off somewhere. For, wherever I may be, I shall endeavour to be useful *to you*." When he had thus spoken, Agesilaus also thought it best to follow this course, and *he* sent him *to the Hellespont*.	without vexing thee." Upon this *he* was sent *to the Hellespont*.

The similarity of words used to express the event suggests the possibility that Plutarch uses Xenophon as his source here. Both Xenophon and Plutarch agree that Lysander hesitantly accepts his mistake of becoming a threat to king Agesilaus and that he is sent to Hellespont based on his request for relocation. Of course, there are some differences as well. For example, according to Plutarch, Lysander came to talk to Agesilaus particularly because he was "deeply pained" having heard what Agesilaus said about him (Plutarch, *Ages.* 8), but Xenophon's Lysander went to Agesilaus "being distressed at his disgrace", that is, the disgrace of not being influential in his relationship to the king. Plutarch's redaction seems to bring contradiction and thus weakens the historical reliability of the story. However, a closer look at the text of Plutarch shows that this apparent discrepancy is introduced because he included a tradition which he believed to be historically reliable and which he uses in his own way. That Plutarch mentions that Agesilaus's hurtful words were said in the hearing of many people, together with the consistency of these words with his tendency to humiliate Lysander, suggests that Plutarch believed the tradition to be historically reliable.[14]

Moreover, Plutarch neither includes Agesilaus's speech concerning those who exalt him nor part of the reason why Lysander asks Agesilaus for a post: "in order that he may not be ashamed." Instead, he presents the reason as serving the king without vexing him. Plutarch does not include what Agesilaus thought when he heard Lysander's request either. Plutarch's redaction may be explained in terms of word economy and emphasis. Plutarch conveys the point that Lysander is sent to Hellespont according to his request for relocation without mentioning Xenophon's remark, "When he had thus spoken, Agesilaus also thought it best to follow this course." Again, this omission may be explained as simple word economy. Xenophon considered the cause of Lysander's request for relocation to be a sense of "shame" and "usefulness," but for Plutarch emphasizes instead "usefulness" and "avoidance of being a threat." This apparent discrepancy might seem contradictory, but it is not. Xenophon views Lysander's request from the point of view of Lysander himself, but Plutarch views it from the point of view of Agesilaus. These views should not be seen as contradictory but complementary.

---

[14] For more examples of Plutarch's use of oral tradition in his biography of Agesilaus see Appendix at the end of this chapter.

What this tells us about ancient biographers is that as long as they believed they were not entering into the realm of contradiction, they were somehow free to retell the story without jeopardizing its essential historical reliability. This has an implication for the study of the Gospels. As biographers of Jesus, they had the same freedom of expressing their story of Jesus within the boundary of non-contradiction. This freedom of expression should not be seen as a reason to dismiss the historicity of the Gospels.

Nepos does not explicitly mention which sources he used for composing his biography of Agesilaus. Instead he mentions the existence of many written sources on Agesilaus (Nepos, *Agesilaus* 17.1). Nevertheless, the fact that he mentioned Xenophon by name as an intimate friend of Agesilaus and a disciple of Socrates (469–399 B.C.), a philosopher, implies that he considers him a particularly reliable source of information. Though Nepos might have had the opportunity to access the sources that Plutarch used to compose his biography of Agesilaus and so could write on both the weaknesses and the strengths of Agesilaus, as was proper in biographies, he chose to elaborate only the virtues of Agesilaus as in Xenophon's encomiastic biography. This sort of imitation suggests that Nepos chose to use Xenophon as his primary source.[15]

The thematic similarity that the biographies exhibit also points to their historical reliability. All of them connect the successes of Agesilaus with his virtuous life. Xenophon comments: "But now I will attempt to show the virtue that was in his soul, the virtue through which he wrought those deeds and loved all that is honourable and put away all that is base"[16] (Xenophon, *Ages.* 3.1). Plutarch also associates his virtuous life with his successes.[17] For example, with regard to his relationship to the authorities, which eventually won him their trust and the right to serve as commander in chief of both the navy and army, he says:

> At that time the ephors and the senators had the greatest power in the state ... to restrain the power of the kings ... the kings were traditionally at feud and variance with them. But Agesilaüs took the opposite course. Instead of colliding and fighting with them ... Consequently, while he was thought to be honouring and exalting the dignity of their office, he was unawares increasing his own influence and adding to the power of the king a greatness which was conceded out of goodwill towards him. (4)

---

[15] For more discussion on this see Stem, *Political Biographies*, 201.

[16] Xenophon describes Agesilaus's virtuous life as generosity (1.18), compassion even to his enemies (1.21), religious piety (3.5; 10.2; 11.1), never defrauds (4.2), non drunkenness (5.1), charity (5.1), frankness (5.2), dedication to his responsibilities (5.1), endurance (5.2), exemplary life (5.3), hate of indolence (5.3), courageousness (6.1), obedience to the law (7.2), justice (8.8), accessibility (9.2), visibility (9.1), adaptability (9.3), self-discipline (10.2), gratefulness to gods (11.2), his respect to the devotee (11.3), peacemaking (1.37), hate of slander (11.5), love for family (11.13).

[17] Some of the virtues of Agesilaus that Plutarch mentions include: harmony with subjects (1), readiness to obey and gentleness (2), sense of honor (2), ambition to be great (2), readiness for task (2), bearing hardship (2), ability to overcome the drawbacks of physical deformity (2), good spirits in every crisis (2), sharing his own with others (1, 4), respect for authorities including gods or goddesses (4, 6), respect for enemies (not injuring them without cause) (5), simple life style (7), keeping his word (9) among others.

Nepos also assigns Agesilaus's success to some of the same virtues mentioned in Xenophon and Plutarch. This agreement of the biographies in theme adds to our confidence in the later writers' commitment to the historicity of the events they report. The same agreement in themes is also observed in the Synoptics. For example, all the evangelists testify that Jesus walked perfectly with God, that he performed miracles, that he proclaimed God's kingdom, that he is the Son of God, that he is the Son of Man, that he died on the cross, that he was raised from among the dead, etc. These facts about Jesus should be embraced as historical because we have good reason to believe that they are ultimately based on eyewitness testimonies, just like the other ancient biographies we are dealing with.[18]

The substantial overlap of the people mentioned in the biographies of Xenophon, Nepos and Plutarch also shows the historical interest of their works. See the table below.[19]

Individuals or groups mentioned in Plutarch's *Agesilaus*	Individuals or groups mentioned in Nepos's *Agesilaus*	Individuals or groups mentioned in Xenophon's *Agesilaus*
Acarnanians (22)[20]		Acarnanians (2.20, 24)
Achaeans (22)		Achaeans (2.20)
Agesilaus (more than 58 citations)	Agesilaus (numerous citations)	Agesilaus (more than 39 citations)
Agis (1; 3; 4; 15; 40)	Agis (1)	Agis (1.5; 4.5)
Arcadians (22; 32; 33)		Arcadians (2.24)
Archers (15)		Archers (1.25)
Archidamus (1; 2; 25; 26; 33; 34; 40)		Archidamus (1.5)
Aristodemus (19)		Aristodemus (8.7)
Athenians (3; 12; 15; 19; 24; 26)	Athenians (4)	Athenians (more than 39 citations)
Boeotians (6; 19; 22)	Boeotians (4)	Boeotians (2.2, 18, 24)
Corinthians (22)		Corinthians (2.6, 18)
Cotys (11)		Cotys (2.26; 3.3)
Cynisca (20)		Cynisca (9.6)
Enemies (5; 7; 9; 10; 12; 16; 20: 31; 32)	Enemy (3; 5; 6)	Enemies (1.20, 29; 2.31; 3.2; 5.6; 6.1, 5, 8; 10.2; 11.10)

---

[18] See e.g., Bauckham, *Eyewitnesses*.

[19] The references are not exhaustive in the sense that there are a number of individuals and groups mentioned in both Plutarch and Nepos that have no overlap with the other biographies. I have not included these for obvious reasons.

[20] In this table, the names of the authors and the titles of their respective works are not indicated for the purpose of saving space.

Epaminondas (19; 26; 30; 31; 32; 34; 35; 38)	Ephaminondas (6)	
Ephors (2; 4; 15; 27; 29; 32; 34)	Ephors (4)	Ephors (1.36)
Herippidas (11)		Herippidas (2.10)
[King] Nectanabis (37; 38; 39)	King Nectenebis (8)	
King of Persia (23)	The great king (7)	The great king (3.4, 5; 7.7; 8.3)
Lacedaemonians (1; 23; 26; 28; 32; 35; 37)	Lacedaemonians (1; 2; 4; 6; 7)	Lacedaemonians (more than 39 citations)
Leotychides (3)	Leotychides (1)	
Lysander (2; 3; 6; 7; 8; 20)	Lysander (1)	
magistrates (5; 6;16; 17; 24; 32; 33)	Magistrates (4)	
Megabates (11)		Megabates (5.4, 5)
Orchomenians (18)		Orchomenians 2.7, 9, 11)
Pharnabazus (7; 8; 11; 13; 17)		Pharnabazus 1.23; 3.3, 5)
Spartans (more than 18 citations)		Spartans (1.7)
Spithridates (8; 11)		Spithridates (3. 2, 3; 5.4)
Targeteers (11; 22)		Targeteers (1.31, 32; 3.4, 25)
The Barbarian (7; 9; 36)	The Barbarian (3)	The Barbarian (1.12, 28, 35; 7.5, 6)
The gods (9; 14; 33)	The gods (2; 4)	The gods (1.13, 34; 2.13; 5.5; 11.1, 2, 13)
The Greeks (more than 14 citations)	The Greeks (5)	The Greeks (more than 11 citations)
	The Persians (4; 5)	The Persians (1.6, 32, 33; 5.4)
Thebans (more than 18 citations)	Thebans (6)	Thebans (2.6, 9, 10, 11, 12, 16, 22)
Tisaphernes (9; 10)	Tissaphernes (2; 3)	
Tithraustes (10)		Tithraustes (1.35; 5.6)
Xenophon (9; 18; 19; 20, 29)	Xenophon (1)	

Every individual or group mentioned in Xenophon (the eyewitness), is mentioned by Plutarch, and nearly half are mentioned in Nepos. In light of the very selective nature of Nepos such a percentage should be considered as fairly high. What this implies is that both Nepos and Plutarch attempted to base their biography upon an eyewitness account to establish the historicity of their accounts while at the same time including or omitting other accounts in order to suit their purposes.[21]

Although both Plutarch and Nepos used Xenophon as their primary source, as argued above, they do differ from it as well. Plutarch's access to various sources and his intellectual ability to interact with his sources has enabled him not only to include stories that are not included in Xenophon, but also to expand and clarify his sources more profoundly. For example, he explains what he thought Xenophon left unexplained: "As for Xenophon's statement that by obeying his country in everything he won very great power, so that he did what he pleased, the case is as follows" (Plutarch, *Ages.* 4). Furthermore, there are a number of places where Plutarch both includes a substantial amount of information beyond Xenophon and excludes some of Xenophon's information.[22] For example, Plutarch records more events in Asia, Boeotia, Corinth, Sparta, and Thebes than the other two (see the table below). By contrast, he has no report of events in Pras, Narthaium, Phthia, Peiraeum, and Acarnanians. Meanwhile, Nepos omits a number of stories from Xenophon, clearly seen in the table below,[23] but also includes information that is not reported in Xenophon. For example, in his prologue, Nepos explains the tradition of king succession of the Lacedaemonians as a background for Agesilaus's succession to the throne (Nepos, *Ages.* 17.1).

---

[21] I will discuss the purposes of the biographers below.

[22] Among his first eight sections alone, Plutarch included a vast amount of information concerning: the wives of Archidamus (1); Agesilaus's public training (1); Agesilaus's early friendship with Lysander (2); Agesilaus's lameness and its contribution to his success (2); Archidamus's fine for marrying a little woman (2); Agis's rejection of Leotychides as his son (3); The kings' declaration of Leotychides as his son (3); Lysander's intention to advance Agesilaus to the throne and his reason for that (3); The challenge from Diopeithes (3); Lysander's reaction to the diviner's prophecy (3); Agesilaus's charity (4); Agesilaus's relationship with the ephors and the senators (4); the ephors' fine against Agesilaus (5); Lysander's role in the Asian war and Agesilaus's precondition to accept the duty (6); The vision Agesilaus saw before he waged war (6); The Boetians disappointment over Agesilaus's order of sacrifice and the Boetians' reaction (6); Agesilaus's fued with Lysander (7; 8); Agesilaus's call in Ephesus for horses and riders in exchange for military service (9); Agesilaus's conference with Pharanazus (7); Agesilaus's conspiracy with Pharanabazus (8).

[23] This table shows the places the biographers used to indicate where events in their biographies happened.

Targeted Comparison of Biographies of Agesilaus   225

Places mentioned in Xenophon	Places mentioned in Nepos	Places mentioned in Plutarch
		Acarnania (22); Acropolis (23; 27); Aulis (6); Caria (9; 10); Chaeroneia (17); Cnidus (17); Conon (17; 23); Delphi (19); Ecbatana (15); Eurotas (19; 31; 32; 34); Geraestus (6); Hellas (6; 16; 27; 28; 36; 40); Heraeum (22); Iphicrates (22); Laconia (23; 28; 31; 32); Larissa (16; 17); Lydia (10); Narthacium (16); Paphlagonia (11); Pythian (19); Sicily (3; 33), Susa (15); Thermopylae (17); Thessaly (16); Tiribazus (23)
Phrygia (1.16, 23)	Phrygia (3)	Phrygia (9; 10; 11)
Asia (1.7, 8, 10, 13, 33, 38; 2.16, 29)		Asia (more than 11 citations)
Ephesus (1.14, 25)		Ephesus (7; 9)
Sardis (1.29, 33)	Sardis (3)	Sardis (10; 11)
Hellespont (1.14; 2.1)		Hellespont (8; 16)
Macedonia (2.1)		
Pras and Narthaium (2.5)		
Phthia (2.5)		
Boeotia (2.2, 18, 24)		Boeotia (8; 17; 23; 24; 26; 28)
Coronea (2.9)	Coronea (4)	Coroneia (15; 18)
Corinth (2.17, 21; 7.5)	Corinth (5)	Corinth (15; 16; 21; 22)
Peiraeum (2.18, 19)		

Sparta (1.35; 2.24, 26, 27, 29; 3.31)		Sparta (more than 21 citations)
Acarnania (2.20)		
Thebes (2.21, 22)		Thebes (15; 22; 23; 24; 27; 28; 34)
Leuctra (2.23, 24)	Leuctra (6; 7)	Leuctra (15; 28; 29; 40)

The redactions of Plutarch and Nepos could be explained in terms of their purposes for writing.[24] Nepos wrote his biographies to introduce his Roman readers to foreign famous people so that they would draw moral lessons. This purpose is indicated in his only editorial comment:[25] "He showed as much deference in obeying the orders of the magistrates, far away as they were, as if he had been a private citizen in the Ephoreium at Sparta. An example that I only wish our generals had been willing to follow!" (Nepos, *Ages.* 17.4 [Rolfe, LCL]).[26] He selects the historical and cultural background information he provides with his audience in mind, seeking to help his readers understand his subject better. Because of these reasons, as one can see from the table above, Nepos focused only on the high points of the biography of Agesilaus.[27] In light of the distinction he makes about reputation by good fortune and by merit in his biography of Lysander (Nepos, *Lys.* 1.1)[28], his mention of the unanimous praise of Agesilaus by all historians, including himself (Nepos, *Ages.* 1.1), could also be his way of defending Agesilaus's honor as he believed it merited. Thus, there is an apologetic purpose as well.

Plutarch's primarily moral purpose for writing is also indicated in one of his editorial comments: "For even though Lysander was troublesome … Agesilaus must surely have known another and more blameless way of correcting a man of high repute and ambition when he erred" (Plutarch, *Ages.* (8).[29] Plutarch's purpose is to inform as well, as his explanations suggest.

Xenophon, meanwhile, portrays the nature of his work as "the virtue and glory of Agesilaus" and its purpose as "tributes of praise" of Agesilaus. This indicates

---

[24] For more information on the purposes of biographies see Burridge, *Gospels?* (2004), 149–52.

[25] Mellor, *Roman Historians*, 139.

[26] Agesilaus should be emulated for his submission to authorities who were above him including gods (17.4), his desire to avoid war with fellow Greeks when possible (17.5), his military genius (17.6) and for his contentment in life (17.7), et al.

[27] Nepos discusses his strategy of writing about the high points of a person's life, together with some historical background, in his biography of Pelopidas; see Nepos, *Pel.* 1 (Rolfe).

[28] Unless otherwise indicated, all the citations taken from Nepos are translated by Rolfe.

[29] See also John Hazel, *Who's Who*, 196.

that Xenophon's primary purpose is encomiastic.[30] However, it has an apologetic purpose as well since he defends Agesilaus from those who blame him for wrong doing (Xenophon, *Ages*. 2.21; 4.4; and 5.6). Moreover, Xenophon has exemplary and moral purposes as well: "I think that the virtue of Agesilaus may well stand as a noble example for those to follow who wish to make moral goodness a habit" (Xenophon, *Ages*. 10.2).

Such observations have implications for the study of the Synoptics in that one should consider the purpose for writing of each gospel together with their intended audience. For example, the explanations of Jewish customs in the Gospel of Mark is a clear indication that this gospel was not written for a Jewish audience. The extensive use of the Old Testament and Jesus's heated interaction with the Jewish religious and political leaders in the Gospel of Matthew also suggest this gospel's polemical nature. So, the differences in the presentation of the story of Jesus in the Gospels, due to the difference in their purposes of writing, should not cause us to think that they do not base their accounts on historical information.

Sample Discrepancies

Due to differences in purpose and the related adaptation/selectivity of material, we have different presentations of the life of Agesilaus, which sometimes introduces apparent discrepancies. However, these discrepancies, which are perceived by some as contradictions, can be explained, as can been seen in the following examples.

In his typical encomiastic fashion Xenophon presents Agesilaus as one who puts his fatherland before his own interests: "His conduct at this juncture also merits unstinted admiration ... he suppressed all thought of these things, and as soon as he received a request from the home government to come to the aid of his fatherland, he obeyed the call of the state" (Xenophon, Ages. 1.36). Plutarch however, presents the perspectives of others who viewed Agesilaus's appointment of his brother-in-law, Peisander, to head naval commander, as an irresponsible act against his fatherland (10). Because of this one may think that Xenophon sacrificed historicity for the sake of achieving his rhetorical purpose.

However, in the absence of concrete evidence that shows Agesilaus's action was indeed nepotism, it is hardly fair to question the historicity of the reports. Biographers today vary widely in their perspectives regarding their subjects' motivations. Moreover, if Xenophon's comment is seen in its context, it does not

---

[30] Xenophon admires Agesilaus for his ability to build military power (2.24; 2.7-8), his willingness to put the needs of his fatherland above his own (1.36), that he brought peace, harmony, and prosperity among people who otherwise would be in conflict (2.37), his ability to bring about success without bloodshed (2.27–28), his wisdom in controlling his personal relationships (5.3-4), his simple life (8.6-7), his high self-esteem (8.4). Xenophon does not present Agesilaus as a failure in any way. In fact, he likes to refer to him as his "hero" (3.1; 5.7; 11.1).

in any way suggest that Agesilaus never made mistakes at all. In fact, Xenophon's remark was intended to highlight the sacrifice that Agesilaus took to return back to his home and help when he could have advanced and subdued the Persians and received the honor associated with such a feat. So, by considering the different contexts of the stories, the apparent discrepancies can be resolved.

The introductory sections of all the biographers mention the preparation for war by the king of Persia, whom Nepos identifies as Artaxerxes. However, the objects of the war and its purpose are presented differently.

Xenophon, *Ages*. 1.6	Plutarch, *Ages*. 6	Nepos, *Ages*. 2.1
"The king of the Persians was assembling a great navy and army for an attack on the Greeks."	"The Persian king was preparing a great armament with which to drive the Lacedaemonians from the sea."	"The rumour had gone forth that Artaxerxes was equipping a fleet and land forces to send to Greece."

Xenophon, Plutarch and Nepos agree that the Persian king was building a great armament (Plutarch) or army and navy (Xenophon, Nepos) and the news was leaked. Plutarch, however, presents the purpose of this military buildup differently from the other two. Whereas Xenophon and Nepos agree on the target as the "Greeks" (1.6) or Greece (2.1) respectively, Plutarch specifies it as the Lacedaemonians. This difference would appear contradictory only when seen in terms of an either/ or approach, but it could also be seen in a complementary way. The king might name his expedition as against the Lacedaemonians, because of their emerging power, but in fact intend to send his troops against all the Greeks and their land Greece to make sure his rule over some of the cities were intact. Or it could also be that the land army was to be sent to attack the Greeks but the navy was intended to attack the Lacedaemonians, due to their strength on the sea. Or some reports may generalize whereas Plutarch is more specific. Moreover, we cannot assume that each of the biographers reported all information available to them. So by understanding that the stories are not exhaustive the apparent discrepancies may be reconciled. Who persuaded whom and the subject of persuasion are points of discrepancy. See the table below.

Xenophon, *Ages*. 1.6-7	Plutarch, *Ages*. 6	Nepos, *Ages*. 2.1
"While the Lacedaemonians and their allies were considering the matter, Agesilaus declared, that if they would give him thirty Spartans, two thousand newly enrolled	"He [Lysander] therefore persuaded Agesilaus to undertake the expedition and make war in behalf of Hellas, ... At the same time he wrote to his friends in Asia urging	"He [Agesilaus] persuaded the Lacedaemonians to send out armies to Asia and make war upon the king."

citizens, and a contingent of six thousand allies, he would cross to Asia and try to effect a peace, or, in case the barbarian wanted to fight, would keep him so busy that he would have no time for an attack on the Greeks."	them to send messengers to Sparta and demand Agesilaus as their commander. Accordingly, Agesilaus went before the assembly of the people and agreed to undertake the war if they would grant him thirty Spartans as captains and counsellors, a select corps of two thousand enfranchised Helots, and a force of allies amounting to six thousand."	

Plutarch and Nepos provide varying reports. For Xenophon, the Lacedaemonians and their allies did not need to be persuaded about the need to defend themselves against the Persians, they were already discussing doing something about it. Nepos claims that Agesilaus was the one who persuaded the Lacedaemonians, without the allies, to send troops to Asia and make war against Artaxerxes. Plutarch has yet another version. He claims that it all started with Lysander, who persuaded Agesilaus to make war on behalf of Hellas (Greece), who in turn persuaded the assembly of the people from both the Spartans and their allies to give him the troops he needed if they wanted him to defend them against Persia. Again, the reports could be complementary, given that each biographer did not intend to tell the whole story, but rather his own perspective. The divergences could also represent different sources or minor creative variations by one of the later writers.

Agesilaus's goal for the expedition to Asia is also presented differently. For Xenophon, Agesilaus's goal was to try to make peace or, if that was not possible, to attack the Persians so that they would be busy defending instead of attacking the Greeks (1.7). For Plutarch and Nepos, it was to make war against Persia (Plutarch, *Ages.* 6; Nepos, *Ages.* 2.1). Again, the difference could reflect the writers different interests and selective reporting; since peace did not ensue, later biographers could omit peacemaking potential as irrelevant to their narrations.

Conclusion and Implications

Keener has rightly argued that ancient biographies written at a time closer to the person's death exhibit "substantial historical information"; they do not freely invent their outlines of events but "depended heavily on preexisting historical information." This paper furthers Keener's argument by demonstrating that when a biography written by an eyewitness is accessible to later biographers, we can still expect substantial historical information from them. The biographers' preference for eyewitness testimony, their use of other sources based on their best judgments concerning the historical reliability of those sources, and the overlap their works exhibit regarding places, people and events of the biographies all invite us to expect "substantial historical information" from them.

Ancient biographers wrote with different purposes, emphases and perspectives and they made redactional changes to their sources in ways that best suited their purposes. Consequently, when some of their redactional changes are compared to other biographies covering the same subject the differences might appear to discredit their historical reliability. However, it is important to note that even though ancient biographers redacted freely, they did so within the boundaries of what they believed to be historical events. Thus we should view apparent discrepancies in light of the freedoms and limitations of the biographic genre.

Since the Synoptics are ancient biographies, and it can be argued that they are based on the eyewitness testimonies, we should expect them to provide historically reliable information even where they record the words and deeds of Jesus including miracles (I believe that miracles happen even today). It is true that the Synoptics exhibit differences that seem to be contradictory; however, when the right methods are applied, the differences can be explained in ways that fit the biographic genre. Consistent with other ancient biographers, the evangelists aimed to pass on historically reliable information while also selecting and adapting their sources to fit their purposes.

Appendix

Plutarch's Sources[31]	Context[32]	Details of writers
Cleon of Halicarnassus	Cleon of Halicarnasssus's letter which he had composed for Lysander and Agesilaus later wished to publish (20).	Perhaps from oral tradition
Dicaearchus	Dicaearchus's indignation on the historians failure to mention both the names of Agesilaus's daughters and the mother of Epaminodas (19).	(326-296 BC) A philosopher of the Peripatetic school from Messene who spent much of his life in Sparta. Wrote perhaps 60 years after the death of Agesilaus.
Duris	Duris's report of Timaea's admission of Leotychides as the son of Alchibiades (3).	A historian, and a pupil of Theophreastus. He was a prolific writer of sensationalized history. Wrote approximately 40 years after the death of Agesilaus.
Erasistratus the son of Phaeax	Erasistratus's comparison of the private and public life of the Lacedaemonians and the Athenians (15).	(315-240 BC) A physician of early third century BC from Iulis in Ceos. Wrote probably 70 years after the death of Agesilaus.
Hidrieus the Carian	"At any rate, there is in circulation a letter of his to Hidrieus the Carian, which runs as follows: "As for Nicias, if he is innocent, acquit	

---

[31] For more information on the figures mentioned here see Hazel, *Who's Who*.
[32] In this table, the names of the authors and the titles of their respective works are not indicated for the purpose of saving space.

	him; if he is guilty, acquit him for my sake; but in any case acquit him" (33).	
Hieronymus the philosopher.	Hieronymus's report of how Agesilaus disregarded his aids, who were in critical situation, when he has to make a sacrifice for helping (13).	(364-260 BC) A soldier and historian from Cardia in the Thracian Chersonese. He wrote probably 30 years after the death of Agesilaus.
Lacedaemonian records	The Lacedaemonian records which states the names of Agesilaus's wife and daughters (19).	
Life of Lycurgus	The power and term of office of the ephors and the senators as described in Plutarch's *Life of Lycurgus* (4).	Plutarch's own work, which depended on eyewitness testimonies including Xenophon (Plutarch, *Lyc.* 1).
Life of Lycurgus	Agesilus's sharing of Spartan love affairs with Agesipolis as described in Plutarch's *Life of Lycurgus* (20).	
Natural philosophers	Natural philosophers' view on the necessity of strife and discord to keep all the hosts of the universe going (5).	
Oral tradition	The Legacy of the Simonides in passing the epithet of "man-subduing" over to the Sparta (34; emphasis added).	
Oral tradition	Agesilaus's contemptuous actions against Lysander (8; emphasis added).	

Targeted Comparison of Biographies of Agesilaus   233

Oral tradition	The support and challenges Agesilaus experienced from the Greeks on his way back home to Sparta from Asia (16; emphasis added).	
Oral tradition	Agesilaus's technique to refute his allies who were declining to support him because of the unfair expectations from them (26; emphasis added).	
Oral tradition	Agesilau's comment on Ephaminodas's failure to drag him into a battle that suits his intentions (32; emphasis added).	
Oral tradition	The way Archidamus was welcomed when he returned home after he conquered the Arcadians (33).	
Theopompus	Theopompus's reflection on Agesilaus's view of virtue versus power (10).	(378-320 BC) A historian from Chios. He studied under Isocrates, who had lived in Chios. A contemporary of Xenophon's and Agesilaus's.
Timotheus	Timotheus's quotation which people used to express Agesilaus's irresistible dominance over his powerful enemies (14).	(415-354 BC) An Athenian General, the son of Conon and a friend of Plato. A contemporary of Xenophon's and Agesilaus's.
Xenophon	Xenophon's statement of how Agesilaus's obedience to his country won him the power he earned (4).	(428-354 BC) An Athenian writer and military man.

| Xenophon | Xenophon's testimony of the battle of Coroneia (18). | |
| Xenophon | Xenophon's testimony that Agesialus's daughter never looked more elaborate than other maids around (19). | |

Chapter 10

An Initial Exploration of the Historical Reliability of Ancient Biographies

Edward T. Wright
Asbury Theological Seminary

Introduction

In his work *What Are the Gospels?* Richard Burridge argues that, in regards to their genre, the four canonical Gospels most closely resemble ancient biographies (Gk. *bioi*; Lat. *vitae*). This is primarily demonstrated through the following: Burridge analyzes ten ancient biographies (AB(s) henceforth) noting the generic features they possess and the ways in which they display them[1]; he then evaluates Matthew, Mark, Luke and John in similar fashion; through this he demonstrates that these fourteen works are congruous *enough* in the features they both possess and ways in which they display them to conclude that they belong to the same genre.[2] His work has been invaluable for understanding the nature and flexibility of ABs and the extent to which the Gospels overlap with works in this genre.

What is not found in Burridge's work is an extensive discussion on the degree of historicity of ABs.[3] One might have hoped to find more on the matter given his conclusion that the Gospels are in fact a type of AB and the degree to which concerns of historicity occupy the minds of a large number of NT scholars. Because of this lacuna, the focus of this essay then is to supplement Burridge's work in this particular area.

Although it would be helpful to thoroughly analyze all ten non-biblical ABs for their level of historical reliability, the scope of this essay must be much narrower.[4] Because of limited space, I have chosen to apply two filters to the ten ABs Burridge has evaluated: first, instead of trying to establish the level of historical reliability for the entire biography, the focus will be on evaluating a specific topic, in this case the death of the subject; and second, only those ABs that were written

---

[1] For the features see Burridge, *Gospels?* (2004), 105-23.

[2] Ibid., 105-232.

[3] This limitation is certainly not an oversight by him, but simply an aspect or element of *bioi* that he chose not to fully explore. He offers a few comments on historicity in Ibid., 259-60, 278, 281.

[4] For clarification, 'their level of historical reliability' means the amount or degree of information they report that is accurate (congruent with events that actually occurred). So a 'high' level of historical reliability would mean that the document under consideration contains a substantial amount of accurate information. I use a 'high level of historical reliability' and (more concisely) a 'high degree of historicity' as synonymous judgments.

by individuals who were contemporaries with their subject will be considered.[5] In applying the first filter, it is found that all but one of the ABs Burridge has surveyed provide treatment of this area of their subject's life: Xenophon's *Agesilaus*, Philo's *Moses*, Satyrus's *Euripides*, Cornelius Nepos's *Atticus*, Tacitus's *Agricola*, Plutarch's *Cato Minor*, Suetonius's *Divus Augustus*, Lucian's *Demonax* and Philostratus's *Apollonius of Tyana*.[6] In applying the second filter, it is found that only four of the remaining ABs were written by individuals who were contemporaries of their subjects: Xenophon's *Agesilaus*, Cornelius Nepos's *Atticus*, Tacitus's *Agricola* and Lucian's *Demonax*.

The remainder of the essay will proceed in the following way: part one will discuss the methodology that will be used for evaluating these ancient documents for their historicity; part two will analyze the death of the subject in the four ABs listed above; the final section will discuss the implications of the findings in part two as well as whether or not those same findings should influence our expectations when we approach similar material in other ancient biographies, such as the Gospels.

A qualification before we proceed: I am not attempting to argue for a predetermined degree of accuracy for any of the works that will be evaluated. I do not have a hypothesis I am trying to prove or disprove, but I do have a research question: Are ABs historically reliable and to what degree and in what specific areas or topics are they most reliable? As has already been suggested, it is not possible to answer the question in full in the space below, but this research may play a small role in answering this much larger, overarching question.

Part One: How Do You Evaluate an Ancient Document for Its Degree of Historicity?

In his recent work *The Resurrection of Jesus* Michael R. Licona writes the following, which is an appropriate notice to those interested in conducting this kind of research:

> The past only survives in fragments preserved in texts, artifacts and the effects of past causes. The documents were written by biased authors, who had an agenda, who were shaped by the cultures in which they lived (and that are often foreign to us), who varied in both their personal integrity and the accuracy of their memories, who had access to a cache of incomplete information that varied in its accuracy,

---

[5] The reason for the latter filter is that one would expect to find the greatest or highest degree of historically reliable material here and I was interested to see if this was in fact the case.

[6] A helpful feature of Burridge's work is the content analysis he provides for each of the works he surveys. He provides a table for each work with the headers 'Chapters', 'Topic' and 'Percentage of work'. The only work that does not cover the death of its subject is Isocrates's *Evagoras*; see Burridge, *Gospels?* (2004), 142.

and who selected from that cache only information relevant to their purpose in writing. Accordingly, all sources must be viewed and employed with prudence.[7]

If Licona is right, the question that needs answering is *how*. How does one get behind the bias and agenda of the author, the cultural influences impinging upon the author, the human imperfections and the limited access the author had to the past to recover the historical content that a document holds? Is it even possible? I believe so. Simply because a document is incomplete or partial in what it reports does not mean that it is entirely inaccurate.[8] The historian's task then is to employ an effective methodology that will aid him or her in differentiating between the historical and the fictitious in what was recorded. That being said, regardless of how effective the methodology is, modern historians stand at a much greater distance from the subject than the ancient author and are always at risk of deeming elements fictitious when the opposite is true.[9] Nevertheless, the task must be attempted.

In order to arrive at a conclusion as to how accurate the ancient author is in his description of the death of his subject I will proceed along the following lines:[10]

1. Gather all the ancient sources that record the event or phenomena under investigation
2. Ask questions of the author and the source.[11]
   a. Author
      i. Who wrote the source?
      ii. What is his[12] relationship to the subject?[13] What position is he in to know the events that he records? Was

---

[7] Licona, *Resurrection*, 38.
[8] Fischer, *Fallacies*, 42 n.4.
[9] For example, various causes of events, including the supernatural, could very well be historical yet deemed fictitious by a historian who does not permit such causes as appropriate explanations given his or her own worldview or bias.
[10] These questions are very similar to and rely upon what is found in David deSilva's NT introduction. See deSilva, *Introduction*, 372-3.
[11] DeSilva is relying here upon the work of Edgar Krentz. Krentz (*Historical-Critical*, 44) emphasizes the value of these types of questions in determining the accuracy of a source: "The writer's position as an observer, his internal consistency, his bias or prejudices, and his abilities as a writer all affect the accuracy of what he knows and the competence of the report." In addition, although I believe the reliability of an author's sources to be very significant in evaluating a work's historical reliability, this essay will not ask questions of the *source*; i.e., textual reliability will be assumed. All ancient sources cited here are from the LCL.
[12] I use exclusively masculine pronouns here because all known authors of AB, unlike many modern biographers, were male.
[13] This could cut both ways. In our case, the author could be so close to his subject that he provides too favorable of a portrait or he restricts some of the more negative elements of his death, or, he could be so close to his subject that he can provide the most accurate depiction of what took place at the time of his subject's death. I am of the opinion that there are elements of both in every AB treated here.

he an eyewitness? Was he even alive during the events he records?[14]

    iii. Are there any outstanding social or political influences that might disrupt his ability to report the truth?[15]

3. Compare the reports in each of the ancient sources and weigh their similarities and differences. Take into account the credibility of each source.

In regards to this last step, Martha Howell and Walter Prevenier's work *From Reliable Sources* provides a set of seven criteria capable of guiding this evaluative effort:

1. If the sources all agree about an event, historians can consider the event proved.[16]
2. However, majority does not rule; even if most sources relate events in one way, that version will not prevail unless it passes the tests of critical textual analysis.[17]
3. The source whose account can be confirmed by reference to outside authorities in some of its parts can be trusted in its entirety if it is impossible similarly to confirm the entire text.[18]
4. When two sources disagree on a particular point, the historian will prefer the source with the most "authority" – i.e., the source created by the expert or the eyewitness.
5. Eyewitnesses are, in general, to be preferred, especially in circumstances where the ordinary observer could have accurately reported what transpired and, more specifically, when they deal with facts known by most contemporaries.
6. If two independently created sources agree on a matter, the reliability of each is measurably enhanced.

---

[14] The latter two questions come from Howell and Prevenier, *Reliable Sources*, 65.

[15] What I have in mind here is something akin to what is found in Tacitus's *Annales*, "The histories of Tiberius and Caligula, of Claudius and Nero, were falsified through cowardice while they flourished, and composed, when they fell, under the influence of still rankling hatreds" (Tacitus, *Ann.* 1.1 [Jackson, LCL]).

[16] "Proved," that is, by historiographic standards, not the sort of absolute proof available in mathematics.

[17] By "critical textual analysis" Howell and Prevenier are referring to what NT scholars would call a mix between textual and source criticism. Howell and Prevenier simply refer to it as 'Source Criticism.' For Howell and Prevenier's description of what critical textual analysis entails, see Howell and Prevenier, *Reliable Sources*, 60-8.

[18] This seems to be a bit generous. It may depend on what Howell and Prevenier mean by "some." Obviously, this means more than one, but how much more? If a document has two parts that can be confirmed, but no more, should we consider the remainder to be historically reliable? Ultimately, the point made by Howell and Prevenier is similar to one made by Colin Hemer, that when a source is reliable where we can check it, that same source should be deemed reliable where we cannot check it; see Hemer, *Acts in History*, 217-18 (courtesy of Kevin Burr).

7. When two sources disagree (and there is no other means of evaluation), then historians take the source which seems to accord best with common sense.[19]

The evaluation of the four ABs previously mentioned will proceed along these lines. The objective is to determine to what degree they are historically reliable in the reporting of their subject's death.

Part Two: Evaluating the Ancient Biographies

The methodology laid out in the previous section will now be applied to the four ABs mentioned above: Xenophon's *Agesilaus*, Cornelius Nepos's *Atticus*, Tacitus's *Agricola* and Lucian's *Demonax*.

Xenophon's *Agesilaus*

Xenophon (ca. 430-ca. 354 BCE) was born into a wealthy family of the Equestrian order who lived in the Athenian deme of Erchia.[20] He was a contemporary of Agesilaus (ca. 445-ca. 359 BCE), Thucydides (ca. 460-ca. 399 BCE) and Socrates (469-399 BCE).[21] One of the more well-known aspects of his life is his military exploits. For example, in modern biographical sketches of his life historians are quick to note that he allied himself, and ten thousand other Greek mercenaries,[22] with Cyrus in his attempt to overthrow Cyrus's brother King Artaxerxes II.[23] Cyrus was killed in the attack (401 BCE) and the remaining troops were allowed to return to their homeland. Xenophon was selected, along with a Spartan by the name of Chirisophus,[24] to lead the evacuation. His work titled *Anabasis* is an account of their expedition home.[25]

Although disagreement[26] exists, it would appear that Xenophon connected with Agesilaus I, King of Sparta, around 396 BCE following Agesilaus's fight

---

[19] Howell and Prevenier, *Reliable Sources*, 70-1.
[20] For helpful biographical sketches of Xenophon's life, which the following information is based on, see Roberts, "Xenophon," 827-30; Sorek, *Ancient Historians*, 37-8; Gray, "Xenophon," 7:266-71; Nesselrath, "Xenophon," 15:824-33.
[21] Along with Agesilaus, apparently he also knew Socrates on a personal level. Diog. Laert., *Lives* 2.6.48.
[22] Gray, "Xenophon," 7:266.
[23] Apparently Xenophon did not take part in the actual fighting. Nesselrath, "Xenophon," 15:824.
[24] Nesselrath, "Xenophon," 15:824.
[25] Sorek, *Ancient Historians*, 37.
[26] The disagreement being whether or not Xenophon was present for the battle against Tissaphernes or joined Agesilaus afterwards. In his description of their preparation for the battle Xenophon writes, "An aspiring sight *it would have been* to watch Agesilaus and all his soldiers behind him returning garlanded from the gymnasium and dedicating their garlands to Artemis" (Xenophon, *Ages.* 1.27 [Marchant, LCL]); emphasis mine. This would

against the Persian viceroys Pharnabazus and Tissaphernes.²⁷ Upon their return to Greece, Xenophon fought against a group of rebellious Greeks at Coronea (394 BCE), including some of his fellow Athenians.²⁸ Ultimately Xenophon was banished from Athens for his involvement in the war. His latter life was spent writing a number of works while living in Scillus, near Olympia, Corinth and, possibly due to a later reprieve of his banishment, Athens.²⁹

The nature of Xenophon's relationship with Agesilaus is what truly concerns us for this would supply many of the answers to the above questions in 2.a.i-iii. Unfortunately, ancient sources offer very little information other than telling us that Xenophon enlisted the troops of Cyrus in the service of Agesilaus, "the Spartan king, to whom he was devoted beyond measure" (Diog. Laert. *Lives* 2.6.51 [Hicks, LCL]). Even if we could place Xenophon in the presence of Agesilaus as early as 396, this merely establishes the fact that they were in close proximity to one another *at that time* and it does not allow for any conclusions to be drawn about the nature of their relationship for the remainder of their lives, nor does it answer the question of whether or not Xenophon was present at or familiar with the manner in which Agesilaus died. That being said, Agesilaus was the *king* and the details of his death would have been widely circulated and difficult to fabricate given how popular he was *and* the fact that Xenophon wrote so closely to the time of his death.³⁰

The details Xenophon provides concerning the death of Agesilaus are sparse. The final words of his account include, "he was brought home to be laid in his eternal resting-place, and, ... was buried with royal ceremony in his own land"

---

seem to give the impression that Xenophon was *not* there. In addition, Merchant writes the following regarding the uncertainty of Xenophon's record of the battle against Tissaphernes, "Xenophon's account of the campaign is utterly different from that which may now be read in a fragment of another history" Marchant, introduction, xvii. This remark, found in Xenophon's *Anab.* only adds to the ambiguity, "at the time he [Xenophon] was returning from Asia with Agesilaus to take part in the campaign against Boeotia" (Xenophon, *Anab.* 5.3.6 [Brownson, LCL]).

²⁷ Cartledge, "Agesilaus II," 39-40.

²⁸ Nesselrath, "Xenophon," 15:824. The language Xenophon uses to describe the battle at Coronea may suggest that he was present and/or actively involved rather than just reproducing the testimony of a source. For one, he begins his description of the battle in a much different way: "I will describe the battle" (Xenophon, *Ages.* 2.9 [Marchant, LCL]). The previous battle reported is void of this introductory remark. In addition, he provides the reader with descriptions that, while they certainly could be from an outside source, do not give that impression, "There was no shouting, nor was there silence, but the strange noise that wrath and battle together will produce" (Xenophon, *Ages.* 2.12 [Marchant, LCL]). Furthermore, he writes, "Now that the fighting was at an end, a weird spectacle met the eye, as one surveyed the scene of the conflict" (Xenophon, *Ages.* 2.14 [Marchant, LCL]). Taken together, and when compared to the fact that the other battle accounts lack such language, they give the impression that Xenophon was present at Coronea. All future translations of Xenophon's *Ages.* will come from Merchant's work in the LCL unless noted otherwise.

²⁹ Gray, "Xenophon," 7:266.

³⁰ As noted above, Xenophon and Agesilaus were contemporaries and while exact dates cannot be known regarding the birth or death of either one, if Agesilaus died ca. 360 BCE Xenophon would have written his *bios* sometime in the next five years.

(Xenophon, *Ages.* 11.16). The only controversial aspect of Xenophon's account of Agesilaus's death is that this sentence comes completely disconnected from where his reader might have expected to find it.

Xenophon's AB of Agesilaus is comprised of two parts, his deeds and virtues. Towards the end of the first part Xenophon gives an account of the then elderly Agesilaus's journey to aid the Egyptian king in a war against Persia.[31] Agesilaus was summoned so that he could command the campaign against Persia, however, the end result was much different than what he was expecting.[32] Agesilaus ultimately did end up fighting "the enemy of the Greeks" and received a large portion of money for his efforts. According to Xenophon, he then "sailed home, though it was mid winter, with all haste, in order that the state might be in a position to take action against her enemies in the coming summer" (Xenophon, *Ages.* 2.31). When compared to the ABs of Agesilaus written by Cornelius Nepos (110-24 BCE) and Plutarch (ca. 50-ca. 120 CE), it becomes apparent that Xenophon has either purposefully left out the above note about Agesilaus's death at the appropriate point or is unaware of the report that the point at which Agesilaus died was during his return trip from Egypt.

Cornelius Nepos, *On Great Generals* 17.8 [Rolfe, LCL]	Plutarch, *Ages.* 40 [Perrin, LCL]
When Agesilaus was on his way back from Egypt after having received from King Nectenebis two hundred and twenty talents to give as a gift to his country, on arriving at the place called the Port of Menelaus, situated between Cyrene and Egypt, he fell ill and died. Thereupon his friends, in order that his body might the more readily be taken to Sparta, having no honey, covered it with wax and thus bore it to his native land.	After this, the Egyptian succeeded in establishing himself firmly and securely in power, and showed his friendliness and affection by begging Agesilaus to remain and spend the winter with him. But Agesilaus was eager to return to the war at home, knowing that his city needed money and was hiring mercenaries. He was therefore dismissed with great honor and ceremony, taking with him, besides other honors and gifts, two hundred and thirty talents of silver for the war at home. But since it was now winter, he kept close to shore with his ships, and was borne along the coast of Libya to an uninhabited spot called the

---

[31] At the time of the journey Agesilaus was eighty; see Xenophon, *Ages.* 2.28. Xenophon's account of the journey can be found in *Ages.* 2.28-31.

[32] He was not given the command and Xenophon does not tell us why. Plutarch tells us that he was relegated to the command of only the mercenaries, not the entire force, and this might have had something to do with Agesilaus's appearance, for at the time he was eighty years old and his body bore the effects of old age and war; see Plutarch, *Ages.* 36-37.

Harbour of Menelaus. Here he died, at the age of eighty-four years. He had been king of Sparta forty-one years, and for more than thirty of these he was the greatest and most influential of all Hellenes, having been looked upon as leader and king of almost all Hellas, down to the battle of Leuctra.

It was Spartan custom, when men of ordinary rank died in a foreign country, to give their bodies funeral rites and burial there, but to carry the bodies of their kings home. So the Spartans who were with Agesilaus enclosed his dead body in melted wax, since they had no honey, and carried it back to Lacedaemon. The kingdom devolved upon Archidamus his son, and remained in his family down to Agis, who was slain by Leonidas for attempting to restore the ancient constitution, being the fifth in descent from Agesilaus.

When read in their larger contexts, without question Cornelius Nepos and Plutarch are describing the same event in Agesilaus's life; the same event that Xenophon narrates at the end of part one of his work. Why, then, did Xenophon give the impression that Agesilaus made it home safely when both Nepos and Plutarch claim that he died on the voyage home? Was there something embarrassing about the nature of his hero's death that swayed him to leave out these details? Was it for literary purposes? Can the three (or two)[33] accounts be harmonized? He does state that "he was *brought home* to be laid in his eternal resting-place" at the closing of his work, so it would appear that he knew of the manner in which Agesilaus died. It is possible that his description of the return voyage could be viewed as inconclusive; "sailed home, with haste" does not necessitate concluding that he actually *made* it home, but again this is not the impression it gives. One would

---

[33] Nepos's and Plutarch's accounts are similar enough in the details about Agesilaus's death to conclude that Plutarch may have been using Nepos as a source. If this were the case, then we would only be dealing with two sources not three as these would no longer be independent attestations. That being said, Plutarch's account is considerably longer than Nepos's. One might suggest that Plutarch is handling a number of different sources, or at least more than one, and more than one of these may have had the information about Agesilaus's death that Nepos had. If this were the case, then we could be dealing with at least three sources, maybe more.

expect that Xenophon, writing so close to the death of his hero, would not make such a noticeable error. Wouldn't those who read Xenophon's work have known that Agesilaus did *not* make it home? The following are three potential explanations for the differences between Xenophon's, Nepos's and Plutarch's accounts of Agesilaus's return voyage from Egypt:

1. Xenophon's account of Agesilaus's return voyage is inaccurate. He has omitted, or was unaware, of the fact that Agesilaus died at the Port of Menelaus. His later statement about Agesilaus being brought home to be laid to rest is unrelated and/or a generic statement about the death of his hero. Implicit in this conclusion is that both Cornelius Nepos and Plutarch, although writing 300-400 years later, are accurate in the details they report.
2. It is possible that Nepos and Plutarch are entirely wrong about the matter. This does, however, seem a curious death for legend or literary artifice to have contrived.
3. Xenophon's account of Agesilaus's return voyage is intentionally inconclusive. His intentions as to why this is the case are unknowable, but a possible explanation could be that he was not interested in describing the details of Agesilaus's death at this point, only in presenting his hero as a committed citizen and fearless leader. As noted above, he provides a reason for why Agesilaus made his way home in haste: "in order that the state might be in a position to take action against her enemies in the coming summer." Although the reader most likely would have been familiar with the fact that Agesilaus died on his way home, instead he is provided a more positive image of the hero, one of determination and commitment to the state. Had Xenophon concluded this section with Agesilaus's death, which was apparently due to illness in old age, the reader might have ignored the reason *why* he was travelling home and been left with a sense of Agesilaus's failure to complete his journey and the finite/limited nature of life itself.

So is he inaccurate or is he intentional? The latter of the two would seem to be the more plausible explanation. It appears that Xenophon has constructed the earlier part of his narrative with rhetorical effect in mind, not to provide a detailed historical account. Furthermore, as already pointed out, Xenophon showed that he was aware of the way Agesilaus died when he included the following at the conclusion of the second half of his biography, "he was brought home to be laid in his eternal resting-place." This sort of purposeful arrangement of his material does not ultimately detract from his reliability.[34] However, it does exemplify the limitations on how much information we should expect from ancient biographers; biographers such as Xenophon arranged material in order to suit a purpose other than strictly providing a historically accurate account.

---

[34] See Michael Licona's chapter in this same book.

Cornelius Nepos's *Atticus*

Although exact dates for Nepos's birth and death are unknown, we learn from his own work that he was a contemporary of Atticus (b. 110 BCE)[35] and a survivor of him as well.[36] Best estimates put Nepos's birth anywhere between 110-100 BCE and his death ca. 24 BCE.[37] He was a native of Transpadane or Cisalpine Gaul, possibly from the city of Ticinum,[38] but by 65 BCE he was living in Rome[39] and had made acquaintance with Atticus, "whose return to Rome from Athens Nepos, with slight hesitation, dates to that year."[40]

As for Cornelius Nepos's professional life, he was an accomplished author capable of producing works in a number of genres; history, biography, geography, moral *exempla* and love poetry.[41] Much of his work exists either in fragments or has been lost altogether.[42]

---

[35] Nepos tells us that Atticus was seventy-seven years of age when he died and that he passed on "the thirty-first of March, in the consulship of Gnaeus Domitus and Gaius Sosius", which would have been in 32 BCE (Nepos, *Att.* 22.3 [Rolfe, LCL]); for his age at the time of death see Nepos, *Att.* 21.1. For a helpful biographical sketch of Cornelius Nepos, upon which most of my knowledge of his life rests, see Briscoe and Drummond, "Cornelius Nepos," 395-401.

[36] Cornelius Nepos, *Att.* 19.1 (Rolfe, LCL), "Here ends what I wrote during the lifetime of Atticus. Now, since it was Fortune's decree that I should survive him." All future English translations from *Att.* will be from Rolfe's translation.

[37] Townend and Spawforth, "Cornelius Nepos," 396. They estimate 110-24 BCE. All we know for certain about his death is found in Pliny, "Cornelius Nepos, who died in the Principate of the late lamented Augustus" (Pliny, *Nat.* 9.137 [Rackham, LCL]). Nepos's death could be no earlier than 27 BCE, the first year of Augustus's reign as Emperor.

[38] Briscoe and Drummond write, "The elder Pliny (Pliny, *Nat.* 3.127) says that he was a 'neighbor of the Po', the younger that he was a *municeps* ('fellow townsman') of Titus Catius, described by Cicero (*Fam.* 15.16.1) as an Insubrian. From this Mommsen (*Hermes* 3 (1869), 62 n.1) argued that he came from Ticinum, since the other Insubrian cities … were too far from the Po to fit Pliny's language. Sherwin-White prefers Mediolanum [present day Milan, another Insubrian city], presumably thinking that the elder's language should not be pressed." See Briscoe and Drummond, "Cornelius Nepos," 395n2.

[39] Hier. *c. Ioh.* 12, "For Cornelius Nepos relates that he was present when Cicero brought to a conclusion his defence of Cornelius, a revolutionary tribune, in virtually the same words as those of the published version." Although Jerome was writing some three hundred years later, this reference to an event that occurred in 65 BCE seems to be taken by scholars as solid evidence for placing Nepos in Rome at 65 BCE. The translation is from an excerpt in Cornell, "Cornelius Nepos," 798-815. For others who rely on this evidence see Townend and Spawforth, "Cornelius Nepos," 396; Briscoe and Drummond, "Cornelius Nepos," 395.

[40] Briscoe and Drummond, "Cornelius Nepos," 395. Nepos writes, "After calm had been established at Rome he returned to the city, in the consulship, I believe, of Lucius Cotta and Lucius Torquatus" (Cornelius Nepos, *Att.* 4.5). Their consulship is dated to 65 BCE.

[41] Burridge, *Gospels?* (2004), 127.

[42] These works include *Love Poems, Chronica, Exempla, Life of Cato, Life of Cicero,* a treatise on Geography. For a brief overview of these works see Rolfe, "Introduction,"

What has survived is a portion of his *De Viris Illustribus*, a group of biographies written in at least sixteen books.[43] Of these sixteen, the entire book *De Excellentibus Ducibus Exterarum Gentium* and two lives from *De Historicis Latinis* (Cato and Atticus) are extant.[44] He was known for his historical acumen, as can be seen by outright praise from other ancient authors[45] and can also be deduced from the fact he is cited as an authoritative source for a large portion of information in Pliny's *Natural History*.[46] Helpful in understanding Nepos's competency as an author is the following distinction he makes between his work as a historian and his work as a biographer in his work titled *Pelopidas*. He writes,

> I am in doubt how to give an account of his merits; for I fear that if I undertake to tell of his deeds, I shall seem to be writing a history rather than a biography; but if I merely touch upon the high points, I am afraid that to those unfamiliar with Grecian literature it will not be perfectly clear how great a man he was. Therefore I shall meet both difficulties as well as I can, having regard both for the weariness and the lack of information of my readers. (Cornelius Nepos, *Pelopidas*, 1.1 [Rolfe, LCL])

Nepos recognizes that a plain record of what an individual said and accomplished is a work of history, not biography, but struggles in knowing how much of the former to incorporate into the latter. This implies that there was a definite distinction between the two genres in antiquity, but also that they both contain elements of the other. Nepos also shows that he is aware of his audience and their limitations and plans to write accordingly. Information such as this should help to establish the fact that he was a professional historian/biographer, aware of current literary conventions and capable of producing works that cater to a number of different audiences.

Cornelius Nepos's relationship to Atticus is thought by Burridge to have been one of the patron/client type, but he offers no support for this view and Nepos does not mention it in his biography of the Roman knight.[47] Regarding how close the two were, however, Nepos does note, "We know from entries in his day-book that he consistently limited his expenses to not more than three thousand sesterces

---

viii. The *Life of Cato* is separate from the biography of Cato in *De Historicis Latinis*, see Cornelius Nepos, *Cato* 3.5.

[43] Rolfe, "Introduction," ix.

[44] Ibid.

[45] Two fragmentary works are translated and cited in Cornell, *Fragments*, 803. Those excerpts are 1) "Cornelius Nepos was both careful in regard to historical facts and as close a friend of Cicero as anyone" (Gell. 15.28.1), and 2) "Cornelius Nepos the historian was regarded as distinguished" (Hier., *chron.* 159). Briscoe and Drummond are quick to point out that Gellius's claim that Cicero and Nepos were close is probably an exaggeration or just simply inaccurate, see Briscoe and Drummond, "Cornelius Nepos," 395-6 for their explanation and the ancient sources referenced for support.

[46] Pliny, *Nat.* 1; following the Preface, Book I is a list of contents and authorities for each of the other books. Nepos is cited as an authority for Book 2, 3, 4, et al. acc. to Cornell, "Cornelius Nepos," 801.

[47] Burridge, *Gospels?* (2004), 127.

each month. And this I state not from hearsay, but from actual knowledge; for because of our intimacy I was often familiar with the details of his domestic life" (Cornelius Nepos, *Att.* 13.6-7). Should this be considered an actual indication of how familiar the two were (and not a fabricated detail), then it would seem likely that Nepos would have also been in a position to know the details surrounding the death of Atticus. The following excerpt from Nepos's biography of Atticus details his subject's death:

> In this fashion Atticus completed seventy-seven years, and up to that advanced age increased in dignity, as well as in importance and fortune – for he acquired many inheritances through no other cause than his good qualities. He also enjoyed such excellent health that for thirty years he required no medical treatment. But just at that time he fell ill of a complaint of which at first both he himself and his physicians made light; for they thought it was a dysentery ... When he had suffered from this trouble for three months without any pain except what was caused by his treatment, suddenly such a violent from of the disease attacked his rectum, that finally fistulas discharging pus broke out through the lower part of his back.
>
> Even before this occurred ... he gave orders that his son-in-law Agrippa should be summoned, and with him Lucius Cornelius Balbus and Sextus Peducaeus. As soon as he saw that they had arrived, raising himself upon his elbow, he said: "How much care and attention I have devoted to trying to restore my health at this time, it is not necessary for me to tell you at more length, since you have been witnesses to my efforts. Having by these, as I hope, satisfied you that I have nothing undone which would tend to restore me, it remains for me to consider my own welfare. I did not wish you to be ignorant of my purpose; for I am resolved to cease to nourish my malady. As a matter of fact, whatever food I have taken during these last days, by prolonging my life has increased my suffering without hope of a cure. Therefore I beg you, first, that you approve my resolution; then, that you do not try by useless exhortations to shake it."
>
> When he had finished this speech ... Agrippa for his part with tears and kisses begged and implored him not to hasten by his own act the decree of nature, but ... to preserve his life for his own sake and that of his loved ones; but Atticus discouraged his prayers by his obstinate silence. Accordingly, when he had abstained from food for two days, on a sudden the fever abated and the disease began to be less violent. Nevertheless, he persisted in his resolution, and so died, on the fifth day after he had made his decision, which was the thirty-first of March, in the consulship of Gnaeus Domitius and Gaius Sosius. He was carried to the grave in a modest litter, as he himself had directed, without any funeral procession, but attended by all the good citizens and a great throng of the commons. He was buried near the fifth milestone of the Appian Way in the tomb of Quintus Caecilius, his maternal uncle. (Cornelius Nepos, *Att.* 21.1-22.4)

According to the methodology laid out above, ideally one would check Nepos's account of Atticus's death against all other extant versions. Unfortunately, unlike Xenophon's *Agesilaus*, there are no other extant records of Atticus's death. This requires us to evaluate the historicity of Nepos's account by alternate means. In looking back at the seven criteria listed above, number three would appear to be the most applicable in this situation: *The source whose account can be confirmed by reference to outside authorities in some of its parts can be trusted in its entirety if it is impossible similarly to confirm the entire text.* There are references within the death account, i.e., names of people, places, dates, relationships, etc., that might be able to be verified in other ancient sources. If Nepos is accurate in these details, then this will *help* to establish the historical reliability of the *death account*.[48] If he is not, a judgment regarding the accuracy of the death account cannot be made until additional content in the remainder of his biography is checked in a similar fashion. The following are a few of the data points from Nepos's account of Atticus's death that were (or were unable to be) verified in other sources:

- *Was he truly void of illness for thirty years prior to his death?* The first thing to consider is what Nepos meant by "He also enjoyed such excellent health that for thirty years he required *no medical treatment*" (emphasis own). Was this thirty years prior to and *leading up to* his death, i.e., from 62-32 BCE? It would appear so, especially given what is stated immediately after, "But just at that time he fell ill …" If it is taken as a reference to the thirty years leading up to his death, the following two excerpts from Cicero's letters to Atticus may negate what Nepos has said about Atticus's clean bill of health. In one of Cicero's letters to Atticus he writes the following, "I am greatly perturbed about your health, for your letter indicates that you are really unwell. And knowing how brave you are I suspect it must be something truly severe that makes you give way and almost breaks you down" (Cicero, *Att.* 7.2.2 [Shackleton Bailey, LCL]).[49] A year later he writes, "I am glad to hear that your health is now fully restored, both from the old complaint and the recent attacks" (Cicero, *Att.* 10.17.2). The first letter of Cicero's is commonly dated to late November of 50 BCE, while the second is commonly dated to mid-May of 49 BCE. If the dating of these letters is correct, this would place them both well within the thirty-year period of 62-32 BCE and force us to conclude that Nepos has made an exaggerative claim that should be dismissed. Had Nepos had in mind some other thirty-year span, given the dating of the letters, it would have had to have been from 81-51 BCE or earlier. While this could have been the case and he certainly could have been made aware of this during his time with Atticus, it would appear that this is a point at which Nepos is incorrect. There is always the possibility that Nepos made the statement about Atticus's clean bill of health in ignorance, but that does not change the falsity of his statement.
- *What is his relationship with Agrippa?* Nepos writes that Atticus "had a grand-daughter by Agrippa, to whom he had united his daughter in her first marriage" (Cornelius Nepos, *Att.* 19.4). Atticus's daughter was named Caecilia Attica and was in fact married to Agrippa ca. 37 BCE.[50] Their marriage did not last long as she was apparently involved or at least

---

[48] Not the entire biography; see n.16 above. I think Howell and Prevenier are being a touch too generous here.

[49] All English translations of Cicero's *Att.* will come from D. R. Shackleton Bailey's translation in the LCL.

[50] At least according to the *OCD*, see Cadoux and Badian, "Caecilia Attica," 267.

accused of being involved in an extramarital affair with her tutor Caecilius Epirota.⁵¹ Agrippa remarried ca. 28 BCE.⁵² Given the fact that Agrippa did not remarry until after Atticus's death, it is certainly reasonable to conclude that he and Atticus were in good standing at the time of the latter's death and that Agrippa would have been present had Atticus requested it.

- *Who were Lucius Cornelius Balbus and Sextus Peducaeus? Were they known affiliates of Atticus?* According to the *Oxford Classical Dictionary* there are two known men named Lucius Cornelius Balbus in antiquity; the first was the famed consul of Octavian who was defended by Cicero in his *Pro Balbo*.⁵³ The other was the nephew of the elder Balbus.⁵⁴ The elder Balbus was born in Gades, obtained Roman citizenship from Pompey in 72 BCE and served Julius Caesar as one of his most trusted advisors from ca. 60 BCE to the time of his death.⁵⁵ He is mentioned in Cicero's *Att.* on numerous occasions: as being with Atticus,⁵⁶ as being present with Cicero in Puteoli,⁵⁷ and several times in passing. While certainty eludes us, it would appear that Atticus and Balbus had a close enough relationship to conclude that Balbus could have been present at the death of Atticus. Even less can be said about Sextus Peducaeus. He is mentioned throughout Cicero's works, including his letters to Atticus.⁵⁸ The contexts in which he is mentioned in Cicero's letters to Atticus show that the three of them had a friendship and a lengthy one at that, considering the letters where Peducaeus is mentioned are dated 68–44BCE. Overall, the evidence is minimal, but there is little reason to doubt both Balbus's and Peducaeus's presence at the time of Atticus's death.

- *Would Nepos have been able to acquire/verify the testimony of the three (Agrippa, Balbus and Peducaeus) individuals mentioned? Did he have a known relationship with any of them?* This is the only time in all of Nepos's extant works that these three individuals are mentioned so it is difficult to determine whether or not Nepos knew them or if he would have had access to their testimony following Atticus's death. That being said, if Atticus and Nepos were as close as the latter said they were, then it would seem likely that Nepos would have also been in contact with Atticus's friends, but to what degree and whether or not it was cordial is unknowable. Furthermore, Nepos is known to have corresponded with

---

⁵¹ Ibid.
⁵² Richardson, et al., "Vipsanius Agrippa, Marcus," 1601-1602.
⁵³ Chilver and Seager, "Cornelius Balbus (1), Lucius," 392.
⁵⁴ Cadoux and Seager, "Cornelius Balbus (2), Lucius," 392.
⁵⁵ Smith and Cornell, "L. Cornelius Balbus," 383-4.
⁵⁶ Cicero, *Att.* 10.18.3.
⁵⁷ Ibid., 14.10.3.
⁵⁸ Ibid., 1.5.4; 7.13.3; 15.13.3 etc.

Cicero[59] and while the nature of their relationship is debated[60] this would further demonstrate the interconnectedness of all the individuals under consideration (Cicero, Atticus, Balbus, Peducaeus and Nepos)[61] and the likelihood that Nepos would have had access to their testimony.

- *Who were Gnaeus Domitius and Gaius Sosius? Were they in office during this time?* Gnaeus Domitius Ahenobarbus and Gaius Sosius were in fact both consuls in 32 BCE.[62] Even without the witness of Dio Cassius (150-235 CE), it would be difficult to fathom that a biographer/historian would be incorrect on a detail like this considering how easily verifiable a fact like this would have been for his audience in public Roman archives.

- *Was his uncle Quintus Caecilius?* Earlier in the biography Nepos tells his reader that Quintus Caecilius was a Roman knight, a friend of Lucius Lucullus, and that he was very wealthy and very hard to please. Atticus was able to endear his uncle towards him and as a result was officially adopted by Caecilius. This ultimately resulted in Atticus acquiring three-quarters of his estate upon his passing, valued at nearly ten million sesterces. This, Rolfe, the modern translator of Nepos's work, tells us, took place in 58 BCE.[63] Interestingly enough we do find confirmation of Atticus's relationship to Caecilius in a letter from Cicero to Atticus. Cicero calls Caecilius his uncle and refers to him on multiple occasions.[64]

Aside from the inaccurate information Nepos provides concerning the clean bill of health that Atticus had prior to his death, the account that Nepos provides appears to include a considerable amount of accurate information. The names, dates and relationships he has chosen to highlight are all congruent with what we know from outside authorities. Some aspects of the story are embellished, and it would be difficult to say with certainty that the recorded speech of both Atticus and Agrippa are a record of what was actually said. Nevertheless, given the criteria we are using to evaluate these documents it seems reasonable to conclude that Nepos has generally accurately reported the death of his subject.

---

[59] Cicero, *Lett. Fr.* 2.1-2.5; 2A.
[60] Briscoe and Drummond, "Cornelius Nepos," 395-6.
[61] Cicero corresponded frequently with Atticus and mentions both Balbus and Peducaeus, the former in a very positive manner. Nepos claims that he is intimately associated with Atticus and also mentions both Balbus and Peducaeus as being bed side at the death of Atticus. Finally, Nepos's correspondence with Cicero shows how all five of them are in some manner a part of the same social network.
[62] Dio Cassius, *Rom. Hist.* 5.50.1.
[63] Cornelius Nepos, *Att.* 5.1-5.2.
[64] Cicero, *Att.* 1.1.3-1.1.4.

Tacitus's *Agricola*

Cornelius Tacitus (ca. 55-ca. 120 CE)[65] was known for his accomplishments in both the political and literary spheres of his day. In regards to the latter, Tacitus's complete oeuvre includes the following: *Agricola, Germania, Dialogus de oratoribus, Historiae* and *Annales*.[66] Both *Annales* and *Historiae* are works of ancient historiography. *Annales* covers the period from Tiberius's accession (14 CE) to the death of Nero (68 CE), while *Historiae*, although written prior to *Annales*, covers a later time period of 69 CE to the downfall of Domitian in 96 CE.[67] Unfortunately, with regards to both, what remains of these two works is only a fraction of what was originally written.[68] That being said, Woodman notes that because of these two works Tacitus is "more responsible for our view of the early Roman Empire than any other ancient historian."[69]

As for his political career Tacitus flourished throughout the Flavian dynasty and the reigns of both Nerva and Trajan as he was asked to serve in a number of different capacities. He states in his *Historiae*, "I cannot deny that my political career owed its beginning to Vespasian; that Titus advanced it; and that Domitian carried it further" (Tacitus, *Historiae* 1.1 [Moore, LCL]). Most likely, Tacitus is referring to his roles as quaestor (81 CE), praetor (88 CE), quindecimuiri (88 CE) and suffect consul (97 CE).[70] The pinnacle of his political career came in 112 CE when he was named proconsul of Asia.[71]

While the above material is certainly relevant to our discussion, our concern is with the nature of his relationship with Agricola, who was also a very powerful figure in the political arena during his day (40-93 CE). Their connection is distinctive in comparison to the other author/subject relationships under consideration, for Tacitus married the daughter of Agricola ca. 76/77 CE.[72] This connection

---

[65] Woodman, "Tacitus," 6:419-23, Woodman notes ca. 56 CE as the date of his birth; Flaig, "Tacitus," 14:105-11.

[66] The works listed above are in the order purportedly to have been written. Dates according to Woodman: *Agricola* (began in 97-98 CE, roughly five years after the death of Agricola); *Germania* (appeared ca. 98 CE); *Dialogus de oratoribus* (date unknown, Woodman suggests 102 CE when "Fabius Justus, to whom the work was dedicated, was consul"); *Historiae* (Tacitus was at work on the project in 105-106 CE); *Annales* (at work on the project in 114-155 CE). Dates can be found in Woodman, "Tacitus," 6:419-21.

[67] Flaig, "Tacitus," 14:106.

[68] Of the *Historiae*, the first four books and a part of the fifth, out of twelve or fourteen books, survive today. Of the *Annales*, books 1-4, 12-15, and fragments of book 5, 6, 11 and 16 survive; Flaig, "Tacitus," 14:106.

[69] Woodman, "Tacitus," 6:422.

[70] These offices and their dates are recorded in a number of secondary sources; Woodman, "Tacitus," 6:419; Flaig, "Tacitus," 14:105; Martin, "Tacitus," 1469-1471.

[71] Woodman, "Tacitus," 6:419.

[72] Tacitus writes, "The consul betrothed his daughter, already a girl of great promise, to me, then in my youth. On the conclusion of his office he placed her hand in mine, and immediately afterwards was gazette to Britain, the priestly office of pontiff accompanying his promotion" (Tacitus, *Agr.* 9.6 [Hutton and Ogilvie, LCL]). Agricola was governor of

should have provided Tacitus with unique access to the details surrounding Agricola's life that others may not have had and it should allow for the modern observer to view Tacitus's biography as trustworthy unless proven otherwise. This does not excuse the modern historian from distinguishing between what is overly encomiastic or biased and what is historical bedrock, but in a similar vein it should prohibit the modern historian from approaching Tacitus's biography with a high degree of skepticism. What is interesting, however, is that neither Tacitus nor his wife were present at the time of death of Agricola, the one aspect of Tacitus's biography that most concerns us. Tacitus writes,

> Yet to me and to his daughter, besides the bitterness of a father's loss, it is an added grief that it was denied us to sit beside his bed of sickness, to comfort his fainting spirit, to take our fill of gazing and embrace. At least we had then received some message, some utterance to lay deeply to heart. This grief was peculiarly ours ... that by the circumstance of our long absence he was lost to us four years too soon. (Tacitus, *Agr.* 45.4).

Where one would have hoped to have found eyewitness testimony by the author himself, instead what *is* found is that Tacitus and his wife were quite removed from the event only to be aware of it through "some message". That being said, it still seems safe to assume that Tacitus was well-informed or even had access to other eyewitness testimony concerning the passing of Agricola, especially if one considers true what Tacitus writes about Agricola's wife being at Agricola's bedside at the time of the latter's death (Tacitus, *Agr.* 45.5). The following excerpt from Tacitus's *Agricola* details what Tacitus knew about the death of his father-in-law:

> The end of his life brought mourning to us, melancholy to his friends, anxiety even to the bystander and those who knew him not; the great public itself and this busy, preoccupied city came repeatedly to his doors, and talked of him in public gatherings and private circles. No one, on hearing of Agricola's death, was glad, nor – at once – forgetful. Commiseration was enhanced by the persistent rumor that he had been put out of the way by poison. I would not venture to assert that we have any firm evidence.
>
> However it be, throughout his illness came the chief freedmen and the confidential physicians of the Palace with a regularity unusual in a prince who visits by deputy, whether this was interest or espionage.
>
> When the end came, every flicker of the failing life, it was well known, was chronicled by relays of runners, and nobody believed that this news was hurried up in this way in order that Domitian should be sad when he heard it. Yet in his manner and in his features he did show an appearance of grief; his hate was now no longer anxious, and it was his temperament to hide joy more easily than fear. It was well ascertained that on reading the will of Agricola, which named Domitian co-heir with the best of wives, the most dutiful of daughters, he was delighted at the honor and approval. So blinded, so perverted was his intelligence by unremitting flattery that he did not see that it is the bad prince who is made heir by good fathers.

Britain for seven years from 77-84 CE; Martin, "Tacitus," 1469 All future English translations of Tacitus's *Agr.* will come from the LCL edition.

Agricola was born on 13 June, in the third consulship of Gaius Caesar; he died in his fifty-fourth year on 23 August, in the consulship of Collega and Priscinus. (Tacitus, *Agr.* 43.1-44.1)

Unfortunately, the limited information on Agricola's death presents us with a situation similar to that of Cornelius Nepos's *Atticus*. The only other ancient author that even mentions Agricola is Dio Cassius (ca. 164-ca. 229 CE) in his *Roman History*. He notes that Agricola was the first to discover that Britain was an island[73] and in the subsequent paragraph offers the following verdict about Agricola's death, "Finally, he was murdered by Domitian for no other reason than this,[74] in spite of his having received triumphal honors from Titus" (Dio Cassius, *Rom. Hist.* 66.20.3 [Cary, LCL]).

This statement about Agricola's death is of obvious importance and while it does not contradict what Tacitus has said, there is a noticeable difference. In Tacitus's statement about Agricola being poisoned he makes clear that he has decided to reserve judgment on the matter due to lack of evidence. Dio Cassius does no such thing and claims outright that Agricola was murdered. Would Tacitus really have had to reserve judgment on the matter due to concerns over lack of evidence when he wrote nearly four to five years after the fact? Furthermore, given the fact that Domitian was murdered in 96 CE, shortly before *Agricola* was written, and the negative perception of that emperor commonly held by members of the Roman upper class, it would seem reasonable to conclude that Tacitus was free to write the truth if in fact Domitian had murdered Agricola.[75]

Instead, Tacitus refrains and we are left wondering if there really was indeed a lack of evidence or if Tacitus has backed away from labeling Domitian as the murderer of his father-in-law for some other reason, possibly an act of political expediency. Another possible explanation could be that because Tacitus was writing biography, not history, and since a major purpose of a biography was to offer a positive portrayal of your subject, including a detail about his assassination might have led some remaining supporters of Domitian to believe that Agricola deserved it, thereby polluting the portrayal and making it negative. Likeliest of

---

[73] This is noted in both Tacitus and Dio Cassius, although it should not be assumed that Dio was an independent witness to this fact. He was undoubtedly working with a source, which may have even been Tacitus's *Agricola*. See Tacitus, *Agr.* 10.5 and Dio Cassius, *Rom. Hist.* 66.20.1.

[74] The "this" refers to the previous line where Dio writes, "But Agricola for the rest of his life lived not only in disgrace but in actual want, because the deeds which he had wrought were too great for a mere general" (Dio Cassius, *Rom. Hist.* 66.20.1 [Cary, LCL]).

[75] My assessment that the upper class's perception of Domitian was negative is based on the fact that his memory was condemned by the senate, an action commonly labeled *damnatio memoriae*. Suetonius writes of Domitian, "The senators on the contrary were so overjoyed that they raced to fill the House, where they did not refrain from assailing the dead emperor with the most insulting and stinging kind of outcries. They even had ladders brought and his shields and images torn down before their eyes and dashed upon the ground; finally they passed a decree that his inscriptions should everywhere be erased, and all record of him obliterated" (Suetonius, *Dom.* 23 [Rolfe, LCL]). For a further explanation of the *damnatio memoriae*, see Balsdon and Levick, "damnatio memoriae," 427.

all, however, is that public hostility toward Domitian's memory solidified suspicion in the years that followed, or that Dio regards the report of Agricola's murder too in keeping with Domitian's character to admit of reasonable doubt.

Aside from this difference in what is recorded concerning Agricola's death, there are no other elements of Tacitus's brief account that could not have been supplied by his mother-in-law who, as previously mentioned, was present at the bedside of Agricola when he passed. In addition, Tacitus also mentions that the end of Agricola's life was "chronicled by relays of runners." The knowledge these informants had of Agricola's death could easily have been accessed by Tacitus given his political influence and, furthermore, given that he was writing so close to the time of his subject's death, these informants were most likely still alive. Considering what Howell and Prevenier have said about eyewitness testimony (see number 5 above), and given the likelihood that Tacitus had access to it, there is little reason to conclude that Tacitus does not provide an accurate account of Agricola's death and the events that immediately surrounded it.

Lucian's *Demonax*

Very little is known about our final author and what is recorded in modern encyclopedias and dictionaries is often fronted with the language of uncertainty. The common dates given for his life are b. ca. 115-125 CE and d. ca. 180-190 CE. Recent biographical sketches cover much of the same ground: he was born in Samosata on the Euphrates river; educated at Ionia; travelled extensively as a professional rhetorician; was a known satirist; spent considerable time in Athens; and possibly took on a post in the government of Egypt latter in life.[76] Lucian is best known for the eighty-two pieces of literature that were attributed to him in antiquity, although many are considered spurious.[77] What is most impressive concerning Lucian's catalogue of literary works is the range he displays in the different genres he navigates: fictional works, non-fictional works, rhetorical declamations, rhetorical introductions, moralizing texts, satires, romances and dialogues.[78] Our concern obviously lies with his non-fictional works, specifically his biography of Demonax, and the relationship the two of them had. Eunapius's (b. 347 CE) comments on Lucian's *Demonax* may be relevant. He reports, "Lucian of Samosata,

---

[76] Helpful sketches of Lucian's life can be found in Whitmarsh, "Lucian of Samosata," 4:288-291; Nesselrath, "Lucianus," 7:836-845; Harmon, "Introduction," ix-xii. All English translations of *Demonax* will come from Harmon's LCL edition unless noted otherwise.

[77] Harmon notes the following, "Among the eighty-two pieces that have come down to us under the name of Lucian, there are not a few of which his authorship has been disputed. Certainly spurious are *Halcyon, Nero, Philopatris,* and *Astrology*; and to these, it seems to me, the *Consonants at Law* should be added. Furthermore, *Demosthenes, Charidemus, Cynic, Love, Octogenarians, Hippias, Ungrammatical Man, Swiftfoot,* and the epigrams are generally considered spurious, and there are several others (*Disowned* and *My Country* in particular) which, to say the least, are of doubtful authenticity." See Harmon, "Introduction," xi.

[78] Whitmarsh breaks down Lucian's works into these categories; Whitmarsh, "Lucian of Samosata," 4:288.

who usually took serious pains to raise a laugh, wrote a life of Demonax, a philosopher of his own time, and in that book and a very few others was wholly serious throughout" (Eunapius, *Lives of the Philosophers* 454 [Wright, LCL]). Evaluative comments such as these, from relative contemporaries, are helpful in determining how readers even further removed from the time of writing should approach the book.

Lucian begins his biography of Demonax (b. ca. 70-80 CE – d. ca. 170-180 CE)[79] by introducing him as a man of "enormous physical prowess and a philosophic mind" and telling his audience that Demonax was his tutor for an apparently extended period of time (Lucian, *Dem.* 1). Overall, his work is neatly framed by his stated purposes for writing. He notes at the outset:

> It is now fitting to tell of Demonax for two reasons – that he may be retained in memory by men of culture as far as I can bring it about, and that young men of good instincts who aspire to philosophy may not have to shape themselves by ancient precedents alone, but may be able to set themselves a pattern from our modern world and to copy that man, the best of all the philosophers whom I know about. (Lucian, *Dem.* 1)

At the end of his book he writes, "These are a very few things out of many which I might have mentioned, but they will suffice to give my readers a notion of the sort of man he was" (Lucian, *Dem.* 67). Within this framework Lucian paints a portrait of Demonax by highlighting his positive attributes, actions, and elements of his philosophy. Lucian portrays Demonax as someone who was kind, gentle, selfless, free from materialistic concerns, a friend to all, honest, etc. (Lucian, *Dem.* passim). In addition to outright declarations about Demonax' character, Lucian offers a portrayal of his subject through a continuous stream of *chreiai* or apothegms.[80] Through these we get a sense of Demonax' wit and one reason why his student Lucian was so successful as a satirist. For instance, Lucian records the following, "A Roman senator in Athens introduced his son to him, a handsome boy, but girlish and neurasthenic, saying: 'My son here pays his respects to you.' 'A dear boy,' said Demonax, 'worthy of you and like his mother!'" (Lucian, *Dem.*

---

[79] These dates are very tentatively held. Lucian tells us that he lived to be about one hundred years old (*Dem.* 63) and that they were contemporaries for a rather lengthy period of time (*Dem.* 1). Lucian tells his audience about an interaction Demonax had with Herodes, the father of Polydeuces, who was mourning the death of his son. Others have suggested that Polydeuces died ca. 174 CE, which would require, if the story recorded by Lucian is factual, the death of Demonax and the writing of this biography to have happened post 174. See Jones, *Lucian*, 91n5.

[80] For those unfamiliar with the term, a *chreia* is best described as "a saying or action that is expressed concisely, attributed to a character [i.e., a person], and regarded as useful for living." See Hock and O'Neil, *Chreia*, 26. This definition is somewhat of a representative definition as they are emphasizing those features that are absolutely essential to the form when looking at extant examples of *chreiai* and the discussions on the form in the *Progymnasmata*. In his *Progymnasmata*, Theon does provide the caveat that a *chreia* can be attributed to "something analogous to a person", i.e., a more general designation like 'Roman,' or 'Laodicean.'

18). Unfortunately, while there are roughly fifty episodes similar to the one above, along with other outright evaluations of Demonax' character as previously mentioned, there is very little said about his death. There are two places where his death is mentioned, both reporting the same thing, namely, that he voluntarily took his own life when he realized he no longer could take care of himself (Lucian, *Dem.* 4, 65-67). The latter mention also includes the following *chreia*:

> A short time before the end he was asked: "What orders have you to give about your burial?" and replied: "Don't borrow trouble! The stench will get me buried!" The ma said: "Why, isn't it disgraceful that the body of such a man should be exposed for birds and dogs to devour?" "I see nothing out of the way in it," said he [Demonax], "if even in death I am going to be of service to living things." (Lucian, *Dem.* 66)

Lucian follows this by briefly describing the funeral he was in fact given, the extent of the mourning by the Athenians and the way the showed respect to Demonax once he had passed by putting garlands on the park bench where he used to rest (Lucian, *Dem.* 67).

The difficulty in evaluating any of this content for its historical reliability comes in finding other material to compare it to or with. C. P. Jones notes that there are roughly thirty of Demonax' sayings found throughout other ancient works of literature, many of which are not in Lucian's work.[81] For Jones, these additional sayings show that there was more to Demonax that what was recorded in Lucian,[82] mainly that he might have been more Cynic in his philosophical outlook than Lucian leads us to believe.[83] While these additional sayings do not corroborate Lucian's biography at every turn,[84] they do not detract from the reliability of Lucian's work either. Much in the same way we went about determining the historical reliability of Nepos's work, the following are a few of the places in Lucian's biography that were able to be verified by outside authorities:

- *Demonax refused to sacrifice to the gods and go through initiation into the local mystery cult (Dem.* 11). On this Jones writes that other Cynic philosophers were known to have done the same. Socrates and Diogenes, both Cynic, refused to either recognize the established gods, in the case of the former, or go through initiation into the mystery cult as in the case of the latter.[85]
- *Demonax's interaction with Herodes is consistent with archaeological evidence.* The following anecdote is found in *Dem.* 24: "When Herodes

---

[81] Jones, *Lucian*, 91. Jones does note that some are certainly spurious.

[82] Ibid., 92. Jones is under the impression that several of these additional sayings may have come from works of literature written by Demonax himself.

[83] Lucian portrays Demonax as being more eclectic. For instance, Lucian writes, "He did not mark out for himself a single form of philosophy but combined many of them, and never would quite reveal which one he favored" (*Dem.* 5).

[84] Some do, especially those concerning Demonax' views on friendship; see Jones, *Lucian*, 92.

[85] Ibid., 93.

... was mourning the premature death of Polydeuces and wanted a chariot regularly made ready and horses put to it just as if the boy were going for a drive, and dinner regularly served for him, Demonax went to him and said: 'I am bringing you a message from Polydeuces.' Herodes was pleased and thought that Demonax ... was falling in with his humour; so he said: 'Well what does Polydeuces want, Demonax?' 'He finds fault with you,' said he, 'for not going to join him at once!' Jones writes, "A memorial recently discovered at the rustic sanctuary of Artemis at Brauron in eastern Attica exactly illustrates Lucian's anecdote, since the "hero" Polydeuces is shown reclining on a banqueting couch while a horse stands nearby."[86]

- *The majority of Demonax's interlocutors are philosophers.* This is consistent with the fact that Athens, the setting for the sayings portion of Lucian's biography, still enjoyed preeminence in the field at this time.[87]

- *Lucian's depiction of certain aspects of his setting, Athens, is consistent with what is known about the city from other ancient sources.* Lucian tells of Demonax entering the assembly in order to dissuade them from instituting gladiatorial games similar to what was held in Corinth.[88] Philostratus speaks of a similar incident involving Apollonius of Tyana where Apollonius also attempted to persuade Athenians to discontinue the horrid practice of paying to watch human slaughter.[89] In addition, Demonax is portrayed as dispelling a riot simply by appearing to the crowd. Jones notes, "it is known that Athenian politics of the 160's were exceptionally turbulent."[90] Furthermore, in regards to Athenian beliefs about the supernatural, Lucian includes anecdotes involving Demonax and Asclepius, Choran and the Athenian belief in spirits or demons, all of which show congruence with the known spiritual milieu of Athens at the time.[91]

- *Demonax's funeral/burial was public and also included him being carried on the shoulders of fellow philosophers (Dem. 67).* Jones notes that both the public burial and his bier being born by fellow philosophers were "two honors which are often attested in literature and inscriptions."[92]

---

[86] Jones, *Lucian*, 94.

[87] Ibid., 95. Other sources show that other cities may have surpassed Athens as centers of philosophy by this period (see e.g., Argyle, "University"; on its decline in other respects, see Engels, *Roman Corinth*, 113); nevertheless, Athens retained the reputation and continued significant philosophic training (Lucian, *Nigrinus* 12-14).

[88] Lucian, *Dem.* 57.

[89] Philostratus, *Vit. Apoll.* 4.22.

[90] Jones, *Lucian*, 97.

[91] For the anecdote concerning Asclepius, see *Dem.* 27; for Charon see *Dem.* 45; for the Athenians believing that Demonax was a sort of spirit or demon, see *Dem.* 63. For Jones's discussion on this particular matter, see Jones, *Lucian*, 97-98.

[92] Ibid., 97.

The last point of contact, the burial of Demonax, is of especial importance because of its subject matter. Taking this information into consideration, and the other abovementioned points of contact with the known social, religious and political aspects of life in Athens, there is little reason to believe that Lucian has not provided his reader with a reliable description of both the death of Demonax, i.e., the manner in which he passed, and the events immediately following. The impression given by Lucian's work is that, while he was certainly encomiastic in his portrayal of Demonax, he intended to portray both his subject and the setting of his biography in an accurate manner.

Part Three: Implications and Conclusions

In the previous section the goal was to determine to what degree four ancient biographies were historically reliable in what they reported concerning the death of their subjects. An account was for the most part considered historically reliable when its details were either directly or indirectly corroborated in other ancient sources.[93] While there were a few elements that detracted from the historical reliability of some of the biographies,[94] it was consistently found that the accounts of the death of the subject in the biographies were reliable.

As stated in the introduction the overarching question driving this research is: Are ABs historically reliable and to what degree and in what specific areas or topics are they most reliable? The question that now needs to be answered is: What role do the above results play in answering this larger question? It is difficult to determine to what degree the results above are indicative of what might be found in other ancient biographies. This is obviously too small of a subset in order to make declarations about the genre as a whole. Nevertheless, the sample might be representative of biographies written by authors who were contemporaries with their subjects. That being said, I would need to find similar results after analyzing several more biographies that fit into this same category before concluding more firmly that ancient biographies were typically historically reliable in this particular area.

Furthermore, a possible reason why the above biographies all appeared to be relatively historically reliable in their accounts of their subjects' deaths might have been due to the lack of competing data. The picture could have looked much different had there been as many ancient sources that reported the death of any

---

[93] By "directly" I mean other sources contained information about the death of the subject and they were similar; by "indirectly" I mean details not concerning the death of the subject were verifiable in other ancient sources.

[94] Xenophon's *Agesilaus* (rearrangement of material for rhetorical effect), Cornelius Nepos's *Atticus* (the note about Atticus's health), and Tacitus's *Agricola* (decision to withhold judgment on whether or not his father-in-law was poisoned when it could be reasonably assumed that he knew one way or the other) both contained elements that some modern critics might claim calls into question the reliability of their accounts. As for Tacitus, it could also be the case that he withheld judgment because he was unwilling to claim more than he knew.

one of the subjects as there are, say, for the death of Jesus. For our analysis of Xenophon's record of the death of Agesilaus we looked at two other accounts from individuals who wrote 300-400 years after the fact. Perhaps early accounts of Socrates's death would be more comparable. In particular, if we were to include sources within a similar chronological range in an analysis of the death of Jesus as found in the Gospel of Matthew there would be a considerably larger amount of data to sift through. The following list would be a starting point for the comparative work:

- The Gospel of Mark
- L – material unique to Luke that is not in Mark
- The Gospel of John
- The Gospel of Peter
- Pauline Literature[95]
    o Testimony before Pontius Pilate: 1 Timothy 6:13
    o Jesus suffered and was killed at the hand of the Jews: 1 Thessalonians 2:14-16
    o Jesus was killed by the "rulers of this age": 1 Corinthians 2:8
    o Jesus's death and/or burial: Romans 5:6, 8, 10; 8:34; 1 Corinthians 15:3-4;
    o Jesus's death on a cross: 1 Corinthians 1:17-18, 23; 2:2; 2 Corinthians 13:4; Galatians 3:1, 13; 6:12, 14; Philippians 2:8; Colossians 1:19-20;
- Jewish sources
    o Josephus, *Antiquities* 18.3.3 (*Testimonium Flavium*)
    o b. Sanh. 43a.
- Pagan sources[96]
    o Tacitus, *Annals* 15.44
    o frg. 18 of Julius Africanus's *Chronology* as preserved in Georgius Syncellus's *Chronology* – a statement by Thallus about the darkness at the time of Jesus (Mark 15:33)
    o A letter from Mara bar Serapion to his son reports the death of Jesus ("their wise king") at the hand of the Jews
    o Lucian, *Peregr.* 11

This is just one of the issues one would need to navigate if he or she was to provide an analysis of the death account of Jesus similar to what has been done above. While this issue does not present any insurmountable obstacles, it would require a much lengthier discussion than space will allow. It would, however, be

---

[95] This list is not intended to be exhaustive, merely representative of Pauline tradition concerning the death of Jesus. For more references and the resource relied on here, see Kierspel, *Charts*, 160.

[96] For this list and further bibliography on each, see Evans, *Ancient Texts*, 298-302; also Theissen and Merz, *Historical Jesus*, 89.

an appropriate next step in answering the overarching research question stated at the outset.

Chapter 11

A Comparison of Josephus' *Life* and *Jewish War*: An Attempt at Establishing the Acceptable Outer Limits of Biographies' Historical Reliability

John Jordan Henderson
Asbury Theological Seminary

Although scholars debated the genre of the Synoptics through most of the twentieth century, an increasing number of scholars today view them as a type of ancient biography. Richard Burridge, among others, has argued that our focus, as we study the Synoptics, should be on the subject of the biographies – Jesus[1] – rather than on hypothetical communities supposedly responsible for creating them.[2] Even if we accept the premise that the Gospels are ancient biographies, the question still remains: How much historically reliable information can we expect from ancient biographies? Furthermore, when we consider the differences among the Synoptics: What range of variation would have been accepted, and therefore expected, by those first century hearers/readers of ancient biographies?

Two of Josephus' works offer a test case to explore this question: his autobiographical *Life* and his *Jewish War*, which contains autobiographical information overlapping with that in his *Life*. In examining the common material between the two works, specifically the discrepancies, we can establish a baseline by which to compare the differences among the biographies of Jesus by Matthew, Mark, and Luke.[3] In looking at this material, I will argue that no one overarching theory accounts for all the discrepancies between Josephus' two works; rather, I will arrange the types of discrepancies in *Life* and *War* topically and use a multifaceted approach in addressing them. I will then briefly reflect on what this might tell us about the similar discrepancies found in the Synoptic Gospels.

---

[1] Burridge, *Gospels?* (2004), 249: "This emphasis on the centrality of the person of Jesus is a hermeneutical consequence of the gospels being *bioi*." (See pp. 233-251.) Cf. Bauckham, *Gospels*; Burridge, "Reading the Gospels," 31-49.

[2] For instance, Michael Grant writes regarding Suetonius' biographies, "It is only from Suetonius that we get a plausible idea of what sort of people [the twelve Caesars] were" (Grant, "Foreward," 10). He does not posit a community that read its experiences back into the lives of the Caesars, then assert that in reading Suetonius' work, all we can really know about is this community.

[3] We will limit our study to the Synoptics and will not discuss the differences between the Synoptics and John.

Scope, Strengths, and Limitations

As previously stated, this chapter will focus especially on the differences between common material in Josephus' *Life* and *War*.[4] These works provide a worthwhile analogy to the Synoptics in that they fall within the same range of time between the life of the subject and the writing of the biography.[5] It is important, however, to note some limitations in this comparative study. Craig Keener has conducted a similar study on the Roman emperor Otho, comparing the material in the biographies of Suetonius and Plutarch with information about him in Tacitus' *Histories*.[6] He notes the importance of examining "a biography about a then-recent historical figure to demonstrate that numerous elements match elements about that figure in a historical work of comparable date."[7] As this study will follow a similar line of argument, it is worth noting a significant difference and limitation: with Josephus' *Life*, we are examining an *auto*-biography, and the historical work (*War*) is written by the same person.

This limits our ability in this case to examine ancient biographers' use of sources as Keener has done with Otho because "we would expect the same author to have access to the same accounts."[8] We are further limited by the fact that we have no work of history in the same time period focusing on the ministry of Jesus that would be analogous to *War* as the Synoptic Gospels are analogous to *Life*. Nevertheless, although none of the evangelists wrote an autobiography, Josephus' *Life* still stands as a sub-type of the common genre of biography shared with the gospels, just as the genre of biography is a sub-type of ancient historiography. This comparison will therefore serve as a case study to examine the outer range of variation that might have been accepted in a work of autobiography and a work of history covering the same historical figure.

---

[4] Quotations of *War* are taken from Whiston's translation, while quotations from *Life* are from the newer translation by Steve Mason.

[5] I accept the standard dating for the Gospel of Mark, ca. 70 CE, separating the earliest extant biography of Jesus from his crucifixion by roughly one generation. Josephus' *Life* "focuses almost entirely on the five or six months from his commission in the Galilee to the period before the siege of Iotapata, thus apparently from about December 66 to mid-May 67" (Mason, *Life*, xxi). If *Life* was originally an epilogue to *Ant.*, that would put the work roughly ca. 93-94, or 26-28 years after the bulk of the subject matter occurred, with his earlier *War* having been composed ca. 75-79, approximately 8-13 years after most of the common events recorded in both works.

[6] Keener, "Otho."

[7] Ibid., 334.

[8] Ibid., 335.

Literature Review

Reading the Synoptic Gospels as Ancient Biographies

Though he was not the first to make the case that the canonical gospels best fit the genre of ancient biography, Burridge's *What are the Gospels?* has proven definitive in arguing this point. Graham Stanton notes, "I do not think it is now possible to deny that the gospels are a sub-set of the broad ancient literary genre of 'lives,' that is, biographies."[9] The key word in Stanton's statement is "broad," which may account for some scholars' hesitance to accept this generic classification. For instance, Eddy and Boyd note that "everyone concedes [the gospels] have elements that are not typical of this genre," and that those who apply this generic classification "have to stretch the definition of the genre to the point that, it could be argued, its distinctiveness as a genre is threatened."[10] This seems to be an overstatement. While the Gospels certainly have a number of unique elements, this may be more the result of the unique character of their subject than their being a *sui generis*.[11] Furthermore, Burridge makes the case before looking specifically at the Gospels, that ancient biography is best seen as a flexible genre "nestling between history, encomium and moral philosophy, with overlaps and relationships in all directions."[12] This leaves room for the unique features found in the Gospels without threatening their classification as ancient biographies: "Using the idea of 'family resemblance', we may compare the gospels to children of the same family: each child is indeed different, unique and special in its own right, but intimate knowledge of them from the inside and comparison with others outside the family show their shared family features arising from a common ancestry."[13]

Given the broad generic similarities noted by Burridge, Raymond Brown is likely correct in saying that "1st-century hearers/readers familiar with Greco-Roman biographies would not have been so precise"[14] in noticing the differences between the Synoptic Gospels to assign them to a new, unique genre. As Mark Allan Powell notes, "a Roman bookstore or library probably would have put our New Testament Gospels on the same shelf as *Lives of Eminent Philosophers* by Diogenes Laertius and *Life of Apollonius of Tyana* by Philostratus."[15] Based on these points and others, I subscribe to the theory that the Synoptic Gospels are ancient biographies and hence analogous to Josephus' *Life*.

---

[9] Stanton, "Foreword," ix.
[10] Eddy and Boyd, *The Jesus Legend*, 323.
[11] Ibid., 360.
[12] Burridge, *Gospels?* (2004), 65; see pp. 59-67.
[13] Ibid., 236.
[14] Brown, *Introduction*, 103.
[15] Powell, *Introducing*, 82-83.

Past Attempts to Account for Contradictions Between Josephus' Life and Jewish War

The ninth century Patriarch of Constantinople St. Photius the Great includes two entries pertinent to our study in his encyclopedic *Bibliotheca*: Josephus' *Jewish War*, known to Photius as *The Suffering of the Jews*,[16] and Justus of Tiberias' *Chronicles of the Kings of the Jews who are in the Pedigrees*. This Justus appears as Josephus' rival in *Life*, but nowhere else in Josephus' extant works. While Photius praises Josephus as having a "pure style, and...[being] apt at expressing his meaning with dignity,"[17] he accuses Justus of "omit[ting] a great deal that is of the utmost importance" in his history. He notes that Justus was a political opponent of Josephus and that his history is "in great part fictitious, especially where he describes the Judaeo-Roman war and the capture of Jerusalem."[18] This disagreement between Justus and Josephus, as summarized by Photius, the latest extant writer to have known both works independently, is significant because "it remains the starting point in almost all research" concerning Josephus' *Life*, including attempts to explain the discrepancies with *War*.[19]

Though Josephus' works were preserved and appreciated by Christians for centuries, largely because of his mentioning Jesus[20] and his attributing the destruction of the Temple to God's wrath visited upon the Jews,[21] nevertheless, the glaring contradictions between the *Life* and *War* do not seem to have garnered much attention until the nineteenth century. Shaye Cohen points out that "pre-nineteenth century scholars noted that [*Life*] and [*War*] were parallel, and that the two texts frequently disagreed, but they were unable to come to grips with the issue."[22] For instance, an annotated German translation of *Life* in 1806 often has "cf. BJ [*Bellum Judaicum*]" in the notes, but no further analysis of the contradictions.[23]

Nineteenth Century Attempts[24]

The first to deal seriously with the differences between the two accounts was the great Jewish historian I. M. Jost, who attempts to harmonize the two accounts by surmising that Josephus did not have a copy of *War* available to him to consult

---

[16] Photius, *Bibl.* 47: *Anegnōsthē Iosepou Ioudaiou ta kata Ioudaious pathē*.
[17] Ibid.
[18] Ibid. 33.
[19] Mason, *Life*, xxvii.
[20] Note that Photius chides Justus of Tiberius because, in contrast to Josephus, "he does not even mention the coming of Christ, the events of His life, or the miracles performed by Him" (Photius, *Bibl.* 33).
[21] Josephus, *War* 4.323; Josephus, *Ant.* 20.164-166.
[22] Cohen, *Josephus*, 8.
[23] Ibid., 9 n.21.
[24] This is by no means an exhaustive survey. As I do not have access to many of these works, I am relying heavily on the literature review of Cohen, *Josephus*, 8-16 for works from the nineteenth century.

when he composed *Life*, and he had simply forgotten many of the details.²⁵ Twenty-five years later, J. Salvador argued that both *Life* and *War* taken together reflect an "inherently contradictory situation" between Josephus' "covert and declared purposes."²⁶ Both Jost and Salvador essentially "combined [*Life*] and [*War*] by accepting [the account in *Life*]."²⁷ This was challenged in the next major contribution to the subject by E. Reuss, who saw *War* and *Life* to be fundamentally incompatible and viewed *Life* as "more an apology against Justus" than a biography, thus paving the way for future discussions on the topic.²⁸ That being said, nineteenth century scholars tended to favor the attempts of Jost and Salvador to harmonize the two accounts rather than follow the suggestions of Reuss.²⁹

Modern Attempts at a Solution

At the end of the nineteenth century, Emil Schürer expanded upon Reuss' view of *Life* as primarily an apology against Justus of Tiberias, and most scholars of the twentieth century have followed his lead.³⁰ This argument is summarized by Mason as follows:

> Josephus introduces Iustus [Justus] early and at some length (*Life* 36-42). In that passage, he mentions Iustus' competing account of the war, blames the Tiberian and his brother for most of the problems in Galilee, and promises to elaborate upon this "as the story unfolds" (41). Not much later, Josephus' chief opponent in Galilee, Ioannes [John] of Gischala, wins over Iustus as his ally (87-88). One might hypothesize, therefore, that whenever Josephus attacks Ioannes and his associates, which he often does, he is tacitly attacking Iustus' account, which would have told Ioannes' side of the story. When Josephus finally opens his formal digression on Iustus (336-367), and notes that Iustus' work concerned "these things" (i.e., the events of the foregoing narrative), we should understand that he has been implicitly responding to Iustus all along.³¹

As previously mentioned, this argument has been followed, to some degree or another, by scholars addressing the problem in the twentieth century. An exception, however, can be seen in Richard Laqueur's 1920 biography of Josephus. In reacting against some of the excesses of source criticism so popular at the time, "Laqueur was especially interested in contradictions and shifts in opinion [in the time between the writing of both works], because these would reveal the development of Josephus' attitudes and, by extrapolation, the evolution of the circumstances in which he worked...The numerous contradictions between [*Life*] and [*War*] resulted when one work had a purpose or point of view different from the

---

²⁵ Ibid., 9. See Jost, *Geschichte*.
²⁶ Ibid., 10. See Salvador, *Histoire*.
²⁷ Ibid.
²⁸ Ibid., 11. See Reuss, *Nouvelle*.
²⁹ Ibid., 11-16.
³⁰ Mason, *Life*, xxvii. See Schürer, *Geschichte*.
³¹ Mason, *Life*, xxvii-xxviii.

other's."³² Laqueur proposed that the kernel of *Life* was actually written prior to *War* when Josephus was in Galilee in 67 CE, and was a response "to complaints made by the Galileans under his control" at the time, rather than later criticisms of Justus.³³ He later added references to Justus in his second edition of the *Life* and appended it to *Ant.* Though this highly hypothetical reconstruction received much criticism, it also gained widespread support.³⁴

Shaye Cohen's *Josephus in Galilee and Rome* remains the most comprehensive modern study of the problem. In his work, Cohen examines Josephus' use of sources by looking at the use of biblical materials in *Ant.*, noting that "on the whole Josephus was faithful to his sources ... However, he did not confuse fidelity with slavish imitation. Like all ancient historians, he molded his material to suit his own ... aims."³⁵ With regard to overlapping material between *Ant.* and *War*, Cohen detects a "Josephan technique of self-paraphrase ... identical with the Josephan technique of paraphrasing other sources," although he finds Josephus inconsistent in his approach.³⁶ In then looking at the *War-Life* parallels, he finds a similar relationship: *War* "thematically arranges the chronological sequence found in [*Life*]."³⁷ In other words, Cohen agrees with the basic premise of Laqueur noted above: *Life* was composed in some form prior to *War*, perhaps even as notes for this forthcoming composition. In *War* Josephus then arranged this material thematically. Then when Josephus later revises *Life* in response to Justus of Tiberias, he uses the already thematically organized material from *War*, along with his original version of the *Life*, and organizes it chronologically.

Since Cohen's study, Bilde³⁸ and Rajak³⁹ have each argued against the idea that *Life* should be read primarily as a response to Justus, and that the apologetic sections specifically dealing with Justus of Tiberias should not be read back into the rest of the text. Bilde in particular argues that we should read this text primarily as what it claims to be – an autobiography – thus challenging the views first set forth by Reuss and Schürer that Josephus' apologetic aims obscured his autobiographical purposes.⁴⁰ Bilde, who notes that Josephus' accounts in the two works "vary a great deal,"⁴¹ nevertheless offers a "comparatively positive interpretation of Josephus' person, life and goals"⁴² and tries to harmonize the varying accounts when possible. Additionally, Steve Mason argues, on the grounds of placing the *Life* in its proper historical and literary contexts, that Josephus in this

---

³² Cohen, *Josephus*, 16. See Laqueur, *Historiker*.
³³ Mason, *Life*, xxx.
³⁴ For a survey of both supportive and contrary perspectives, see Cohen, *Josephus*, 16-23; Mason, *Life*, xxx-xxxii
³⁵ Cohen, *Josephus*, 47. See pp. 24-47 for his full argument.
³⁶ Ibid., 65. See pp. 48-66.
³⁷ Ibid., 83.
³⁸ Bilde, *Josephus*.
³⁹ Rajak, *Josephus*.
⁴⁰ Bilde, *Josephus*, 108-110.
⁴¹ Ibid., 38.
⁴² Ibid., 28.

work is less concerned with historical accuracy and more concerned with displaying his own character while also vilifying his enemies by means of contemporary Roman rhetoric.[43]

Historical Background

As Berlin and Overman note, "Neither Judea nor trouble in Judea were new to Rome in 66 CE."[44] Since the Hasmoneans established relations with Rome in the second century BCE, Judea had been "officially part of Rome's orbit, concern, and propriety."[45] However, this relationship had weakened substantially since Pompey's invasion of Jerusalem in 63 BCE. The tension with Rome, felt throughout the first century CE, came to a boiling point during the reign of Nero in 66 CE when revolt broke out in Judea and Nero sent Vespasian to deal with it. He arrived with his son Titus, who would also eventually become emperor. Following the first victory over the Jewish rebels at Jotapata, the revolt would last only a few short years before Rome proved victorious in 70 CE. Their triumphant victory was symbolized in the destruction of the temple in Jerusalem.

Josephus had become involved in Roman affairs when, at twenty-six years old, he worked successfully to secure the release of several priests who had been imprisoned by Felix the Procurator.[46] This incident brought him into prominence among his countrymen.[47] The revolt was just beginning when Josephus returned from this mission to Rome.[48] He initially fought on the side of the rebels at their defeat at Jotapata before switching sides and predicting Vespasian would succeed Nero as emperor.[49]

Roughly eight years later, "while he was in Rome enjoying the benefits granted him by his patron,"[50] he composed *War*, first in Aramaic, then in Greek.[51] This seven-volume work begins with the Jewish conflicts with Antiochus IV Epiphanes in the second century BCE and concludes with the aftermath of the revolt in 66-70 CE. In addition, during this time period, Josephus also "was contemplating writing the complete history of the Jews from the creation to his own time."[52] Towards the end of the first century, he received encouragement from his

---

[43] Mason, *Life*, xxxiv-l. See also Rodgers, "Justice for Justus," 169-192.
[44] Berlin and Overman, *Revolt*, 2.
[45] Ibid. The initial establishment of relations between the Hasmoneans and Rome is described in 1 Macc. 8.
[46] Josephus, *Life* 13-16.
[47] Shutt, *Studies*, 2. Shutt writes, "either officially or unofficially Josephus became their champion."
[48] Josephus, *Life* 17.
[49] Josephus, *War* 3.399-408. However, both Tacitus (*Histories* 2.79) and Suetonius (*Vespasian* 2) have Vespasian hailed as emperor earlier in Egypt.
[50] Shutt, *Studies*, 7.
[51] Josephus, *War* 1.3.
[52] Bilde, *Josephus*, 80. See Josephus, *Ant.* 1.6-7. Bilde notes objections to whether such a project had actually been planned that far back.

268   Biographies and Jesus: What Does It Mean for the Gospels to be Biographies?

patron Epaphroditus and "finally succeeded in completing his great project,"[53] which he entitled *Antiquities of the Jews*. He notes at the conclusion of this massive twenty-volume work, "And now it will not be perhaps an invidious thing if I treat briefly of my own family, and of the actions of my own life,"[54] thus segueing into his *Life* which was appended as an epilogue. Thus, for instance, when Eusebius later quotes from *Life*, he does not treat it as a separate work, but as "words attached to the end of *Antiquities*."[55]

Examination of Parallel Accounts in *War* and *Life*

Rather than providing an additional comparison chart of the parallels between the *War* and *Life*, I will instead rely on and comment upon the detailed chart of Steve Mason.[56] I will arrange the following material topically and I will begin with what I consider to be the more easily reconcilable differences between the two works and proceed towards the more difficult contradictions. After considering the differences, I will present my proposed solutions, again topically, in the same order as they are listed in this section.

Proper Names

A number of people and places are mentioned in both works but called by slightly different names. For example, in *Life* 48, we are introduced to Varus who is said to have been governing the kingdom at that time.[57] He is referred to as Noarus in *War* 2.481. In *Life* 131, Josephus sends for "the two principal men, Dassion and Ianneus the son of Levis." In *War* 2.597, Josephus does not mention Dassion, but refers to Ianneus as Eneas. He mentions the fortified cities in Upper Galilee of Iamnia, Ameroth, and Acharabe in *Life* 187-88, which has been changed from Achabari, Jamnith, and Meroth, in *War* 2.574. Also, in *War* 2.574 he mentions Seth, but fails to mention him in *Life* 187-88. Likewise, the members of the delegation from Jerusalem in *Life* 197 (Ionathes, Ananias, Simon, and Iozar) differ from the parallel passage of *War* 2.628 (Ioesdrus [=Iozar] and Ananias; no mention of Ionathes being part of the delegation. Instead, Simon and Judas are included and are said to be sons of Ionathes).

---

[53] Ibid.
[54] Josephus, *Ant.* 20.266.
[55] Eusebius, *Hist. Eccl.* 3.10.8-11.
[56] "Appendix C: Synopsis: Parallel Episodes in Josephus' *Life* and *War*," in Mason, *Life*, 213-222. For an excellent survey of the differences, see Cohen, *Josephus*, 3-8, which includes a comparison chart I also consulted in compiling these differences.
[57] Josephus, *Life* 49-53.

Varying Numbers[58]

There are numerous discrepancies here. *Life* 127 records five hundred gold pieces taken at Dabaritta, while *War* 2.595 has six hundred. Six hundred soldiers surround Josephus' house in *Life* 145, while in *War* 2.610 it is two thousand.[59] In *Life* 200-1, John of Gischala receives one thousand reinforcements from Jerusalem, while in *War* 2.628 he receives two thousand five hundred. In the ultimatum to John's followers in *Life* 370, they are given a time limit of twenty days, while in *War* 2.624 they are given a limit of five days. In *Life* 371-372, four thousand soldiers desert John of Gischala while one thousand five hundred remain. In *War* 2.625, three thousand desert while two thousand remain.

Chronology

Though it is not readily apparent in Mason's comparison chart, there are a number of chronological differences between the two accounts. In *War* 2.570-71, Josephus establishes a supreme council, "as he chose seven judges in every city to hear the lesser quarrels; for as to the greater causes, and those wherein life and death were concerned, he directed they should be brought to him and the seventy elders." This is immediately followed by and connected to the fortifications of the Galilean cities in *War* 2.572-75. However, the establishment of the council and the fortifications are separated in *Life* 79 (supreme council) and 187-189 (fortifications). Similarly, *Life* 85 has John of Gischala go to Tiberias. This precedes the episode in *Life* 126-148 where "some audacious young men of Dabarittan origin" rob Ptolemy's wife, leading to Josephus being accused of being a traitor. In *War* 2.595-613, these two events happen in the opposite chronology and are joined together, whereas they are separated in *Life*. Likewise, the delegation from Jerusalem in *Life* 190-335 comes before the dispersal of John's followers in 368-72, whereas the order of these two events are reversed in *War* 2.624-25 (dispersal of John's followers) and 2.626-31 (delegation from Jerusalem).

Unique Elements in Life

Perhaps most significantly, Justus of Tiberias is completely missing from *War*, as well as Josephus' other works, whereas he occupies a prominent enough place in *Life* to convince numerous scholars that the entire work is an apologetic against him.[60] Also notable is the material on Gamala and Philip son of Iacimus in *Life* 46-61. Cohen also notes that, although neither work is friendly to John of Gischala, only the *War* "vilifies him."[61]

---

[58] Each of the examples here are noted in Cohen, *Josephus*, 7.

[59] In this and the following example, it is interesting that he has decreased the number in the later work rather than expanding it.

[60] See "Literature Review" above.

[61] Cohen, *Josephus*, 8.

Contradictions in Various Details

Soemus is mentioned in *Life* 45 as a tetrarch, but in *War* 2.481 as a king. In *War* 2.592, John of Gischala buys four amphorae of oil for the equivalent of four drachmas, whereas in *Life* 75, he can buy eighty amphorae for four drachmas.[62] Additionally, the oil is for the Jews of Caesarea Philippi in *Life* and for the Jews of Syria in *War*. In the "Dabaritta affair" mentioned above,[63] Ptolemy is attacked in *War* 2.595, whereas his wife is attacked in *Life* 126. Josephus is counseled to commit suicide by four bodyguards in *War* 2.600-1, but only by one in *Life* 137. In *War* 2.612, following the "Dabaritta affair," Josephus whips a group of people, "until every one of their inward parts appeared naked." By contrast, in the parallel account in *Life* 147, he only whips one man,[64] then forces him to cut off his own hand and hang it around his neck, a detail absent from the account in *War*.

Nature of the Galilee Mission

In *War*, Josephus describes Cestius' unsuccessful attack upon Jerusalem, which resulted in the deaths of many Roman soldiers. Cestius was able to flee the Jews he had attacked, though they pursued him as far as Antipatris and killed thousands of his men. Soon afterward, Cestius informed Nero of the situation.[65] Josephus then writes of himself in the third person as one of several generals (*strategoi*) appointed by the Jewish revolutionaries in Jerusalem who had pursued Cestius in preparation for an expected counterattack by the Romans.[66] Josephus then went to Galilee, where he appointed rulers of the people there and set about to "make provisions for their safety against external violence."[67]

By contrast, Josephus writes in *Life* that he was sent to Galilee by "principle men of Jerusalem" who *feared* the Jewish revolutionaries in order to convince the Galileans to lay down their arms and "wait to see what the Romans would do."[68] Upon his arrival in Galilee, he went to Sepphoris and immediately began to pacify those in fear of the Romans.[69]

This is by far the most significant of the differences between the two works. Reuss' pertinent questions emphasize his reason for declaring the two works incompatible and unable to be harmonized:

> In whose name, with what intention, for the defense of what interest did [Josephus] go to Galilee? Was it to pacify the spirits and reconcile the parties, or was

---

[62] As Mason notes, that is a rate of .05 drachmas per amphora in *Life* vs. one drachma for one amphora in *War*. Mason, *Life*, 64 n.414.

[63] See "Chronology" above.

[64] This discrepancy is similar to the different number of angels at Christ's tomb in the various gospels.

[65] Josephus, *War* 2.513-58.

[66] Josephus, *War* 2.566-68.

[67] Josephus, *War* 2.572.

[68] Josephus, *Life* 28-29.

[69] Josephus, *Life* 30-31.

it to excite the passions and organize the resistance? Was he the agent of the moderates or the demagogues? What were all those interminable quarrels which absorbed him there, which he recounts with so much emphasis, but whose origin and resolution we do not understand?[70]

Making Sense of the Differences: A Synthetic Approach

The work of Per Bilde has provided a refreshing shift in Josephan scholarship on the *Life*, suggesting that it be read "as what it purports to be, namely, an autobiography."[71] In other words, rather than detecting apologetic arguments against Justus of Tiberius behind every text throughout *Life*,[72] those passages which directly address Justus are allowed to function apologetically as they were intended, while the rest of the text that purports to give autobiographical information is allowed to function as just that, autobiography. Steve Mason helpfully critiques Bilde's position by taking into account practices of ancient rhetoric, features of Graeco-Roman biography, and "advice to the public figure" as found in Plato, Aristotle, and Xenophon among others, and finally, models for the military leader as seen in the *Commentarii* of Julius Caesar.[73] In light of rhetorical practice of the day, he cautions against "anticipating simple truth anywhere in his writing, and against simplistic assessments of his 'lies.' Like all ancient writers, Josephus was concerned not to tell the truth for the truth's sake but to make a point – in this case, about his character."[74] However, a work can be both apologetic *and* autobiographical (cf. Gal. 1), as apologetic is not a genre, but a motive. These two are not mutually exclusive categories.

I arranged the discrepancies between *Life* and *War* above in descending order of complexity to make a point: the types of discrepancies we see in the two works vary greatly. Therefore, rather than construct an argument that tries to account for everything from spelling differences to the nature of Josephus' mission to Galilee on the basis of one overarching thesis, I have found that an approach that takes into account various reasons for different types of discrepancies offers greater explanatory scope.

Proper Names

The variation in proper names can be accounted for in a number of ways. For instance, in the discrepancy between Varus/Noarus noted above, Mason opines that Noarus may indicate his native name.[75] In the case of Ianneus/Eneas, when

---

[70] Quoted in Cohen, *Josephus*, 11.
[71] Bilde, *Josephus*, 109.
[72] Ibid., 108.
[73] Mason, *Life*, xxxvi-xlvii
[74] Ibid., xxxviii.
[75] Ibid., 52 n.291.

we consider that this is already a Hebrew name which has been transliterated into Greek, such "errors" do not really amount to much.

Varying Numbers

The discrepancies between numbers could result from not consulting his sources and relying on memory, as first suggested by Jost in the nineteenth century.[76] They also could have been changed for rhetorical purposes, but this is probably not the case. For example, in the episode noted above we might expect the two thousand troops surrounding Josephus' house in *War* to be inflated over time between the two writings, instead it has been deflated to six hundred in *Life*. While rhetorical purposes may account for some of the discrepancies in the numbers, it seems more likely that the discrepancies are due to sloppiness on the part of Josephus, whether due to not having access to certain sources while writing *Life* or not consulting them.

Chronology

With regard to chronology, although it is interesting to note the discrepancies between the two works, the differences can be accounted for by reading *Life* as a sub-type of ancient biography which "did not need to follow a chronological sequence," with most biographers feeling "free to rearrange their material topically."[77] I do find plausible the theory first proposed by Laqueur, and modified by so many, that Josephus had written a version of the *Life* prior to *War*, used it as a source and organized the material topically, then used both as sources for the revised *Life* later.[78] However, I think such a complicated theory is not entirely necessary to account for discrepancies in chronology.

Unique Elements in *Life*

Any attempt to account for the material unique to *Life* will be highly theoretical, as it is impossible to determine precisely why an author chose to include certain things at one time and not another, short of the author explicitly explaining his or her motivations. At the risk of claiming more than I am able to prove, I will simply state the obvious: the circumstances which called forth Josephus' writing of *The Jewish War* did not necessitate his mentioning Justus of Tiberias, Philip, or Gamala, whereas in *Life* he felt the need to include them. In the case of Justus, we can say that his criticism of and rivalry with Josephus was much more pertinent when *Life* was written, and that Josephus felt the need to respond to his public criticisms, with which the members of his audience were likely familiar.

---

[76] See Cohen, *Josephus*, 9-10.
[77] Keener, *Historical Jesus*, 82.
[78] See "Literature Review" above.

Contradictions in Various Details

Much of what was said under "Varying Numbers" above can also be applied when we consider contradictions in various details between *Life* and *War* (e.g. whether Ptolemy or his wife was attacked). Rhetoric can account for some of these, but this explanation often obscures rather than clarifies. Why, for instance, would Josephus have four bodyguards try to convince him to commit suicide in *War* then later reduce the number of bodyguards to one for rhetorical purposes? It seems that in such cases he had inflated the number in *War* but was now writing for an audience that had first-hand knowledge of the event. This approach, however, goes against the general trend of presuming a friendly audience for *Ant.* and *Life*.[79]

Nature of the Galilean Mission

Finally, the most difficult contradiction to account for are the differences between *Life* and *War* in regards to the aims of Josephus' Galilean mission. *War* clearly portrays Josephus as a "general selected by an assembly to carry on the war against Rome," while *Life* "claims that Josephus and two others were sent as emissaries of the Jerusalem aristocracy to maintain peace in Galilee."[80] Even with a sympathetic reading of Josephus, giving the text the benefit of the doubt, we are left with a glaring contradiction here and a reason to doubt the truthfulness of at least one account. A possible solution is to assume that the differences are rhetorical in nature and then read each work against the political and social backgrounds in which they were written. Along with the current trend in Josephan scholarship, we can maintain "that Josephus consistently concerned himself with the issues surrounding Jewish existence in the Roman Empire and the preservation of Jewish rights."[81] Keeping this consistent aim in mind, circumstances when he wrote the *War* demanded (at least to his mind) that he portray himself as a general while the audience of *Ant./Life* necessitated (again, at least to his own mind) that he be portrayed as a pacifist in this account.

What prompted such a change? Perhaps the most significant factor in the intervening years between the two works was the accession of Domitian as Roman Emperor. Josephus had remained in the good graces of the Flavians since his surrender to Vespasian, especially given his prediction that the latter would become emperor. This eventually prompted Vespasian not only to grant Josephus his freedom, but the name Flavius as well. This close relationship was maintained with Vespasian's son Titus, for whom Josephus pleaded with the Jews in Jerusalem just prior to the destruction of the Temple.[82]

However, we might ask whether this close relationship was maintained with Vespasian's other son Domitian. Vespasian had gained fame and prestige serving

---

[79] See Rodgers, "Justice for Justus," 174.
[80] Cohen, *Josephus*, 8.
[81] Rodgers, "Justice for Justus," 169.
[82] Josephus, *War* 6.93-176.

as commander of the Roman forces which subjugated Judea, as did Titus who valiantly fought under his father's command. Josephus demonstrated his loyalty to both of these men in this revolt. Domitian, however, did not take part in this fight, having been placed under the care of his uncle in Rome.

Furthermore, according to Suetonius, the close relationship between Vespasian and Titus, as well as their shared victories in battle, bred jealousy in Domitian: "Whenever Vespasian and Titus now appeared seated in their official chairs, [Domitian] had to be content with following behind in a litter."[83] This jealousy extended to Domitian ordering Titus' attendants to abandon him to die when he was bitterly ill, but had not breathed his last. Following his death, Domitian "often slighted Titus' memory by the use of ambiguous terms in speeches and edicts."[84] Suffice it to say, following both Vespasian's and Titus' deaths, it could not be assumed that Domitian would share their loyalty to Josephus.

In addition to Domitian's complex family relationships, we note the general paranoia and cruelty that characterized his reign, he being "not merely cruel, but cunning and sudden into the bargain."[85] Of course, one group of people who particularly felt the wrath of his reign were the Jews, although the extent of their persecution is uncertain. Eusebius, drawing on Hegesippus, records that Domitian ordered the execution of all Jews.[86] Though this seems an exaggeration, Suetonius also records the peculiar cruelty with which Domitian collected taxes from the Jews.[87] Josephus' good relations with the Flavians would not have spared him Domitian's wrath, as can be seen in the case of Domitian's cousin Flavius Clemens, whom Domitian had executed. Nor should we assume that Domitian would be unconcerned with a work of history such as Josephus' *Jewish War*, as both Hermogenes of Tarsus and several slaves who served as his copyists were executed because of some historical allusions in one of his writings.[88]

While Josephus' earlier account in *War* of having been a *strategos* sent to fight the Romans did not presumably bother Vespasian and Titus, to whom he also accounted in the same work his pledge of loyalty, he would have had reason to fear that Domitian would not have been so understanding, given all that is mentioned above. Although Josephus makes a point to note Domitian's kindness to him at the conclusion of *Life*, I believe this justifiable fear of Domitian caused him to rewrite the story of his role in the Jewish rebellion three decades before, changing the motivation of his initial arrival in Galilee from resistance fighter to pacifist.

---

[83] Suetonius, *Domitian* 2 (trans. Graves). All translations of Suetonius are from Graves' translation.

[84] Suetonius, *Domitian* 2.

[85] Suetonius, *Domitian* 11.

[86] Eusebius, *Hist. Eccl.*, 3.19-20.

[87] Suetonius, *Domitian* 12.

[88] Suetonius, *Domitian* 10.

Conclusion

This chapter has explored the discrepancies between Josephus' *Life* and *War*. I have found that each of the different types of discrepancies need to be addressed individually because there is no single overarching theory that explains them all. I have attempted to reconcile differences where possible, but we are still left with some notable contradictions.

Many of the differences noted above have parallels in the Synoptic Gospels, such as discrepancies in numbers (how many angels were at the tomb?), names (e.g. variations in the lists of the apostles), details of stories, chronology, and material unique to only one writer (e.g. the birth narratives of Matthew and Luke). When we consider the fact that Josephus, writing about his own life in two separate works, can have discrepancies and even glaring contradictions, we get a sense of the *possible* outer range of variation that might have been acceptable in antiquity. Given the number of discrepancies noted above, whatever the reason behind them, we can see that the Synoptic Gospels fall well within this broad range of variation. One could even argue that no contradiction occurs in the Synoptic Gospels comparable to Josephus' contradictory claims about the aim of his own mission to Galilee.

Josephus' work therefore stands as an example of the range of variation that might have been accepted in the genre of ancient biography, though we cannot say for certain whether he would have been seen to exceed the limits of this range. The need remains for continued examination of other ancient biographical works in order to completely establish the outer limits of the historical reliability of the genre.

Chapter 12

A Redaction-Critical Study on Philo's *On the Life of Moses*, Book One

Esteban Hidalgo
Asbury Theological Seminary

Philo's *On the life of Moses* (*Moses* henceforth), as distinct from his philosophical and allegorical treatises, is a straightforward, rewritten story of Judaism's most looming figure from the Pentateuch. It is addressed primarily to non-Jews as an official ancient Greco-Roman biography with the hope of winning some Gentiles over to Judaism (*Moses* 2.25–44).[1] The two-part work, with a possible lacuna after 2.65, describes Moses as a king, chief-priest, lawgiver, and prophet (*Moses* 1.334). The flattering account of Moses' career highlights respected Greco-Roman virtues, perhaps as a basis for moral instruction.[2]

When this text is approached from a redaction-critical perspective a few questions surface for consideration: How do Philo's interests influence his selections of which accounts to include and the way they are presented from the Pentateuchal sources? What characteristics of his writing style may be observed when compared to the sources he uses? How does this case study of a portion of a single Hellenistic Jewish writer illuminate the way ancient biographers appropriated their sources and incorporated them to their assumed historical composition? The following brief study is a redaction-critical comparison between Philo's *Moses* and the Pentateuch, analyzing the way Philo uses his sources and incorporates them to create a distinct work, a biography on the life of Moses.[3]

According to Louis H. Feldman, to whom much credit for the observations below is given, "Book 1 is factual history, Plutarchian in style, while Book 2 is a biography, Suetonian in style, systematically ordered and concentrating on Moses' virtues."[4] Due to space limitations, this study is confined to Book 1, selected because it serves as a foil to discuss how a biographer interested in "factual history" would embrace his redactional rights to freely develop the accounts from textual sources according to his purposes yet consistently refrain from misrepresenting those sources.

---

[1] See Feldman, *Philo's Portrayal*, 13–16.
[2] Ibid., 16. Other ancient Greco-Roman *bioi* that exhibit aretological features include Diogenes Laertius, *Lives of Eminent Philosophers* and Philostratus, *Life of Apollonius of Tyana* (if the latter is a true *bios*).
[3] Distinct, that is, from the narratives of Moses in the LXX, which was available to his contemporaries.
[4] Feldman, *Philo's Portrayal*, 361.

The study is divided into three parts. Part one, Philo's Use of Sources, demonstrates how he is heavily dependent upon a textual tradition: The Pentateuch. To illustrate, a chart that surveys Book 1 section-by-section in summary form showing which biblical passages have been consulted and alluded to, is provided in full. The second part, Redactional Characteristics, is an exploration of Philo's use of his sources. Some areas considered include: (1) thematic arrangements; (2) interpretative adaptations, especially for instruction in theological or moral aims; (3) additions based on psychological analysis; (4) transmission of historical details; and (5) descriptive expansions. It is beyond the scope of this chapter to be exhaustive, so representative examples will have to suffice in order to demonstrate the standard features throughout the work. Part three, Philo's Use of Discourses, is a heuristic attempt to understand how speeches in the Pentateuch are represented in the biography and how Philo uses discourses to describe his interpretation of a historical account. This study concludes with a few stated implications of how this analysis may illuminate research into the Gospels as ancient biographies.

Philo's Use of Sources

From his introduction, Philo plainly states what are his two major sources that he uses in order to considers himself well "acquainted with the history of [Moses'] life," these are: (1) "those sacred Scriptures which he has left" and (2) the oral tradition which he often heard "from the elders of [the Jewish] nation" (*Moses* 1.1.4). It is evident, as the chart below illustrates, that Philo is clearly dependent upon the Pentateuch; it is less clear, however, when the oral tradition influences his composition. After all, he confesses that he has "continually connected together what I have heard with what I have read" (1.1.4), so that it is difficult to determine the difference between his redaction of the text, that seeks to emphasize Moses' virtues, and between how he must have heard those accounts (the way the Jewish elders would have narrated them).

Even when he introduces an unattributed oral source, with the use of *phēmi* ("they say"), it may well be describing exactly what can be logically inferred from the Pentateuch, so there is no consistent form, like an introductory formula, to distinguish his oral sources from his own reconstruction of the text. Below are representative examples comparing the written source with Philo's use of introductory formula for oral sources (italicized):[5]

Account with Unattributed Oral Source	Biblical Source
Accordingly, *they say* that for three months continuously they kept him	They hid it three months (Exod 2:2b)

---

[5] The texts used in these charts to compare Philo's *Moses* to the LXX are from *The Lexham English Septuagint* and Yonge, trans. *The Works of Philo*, 459–490.

at home, feeding him on milk, without its coming to the knowledge of the multitude (*Moses* 1.3.9)	
Now the king of the country had an only daughter, whom he tenderly loved, and *they say* that she, although she had been married a long time, had never had any children, and therefore, as was natural, was very desirous of children ... on that particular day was she overcome by the weight of her anxiety, that, though it was her ordinary custom to stay indoors ... yet now she went forth with her handmaidens down to the river, where the infant was lying. And there, as she was about to indulge in a bath (*Moses* 1.4.13-14).	The daughter of Pharaoh came down to bathe at the Nile, with her maidens walking alongside the Nile; and she saw the basket among the reeds and sent her maid, and she brought it *to her* (Exod 2:5a).
And at this time *they say* that some persons threw themselves on their beds, and did not venture to rise up, and that some, when any of the necessities of nature overtook them, could only move with difficulty by feeling their way along the walls or whatever else they could lay hold of, like so many blind men; for even the light of the fire lit for necessary uses was either extinguished by the violence of the storm, or else it was made invisible and overwhelmed by the density of the darkness (*Moses* 1.21.24).	Moses stretched out his hand toward the heaven, and there was darkness—a dark, dense storm—over the whole land of Egypt *for* three days and no one saw his neighbor *for* three days, and no one arose from off of his couch *for* three days (Exod 10:22–23a).
And *they say* that there was not a single house in the whole land which was exempt from the visitation (*Moses* 1.24.135).	for *there* was not a house in which there was not a dead person in it (Exod 12:30b)
And *they say*, that a most portentous miracle happened at that time, a prodigy of nature, which no one anywhere recollects to have ever happened before; for a cloud, fashioned into the form of a vast pillar, went before the multitude by day,	Now God was leading them by day by a pillar of cloud to show them the way, but during the night by a pillar of fire. And the pillar of cloud did not leave by day, nor the pillar of fire by night, from right in front of all the people (Exod 13:21–22).

giving forth a light like that of the sun, but by night it displayed a fiery blaze, in order that the Hebrews might not wander on their journey, but might follow the guidance of their leader along the road, without any deviation. (*Moses* 1.29.165–66).

Perhaps Philo employs "they say" as a rhetorical device to catch the attention of his audience or give credibility to his narrative.[6] Maybe he remembers it being repeated in oral performances, even if the tradition was dependent on the written text. In any case, he never employs a quotation formula to cite the Pentateuch,[7] presumably since his non-Jewish audience would derive no benefit from a stated "it is written." However, because of the availability of the LXX, it was assumed that Philo derived most of his data from it. Except for some rare examples (e.g., what is known about Balaam outside of Scripture, cf. *Moses* 1.48.264–65)[8] and contemporary illustrations or sayings, Philo does not use sources outside of the Pentateuch to relate material about Moses' life.

---

[6] For instance, in *Moses* 1.211, Philo uses "I say" instead of employing "they say" to emphasize the wonder of this historical event: "at all events the rock, I say, was cleft open by the force of the blow and poured forth water in a stream ... a relief from thirst" (cf. Exod 17:6).

[7] Perhaps the only one exception in Book 1 may be: "For he also was called the god and king of the whole nation, and he is said to have entered into the darkness where God was" (*Moses* 1.28.158; cf. Exod 7:1; 20:21)

[8] "Now there was a man at that time very celebrated for his skill in divination, dwelling in Mesopotamia, who was initiated in every branch of the soothsayers' art. And he was celebrated and renowned above all men for his experience as a diviner and prophet, as he had in many instances foretold to many people incredible and most important events; for, on one occasion, he had predicted heavy rain to one nation at the height of summer; to another he had foretold a drought and burning heat in the middle of winter. Others he had forewarned of a dearth which should follow a season of abundance; and, on the other hand, plenty after famine. In some instances, he had predicted the inundations of rivers; or, on the contrary, their falling greatly and becoming dried up; and the departure of pestilential diseases, and ten thousand other things. From all which he had obtained a name of wide celebrity, as he was believed to have foreseen them all, and so he had attained to great renown and his glory had spread everywhere and was continually increasing" (*Moses* 1.48.264–65).

The dependence of the biography on the Pentateuch is illustrated through the chart below, which identifies the biblical sources used in each section.

Summary of Book 1 by Sections:	Biblical References:
I. Introduction to the life of Moses (1-4)	Moses, "the most perfect man that ever lived" (cf. Num 12:3); His law envied by other nations (cf. Deut 4:6–8, 44)
II. Moses' lineage and upbringing (5-7)	Egyptian upbringing (cf. Exod 2:10a); Hebrew lineage (Exod 1:1a; 2:1–2; cf. Gen 35:28–29; 47:28; Exod 6:14–27).[9]
III. Baby Moses hidden from massacre[10] (8-11)	Rationale for King's decree to kill male babies (Exod 1:8–10, 22). Moses hidden (2:2–3).[11]
IV. Moses found in Nile by Egyptian princess (12-17)	Account closely follows Exod 2:4–10
V. Moses adopted by Egyptian princess (18-24) VI. Education of Moses[12] (25-31)	Allusion to Exod 2:10a
VII. Moses senses injustice of Hebrew oppression (32-39)	Allusion to Exod 1:11, 14; 2:11a
VIII. Moses kills an Egyptian (40-45)	Allusion to Exod 2:11b–15a).[13]
IX. Moses flees to Arabia (46-50)	Allusion to Exod 2:15b.

---

[9] Philo does not mention Abraham nor Moses' parents by name, in fact, the name of the LORD is only referenced once, on the lips of Pharaoh who doubts his existence: "Who is it whom I am to obey? I know not this new Lord of whom you are speaking" (*Moses* 1.88). The focus throughout the biography seems to be exclusively on Moses.

[10] A psychological portrait of the grief of Moses' parents adds descriptive elements to the biblical account. This kind of analysis is often developed throughout the Book, "perhaps under the influence of the tragedians, notably Euripides, with whose works he [Philo] was so well acquainted" (Feldman, *Philo's Portrayal*, 363).

[11] Philo omits the account of the midwives (Exod 1:15–21) and makes no mention of the basket (2:3).

[12] "The greatest changes from the biblical narrative are to be found in Philo's account of Moses' education ... Moses is said to have had Egyptian teachers in mathematics, music, philosophy, and even to have been taught regard for animals ... teachers were imported from Greece to teach him the liberal arts, the very curriculum that Plato prescribes for the higher education of the philosopher-kings in his *Republic* – notably grammar, geometry, astronomy, rhetoric, and music – and which, most likely, reflects Philo's own education" (Feldman, *Philo's Portrayal*, 363, cf. 47–55).

[13] The account of the Hebrews quarreling and response to Moses' intervention is omitted (Exod 2:13–14).

X. Moses rescues damsels by the well.[14] (51-57)	Closely follows Exod 2:16–17.
XI. Moses settles as a Shepherd (58-62)	Allusion to Exod 2:18–21
XII. Moses encounters burning bush[15] (63-67)	Allusion to Exod 3:1–2a.
XIII. Allegorical interpretations[16] (68-70)	
XIV. The Call of Moses[17] (71-84)	Closely follows Exod 3:7, 9–10a, 15–16a, 18; Alludes to Exod 2:23a; 3:13–14; 4:1–4, 6–16, 19.
XV. Moses confronts Pharaoh[18] (85-91)	Allusion to Exod 4:18a, 20, 27–31 (cf. 7:1–2); 5:1–21
XVI. Rods into serpents (91-96)	Allusion to Exod 7:8–13
XVII. Analysis of 10 Plagues. Those assigned to Aaron: (1) Water into blood[19] (96-101)	Follows closely Exod 7:19–21, 24–25
XVIII. (2) Plague of Frogs (102-5)	Discipline of a father (cf. Prov 3:11–12) *Analysis of Egyptian stubbornness of heart.* Follows closely

---

[14] Includes a virtuous discourse which is absent from the biblical narrative (cf. Exod 2:16–17). The intent behind the discourse is given: "I will also mention one action which was done by him at that time, even although it may be but a trifling one in appearance, but still it proceeded from a lofty spirit" (*Moses* 1.10.51).

[15] Instead of leading his sheep to a wilderness location, a mountainous region around Mt. Horeb (Exod 3:1), Philo apparently knows better: Moses as "the most skillful herdsman of his time" must have led his sheep to a shaded valley "full of good water and good grass, where there was also a great deal of herbage especially suitable for sheep" (*Moses* 1.12.63–65).

[16] Philo cannot resist making an allegorical interpretation in this episode.

[17] The Lord's rebuke of Moses' curiosity and command to remove his sandals is omitted (cf. Exod 3:3-6); the reference of the promised land is omitted (cf. 3:8); Moses' humble reply, "who am I," is omitted (3:11–12); and the repetition of the command as worded in the Pentateuch is also omitted (4:5). However, an elaborate interpretation of God's name is included.

[18] Encounter with angel because of their neglect to circumcise their children is omitted (Exod 4:24–25).

[19] An interpretative (allegorical) analysis, dividing the 10 plagues based on who was the agent (performer) of the miracle and how they represent the elements of the earth. The order of the plagues follows this analytical approach, first to those assigned to Aaron (3), then Moses (3), both (1), and those by the LORD (3). The biblical order of the plagues and reference to the performer are thus: (1) Exod 7:19 – water into blood (by Aaron); (2) Exod 8:5 – frogs over the land (by Aaron); (3) Exod 8:16 – dust as gnats (by Aaron); (4) Exod 8:21 – swarm of flies (the LORD); (5) Exod 9:5 – cattle die (the LORD); (6) Exod 9:8 – boils (Moses and Aaron); (7) Exod 9:22 – Hail (Moses); (8) Exod 10:12 – Locust (Moses); (9) Exod 10:21 – Darkness (Moses); (10) Exod 12:29 – Death of firstborn (the LORD).

	Exod 8:5–6, 8, 11, 13b–14 (expanded).
XIX. (3) Plague of gnats (106-12)	Alludes to Exod 8:15; follows closely 8:16–17, 19b.
XX. Plagues by Moses: (4) Hailstorm[20] (113-19)	Allusion to Exod 9:18, 22–25.
XXI. (5) Plagues of locusts and (6) dense darkness (120-25)	Allusion to Exod 9:34; follows closely Exod 10:12–15 (Change of order), 7; continues allusion to 10:16–20, and relies heavily on 10:21–23a.
XXII. Plague by both Moses and Aaron: (7) Painful sores (126-29)	Follows closely Exod 9:8–11
XXIII. Plagues by the LORD: (8) The dog-fly and (9) death of cattle (130-33)	Allusion to Exod 8:21, 24; 9:3, 5–6a
XXIV. (10) Death of Firstborn (134-39)	Follows closely Exod 11:4–6; 12:12; alludes to 12:12, 29–30
XXV. The Israelites plunder the Egyptians[21] (140-42)	Allusion to Exod 12:35–36.
XXVI. Analysis of distinction between Israelites and Egyptians during plagues (143-46)	Allusion to Exod 8:22–23a; 9:4, 6b, 25–26; 10:22–23; 11:5a, 7.
XXVII. Israel leaves Egypt:[22] Moses is elected leader[23] (147-54)	Follows Exod 12:37–38; alludes to 12:43–45, 51. Analysis of Israelite election (cf. Gen 12:2–3; Exod 19:5b–6a)
XXVIII. Analysis of Moses' leadership privileges[24] and virtues (155-62)	Moses' virtues extolled: He was as god and king (cf. Exod 7:1; 32:1; cf.

---

[20] Scientific analysis of the weather patterns in Egypt to highlight the miracle.

[21] Moral justification for despoiling the Egyptians: (1) these were their wages for having worked as slaves; (2) this was their recompense for having suffered under them; (3) they were treated as prisoners of war, now they were the conquerors so they despoiled their enemies.

[22] Quantitative and character analysis of the multitudes involved in the Exodus.

[23] Justification of Moses' leadership to extol his virtues once more: He abandoned Egyptian privileges for faith in God's promises (cf. Heb 11:24–26). Character analysis of Moses, deduced from what he did not do in comparison to other rulers and monarchs. Concludes with a catalogue of virtues.

[24] When analyzing Moses' inheritance, a use of a syllogism is employed: If friends hold all things in common and Moses was a friend of God (cf. Exod 33:11a), then all things which are God's were under Moses' authority.

	"king" in Deut 33:5); Moses entered darkness of God (cf. Exod 20:21) and was appointed lawgiver.
XXIX. Moses leads Israel aided by a Messenger in a pillar of cloud[25] (163-66)	Allusion to Exod 13:17–18; follows closely 21–22.
XXX. Pharaoh pursues Israel (167-69)	Alludes to Exod 14:3–7, 9–10a.
XXXI. Moses encourages frightened Israel (170-75)	Follows closely Exod 14:10b–12; alludes to 14:13–14.
XXXII. Crossing the sea; defeating Egypt (176-80)	Alludes to Exod 14:15–16, 20b–22 (change of order), 19–20, 24–25, 27–29, 31–15:1, 20–21a.
XXXIII. Bitter springs turned sweet[26] (181-86)	Alludes to Exod 15:22–24 (cf. 16:3; 17:3b); follows closely 15:25
XXXIV. Allegorical analysis of the 12 springs and 70 palm trees[27] (187-90)	Alludes to Exod 15:27.
XXXV. Israel's complaint for having no food[28] (191-95)	Alludes to Exod 16:1–3
XXXVI. Provision of Manna[29] (196-205)	Allusion to Exod 16: 3–4, 12, 13b–20, 22–30.
XXXVII. Analysis of miraculous provision of food (206-9)	Miracle throughout the 40 years (16:35); Sabbath instruction (16:23 Al); food prepared from "manna" (16:31); evening meat (16:12b, 13a).
XXXVIII. Water from the rock: Theological analysis of miracles (210-13)	Alludes to Exod 17:1b–2a, 5–6.
XXXIX. Joshua's victory in battle: Moses procures alliance with God[30] (214-219)	Alludes to Exod 17:8–11, 13, 15 (victory against Amalek)

---

[25] Contemporizes geographical locations, the text mentions the Philistines, but Philo identifies that land as Phoenicia, Coele-Syria and Palestine.

[26] The commandments pronounced at Marah are omitted (cf. Exod 15:26–27)

[27] Allegorical analysis: twelve fountains = twelve pious tribes; 70 palm trees = 70 elders; palm tree = wise and pious person.

[28] Includes an expanded discourse.

[29] Omission of Moses' commands and anger towards the disobedient ones.

[30] Omission of Aaron and Hur upholding Moses' arms; replaced with comparison of Moses' hands as heavenly wings in seeking alliance with God.

XL. Analysis of the decision to spy out the land (220-26)	Alludes to Num 13:2–3a (cf. Deut 1:20–25 *Al*); follows closely 13:3b; alludes to 13:18–21.
XLI. Reconnaissance mission of the twelve (227-31)	Allusion to Num 13:22–25.
XLII. Report of the spies and results (232-36)	Allusion to Num 13:26–34.
XLIII. Analysis of Edom's rejection of Israel[31] (237-43)	Allusion to Num 20:14–21.
XLIV. Moses wisely restrains war[32] (244-49)	Israel takes a different route (cf. Judg 11:16–18).
XLV. Canaanites attack: Israel avenged[33] (250-54)	Allusion to Num 21:1–3.
XLVI. Rejoicing by the well[34] (255-57)	Allusion to Num 21:16–18.
XLVII. Victory over Sihon and his country (258-62)	Allusion to Num 21:21–25.
XLVIII. Balak sends for Balaam[35] (263-68)	Allusion to Num 22:2–5, 7–8, 13, 15–19, 21.
XLIX. Analysis of the visions of Balaam and his decision to curse Israel[36] (269-74)	Allusion to Num 22:22–35
L. Balak receives Balaam: Balaam blesses Israel in divination (275-79)	Follows closely Num 22:36–41 and 23:1–10.
LI. Balaam blesses Israel again (280-84)	Follows closely Num 23:13–24.
LII. Balaam blesses Israel a third time (285-91)	Follows closely Num 23:25–30; 24:1–9.
LIII. Balak's angry response: Balaam excuses his oracles but advises Balak (292-94)	Follows closely Num 24:10–14.

---

[31] Jacob and Esau contrasted through their descendants.

[32] Includes a valiant discourse.

[33] Explanation or justification for total destruction or anathema of their enemies; First-fruits of the plunder of the land is given to God.

[34] Military analysis derived from the location of their encampment towards the borders of enemy territory.

[35] Philo includes some other source of information for Balaam son of Beor (see no. 7 above).

[36] Explains narrative puns: A beast can see the vision that the seer boasts to see but does not. A character analysis is provided by explaining the rationale for permitting Balaam to go against the will of God.

LIV. Balaam's advice: Send harlots to make Israel break their covenant law (295-99)	Interpretative allusion to Num 25:1–3, 16–18.
LV. Balak sends women to make Israel sin: Phinehas leads others to eliminate the evil[37] (300-4)	Alludes to Num 25:1–13.
LVI. Moses commissions war against Balak[38] (305-8)	Alludes to Num 31:1–7.
LVII. Victory and sharing of spoils[39] (309-14)	Alludes to Num 31:7–24.
LVIII. Analysis of the division of spoils (315-18)	Alludes to Num 31:25–54.
LIX. Moses reproaches two tribes for asking for their inheritance ahead of time (319-27)	Alludes to Num 32:1–15.
LX. Tribes promise to go to war: Moses permits their inheritance (328-34)	Alludes to Num 32:16–24, 33–38.

Redactional Characteristics

Thematic Arrangements

From the evidence above, one observes how Philo is heavily dependent on the Pentateuch as the source for chronicling the events surrounding Moses' life. Rarely does it deviate from the general sequential order from Exodus (1:1–17:15), except after ch. 17; from there the narrative skips to selections from the book of Numbers (13; 20–25; 31–32). This change reflects the intentional thematic arrangement in order to emphasize Moses' leadership abilities as a model of kingship. He leaves the other accounts of Exodus for Book 2, where Moses' roles as priest and lawgiver are stressed. The arrangement of Book 1 commences with Moses' qualifications and preparation to become a fitful king (e.g., beautiful appearance, virtuous character, royal education, discipline of a shepherd) and, after discussing the historical events that led him to renounce the Egyptian crown and choose to serve Israel instead, Moses is officially elected king at the conclusion of the ten plagues (*Moses* 1.27.148). At this juncture Philo is free to analyze Moses' leadership as a basis for instruction in kingly behavior.[40] Indeed, not only is

---

[37] The plague is interpreted as the destruction of Israelite offenders by faithful zealots.

[38] Discourse expansion from 31:3. Implications for military expeditions from Moses' kingly example.

[39] Moral analysis of taking spoils of war. Omission of geographical locations, the death of Balaam, and Moses' anger.

[40] He includes accounts of how he selflessly lead Israel, provided for their necessities, sought a diplomatic alliance with God, sent reconnaissance missions, engaged in battles,

Philo's broad use of sources affected by his thematic arrangement, but individual *chreia* are organized differently to reflect an interpretative analysis.[41] Further observations of other redactional characteristics are analyzed below.

Interpretative Adaptations

According to his stated purposes, Philo is interested in demonstrating Moses' virtues as a model of instruction for righteous behavior. Therefore, he generously xpands the accounts that extol his virtues, sometimes making analytical arguments from silence.[42] At other times he will minimize apparent failures by omission or

---

and fairly divided the spoils and the land of inheritance. Although Moses is generally absent when the accounts of Balaam are narrated (secs. 48–56), in keeping with Philo's purposes, they set the stage to uplift Israel's glory and serve as a background for Moses' actions in response.

[41] As a principal example stands the sequence of the ten plagues as arranged by Philo and subsequent analysis of why the Egyptians were affected but not Israel (*Moses* 1.17.96–24.139). According to Feldman, "his reclassified order takes into account his analysis of the elements—earth, water, air, and fire—and the agents—Aaron, Moses, the two together, and G-d—through whom the plagues were carried out" (*Philo's Portrayal*, 361). What might be another reason behind the changes to the biblical narrative? Feldman's response: "To respond to logical objections that readers might make." For example, Philo changes the biblical order--first killing male babies, then enslaving them—because "a slave master would normally be interested in increasing the number of slaves and if decreasing them was his goal, why not put the female babies to death?" (Ibid., 361-62).

[42] An entire section with an extended discourse is provided to elaborate on Moses' virtue for rescuing the seven daughters of the priest of Midian, introduced with the following statement: "I will also mention one action which was done by him at that time, even although it may be but a trifling one in appearance, but still it proceeded from a lofty spirit" (*Moses* 1.10.51–57; cf. Exod 2:16–17). Another section that affords Philo an opportunity to exalt Moses' virtues is not based on some of Moses actions as stated in the Pentateuch, but on his abstention of kingly privileges, which is deduced from the lack of such actions in the Pentateuch. The following extended example uplifts Moses' virtues by interpreting positively what is not explicit, or even absent, in the text: "And when he had received this authority, he did not show anxiety, as some persons do, to increase the power of his own family, and promote his sons ... for he kept one most invariable object always steadily before him, namely, that of benefiting those who were subjected to his authority ... Therefore he alone of all the persons who have ever enjoyed supreme authority, neither accumulated treasures of silver and gold, nor levied taxes, nor acquired possession ... which has reference to magnificence and superfluity, although he might have acquired an unlimited abundance of them all ... not indulging in any theatrical affectation of pomp and magnificence, but cultivating the simplicity and unpretending affable plainness of a private individual, but a sumptuousness which was truly royal, in those things which it is becoming for a ruler to desire and to abound in ... and these things are, temperance, and fortitude, and continence, and presence of mind, and acuteness, and knowledge, and industry, and patience under evil, and contempt of pleasure, and justice, and exhortations to virtue and blame, and lawful punishment of offenders, and, on the contrary, praise and honor to those who did well in accordance with law" (*Moses* 1.27.150–54).

justification.⁴³ Another kind of interpretative analysis is that which is theological in nature.⁴⁴ These may be expressed through allegorical interpretations that at times may adapt the way the event is narrated from what is present in the Pentateuch.⁴⁵ The Balaam episode affords an example of an inferential, although traditional, interpretative analysis whereby Philo makes explicit what may be speculative.⁴⁶ Philo is interested in developing a historical biography, but by observing

---

⁴³ Two anecdotes demonstrate both the use of omission and justification which alter the account: (1) In *Moses* 1.8.44–45 Philo omits Moses' concealment of the murder or how it was found out (cf. Exod 2:12–14) since the murder was justified as a "pious action to destroy one who only lived for the destruction of others;" and (2) in *Moses* 1.14.71–84 he does not include the Lord's anger or hints of rebuke over Moses' lack of respect over a holy place or his reluctance when called (cf. Exod 3:3–4:16), instead his hesitancy is approved by God as "modesty." Outside of justifying Moses, in another example Philo gives the moral rationale for the Israelites despoiling the Egyptians (*Moses* 1.25.140-42).

⁴⁴ Not that morality can be separated from theology in Philo's view, but that the Scripture is analyzed with a theological intent. Consider the following example which characteristically includes a demonstration of Moses' virtues, a description of the superiority of the Jewish nation, and a final theological statement concerning God's intent with the election of Israel: "Of all these men, Moses was elected the leader ... appointed for the sake of his virtue and excellence and that benevolence towards all men which he was always feeling and exhibiting ... For, as he had abandoned the chief authority in Egypt ... it seemed good to the Ruler and Governor of the universe to recompense him with the sovereign authority over a more populous and more powerful nation, which he was about to take to himself out of all other nations and to consecrate to the priesthood, that it might forever offer up prayers for the whole universal race of mankind, for the sake of averting evil from them and procuring them a participation in blessings" (*Moses* 1.27.148; cf. Gen 12:1–3; Exod 19:5b–6a). For a theological analysis of God's power through the things of nature see *Moses* 1.38.212–13.

⁴⁵ Below are a few examples of allegorical interpretations: "For the burning bush was a symbol of the oppressed people, and the burning fire was a symbol of the oppressors; and the circumstance of the burning bush not being consumed was an emblem of the fact that the people thus oppressed would not be destroyed ... The angel, again, was the emblem of the providence of God ... All these circumstances are an allegory." (*Moses* 1.12.67; cf. 13.68–70). Elsewhere, he analyzes allegorically the scene at Elim: "The twelve fountains represent the twelve tribes of Israel; the 70 palm trees refer to the 70 elders, because palm trees, which are the most excellent of all trees," have their fruit "situated high up like the heart of a man ... And like the intellect [of virtuous persons] it has learned to look upwards and to soar on high, and is continually keeping its eye fixed on sublime objects" (*Moses* 1.34.187 – 90; cf. Exod 15:27). When analyzing 17:11 – "It happened that whenever Moses raised up his hands, Israel prevailed, but whenever he lowered his hands, Amalek prevailed" – Philo allegorically interprets: "God showing thus by a figure that the earth and all the extremities of it were the appropriate inheritance of the one party, and the most sacred air the inheritance of the other. And as the heaven is in every respect supreme to and superior over the earth, so also shall the nation which has heaven for its inheritance be superior to their enemies." Instead of relating how Aaron and Hur assisted Moses, Philo mentions that his "fingers as if they were wings ... were raised to a lofty height, like winged birds who traverse the heaven, and they continued at this height until the Hebrews had gained an unquestionable victory" (*Moses* 1.39.217–18).

⁴⁶ That is, Balaam's advice to Balak on how to sabotage Israel's covenant with the LORD through harlotry is a traditional interpretation (*Moses* 1.53.294–55.300; cf. b. Sanh.

his use of the Pentateuch, he remains foremost a biblical interpreter, thus, one may agree with Feldman's assertion that when dealing with the biblical text in general, "Philo's purpose is to present not a paraphrase but rather an analysis."[47]

Details such as Names and Numbers

Although Philo follows good rhetorical practices of expanding the original *chreia*, he remains faithful in communicating the historicity of a text. When mentioning place names, he will at times mention both the biblical name and his contemporary geographical location (cf. *Moses* 1.29.163).[48] Philo seldom uses personal names of secondary characters,[49] but is precise in the reapplication of numbers.[50]

106a; Josephus, *A.J.* 4.129–30; Rev 2:14), but it may be based on an inferential analysis of the text. Apparently, Balaam's "advice" in Num 24:14 is reapplied, for although the text has Balaam "advising" Balak with more prophetic oracles against the Midianites in Israel's favor, this "advice" is interpreted as the cause of the evil suggested in Num 25:1–3 and 31:2 to render Balaam as it's instigator. Compare the following: "Whatever things God may say, these things I will speak'. And now, behold, I am about to depart to my territory. Come! I will *advise* you concerning what this people will do *to* your people during the latter days." (Num 24:13-14; italics added); "And Balaam replied: 'All that I have hitherto uttered have been oracles and words of God; but what I am going to say are merely the suggestions of my own mind: And taking him by the right hand, he, while they two were alone, gave him *advice* ... As he knew that the only way by which the Hebrews could be subdued was by leading them to violate the law, he endeavored to seduce them by means of debauchery and intemperance ... This, then, was the *advice* which Balaam gave to Balak'" (*Moses* 1.53.294; 54.295; 55.300; italics added).

[47] Feldman, *Philo's Portrayal*, 361. Although many examples may be reproduced, the following one explicitly portrays the author's reflection included in the narrative with the use of the first person to develop the theme of virtue and piety: "And it seems to me that ... they were also there for the purpose of being taught that most beautiful and beneficial of all lessons, namely, piety. For a distinction could otherwise have never been made so decidedly between the good and the bad, giving destruction to the one and salvation to the other" (*Moses* 1.26.146).

[48] The Bible states that Moses fled into the land of Midian (Exod 2:15b), however, Philo interprets that "he retreated to the contiguous country of Arabia" (*Moses* 1.9.47). He transliterates the named location of the oasis: Aileem (*Moses* 1.34.188); and describes the wilderness of Zin: "For all around were rugged and precipitous rocks, or else a salt and brackish plain, and stony mountains, or deep sands reaching up and forming mountains of inaccessible height; and moreover there was no river, neither winter torrent nor ever-flowing stream" (*Moses* 1.35.192). Furthermore, he generalizes the provenance of Balak, as a "neighboring king" of the "Asiatic nations," and Balaam, proceeding from Mesopotamia (*Moses* 1.48.263–64; cf. Num 22:2–5).

[49] He mentions Aaron, Joshua, and Phineas, but omits Caleb, Miriam, or Moses' lineage, including his parents.

[50] Whether it is mentioning the 600 chariots, the 40 years in the wilderness, the three days of darkness, the seven daughters, or the percentages for the divisions of spoils, etc., he does not deviate from the Pentateuch's numerical details.

Descriptive Expansions

When adapting his source into his biography, Philo is careful not to copy word-for-word what is stated in his source. The changes generally relate to descriptive expansions that serve rhetorical purposes. These expansions do not contradict the account, instead they are logical deductions from the text, sometimes based on ideological or theological interpretations. The following few examples should suffice:

Philo's Descriptive Expansion:	Pentateuchal Source:
Accordingly, he took all his force of cavalry, and his darters, and his slingers, and his equestrian archers, and all the rest of his light-armed troops, and he gave his commanders six hundred of the finest of his scythe-bearing chariots, that with all becoming dignity and display they might pursue these men, and join in the expedition and so suing all possible speed, he sallied forth after them and hastened and pressed on the march, wishing to come upon them suddenly before they had any expectation of him (*Moses* 1.30.168).	Therefore, Pharaoh made ready his chariot and took all his people with himself. And he took six hundred select chariots and all the horsemen of the Egyptians and attending officers on each one. And the Lord hardened the heart of Pharaoh, king of Egypt, and of his attendants, and he pursued hard after the children of Israel (Exod 14:6–8).
For again, the brother of Moses, being ordered to do so, stretched out his hand and held his rod over all the canals, and lakes, and marches; and at the holding forth of his rod, so immense a multitude of frogs came up, that not only the marketplace, and all the spots open to the air, were filled with them, but likewise all the stables for cattle, the houses, and all the temples, and every building, public or private, as if nature had designed to send forth one race of aquatic animals into the opposite region of earth, to form a colony there, for the opposite region to water is earth. (104) Inasmuch then as they could not go out of doors, because all the passages	And the Lord said to Moses, "Say to Aaron, your brother, 'Stretch out in your hand your staff over the rivers and over the irrigation channels and over the ponds and bring up the frogs.'" Aaron stretched out his hand over the waters of Egypt and brought up the frogs. And the frogs came up and covered the land of Egypt (Exod 8:5–6).

were blocked up, and could not remain in-doors, for the frogs had already occupied all the recesses, and had crawled up to the very highest parts of the houses, they were now in the very greatest distress, and in complete despair of safety (*Moses* 1.18.103–4).	

Psychological Analysis

Similar to Euripides's tragedies, "Philo adds to the accounts psychological portraits,"[51] but these additions do not contradict the source text, they can be easily inferred. Although much psychological analysis is employed, sometimes a scientific treatment is presented to explain the reliability of a miracle to a sophisticated first-century Alexandrian audience.[52]

Philo's Use of Discourses

There are at least four ways of categorizing Philo's use of discourses: First, a summarization of a speech as it appears in the narrative of the Pentateuch; Second, a straightforward reapplication of a discourse or saying into his biography (although never verbatim, yet closely approximating in length and content); Third, an expanded and elaborated reapplication of a discourse or dialogue which has as a final result a more extended speech, which includes additional analysis; and Fourth, a discourse in the biography that is not recorded as such in the Pentateuch.

---

[51] Feldman, *Philo's Portrayal*, 364. For example, after the death of the firstborn, Philo includes this moving description of the grief born by the Egyptians: "And, for a while, they remained in their houses, no one being aware of the misfortune which had befallen his neighbour, but lamenting only for his individual loss. But when any one went out of doors and learnt the misfortunes of others also, he at once felt a double sorrow, grieving for the common calamity, in addition to his own private misfortune, a greater and more grievous sorrow being thus added to the lesser and lighter one, so that everyone felt deprived of all hope of consolation. For who was likely to comfort another when he himself stood in need of the same consolation?" (*Moses* 1.24.137).

[52] Two examples are set forth: (1) "And the rock being struck this seasonable blow, whether it was that there was a spring previously concealed beneath it, or whether water was then for the first time conveyed into it by invisible channels pouring in all together and being forced out with violence, [...] poured forth water in a stream" (*Moses* 1.38.211); (2) "Such, then, were the afflictions and punishments by which Egypt was corrected [...] touching the same earth and water, and air and fire, which are all component parts of nature, and which it is impossible to escape from. And this is the most extraordinary and almost incredible thing, that, by the very same events happening in the same place and at the same time, one people was destroyed and the other people was preserved" (*Moses* 1.26.143).

The following charts provide representative examples of each in the order assigned above:

Philo's Summarization	Speeches Present in the Pentateuch
God commanded him to put one of his hands in his bosom and hide it there, and a moment afterwards to draw it out again. And when he had done what he was commanded, his hand in a moment appeared whiter than snow. Again, when he had put his hand a second time into his bosom, and had a second time drawn it forth, it returned to its original complexion, and resumed its proper appearance (*Moses* 1.14.79).	And the Lord said to him again, "Bring in your hand into your bosom!" And so he brought in his hand into his bosom, and he brought forth his hand out of his bosom, and his hand had become as though *it were* snow. And he said again, "Bring your hand into your bosom." And he put his hand into his bosom, and he brought it forth from his bosom, and again it was reestablished as the skin of its flesh (Exod 4:6–7).
But though he believed the words of God, nevertheless he tried to avoid the office to which God was appointing him, urging that he was a man of a weak voice, and slow of speech, and not eloquent, and especially so ever since he had heard God himself speaking (*Moses* 1.14.83).	But Moses said to the Lord, "I beseech *you*, O Lord, I am not adequate before yesterday nor before the previous day nor from the time when you began to speak to your attendant. I am weak-voiced and slow of tongue" (Exod 4:10).
Again, therefore, they have recourse to the same means of escape by entreating Moses, and the king now promised to permit the Hebrews to depart, and they propitiated God with prayers (*Moses* 1.18.105).	And so Pharaoh summoned Moses and Aaron and said, "Entreat the Lord for me, and let him remove the frogs from me and also from my people. And I shall release them so that they may sacrifice to the Lord" (Exod 8:8).
And, as he repented of having let them go, he determined to pursue them (*Moses* 1.30.167).	and the heart of Pharaoh and the heart his of attendants was changed toward the people. Then they said, "What *is* this we have done by sending forth the children of Israel from not serving us?" (Exod 14:5).
But with great courtesy and civility [Balaam] evaded their request, as if he were one of the most celebrated prophets, and as such was accustomed to do nothing whatever without first consulting the oracle, and	Then he said to them, "Remain here during the night, and I will give an answer to you concerning the things that the Lord may speak to me." And the leaders of Moab remained with Balaam... And when

so he declined, saying that the Deity would not permit him to go with them (*Moses* 1.48.266).	Balaam arose in the morning, he said to the leaders of Balak, "Depart to your ruler; God is not permitting me to go along with you" (Num 22:8, 13).

Philo's Straightforward Reapplication	Speeches Present in the Pentateuch
And then at length the men in authority came ... and said to the king, "How long wilt thou refuse to permit the men to depart? Dost thou not understand, from what has already taken place, that Egypt is destroyed?" (*Moses* 1.21.122)	[7] And the attendants of Pharaoh said to him, "How long will this one be a snare to us? Send forth the men so that they may worship their God! Or are you willing to know that Egypt is destroyed?" (Exod 10:7).
And he when he beheld it said: "Do thou, O king, build here seven altars, and offer upon every one of them a bullock and a ram. And I will turn aside and inquire of God what I am to say." (*Moses* 1.50.277)	And Balaam instructed Balak, "Construct for me here seven altars and prepare for me here seven oxen and seven rams" (Num 23:1).
And spoke in prophetic strain as follows: "Balak has sent for me from Mesopotamia, having caused me to take a long journey from the east, that he might chastise the Hebrews by means of curses. But in what manner shall I be able to curse those who have not been cursed by God? For I shall behold them with my eyes from the loftiest mountains, and I shall see them with my mind; and I shall never be able to injure the people which shall dwell alone, not being numbered among the other nations, not in accordance with the inheritance of any particular places, or any apportionment of lands, but by reason of the peculiar nature of their remarkable customs, as they will never mingle with any other nation so as to depart from their national and ancestral ways.	And taking up his poetic discourse, he said, "Out from Paddan-aram Balak sent for me, the king of Moab, out of the mountainous hill country of the east, saying, 'Come, curse Jacob for me, and come entreat curses *against* Israel for me.' How may I curse whom the Lord has not cursed? Or how may I condemn whom God has not condemned? For from the height of the mountainous hill country I will see him, and from high places I will perceive him. Behold a people will dwell alone and will not be reckoned among the nations. Who can calculate the seed of Jacob? And who can number the multitude of Israel? May my soul die among the souls of the righteous, and may my seed be as the seed of these people" (Num 23:1–10).

Who has ever discovered with accuracy the first origin of the birth of these people? Their bodies, indeed, may have been fashioned according to human means of propagation; but their souls have been brought forth by divine agency, wherefore they are nearly related to God. May my soul die as to the death of the body, that it may be remembered among the souls of the righteous, such as the souls of these men are." (*Moses* 1.50.278-79)	
But Balak, being very indignant… said: "O man, neither curse them at all, nor bless them at all; for silence, which is free from danger, is better than unpleasant speeches." (*Moses* 1.52.285).	And Balak responded to Balaam, "*Do* not curse him with curses for me, neither bless him by blessing" (Num 23:25).

Philo's Expanded Use of Discourse	Original Discourse as in the Pentateuch
"Because there were no graves in Egypt in which we could be buried after we were dead, have you brought us out hither to kill and bury us here? Or, is not even slavery a lighter evil than death? Having allured the multitude with the hope of liberty, you have caused them to incur a still more grievous danger than slavery, namely, the risk of the loss of life. Did you not know our simplicity, and the bitterness and cruel anger of the Egyptians? Do you not see the magnitude of the evils which surround us, and from which we cannot escape? What are we to do? Are we, unarmed, to fight against men in complete armor? or shall we flee now that we are hemmed in as by nets cast all around us by our pitiless enemies—hemmed in by pathless deserts and impassable seas? Or,	And he (sic.) said to Moses, "Since there are no graves in the land of Egypt, you are leading us out to be put to death in the wilderness! What *is* this you are doing to us, bringing us out of Egypt? Was this not the thing that we spoke to you in Egypt, saying, 'Leave us alone so that we may serve the Egyptians. For *it is* better for us to be slaves to the Egyptians than to die in this wilderness'" (Exod 14:11–12).

even, if the sea was navigable, how are we to get any vessels to cross over it?" (*Moses* 1.31.171–72).	
[Moses] encouraged and comforted those who cried out to him, saying: "Do not faint and despair. God does not deliver in the same way that man does. Why do you only trust such means of deliverance as seem probable and likely? God, when he comes as an assistant, stands in need of no adventitious preparations. It is his peculiar attribute to find a path amid inextricable perplexities. What is impossible to every created being is possible and easy to him above." Thus he spoke to them while yet standing still. But after a short time he became inspired by God, and being full of the divine spirit and under the influence of that spirit which was accustomed to enter into him, he prophesied and animated them thus: "This army which you behold so splendidly equipped with arms, you shall no more see arrayed against you; for it shall fall, utterly and completely overthrown, so that not a relic shall be seen any more upon the earth, and that not at any distance of time, but this very next night" (*Moses* 1.31.173–75).	Now Moses said to the people, "Be courageous, stand firm! And observe the salvation that *is* from God, which he will perform for you today … For in the manner which you behold the Egyptians today, you will not continue any longer to see them ₁forever₁. ¹⁴ The Lord will do battle for you. You keep silent!" (Exod 14:13–14).
And when he had selected the men he spoke to them as follows: "The inheritance which is before us is the prize of those labours and dangers which we have endured hitherto, and are still enduring, and let us not lose the hope of these things, we who are thus conducting a most populous nation to a new settlement. But the knowledge of the places, and of the men, and of the circumstances, is most useful, just	And so Moses sent them to seek out the land of Canaan and said to them, "Go up through the wilderness and go on up into the hill country (Num 13:18). And now look over the land, what it is *like*, and the people who dwell upon it, whether they are quite

as ignorance of these particulars is most injurious. We have therefore appointed you as spies, that we, by your eyes and by your intellects, may see the state of things there; ye, therefore, must be the ears and eyes of all these myriads of people, that thus they may arrive at an accurate comprehension of what is indispensable to be known.

"Now what we wish to know consists of three points; the number of the inhabitants, and the strength of their cities, whether they are planted in favourable situations, whether they are strongly built and fortified, or the contrary. As to the country, we wish to know whether it has a deep and rich soil, whether it is good to bear all kinds of fruits, both of such plants as are raised from seed and of fruit-trees; or whether, on the contrary, it has a shallow soil; that so we may be prepared against the power and numbers of the inhabitants with equal forces, and against the fortified state of buildings and cities by means of engines and machines, for the destruction of cities.

"And it is indispensable to understand the nature of the country, and whether it is a good land or not; for to encounter voluntary dangers for a poor and bad land is an act of folly; and our weapons, and our engines, and all our power, consist solely in our trust and confidence in God. Having this preparation we will yield to no danger or fear, for this is sufficient with great superfluity of power to subdue otherwise invincible strength, which relies only on bodily vigour and on armies, and on courage, and skill, and numbers; since to that too we owe

strong or weak, whether they are few or many. [20] And *see* what the land, upon which these *people* who are dwelling upon it, whether it is good or bad, and what the cities, which these *people* are dwelling in them, whether with walls or without walls. [21] And *see* what the land *is like*, whether rich and fertile or infertile and poor, whether there are in it trees or not" (Num 13:19–21a).

… and putting forth great care and effort, take some of the fruit of the land." Now the season *was* the season of spring, heralding the grape season (Num 13:21b).

it, that even in a vast wilderness we have full supplies of everything, as if we were in well-stocked cities; and the time in which it is most easy to come to a proper understanding of the good qualities of the land is the spring, the season which is now present; for in the season of spring what has been sown is coming to perfection, and the natures of the trees are beginning to propagate themselves further. It will be better, therefore, for you to enter the land now, and to remain till the middle of the summer, and to bring back with you fruits, as samples of what is to be procured from a prosperous and fertile country" (*Moses* 1.40.222-26).	

Philo's Added Discourses Not Present in Pentateuch	Alluded Source
But all the sophists and magicians who were present said, "Why are you thus alarmed? we also are not unpracticed in such tricks as these, and we are skilled in an art which can produce similar effects" (*Moses* 1.16.92).	And the magicians of the Egyptians also did likewise by their spells (Exod 7:11b).
But Moses, seeing what was done … ran up; and … said: "Will not you desist from behaving thus unjustly thinking this solitary place a fitting field for the exercise of your covetousness? Are you not ashamed to have such cowardly arms and hands? You are long-haired people, female flesh, and not men. The damsels behave like vigorous youths, hesitating about nothing that they ought to do; but you, young men, are now behaving lazily, like girls. Will you not depart? Will you not be off and give place to those who arrived first, to whom	The shepherds, coming by, drove them out; but Moses rose up and rescued them (Exod 2:17a).

the water belongs, and who are entitled to it; when you ought rather to have drawn water for them, that so they might have had it in greater abundance? And are you, on the contrary, endeavouring to take away from them what they themselves have got ready? "But I swear, by the celestial eye of justice, which sees what is done even in the most solitary places, that you shall not take it from them. And at all events, now justice has sent me and appointed me to bring them assistance who never expected such an officer; for I am an ally to these damsels who are thus injured by violence, and I come with a might which you evil-doers and covetous people cannot face, but you shall feel it wounding you in an invisible manner, if you do not change your ways" (*Moses* 1.10.54).	
But as the Hebrews received their answer with great indignation, and prepared at once to oppose them, Moses stood in a place from whence he would be well heard, and said, "O men, your indignation is reasonable and just; for though we, in a peaceable disposition, have made them good and friendly offers, they have made us an evil reply out of their evil and perverse disposition. But it does not follow that because they deserve to pay the penalty for their cruelty, therefore it is desirable for us to proceed to take vengeance upon them, by reason of the honor due to our own nation, that we may show that in this particular we are good and different from wicked men, inasmuch as we consider not only whether such and	And Edom was not willing to permit Israel to pass through their territory; and Israel turned away from them (Num 20:21).

such persons deserve to be punished, but whether also it is proper that they should receive their punishment from us." On this he turned aside and led his army by another road (*Moses* 1.44.244-46).	
Come, then, let us examine into [Balaam's] fine recommendations ... for, said he, "O king! the women of the country surpass all other women in beauty, and there are no means by which a man is more easily subdued than by the beauty of a woman; therefore, if you enjoin the most beautiful of them to grant their favors to them and to prostitute themselves to them, they will allure and overcome the youth of your enemies. But you must warn them not to surrender their beauty to those who desire them with too great facility and too speedily, for resistance and coyness will stimulate the passions and excite them more, and will kindle a more impetuous desire; and so, being wholly subdued by their appetites, they will endure to do and to suffer anything. "And let any damsel who is thus prepared for the sport resist, and say, wantonly, to a lover who is thus influenced, "It is not fitting for you to enjoy my society till you have first abandoned your native habits, and have changed, and learnt to honor the same practices that I do. And I must have a conspicuous proof of your real change, which I can only have by your consenting to join me in the same sacrifices and libations which I use, and which we may then offer together at the same images and statues, and other erections in honor of my gods. And the lover being, as it	Now Israel stayed in Shittim, and the people were profaned by committing harlotry with the women of Moab. They called them to the sacrifices for their idols, and the people ate their offerings and bowed down and worshiped their idols, and Israel was consecrated to Baal-peor. And the Lord was incensed with wrath against Israel (Num 25:1–3).

were, taken in the net of her manifold and multiform snares, not being able to resist her beauty and seductive conversation, will become wholly subdued in his reason, and, like a miserable man, will obey all the commands which she lays upon him, and will be enrolled as the salve of passion" (*Moses* 1.53.295–99).

Implications for the Study of the Gospels

The selections above and observations throughout this study have not been exhaustive but a representative analysis of Philo's use of sources in the whole of Book 1. In summary, it has been shown that Philo is dependent on the Pentateuch throughout his work, although he never introduces a quotation. He analyzes the text as an interpreter although he is interested in writing a biography that conforms to the historical facts. In keeping with the style of ancient Greco-Roman writers, Philo is careful not to repeat verbatim any part of the written document, neither does he invent an account on Moses' life that cannot be deduced from careful analysis of his source. Whether he employs discourse expansions, psychological analysis, interpretative additions, or thematic arrangement (influenced by the author's stated purposes), all the *chreia* surrounding the life of Moses depend on the Pentateuch as a historical source. The reader is not left questioning the historical veracity of the subject matter, it is assumed that one would be able to examine the evidence in the LXX and compare it with the biography.

Concerning discourses, it is not assumed that a statement that is narratively placed on the lips of another must have been the *ipsissima verba* of that individual. What characters say, as well as the specific descriptions of how events occur, are not so important to demonstrate the historical veracity of a work; instead, it is part of the author's literary rights to freely display his skillful abilities as a rhetorician or interpreter of history by analyzing and highlighting certain features from a historical record.

How would this analysis help us in the study of the Gospels? By admitting to their genre as ancient Greco-Roman biographies, one may deduce that one of their assumed interests is to maintain a certain degree of historical reliability. Notwithstanding, like Book 1 of Philo's *Moses*, the evangelists may have adapted their sources on the life of Jesus by arranging individual *chreia* thematically, adding theological interpretations and including descriptive expansions, such as psychological analysis. The aretological goals which influenced Philo's portrayal of Moses may be compared to those of the Gospel writers in their depiction of Jesus. The examples provided of Philo's use of discourses may provide additional models to further study the sayings and discourses of Jesus as depicted in the Gospels, specifically in the Fourth Gospel.

Chapter 13

Comparing First and Second Maccabees: Do Their Differences Make Them Unreliable?

Adrian Reynolds
Asbury Theological Seminary

Introduction

This chapter aims to determine the impact that a comparison between 1 and 2 Maccabees might have on the question of the historical reliability of the Greco-Jewish historiographic tradition, and hence possibly on the Synoptic Gospels.[1] The endeavor proposes that certain kinds of difference between 1 and 2 Maccabees indicate 1) that there were, during the Greco-Roman period, accepted ways of presenting historical material in Jewish circles that did not require exact agreement between descriptions of events;[2] and 2) that there was a widely accepted convention within the genre of history writing that allowed for adaptations which are best attributed to the historian's *interpretation* of events.[3] This act of interpreting history can account for many differences between disparate versions of events.

A comparison of the two Maccabean histories should shed light on the Synoptics as ancient biographies (a sub-genre of history), and their historical reliability.[4] In pursuit of this overarching goal, I will survey differences between 1 and 2 Maccabees that should highlight three outcomes.

---

[1] I am working in general within Huizinga's somewhat broad definition of history: "History is the intellectual form in which a civilization renders account to itself of its past," in Huizinga, "Concept," 9. Documents like 1 and 2 Maccabees and the Synoptic Gospels fit this definition of "history" in certain ways, and can be relied upon to some extent for significant information about the Jewish past. That they fit the definition is underscored by a perusal of Van Seters's five criteria: Van Seters, *Historiography*, 4-5.

[2] Grabbe recognizes that 1 and 2 Maccabees are indeed Jewish Hellenistic compositions. See Grabbe, "Jewish Historiography," 152.

[3] For a discussion of how the Deuteronomist, the first historian in Van Seters's view, used the past, see Van Seters, *Historiography*, 356-62.

[4] For important studies on the Gospels as ancient biographies, see Talbert, *What is a Gospel?*; Shuler, *Genre*; Aune, "Greco-Roman Biography," 107-26; and Burridge, *Gospels?* (2004); also, briefly, see Keener, *Historical Jesus*, 73-84.

First, I will argue that the two books of Maccabees are best seen as "the same yet different," a label that James Dunn has applied to the Synoptics.[5] The relevant implication is that the Synoptics are therefore not unique in this regard; they belong to an accepted kind of historiography that was well established by the time they were written.[6] This pattern of historiographical writing had been in place for at least two hundred years prior to the Gospels' formation.

Second, the authors of 1 and 2 Macc did in fact make critical choices about what they wrote and there is little evidence to suggest that they did not.[7] I am, in this regard, in agreement with Van Seters's claim that the Deuteronomist was in fact the first real historian and that Greek influence is apparent in comparatively later Jewish history writing.[8] Despite obvious Greek influences, both 1 and 2 Maccabees and the Synoptic Gospels reported the past for Jewish reasons.[9] That is, they critically engaged their subject matter in Jewish ways.

Third, I will show that differences between 1 and 2 Maccabees actually serve to suggest that the two are useful histories. At the very least many of their divergences can be explained satisfactorily and at most they serve to increase the level of confidence we can have in partially disparate accounts as witnesses to the past. This is partly because, in view of the criterion of multiple attestation, similarities between historical portrayals are much more significant for establishing reliable data than are differences. My conclusion will discuss the bearing all this has on how we should evaluate the historical reliability of the Synoptics.

1 Maccabees 4:1-61 and 2 Maccabees 8:1-10:9

In this paper I treat 1 and 2 Macc as documents that record the same events in history, but do not have any known connection besides that.[10] They record well-known major events, yet differ in many of the details. In this section, then, I will take samples from 1 Macc 3:1-6:16 and 2 Macc 8:1-10:9 and examine the major

---

[5] Dunn, *Social Memory*, 179-94.

[6] For an argument for the historiographic nature of 1 and 2 Maccabees, see Lichtenberger, "History-Telling," 95–110. For a similarly balanced, but more optimistic view of the historical value of 2 Macc, see Schwartz, *2 Maccabees*, 56.

[7] Contra Lester Grabbe: "It seems doubtful that true critical investigation is found in either 1 or 2 Maccabees" and that the first "real historians" were not Israelites but Greeks; see Grabbe, "Real Historians," 178-81.

[8] Van Seters, *Historiography*, 362.

[9] For a discussion of one kind of Greek influence on 2 Macc, see Simkovich, "Greek Influence," 293–310.

[10] This sets 1 and 2 Maccabees apart from the Gospels in that sense, but their common Jewish Hellenistic character suggests a great many more points of connection than of contrast. Carroll argues that this phenomenon of Jewish/Greek mutual influence can be seen in the OT, indicating that it had a significant length of time in which to take root in Judean historiography. Carroll, *Jewgreek Greekjew*, 91-107. Also see Van Seters, *Historiography*, 8-54, for further discussion of the influence of Greek historiography on Israelite historiography.

differences to display the relationship between the two. I will argue that an examination of these differences will expose the ideas each author sought to emphasize, and that such differences in presentation do not undermine the substantial historical reliability value of each work.

The Books

1 Maccabees 3:27-6:16 tells the story of a Seleucid campaign against Judea that ultimately resulted in Judea's successful defense by Judas Maccabaeus and his brothers, the purification of the temple, and the death of Antiochus Epiphanes.[11] 2 Macc 8:1-10:9 tells the same story but in a different way. 1 Maccabees as a whole makes no explicit claim to a particular theological or rhetorical agenda. The book plainly describes the events of the period with which it is concerned.[12] This does not mean that the author of 1 Macc did not make any theological claims or have a rhetorical agenda, but rather that he leaves his readers to draw such conclusions from the account. This will become increasingly apparent as this project proceeds. The following is an outline of the section of 1 Macc (1:1—7:50) that corresponds to the whole of 2 Macc:

    1:1-64 – Jerusalem defiled
    2:1-70 – The Jewish resistance begins
    3:1-3:26 – Antiochus reacts to Judas' successes
    3:27-60 – Lysias attacks Jerusalem
    4:1-61 – Hanukkah inaugurated
    5:1-6:16 – Death of Antiochus IV
    6:17-7:50 – Nicanor's day inaugurated

2 Maccabees describes itself as a summary of a much longer work, and its compiler is candid about his rhetorical agenda. His purpose is to persuade Egyptian Jews to celebrate the purification of the temple (Hanukkah) on the 25th of Chislev every year.[13] This is clear from the two embedded letters with which it begins and the subsequent account of the temple's purification which ends in 10:9.[14] Here is an outline of the book:

---

[11] Some have thought that 1 Macc was written by an eyewitness of some of the events and that as a result it is more reliable than 2 Macc. This is not a widely held view now, but should be noted here. For an example of this older view, see Bar-Kochva, *Judas Maccabaeus*, 403.

[12] For an examination of the claim that 1 Macc records the Hasmoneans' "reclaiming of the promised land," see Berthelot, "Reclaiming the Land," 539–59.

[13] Frenkel argues that 2 Macc was written in part to counter the Epicurean ideas of Antiochus IV. While I do not agree fully, the article illustrates the important point that 2 Macc was written with a rhetorical purpose. See Frenkel, "Debate Filosófico," 123–33.

[14] For the purposes of this paper the "author" of 2 Macc is Jason of Cyrene (2:23), the "abridger" summarized Jason's work and the "compiler" is the Jerusalemite who wrote the introductory letters and put the book in the present form. See Parker, "Letters in II Maccabees," 386–402, for a discussion of the roles of these three characters in the book's composition.

1:1-2:18 – Letters urging Jews in Egypt to celebrate purification of the Temple
2:19-32 – Introductory explanation of aims and method and scope
3:1-4:50 – Sanctity of temple protected by God then betrayed by Jews
5:1-7:42 – Temple violated; fFaithful Jews martyred
8:1-10:9 – Hanukkah inaugurated
10:10-15:37 – Nicanor's day inaugurated
15:38-39 – Closing remarks

The section of most interest to the current project is 2 Macc 8:1-10:9 in which the narrative shows how the fortunes of Jerusalem changed for the better, and how Hanukkah came to be celebrated as a national holiday.[15] Within this section I have chosen 9:28-10:9, the description of the temple purification, for comparison with the parallel section of 1 Macc (1 Macc 3:35-59). Some see 2 Macc 10:1-8 as an interpolation by the Jerusalemites who wrote the letters to which the abridged history is attached.[16] I do not consider this to be the case. On the contrary, the following comparison will demonstrate how that section's concern for Jews in the diaspora is a characteristic it shares with most, if not all, of the rest of the book and is therefore of a piece with the work as a whole.

1 Maccabees 4:35-59 and 2 Maccabees 9:28-10:9

This section includes both a presentation and explanation of the similarities and differences between 1 Macc 4:35-59 and 2 Macc 9:28-10:9. Within the explanation the focus will be on how the differences impact our view of the historical reliability of the two documents.[17] If attention to what we know of the situation explains the differences, then we can entertain one level of certainty. The absence of an explanation will result, of course, in a lower level of confidence. The table below juxtaposes the two renditions.

Legend:
Literary setting: []
Material unique to 1 or 2 Macc: {}
Material in both worded differently: Underline
Material in both worded similarly: *Italics*
Pertinent vocabulary differences: ()

---

[15] For an examination of Hanukkah and its relation to 2 Macc, see Wheaton, "The Festival," 247–62.

[16] Schwartz, *2 Maccabees*, 8.

[17] By "historical reliability" I mean the degree to which the recorded events actually took place.

Comparing First and Second Maccabees 305

1 Maccabees 4:35-59	2 Maccabees 9:28-10:9
[³⁵ Seeing the rout of his army and the courage of Judas' troops and their readiness to live or die nobly, Lysias withdrew to Antioch, where he recruited mercenaries for a further invasion of Judaea in even greater strength. ³⁶ Judas and his brothers then said, 'Now that our enemies have been defeated, let us go up to purify the sanctuary and dedicate it.']	[⁸ And so this murderer and blasphemer [Antiochus IV], having endured sufferings as terrible as those which he had made others endure, met his pitiable fate, and ended his life in the mountains far from his home. ²⁹ His comrade Philip brought back his body, and then, fearing Antiochus' son, withdrew to Egypt, to the court of Ptolemy Philometor.]
... ⁴¹ Judas {then ordered his men to keep the Citadel garrison engaged until he had purified the sanctuary (*hagia*). ⁴² Next,} he selected priests who were blameless and zealous for the Law ⁴³ to purify the sanctuary (*hagia*) {and remove the stones of the 'Pollution' to some unclean place. ⁴⁴ They discussed what should be done about the altar of burnt offering which had been profaned,}	¹ Maccabaeus {and his companions, under the} Lord's guidance, restored the Temple (*neō*) {and the city,}
⁴⁵ and {very properly decided} to pull it down, {rather than later be embarrassed about it since it had been defiled by the gentiles (*ethnē*). They therefore demolished it ⁴⁶ and deposited the stones in a suitable place on the hill of the Dwelling to await the appearance of a prophet who should give a ruling about them.}	² and pulled down the altars {erected by the foreigners (*allophylōn*) in the market place, as well as the shrines.}

{⁴⁷ They took unhewn stones, as the Law prescribed}, *and built (ōkodomēsan)* <u>a new</u> *altar* {on the lines of the old one.} ⁴⁸ {They} *restored (ōkodomēsan) the Holy Place* {and the interior of the Dwelling, and purified the courts. ⁴⁹ They made new sacred vessels, and brought the lamp-stand, the altar of incense, and the table into the Temple.} ⁵⁰ *They burned incense* {on the altar and} *lit the lamps* {on the lamp-stand, and these shone inside the Temple.} ⁵¹ *They placed the loaves on the table* {and hung the curtains and completed all the tasks they had undertaken.}	³ *They purified (katharisantes) the sanctuary (<u>neō</u>) and built (epoiēsan)* <u>another</u> *altar*; *then*, {striking fire from flints and using this fire}, *they offered* {the first} *sacrifice* {for two years}, *burning incense, lighting the lamps and setting out the loaves.*
⁵² *On the twenty-fifth of the* <u>ninth</u> *month, Chislev,* {in the year 148 they rose at dawn} ⁵³ *and offered a* {lawful} *sacrifice* {on the new altar of burnt offering which they had made. ⁵⁴ The altar was dedicated, to the sound of hymns, zithers, lyres and cymbals}, *at the same time of year and on the same day on which the gentiles (ethnē) had originally profaned it.*	{⁴ When they had done this}, *prostrating themselves (pesontes epi koilian) on the ground,* {they implored the Lord never again to let them fall into such adversity, but if they should ever sin, to correct them with moderation and not to deliver them over to blasphemous and barbarous nations. ⁵ This day of the purification of the Temple fell} *on the very day on which the Temple had been profaned by the foreigners (ethnesin), the twenty-fifth of the* <u>same</u> *month, Chislev.*
{⁵⁵ The whole people} *fell prostrate (epesen ... epi prosōpon)* {in adoration and then praised Heaven who had granted them success.} ⁵⁶ *For eight days they celebrated* {the dedication of the altar, joyfully offering burnt offerings, communion and thanksgiving sacrifices.}	⁶ *They kept eight festal days with rejoicing,* {in the manner of the feast of Shelters, remembering how, not long before at the time of the feast of Shelters, they had been living in the mountains and caverns like wild beasts.}

{⁵⁷ They ornamented the front of the Temple with crowns and bosses of gold, renovated the gates and storerooms, providing the latter with doors.} ⁵⁸ *There was no end to the rejoicing among the people*, {since the disgrace inflicted by the gentiles had been effaced.}	{⁷ Then, carrying thyrsuses, leafy boughs and palms, they offered hymns to him who had brought the cleansing of his own holy place to a happy outcome.}
⁵⁹ <u>Judas, with his brothers and the whole assembly of Israel,</u> made it a law *that* {the days of the dedication of the altar} *should be celebrated yearly* {at the proper season, for eight days beginning on the twenty-fifth of the month of Chislev, with rejoicing and gladness.}	⁸ <u>They also decreed</u> {by public edict, ratified by vote}, *that* {the whole Jewish nation} *should celebrate those same days every year.*
	[⁹ Such were the circumstances attending the death of Antiochus styled Epiphanes.]

Purification of the Temple: Similarities

The following broad outline of the Temple's purification is discernible in both accounts. It took place in Jerusalem in a period of relative peace following a victory over invading gentiles. Judas Maccabaeus led the Judean military's defensive effort operating according to Jewish norms and in consultation with the Jewish God. The altar of burnt offering which had been defiled was torn down and replaced in an acceptable manner. Upon the altar's restoration, incense and a "lawful" burnt offering were ignited upon it. This was all accompanied by the lighting of lamps, the setting out of loaves, and prayer. The celebration lasted eight days and ended with a widely accepted declaration that it should take place yearly in perpetuity.

Although the actual volume of material that is common to both works is relatively small, it does include the most important elements of the plot.[18] The fact that the two versions are different (stylistically and in other ways) but agree on the main story line suggests that the major features are reliable. In general, because similarities between accounts should count for significantly more than

---

[18] There is a significant sense in which in might be said that were any of the noted elements (with the exception perhaps of the lighting of the lamps/the setting out of the loaves) excluded from either telling of the story its plot would change significantly and it would be difficult to maintain that the two accounts do indeed record the same event. The exclusion of other, less central, details would not have the same dislocating effect.

dissimilarities when reconstructing events,[19] the fact that agreement over major details exists suggests the overall trustworthiness of their essential substance.

Purification of the Temple: Differences

A primary difference between the two records is their literary setting. 1 Macc places the temple purification after battles won by Judas over Gorgias and Lysias. In doing so the author emphasizes the extent to which Judea is defiled by the pagan invaders and their insider allies, thus providing more than sufficient warrant for Judas' actions. So the purification of the temple here represents Judas's able and proper correction of pagan indiscretions. 2 Maccabees, on the other hand, places the temple purification at the death of Antiochus IV. It is, in fact, said to be one of its attending circumstances (2 Macc 10:9).[20] This highlights both the event of the temple cleansing and the fact that Israel's God took Antiochus' life for his sins.

Secondly, the theme of God's overt intervention in Israel's affairs is generally much starker in 2 Macc than in 1 Macc. In fact, many of the major theological differences between the two center on the extent to which each writer accentuates God's activity.[21] In the current instance, while both recognize the importance of the temple's purification, 1 Macc uses it to lend credibility to purported Maccabean prowess, and 2 Macc to show God's action on Israel's (not just Jerusalem's or the temple's) behalf.

Thirdly, a diasporic emphasis is apparent in 2 Macc but not discernible in 1 Macc. 2 Macc presents God as the deliverer of *all* Israel in order to urge unity between Jews in the diaspora and Jerusalemites through mutual celebration of Hanukkah as God's people. 1 Macc depicts temple ritual correctness to promote Judas and his descendants, a much narrower interest.[22]

The divergences noted so far do not necessarily have a negative impact on the reliability of 1 and 2 Macc. They can be readily explained in terms of the author's rhetorical agenda and theological outlook, both of which were typical aspects of ancient Greek-influenced Jewish historiography. Other differences, however, impact the inquiry to varying extents and in distinct ways. I have used the following categories to organize some of them: 1) Order of Events; 2) Extent

---

[19] As noted earlier, this notion that similarities are especially pertinent to an assessment of a document's reliability will be supported below.

[20] For argumentation that this is indeed the more accurate historical placement for the death of Antiochus IV, see Williams, "1 Maccabees," 71.

[21] The interest in the miraculous shown by the author of 2 Maccabees is often cited as a reason to doubt his historical interest and reliability. See, Lichtenberger, "History-Telling," 109. However, that a priori line of reasoning is now questionable in view of Keener, *Miracles*.

[22] It is of course true that Jerusalemite leaders of some kind put 2 Macc into its present form. This is shown by the letters attached to it. The result is a Jerusalemite correspondence attached to an abridged history the long version of which was written by a diasporan Jew.

of Abridgment; 3) Descriptive Detail; 4) Vocabulary Use; and 5) Unequivocal Contradiction.

Order of Events

Both accounts contain descriptions of the same events, i.e. attacks by Lysias, victory for Judas and the Jews, the death of Antiochus IV, and the temple purification. They are, however, in a different order in each document:

1 Maccabees	2 Maccabees
Judas defeats Lysias	Antiochus IV dies in route from Persia
Judas cleanses temple and institutes Hanukkah	Judas cleanses temple and institutes Hanukkah
Intervening battles	Intervening battles
Antiochus IV dies in route from Persia	Judas defeats Lysias

There are ways of explaining these differences. For example, the writers or their respective sources simply remembered the order differently. Of course, without an alternative, third-party account of the events, there is no way to settle the matter. It is not possible to discover who remembered what and with what degree of accuracy.

It is helpful, however, to note that the order of events in 1 Macc emphasizes Judas' prowess whereas in 2 Macc the order emphasizes God's supernatural intervention. This undergirds the theological/rhetorical contrast already noted.[23] By placing the purification within the account of Antiochus' death 2 Macc accentuates the supernatural deliverance of the temple. 1 Macc highlights Judas's role and disassociates Antiochus's punishment from the temple's emancipation.[24] This does not help with deciding which version is more "accurate," but it accounts for the variations. Also, the fact that both accounts record the same events indicates that the episodes took place in some order.

---

[23] Bar-Kochva, in a similar way, explains the different placements of Lysias's campaign in terms of theological divergence between authors. See Bar-Kochva, *Judas Maccabaeus*, 276-77. One might compare the Synoptic versus Johannine chronologies for Jesus's temple cleansing (though biographies, unlike larger histories, were less concerned with historical sequence).

[24] For a discussion of how the apparently conflicting dates for the death of Antiochus IV's death may be explained in light of recent scholarly opinion, see Williams, "1 Maccabees," 171.

Extent of Abridgment

2 Maccabees uses shorter and more general descriptors than 1 Macc. This is displayed in the table below.

1 Maccabees 4:42	2 Maccabees 10:1
...he selected priests who were blameless and zealous for the law...	...under the Lord's guidance...
...to purify the sanctuary and remove the stones of the 'Pollution' to some unclean place...	...restored the temple and the city...
1 Maccabees 4:45-46	**2 Maccabees 10:2**
They very properly decided to pull it down, rather than later be embarrassed about it since it had been defiled by the gentiles. They therefore demolished it [46] and deposited the stones in a suitable place on the hill of the Dwelling to await the appearance of a prophet who should give a ruling about them.	They pulled down the altars erected by the foreigners in the market place, as well as the shrines.

These differences do not pose problems for reconciling the accounts, but they do indicate varying perspectives. 1 Macc points out the correctness of the procedure used for purification, specifically of the temple. 2 Macc is concerned to show summarily that God was directly involved in the events described, and that Jerusalem as a whole was cleansed as well as the temple.[25] The shorter, more general descriptions in 2 Macc are consistent with the abridger's stated method (2:24-25).

On the one hand, 1 Macc shows that Judas is both an able defender of Israel on the battlefield and a religious leader worthy of the nation's trust on ritual matters. The author may therefore be an observant Jew who values the law, a Jerusalemite living in close proximity to the temple. 2 Macc, on the other hand, displays a much broader perspective, one less tied to the temple. Its author is concerned for the whole city, which might suggest that he is a Jew living in the diaspora concerned with the scattered Jewish people.[26] This further indicates that the account of the temple's purification in 2 Macc is not a Jerusalemite addition,

---

[25] For a thoughtful discussion of the variant views of the temple displayed in 1 and 2 Maccabees, see Zsengellér, "Temple Propaganda," 181-95.

[26] de Wet, "O Woman," 33–56. To undergird the diasporan nature of 2 Macc, de Wet argues that the suffering mother in 2 Macc 7 offers a diasporan perspective on the problems of hellenization in the diaspora.

as suggested by some.²⁷ Rather, its viewpoint is consistent with the widely acknowledged diasporic outlook of most of the rest of the book.²⁸

Clearly, then, it is difficult to argue that either the abridger of 2 Macc or the authors of 1 and 2 Macc were as uncritical as Grabbe suggests. On the contrary, it seems reasonable to deduce that the authors depicted events in a way that evidences a critical eye, and that even the abridger of 2 Macc evaluated information in a particular way that certainly did not exclude a consciousness of historical accuracy.²⁹ The mere absence of explicit claims to critical engagement with the question of historicity does not indicate its absence. To this extent, Grabbe's argument against the works' reliability is an argument from silence.

Descriptive Detail

As illustrated below, the lion's share of each excerpt is unique to that account. The following table represents a sample from the two accounts that illustrates just how different they can be when covering the same ground. I have marked the material found only in 1 Macc with [], and that found only in 2 Macc with {}, and when the same idea is described but with different wording, it is in *italics* type:

1 Macc 4:52-54	2 Macc 10:4-5
On the twenty-fifth of the *ninth* month, Chislev, [in the year 148 they rose at dawn ⁵³ and offered a lawful sacrifice on the new altar of burnt offering which they had made. ⁵⁴ The altar was dedicated, to the sound of hymns, zithers, lyres and cymbals,] at the same time of year and on the same day on which the gentiles had originally profaned it. ⁵⁵ [The whole people] fell prostrate [in adoration and then praised Heaven who had granted them success.] ⁵⁶ For eight days they celebrated [the dedication of the altar, joyfully offering burnt offerings, communion and thanksgiving sacrifices.]	{When they had done this,} prostrating themselves on the ground, {they implored the Lord never again to let them fall into such adversity, but if they should ever sin, to correct them with moderation and not to deliver them over to blasphemous and barbarous nations. ⁵ This day of the purification of the Temple fell} on the very day on which the Temple had been profaned by the foreigners, the twenty-fifth of the *same* month, Chislev. ⁶ They kept eight festal days with rejoicing, {in the manner of the feast of Shelters, remembering how, not long before at the time of the feast of Shelters, they had been living in the

---

²⁷ Schwartz, *2 Maccabees*, 8-10.
²⁸ Schwartz, *2 Maccabees*, 45.
²⁹ T. Nisula has argued that the letter writing style of the 2 Macc compiler shows a high level of competence and familiarity with Greek letter writing. This, he says, bodes well for the reliability of the document as a whole (Nisula, "Time Has Passed," 201–22).

	mountains and caverns like wild beasts.}

One of the most striking differences between these two passages, aside from the volume of material unique to each, is the content of their prayers. 1 Macc records adoration and praise of "Heaven." 2 Macc says that they implored "the Lord." 1 Macc highlights the act of offering "lawful" sacrifices significantly more vigorously than it emphasizes acts of offering prayer and praise. 2 Macc does the opposite. So they not only label the object of the prayers and sacrifices differently, but the worship activity they record varies as well.[30]

1 Macc does not make use of either *kyrios* or *theos* at all in relation to the Israelite God. This absence might indicate (especially when understood in light of other matters discussed) a rather distant notion of him that does not expect his intervention in human affairs, but that does see value in the perpetuation of religious tradition. 2 Macc uses both *kyrios* and *theos* copiously in keeping with its persistent concern for God's personal and consistent activity in the story. This difference in convention could indicate different perspectives or even distinct sects within Judaism. Certain aspects of 2 Macc bring parts of Josephus' description of Pharisees and Essenes to mind. It is even conceivable that 2 Macc was written by a Pharisee with some Essene-like ideas, although this suggestion is weakened by Jason's Cyrenian background.[31]

In addition, the evident emphasis on sacrificial offerings in 1 Macc over against on prayer and praise in 2 Macc represents theological distinctions consistent with those already noted.[32] It also implies that the author of 1 Macc had a personal connection to sacrificial rites in the temple. He is careful to assert that a "lawful" sacrifice was offered and adds details of instruments played and other accompanying activities. The details themselves could have been widely known, but their manner of inclusion (with an apologetic air) suggests the status of their author as one of the elite in temple administration circles.[33] A Sadducee could perhaps have written 1 Macc.[34]

Moreover, 2 Macc declares that God punished his people for their sins by allowing the temple defilement. The work even suggests that the sufferings of God's people at the hands of gentiles (also expressed elsewhere in the book ex. 6:12-16) are actually a sign of God's mercy because they represent His loving

---

[30] For a discussion of the rhetorical (and political) power and function of prayer accounts toward unifying diasporan Jews in 2 Macc, see, de Wet, "Power and Priestcraft," 150–61.

[31] For instance, Josephus, *War* 2.119-166, and *Ant.* 18.12-15, and 18.18-22 show both the Pharisaic concern for the supernatural and the Essene ideas on divine punishment.

[32] See, Simkovich, "Greek Influence," 293–310, for argumentation that 2 Macc is less familiar than 1 Macc with the temple because it is diasporan.

[33] 1 Maccabees is significantly nationalistic. F.M. Abel argues that this is based on "La conviction qu'Israel est le peuple de Dieu"; see Abel, "Livres Des Maccabees," 11.

[34] Josephus, *War* 2.164-165 and *Ant.* 18.16-17 show the Sadducean lack of belief in the immanence of the supernatural among other traits, several of which are evident in 1 Macc. For agreement on this point, see Dancy, *1 Maccabees*, 3.

discipline. The prayer itself is an acknowledgement of Israel's corporate sin (another important aspect of 2 Macc theology) and a request to punish them more gently in the future without handing them over to another nation. The writer of this work thus believes both that God will intervene in affairs of this world on behalf of his people, and that he will refrain from doing so in order to discipline them.[35] None of this is noticeable in 1 Macc.

These increasingly evident theological differences between the books suggest ever more strongly that 1 and 2 Macc were written by Jews of significantly different perspectives.[36] It would also indicate that they worked independently of one another and probably did not share sources. If they did use common sources they changed them so thoroughly towards their own ends that traces of that common origin are difficult to find. This point will be substantiated further in the next section. If, then, these variant versions of history agree on major details, they evidently depend on reports of events that probably significantly predate either version. The similarities show themselves, then, to be especially pertinent.

Vocabulary Use

Significant differences in style exhibited by the two authors further emphasize a lack of contact between them.[37] This is manifested in their vocabularies. Here is a small sampling of poignant disparities:

1 Maccabees	2 Maccabees
hagia - temple (holy place)	*neō* - temple
ethnē - gentiles/nations	*allophylōn* - gentiles/foreigners
ōkodomēsan - built (an altar)	*epoiēsan* – built/made (as altar)
ōkodomēsan – restored (the Holy Place)	*katharisantes* - purified (the sanctuary)
epesen ... epi prosōpon - prostrating themselves (on faces)	*pesontes epi koilian* - prostrating themselves (on stomach)

These divergences in vocabulary are notable because they are found in crucially important words.[38] The story line itself is not greatly affected by the

---

[35] This seems to be a slightly more "for the people" theology than that which appears in 1 Macc, so it is relevant that Josephus claimed the Pharisees were indeed much more in touch with the community than were the Sadducees. See Josephus, *War* 2.166, and *Ant.* 18.15.

[36] To further substantiate this claim Schmitz has argued that resurrection plays a very prominent role in 2 Macc theology. See Schmitz, *Auferstehung und Epiphanie*, 105–42. Resurrection is not at all prominent in 1 Macc.

[37] Williams, "2 Maccabees," 74. Comments here confirm that this position is generally held among scholars.

word choices, but the selections surely hold clues to the authors' respective outlooks. This difference in vocabulary also supports the idea that the two Maccabaean books are independent histories, which lends weight to the idea that where they agree we can have a significant level of confidence that agreed-upon events took place. That is, it illustrates the somewhat unintuitive larger proposal of this essay that, in a rather interesting way, the very differences between the accounts have the effect of increasing our confidence in their substantial reliability rather than the opposite. One more set of distinctions warrants attention.

Unequivocal Contradiction

There are several obvious discrepancies between the two works. The table below is intended to show a sampling of some of the more significant ones.

1 Maccabes 3:27-39	2 Maccabees 8:8-11
[The news of these events infuriated]. Antiochus, and he ordered mobilization of all the forces in his kingdom, a very powerful army ... He therefore left Lysias, a nobleman and member of the royal family, to manage the royal affairs between the River Euphrates and the Egyptian frontier ... To him Antiochus made over half his forces, with the elephants, giving him instructions about what he wanted done, particularly with regard to the inhabitants of Judaea and Jerusalem, against whom he was to send a force, to crush and destroy the power of Israel and the remnant of Jerusalem. Lysias chose Ptolemy son of Dorymenes, with Nicanor and Gorgias, influential men from among the Friends of the King, and, under their command, despatched forty thousand foot and seven thousand horse to invade the land of Judah and devastate it, as the king had	When Philip saw Judas was making steady progress and winning more and more frequent successes, he wrote to Ptolemy, the general officer commanding Coele-Syria and Phoenicia, asking for reinforcements in the royal interest. Ptolemy chose Nicanor son of Patroclus, one of the king's First Friends, and sent him without delay at the head of an international force of at least twenty thousand men to exterminate the entire Jewish race. As his associate he appointed Gorgias, a professional general of wide military experience. Nicanor for his part proposed, by the sale of Jewish prisoners of war, to raise the two thousand talents of tribute money owed by the king to the Romans. He lost no time in sending the seaboard towns an invitation to come and buy Jewish manpower, promising delivery of ninety head for one talent; but he did not reckon on the judgement

---

[38] These are but a few examples, many more could have been provided, but space did not permit.

ordered ... The local merchants, hearing the news of this, arrived at the camp, bringing with them a large amount of gold and silver, and fetters as well, proposing to buy the Israelites as slaves; they were accompanied by a company from Idumaea and the Philistine country.	from the Almighty that was soon to overtake him.

As mentioned above, there are several notable differences here. The author of 2 Macc has named a different Ptolemy to the one in 1 Macc, and has described the process of sending armies into Judea differently. 1 Macc is much longer (my selection has been redacted to display the more relevant portions), and claims that 47,000 troops were sent to invade Judah, whereas 2 Macc is shorter, and refers to only 20,000 soldiers.[39] Additionally, 2 Macc places Nicanor, having been appointed by Ptolemy, at the head of the named Seleucid commanders and puts the proposal to sell Jewish prisoners and the invitation to slave buyers into his mouth. 2 Macc also asserts that Nicanor's action is the cause of his imminent demise. 1 Macc places Ptolemy, having been appointed by Lysias, at the head of the Seleucid forces in conjunction with Gorgias and Nicanor and describes the whole process differently. The versions are difficult, if not impossible, to reconcile.

I would suggest that these variations, in light of the substantial agreement on crucial detail, support the essential independence of the works in a way that actually reinforces the credibility of the points on which they do agree. Substantial differences like those displayed above are disconcerting to the modern reader, but the major details, recorded from widely differing perspectives, still remain intact. The best way to explain this is to remember the role interpretation of events plays in determining how the material is presented. The main events are agreed upon even by two widely different authors with differing agendas.

While such flexibility on the part of one or both authors or of some of their traditions precludes determining certain particulars on the basis of the testimony we have before us, it does not warrant a rejection of the key events to which both our documents bear witness.[40] Such results ought to provide a caution both the unduly pessimistic reader who dismisses these sources' historical testimony and for the overly optimistic reader who wants to embrace all their details

---

[39] Most scholars see 2 Macc as recording the more likely accurate number here, but for a discussion on the relationship between 1 and 2 Maccabees in regards to the numbers they use see, Hilbert, "185,000 Slain," 102–106.

[40] For general agreement and a discussion of this very issue see, Aguilar, "Judean Past," 58-67.

uncritically. In spite of the likely essential reliability of 1 and 2 Macc uncertainties on some of the more minor details still obviously remain.⁴¹

Conclusion

This essay suggests, first, that, when assessing reconstructing historical reliability information, similarities between the two books carry much more weight than do dissimilarities. This is because, in general, similarities can only be accounted for in a limited number of ways. They occur either because writers have first-hand knowledge of actual events or because they acquire it from sources. If the accounts are independent *and* they describe the same stories then it is highly likely that both reflect earlier testimonies that may well reflect events that actually happened.⁴² Similarity in accounts of the fairly recent past suggests that agreed upon events did happen⁴³ especially when agreement occurs amidst varied style and rhetorical impact that can suggest independent sources.⁴⁴ A comparable level of dissimilarity does not have an equal impact toward indicating general unreliability of key events.⁴⁵

Secondly, the theological differences between 1 and 2 Macc are evident and show that 1 Macc was written by a Jerusalem temple insider with a more elite perspective. 2 Macc, on the other hand, was written largely by a Jew (Jason of Cyrene) with a concern for Israelites in the diaspora and a more popular outlook. The differences are of the kind that might be expected to manifest between a Sadducee (1 Macc) and a Pharisee with diasporic concerns (2 Macc). The opening letters in 2 Macc are clearly written by Jerusalemites who presumably shared at least some theological assumptions with Jason and the abridger.⁴⁶ The

---

⁴¹ An example of an overly optimistic perspective, in my opinion, is Dancy's: "Internal evidence makes it *certain* [emphasis mine] that the narrative of 1M is in many cases based on first-hand reports"; see Dancy, *1 Maccabees*, 3.

⁴² When dealing with legends the outcome is undoubtedly different, and it is true that sections fitting this label seem to occur in both books. But these portions are where rhetorical differences between accounts are starkest and do not generally include the major details of commonly described historical events. In these cases, ambiguity must be acknowledged.

⁴³ Not, of course, always with absolute certainty. But history works on the principle of probability rather than the sorts of certainties applicable to mathematics.

⁴⁴ The likelihood that similarities between the works are the result of their author's knowledge of actual events is noted in Grabbe, *Cyrus to Hadrian*, 225.

⁴⁵ That is not to say that dissimilarities are irrelevant to the question. Rather they impact it differently. In cases of blatant disagreement, one account is probably less accurate than the other, but this does not call into question the essential historical thrust of the whole work.

⁴⁶ Their level of theological commonality is difficult to ascertain. Schwartz suggests that Hasmonean leadership sent the letters to Egypt. See, Schwartz, *2 Macc*, 37. This idea is undergirded by Schorch, "Libraries in 2 Macc," 169–80. He suggests that the second festal letter shows the author valued the Torah above all other books of the Hebrew Bible.

fact that the authors had differing perspectives satisfactorily accounts for the majority of key differences between the two books. This is not surprising in that interpretation of history was an acceptable activity among historians in these settings.[47] So the relationship between 1 and 2 Macc is one of historical general agreement presented in a framework of theological and rhetorical difference. As Becking notes, 1 and 2 Macc both "relate the events… [and] reveal their writer's perception of the events."[48]

All of this bears on the question of the historical reliability of the Synoptics by showing that differences among examples of ancient, partially Hellenized, Jewish historiography (including biographies like the Synoptic Gospels) can be satisfactorily explained as interpretations of the events described.[49] This was acceptable, useful, history writing in that ancient setting. An amount of uncertainty in exact detail cannot be ignored, but that does not warrant a thoroughgoing skepticism with regard to the works in their entirety. On the contrary, where differences in style and perspective are most poignant and agreement on important detail exists, reliability is likely to be at its highest.

The phenomenon of interpreted history is as thoroughly evident in the Synoptics as it is in the Maccabean accounts, and that is in part my point. The relationship between the Synoptics is, of course, in one way different to that between 1 and 2 Macc. They clearly relied on common sources for some of their information whereas 1 and 2 Macc seemingly did not.[50] Yet, the events and characters of the Gospels are viewed from varying perspectives and highlighted for differing rhetorical reasons, just as they are in 1 and 2 Maccabees.[51] The likelihood that the key events they describe happened is similarly high. If this positive attitude is valid in regard to major agreed upon events, then it is reasonable to suggest that more minor uniquely attested events be viewed with a similarly increased level of trust, especially (but not only) where they are not contradicted elsewhere.[52] This would invite a rather optimistic view of the strong majority of the Synoptic material.

Illustration of Dunn's "same yet different" concept is not unique to the Gospels; it can be demonstrated in other Jewish literature of the Greco-

---

This could indicate that a Sadducee wrote the letter, which would likely occur under Hasmonean leadership.

[47] For a discussion linking history reporting and interpreting, theology and eyewitness testimony see, Richard Bauckham, *Eyewitnesses*, 505-8.

[48] Becking, "Hellenistic Period," 78-90.

[49] See Keener, "Otho," 331–55, for a project similar to this in certain ways, but that article emphasizes the fact that ancient biographies generally relied on historically sensitive sources like the Synoptic writers did. Keener appeals to this similarity as evidence for the Gospels' historical reliability. I am appealing to a different kind of similarity between the Synoptics and other ancient literature, but to the same end and with a similar result.

[50] Lichtenberger, "History-Telling," 97.

[51] It should be parenthetically noted that a certain richness is available to the historian in the presence of varying accounts of the same events. See Stein, *Synoptic Gospels*, 278.

[52] Schwartz, *2 Maccabees*, 38-44, displays a properly optimistic view of the historical usefulness of 2 Macc.

hellenistic and Roman periods.[53] Grabbe's assertion that 1 and 2 Macc lack evidence for critical investigative engagement by their authors with the subject material appears unwarranted. Critical historical inquiry, albeit influenced also by theological/rhetorical concerns, is evident in both Maccabean accounts.[54] In the end, differences of the kind that occur most often have been shown to lend a kind of increased reliability to Greek-influenced Jewish historical accounts where more than one version of the same event exists.[55] Surely this observation calls for a generally less, rather than a more, suspicious approach to the question of whether the Synoptics are historically reliable.

---

[53] Dunn's reasoning is relevant here as well though there is not space to discuss it. See particularly the discussion on the impact Jesus had on the community, Dunn, "Social Memory," 187-89, and in Dunn, *Jesus Remembered*, 129-34, 239-42, 327-29.

[54] As shown this is evidenced by the likely accuracy of much of the information presented in the books. In the case of 2 Macc it should be noted that it applies to Jason particularly and not so much to the abridger because the accounts are in fact mostly Jason's.

[55] Stein has noted the impressiveness of agreement in the Synoptics; see Stein, *Synoptic Gospels*, 279.

Chapter 14

The Importance of the "How" and "Why" in Ancient Biographies

Holly J. Carey
Point University

In any biography, the focus of the reader is naturally on the protagonist. The protagonist is the one who inspires the writing in the first place, and all events, narration, and dialogue centers on him or her. The obvious elements of a biography are the "what" elements – what did the protagonist do, what did the protagonist say, what was the response of his or her disciples, enemies, or audience in the story? These are crucial to understanding the narrative, and these are the aspects of the story that drive it in the direction that the author is headed.

But equally important are the "how" elements of a biography. These tend to be more subtle and require the reader to look beyond the action of the story and consider the way an author treats the hero of the story. Is he ever critical of the protagonist? Is he willing to share potentially embarrassing incidents of his or her life? Is there an extent to which the author wants the audience to emulate the hero, or is he merely telling an entertaining story? When dealing with embarrassing material, does the author feel the need to defend the actions or reactions of the protagonist? How does the author use antagonists in the story to underscore the strengths of his protagonist?

These "how" questions are particularly interesting when examining ancient biographies that are relatively contemporary to the Gospels. Biographies written roughly 150 years before or after the Gospels provide a good comparison for understanding the expectations of biographical writing at this time, recognizing trends in this material, and giving us a cultural perspective from which to note similarities and differences in the treatment of Jesus and the leaders of the early church in the Gospels.[1] This reminds us that the evangelists were not composing their narratives of Jesus in a vacuum, but were most certainly influenced by and were in dialogue with their environment.[2]

---

[1] Here I include not just strict biographies, but writings which contain a significant amount of biographical material. An example of this would be the collective presentation of biographical information on "The Teacher of Righteousness" in the Damascus Document, Pesher Habakkuk, Pesher Psalms[a], Pesher Psalms[b], and Pesher Micah from the Qumran Community.

[2] See, for example, Burridge, *Gospels?* (2004).

Let us take one area where attention to the "how" might be useful in our study of ancient biography and its relationship to the Gospels. How do ancient biographies deal with potential critique of their protagonists? Do the authors include criticism of their heroes, and if so, how do they deal with it?

More often than not, these biographies tend to shy away from critiquing their heroes. One strategy is to avoid including potentially embarrassing facts or stories altogether, especially if it there is no way to overcome the embarrassment or if the story demonstrates attitudes or values that conflict with the aim of the author. For example, in *On the Life of Moses*, Philo of Alexandria wants to demonstrate that the Law and Judaism represent the ideals of Greek philosophy. He does this by presenting Moses as the ideal Jew and therefore a representative of his religion. Moses's costly blunder at Meribah and the resulting ban from entering the Promised Land is never mentioned in Philo's biography. It was a part of Moses's story that was apparently too difficult to justify and so therefore was simply ignored.[3]

Rather than ignoring potential criticisms of their protagonist, sometimes the author will meet those criticisms head-on and explain them away or justify them so as to preserve the reputation of their hero. In the biography of the Grecian king Cleomenes in Plutarch's *Lives*, the protagonist's perceived faults are justified by a combination of explanation from the author and by providing Cleomenes's inner monologue for the reader. His initiation of war is not war-mongering, but is fueled by his desire to reform Sparta. The mockery of his dead enemy is justified because it was Lydiadas who began the revolt in the first place. Additionally, although he slaughters the leaders of the city who opposed him, Cleomenes shows mercy to one who was wounded.[4] At every point, what would seem selfish and even heinous behavior is motivated by Cleomenes's selflessness and honor. Similarly, in Philo's *Life of Moses*, this is accomplished by embellishing the biblical story of Moses and altering problematic texts. In narrating Moses's murder of the Egyptian overseer, for example, Philo justifies his actions by depicting the overseers as animals and the one Moses murders as the worst of these.[5] Moses's action, then, is righteous and controlled (rather than impulsive and demonstrative of an anger management problem). He ends this account by appealing to the "eye for an eye" principle: "And righteous it was that one who only lived to destroy men should himself be destroyed."[6]

These observations are all the more interesting when compared to the evangelists' treatment of Jesus and his followers. The Gospels do not shy away from including potentially embarrassing information about Jesus - rather they embrace it. How much easier would it have been to leave out, for instance, his association with prostitutes and tax-collectors (a potentially devastating social association at that time, and clearly used as ammunition against him by his enemies)?[7] He has very positive interactions with Gentiles, including Romans of high standing and

---

[3] Philo, *Moses*, 1.210-213.
[4] Plutarch, *Cleom.*, 1.4; 6.4; 8.2.
[5] Philo, *Moses*, 1.43.
[6] Philo, *Moses*, 1.44.
[7] Mark 2:15-17.

a woman who seems to best him in witty combat.[8] His last words from the cross in Matthew and Mark are unsettling.[9] And the trustworthiness of the first witnesses to the tomb would have been culturally questionable simply because they were women.[10]

The gospel writers even seem to embrace – rather than defend or explain away – his ignominious death (as crucifixion would have been regarded at the time), and they certainly do not ignore it. The cross is the climactic part of each of the Gospels – everything that Jesus does and says is leading to this point. In fact, it is the "taking up of the cross" which becomes the primary feature of the Kingdom.[11] And when Jesus is finally crucified, his death has a very raw, real feel to it – it is not sanitized and there is no apology or cover-up.[12] His suffering and shame is on full display for all to see and it is clear that he feels it all deeply. Yet this path through suffering and shame ultimately leads to vindication – this is the irony of the cross.[13]

The general lack of criticism of the heroes in ancient biographies contemporary with the Gospels also stands in contrast with the Gospels' treatment of the apostles and other leaders of the church. Discipleship is a crucial theme in the Gospels, and Jesus's earliest followers were the first examples of this. The audience, then, learns from the successes and failures of these early church leaders – their stories serve as a primer for what to do and what not to do, as they become the pioneers for living in the community of "The Way." It is interesting to see that the storylines of some key leaders include quite negative aspects of their personalities, shortcomings, and even unbelief. Some of these, as in the case of Peter's denial, carry with them quite embarrassing elements that would have been easier to leave out altogether.

Answering the "how" question then leads us to the "why." Why do the authors tend to portray their protagonists the way that they do? Why are they writing their stories in the first place? What does the "how" of the characterization of protagonists in ancient biographies tell us about the values of the author, his audience, and the culture in which they lived? More specifically, why must the author communicate those values in that particular way?

This question, in turn, must be asked of the Gospels and their portrayal of Jesus. What does all of this tell us about Jesus, discipleship, and the Church? Although space will not allow a full answer here, one can at the very least note that the "how" of the gospel narratives points to a Jesus that is grounded – he is relatable, he is human, he is less distant than might be expected of the Son of God. His

---

[8] Mark 7:24-30.
[9] Matthew 27:46; Mark 15:34.
[10] Mark 16:1-8.
[11] Mark 8:34.
[12] I think here, by contrast, of the apocryphal accounts of Jewish martyrdom such as Eleazar (2 Macc 6:18-31; 4 Macc 5-7) or some later accounts of Christian martyrdom such as that of Polycarp (*Mart. Pol.* 9-19), which depict an almost ethereal experience for the faithful in their tortures.
[13] Mark 15:38 (see Carey, *Jesus' Cry* for a discussion of the vindication motif in the tearing of the Temple veil); 1 Corinthians 15.

disciples, in all of their flaws and failings, provide a connection for the audience as well. Following Jesus does not mean perfection, it means authenticity even at the cost of embarrassment or difficulty. Perhaps more than anything else, the criticisms of those earliest followers of Jesus call the audience to "do something with" their stories, motivating them to action in their discipleship, even when they fall short.

Chapter 15

Viewing the Gospels as Ancient Biographies Resolves Many Perceived Contradictions[1]

Michael R. Licona
Houston Baptist University

Richard Burridge's book *What are the Gospels?* has been largely influential in persuading a majority of New Testament scholars to regard the Gospels as belonging to the genre of Greco-Roman biography.[2] Viewing the Gospels in this sense impacts how we interpret them and provides illumination in an area of great interest for many Christians: differences in the Gospels. In this essay, I will be proposing that understanding the Gospels as Greco-Roman biographies sheds light on some of the more stubborn differences between them.

Plutarch wrote more than sixty *Lives* (i.e., biographies) between the years 70-120. Fifty of them have survived. Of these, nine feature main characters who had lived at the same time and had participated in many of the same events. As a result, Plutarch often narrates the same story in two or more of the *Lives*. This provides us with a rare opportunity to observe how an ancient author would tell the same story differently. Since Plutarch simultaneously wrote six of the nine *Lives* we will be considering as a set, it is probable that he was using the same sources.[3] Accordingly, differences between parallel accounts in the *Lives* can often be plausibly explained as resulting from the use of compositional devices. And if we view similar differences appearing in parallel pericopes in the Gospels, we may plausibly explain them as the result of compositional devices similar to those employed by Plutarch.

Christopher Pelling is perhaps today's foremost authority on Plutarch. As of the end of 2015, Pelling has written the most extensive treatment comparing how Plutarch narrates the same events differently.[4] He examines a few parallel pericopes in Plutarch's *Lives*, then identifies six types of compositional devices Plutarch employed when writing them. In what follows I will focus on three of the

---

[1] This essay is derived from a more robust chapter that is to appear later; see Licona "Compositional Techniques."

[2] Burridge, *Gospels?* (2004).

[3] These are Plutarch's *Lives* of *Caesar, Crassus, Pompey, Cato Minor, Brutus,* and *Antony*.

[4] See Pelling, *Plutarch*, 58-71. For what will be a more extensive treatment, this author (i.e., Licona) is presently writing a volume with Oxford University Press (New York) that is scheduled for publication in late 2016.

six devices, providing examples from Plutarch and from the Gospels where the evangelists appear to be employing similar compositional devices.

Compression

When an author knowingly portrays events as though they had occurred over a shorter period of time than they had actually occurred, he may be said to compress the story.

We might refer to this as the guy version of a story. Those of us who are married can immediately recognize how, generally speaking, in Western culture, men and women tell stories differently. Women like details, and lots of them. First we must hear of the background in which the event occurred in order to give us a proper context in which to understand the event. Then we must hear the story with vivid details in order to allow us to experience it. What occurred? When did it occur? Why did it occur? How did it occur? What were the thoughts and feelings of the victims afterward? Then the storyteller may share her thoughts and feelings about the matter. And finally, the storyteller may ask for the listener's thoughts and feelings now that s/he knows the story. On the other hand, men usually like succinct accounts, bullet points. "Let's have the bottom line, please." They often compress stories by eliminating details they may regard as insignificant.

Let's look at an example of compression in Plutarch. In 63 BC, the Roman politician Lucius Sergius Catilina (aka Catiline) mounted an unsuccessful revolt against Rome. This is known as the Catilinarian Conspiracy. After Catiline's revolt had begun, a few of his co-conspirators were arrested, tried and executed. When Plutarch narrates what occurred in his *Life of Cicero* and *Life of Crassus*, the Catilinarians are exposed one day, tried on another, and their punishment decided still later.[5] However, in his *Life of Caesar*, Plutarch gives the impression that the Catilinarians were convicted, condemned and executed on the same day.[6] If the events had been video-recorded and we were viewing them, we would undoubtedly observe them unfolding over a period of several days.

There are three very clear examples of compression in the Gospels: The raising of Jairus's daughter,[7] Jesus's cursing the fig tree,[8] and Luke's account of Jesus's resurrection appearances and ascension. Let's take a look at the third. John reports that Jesus appeared to his disciples over a period of time that was well over a week. Luke on the other hand reports that Jesus rose from the dead, appeared to some of his disciples on the Emmaeus road, then appeared to all of them in Jerusalem, then ascended to heaven, and that all of this had occurred on Easter. So, did all of Jesus's resurrection appearances and his ascension all occur on the

---

[5] Plut. *Cic.* 19.1-4, 20.4-21.5; Plut. *Crass.* 13.3.
[6] Plut. *Caes.* 7.3-8.1. See Pelling, *Plutarch*, 91. The reference numbering Pelling provides is that of Teubner whereas I have incorporated the reference numbering found in Loeb.
[7] Matt 9:18-26 // Mark 5:21-43; Luke 8:40-56.
[8] Matt 21:18-22 // Mark 11:11-14, 19-21.

same day per Luke or did they stretch out over a longer period of time per the other Gospels?

This tension is easily resolved when we recognize that Luke is compressing the story. He is taking events that he knows had occurred over a longer period and telling them as though they had occurred on a single day. We know Luke has done this, because in Acts 1:3 he reported that Jesus had appeared to his disciples over a period of forty days. Thus, compression rather than contradiction is responsible for the difference.

Transferal

When an author knowingly attributes words or deeds to a person that he knows belonged to another, that author has transferred them.

At the meeting in Luca in 56 BC, Caesar, Pompey and Crassus made an agreement. Caesar would assist Pompey and Crassus in getting elected consuls while in return they would grant him another five years as proconsul in charge of Gaul. Caesar kept his promise. And once Pompey and Crassus were elected, they had a law passed extending Caesar's proconsulship for five years. In Plutarch's *Life of Pompey* and *Life of Cato Minor*, they do so through the tribune Trebonius who proposes the measure to the senate.[9] However, in the *Life of Crassus*, it is Pompey and Crassus themselves who have the measure passed with no mention of Trebonius.[10] If the event had been video-recorded and we were viewing it, we surely would have seen Trebonius making the suggestion, since it would have been his responsibility as tribune to propose the measures before the senate. Because Pompey and Crassus were certainly behind the proposal, Plutarch simply omits Trebonius in his *Life of Crassus*.

We find the Evangelists employing transferal in the Synoptics. In Matthew, the mother of James and John approach Jesus with her two sons and requests that each of them sit on Jesus's right and left when he establishes his kingdom. In Mark, however, it is James and John who come to Jesus and make the request and no mention is made of their mother being present.[11]

If the event had been video-recorded and we were viewing it, what would we observe? It is obvious that either Matthew or Mark has redacted the story. One may only guess. But I suspect that Mark knew the mother had made the request with her two sons present and transferred the request to James and John, since they were ultimately behind it, just as Pompey and Crassus were behind the proposal made by Trebonius. Thus, transferal rather than contradiction is responsible for the difference.

---

[9] Plut. *Pomp.* 52.3; Plut. *Cat. Min.* 43.1-6.
[10] Plut. *Crass.* 15.5.
[11] Matt 20:20-28 // Mark 10:35-45.

Displacement

Displacement occurs when an author knowingly removes an event from its original context and places it in another.

In his *Life of Caesar*, Plutarch narrates an occasion on which a group of senators approached Caesar in a processional in order to honor him. When in turn Caesar refused to stand in respect, many of the senators left humiliated and the crowds frowned upon Caesar for his act. Caesar realized his error, pulled back his toga exposing his neck and invited anyone to strike and kill him who wished. On another occasion, Caesar was seated at the Lupercalia festival when a number of men who had just completed a traditional run through the city lifted up Antony who then attempted to place a wreath on Caesar's head, a gesture suggesting Caesar should be made king. When only a few applauded Antony, Caesar declined the wreath, pushing it away. This elicited hardy applause from the crowd. Antony again offered the wreath to Caesar, which was again met by weak applause. Once more, Caesar declined to allow Antony to place it on his head, pushing it away. And, once more, this was met by hardy applause. At this, Caesar left the event greatly disappointed.[12]

Both of these events are described in Plutarch's *Life of Caesar*. But in his *Life of Antony*, Plutarch omits the processional. However, he appears to like the element of Caesar offering his neck. So, he displaces it from the procession and transplants it in the context of the Lupercalia festival so that Caesar offers his neck when the people respond unfavorably to the suggestion that he be made king.

The evangelists also displaced events. An example that immediately presents itself is the pericope of Jesus overturning tables in the temple. In John, the event occurs at the beginning of Jesus's ministry, whereas in the Synoptics it occurs at its end, on Palm Sunday. While it is possible Jesus performed the act twice, it is also possible that John has displaced the event from its original context and placed it at the beginning of Jesus's ministry.

Another possible occasion of displacement in the Gospels concerns the day and time on which Jesus was crucified. The Passover meal was distinct from other meals eaten during the week of that feast. According to Exodus 12, the Feast of Unleavened Bread lasted for seven days and the Passover meal was to be eaten on the first evening. Any food left over from that meal was to be burned the next morning. So, there were to be no leftovers when it came to the Passover meal.

According to all three Synoptics, Jesus was crucified on the day after they had eaten the Passover meal.[13] However, John's Gospel creates a tension. Just as the Synoptics report, Jesus eats his last meal with his disciples where he tells them one of them is about to betray Him. He identifies Judas as the betrayer who then leaves and the rest is history. So, this is the same event reported as the Passover meal in the Synoptics. However, there is nothing in John's account suggesting it

---

[12] Plut. *Caes.* 60.6. Pelling, *Plutarch*, 37n88.
[13] Especially clear is Matt 26:17-20. But see also Mark 14:12-18 // Luke 22:7-15.

was the Passover meal. In fact, John's Last Supper could not have been the Passover meal, since it is introduced in 13:1-2 with the words, "Now before the Feast of the Passover." Moreover, in John 18:28, Jesus has been arrested and John reports, "Then they led Jesus from the house of Caiaphas to the praetorium. It was early. They themselves did not enter the praetorium, so that they might not be defiled, but might eat the Passover." Pilate then proceeds to condemn and execute Jesus. So, while the Synoptics report that Jesus was crucified *after* the Passover meal had been eaten, John reports that he was crucified before the Passover meal was to be eaten.

Robert Stein considers several of the leading proposals to explain the difference then comments, "it is doubtful that any of the explanations has a particularly high degree of certainty."[14] Not included in Stein's analysis is the proposal of Craig Keener who notes the teaching in the Mishnah that when the Passover fell on the eve of a Sabbath, the evening burnt-offering would be moved back two hours and the paschal lamb was slaughtered afterward. Since the burnt offerings were normally slaughtered around 2:30 in the afternoon, they would be moved back to around 12:30. It is, therefore, of additional interest that John reports Pilate delivered Jesus over to be crucified around the sixth hour or noon whereas Mark reports that it was the third hour or 9 am.[15] Those attempting to harmonize the accounts sometimes talk about the possibility of one author referring to Roman time while the other is referring to Jewish time. While this is possible, it does not account for the different days. Keener's proposal accounts for both the day and time of Jesus's crucifixion by suggesting John may have displaced the day and time in order to make a theological point recognized decades earlier by Paul: Jesus is our Passover Lamb and the burnt offering for our sins.[16] This is quite plausible. For the overriding objective of ancient biography was to illuminate the character of the person who is the subject of that biography. This was certainly Plutarch's objective as he states in his *Lives* of *Alexander*, *Nicias* and *Pompey*.[17] Thus, Keener's proposal is not only plausible, it possesses great explanatory scope by accounting for both the differences in the day and time at which Jesus was crucified.

If Keener's solution is correct and the event had been video-recorded, we would have seen Jesus crucified after the Passover meal, just as the Synoptics report. Did John then get it wrong? Only if one measures accuracy according to the expectations of *modern* biography. But that would be anachronistic, since the Gospels belong to Greco-Roman biography and did not always have the modern objective of raw or untouched photographic accuracy. Indeed, even modern biography often sacrifices that degree of accuracy. Accordingly, if Keener is correct, displacement by John rather than contradiction is responsible for the differences.

---

[14] Stein, *Difficult Passages*, 65.
[15] Mark 15:25; John 19:14.
[16] See Rom 8:3 and 1 Cor 5:7. Also Eph 5:2; Heb 10:10, 14; 13:11-12.
[17] Plut. *Alex.* 1.1-3; Plut. *Nic.* 1.5; cf. Plut. *Pomp.* 8.7.

Conclusion

Amateur photography is my hobby. I love the challenge of getting great shots. But it is very frustrating when I have framed the picture well, set the aperture, shutter speed, and white balance correctly, only to have the photograph being out of focus. I missed the shot. The same can occur when we are studying the Bible. We love the challenge of accurately interpreting difficult texts. After a lot of work, we seem to have things figured out. But oftentimes, a fuzziness lingers informing us we missed the shot.

Matthew, Mark, Luke, and John wrote biographies of Jesus using the literary conventions of their day. Occasionally, the compositional devices they employed may make us uncomfortable. But we must learn to read ancient literature in light of the literary rules of its day rather than impose our modern ideas of precision upon them.

Scholars will remain puzzled over many ancient texts. In this essay, I have proposed that Gospel differences are often present because the lens through which we peer into the distant past is set to examine ancient texts using modern rules. But when we adjust our lens to view the distant past using their rules, a lot more comes into focus.

Appendix

Before Biographies: Memory and Oral Tradition[1]

Craig S. Keener
Asbury Theological Seminary

Studies of ancient biography lead us to expect both some consistency on matters of primary substance and some flexibility in how it is recounted. Ancient biographers were familiar enough with their sources to understand that they could not write otherwise: even their accounts from nearest the events already included both consistency and adaptation, comporting with the nature of individual and social memory in general.

Some scholars may grant that as biographers the Gospel writers preserve substantial oral tradition about Jesus, and yet question whether the oral tradition on which they depended was historically reliable. To some extent this is a question that our documentary sources cannot answer, given the limitations of normal historical method.[2] It also is a question that affects not only the Gospels but all ancient biographic and historical accounts not derived directly from eyewitnesses. Given ancient descriptions of conventional practices, however, the survival of significant testimony is normally far more likely than not.

The Gospels were written much sooner after the events they describe than were most ancient biographies, so, to be consistent, those who dismiss the Jesus tradition because they doubt the survivability of oral tradition ought to be equally agnostic or negative regarding most of what we know about ancient history. One can of course reasonably object here that perhaps we do *not* know much about ancient history.

Nevertheless, our information about ancient Mediterranean memory[3] and oral tradition, reflecting a significant geographic and chronological range of

---

[1] Much of this appendix adapts a paper (Keener, "Dependability") presented at an interdisciplinary forum on orality, April 3, 2014, which is included in a different form in a forthcoming digibook produced by Seedbed.

[2] Orality markers may provide clues to pre-Markan material (see helpfully and cautiously Zwiep, "Orality," though warning that the identification of such markers remains in its infancy), but such markers could in principle reflect Mark's as well as Peter's storytelling style. Like the careful redactional work of Pryke, *Style*, specific explorations in pre-Markan tradition necessarily remain somewhat speculative at this point. Such a situation makes all the more valuable an understanding of ancient biographic practice, since ancient convention provides a range of default expectation to be dismissed in any given case only where strong evidence supports a particular document's idiosyncratic character.

[3] Here I refer to psychological and social memory, and to an extent collective memory. My focus in this essay is not on cultural memory because that discussion is

sources, is considerable. As in other eras, we cannot depend on memory to provide precision in all details; moreover, even if we could, the ancient rhetorical emphasis on paraphrase and biographic preference for coherent stories would significantly mitigate such precision, as noted in this volume's discussions of ancient biography. Where we can normally be most confident historically is in the general events in the traditions—especially when the reports stem from within a generation or two of the events.

At the very start of his Gospel, Luke notes that in writing about Jesus he was following the path of many before him who "set about to organize a narrative of the matters completed among us, just as those who were from the beginning eyewitnesses and servants of the message have handed them down to us" (Luke 1:1-2). How accurately might the message have been handed down until the time it began to be written?

Introductory Issues

After noting earlier scholars' appeal to folk traditions and more recent scholars' use of psychological memory studies, this appendix turns to concrete evidence for the character of ancient Mediterranean memory. Here I will address first widespread evidence for psychological memory in literate circles (because most surviving concrete evidence comes from these circles), including among speakers and in education. With regard to education, I will give special attention to the matter of disciples (not all of whom were literate), which is what Jesus's closest followers were. After this I will address the more limited yet valuable extant evidence for memory in exclusively oral settings. Finally, I will briefly survey some characteristics of the tradition about Jesus preserved in the Gospels, although I have treated that subject much more extensively elsewhere.

Western Scholars' Questions

Some scholars have doubted the possibility of significant, accurate oral transmission before the first written sources about Jesus. By contrast, that such radical amnesia should have obliterated the memories of just a few decades strikes as counterintuitive those who trust the memories of even Westerners today about events a comparable distance from us. This observation is not meant to deny that witnesses remember events in very different ways until memories become culturally standardized; it is simply to affirm that the various recollec-

---

relevant especially to a period beyond living memory of eyewitnesses. (I am grateful to Prof. Sandra Hübenthal ["Another Jesus Remembered"] for bringing these distinctions to my attention; my focus here is oral tradition with historical interest, rather than the no less important subject of memory theory and cultural memory.) With a majority of scholars, I believe that all the Gospels, including Luke, date from fewer than seven decades after Jesus's public ministry (see Keener, *Acts*, 1:383-401).

tions are substantially referential: that is, they normally depend on concrete events.

The Gospel of Mark is usually dated between 64 and 75 CE. (some 34 to 45 years after Jesus's ministry), and the probable source that most scholars call Q is probably even earlier,[4] though its contours are debated.[5] Other written sources, probably noted in Luke 1:1, may have been circulating in the same period. We do not know when the first gospel sources were written, but a finished Gospel was completed within a generation, at the latest.[6] By comparison, most of what we know of other ancient history comes from historical and biographic sources written far more than four decades after the events that they narrate.

Early twentieth-century skepticism about accurate memories of Jesus often stemmed from comparing the gospel traditions with European folk traditions believed to have developed over the course of centuries. No one disputes that centuries of oral tradition breeds variants, even in poetry; the ancients themselves recognized as much.[7] Given the brief span of time involved in gospel transmission, however, the analogy with centuries-old folktales is limited in its value.[8] This comparison is especially inappropriate with regard to leaders who were Jesus's disciples, who presumably needed to recount stories about Jesus over and over again.[9] By way of comparison, even today, professors who teach a course repeatedly can often recount much of its content from memory.

None of this is to deny that some diverse traditions about Jesus arose by the later decades of the first century. Even if we explain many Johannine divergences from the Synoptics as homiletical and theological extrapolations that ancient Christian auditors might recognize as such, divergent traditions about the specifics of Judas's grisly death[10] or Jesus's genealogy (Matt 1:2-16; Luke 3:24-38) reveal some significant variation. Yet the bulk of the tradition in our first-century sources appears remarkably stable, no doubt in part because our written sources derive from the period of living memory of Jesus.

---

[4] See Theissen, *Gospels*, 220-21, 230-32.

[5] See e.g., recent careful suggestions in Sloan, "Similitudes," which suggest a larger Q than traditionally thought. Some other scholars challenge the existence of Q (see e.g., Goodacre and Perrin, *Questioning*).

[6] Even aside from the tradition in Papias, scholars date Mark this early partly because Matthew and Luke most likely depend on Mark, and Matthew, at least, must be sufficiently early for its widespread use in the earliest of the Apostolic Fathers.

[7] On Homer, see Josephus, *Apion* 1.12; Diogenes Laertius 9.12.113.

[8] See this complaint already in Davies, *Invitation*, 115-16; Benoit, *Gospel*, 33.

[9] Repetition helps cement the memory (Stock, Gajsar, and Güntürkün, "Neuroscience of Memory," 375), although standardizing its form (Redman, "Eyewitnesses," 189) and modifying the memory by its association with the new contexts (Stock, Gajsar, and Güntürkün, "Neuroscience of Memory," 385).

[10] Matt 27:5; Acts 1:18; Papias frg. 18.1-7 Holmes; cf. *Mart. Pol.* 6.2. See discussion in Keener, *Matthew*, 657-60; and *Acts*, 1:760-65, where parallels among the accounts are noted and preference on details (from the standpoint of modern historical method) is given in both cases to Luke's account.

Memory Studies

A different sort of question is related to psychological memory studies, which can provide a useful control regarding memory.[11] Most memory studies so far involve contemporary western memories—which are usually considered less rigorous than ancient Mediterranean ones[12]—but they at least provide some basis for thinking about the nature of recall. Although the scholars I cite here reflect a range of perspectives, they all agree on the central (and not very counterintuitive) point for which I contend: memories can include both a degree of fixity and fluidity. Scholars who therefore dismiss the possibility of memories of Jesus's teachings a few decades after Jesus's ministry, based on the fluidity of memory and tradition, emphasize only one side of the data.

Memory studies show that interpretive grids affect what is remembered and how it is remembered,[13] though interpretive structures can arise early in the recollection process.[14] Likewise, similar memories can be conflated.[15] Moreover, memories are normally piecemeal and may be organized interpretively rather than chronologically.[16] Setting sayings in new contexts certainly can change their application,[17] but this was a common and understood rhetorical practice in no way limited to the Gospels.[18]

Such limits would not trouble ancient hearers of the gospel tradition; its contemporaries did not expect chronological arrangement for the anecdotes in most biographies.[19] Moreover, not only in ancient practice but in human memory in

---

[11] Memory studies in psychology have tended to emphasize memory's imprecision, whereas oral historiography has (even if by virtue of necessity) emphasized its value; see Eddy and Boyd, *The Jesus Legend*, 280. Both approaches offer valuable perspective, challenging both our intuitive confidence in individual memory and our frequent skepticism about any value in social memory. For a survey of research in orality and Gospels studies to 2009, see Iverson, "Orality"; earlier, Byrskog, *Story as History*, 33-40; for a survey of literacy studies in classics, see Werner, "Studies."

[12] Cf. Galinsky, "Introduction," 17: "Ancient Rome was a memory culture par excellence." Cf. also the concessions in Redman, "Eyewitnesses," 179, 192-93. Ready access to bites of information in the wired West may often deprive our memories of rigorous exercise in a manner analogous to how calculators enable our arithmetic skills to atrophy.

[13] Redman, "Eyewitnesses," 180-82.

[14] Bauckham, *Eyewitnesses*, 330, 334-38, 350. "Prejudices and stereotypes" can shape memories (Stock, Gajsar, and Güntürkün, "Neuroscience of Memory," 388).

[15] Kirk, "Memory," 166; Kloppenborg, "Memory," 289.

[16] Bauckham, *Eyewitnesses*, 326, 333, 344. For topical associations, semantic substitutions, schematization according to relevance, and so forth, see Kloppenborg, "Memory," 289 (here following Schacter, Norman and Koutstaal, "Neuroscience," 294; and Schacter and Addis, "Neuroscience," 778).

[17] With e.g., Kloppenborg, "Memory," 304.

[18] See e.g., Theon *Progymn.* 4.73-79; cf. 5.388-441. Preaching continues to recontextualize Jesus's teachings for new contexts (cf. Keener, *Spirit Hermeneutics*); for that matter, some sorts of teaching, including often proverbs, were meant to be applied in diverse settings.

[19] Stanton, *Preaching*, 119–21; Aune, *Literary Environment*, 31–34, 63–64; on the

general we must expect some flexibility. Paraphrase, substitution of synonyms, as well as abbreviation and conformity to one's interpretive grid are far more common than verbatim recall, especially for narratives.[20]

The critique that memory studies accurately offer, however, is primarily against the preservation of precise wording and details, matters generally of less concern in oral cultures in any case. Repeatedly telling the stories about Jesus would likely produce patterns of recitation over time, but no one expected verbatim preservation of wording (despite probable echoes of Jesus remaining).[21] Even in elite rhetorical training, paraphrase was a standard practice,[22] and variation in wording plainly appears in our current Gospels. Ancient orators themselves recognized that recollections were often random.[23]

What is significant in the Jesus tradition, however, is the preservation of much of the original substance, including persistent themes, stories, the substance of climactic key sayings, and the like.[24] Wording is rarely preserved verbatim, especially in long-term memory, but central images and concepts are more stable.[25] Memory usually preserves the gist of events it includes,[26] which is all that ancient readers of biographies would ask. Richard Bauckham lists the following among factors that often facilitate witnesses' long-range recollection:

- Important or unusual experiences[27]
- Vivid and emotionally charged experiences[28]

Gospels, cf. Papias frg. 3.15 (although ancient usage may suggest that Papias's language refers to rhetorical rather than to chronological *taxis*; see Moessner, "Voice"); Augustine *Harm. G.* 21.51.

[20] See here Kloppenborg, "Memory," 291, following helpfully DeConick, "Memory." Cf. again Kloppenborg, "Memory," 318: "the Jesus tradition was" likely "condensed, schematized, paraphrased, and occasionally elaborated in the course of transmission."

[21] Comparing Jesus's sayings in parallel gospel accounts should readily dispel assumptions that the writers sought verbatim representation (Sanders, *Paul*, 211n22). Indeed, anyone who recognizes that Jesus usually taught in Aramaic and who has a rudimentary understanding of translation must recognize that our current Gospels in Greek cannot offer verbatim renderings of Jesus's teachings.

[22] See e.g., Theon *Progymn.* 1.93-171.

[23] Sen. *Controv.* 1.pref.4.

[24] See the varied discussions in Allison, *Constructing*; Bauckham, "Eyewitnesses"; idem, *Eyewitnesses,* 325-41 (esp. on gist in 333-34); Redman, "Eyewitnesses"; McIver, "Eyewitnesses."

[25] See Kloppenborg, "Memory," 291 (again summarizing DeConick, "Memory").

[26] Bauckham, *Eyewitnesses,* 327, 333-34, 345; Allison, *Constructing*, 11-13; Kloppenborg, "Memory," 289, 293-94.

[27] Bauckham, *Eyewitnesses,* 331; cf. Redman, "Eyewitnesses," 182-83; Galinsky, "Introduction," 18.

[28] Bauckham, *Eyewitnesses,* 331-32, 492-505; Redman, "Eyewitnesses," 184. "Flashbulb memories," however, remain fallible; see Allison, *Constructing*, 7n40; Redman, "Eyewitnesses," 184; in cases of trauma, cf. Stock, Gajsar, and Güntürkün, "Neuroscience of Memory," 384. Emotion helps imprint memories by creating multiple associations (Stock, Gajsar, and Güntürkün, "Neuroscience of Memory," 379-80); ancient rhetoricians recognized and even played on this feature of memory (see *Rhet. Her.* 3.22;

- Repetition or rehearsal[29]

Bauckham shows the relevance of such factors for Jesus's disciples.[30] Likewise, as Dale Allison observes, memory can be especially reliable when handling atypical events that one personally participated in, found mentally engaging, experienced as emotionally intense, and then later rehearsed."[31] Were it otherwise, we could never trust memoirs.

Some scholars who appeal to modern Western psychological memory studies emphasize the deficiencies of individual memory.[32] Certainly memory studies rightly lead us to expect eyewitnesses' recollection to be selective. But whereas based on such studies we would expect inaccuracy in as much as "20 percent of the details" of eyewitness reports behind the gospel tradition, such errors would not negate substantial memory.[33] Moreover, even these details "are almost always consistent with the broader picture of what actually happened, even if, strictly speaking, they are errors of detail."[34] In general, memory is more reliable than unreliable.[35]

We typically respect modern memoirs, despite their tendencies and imperfections; why would we dismiss ancient ones?[36] As N. T. Wright puts it, Jesus

---

Galinsky, "Introduction," 17).

[29] Bauckham, *Eyewitnesses*, 334. Repetition consolidates memories, though it can also contaminate them (Stock, Gajsar, and Güntürkün, "Neuroscience of Memory," 385).

[30] Bauckham, *Eyewitnesses*, 341-46; cf. Redman, "Eyewitnesses," 183-84; Elliott, *Feelings*, 44-45; though cf. limitations in Woodman, *Rhetoric*, 18-22; Allison, *Constructing*, 7n40.

[31] Allison, *Constructing*, 9n46. Allison urges caution rather than "hyperskepticism"; he doubts that the disciples were "amnesiacs" (9n47).

[32] Redman's article, which critiques Bauckham, is highly informative, but it overlaps with Bauckham's observations and Redman seems to regard Bauckham as claiming more than he actually claims; see further discussion in Keener *Acts*, 1:299n357, and especially the balanced conclusions in McIver, "Eyewitnesses" (see esp. 535, 540-41, 545-46). Allison, who does note limitations (*Constructing*, 1-7; but cf. 8-9 and the gist on 11-13, 28), believes that a motivated tradent could have naturally recalled even a passage such as the Q version behind Lk 6:27-42 (*Constructing*, 374).

[33] McIver, "Eyewitnesses," 545.

[34] McIver, "Eyewitnesses," 545-56.

[35] See Allison, *Constructing*, 8n46.

[36] Already in the second century the Gospels were viewed as "memoirs" (*apomnēmoneuta*) of the apostles; see Justin *1 Apol.* 66; 67; *Dial.* 103.8; 106.3 (with Stanton, *New People*, 62-63; Abramowski, "Memoirs"; Kennedy, "Source Criticism," 136; cf. discussion in Robbins, *Teacher*, 62-67). Cf. perhaps Papias frg. 3.16 (Holmes; Euseb. *H.E.* 3.39.1), if Papias's "Matthew" is our "Q" (cf. e.g., Filson, *History*, 83; Hill, *Matthew*, 23-27, 53; Bruce, *Documents*, 40; cf. Hagner, *Matthew*, xliv, citing also Schleiermacher, T. W. Manson, M. Black, and B. de Solages; rejected by e.g., Jeremias, *Theology*, 38). Papias's *logia* could refer to something dominated by sayings (such as Q), fitting common usage (see e.g., BDF), and explaining the contextual contrast with Mark if (and Eusebius's selectivity with Papias leaves this uncertain) his treatment of Matthew followed in the original (Papias frg. 3.14-16); but the term may not be used so narrowly in Papias frg. 3.1, 15; 5.1; 6.3; cf. Stanton, *New People*, 117n1.

impacted people's memories no less than do other significant figures: "just as the friends of C. S. Lewis still bring out books of reminiscences about the great man forty or fifty years after his death, and people who worked with Winston Churchill during the war still dine out on their memories of his temper, his wit and his prodigious intake of alcohol."[37]

Presumably most of us in our fifties or sixties can recall memorable incidents and information that we learned from four decades ago. I can personally attest to all the sorts of memory lapses noted in memory studies, and that many of my rarely recalled memories have faded over time. Nevertheless, I can recount various anecdotes and significant information from forty years ago, with many names and other details. Stories that I have recounted often are frequently condensed and patterned for their retelling and sometimes even less personally vivid than other ones, since I remember the frequently retold form; nevertheless, these patterned versions are seared deeply in my memory. Moreover, I can recall additional details that I deem less relevant to the stories hence do not ordinarily recount. In my own case, because I am literate, I can often confirm the substance of such experiences, even including conversations, by consulting my journals or other written renditions of my experiences.[38] I offer my own example for a pattern that I believe to be fairly representative, at least for those who treasure and sometimes share particularly significant memories.

If distracted western hearers can recall many experiences under the conditions noted above, committed individuals in cultures that value repeated recounting of experiences may be expected to do so more fully, despite the likely greater propensity toward also establishing more intriguing narrative frameworks.

Ancient Mediterranean Memory

My focus here will be on some concrete evidence for the character of ancient Mediterranean individual (and to some extent social) memory. Given the nature of extant sources, much of this concrete ancient evidence comes from literary sources depicting literate persons, which does not likely describe most of Jesus's

---

[37] Wright, *Faithfulness*, 649. Ancient historiographically-oriented writers also consulted memoirs; see e.g., Polybius 12.25e.1; Plutarch *Demosth.* 5.5; Laistner, *Historians*, 35; earlier, on Xenophon's memoirs of Socrates, despite their limitations, cf. Kennedy, "Source Criticism," 137; Hägg, *Biography*, 23-30. For Cicero's memoirs, see Cicero *Att.* 2.1.

[38] When I do consult detailed written accounts, even decades later, they inevitably preserve some details that I have forgotten; in the vast majority of cases, however, what I do recollect is fully consistent with the written accounts. I cut roughly 45 percent of the original draft for Keener and Keener, *Impossible Love*, retaining what seemed most useful to the basic thread of our stories that we chose to emphasize. The content, however, consists entirely of actual events; our source material constrained our telling in ways not necessary to a novel. Indeed, a well-written novel would be able to appeal to popular interest better by seeking fewer main characters and far fewer toponyms and names unfamiliar to our audience.

Galilean hearers. Nevertheless, the evidence that we do have is not limited to the literate (as noted in a later section), and it is consistent over a wide geographic range (against those who raise the uninformed objection that it appears only in later rabbinic sources).

In the brief space permitted here, I can only survey some of the relevant evidence, which I have treated elsewhere in greater detail.[39]

Some object that the gospel tradents and writers would not give preference to eyewitnesses as sources;[40] even if we neglect the position of Jesus's own disciples in leadership positions in the church, however (Gal 1:18-19; 2:9; cf. 1 Cor 15:5-7), actual hard data from antiquity demonstrates that ancients did regularly prefer eyewitnesses. Historians and biographers in the eastern Mediterranean regularly consulted eyewitnesses or those who passed on traditions thought to go back to eyewitnesses.[41] Of course, even eyewitnesses might differ regarding details; historians recognized that they had to evaluate testimonies (Thucydides 1.22.3). Likewise, they understood that oral sources lacked the fixity offered in the written medium (Eunapius *Lives* 453).

Nevertheless, informants within living memory of the eyewitnesses could provide significant information. Thucydides indeed lamented that eyewitness reports of some events varied according to partisan leanings or varied recollections (1.22.2-3), but still believed that he could provide a reasonably accurate account by building on common elements among these sources.

Oral memory was highly valued,[42] and ancient emphasis on memory sometimes augmented this preference for orality. To a friend who had lost his notes, a philosopher is said to have responded, "You should have inscribed them ... on your mind instead of on paper" (Diogenes Laertius 6.1.5). Thus even in the early second century some Christians still preferred oral to written memories about Jesus: "I did not suppose that matters written in books would benefit me as much as matters from a living and remaining voice" of eyewitnesses or those who heard them (Papias frg. 3.4).[43] Certainly more oral traditions circulated in

---

[39] Keener, *Historical Jesus*, 139-64; idem, "Assumptions"; idem, "Biographies of a Sage." I draw especially here on my work in Keener, *Historical Jesus*.

[40] Kloppenborg, "Memory," 296.

[41] See e.g., E.g., Xenophon *Apol*. 2; *Ages*. 3.1; Dionysius of Halicarnassus *Thuc*. 7; Plutarch *Demosth*. 11.1; Arrian *Alex*. 1, pref. 2-3; 6.11.8; Cornelius Nepos 23 (Hannibal), 13.3; 25 (Atticus), 13.7; 17.1; Josephus *Life* 357; *Ag. Ap.* 1.45-49, 56; *War* 1.2-3. This was true as early as Herodotus; see Meister, "Herodotus," 267-68; Byrskog, "History," 279. See further Aune, *Literary Environment*, 81.

[42] Harvey, *Listening*, 53.

[43] Papias's "elders" in 3.4 seems to refer especially to apostles past and (for Aristion and John) still living into his own time (taking his knowledge of the "elders" in 3.3 as indirect; but "elders" applies to those who knew John in 14.1); I take the distinction between the two Johns in 3.5-6 as Eusebius's interpretation based on later tradition and Eusebius's negative view on Revelation. Plato's preference for oral instruction persisted in the early empire; cf. Plutarch's Middle Platonic adaptation in Zadorojnyi, "Ethico-Politics."

the first century than those that have survived (cf. Acts 20:35; John 20:30; 21:23).[44]

Feats of Memory

Modern Western readers often find claims of ancient feats of memory astonishing. While some reports seem exaggerated,[45] others are plausible in light of ancient mnemonic practices.[46] The elder Seneca, for example, purported to recount long sections of more than a hundred declamations from his youth (*Controv.* passim). He even reports that in his younger days he could repeat back 2000 names in exactly the sequence in which he had just heard them, or recite up to 200 verses given to him, in reverse (*Controv.* 1.pref.2).

Although Seneca's claims about himself are exceptional (and thus depict the higher end of memory skills, not what was typical), he was not alone in cultivating memory. In *Controv.* 1.pref.19, he reports that another man, hearing a poem recited by its author, recited it back to the author verbatim (facetiously claiming the poem to be his own). He also recalls the famous Hortensius, who listed back every purchaser and price at the end of a day-long auction, his accuracy attested by the bankers. Nor were such practices purely Roman; in the same passage Seneca notes an ambassador who the next day greeted all the members of the Senate and the gathered townspeople by name.

A biographer writing about orators notes one who even in his old age could repeat back fifty names in sequence after hearing them just once (Philostratus *Vit. soph.* 1.11.495). My point in recounting such feats is not to imply that they were typical, but that the ancient Mediterranean world valued memory skills in ways that are often foreign to modern Western readers.[47]

Rhetoricians believed that artificial memory, augmented by discipline and training, could move far beyond natural (i.e., untrained) memory (*Rhet. Her.* 3.16.28), and ancients developed mnemonic techniques to help them recall blocks of data astonishing to modern readers dependent on a continuous flow of information.[48] Jocelyn Penny Small observes, for example, that one could memorize a work one part at a time (Quintilian *Inst.* 11.2.27); practice and then quiz oneself (11.2.34-35); and repeat the lines orally (11.2.33).[49]

---

[44] Some eyewitnesses survived for many years; see Quadratus in Eusebius *H.E.* 4.3.1-2; Evans, *World*, 7-8.

[45] E.g., Valerius Maximus 8.7.ext. 16; Pliny the Elder, *Nat.* 7.24.88.

[46] Kennedy, "Source Criticism," 143; Small, "Memory," 204.

[47] Cf. even personified, divine Mnemosyne (see Walde, "Mnemosyne"); more moderately, Arius Didymus 2.7.7b, p. 44.26. On the importance and nature of memory in antiquity, see also Byrskog, *Story as History*, 160-65; on Roman theory of memory, see e.g., Farrell, "Phenomenology."

[48] Cf. Cicero *De or.* 2.351 (and Olbricht, "Delivery," 163); *Rhetorica ad Herennium* 3.22.35; Small, *Wax Tablets*; idem, "Memory," 196; Byrskog, *Story as History*, 82-83, 110-11, 163-65; Walde, "Mnemonics"; Gaines, "Handbooks," 167; Galinsky, "Introduction," 17. Such practices appear as early as the fifth century BCE (Kennedy, "Source Criticism," 98).

[49] Small, "Memory," 202-3. Cf. other sorts of mental exercises in Sorabji, *Emotion*,

Orators would memorize their speeches,[50] despite these speeches often being hours long.[51] Orators advised reciting model speeches from memory, if possible (Dio Chrysostom *Or.* 18.19). *Memoria*, "learning the speech by heart in preparation for delivery," was one of the five basic tasks of an orator,[52] and ancient rhetoricians praised this skill (cf. Aeschines *Embassy* 48, 112).

Rhetorical students practiced declamation, offering their practice speeches "from memory."[53] Indeed, Pliny the Younger praises a rhetorician so skillful that he could repeat verbatim even speeches that he had delivered extemporaneously (*Ep.* 2.3.3). One orator could remember every declamation he had ever delivered, word for word, making written accounts unnecessary (Seneca *Controv.* 1.pref.18). The memory of hearers was also valued. At least rhetorically sensitive hearers could recall elements of speeches, with memory strong enough even to supplement written sources (Lucian *Peregr.* 3; Eunapius *Lives* 494).

Again, I am not implying that any of Jesus's original disciples had rhetorical training. My point is to underline the valuing of ancient memory and the upper ranges of the extent to which it could be developed.

Memory in Basic Ancient Education

Memorization was the most pervasive feature of ancient education.[54] The youngest learned by rote memorization at the elementary level.[55] Even elementary education including memorizing maxims, famous sayings, reused for centuries.[56] Students at various levels also memorized historical examples (Theon *Progymn.* 2.5-8). Judean oral education similarly circulated the sorts of wise sayings (proverbs, parables and the like) also used by Jesus.[57] Such sayings circulated both in collections and independently, and could be combined with stories about the teacher in question.[58]

Although rote memorization was not the focus of higher education (which began in the mid-teens),[59] advanced education continued to build on valued memory skills. I noted already above oratorical students' practice of memorizing

---

211-27. On Quintilian's understanding of how children learn, cf. Bloomer, "Quintilian."

[50] Quintilian *Inst.* 11.2.1-51. Memorized quotations also mattered (Eunapius *Lives* 502).

[51] Cicero *Brutus* 93.324; Tacitus *Dial.* 38.

[52] Satterthwaite, "Background," 344; cf. Olbricht, "Delivery," 159, 163.

[53] Watson, "Education," 310.

[54] See e.g., Quintilian *Inst.* 1.3.1; Plutarch *Educ.* 13, *Mor.* 9E; Musonius Rufus *frg.* 51, p. 144.3-7; Diogenes Laertius 6.2.31; Eunapius *Lives* 481; Carr, *Tablet*, 111-73 (as cited in Ehrensperger, *Dynamics*, 119); Alexander, "Memory," 133; Heath, *Hermogenes*, 11; Watson, "Education," 310, 312.

[55] See Quintilian *Inst.* 2.4.15; Jeffers, *World*, 254, 256; memorizing poets in Aune, *Dictionary*, 143.

[56] Hermogenes *Progymn.* 4.On Maxim, 8-10. Cf. Anderson, *Glossary*, 126-27.

[57] Cf. Pirke Aboth; Vermes, *Jesus the Jew*, 27.

[58] See e.g., Theon *Progymn.* 4.73-79; cf. 5.388-441.

[59] See the sources in Keener, *Acts*, 3:3209-10; esp. Josephus *Life* 10; Pliny *Ep.* 5.8.8; Watson, "Education," 312; Stamps, "Children," 198.

model speeches. Teachers at this level also still demanded students' attentiveness during lectures; thus the philosopher Peregrinus rebuked an equestrian who was yawning (Aulus Gellius 8.3). One sophist struck a hearer for sleeping (Philostratus *Vit. soph.* 2.8.578).

These young adult disciples of teachers (typically in their teens) had to learn what their teacher taught and, if they became teachers themselves, were expected to pass it on. This was true whether the sages were philosophers or Jewish teachers of wisdom. To this subject I now turn.

Disciples and Teachers

With regard to the Gospels and biographies of other sages, observations about memory in general are less relevant than what we know of memory specifically related to discipleship. Virtually all scholars agree that Jesus was a teacher with disciples. Moreover, virtually all scholars agree that Paul genuinely authored the letters that verify that at least some of these disciples remained in key positions of leadership in the early Christian movement in the period not long before gospel sources such as Mark were written (Gal 1:17-19; 2:1-2, 7-10; 1 Cor 15:5-7).

Yet ancient hearers, in contrast to most modern ones, would recognize that these facts have clear implications for the character of the gospel tradition. Disciples were normally adherents of a school[60] or, at the beginning, its founder; they passed on teachings.[61] Thus, for example, Theophrastus became a great philosopher by imitating his teacher Aristotle and passing on his life and teaching.[62] Likewise, as already mentioned, historians normally consulted eyewitnesses when they were available.

Teachers passed on their teachings to others. One familiar term for this practice, *paradidômi*,[63] was also applicable to passing down a founder's teachings[64] or practices,[65] passing down traditional practices from ancestors,[66] and passing down information in a historian.[67] Both Luke and Paul employ this term for the passing on of gospel tradition;[68] the cognate noun applies not only to probably the gospel tradition[69] but to Pharisaic traditions that were believed to be passed on meticulously.[70]

---

[60] Cf. Wilkins, *Discipleship*.

[61] Emphasis remained on the gist, passing on reminiscences, with both fixity and flexibility, as in Bailey's mideast tradition approach; see Alexander, "Memory," 143.

[62] See e.g., Libanius *Anecdote* 4.1. Likewise Isocrates's teaching multiplied his role (Libanius *Anecdote* 3.2).

[63] E.g., in Lucian *Alex.* 61. See additionally many examples in BDAG.

[64] Lucian *Alex.* 61; Iamblichus *Pyth. Life* 28.148.

[65] Iamblichus *Pyth. Life* 28.149.

[66] Thucydides 1.85.1.

[67] Dio Chrysostom *Or.* 18.10.

[68] Luke 1:2; 1 Cor 11:23; 15:3; cf. Papias frg. 3.14; 20.1; 21.1; perhaps *Ep. Diogn.* 11.1.

[69] See 2 Thess 2:15; Papias frg. 3.7, 8, 11, 14; *Ep. Diogn.* 11.6; perhaps *1 Clem.* 7.2.

[70] See Matt 15:2; Mark 7:3, 5; Gal 1:14; Josephus *Ant.* 13.297, 408.

Sayings attributed to founders of Greek schools were transmitted by members of each school from one generation to the next.[71] This practice of transmission seems to have been encouraged by some schools' founders themselves.[72]

Indeed, in all schools "teaching was passed down from master to pupils, who in turn passed it on to their own pupils";[73] the founder's teachings often functioned as canonical for their communities.[74] Many teachers left the matter of publication to their followers.[75] Occasionally students left their philosophic traditions and disagreed with their former teachers, but if they disagreed they said so, rather than falsely attributing their own views to the teacher.[76]

Developing Memory of Teachings and Behavior

Disciples were expected to develop their memories to learn teachings. Pythagoreans provide particularly graphic examples of memorizing a school's teachings.[77] One criterion for prospective Pythagorean disciples was said to be their ability to preserve what they were taught.[78] Pythagoreans allegedly would not rise from bed in the morning until they had recited their previous days' works.[79] They helpfully employed repetition to reinforce memorization.[80]

Although Pythagoreans provide the most graphic example of this practice, all extant Mediterranean evidence for students of sages in the period of the early Roman empire confirms the importance of memory. Thus, for example, another philosophic student could be depicted as rehearsing each of the points of the previous day's lectures in his mind.[81] All schools emphasized memory, though not all to an equal degree.[82] Whether the emphasis was on memorizing texts or the teacher's words depended on the particular ancient school in question;[83] among Jesus's disciples the teacher's words would necessarily be the focus.

---

[71] Culpepper, *School*, 193; Alexander, "Memory," 141; Aulus Gellius 7.10.1; Socrates *Ep.* 20. Other scholars have noted Culpepper's research, though the evidence is less complete for some locations (cf. Mack and Murphy, "Wisdom Literature," 391).

[72] See Diogenes Laertius 10.1.12; Culpepper, *School*, 50.

[73] Alexander, "IPSE DIXIT," 112.

[74] Alexander, "IPSE DIXIT," 112-13; Sedley, "Debate," 149.

[75] Kennedy, "Source Criticism," 129.

[76] See e.g., Valerius Maximus 8.15.ext. 1; Seneca *Ep. Lucil.* 108.17, 20, 22; 110.14, 20; Musonius Rufus 1, 36.6-7; Philostratus *Vit. Apoll.* 7.22; for the emphasis on individualism in Stoic practice, cf. Reydams-Schils, "Authority" (but cf. Epict. *Disc.* 2.19.29). For respect for teachers, see e.g., *Abot R. Nathan* 1A; 25A; *Sipra Shemini Mekhilta deMiluim* 99.5.6; Fronto *Ad Verum Imp.* 2.3; Philostratus *Vit. Apoll.* 5.38.

[77] E.g., Iamblichus *Vita Pyth.* 29.164; 35.256; Philostratus *Vit. Apoll.* 1.14, 19; 2.30; 3.16. Although Iamblichus and Philostratus write after our period, Diodorus Siculus (below) writes in the first century BCE.

[78] Iamblichus *Vita Pyth.* 20.94.

[79] Diodorus Siculus 10.5.1; Iamblichus *Vit. Pyth.* 29.165.

[80] Iamblichus *Vit. Pyth.* 31.188.

[81] Lucian *Hermot.* 1.

[82] Alexander, "Memory," 133, 138.

[83] Culpepper, *School*, 177. The textual focus dominates primarily in later times; see

Although virtually no one insists that the disciples preserved Jesus's Aramaic teachings verbatim, many have noted Aramaisms and characteristic elements of his style remaining in the words attributed to him in the Gospels. The preservation of a teacher's distinctive style appears in collections of other sages' words as well, both in Jewish[84] and Greek[85] sources.[86]

Although the emphasis lay on memorizing teachings, students studied and emulated teachers' behavior as well.[87] Further, they transmitted it: thus, for example, Eunapius learned a story about Iamblichus from Eunapius' teacher Chrysanthius, who learned it from Aedesius the disciple of Iamblichus himself (Eunapius *Lives* 458). Similarly, Philostratus has oral information about a teacher two generations earlier through an expert from the previous generation (*Vit. Soph.* 1.22.524). Both Greek[88] and Jewish[89] disciples sought to imitate their teachers, and later Jewish disciples even used the behavior of earlier rabbis as legal precedent.[90]

Rabbinic Jewish Memory

Although rabbinic sources postdate the Gospels, they provide the fullest concrete examples of Jewish education, and these examples are consistent with the other ancient Mediterranean evidence. Here teachers expected disciples to memorize their teachings by laborious repetition.[91] Thus a rabbi might praise a student who, instead of trying to learn on his own, merely preserved his teacher's wisdom, like a good cistern (*Sipre Deut.* 48.2.6).

Rabbis emphasized the careful passing on of tradition,[92] a point emphasized by some earlier Scandinavian scholars.[93] Although early studies were sometimes exaggerated and generated controversy,[94] subsequent refinement of the approach has allowed some scholars today to build on the early studies' central point.[95]

Blyth, "Cicero," 71-98.

[84] See Keener, *Historical Jesus*, 187-88; *m. Eduyoth* 1:3.

[85] Xenophon *Apol.* 1; Epictetus *Diatr.* 1.preface.

[86] Sayings may have often been transmitted with greater attention to preserving wording than were narratives (Witherington, *Christology*, 28-29; Theissen, *Gospels*, 60).

[87] See e.g., Philostratus *Vit. Apoll.* 5.21; Liefeld, "Preacher," 223; Robbins, *Teacher*, 64.

[88] Xenophon *Mem.* 1.2.3; Seneca *Ep. Lucil.* 108.4.

[89] Josephus *Life* 11.

[90] E.g., *tosefta Piska* 2:15-16; *Sipre Deut.* 221.1.1.

[91] *Sipre Deut.* 48.1.1-4; Goodman, *State*, 79; cf. Zlotnick, "Memory," 229-41.

[92] E.g., *tosefta Yeb.* 3:1; *Mekilta Pisha* 1.135-36; *Sipre Deut.* 48.2.6.

[93] Gerhardsson, *Memory*, 122-70; Gerhardsson, *Origins*, 19-24; Gerhardsson, "Path"; Riesenfeld, *Tradition*, 14-17. Earlier scholars had also drawn analogies between the gospel tradition and rabbinic tradition (Dibelius, *Tradition*, 39).

[94] Gerhardsson (*Memory*) overplayed the analogy, inviting the harsh critique in Smith, "Comparison" (a harshness not uncharacteristic of Smith).

[95] Neusner's earlier critique, based on his literary focus, misunderstood Gerhardsson's oral one (Kelber, "Work," 194); Neusner has since recognized that Gerhardsson's work, though overstated, contains valuable elements (Neusner, "Foreword"). Gerhardsson's

Though early work compared Christianity too closely with ancient schools,[96] churches, like synagogues,[97] could be compared with school by outsiders,[98] a comparison that became fairly common in the second century.[99]

It seems hardly likely, prima facie, that the later rabbinic method simply arose *ex nihilo* after 70 CE.[100] Rabbinic evidence in fact fits the rest of the Jewish and Greco-Roman evidence available.[101] Nevertheless, I have illustrated briefly above that the emphasis on memory fits our other evidence even if we needed to neglect rabbinic evidence.

Well before 70, Pharisees were known for passing on traditions,[102] and Judeans and Galileans in general were known for instructing boys meticulously in the law,[103] probably especially orally and presumably developing memory skills. Many Jews as early as the period of 2 Maccabees apparently liked to memorize details of Jewish history (2 Macc 2:25).[104]

One might dismiss such reports as pure propaganda—though many Gentiles seem to have believed it[105]—but one should be honest about what one is doing. One is explaining away virtually all extant evidence and then complaining that no evidence supports the only position for which we have any substantial evidence—namely, that ancient disciples did normally seek to remember and pass on what they were taught.

Note-Taking

Note-taking as a memory aid[106] was common among those with sufficient literacy to employ it, and it is not impossible that at least one of Jesus's close followers was capable of taking some notes. Hearers of speeches sometimes

---

work, appreciated by rabbinics scholars, recognized both the "conservation" and "mobility" of tradition (Kelber, "Work," 191-92).

[96] Note the criticism in Smith, "Comparison," 174.

[97] Cf. Alexander, "IPSE DIXIT," 105.

[98] Judge, "Scholastic Community," 137; Wilken, "Christians," 107-10; Wilken, "Interpretation"; Aune, *Prophecy*, 229; Meeks, *Moral World*, 114; Stowers, "Resemble Philosophy?" 81-102.

[99] Schmeller, "Gegenwelten"; Wilken, "Interpretation," 444-48; Wilken, "Collegia," 277; Alexander, "IPSE DIXIT," 107.

[100] See Hagner, *Matthew*, xlix.

[101] See comments above and esp. Riesner, *Lehrer*.

[102] Josephus *Ant.* 13.297, 408.

[103] Josephus *Ant.* 4.211; *Apion* 1.60; 2.204. Somewhat later, and perhaps most relevant to the intelligentsia, see *m. Ab.* 5:21. Rabbis believed they continued much earlier discipleship practices (*Mekilta Pisha* 1.150-53), a belief probably relevant for then-recent generations. Cf. perhaps Prov 3:1; Sir 28:7. One hellenistic Jewish tradition allegorically interpreted cud-chewing as memory rehearsal (*Let. Aris.* 154; Philo *Spec. Laws* 4.107).

[104] Hellenistic approaches to education influenced Judean education at an early period; see Clark, "Education"; cf. Koskenniemi, "Moses."

[105] For Jews as a "nation of philosophers," see Gager, *Anti-Semitism*, 39; Stern, *Authors*, 8-11, 46, 50; cf. Mayer, "Abrahambildes," 125-26; Satlow, "Philosophers"; Bosch-Veciana, "Filosofia."

[106] Cf. Montanari, "Hypomnema."

took notes to capture the gist of the speeches,[107] sometimes even during school declamations (Seneca *Suas.* 3.2). Some also took notes from which they later arranged a composition.[108]

It is especially in academic settings, however, that note-taking prevailed. Disciples of advanced Greek teachers, both in philosophy and rhetoric, often took notes during their teachers' lectures.[109] As early as five centuries before the era of Jesus's disciples, such notes were sometimes published,[110] a practice that continued in the period in which the Gospels were published.[111]

Jewish disciples apparently emphasized orality much more highly than most Gentiles. Nevertheless, extant sources suggest that even some of them were able to take rudimentary notes for use as initial mnemonic devices to recall larger blocs of material.[112] Some scholars suggest that at least one of Jesus' followers, a tax-collector (Mark 2:14), would have had the skills to take such notes.[113]

Whether or not any disciples took notes of Jesus's teachings, the taking of notes among those who could take them reinforces the overall portrait of an ancient setting in which the preservation of a master's teachings was heavily emphasized.

General Observations About Memory Among Nonelites

Some critics wish to dismiss the value of all the above evidence, arguing that most of it comes from the ranks of the elite. Such a dismissal often seems designed to support a consequent resort to arguments from silence against where our only extant evidence points, since elite evidence is often nearly the only textual evidence that survives.

Nevertheless, ancient disciples of other sages did *not* all come from the ranks of the educated.[114] Lucian complains that not only many disciples but even their teachers were uneducated members of the working class.[115] In circles that em-

---

[107] Gempf, "Speaking," 299.

[108] Cf. Cicero *Fin.* 3.3.10; 5.5.12; Aulus Gellius *pref.* 2, 22.

[109] Cf. Quintilian *Inst.* 11.2.2, 25; Seneca *Ep. Lucil.* 108.6; Arius Didymus *Epit.* 2.7.11k, p. 80.36—82.1; Lucian *Hermot.* 2; see also Lutz, "Musonius," 7, 10; Kennedy, "Source Criticism," 131; Gempf, "Speaking," 299; cf. Hippolytus *Refutation of All Heresies* 1.15.

[110] Kennedy, *Classical Rhetoric*, 19.

[111] Quintilian *Inst.* 1.pref. 7-8; Epictetus *Diatr.* 1.preface. For the nature of ancient publication, cf. discussion in Keener, *Acts*, 1:43-50.

[112] Cf. Gerhardsson, *Memory*, 160-62; Safrai, "Education," 966.

[113] E.g., Eddy and Boyd, *The Jesus Legend*, 250. For commercial literacy—insufficient for prose composition but adequate for basic needs, see Thomas, "Writing," 25-28 (cf. also officials' literacy versus compositional literacy in 37-41). Other evidence suggests basic literacy without compositional literacy; see esp. Woolf, "Literacy"; Hurtado, "Fixation," 330-33, 339; cf. Milnor, "Literacy."

[114] Among Greeks, cf. e.g., uneducated farmers in Alciphron *Farm.* 11 (Sitalces to Oenopion, his son), 3.14; 38 (Euthydicus to Philiscus), 3.40; among Jewish people, cf. accounts concerning the backgrounds of Hillel and Akiba, e.g., *b. Ned.* 50a; *Pesah.* 49b.

[115] Lucian *Runaways* 12, 14.

phasized oral tradition, in fact, oral memory would be more important for learning than would be the study of texts. Even in Greek schools, some emphasized more one or the other.[116] The examples of oral memory above do not require a specifically literate environment even when they involve literate persons.

Orality and literacy coexisted in much of the Mediterranean world.[117] Although textual literacy was the domain especially of elites,[118] it is unlikely that exercises of memory were limited to them. Some argue from analogies that, in general, oral cultures are particularly adept in memory.[119] This adeptness is not always the case; studies show that literacy tends to improve some kinds of memory, especially verbatim memory, because of access to texts. Oral cultures can, however, retain the gist.[120]

Despite the imperfections of oral tradition,[121] interest in oral historiography has grown in recent decades.[122] Because oral history can supplement written records,[123] oral historiography is valuable, especially for regions where written records are limited.[124] My wife is from Congo and did her PhD in history in France. She notes that the younger generation in Congo, increasingly dependent on texts and electronic sources, is no longer passing on memories about predecessors, memories that had circulated for generations and that she has sometimes gathered from the passing generation.[125] Oral history can also be informative in other societies insofar as memories are valued.[126]

---

[116] Culpepper, *School*, 177.

[117] See e.g., Talbert, "Response"; Aune, *Dictionary*, 325; Gamble, "Literacy," 646; Byrskog, *Story as History*, 107-44; Goldhill, "Anecdote"; Habinek, "Situating Literacy."

[118] See Keith, *Scribal Elite*.

[119] Byrskog, *Story as History*, 110-11.

[120] See Kloppenborg, "Memory," 293-94.

[121] See e.g., Kloppenborg, "Memory," 296-97, noting limitations in Goody and Watt, Goody and Watt, "Consequences," 310; Goody, *Logic*, 9. Kloppenborg nevertheless acknowledges divergent perspectives ("Memory," 297n29, and esp. the balanced approach of Rodriguez, *Memory*, 41-80).

[122] Although some earlier modern historians treated personal involvement as permitting bias (Byrskog, *Story as History*, 19-22; less today, cf. 23-26), oral historiography allows greater appreciation for participation (Byrskog, *Story as History*, 153; for its wider use today, see e.g., Moniot, "Profile," 50). To exclude such sources could undermine any historical reports by eyewitnesses in any traumatic or otherwise emotionally invested situation in history (wars, the Nazi Holocaust, etc.; see Eddy and Boyd, *The Jesus Legend*, 397-98). On the use of and methodologies for oral history in historiography, see Byrskog, *Story as History*, 26-33; on its use in NT scholarship, see 33-40. Whereas modern oral history focuses on "low people" excluded from traditional western history, ancient historians focused on whatever sources gave them best access to the events important to them (*Story as History*, 305).

[123] E.g., Aron-Schnapper and Hanet, "Archives orales"; Hoeree and Hoogbergen, "History."

[124] For Africa, see e.g., Horton, "Types," 14; Moniot, "Profile," 50. Westerners' prior neglect often reflects ethnocentric prejudices (Chrétien, "Exchange," 77).

[125] She has contributed some articles to the online *Dictionary of African Christian Biography*, such as Keener, "Ndoundou"; "Mboungou"; "Moussounga."

[126] My neighbor Anna Gulick, who recently passed at age 96, notes that even in the

Traditional Quranic education in non-Arab societies today shows the potential for extensive rote memorization even among the illiterate,[127] although we should not envision such a textually constrained process for the gospel tradition before the writing of the Gospels. (The Hadith indicate that variants exist even in early Quranic tradition; today, however, Qur'an recitation is widely standardized.) Other highly skilled memories can preserve far more than anyone argues for the early gospel tradition; thus as a girl Pandita Ramabai could recite from memory "for an hour or more," and eventually she "could recite eighteen thousand verses of these sacred texts."[128]

Other analogies further suggest the frequent persistence of the substance in oral memory. Many cultures transmit key elements of their traditions orally for centuries, although details and language remain fluid.[129]

Again, none of this is intended to suggest verbatim preservation of the material in the Gospels; studies of psychological, collective and cultural memory all militate against most verbatim preservation of prose materials. What such examples do challenge is the frequent modern western skepticism that the substance of many traditions could be remembered for a generation. Although such recollections normally involve themes and gist rather than precise wording, they can include epics that westerners today cannot imagine memorizing.[130] Variation is expected in oral performance, which is adapted for its audiences.[131] Such variation may help explain some of the range of differences in the Gospels.[132] The

---

United States families passed on stories before the advent of television; she recounts unpublished anecdotes from nineteenth-century ancestors and some information reaching back to the Revolutionary War (for some examples, see Gulick, *Windows*, 6-8; I was able to independently verify some of this information). For passing on family tales in the modern Mediterranean world, see e.g., Pizzuto-Pomaco, "Shame," 38, 42.

[127] Cf. discussion in e.g., Wagner and Lotfi, "Learning"; Eickelman, *Knowledge*, 41, 50, 63-65, 70 (fading in newer times, 171); Graham, *Beyond*, 79-80, 101-2, 105 (cf. 131 for illiterate Christians memorizing Scripture as a prerequisite for the monastery; cf. also 43, 124); Wagner, *Literacy*, 47, 269 (noting recent decline, 48); Zubaida, *Law*, 27-28; Touati, *Literacy*, 12; Johnson and Musser, *Story*, 101; old Arabic poems in Janin, *Pursuit*, 49. Cf. periodic news stories, e.g., http://www.huffingtonpost.com/2011/07/27/koran-by-heart_n_911454.html; starting from age five, Maariya Aslam in the United Kingdom memorized the entire Qur'an in Arabic over a period of two years ("Eight-year-old memorises the Koran," BBC news, April 27, 2016).

[128] Noll and Nystrom, *Clouds*, 127, 129. Ramabai was at the time a Hindu, although converted to Christian faith as an adult.

[129] Cf. Lord, *Singer*, 138; Lewis, *History*, 43; Vansina, "Afterthoughts," 110; Yamauchi, "Historic Homer." Redman, "Eyewitnesses," 191, agrees, but notes (191-92) that in cases such as Homer and Lord's examples, poetic or musical form aids retention (cf. also Kennedy, "Source Criticism," 143).

[130] Harvey, *Listening*, 41; Noll and Nystrom, *Clouds*, 129.

[131] Bazin, "Past," 70-71. For that matter, perspectives affect differences even in fresh eyewitness testimony, as forensic investigators note; on a popular but informed level, see Wallace, *Christianity*, 80-81

[132] Dunn, *Perspective*, 110, 112, 118, 122. For oral history in NT scholarship, see Byrskog, *Story as History*, 33-40; Eddy and Boyd, *The Jesus Legend*, 239-68 (esp. 252-59).

variation evident there is less than in many traditions, but as noted above the period of purely oral transmission that preceded the first of the Gospels cannot be more than roughly a four-decade generation, i.e., well within living memory.[133] As already suggested, recollection of events within living memory of the first tradents, even to more than a century, can often be accurate to a significant degree.[134] Memory theorists often distinguish "cultural" and "communicative" memory; "the latter is characterized by direct communication with a time frame of three to four generations or some eighty to a hundred years."[135]

Jesus's disciples probably lacked "professional" training other than learning from Jesus, but even those who emphasize this lack recognize that their memory skills probably exceeded those of modern Western critics.[136] Again, ordinary Judean and Galilean boys lacked "professional" training but nevertheless developed memory skills; they were raised remembering their ancestral laws.[137] Illiterate persons would learn stories about Jesus that they heard repeatedly.[138] Not merely elites but a significant proportion of people in some other oral societies can recall extensive shared tradition.[139]

Ancient Reports of Memory Outside Elites

We need not settle for generalized analogies, however. Although the majority of surviving evidence about ancient memory surrounds elites, some concrete evidence also confirms the strength of memory among nonelites. For example, many bards could recite from memory the entire *Iliad* and *Odyssey*, even though the educated often looked down on them as lacking critical skills.[140] Analogies with some memorizers of the Qur'an today even render plausible the ancient claim that one ancient people knew the *Iliad* from memory even though they no longer spoke good Greek.[141]

---

[133] On the accumulation of problems in oral tradition over time, see e.g., Harms, "Tradition"; Raphael, "Travail"; Iglesias, "Reflexoes"; Henige, "History," 103; though cf. Eddy and Boyd, *The Jesus Legend*, 260-64.

[134] Eddy and Boyd, *The Jesus Legend*, 395.

[135] Galinsky, "Introduction," 12. In Hübenthal, "Another Jesus Remembered," social and collective memory is the preferred title for memories within three to four generations.

[136] Redman, "Eyewitnesses," 192-93; cf. also 179.

[137] Cf. Josephus *Ant.* 4.211; *Apion* 1.60; 2.178, 204, even allowing for some likely hyperbole. Cf. also Freyne, *Galilee*, 208.

[138] Dunn, *Perspective*, 119; cf. Byrskog, *Story as History*, 110.

[139] Today, it is said that all "true" Dulong can remember their epics, even though recounting them all fully can take several days (Yamamori and Chan, *Witnesses*, 22).

[140] Xenophon *Symp.* 3.5-6; cf. West, "Rhapsodes." Poetry and song involved memorization (Apollodorus *Bib.* 1.3.1; Seneca *Controv.* 1.pref.2, 19). Various repetition devices aided memory (Harvey, *Listening*, 45, 56).

[141] Dio Chrysostom *Or.* 36.9. External sources confirm at least some of Dio's report (cf. *Corpus inscriptionum graecarum* 2.2077 in the Loeb translator's note). In contrast to poems that varied more flexibly, the *Iliad* persisted in a more pervasive form because it functioned canonically for Greeks (see Finkelberg, "*Cypria*").

Again, Jewish people also valued memory skills; whether or not they could read and (still more rarely) write, Jewish boys learned to recite Torah.[142] Those who were not literate therefore learned Torah orally.[143]

In informal settings, stories and songs were believed passed on for long periods of time,[144] including in Jewish circles.[145] Ancient researchers trusted local oral traditions sufficiently that they often depended on them even when they were centuries old (e.g., Pausanias 1.23.2). Dependence in such centuries-old cases may have sometimes been ill-advised,[146] but all the canonical Gospels, by contrast, were likely composed within a maximum of six and a half decades after the events they narrate.[147]

Memory in Jesus's Earliest Movement

Various considerations support the probability that the disciples and those who heard them would have preserved many reliable oral memories of Jesus before the composition of early sources such as Mark and Q.

Communal Memory

Given the size of Jesus's movement, at least some members probably did have exceptional memory abilities. Even if they did not, however, *communal memory* should have preserved the essential substance of Jesus' message and activity, as well as many examples from these. In communal memory, various hearers bring different points to the recollection of their peers (this could happen among ancient disciples, as in Philostratus *Vit. soph.* 1.22.524). I observed this benefit among eyewitnesses when, for example, in response to my questions my wife's siblings readily supplemented her recollections of the Congolese war.[148]

---

[142] Cf. Riesner, "Education élémentaire"; idem, *Lehrer*.

[143] Kirk, "Memory," 157-58. Some scholars argue against much literacy in Judea and Galilee (e.g., Hezser, *Literacy*); others have been more optimistic (Millard, *Reading*; idem, "Literacy"; Head, "Note"; Evans, *World*, 63-88; cf. Porter, "Reconstructing," 45, citing essays in Beard, *Literacy*). In either case, papyri from Egypt suggest a degree of writing literacy among tax-collectors: not enough to compose literary works, but enough for basic notes (cf. Mark 2:14; Papias 3.16). Literacy was more common in urban areas (Curchin, "Literacy"; cf. Dewey, "Event," 146-47); even in impoverished Egypt, most metropolites (citizens of Greek-speaking nome capitals), in contrast to typical rural agriculturalists, could read and write (Lewis, *Life*, 61-62).

[144] Xenophon *Cyropedia* 1.2.1.

[145] Charlesworth, *Pseudepigrapha*, 1-3; cf. Bailey, "Oral Tradition."

[146] Cf. Pretzler, "Pausanias and Tradition."

[147] A minority of scholars do now date Acts to the second century, but see Keener, *Acts*, 1:383-401; cf. 1:402-22; 3:2350-74.

[148] Memories and journal entries summarized in Keener and Keener, *Impossible Love*; see comment above.

Communal memory is not perfect, but it tends to be more stable than individual memory.[149]

The game of "telephone"[150] involves a single chain of transmission, any fallible link in which can involve significant loss; communities of disciples and others, however, could practice "net" transmission as opposed to merely "chain" transmission.[151] Communal memory is common in older Middle Eastern culture,[152] and is surely relevant for Jesus's movement. There were apparently no less than five hundred followers available for some key events (1 Cor 15:6-7). Some scholars even argue that a number of the persons named in the Gospels may be cited as guarantors of the tradition.[153] Early Christian sources, however, suggest that the Twelve were the most authoritative witnesses, functioning as the communal tradents par excellence (Acts 1:21-22).[154]

Communal memory of events significant for the community, and from the community's perspective,[155] can endure for generations, as is evident in some ethnic conflicts around the world. Megarians, for instance, persisted in hating Athens some seven hundred years after their conflicts (Philostratus *Vit. soph.* 1.24.529).

The Wording of Jesus's Sayings

There is evidence that Jewish teachers sometimes spoke in easily memorizable forms, as Jesus sometimes or often did.[156] Stylistic features of oral tradition

---

[149] Redman, "Eyewitnesses," 186-87.

[150] Notoriously used for an analogy in Ehrman, *Introduction*, 52-53. Like the rest of us, however, Ehrman presumably expects his students to remember some of his teachings, at least for examinations. Content also matters; experiences of events significant to us differ from the typically trivial and less relevant material transmitted in the game of telephone.

[151] Dunn, *Perspective*, 43, 114-15.

[152] Dunn, *Perspective*, 45-46.

[153] Bauckham, "Eyewitnesses," though I have concerns about some of this evidence (see Keener, "Review of Bauckham"). Even the tradition in the Fourth Gospel, which we are not engaging much in this book, rests on the testimony of the "beloved disciple" (who claims to be an eyewitness of at least some of the events; John 13:23; 19:26-27, 35; 21:24); see further Keener, *John*, 81-139; Bauckham, *Testimony*, 33-91. Papias depends on sayings of a John (though frg. 3.1 and 5.1 Holmes might mean indirectly; see frg. 3.4-5; 7.3), or, on Eusebius's view, two Johns (3.5-6, attributing the Gospel to the apostle); the John who authored 1 John (so Papias frg. 3.17) is presumably at least closely connected with the Gospel's author.

[154] On the reliability of the tradition about the Twelve, see e.g., Sanders, *Jesus and Judaism*, 11, 98-101; Meier, "Circle."

[155] Communal memory is not comprehensive but selects what it deems relevant (Kirk, "Memory," 168). Because of suggestibility, a false memory can be injected into collective memory (cf. Redman, "Eyewitnesses," 185-88; Stock, Gajsar, and Güntürkün, "Neuroscience of Memory," 386-88; Kloppenborg, "Memory," 290, following e.g., Schacter, "Sins," 192), but the events depicted normally remain authentic.

[156] Allison, *Constructing*, 375-77; Keener, *Matthew*, 25-29. Greek and Roman philosophers also could do the same (Philostratus *Vit. soph.* 1.22.523), even using poetry to

(and perhaps a teaching style designed to facilitate such transmission) pervade Jesus' teachings recorded in the Gospels.[157] Some studies of rural Middle Eastern oral tradition suggest that the form of news and jokes would have been highly flexible, that of parables and narratives somewhat flexible, and that of proverbs and poems virtually inflexible.[158] Most of Jesus' sayings would thus be conveyed with significant continuity.[159]

Nevertheless, our expectations for the practices of those who passed on the gospel tradition should be consistent with the expectations of their contemporaries. These practices suggest some degree of flexibility.[160] (The passage of generations, especially after living memory of the originator, further amplified the degree of adaptation expected, but again, that duration of time is less relevant for the Gospels.) Early rabbis not only preserved but adapted prior tradition.[161] Teachings could be condensed,[162] and similar sayings could appear in different words.[163]

Among Gentiles, standard rhetorical practice included paraphrasing sayings, as evidenced by the rhetorical exercises in which it features prominently.[164] Thus one biographer praises a sophist who both "received" disciple-instruction accurately and "passed it on" more eloquently (Philostratus *Vit. soph.* 2.29.621). Although expanding narratives usually did not require introducing new information, unless from another source,[165] writers sometimes added details to aug-

---

reinforce their teaching for rudimentary students (Seneca *Ep. Lucil.* 108.9-10).

[157] See Dunn, *Perspective*, 115.

[158] Bailey, "Oral Tradition"; also noted in Aune, *Dictionary*, 326. Weeden's critique of Bailey (Weeden, "Theory") does not overturn Bailey's essential insights about a degree of continuity (see Dunn, "Critiquing"), not unique to him, but it does undermine some of his key examples, which highlight proliferation of rumor rather than controlled tradition (see also Kloppenborg, "Memory," 300-3).

[159] Confusion of other sages' sayings with those of Jesus would, however, be unlikely this early in the process (see fuller discussion in Keener, *Historical Jesus*, 142-44).

[160] E.g., whereas some Q pericopes exhibit more than 80 percent verbal correspondence, more than one third exhibit "less than 40 percent" (Dunn, *Perspective*, 110). (Where close verbal correspondence exists, it probably typically suggests a written source, and even divergences can simply reflect memory rather than consultation of texts; see Kloppenborg, "Memory," 292, 304, following DeConick). Cf. comparable flexibility in Greek traditions in Kennedy, "Source Criticism," 132-33.

[161] Davies, "Reflexions," 156.

[162] Gerhardsson, *Memory*, 136-48, 173; Goulder, *Midrash*, 64-65.

[163] E.g., *m. Shab.* 9:1; *Abod. Zar.* 3:6.

[164] Theon *Progymn.* 1.93-171; cf. also Libanius *Anecdote* 1.4; 2.3; *Maxim* 1.2-5; 2.3; 3.2; Hermogenes *Method* 24.440.

[165] On expanding material rhetorically, see Theon *Progymn.* 3.224-40; 4.80-82; Longin. *Subl.* 11.1; Hermog. *Inv.* 2.7.120; cf. Theon *Progymn.* 2.115-23; Hermog. *Progymn.* 3.On Chreia, 7; Men. Rhet. 2.3, 379.2-4; Aphth. *Progymn.* 3. On Chreia, 23S, 4R; 4.On Maxim, 9-10.

ment dramatic effect.[166] The standard of accuracy for ancient memory was the "gist,"[167] and this is often the best that ordinary memory can offer in any case.[168]

Thus it is not surprising that the exact wording of Jesus's sayings could vary, for instance, from Matthew to Luke to the Didache.[169] E. P. Sanders concludes that "The gospel writers did not wildly invent material," though "they developed it, shaped it and directed it in the ways they wished."[170]

Arrangement was considered more a literary and rhetorical than historical issue. Jesus's sayings sometimes appear in different Gospel frameworks (cf. e.g., Matt 7:13-14//Luke 13:24; Matt 8:11//Luke 13:29). Like most sages, Jesus probably used some sayings in various settings;[171] when narrative contexts were connected with the saying in significant ways, they often circulated together.[172] Sayings could also circulate independently (e.g., Seneca *Ep. Lucil.* 94.27-28), however, being combined with narratives simply to provide a literary or rhetorical location (Theon *Progymn.* 4.73-79; cf. 5.388-441).

Many Synoptic narratives about Jesus fit typical forms that were more easily valued and remembered. The combination of such narratives with anecdotes, sayings, plus an extended account of the protagonist's end, characterizes much of ancient biography in general, so ancient hearers would have recognized these patterns in the Gospels.[173] *Taxis*, or arrangement, was a standard rhetorical concern with narratives; Papias accepts Mark as a legitimate link in tradition while apparently preferring the superior rhetorical arrangement of Mark's Evangelist successors.[174]

---

[166] Plut. *Alex.* 70.3. Even such augmentation elicited some protests; see Lucian *Hist.* 7-13; Shuler, *Genre*, 11-12.

[167] Small, "Artificial Memory."

[168] Bauckham, *Eyewitnesses*, 333-34; cf. Allison, *Constructing*, 11-13; Eddy and Boyd, *The Jesus Legend*, 275-85.

[169] See Draper, "Tradition."

[170] Sanders, *Figure*, 193.

[171] Frye, "Synoptic Problems," 291.

[172] Hermogenes *Progymn.* 3.On Chreia, 6-7; Plutarch *Themist.* 11.2.

[173] Burridge, *Gospels?* (1992), 203; cf. Robbins, *Quotes*. We may, however, contrast, for example, the early third-century CE Diogenes Laertius's collection of chreiai regarding the fourth-century BCE Cynic Diogenes (cf. Hägg, *Biography*, 312)—employing material that had accumulated over the course of more than half a millennium—with the first-century Gospels recounting stories roughly a half-century to seven decades after the events.

[174] See Papias frg. 3.15 (Holmes), as articulated in Moessner, "Voice." On this view, Mark accurately preserved Peter's living voice (7.3-4), but lacked suitable arrangement. Papias was not rhetorically adept, but *taxis* implies proper organization (with beginning and ending) not only in ancient historiography but even in nontechnical contexts. In subsequent discussion (Aug. 3, 2016), Prof. Moessner pointed out that Mark fails roughly half of Theon's criteria for a good plot (by ancient standards, not modern ones).

Misplaced Analogies

Rejecting comparisons with more reliable oral tradition, some compare instead the rapid spread of distortions in the seventeenth-century messianic movement following Sabbatai Sevi or the twentieth-century messianic movement following Simon Kimbangu.[175] Aside from the problem of depending more on subsequent movements when we have more directly relevant ancient evidence (see discussion above), Kimbangu did not train disciples by passing on easily memorizable sayings, disciples who then led the movement and cited his teachings. Indeed, many of Kimbangu's "closest disciples were also arrested."[176] Much more than is evident in our first-century sources about Jesus,[177] views about their movement's founder varied widely among Kimbangu's followers, especially after his son's death some forty years later.[178]

Further, the labels given to Sabbatai Sevi and eventually Kimbangu derived from analogies with Jesus—a claim more difficult to make for Jesus given the lack of contemporary parallels in his day. His early Galilean Jewish followers lacked close models for rapid deification; his later Gentile followers in the Diaspora would hardly have invoked the category of "Messiah."[179] The category fallacy here illustrates that not all possible analogies are equally valuable.

Had early storytellers and writers indulged in free invention in various geographical communities, we would expect Gospels much more diverse than our Synoptics are—more like the later Gnostic materials formed under such conditions.[180] Paul's letters sometimes attest early traditions about Jesus's life and teaching (e.g., 1 Cor 7:10-12; 9:14; 11:23; 15:3; 1 Thess 4:15), and in some of these cases he explicitly distinguishes his teaching from that of Jesus (1 Cor 7:10, 12, 25).[181]

Sayings That Fit Jesus's Environment

Many of Jesus's reported sayings imply a setting relevant only to Jesus's particular geographic or chronological milieu, as opposed to that of later sources.[182] That earliest milieu is relevant to Jesus's disciples as well as to Jesus

---

[175] Price, *Shrinking*, 29.

[176] Gray, "Christianity," 158.

[177] Some early Christian sources say little about matters emphasized in other sources, but this silence differs from widely conflicting views such as found among Kimbanguists. Those who speak of communities of Jesus-followers who denied his messiahship or resurrection always must argue from silence.

[178] Gondola, "Kimbangu," 767. Keep in mind that the basic contours of earliest Christian theology already appear in Paul and Mark, within forty years of the Jesus movement's beginning.

[179] See Keener, "Parallel Figures."

[180] Cf. Hill, *Prophecy*, 163, 172.

[181] On Paul and the Jesus tradition, see e.g., Wenham, *Rediscovery*; idem, "Story"; Richardson and Gooch, "Logia," 52; Taylor, "Quest"; Eddy and Boyd, *The Jesus Legend*, 216-28; Keener, *Historical Jesus*, 361-71; see esp. Dungan, *Sayings*.

[182] See Theissen, *Gospels*, 25-59.

himself, but we should remember that Jesus's disciples were those with the most direct and complete memories of Jesus's ministry. For just several possible examples among many:[183]

- The Pharisees' question about divorce (Mark 10:2; Matt 19:3) reflects a debate among Pharisaic schools from Jesus's generation[184]
- Jesus plays on current Pharisaic debates about purity regarding the inside or outside of cups[185]
- Jesus's warning that it would be "measured" to one as one measured to others echoes a Jewish tradition (Matt 7:2; Luke 6:38)[186]
- Jewish teachers often employed the phrase, "to what shall I/we compare?" (Matt 11:16//Luke 7:31), especially to introduce parables[187]
- The first half of the "Lord's Prayer" (Matt 6:9-10//Luke 11:2) corresponds closely to the language of some early Palestinian Jewish prayers[188]
- Later Jewish teachers, not likely influenced by Jesus, could depict what was almost impossible as a large animal passing through a needle's eye (Mark 10:25)[189]

In the period of the Synoptics, Christians undoubtedly applied their stories to their current setting. Nevertheless, they avoided creating new traditions about Jesus to resolve even burning issues of their day, such as circumcising Gentiles.[190] Mark thus has to include an interpretive aside (Mark 7:14) to address the issue of kosher foods, and his one story about a Gentile involves Jesus first insulting her (7:27).[191]

Many other relevant observations, which I have treated more fully elsewhere,[192] can be mentioned only in passing here. Traditional historical-critical approaches often lend independent support to the antiquity of many traditions about Jesus.[193]

Starting assumptions do shape the standard of evidence that scholars demand, however, and our understanding that memories can persist over the

---

[183] From somewhat fuller treatments in Keener, "Suggestions"; idem, "Assumptions," 49-52.

[184] See *m. Git.* 9:10; *Sipre Deut.* 269.1.1.

[185] Cf. Neusner, "Cleanse," 492-94; McNamara, *Judaism*, 197.

[186] Smith, *Parallels*, 135.

[187] E.g., *m. Ab.* 3:17; *Suk.* 2:10; *tos. Ber.* 1:11; 6:18; *Sanh.* 1:2; 8:9.

[188] Vermes, *World*, 43.

[189] Abrahams, *Studies*, 208.

[190] Theissen and Merz, *Historical Jesus*, 105; Wright, *People*, 421; Stanton, *Truth?*, 60-61.

[191] For one interpretation, see Cotter, *Miracle Stories*, 148-54. On dogs as an insult, see e.g., Homer *Il.* 8.527; 11.362; 20.449; 22.345 (cf. 9.373; 21.394, 421); *Od.* 17.248; 22.35; Callimachus *Hymn* 6 (to Demeter), 63; when addressed to women, it sometimes connoted sexual looseness, Homer *Od.* 11.424; 18.338; 19.91.

[192] Especially in Keener, *Historical Jesus*.

[193] See current discussions in Porter and Holmén, *Handbook*; Charlesworth, Rhea and Pokorny, *Jesus Research*.

course of four decades should support a default setting that gives greater room for optimism than skepticism.[194] I have argued much more fully elsewhere that arguments against tradition because of some apparent elements of high Christology[195] or because of miracle or exorcism accounts[196] are misplaced.

Implications

In light of the foregoing discussion, our starting assumption should be that disciples of Jesus would have learned and transmitted his teachings no less carefully than most ancient disciples transmitted the wisdom of their mentors.[197] If we must start with assumptions either way, should not a heavier burden of proof rest on the approach of radical skeptics, rather than with the assumption that Jesus's disciples were like other disciples in antiquity hence sought to transmit their master's teachings reliably?

The historiographic considerations applicable to ancient sources in general apply here: sources from the first generation are two are likely to have often preserved at least the gist of the events they report. Luke attests his audience's knowledge of many written sources as well as oral sources (Luke 1:1-2), and he believed that his detailed account confirmed the stories that at least some of his audience already knew (1:3-4). Given that he wrote at a time when he had access to such information (Luke 1:2-3; Acts 21:8, 17-18),[198] his claim should count against modern speculation, which often rests on dismissing all the evidence we have and arguing the contrary based on the silence that remains.

Conclusion

Ancient Mediterranean culture valued memory more than modern Western culture does. They could preserve oral traditions and could use collections of sayings in written or oral form, or in both.

We cannot expect disciples to have remembered everything that Jesus said, nor can we expect them to have recalled his words in verbatim form; for that matter, the form often varies even among our current Gospels. Nevertheless, we can expect much of the substance of key teachings to remain. Indeed, many of Jesus' teachings are in the sort of readily memorizable forms in which sages often offered them to facilitate retention. Moreover, Jesus's sayings often reflect their original context in his Galilean ministry far better than they reflect the situations of the churches addressed in the Gospels.

---

[194] Keener, "Assumptions."
[195] Keener, "Parallel Figures"; see more fully e.g., Hurtado, *Lord Jesus Christ*; Hays, *Reading Backwards*; Gathercole, *Preexistent Son*; Tilling, *Christology*.
[196] Keener, "Comparisons"; idem, "Spirit Possession"; idem, *Miracles*; idem, "Reassessment."
[197] Cf. similarly Eddy and Boyd, *The Jesus Legend*, 269-306.
[198] See Keener, *Acts*, 1:51-422; 3:2350-74.

Ancient memories could be highly developed, as illustrated in oratory, storytelling, basic education and advanced education. Disciples normally preserved the substance of their masters' teachings and, where relevant, stories about their behavior. Disciples sometimes took notes that proved highly accurate, but those who could not do so were nevertheless expected to recall their teachers' instruction. To assume that Jesus' disciples acted completely unlike other disciples with regard to transmitting their teachers' sayings—despite the comparatively early publication of sources about Jesus—is to value one's skepticism about Jesus more highly than the concrete comparative evidence. If some scholars exhibit a serious canonical bias, scholars who treat the gospel traditions as significantly less reliable than analogous traditions from antiquity appear to reflect either an anticanonical bias or a lack of direct knowledge of the analogous ancient sources.

Bibliography

Abel, *Livres*. *Les Livres Des Maccabees*. Translated by F. M. Abel. 2d ed. Paris: Les Editions Du Cerf, 1951.
Abrahams, *Studies*. Abrahams, I. *Studies in Pharisaism and the Gospels*. 2nd ser. Cambridge: Cambridge University Press, 1924.
Abramowski, "Memoirs." Abramowski, Luise. "The 'Memoirs of the Apostles' in Justin." Pages 323-35 in *The Gospel and the Gospels*. Edited by Peter Stuhlmacher. Grand Rapids: Eerdmans, 1991.
Achtemeier, *Miracle Tradition*. Achtemeier, Paul J. *Jesus and the Miracle Tradition*. Eugene, Ore.: Cascade, 2008.
Adams, *The Genre of Acts*. Adams, Sean A. *The Genre of Acts and Collected Biography*. SNTSMS 156. Cambridge: Cambridge University Press, 2013.
Aguilar, "Judean Past." Aguilar, Mario I. "Rethinking the Judean Past: Questions of History and a Social Archaeology of Memory in the First Book of the Maccabees." *BTB* 30 (2000): 58-67.
Alexander, "IPSE DIXIT." Alexander, Loveday C. A. "IPSE DIXIT: Citation of Authority in Paul and in the Jewish Hellenistic Schools." Pages 103–27 in *Paul beyond the Judaism/Hellenism Divide*. Edited by Troels Engberg-Pedersen. Louisville: Westminster John Knox, 2001.
Alexander, "Memory." Alexander, Loveday. "Memory and Tradition in the Hellenistic Schools." Pages 113–53 in *Jesus in Memory: Traditions in Oral and Scribal Perspectives*. Edited by Werner H. Kelber and Samuel Byrskog. Waco: Baylor University Press, 2009.
Alexander, *Preface*. Alexander, Loveday C. A. *The Preface to Luke's Gospel: Literary Convention and Social Context in Luke 1.1–4 and Acts 1.1*. SNTSMS 78. Cambridge: Cambridge University Press, 1993.
Alexander, "Rabbinic Biography." Alexander, Philip S. "Rabbinic Biography and the Biography of Jesus: A Survey of the Evidence." Pages 19–50 in *Synoptic Studies: The Ampleforth Conferences of 1982 and 1983*. Edited by Christopher M. Tuckett. JSNTSup 7. Sheffield: JSOT Press, 1984.
Alexander, "Review." Alexander, Loveday. Review of *What are the Gospels? A Comparison with Graeco-Roman Biography* (1992), by Richard A. Burridge. *Evangelical Quarterly* 66 (1994): 73-76.
Allison, *Constructing*. Allison, Dale C. *Constructing Jesus: Memory, Imagination, and History*. Grand Rapids: Baker Academic, 2010.
Allison, *Jesus of Nazareth*. Allison, Dale C. *Jesus of Nazareth: Millenarian Prophet*. Minneapolis: Fortress, 1998.

Anderson, *Glossary.* Anderson, R. Dean, Jr. *Glossary of Greek Rhetorical Terms Connected to Methods of Argumentation, Figures, and Tropes from Anaximenes to Quintilian.* Leuven: Peeters, 2000.

Argyle, "University." Argyle, A. W. "The Ancient University of Alexandria." *CJ* 69 (4, 1974): 348-50.

Aron-Schnapper and Hanet, "Archives orales." Aron-Schnapper, Dominique, and Daniele Hanet. "Archives orales et histoire des institutions sociales." *Revue francaise de sociologie* 19 (2, 1978): 261–75.

Ash, Mossman, and Titchener, *Fame.* Ash, Rhiannon, Judith Mossman, and Frances B. Titchener, eds. *Fame and Infamy: Essays for Christopher Pelling on Characterization in Greek and Roman Biography and Historiography.* Oxford: Oxford University Press, 2015.

Attridge, "Historiography." Attridge, Harold W. "Jewish Historiography." Pages 311–43 in *Early Judaism and Its Modern Interpreters.* Edited by Robert A. Kraft and George W. E. Nickelsburg. SBLBMI 2. Atlanta: Scholars Press, 1986.

Aune, *Dictionary.* Aune, David E. *The Westminster Dictionary of New Testament and Early Christian Literature and Rhetoric.* Louisville: Westminster John Knox, 2003.

Aune, *Literary Environment.* Aune, David E. *The New Testament in Its Literary Environment.* LEC 8. Philadelphia: Westminster, 1987.

Aune, "Greco-Roman Biography." Aune, David E. "Greco-Roman Biography." Pages 107–26 in *Greco-Roman Literature and the New Testament: Selected Forms and Genres.* Atlanta: Scholars Press, 1988.

Aune, "Problem." Aune, David E. "The Problem of the Genre of the Gospels: A Critique of Charles H. Talbert's *What is a Gospel?*" Pages 9-60 in *Gospel Perspectives, vol. II.* Edited by R. T. France and D. Wenham. Sheffield: JSOT, 1981.

Aune, *Prophecy.* Aune, David E. *Prophecy in Early Christianity and the Ancient Mediterranean World.* Grand Rapids: Eerdmans, 1983.

Badian, "Alexander." Badian, Ernst. "Alexander the Great and the Unity of Mankind." *Historia* 7 (1958): 425-444.

Badian, "Skill." Badian, Ernst. "Plutarch's Unconfessed Skill: The Biographer as a Critical Historian." Pages 26-44 in *Laurea internationalis: Festschrift für Jochen Bleicken zum 75. Geburstag.* Edited by Theodora Hantos. Stuttgart: Franz Steiner, 2003.

Bailey, "Oral Tradition." Bailey, Kenneth Ewing. "Informal Controlled Oral Tradition and the Synoptic Gospels." *Asia Journal of Theology* 5 (1, 1991): 34–54.

Balch, "The Genre of Luke-Acts." Balch, David L. "The Genre of Luke-Acts: Individual Biography, Adventure Novel, or Political History?" *SwJT* 33 (1990): 5–19.

Baldwin, *Suetonius.* Baldwin, Barry. *Suetonius.* Amsterdam: Adolf M. Hakkert, 1983.

Balsdon and Levick, "damnatio memoriae." Balsdon, John P.V.D. and Barbara M. Levick. "damnatio memoriae." *OCD*[4] 411.

Bar-Kochva, *Judas Maccabaeus.* Bar-Kochva, Bezalel. *Judas Maccabaeus: The Jewish Struggle against the Seleucids.* Cambridge: Cambridge University Press, 1989.

Barr and Wentling, "Biography and Genre." Barr, David L., and Judith L. Wentling. "The Conventions of Classical Biography and the Genre of Luke-Acts: A Preliminary Study." Pages 63–88 in *Luke-Acts: New Perspectives from the Society of Biblical Literature Seminar.* Edited by Charles H. Talbert. New York: Crossroad, 1984.

Bauckham, "Acts of Paul." Bauckham, Richard. "The Acts of Paul as a Sequel to Acts." Pages 105–52 in *The Book of Acts in Its Ancient Literary Setting.* Edited by Bruce W. Winter and Andrew D. Clark. Vol. 1 of *The Book of Acts in Its First Century Setting.* Edited by Bruce W. Winter. Grand Rapids: Eerdmans; Carlisle, U.K.: Paternoster, 1993.

Bauckham, "Eyewitnesses." Bauckham, Richard. "The Eyewitnesses and the Gospel Traditions." *Journal for the Study of the Historical Jesus* 1 (1, 2003): 28–60.

Bauckham, *Eyewitnesses.* Richard Bauckham, *Jesus and the Eyewitnesses: The Gospels as Eyewitness Testimony.* Grand Rapids: Eerdmans, 2006.

Bauckham, "For Whom." Bauckham, Richard. "For Whom Were the Gospels Written?" Pages 9-48 in *The Gospels for All Christians.* Edited by Richard Bauckham. Edinburgh: T. & T. Clark; Grand Rapids: Eerdmans, 1998.

Bauckham, *Gospels.* Bauckham, Richard, ed. *The Gospels for All Christians.* Edinburgh: T. & T. Clark; Grand Rapids: Eerdmans, 1998.

Bauckham, "Historiographical Characteristics." Bauckham, Richard. "Historiographical Characteristics of the Gospel of John." *NTS* 53 (1, 2007): 17–36.

Bauckham, "Liber antiquitatum." Bauckham, Richard. "The Liber antiquitatum biblicarum of Pseudo-Philo and the Gospels as 'Midrash.'" Pages 33–76 in *Studies in Midrash and Historiography.* Edited by R. T. France and David Wenham. Gospel Perspectives 3. Sheffield, U.K.: JSOT Press, 1983.

Bauckham, *Testimony.* Bauckham, Richard. *The Testimony of the Beloved Disciple: Narrative, History, and Theology in the Gospel of John.* Grand Rapids: Baker Academic, 2007.

Bauckham and Porter, "Apocryphal Gospels." Bauckham, Richard, and Stanley E. Porter, "Apocryphal Gospels," 71-79 in *DNTB.*

Bauernfeind and Michel, "Beiden Eleazarreden." Bauernfeind, Otto, and Otto Michel. "Die beiden Eleazarreden in Jos. bell. 7,323–336; 7,341–388." *ZNW* 58 (3–4, 1967): 267–72.

Baum, "Biographien." Baum, Armin D. "Biographien im alttestamentlich-rabbinischen Stil. Zur Gattung der neu-testamentlichen Evangelien." *Biblica* 94 (4, 2013): 534-64.

Baynham, *Alexander.* Baynham, E. J. *Alexander the Great: The Unique History of Quintus Curtis.* Ann Arbor: University of Michigan Press, 1998.

Baynham, "Quintus Curtius." Baynham, E. J. "Quintus Curtius Rufus on the 'Good King': The Dioxippus Episode in Book 9.7.16–26." Pages 427–33 in *A Companion to Greek and Roman Historiography*. Edited by John Marincola. 2 vols. Oxford: Blackwell, 2007.

Bazin, "Past." Bazin, Jean. "The Past in the Present: Notes on Oral Archaeology." Pages 59–74 in *African Historiographies: What History for Which Africa?* Edited by Bogumil Jewsiewicki and David Newbury. SSAMD 12. Beverly Hills, Calif.; London; and New Delhi: Sage, 1986.

Beard, *Literacy*. Beard, Mary, ed. *Literacy in the Roman World*. Ann Arbor: Journal of Roman Archaeology, University of Michigan, 1991.

Beavis, *Mark's Audience*. Beavis, Mary Ann. *Mark's Audience: The Literary and Social Setting of Mark 4:11-12*. JSNTSup 33. Sheffield: Sheffield Academic Press, 1989.

Becking, "Hellenistic Period." Becking, Bob. "The Hellenistic Period and Ancient Israel: Three Preliminary Statements." Pages 78-90 in *Did Moses Speak Attic?: Jewish Historiography and Scripture in the Hellenistic Period*. Edited by Lester L. Grabbe. JSOTsup317. Sheffield: Sheffield Academic, 2001.

Begg, "Elisha's Deeds." Begg, Christopher T. "Elisha's Great Deeds according to Josephus (*AJ* 9,47–94)." *Hen* 18 (1–2, 1996): 69–110.

Begg, "Jotham." Begg, Christopher T. "Jotham and Amon: Two Minor Kings of Judah according to Josephus." *BBR* 6 (1996): 1–13.

Begg, "Marah Incident." Begg, Christopher T. "The Marah Incident according to Josephus and Philo." *Laurentianum* 49 (2-3, 2008): 321-33.

Begg, "Moves." Begg, Christopher T. "Moses' First Moves (Exod 2:11-22) as Retold by Josephus and Philo." *Polish Journal of Biblical Research* 9 (1-2, 2010): 67-93.

Begg, "Rape of Tamar." Begg, Christopher T. "The Rape of Tamar (2 Samuel 13) according to Josephus." *EstBib* 54 (4, 1996): 465–500.

Begg, "Rephidim Episode." Begg, Christopher T. "The Rephidim Episode according to Josephus and Philo." *Ephemerides Theologicae Lovanienses* 83 (4, 2007): 367-83.

Begg, "Retelling." Begg, Christopher T. "Josephus' and Philo's Retelling of Numbers 31 Compared." *Ephemerides Theologicae Lovanienses* 83 (1, 2007): 81-106.

Begg, "Zedekiah." Begg, Christopher T. "Josephus's Zedekiah." *ETL* 65 (1, 1989): 96–104.

Bellemore, *Nicolaus*. Bellemore, Jane, ed. *Nicolaus of Damascus: Life of Augustus: Edited with Introduction, Commentary, and Translation*. Bristol, UK: Bristol Classical, 1984.

Beneker, "Chaste Caesar." Beneker, Jeffrey. "No Time for Love: Plutarch's Chaste Caesar." *GRBS* 43 (1, 2002–3): 13–29.

Beneker, "Crossing." Beneker, Jeffrey. "The Crossing of the Rubicon and the Outbreak of Civil War in Cicero, Lucan, Plutarch, and Suetonius." *Phoenix* 65 (1–2, 2011): 74–99.

Beneker, "Nepos' Method." Beneker, Jeffrey. "Nepos' Biographical Method in the Lives of Foreign Generals." *CJ* 105 (2009): 109–21.
Beneker, *Statesman*. Beneker, Jeffrey. *The Passionate Statesman. Eros and Politics in Plutarch's Lives*. Oxford: Oxford University Press, 2012.
Benoit, *Gospel*. Benoit, Pierre. *Jesus and the Gospel*. Translated by Benet Weatherhead. 2 vols. Vol. 1: New York: Herder & Herder; London: Darton, Longman & Todd, 1973. Vol. 2: New York: Seabury (Crossroad); London: Darton, Longman & Todd, 1974.
Ben Zeev, "Capitol." Ben Zeev, Miriam Pucci. "Polybius, Josephus, and the Capitol in Rome." *JSJ* 27 (1, 1996): 21–30.
Berchmann, "Arcana Mundi." Berchmann, R. M. "Arcana Mundi: Prophecy and Divination in the *Vita Mosis* of Philo of Alexandria." Pages 385-423 in *Society of Biblical Literature 1988 Seminar Papers*. SBLSPS 27. Edited by David J. Lull. Atlanta: Society of Biblical Literature, 1988.
Bergren, "Nehemiah." Bergren, Theodore A. "Nehemiah in 2 Maccabees 1:10–2:18." *JSJ* 28 (3, 1997): 249–70.
Berlin and Overman, *Revolt*. Berlin, Andrea M. and J. Andrew Overman., eds. *The First Jewish Revolt: Archaeology, History, and Ideology*. London: Routledge, 2002.
Bernal, *Athena*. Bernal, Martin. *Black Athena: The Afroasiatic Roots of Classical Civilization*. 3 vols. London: Free Association; New Brunswick, N.J.: Rutgers University Press, 1987–2006.
Bernheim, *Lehrbuch*. Bernheim, Ernst. *Lehrbuch der historischen Methode und der Geschichtsphilosophie*. Leipzig: Duncker & Humblot, 1908.
Berthelot, "Conquest." Berthelot, Katell. "Philo of Alexandria and the Conquest of Canaan." *JSJ* 38 (1, 2007): 39–56.
Berthelot, "Reclaiming the Land." Berthelot, Katell. "Reclaiming the Land (1 Maccabees 15:28-36): Hasmonean Discourse between Biblical Tradition and Seleucid Rhetoric." *JBL* 133 (2014): 539-59.
Bilde, *Josephus*. Bilde, Per. *Flavius Josephus between Jerusalem and Rome: His Life, his Works, and their Importance*. Journal for the Study of the Pseudepigrapha Supplement Series. Ed. James H. Charlesworth. Sheffield: SJOT Press, 1988.
Bilezikian, *The Liberated Gospel*. Bilezikian, Gilbert G. *The Liberated Gospel: A Comparison of the Gospel of Mark and Greek Tragedy*. BBMS. Grand Rapids: Baker Book House, 1977.
Black, "Oration at Olivet." Black, C. Clifton. "An Oration at Olivet: Some Rhetorical Dimensions of Mark 13." Pages 66–92 in *Persuasive Artistry: Studies in New Testament Rhetoric in Honor of George A. Kennedy*. Edited by Duane F. Watson. JSNTSup 50. Sheffield, U.K.: Sheffield Academic, 1991.
Bloch, "Alexandria." Bloch, René. "Alexandria in Pharaonic Egypt: Projections in De Vita Mosis," *Studia Philonica Annual* 24 (2012): 69-84.
Blomberg, *Historical Reliability*. Blomberg, Craig L. *The Historical Reliability of the Gospels*. 2nd ed. Downers Grove, IL: IVP Academic, 2007.

Bloomer, "Quintilian." Bloomer, W. Martin. "Quintilian on the Child as a Learning Subject." *Classical World* 105 (1, 2011): 109-137.
Blyth, "Cicero." Blyth, Dougal. "Cicero and Philosophy as Text." *ClassJourn* 106 (1, 2010): 71-98.
Borgen, "Reviewing and Rewriting." Borgen, Peder. "Philo of Alexandria: Reviewing and Rewriting Biblical Material." *SPhilA* 9 (1997): 37–53.
Bosch-Veciana, "Filosofia." Bosch-Veciana, A. "La 'filosofia' del judaisme alexandrí com a 'manera de viure.'" *Revista Catalana de Teología* 34 (2, 2009): 503-21.
Bosworth, *Arrian to Alexander*. Bosworth, A. B. *From Arrian to Alexander: Studies in Historical Interpretation.* New York: Oxford University Press, 1988.
Bosworth, "Death." Bosworth, A. B. "The Death of Alexander the Great: Rumour and Propaganda." *The Classical Quarterly* 21 (1971): 112-136.
Bosworth, "Pseudo-Callisthenes." Bosworth, A. B. "Pseudo-Callisthenes." OCD^3 1270.
Bosworth, "Pursuit." Bosworth, A. B. "Arrian, Alexander, and the Pursuit of Glory." Pages 447-53 in *A Companion to Greek and Roman Historiography*. Edited by John Marincola. 2 vols. Oxford: Blackwell, 2007.
Bovon, *Luke*. Bovon, François. *Luke*. 3 vols. Hermeneia. Minneapolis: Fortress, 2002-12.
Bowersock, *Fiction as History*. Bowersock, G. W. *Fiction as History: Nero to Julian*. Berkeley: University of California Press, 1994.
Bowie, "Apollonius." Bowie, Ewen Lyall. "Apollonius of Tyana: Tradition and Reality." *ANRW* 2.16.2:1652-99.
Bowie, "Philostratus." Bowie, Ewen Lyall. "Philostratus: Writer of Fiction." Pages 181-99 in *Greek Fiction: The Greek Novel in Context*. Edited by J. R. Morgan and Richard Stoneman. London: Routledge, 1994.
Bowman, "Prophets." Bowman, John. "Prophets and Prophecy in Talmud and Midrash." *EvQ* 22 (2, 1950): 107–14; (3, 1958): 205–20; (4, 1950): 255–75.
Boyd-Taylor, "Adventure." Boyd-Taylor, Cameron. "Esther's Great Adventure: Reading the LXX Version of the Book of Esther in Light of Its Assimilation to the Conventions of the Greek Romantic Novel." *BIOSCS* 30 (1997): 81–113.
Bradley, "Suetonius." Bradley, Keith R. "Suetonius (Gaius Suetonius Tranquillus)." OCD^3 1451–52.
Bravo, "Antiquarianism." Bravo, Benedetto. "Antiquarianism and History." Pages 515–27 in *A Companion to Greek and Roman Historiography*. Edited by John Marincola. 2 vols. Oxford: Blackwell, 2007.
Briscoe and Drummond, "Cornelius Nepos." Briscoe, John, and Andrew Drummond, "Cornelius Nepos." Pages 395-401 in *The Fragments of the Roman Historians: Introduction*. Edited by T. J. Cornell. Vol. 1 of *The Fragments of the Roman Historians*. Edited by T. J. Cornell. Oxford: Oxford University Press, 2013.

Brown, *Historians.* Brown, Truesdell S. *The Greek Historians.* Lexington, Mass.: D. C. Heath, 1973.
Brown, *Introduction.* Brown, Raymond E. *An Introduction to the New Testament,* The Anchor Bible Reference Library New York: Doubleday, 1997.
Brownson, "Introduction to *Anabasis.***"** Brownson, Carleton L. Introduction to *Anabasis.* Pages 231–38 in vol. 2 of *Xenophon.* Translated by Carleton L. Brownson, O. J. Todd, and E. C. Marchant. 4 vols. LCL. New York: G. P. Putnam's Sons, 1918–23.
Bruce, *Documents.* Bruce, F. F. *The New Testament Documents: Are They Reliable?* 5th rev. ed. Grand Rapids: Eerdmans; Leicester, U.K.: Inter-Varsity, 1981.
Bryan, *Preface to Mark.* Bryan, Christopher. *A Preface to Mark: Notes on the Gospel and its Literary and Cultural Settings.* New York: Oxford University Press, 1993.
Bultmann, *Geschichte.* Bultmann, Rudolf. *Die Geschichte der synoptischen Tradition.* FRLANT. Göttingen: Vandenhoeck & Ruprecht, 1931.
Bultmann, *History.* Bultmann, Rudolf. *The History of the Synoptic Tradition.* 2nd ed. Translated by John Marsh. Oxford: Blackwell, 1968.
Bultmann, "The Gospels (Form)." Bultmann, Rudolf. "The Gospels (Form)." Pages 86–92 in *Twentieth Century Theology in the Making: Themes of Biblical Theology.* Edited by Jaroslav Pelikan, Translated by Richard A. Wilson. London: Fontana, 1969.
Bünker, "Disposition der Eleazarreden." Bünker, Michael. "Die rhetorische Disposition der Eleazarreden (Josephus, Bell. 7,323–388)." *Kairos* 23 (1–2, 1981): 100–107.
Burgersdijk and van Waarden, *Emperors and Historiography.* Burgersdijk, D.W.P. and J.A. van Waarden, eds. *Emperors and Historiography: Collected Essays on the Literature of the Roman Empire by Daniël den Hengst.* Monographs on Greek and Roman Language and Literature 319. Leiden: Brill, 2010.
Burnette-Bletsch, "Jael." Burnette-Bletsch, Rhonda. "At the Hands of a Woman: Rewriting Jael in Pseudo-Philo." *JSP* 17 (1998): 53–64.
Burridge, "About People." Burridge, Richard A. "About People, by People, for People: Gospel Genre and Audiences." Pages 113-45 in *The Gospels for All Christians.* Edited by Richard Bauckham. Edinburgh: T. & T. Clark; Grand Rapids: Eerdmans, 1997.
Burridge, "Absence of Rabbinic Biography." Burridge, Richard A. "Gospel Genre, Christological Controversy and the Absence of Rabbinic Biography: Some Implications of the Biographical Hypothesis." Pages 137–56 in *Christology, Controversy, and Community: New Testament Essays in Honour of David R. Catchpole.* Edited by David G. Horrell and Christopher M. Tuckett. Leiden: Brill, 2000.
Burridge, "Biography." Burridge, Richard A. "Biography." Pages 371–91 in *Handbook of Classical Rhetoric in the Hellenistic Period, 330 B.C.-A.D. 400.* Edited by Stanley E. Porter. Leiden: Brill, 1997.

Burridge, "Biography, Ancient." Burridge, Richard A. "Biography, Ancient." *DNTB* 167–70.

Burridge, *Four Gospels*. Burridge, Richard A. *Four Gospels, One Jesus: A Symbolic Reading.* London: SPCK, 1994.

Burridge, "Genre." Burridge, Richard A. "Biography as the Gospels' Literary Genre." *Revista Catalana de Teología* 38 (1, 2013): 9-30.

Burridge, "Gospel." Burridge, Richard A. "The Gospel of Jesus: Graham Stanton, Biography and the Genre of Matthew." Pages 5-22 in *Jesus, Matthew's Gospel and Early Christianity: Studies in Memory of Graham N. Stanton.* Edited by D. M. Gurtner, J. Willitts and R.A. Burridge. LNTS 435. London: T. & T. Clark, 2011.

Burridge, *Gospels?* (1992). Burridge, Richard A. *What are the Gospels? A Comparison with Græco-Roman Biography.* SNTSMS 70. Cambridge: Cambridge University Press, 1992.

Burridge, *Gospels?* (2004). Burridge, Richard A. *What are the Gospels? A Comparison with Græco-Roman Biography.* 2nd ed. The Biblical Resource Series. Grand Rapids: Eerdmans, 2004.

Burridge, "Gospel: Genre." Burridge, Richard A. 'Gospel: Genre', in J. B. Green, J.K. Brown and N. Perrin (eds), *Dictionary of Jesus and the Gospels* (2nd ed.; Downers Grove: IVP): 335-42.

Burridge, "Reading the Gospels." Burridge, Richard A. "Reading the Gospels as Biography." Pages 31–49 in *The Limits of Ancient Biography.* Edited by Brian McGing and Judith Mossman. Swansea: The Classical Press of Wales, 2006.

Burridge, "Review." Burridge, Richard A. "*The Art of Biography in Antiquity*: A Review." *JSNT* 37 (4, June 2015): 474-79.

Buszard, "Parallel." Buszard, Bradley. "A Plutarchan Parallel to Arrian *Anabasis* 7.1." *GkRomByzStud* 50 (4, 2010): 565-85.

Byrskog, "History." Byrskog, Samuel. "History or Story in Acts—a Middle Way? The "We" Passages, Historical Intertexture, and Oral History." Pages 257–83 in *Contextualizing Acts: Lukan Narrative and Greco-Roman Discourse.* Edited by Todd Penner and Caroline Vander Stichele. SBLSymS 20. Atlanta: Society of Biblical Literature, 2003.

Byrskog, *Story as History*. Byrskog, Samuel. *Story as History—History as Story: The Gospel Tradition in the Context of Ancient Oral History.* Boston: Brill, 2002.

Cadoux and Badian, "Caecilia Attica." Cadoux, Theodore J. and Ernst Badian. "Caecilia Attica." *OCD*[4] 257.

Cadoux and Seager, "Cornelius Balbus (2), Lucius." Cadoux, Theodore J. and Robin J. Seager. "Cornelius Balbus (2), Lucius." *OCD*[4] 376-77.

Caird, *Language*. Caird, G. B. *The Language and Imagery of the Bible.* Philadelphia: Westminster, 1980.

Cancik, "Gattung." Cancik, Hubert. "Die Gattung Evangelium: Das Evangelium des Markus im Rahmen der antiken Historiographie." Pages 85–113 in *Markus-Philologie: Historische, literargeschichtliche, und stilistische Untersuchungen zum zweiten Evangelium*. Edited by Hubert Cancik. WUNT 33. Tübingen: Mohr Siebeck, 1984.
Canevet, "Remarques sur l'utilisation." Canevet, Mariette. "Remarques sur l'utilisation du genre littéraire historique par Philon d'Alexandrie dans la *Vita Moysis*, ou Moïse général en chef-prophète." *RevScRel* 60 (3–4, 1986): 189–206.
Carey, *Jesus' Cry*. Carey, Holly J. *Jesus' Cry from the Cross: Towards a First-Century Understanding of the Intertextual Relationship between Psalm 22 and the Narrative of Mark's Gospel*. LNTS 398. London: T&T Clark, 2009.
Carr, *Tablet*. Carr, David M. *Writing on the Tablet of the Heart: Origins of Scripture and Literature*. New York: Oxford University Press, 2005.
Carroll, "Jewgreek, Greekjew." Carroll, Robert P. "Jewgreek Greekjew: The Hebrew Bible Is all Greek to Me: Reflections on the Problematics of Dating the Origins of the Bible in Relation to Contemporary Discussions of Biblical Historiography." Pages 91-107 in *Did Moses Speak Attic?: Jewish Historiography and Scripture in the Hellenistic Period*. Edited by Lester L. Grabbe. JSOTsup317. Sheffield: Sheffield Academic, 2001.
Cartledge, "Agesilaus II." Cartledge, Paul Anthony. "Agesilaus II." *OCD^4* 38-9.
Champion, "Aetolia." Champion, Craige B. "Polybius and Aetolia: A Historiographical Approach." Pages 356–62 in *A Companion to Greek and Roman Historiography*. Edited by John Marincola. 2 vols. Oxford: Blackwell, 2007.
Chaplin, "Conversations." Chaplin, Jane D. "Conversations in History: Arrian and Herodotus, Parmenio and Alexander." *Greek, Roman and Byzantine Studies* 51 (4, 2011): 613-33.
Charlesworth, *Pseudepigrapha*. Charlesworth, James H. *The Old Testament Pseudepigrapha and the New Testament: Prolegomena for the Study of Christian Origins*. SNTSMS 54. Cambridge: Cambridge University Press, 1985.
Charlesworth and Evans, "Agrapha." Charlesworth, James H., and Craig A. Evans. "Jesus in the Agrapha and Apocryphal Gospels." Pages 479–533 in *Studying the Historical Jesus: Evaluations of the State of Current Research*. Edited by Bruce Chilton and Craig A. Evans. NTTS 19. Leiden: Brill, 1994.
Charlesworth, Rhea and Pokorny, *Jesus Research*. Charlesworth, James H., Brian Rhea and Petr Pokorny, editors. *Jesus Research: New Methodologies and Perceptions. The Second Princeton-Prague Symposium on Jesus Research*. Grand Rapids: Eerdmans, 2014.
Cheon, "Plagues." Cheon, Samuel. "Josephus and the Story of the Plagues: An Appraisal of a Moralising Interpretation." *AJT* 18 (1, 2004): 220–30.
Chilver and Seager, "Cornelius Balbus (1), Lucius." Chilver, Guy E. F. and Robin J. Seager. "Cornelius Balbus (1), Lucius." *OCD^4* 376.

Chiu, "Importance." Chiu, Angeline. "The Importance of Being Julia: Civil War, Historical Revision and the Mutable Past in Lucan's Pharsalia," *Classical Journal* 105 (4, 2010): 343-60.

Chrétien, "Exchange." Chrétien, Jean-Pierre. "Confronting the Unequal Exchange of the Oral and the Written." Pages 75–90 in *African Historiographies: What History for Which Africa?* Edited by Bogumil Jewsiewicki and David Newbury. SSAMD 12. Beverly Hills, Calif.: Sage, 1986.

Clark, "Education." Clark, T. "Jewish Education in the Hellenistic Period and the Old Testament." *St. Vladimir's Theological Quarterly* 54 (3-4, 2010): 281-301.

Clifford, "Moses." Clifford, Hywel. "Moses as Philosopher-Sage in Philo." Pages 151-67 in *Moses in Biblical and Extra-Biblical Traditions*. Edited by Axel Graupner and Michael Wolter. Beihefte zur Zeitschrift für die alttestamentliche Wissenschaft 372. Berlin; New York: de Gruyter, 2007.

Cohen, *Josephus*. Cohen, Shaye J. D. *Josephus in Galilee and Rome: His Vita and Development as a Historian*. Columbia Studies in the Classical Tradition. Ed. William V. Harris. Volume III. Leiden: Brill, 1979.

Cohen, *Maccabees*. Cohen, Shaye J. D. *From the Maccabees to the Mishnah*. LEC 7. Philadelphia: Westminster, 1987.

Cohen, "Masada." Cohen, Shaye J. D. "Masada: Literary Tradition, Archaeological Remains, and the Credibility of Josephus." *JJS* 33 (1982): 385–405.

Cohen, "What Happened?" Cohen, Shaye J. D. "What Really Happened at Masada?" *Moment* 13 (5, 1988): 28–35.

Collins, "Genre and the Gospels." Collins, Adela Yarbro. "Genre and the Gospels." *JR* 75 (1995): 239–46.

Collins, *Mark*. Collins, Adela Yarbro. *Mark: A Commentary*. Hermeneia. Minneapolis: Fortress, 2007.

Collins, *The Beginning of the Gospel*. Collins, Adela Yarbro. *The Beginning of the Gospel: Probings of Mark in Context*. Minneapolis: Fortress, 1992.

Conybeare, "Introduction." Conybeare, F. C. Introduction. Pages v–xv in vol. 1 of Philostratus, *The Life of Apollonius of Tyana*. Translated by F. C. Conybeare. 2 vols. LCL. Cambridge, Mass.: Harvard University Press, 1912.

Conzelmann and Lindemann, *Interpreting*. Conzelmann, Hans and Andreas Lindemann. *Interpreting the New Testament: An Introduction to the Principles and Methods of NT Exegesis*. Peabody, MA: Hendrickson, 1988.

Cook, "Plutarch's Use." Cook, Brad L. "Plutarch's Use of *legetai*: Narrative Design and Source in *Alexander*." *GRBS* 42 (4, 2001): 329–60.

Copeland, *History*. Copeland, Rita, editor. *The Oxford History of Classical Reception*. Vol. 1: 800-1558. Oxford: Oxford University Press, 2016.

Cornell, "Cornelius Nepos." Cornell, T. J. "Cornelius Nepos." Pages 798-815 in *The Fragments of the Roman Historians: Texts and Translations*. Edited by T. J. Cornell. Vol. 2 of *The Fragments of the Roman Historians*. Edited by T. J. Cornell. Oxford: Oxford University Press, 2013.

Cornell, *Fragments*. Cornell, T. J., ed. *The Fragments of the Roman Historians: Texts and Translations.* Vol. 2 of *The Fragments of the Roman Historians.* Edited by T. J. Cornell. Oxford: Oxford University Press, 2013.
Cotter, *Miracle Stories*. Cotter, Wendy J. *The Christ of the Miracle Stories: Portrait through Encounter.* Grand Rapids: Baker Academic, 2010.
Croke, "Historiography." Croke, Brian. "Late Antique Historiography, 250–650 CE." Pages 567–81 in *A Companion to Greek and Roman Historiography.* Edited by John Marincola. 2 vols. Oxford: Blackwell, 2007.
Cross, "Genres." Cross, Anthony R. "Genres of the New Testament." *DNTB* 402–11.
Crossan, *Jesus*. Crossan, John Dominic. *The Historical Jesus: The Life of a Mediterranean Jewish Peasant.* San Francisco: HarperSanFrancisco, 1991.
Crossan, "Necessary." Crossan, John Dominic. "Why Is Historical Jesus Research Necessary?" Pages 7–37 in *Jesus Two Thousand Years Later.* Edited by James H. Charlesworth and Walter P. Weaver. FSCS. Harrisburg, Pa.: Trinity Press International, 2000.
Culpepper, *John*. Culpepper, R. Alan. *The Gospel and Letters of John.* IBT. Nashville: Abingdon, 1998.
Culpepper, *School*. Culpepper, R. Alan. *The Johannine School: An Evaluation of the Johannine-School Hypothesis Based on an Investigation of the Nature of Ancient Schools.* SBLDS 26. Missoula, Mont.: Scholars Press, 1975.
Cunningham and Bock, "Midrash." Cunningham, Scott, and Darrell L. Bock. "Is Matthew Midrash?" *Bibliotheca Sacra* 144 (1987): 157-80.
Curchin, "Literacy." Curchin, Leonard A. "Literacy in the Roman Provinces: Qualitative and Quantitative Data from Central Spain." *AJP* 116 (3, 1995): 461-76.
Damgaard, *Recasting Moses*. Damgaard, Finn. *Recasting Moses: The Memory of Moses in Biographical and Autobiographical Narratives in Ancient Judaism and 4th-Century Christianity.* Early Christianity in the Context of Antiquity 13. Frankfurt: Lang, 2013.
Damon, "Rhetoric." Damon, Cynthia. "Rhetoric and Historiography." Pages 439–50 in *A Companion to Roman Rhetoric.* BCompAW. Edited by William Dominik and Jon Hall. Oxford: Blackwell, 2007.
Damon, "Source to *sermo*." Damon, Cynthia. "From Source to *sermo*: Narrative Technique in Livy 34.54.4–8." *AJP* 118 (2, 1997): 251–66.
Dancy, *1 Maccabees*. Dancy, J. C. *A Commentary on 1 Maccabees.* 2d ed. Oxford: Billing and Sons, 1954.
Darko, "Review." Darko, Daniel K. Review of William den Hollander. *Josephus, the Emperors, and the City of Rome: From Hostage to Historian. BBR* 26 (2, 2016): 277-79.
Davies, *Invitation*. Davies, W. D. *Invitation to the New Testament: A Guide to Its Main Witnesses.* Garden City, N.Y.: Doubleday, 1966.

Davies, "Reflexions." Davies, W. D. "Reflexions on Tradition: The Aboth Revisited." Pages 129–37 in *Christian History and Interpretation: Studies Presented to John Knox*. Edited by W. R. Farmer, C. F. D. Moule, and R. R. Niebuhr. Cambridge: Cambridge University Press, 1967.

Derrenbacker, *Ancient Compositional Practices.* Derrenbacker, Robert A. *Ancient Compositional Practices and the Synoptic Problem*. BETL 186. Leuven: Leuven University Press, 2005.

DeConick, "Memory." DeConick, April D. "Human Memory and the Sayings of Jesus: Contemporary Exercises in the Transmission of Jesus Tradition." Pages 135-79 in *Jesus, the Voice and the Text: Beyond the Oral and the Written Gospel*. Edited by Tom Thatcher. Waco: Baylor University Press, 2008.

DeConick, *Recovering.* DeConick, April D. *Recovering the Original Gospel of Thomas: A History of the Gospel and its Growth*. Library of NT Studies 286. London: T& T Clark, 2005.

deSilva, *Introduction.* deSilva, David A. *An Introduction to the New Testament: Context, Methods & Ministry Formation*. Downers Grove, IL: InterVarsity Press, 2004.

Dewald, "Construction." Dewald, Carolyn. "The Construction of Meaning in the First Three Historians." Pages 89–101 in *A Companion to Greek and Roman Historiography*. Edited by John Marincola. 2 vols. Oxford: Blackwell, 2007.

De Wet, "O Woman." de Wet, Chris L. "'O Woman, Who Alone Gave Birth to Such Complete Devotion!' Some Remarks on the Materfamilias and Other Women of 1-4 Maccabees." *JS* 17 (2008): 33-56.

De Wet, "Power and Priestcraft." de Wet, Chris L. "Between Power and Priestcraft: The Politics of Prayer in 2 Maccabees." *Religion and Theology* 16 (2009): 150-61.

Dewey, "Event." Dewey, Joanna. "The Gospel of Mark as an Oral-Aural Event: Implications for Interpretation." Pages 145-163 in *The New Literary Criticism and the New Testament*. Ed. Edgar V. McKnight and Elizabeth Struthers Malbon. Valley Forge, PA: Trinity Press International, 1994; Sheffield: JSOT Press, 1994.

Dibelius, *Tradition.* Dibelius, Martin. *From Tradition to Gospel*. Translated by Bertram Lee Woolf. Cambridge, U.K.: James Clarke; Greenwood, S.C.: Attic, 1971.

Dihle, "Biography." Dihle, Albrecht. "The Gospels and Greek Biography." Pages 361–86 in *The Gospel and the Gospels*. Edited by Peter Stuhlmacher. Grand Rapids: Eerdmans, 1991.

Dillon and Hershbell, "Introduction." Dillon and Hershbell, "Introduction." Dillon, John M., and Jackson Hershbell. Introduction. Pages 1–29 in Iamblichus, *On the Pythagorean Way of Life: Text, Translation, and Notes*. Edited and translated by John M. Dillon and Jackson Hershbell. SBLTT 29. Graeco-Roman Religion Series 11. Atlanta: Scholars Press, 1991.

Dobbeler, "Geschichte." Dobbeler, Stephanie von. "Geschichte und Geschichten: Der theologische Gehalt und die politische Problematik von 1 und 2 Makkabäer." *BK* 57 (2, 2002): 62–67.
Downing, "A Bas Les Aristos." Downing, F. Gerald. "A Bas Les Aristos: The Relevance of Higher Literature for the Understanding of the Earliest Christian Writings." *NovT* 30 (1988): 212–30.
Downing, "Contemporary Analogies." Downing, F. Gerald. "Contemporary Analogies to the Gospels and Acts: 'Genres' or 'Motifs'?" Pages 51–65 in *Synoptic Studies: The Ampleforth Conferences of 1982 and 1983*. Edited by Christopher M. Tuckett. JSNTSup 7. Sheffield: JSOT Press, 1984.
Downing, "Redaction Criticism." Downing, F. Gerald. "Redaction Criticism: Josephus' Antiquities and the Synoptic Gospels (II)." *JSNT* 9 (1980): 29–48.
Draper, "Tradition." Draper, Jonathan. "The Jesus Tradition in the Didache." Pages 269–87 in *The Jesus Tradition outside the Gospels*. Edited by David Wenham. Gospel Perspectives 5. Sheffield, U.K.: JSOT Press, 1984.
Droge, "Anonymously." Droge, A. J. "Did 'Luke' Write Anonymously? Lingering at the Threshold." Pages 495–518 in *Die Apostelgeschichte im Kontext antiker und frühchristlicher Historiographie*. Edited by Jörg Frey, Clare K. Rothschild, and Jens Schröter, with Bettina Rost. BZNWK 162. Berlin: de Gruyter, 2009.
Droysen, *Geschichte*. Droysen, G. *Geschichte des Hellenismus* Gotha: Friedrich Andreas Perthes, 1877.
Drury, *Design*. Drury, John. *Tradition and Design in Luke's Gospel: A Study in Early Christian Historiography*. London: Darton, Longman & Todd, 1976.
Duff, "Models." Duff, Timothy E. "Models of Education in Plutarch." *JHS* 128 (2008): 1–26.
Duff, *Plutarch's Lives*. Duff, Timothy E. *Plutarch's Lives: Exploring Virtue and Vice*. Oxford: Oxford University Press, 1999.
Dungan, *Sayings*. Dungan, David L. *The Sayings of Jesus in the Churches of Paul: The Use of the Synoptic Tradition in the Regulation of Early Church Life*. Philadelphia: Fortress, 1971.
Dunn, *Acts*. Dunn, James D. G. *The Acts of the Apostles*. Narrative Commentaries. Valley Forge, Pa.: Trinity Press International, 1996.
Dunn, "Critiquing." Dunn, James D. G. "Kenneth Bailey's Theory of Oral Tradition: Critiquing Theodore Weeden's Critique." *Journal for the Study of the Historical Jesus* 7 (2009): 44-62.
Dunn, *Jesus Remembered*. Dunn, James D. G. *Jesus Remembered*. Vol. 1 of *Christianity in the Making*. Grand Rapids: Eerdmans, 2003.
Dunn, *Oral Gospel*. Dunn, James D. G. *The Oral Gospel Tradition*. Grand Rapids: Eerdmans, 2013.
Dunn, *Perspective*. Dunn, James D. G. *A New Perspective on Jesus: What the Quest for the Historical Jesus Missed*. Grand Rapids: Baker, 2005.

Dunn, "Social Memory." Dunn, James. "Social Memory and the Oral Jesus Tradition." Pages 179-94 in *Memory in the Bible and Antiquity*. Edited by Stephen C. Barton, Loren T. Stuckenbruck, and Benjamin G. Wold. WUNT 212. Tübingen: Mohr Siebeck, 2007.

Eddy and Boyd, *The Jesus Legend*. Eddy, Paul Rhodes, and Gregory A. Boyd. *The Jesus Legend: A Case for the Historical Reliability of the Synoptic Jesus Tradition*. Grand Rapids: Baker Academic, 2007.

Edwards, *Mark*. Edwards, James R. *The Gospel according to Mark*. Pillar New Testament Commentary. Grand Rapids: Eerdmans, 2002.

Edwards, "Introduction." Edwards, Catherine. "Introduction." Pages vii–xxx in Suetonius, *Lives of the Caesars*. Trans. Catherine Edwards. Oxford: Oxford University Press, 2000.

Egelhaaf-Gaiser, "Sites." Egelhaaf-Gaiser, Ulrike. "Roman Cult Sites: A Pragmatic Approach." Pages 205–21 in *A Companion to Roman Religion*. Edited by Jörg Rüpke. BCompAW. Oxford: Blackwell, 2011.

Ehrensperger, *Dynamics*. Ehrensperger, Kathy. *Paul and the Dynamics of Power: Communication and Interaction in the Early Christ-Movement*. LNTS 325. New York, London: T&T Clark International, 2007.

Ehrman, *Introduction*. Ehrman, Bart D. *The New Testament: A Historical Introduction to the Early Christian Writings*. 3rd ed. New York and Oxford: Oxford University Press, 2004.

Ehrman, *New Testament*. Ehrman, Bart. *The New Testament: A Historical Introduction to the Early Christian Writings*. Oxford: Oxford University Press, 1997.

Eickelman, *Knowledge*. Eickelman, Dale F. *Knowledge and Power in Morocco: The Education of a Twentieth-Century Notable*. Princeton: Princeton University Press, 1992.

Eisman, "Dio and Josephus." Eisman, M. M. "Dio and Josephus: Parallel Analyses." *Latomus* 36 (3, 1977): 657–73.

Elliott, *Feelings*. Elliott, Matthew. *Faithful Feelings: Emotion in the New Testament*. Leicester, U.K.: Inter-Varsity, 2005.

Endres, *Interpretation*. Endres, John C. *Biblical Interpretation in the Book of Jubilees*. CBQMS 18. Washington, D.C.: Catholic Biblical Association of America, 1987.

England, "Mark as Drama." England, Frank Ernest. "Mark as Drama: A Prolegomenon to Reading the Gospel of Mark as an Aristotelian Tragedy." PhD diss., University of Cape Town, 2010.

Engles, *Roman Corinth*. Engles, Donald W. *Roman Corinth: An Alternative Model for the Classical City*. Chicago: University of Chicago Press, 1990.

Epp and MacRae, *Modern Interpreters*. Epp, Eldon Jay, and George W. MacRae, eds. *The New Testament and Its Modern Interpreters*. Philadelphia: Fortress, 1989.

Eshleman, "Sophists." Eshleman, Kendra. "Defining the Circle of Sophists: Philostratus and the Construction of the Second Sophistic." *CP* 103 (4, 2008): 395–413.

Evans, *Ancient Texts*. Evans, Craig A. *Ancient Texts for New Testament Studies: A Guide to the Background Literature*. Grand Rapids: Baker, 2005.
Evans, *World*. Evans, Craig A. *Jesus and His World: The Archaeological Evidence*. Louisville: Westminster John Knox, 2012.
Évrard, "Polybe." Évrard, Étienne. "Polybe et Tite-Live, à propos d'Antiochus IV." *Latomus* 70 (4, 2011): 977–82.
Fantuzzi, "Historical Epic." Fantuzzi, Marco. "Historical Epic." *BrillPauly* 6:409–11.
Farrell, "Phenomenology." Farrell, Joseph. "The Phenomenology of Memory in Roman Culture." *Classical Journal* 92 (4, 1997): 373-83.
Farrington, "Action." Farrington, Scott T. "Action and Reason: Polybius and the Gap between Encomium and History," *Classical Philology* 106 (4, 2011): 324-42.
Feldman, "'Aqedah." Feldman, Louis H. "Josephus as a Biblical Interpreter: The 'Aqedah." *JQR* 75 (3, 1985): 212–52.
Feldman, "Balaam." Feldman, Louis H. "Philo's Version of Balaam." *Hen* 25 (3, 2003): 301–19.
Feldman, "Birth." Feldman, Louis H. "Philo's View of Moses' Birth and Upbringing," *Catholic Biblical Quarterly* 64 (2, 2002): 258-81.
Feldman, "Calf." Feldman, Louis H. "Philo's Account of the Golden Calf Incident." *JJS* 56 (2, 2005): 245–64.
Feldman, "Command." Feldman, Louis H. "The Command, according to Philo, Pseudo-Philo, and Josephus, to Annihilate the Seven Nations of Canaan." *AUSS* 41 (1, 2003): 13–29.
Feldman, "Concubine." Feldman, Louis H. "Josephus' Portrayal (*Antiquities* 5.136–174) of the Benjaminite Affair of the Concubine and Its Repercussions (Judges 19–21)." *JQR* 90 (3–4, 2000): 255–92.
Feldman, "General." Feldman, Louis H. "Moses the General and the Battle against Midian in Philo." *Jewish Studies Quarterly* 14 (1, 2007): 1-17.
Feldman, "Jehoram." Feldman, Louis H. "Josephus's Portrait of Jehoram, King of Israel." *BJRL* 76 (1, 1994): 3-20.
Feldman, "Jacob." Feldman, Louis H. "Josephus' Portrait of Jacob." *JQR* 79 (2–3, 1988–89): 101–51.
Feldman, "Jehu." Feldman, Louis H. "Josephus' Portrait of Jehu." *JSQ* 4 (1, 1997): 12–32.
Feldman, "Joshua." Feldman, Louis H. "Josephus's Portrait of Joshua." *HTR* 82 (4, 1989): 351–76.
Feldman, "Korah." Feldman, Louis H. "Philo's Interpretation of Korah." *Revue des Études Juives* 162 (1-2, 2003): 1-15.
Feldman, "Levites." Feldman, Louis H. "The Levites in Josephus." *Hen* 28 (2, 2006): 91–102.
Feldman, "Philo's Interpretation of Joshua." Feldman, Louis H. "Philo's Interpretation of Joshua," *Journal for the Study of the Pseudepigrapha* 12 (2, 2001): 165-78.

Feldman, *Portrayal*. Feldman, Louis H. *Philo's Portrayal of Moses in the Context of Ancient Judaism*. Christianity and Judaism in Antiquity, 15. Notre Dame: University of Notre Dame, 2007.
Feldman, "Roncace's Portraits." Feldman, Louis H. "On Professor Mark Roncace's Portraits of Deborah and Gideon in Josephus." *JSJ* 32 (2, 2001): 193–220.
Feldman, "Samson." Feldman, Louis H. "Josephus' Version of Samson." *JSJ* 19 (2, 1988): 171–214.
Feldman, "Saul." Feldman, Louis H. "Josephus' Portrait of Saul." *HUCA* 53 (1982): 45–99.
Feldman, "Solomon." Feldman, Louis H. "Josephus' Portrait of Solomon." *HUCA* 66 (1995): 103–67.
Feldman, "Spies." Feldman, Louis H. "Philo's Version of the Biblical Episode of the Spies," *Hebrew Union College Annual* 73 (2002): 29-48.
Filson, *History*. Filson, Floyd V. *A New Testament History*. Philadelphia: The Westminster Press, W. L. Jenkins, 1964.
Finkelberg, "*Cypria*." Finkelberg, Margalit. "The *Cypria*, the *Iliad*, and the Problem of Multiformity in Oral and Written Tradition." *Classical Philology* 95 (1, 2000): 1–11.
Fischer, *Fallacies*. Fischer, David Hackett. *Historians' Fallacies: Toward a Logic of Historical Thought*. New York: Harper & Row, 1970.
Fisk, "Bible." Fisk, Bruce N. "Rewritten Bible in Pseudepigrapha and Qumran." *DNTB* 947–53.
Fisk, "Scripture." Fisk, Bruce N. "Scripture Shaping Scripture: The Interpretive Role of Biblical Citations in Pseudo-Philo's Episode of the Golden Calf." *JSP* 17 (1998): 3–23.
Fitzgerald, "The Ancient Lives." Fitzgerald, John. "The Ancient Lives of Aristotle and the Modern Debate about the Genre of the Gospels." *ResQ* 36 (1994): 209–21.
Flaig, "Tacitus." Flaig, Egon. "Tacitus." 14:105-11 in *Brill's New Pauly*. Leiden, Boston: Brill, 2005.
Fornara, *Nature of History*. Fornara, C. W. *The Nature of History in Ancient Greece and Rome*. Berkeley: University of California Press, 1983.
Forsythe, "Quadrigarius." Forsythe, Gary. "Claudius Quadrigarius and Livy's Second Pentad." Pages 391–96 in *A Companion to Greek and Roman Historiography*. Edited by John Marincola. 2 vols. Oxford: Blackwell, 2007.
Fox, *Alexander*. Fox, Robin Lane. *Alexander the Great*. London: Folio Society, 1997.
France, *Mark*. France, R. T. *The Gospel of Mark*. NIGTC. Carlisle, U.K.: Paternoster Press, 2002.
Fredricksmeyer, "Alexander." Fredricksmeyer, E. A. "Alexander the Philip: Emulation and Resentment," *Classical Journal* 85 (1990): 300-315.
Frenkel, "Debate Filosófico." Frenkel, Diana. "Un Debate Filosófico En II Macabeos." *Circe De clásicos Y modernos* 11 (2007): 123-33.

Freyne, "Imagination." Freyne, Sean. "Early Christian Imagination and the Gospels." Pages 2-12 in *The Earliest Gospels: The Origins and Transmission of the Earliest Christian Gospels*. Edited by Charles Horton. London: T&T Clark, 2010.

Freyne, *Galilee*. Freyne, Sean. *Galilee, Jesus and the Gospels: Literary Approaches and Historical Investigations*. Philadelphia: Fortress Press, 1988.

Frickenschmidt, *Evangelium*. Frickenschmidt, Dirk. *Evangelium Als Biographie: Die Vier Evangelien Im Rahmen Antiker Erzählkunst*. TANZ 22. Tübingen: Francke, 1997.

Frye, "Synoptic Problems." Frye, Roland Mushat. "The Synoptic Problems and Analogies in Other Literatures." 261-302 in *The Relationships Among the Gospels: An Interdisciplinary Dialogue*. Ed. William O. Walker, Jr. San Antonio: Trinity University Press, 1978.

Gafni, "Josephus and Maccabees." Gafni, Isaiah M. "Josephus and 1 Maccabees." Pages 116–31 in *Josephus, the Bible, and History*. Edited by Louis H. Feldman and Gohei Hata. Detroit: Wayne State University Press, 1989.

Gager, *Anti-Semitism*. Gager, John G. *The Origins of Anti-Semitism: Attitudes toward Judaism in Pagan and Christian Antiquity*. New York: Oxford University Press, 1983.

Gaines, "Handbooks." Gaines, Robert N. "Roman Rhetorical Handbooks." Pages 163–80 in *A Companion to Roman Rhetoric*. Edited by William Dominik and Jon Hall. Oxford: Blackwell, 2007.

Galinsky, "Introduction." Galinsky, Karl. "Introduction." Pages 1-39 in *Memory in Ancient Rome and Early Christianity*. Edited by Karl Galinsky. Oxford: Oxford University Press, 2016.

Gamble, "Literacy." Gamble, Harry. "Literacy and Book Culture." Pages 644–48 in *Dictionary of New Testament Background*. Edited by Craig A. Evans and Stanley E. Porter. Downers Grove, IL: InterVarsity Press, 2000.

Gathercole, *Preexistent Son*. Gathercole, Simon J. *The preexistent Son: recovering the Christologies of Matthew, Mark, and Luke*. Grand Rapids: Eerdmans, 2006.

Geiger, *Cornelius Nepos*. Geiger, Joseph. *Cornelius Nepos and Ancient Political Biography*. Stuttgart: Historia Einzelschriften, 1985.

Geljon, *Exegesis*. Geljon, Albert C. *Philonic exegesis in Gregory of Nyssa's De vita Moysis*. Brown Judaic Studies, 333.; Studia Philonica monographs, 5. Providence, RI : Brown Judaic Studies, 2002.

Gempf, "Speaking." Gempf, Conrad. "Public Speaking and Published Accounts." Pages 259–303 in *The Book of Acts in Its Ancient Literary Setting*. Edited by Bruce W. Winter and Andrew D. Clarke. Vol. 1 of *The Book of Acts in Its First Century Setting*. Edited by Bruce W. Winter. Grand Rapids: Eerdmans; Carlisle, U.K.: Paternoster, 1993.

Georgiadou, "Lives of the Caesars." Georgiadou, Aristoula. "The Lives of the Caesars and Plutarch's Other Lives." *ICS* 13 (1988): 349–56.

Gera, "Olympiodoros." Gera, Dov. "Olympiodoros, Heliodoros and the Temples of Koile Syria and Phoinike." *ZPE* 169 (2009): 125–55.

Gerhardsson, *Memory*. Gerhardsson, Birger. *Memory and Manuscript: Oral Tradition and Written Transmission in Rabbinic Judaism and Early Christianity*. ASNU 22. Uppsala: C. W. K. Gleerup, 1961.

Gerhardsson, *Origins*. Gerhardsson, Birger. *The Origins of the Gospel Traditions*. Philadelphia: Fortress, 1979.

Gerhardsson, "Path." Gerhardsson, Birger. "The Path of the Gospel Tradition." Pages 75–96 in *The Gospel and the Gospels*. Edited by Peter Stuhlmacher. Grand Rapids: Eerdmans, 1991.

Goldhill, "Anecdote." Goldhill, Simon. "The Anecdote: Exploring the Boundaries between Oral and Literate Performance in the Second Sophistic." Pages 96-113 in *Ancient Literacies: The Culture of Reading in Greece and Rome*. Edited by William A. Johnson and Holt N. Parker. New York: Oxford University Press, 2009.

Gondola, "Kimbangu." Gondola, Charles Didier. "Kimbangu, Simon, and Kimbanguism." 2:766-67 in *Encyclopedia of African History*. 3 vols. Ed. Kevin Shillington. New York, London: Fitzroy Dearborn (Taylor & Francis Group), 2005.

Goodacre and Perrin, *Questioning*. Goodacre, Mark, and Nicholas Perrin, ed. *Questioning Q: A Multidimensional Critique*. Foreword by N. T. Wright. Downers Grove, IL: InterVarsity, 2014.

Goodenough, "Exposition." Goodenough, E. R. "Philo's Exposition of the Law and his *De Vita Mosis*." *HTR* 27 (2, April 1933): 109-25.

Goodman, *State*. Goodman, Martin. *State and Society in Roman Galilee, A.D. 132–212*. Oxford Centre for Postgraduate Hebrew Studies. Totowa, N.J.: Rowman & Allanheld, 1983.

Goody, *Logic*. Goody, Jack. *The Logic of Writing and the Organization of Society*. Studies in Literacy, Family, Culture, and the State. Cambridge: Cambridge University Press, 1986.

Goody and Watt, "Consequences." Goody, Jack, and I. Watt. "The Consequences of Literacy." *Comparative Studies in Society and History* 5 (1963): 304-45.

Görgemanns, "Biography: Greek." Görgemanns, Herwig. "Biography: Greek." 2:648-51 in *Brill's New Pauly*. Leiden, Boston: Brill, 2005.

Goshen-Gottstein, "Hillel and Jesus." Goshen-Gottstein, Alon. "Hillel and Jesus: Are Comparisons Possible?" Pages 31–55 in *Hillel and Jesus: Comparative Studies of Two Major Religious Leaders*. Edited by James H. Charlesworth and Loren L. Johns. Minneapolis: Fortress, 1997.

Gossage, "Plutarch." Gossage, A. J. "Plutarch." Pages 45-77 in *Latin Biography*. Edited by T. A. Dorey. New York: Basic, 1967.

Goulder, *Midrash*. Goulder, M. D. *Midrash and Lection in Matthew*. London: SPCK, 1974.

Gowing, "Memory." Gowing, Alain M. "Memory as Motive in Tacitus." Pages 43-64 in *Memory in Ancient Rome and Early Christianity*. Edited by Karl Galinsky. Oxford: Oxford University Press, 2016.

Grabbe, *Cyrus to Hadrian.* Grabbe, Lester L. *Judaism from Cyrus to Hadrian.* 2 vols. Minneapolis: Fortress, 1992.

Grabbe, "Jewish Historiography." Grabbe, Lester L. "Jewish Historiography and Scripture in the Hellenistic Period." Pages 129-55 in *Did Moses Speak Attic?: Jewish Historiography and Scripture in the Hellenistic Period.* Edited by Lester L. Grabbe. JSOTsup317. Sheffield: Sheffield Academic, 2001.

Grabbe, "Real Historians." Grabbe, Lester. "Who Were the First Real Historians? On the Origins of Critical Historiography." Pages 156-81 in *Did Moses Speak Attic?: Jewish Historiography and Scripture in the Hellenistic Period.* Edited by Lester L. Grabbe. JSOTsup317. Sheffield: Sheffield Academic, 2001.

Graham, *Beyond.* Graham, William Albert. *Beyond the Written Word: Oral Aspects of Scripture in the History of Religion.* Cambridge: Cambridge University Press, 1993.

Granata, "Introduzione." Granata, Giovanna. "Introduzione allo studio del *De Vita Mosis* di Filone Alessandrino." PhD dissertation, Piso, 1995.

Grant, "Foreward." Grant, Michael. Foreward to *The Twelve Caesars*, by Suetonius. Translated by Robert Graves. New York: Penguin, 1979.

Gray, "Christianity." Gray, Richard. "Christianity." 140-90 in *The Cambridge History of Africa*. 8 vols. Ed. J. D. Fage and Roland Oliver. Vol. 7: from 1905-1940. Ed. A. D. Roberts. Cambridge: Cambridge University Press 1986.

Gray, "Xenophon." Gray, Vivenne. "Xenophon." *OEAGR* 7:266-71.

Gregory, "Literary Dependence." Gregory, Andrew. "What Is Literary Dependence?" Pages 87–114 in *New Studies in the Synoptic Problem: Oxford Conference, April 2008: Essays in Honour of Christopher M. Tuckett.* Edited by Paul Foster, Andrew Gregory, John S. Kloppenborg, and Jos Verheyden. BETL 239. Leuven: Peeters, 2011.

Griffin, "Tacitus." Griffin, Miriam T. "Tacitus as a historian." In *The Cambridge Companion to Tacitus.* Edited by A.J. Woodman. Cambridge: Cambridge University Press, 2009.

Gulick, *Windows.* Gulick, Anna. *Windows on a Different World.* Lexington: Emeth, 2014.

Gundry, "Genre." Gundry, Robert H. "Recent Investigations into the Literary Genre 'Gospel.'" Pages 97–114 in *New Dimensions in New Testament Study.* Edited by Richard N. Longenecker and Merrill C. Tenney. Grand Rapids: Zondervan, 1974.

Gundry, *Matthew.* Gundry, Robert H. *Matthew: A Commentary on His Literary and Theological Art.* Grand Rapids: Eerdmans, 1982.

Gyselinck and Demoen, "Author." Gyselinck, Wannes, and Kristoffel Demoen. "Author and Narrator: Fiction and Metafiction in Philostratus' *Vita Apollonii.*" Pages 95-127 in *Theios Sophistes: Essays on Flavius Philostratus' Vita Apollonii.* Edited by Kristoffel Demoen and Danny Praet. Mneomsyne Supplements 305. Leiden: Brill, 2009.

Habinek, "Situating Literacy." Habinek, Thomas. "Situating Literacy at Rome." Pages 114-140 in *Ancient Literacies: The Culture of Reading in Greece and Rome*. Edited by William A. Johnson and Holt N. Parker. New York: Oxford University Press, 2009.

Hacham, "Polemic." Hacham, Noah. "3 Maccabees: An Anti-Dionysian Polemic." Pages 167–83 in *Ancient Fiction: The Matrix of Early Christian and Jewish Narrative*. Edited by Jo-Ann A. Brant, Charles W. Hedrick, and Chris Shea. SBLSymS 32. Atlanta: SBL, 2005.

Hack, "Literary Forms." Hack, R. K. "The Doctrine of Literary Forms." *HSCP* 27 (1916): 1–65.

Hadas, "Introduction." Hadas, Moses. Introduction. Pages ix–xxiii in *The Complete Works of Tacitus*. Edited by Moses Hadas. Translated by Alfred John Church and William Jackson Brodribb. New York: Random House, 1942.

Hadas and Smith, *Heroes and Gods*. Hadas, Moses, and Morton Smith. *Heroes and Gods: Spiritual Biographies in Antiquity*. New York: Harper & Row, 1965.

Hägg, *Biography*. Hägg, Tomas. *The Art of Biography in Antiquity*. Cambridge: Cambridge University Press, 2012.

Hagner, *Matthew*. Hagner, Donald A. *Matthew*. 2 vols. WBC 33AB. Dallas: Word, 1993–95.

Hamilton, *Plutarch, Alexander*. Hamilton, J. R. *Plutarch, Alexander: A Commentary*. Oxford: Clarendon Press, 1969.

Hammond, *Three Historians*. Hammond, N. G. L. *Three Historians of Alexander the Great: The so-Called Vulgate Authors, Diodorus, Justin, and Curtius*, Cambridge classical studies. Cambridge: Cambridge University Press, 1983.

Hanson, "Agricola." Hanson, William S. "Tacitus' 'Agricola': An Archaeological and Historical Study." *ANRW* 2.33.3:1741-84.

Harmon, "Introduction." Harmon, A. M. Introduction. Pages ix-xii in vol. 1 of *Lucian*. Translated by A. M. Harmon et al. 8 vols. LCL. Cambridge: Harvard University Press, 1913-67.

Harms, "Tradition." Harms, Robert. "Oral Tradition and Ethnicity." *Journal of Interdisciplinary History* 10 (1, summer 1979): 61-85.

Harrington, "Bible." Harrington, Daniel J. "The Bible Rewritten (Narratives)." Pages 239–47 in *Early Judaism and Its Modern Interpreters*. Edited by Robert A. Kraft and George W. E. Nickelsburg. SBLBMI 2. Atlanta: Scholars Press, 1986.

Hartman, "Reflections." Hartman, Lars. "Some Reflections on the Problem of the Literary Genre of the Gospels." Pages 3-23 in Lars Hartman. *Text-Centered New Testament Studies*. Edited by David Hellholm. WUNT 102. Tübingen: Mohr Siebeck, 1997.

Harvey, *Listening*. Harvey, John D. *Listening to the Text: Oral Patterning in Paul's Letters*. Foreword by Richard N. Longenecker. Grand Rapids: Baker; Leicester, U.K.: Apollos, 1998.

Hays, *Reading Backwards*. Hays, Richard B. *Reading Backwards: Figural Christology and the Fourfold Gospel Witness.* Waco: Baylor University Press, 2014.
Hazel, *Who's Who*. Hazel, John. *Who's Who in the Greek World.* London: Routledge, 2000.
Head, "Note." Head, Peter M. "A further note on *Reading and Writing in the Time of Jesus*." *Evangelical Quarterly* 75 (4, 2003): 343-45.
Heath, *Hermogenes*. Heath, Malcolm, ed. and trans. *Hermogenes On Issues: Strategies of Argument in Later Greek Rhetoric.* Oxford: Clarendon, 1995.
Helms, *Gospel Fictions*. Helms, Randel. *Gospel Fictions.* Buffalo, NY: Prometheus, 1988.
Hemer, *Acts in History*. Hemer, Colin J. *The Book of Acts in the Setting of Hellenistic History.* Edited by Conrad H. Gempf. WUNT 49. Tübingen: Mohr Siebeck, 1989.
Henderson, "*Life* and *War*." Henderson, Jordan. "Josephus's *Life* and *Jewish War* compared to the Synoptic Gospels." *JGRChJ* 10 (2014): 113-31.
Hendricks, "Comparison." Hendricks, William N., III. "A Comparison of Diodorus' and Curtius' Accounts of Alexander the Great." PhD diss., Duke University, 1974.
Hengel, "Aufgaben." Hengel, Martin. "Aufgaben der neutestamentlichen Wissenschaft." *NTS* 40 (1994): 321-57.
Hengel, "Eye-Witness Memory." Hengel, Martin. "Eye-Witness Memory and the Writing of the Gospels: Form Criticism, Community Tradition and the Authority of the Authors." Pages 70–96 in *The Written Gospel*. Edited by Markus Bockmuehl and Donald A. Hagner. Cambridge: Cambridge University Press, 2005.
Hengel, "Geography." Hengel, Martin. "The Geography of Palestine in Acts." Pages 27–78 in *The Book of Acts in Its Palestinian Setting*. Edited by Richard Bauckham. Vol. 4 of *The Book of Acts in Its First Century Setting*. Edited by Bruce W. Winter. Grand Rapids: Eerdmans; Carlisle, U.K.: Paternoster, 1995.
Hengel, "Tasks." Hengel, Martin. "Tasks of New Testament Scholarship." Translated by P. E. Devenish and Craig Evans. *BBR* 6 (1996): 67-86.
Hengel and Schwemer, *Damascus and Antioch*. Hengel, Martin, and Anna Maria Schwemer. *Paul between Damascus and Antioch: The Unknown Years.* Translated by John Bowden. London: SCM; Louisville: Westminster John Knox, 1997.
Henige, "History." Henige, David. "African History and the Rule of Evidence: Is Declaring Victory Enough." 91-104 in *African Historiographies: What History for Which Africa?* Ed. Bogumil Jewsiewicki and David Newbury. SSAMD 12. Beverly Hills, London, New Delhi: Sage, 1986.
Heyer, *Jesus Matters*. Heyer, C. J. den. *Jesus Matters: 150 Years of Research.* Valley Forge: Trinity Press International, 1997.
Hezser, *Literacy*. Hezser, Catherine. *Jewish Literacy in Roman Palestine.* TSAJ 81. Tübingen: Mohr-Siebeck, 2001.

Hilbert, "185,000 Slain." Hilbert, Benjamin D. H. "185,000 Slain Maccabean Enemies (Times Two) Hyperbole in the Books of Maccabees." *ZAW* 122 (2010): 102-06.

Hill, *Matthew*. Hill, David. *The Gospel of Matthew*. NCBC. Grand Rapids: Eerdmans; London: Marshall, Morgan & Scott, 1972.

Hill, *Prophecy*. Hill, David. *New Testament Prophecy*. NFTL. Atlanta: John Knox, 1979.

Hock, "Paul and Education." Hock, Ronald F. "Paul and Greco-Roman Education." Pages 198–227 in *Paul in the Greco-Roman World: A Handbook*. Edited by J. Paul Sampley. Harrisburg, Pa.: Trinity Press International, 2003.

Hock and O'Neil, *Chreia*. Hock, Ronald F. and Edward N. O'Neil. *The Chreia in Ancient Rhetoric. Volume 1: The Progymnasmata*. 3 vols. SBL Texts and Translations 27. SBL Greco-Roman Religion Series 9. Atlanta: Scholars Press, 1986.

Hoeree and Hoogbergen, "History." Hoeree, Joris, and Wim Hoogbergen. "Oral History and Archival Data Combined: The Removal of the Saramakan Granman Kofi Bosuman as an Epistemological Problem." *Communication and Cognition* 17 (2–3, 1984): 245–89.

Höffken, "Hiskija." Höffken, Peter. "Hiskija und Jesaja bei Josephus." *JSJ* 29 (1, 1998): 37–48.

Hofmann, "Novels: Christian." Hofmann, Heinz. "Novels: Christian." *BrillPauly* 9:846–49.

Hollander, *Josephus*. Hollander, William den. *Josephus, the Emperors, and the City of Rome: From Hostage to Historian*. Ancient Judaism and Early Christianity 86. Leiden: Brill, 2014.

Hooker, *Gospel*. Hooker, Morna D. *The Gospel according to Saint Mark*. BNTC 2. Peabody, MA: Hendrickson, 1991.

Horton, "Types." Horton, Robin. "Types of Spirit Possession in Kalabari Religion." Pages 14–49 in *Spirit Mediumship and Society in Africa*. Edited by John Beattie and John Middleton. Foreword by Raymond Firth. New York: Africana, 1969.

Hose, "Cassius Dio." Hose, Martin. "Cassius Dio: A Senator and Historian in the Age of Anxiety." Pages 461–67 in *A Companion to Greek and Roman Historiography*. Edited by John Marincola. 2 vols. Oxford: Blackwell, 2007.

Hose, "Historiography: Rome." Hose, Martin. "Historiography: Rome." *BrillPauly* 6:422–26.

Houston, "Library." Houston, George W. "How Did You Get Hold of a Book in a Roman Library? Three Second-Century Scenarios." *CBull* 80 (1, 2004): 5–13.

Howell and Prevenier, *Reliable Sources*. Howell, Martha and Walter Prevenier. *From Reliable Sources: An Introduction to Historical Methods*. Ithaca, NY: Cornell University Press, 2001.

Hübenthal, "Another Jesus Remembered." Hübenthal, Sandra. "Another Jesus Remembered: Reading Luke's Narration through a Memory-Theory-Lens." Paper presented in the "Memory, Narrative, and Christology in the Synoptic Gospels" Seminar at the Annual Meeting of the Society for New Testament Studies. Montreal, Canada, 5 August 2016.

Huizinga, "Concept." Huizinga, Johan. "A Definition of the Concept of History." Pages 1-10 in *Philosophy and History: Essays Presented to Ernst Cassirer*. Edited by Raymond Klibansky and H. J. Paton. Oxford: Clarendon,1936; Repr., Gloucester, MA: Peter Smith, 1975.

Hunt, *History and Legacy*. Hunt, Rosalie Hall. *Bless God and Take Courage: The Judson History and Legacy*. Valley Forge, Pa.: Judson, 2005.

Hurtado, "Fixation." Hurtado, Larry W. "Oral Fixation and New Testament Studies? 'Orality', 'Performance' and Reading Texts in Early Christianity." *NTS* 60 (3, July 2014): 321-40.

Hurtado, "Gospel (genre)." Hurtado, Larry W. "Gospel (genre)." Pages 276-82 in *Dictionary of Jesus and the Gospels*. Edited by Joel B. Green, S. McKnight and I.H. Marshall. Downers Grove, IL: InterVarsity Press, 1992.

Hurtado, *Lord Jesus Christ*. Hurtado, Larry W. *Lord Jesus Christ: Devotion to Jesus in Earliest Christianity*. Grand Rapids: Eerdmans, 2003.

Iglesias, "Reflexoes." Iglesias, Esther. "Reflexoes sobre o quefazer da historia oral no mundo rural." *Dados* 27 (1, 1984): 59-70.

Iverson, "Orality." Iverson, Kelly R. "Orality and the Gospels: A Survey of Recent Research." *Currents in Biblical Research* 8 (1, 2009): 71-106.

Jackson, *Quest*. Jackson, Bill. *The Quest for the Radical Middle: A History of the Vineyard*. Foreword by Todd Hunter. Cape Town: Vineyard International, 1999.

Jacoby, *Die Fragmente*. Jacoby, Felix. *Die Fragmente der griechischen Historiker*, ii.B. Berlin: Weidmann, 1927.

Janin, *Pursuit*. Janin, Hunt. *The Pursuit of Learning in the Islamic World*. Jefferson, NC: McFarland, 2005.

Jeffers, *World*. Jeffers, James S. *The Greco-Roman World of the New Testament Era: Exploring the Background of Early Christianity*. Downers Grove, Ill.: InterVarsity, 1999.

Jenkinson, "Nepos." Jenkinson, Edna. "Nepos: An Introduction to Latin Biography." Pages 1-15 in *Latin Biography*. Edited by T. A. Dorey. Studies in Latin Literature and its Influence. New York: Basic Books, 1967.

Jeremias, "Pap. Egerton." Jeremias, Joachim. Introduction to "Pap. Egerton 2." Pages 94–96 in *Gospels and Related Writings*. Vol. 1 of *New Testament Apocrypha*. Edited by Edgar Hennecke, Wilhelm Schneemelcher, and R. McL. Wilson. Philadelphia: Westminster, 1963.

Jeremias, *Theology*. Jeremias, Joachim. *New Testament Theology*. New York: Charles Scribner's Sons, 1971.

Jervell, "Future." Jervell, Jacob. "The Future of the Past: Luke's Vision of Salvation History and Its Bearing on His Writing of History." Pages 104–26 in *History, Literature, and Society in the Book of Acts*. Edited by Ben Witherington III. Cambridge: Cambridge University Press, 1996.

Johnson, *Acts*. Johnson, Luke Timothy. *The Acts of the Apostles*. SP 5. Collegeville, Minn.: Liturgical Press, 1992.

Johnson, "Fictions." Johnson, Sara. "Third Maccabees: Historical Fictions and the Shaping of Jewish Identity in the Hellenistic Period." Pages 185–97 in *Ancient Fiction: The Matrix of Early Christian and Jewish Narrative*. Edited by Jo-Ann A. Brant, Charles W. Hedrick, and Chris Shea. SBLSymS 32. Atlanta: SBL, 2005.

Johnson and Musser, *Story*. Johnson, Dennis, and Joe Musser. *Tell Me a Story. Orality: How the World Learns*. Colorado Springs: David C. Cook, 2012.

Jones, "Apollonius' Passage." Jones, C. P. "Apollonius of Tyana's Passage to India." *GRBS* 42 (2, 2001): 185–99.

Jones, "Inscription." Jones, C. P. "The Inscription from Tel Maresha for Olympiodoros," *Zeitschrift für Papyrologie und Epigraphik* 171 (2009): 100-104.

Jones, *Lucian*. Jones, C. P. *Culture and Society in Lucia*. Cambridge: Harvard University Press, 1986.

Jost, *Geschichte*. Jost, I. M. *Geschichte der Israeliten*. Vol. 2. Berlin: 1820-1828.

Judge, *First Christians*. Judge, Edwin A. *The First Christians in the Roman World: Augustan and New Testament Essays*. Edited by James R. Harrison. WUNT 229. Tübingen: Mohr Siebeck, 2008.

Judge, "Scholastic Community." Judge, Edwin A. "The Early Christians as a Scholastic Community." *JRH* 1 (1, 1960): 4–15; (3): 125–37. Reprinted in Judge, *First Christians*, 526–52.

Judge, "Sources." Judge, Edwin A. "Biblical Sources of Historical Method." Pages 276–81 in *Jerusalem and Athens: Cultural Transformation in Late Antiquity*. Edited by Alanna Nobbs. Tübingen: Mohr Siebeck, 2010.

Kaesser, "Tweaking." Kaesser, Christian. "Tweaking the Real: Art Theory and the Borderline between History and Morality in Plutarch's *Lives*." *GRBS* 44 (4, 2004): 361–74.

Keane, "Satiric Memories." Keane, Catherine. "Satiric Memories: Autobiography and the Construction of Genre." *CJ* 97 (3, 2002): 215–31.

Kee, *Origins*. Kee, Howard Clark. *Christian Origins in Sociological Perspective: Methods and Resources*. Philadelphia: Westminster, 1980.

Keener, *Acts*. Keener, Craig S. *Acts: An Exegetical Commentary*. 4 vols. Grand Rapids: Baker Academic, 2012–15.

Keener, "Assumptions." Keener, Craig S. "Assumptions in Historical-Jesus Research: Using Ancient Biographies and Disciples' Traditioning as a Control." *JSHJ* 9 (2011): 26–58.

Keener, "Biographies of a Sage." Keener, Craig S. "Reading the Gospels as Biographies of a Sage." *Buried History* 47 (2011): 59–66.

Keener, "Comparisons." Keener, Craig S. "Cultural Comparisons for Healing and Exorcism Narratives in Matthew's Gospel." *HTS Theological Studies* 66 (1, 2010).

Keener, "Dependability." Keener, Craig S. "First-Century Gospels and the Dependability of the Oral Tradition." Paper presented at the International Orality Network Forum, Asbury Theological Seminary, April 3, 2014.
Keener, *Historical Jesus*. Keener, Craig S. *The Historical Jesus of the Gospels.* Grand Rapids: Eerdmans, 2009.
Keener, *Introduction*. Keener, Craig S. *Introduction and 1:1-2:47.* Vol. 1 of *Acts: An Exegetical Commentary.* Grand Rapids, MI: Baker Academic, 2012.
Keener, *John*. Keener, Craig S. *The Gospel of John: A Commentary.* 2 vols. Peabody, MA: Hendrickson, 2003.
Keener, "Luke-Acts." Keener, Craig S. "Luke-Acts and the Historical Jesus." Pages 600–623 in *Jesus Research: New Methodologies and Perceptions – The Second Princeton-Prague Symposium on Jesus Research, Princeton 2007*. Edited by James H. Charlesworth, Brian Rhea, and Petr Pokorný. Grand Rapids: Eerdmans, 2014.
Keener, *Matthew*. Keener, Craig S. *A Commentary on the Gospel of Matthew.* Grand Rapids: Eerdmans, 1999.
Keener, "Mboungou." Keener, Médine Moussounga. "Jean Mboungou." No pages. *DACB.* Online: http://www.dacb.org/stories/congo/f-mboungou_john.html.
Keener, *Miracles*. Keener, Craig S. *Miracles: The Credibility of the New Testament Accounts.* Grand Rapids: Baker Academic, 2011.
Keener, "Moussounga." Keener, Médine Moussounga. "Jacques Moussounga." No pages. *DACB.* Online: http://www.dacb.org/stories/congo/f-moussounga_jacques.html.
Keener, "Ndoundou." Keener, Médine Moussounga. "Daniel Ndoundou." No pages. *DACB.* Online:http://www.dacb.org/stories/congo/Ndoundou_daniel.html.
Keener, "Otho." Keener, Craig S. "Otho: A Targeted Comparison of Suetonius's Biography and Tacitus's History, with Implications for the Gospels' Historical Reliability." *BBR* 21 (2011): 331–56.
Keener, "Parallel Figures." Keener, Craig S. "Jesus and Parallel Jewish and Greco-Roman Figures." Pages 85-111 in *Christian Origins and Greco-Roman Culture: Social and Literary Contexts for the New Testament.* Edited by Stanley Porter and Andrew W. Pitts. Vol. 1 of Early Christianity in its Hellenistic Context. Vol. 9 in Texts and Editions for New Testament Study. Leiden: Brill, 2013.
Keener, "Reassessment." Keener, Craig S. "A Reassessment of Hume's Case against Miracles in Light of Testimony from the Majority World Today." *Perspectives in Religious Studies* 38 (3, Fall 2011): 289–310.
Keener, "Review of Bauckham." Keener, Craig S. Review of Richard Bauckham, *Jesus and the Eyewitnesses. Bulletin for Biblical Research* 19 (2009): 130-32.
Keener, *Spirit Hermeneutics*. Keener, Craig S. *Spirit Hermeneutics: Reading Scripture in Light of Pentecost.* Foreword by Amos Yong. Grand Rapids: Eerdmans, 2016.

Keener, "Spirit Possession." Keener, Craig S. "Spirit Possession as a Cross-Cultural Experience." *Bulletin for Biblical Research* 20 (2010): 215–36.

Keener, "Suggestions." Keener, Craig S. "Suggestions for Future Study of Rhetoric and Matthew's Gospel." *HTS Theological Studies* 66 (1, 2010): Art. 812.

Keener and Keener, *Impossible Love*. Keener, Craig S., and Médine Moussounga Keener. *Impossible Love: The true story of an African civil war, miracles, and hope against all odds*. Grand Rapids: Chosen, 2016.

Keith, *Scribal Elite*. Keith, Chris. *Jesus against the Scribal Elite: The Origins of the Conflict*. Grand Rapids: Baker Academic, 2014.

Kelber, "Work." Kelber, Werner H. "The Work of Birger Gerhardsson in Perspective." Pages 173–206 in *Jesus in Memory: Traditions in Oral and Scribal Perspectives*. Edited by Werner H. Kelber and Samuel Byrskog. Waco: Baylor University Press, 2009.

Kelhoffer, "Maccabees at Prayer." Kelhoffer, James A. "The Maccabees at Prayer: Pro- and Anti-Hasmonean Tendencies in the Prayers of First and Second Maccabees." *Early Christianity* 2 (2, 2011): 198-218.

Kennedy, "Source Criticism." Kennedy, George A. "Classical and Christian Source Criticism." Pages 125–55 in *The Relationships among the Gospels: An Interdisciplinary Dialogue*. Edited by William O. Walker, Jr. San Antonio, TX: Trinity University Press, 1978.

Kennedy, *Classical Rhetoric*. Kennedy, George A. *Classical Rhetoric and Its Christian and Secular Tradition from Ancient to Modern Times*. Chapel Hill: University of North Carolina Press, 1980.

Keylock, "Distinctness." Keylock, Leslie R. "Bultmann's Law of Increasing Distinctness." Pages 193–210 in *Current Issues in Biblical and Patristic Interpretation: Studies in Honor of Merrill C. Tenney Presented by His Former Students*. Edited by Gerald F. Hawthorne. Grand Rapids: Eerdmans, 1975.

Kierspel, *Charts*. Kierspel, Lars. *Charts on the Life, Letters, and Theology of Paul*. Grand Rapids: Kregel Publications, 2012.

Kirk, "Memory." Kirk, Alan. "Memory." Pages 155–72 in *Jesus in Memory: Traditions in Oral and Scribal Perspectives*. Edited by Werner H. Kelber and Samuel Byrskog. Waco: Baylor University Press, 2009.

Klauck, *Context*. Klauck, Hans-Josef. *The Religious Context of Early Christianity: A Guide to Graeco-Roman Religions*. Translated by Brian McNeil. Minneapolis: Fortress, 2003.

Kloppenborg, "Memory." Kloppenborg, John S. "Memory, Performance, and the Sayings of Jesus." Pages 286-323 in *Memory in Ancient Rome and Early Christianity*. Edited by Karl Galinsky. Oxford: Oxford University Press, 2016.

Koester, *Introduction*. Koester, Helmut. *Introduction to the New Testament*. 2 vols. Philadelphia: Fortress, 1982.

Koskenniemi, "Moses." Koskenniemi, Erkki. "Moses—A Well-Educated Man: A Look at the Educational Idea in Early Judaism," *Journal for the Study of the Pseudepigrapha* 17 (4, 2008): 281-96.

Krasser, "Reading." Krasser, Helmut. "Light Reading." *BrillPauly* 7:553–55.
Krentz, *Historical-Critical*. Krentz, Edgar. *The Historical-Critical Method.* Minneapolis: Augsburg Fortress, 1975; Eugene, OR: Wipf & Stock, 2002.
Kümmel, *Introduction*. Kümmel, Werner George. *Introduction to the New Testament.* London: SCM, 1965.
Kurz, "Models." Kurz, William S. "Narrative Models for Imitation in Luke-Acts." Pages 171–89 in *Greeks, Romans, and Christians: Essays in Honor of Abraham J. Malherbe.* Edited by David L. Balch, Everett Ferguson, and Wayne A. Meeks. Minneapolis: Fortress, 1990.
Ladouceur, "Josephus." Ladouceur, David J. "Josephus and Masada." Pages 95–113 in *Josephus, Judaism, and Christianity.* Edited by Louis H. Feldman and Gohei Hata. Detroit: Wayne State University Press, 1987.
Ladouceur, "Masada." Ladouceur, David J. "Masada: A Consideration of the Literary Evidence." *GRBS* 21 (3, 1980): 245–60.
Laistner, *Historians*. Laistner, M. L. W. *The Greater Roman Historians.* Berkeley: University of California Press; London: Cambridge University Press, 1947.
Lalleman, "Apocryphal Acts." Lalleman, Pieter J. "Apocryphal Acts and Epistles." *DNTB* 66–69.
Lamour, "Organisation." Lamour, Denis. "L'organisation du récit dans l'*Autobiographie* de Flavius Josèphe." *BAGB* 55 (2, 1996): 141–50.
Lanfranchi, "Reminiscences." Lanfranchi, Pierluigi. "Reminiscences of Ezekiel's *Exagoge* in Philo's *De Vita Mosis*." Pages 144-50 in *Moses in Biblical and Extra-Biblical Traditions.* Edited by Axel Graupner and Michael Wolter. Beihefte zur Zeitschrift für die alttestamentliche Wissenschaft 372. Berlin; New York: de Gruyter, 2007.
Lang, *Kunst*. Lang, Manfred. *Die Kunst des christlichen Lebens: Rezeptionsästhetische Studien zum lukanischen Paulusbild.* ABIG 29. Lepizig: Evangelische Verlagsanstalt, 2008.
Laqueur, *Historiker*. Laqueur, Richard. *Der Jüdische Historiker Flavius Josephus: Ein Biographischer Versuch Auf Neuer Quellenkritischer Grundlage.* Darmstadt: Wissenschaftliche Buchgesellschaft, 1970 (reprinted from 1920).
Lavery, "*Lucullus*." Lavery, Gerald B. "Plutarch's Lucullus and the Living Bond of Biography." *Classical Journal* 89 (3, 1994): 262-73.
Levene, "Speeches." Levene, D. S. "Speeches in the *Histories*." In *The Cambridge Companion to Tacitus.* Edited by A.J. Woodman. Cambridge: Cambridge University Press, 2009.
Levine, "Christian Faith." Levine, Amy-Jill. "Christian Faith and the Study of the Historical Jesus: A Response to Bock, Keener, and Webb." *JSHJ* 9 (1, 2011): 96-106.
Lewis, *History*. Lewis, Bernard. *History Remembered, Recovered, Invented.* New York: Simon & Schuster, 1975.
Lewis, *Life*. Lewis, Naphtali. *Life in Egypt Under Roman Rule.* Oxford: Clarendon Press, 1983.

Lichtenberger, "History-writing." Lichtenberger, Hermann. "History-writing and History-telling in First and Second Maccabees." Pages 95-110 in *Memory in the Bible and Antiquity*. Edited by Stephen C. Barton, Loren T. Stuckenbruck, and Benjamin G. Wold. WUNT 212. Tübingen: Mohr Siebeck, 2007.

Licona, "Compositional Techniques." Licona, Michael R. "Compositional Techniques within Plutarch and the Gospel Tradition." In *Christian Origins and the Establishment of the Early Jesus Movement*. Edited by Stanley E. Porter and Andrew W. Pitts. TENTSL ECHC 4. Leiden: Brill, forthcoming 2016.

Licona, "Contradictions." Licona, Michael R. "Viewing the Gospels as Ancient Biographies Resolves Many Perceived Contradictions." Paper presented at the Annual Meeting of the ETS. Milwaukee, WI, 15 November 2012.

Licona, "Differences." Licona, Michael R. "Viewing the Gospels as Ancient Biographies Explains Many of the Differences." Unpublished Paper.

Licona, *Resurrection*. Licona, Michael R. *The Resurrection of Jesus: A New Historiographical Approach*. Downers Grove, IL: InterVarsity Press, 2010.

Licona, "Using Plutarch's Biographies." Licona, Michael R. "Using Plutarch's Biographies to Help Resolve Differences in Parallel Gospel Accounts." Paper presented at the Annual Meeting of the ETS. Baltimore, MD, 21 November 2013.

Licona, *Why Differences*. Licona, Michael R. *Why Are There Differences in the Gospels?* New York: Oxford University Press, forthcoming.

Liefeld, "Preacher." Liefeld, Walter Lewis. "The Wandering Preacher as a Social Figure in the Roman Empire." PhD diss., Columbia University, 1967.

Lincoln, *Saint John*. Lincoln, Andrew T. *The Gospel according to Saint John*. BNTC 4. London: Continuum, 2005.

Long, "Samuel." Long, V. Phillips. "1 Samuel." Pages 267–411 in vol. 2 of *Zondervan Illustrated Bible Backgrounds Commentary: Old Testament*. Edited by John Walton. 5 vols. Grand Rapids: Zondervan, 2009.

Lord, *Singer*. Lord, Albert B. *The Singer of Tales*. New York: Atheneum, 1965.

Lutz, "Musonius." Lutz, Cora E. "Musonius Rufus: The Roman Socrates." *Yale Classical Studies* 10 (1947): 3–147.

Luz, "Masada." Luz, Menahem. "Eleazar's Second Speech on Masada and Its Literary Precedents." *RMPhil* 126 (1, 1983): 25–43.

Luz, *Matthew*. Luz, Ulrich. *Matthew 1–7: A Commentary*. Rev. ed. Hermeneia. Minneapolis: Fortress, 2007.

Lyons, *Autobiography*. Lyons, George. *Pauline Autobiography: Toward a New Understanding*. SBLDS 73. Atlanta: Scholars Press, 1985.

Mack and Murphy, "Wisdom Literature." Mack, Burton L., and Roland E. Murphy. "Wisdom Literature." Pages 371-410 in *Early Judaism and Its Modern Interpreters*. Edited by Robert A. Kraft and George W. E. Nickelsburg. Society of Biblical Literature and Its Modern Interpreters Series 2. Atlanta: Scholars Press, 1986.

Maclean and Aitken, *Heroikos*. Maclean, Jennifer K. Berenson, and Ellen Bradshaw Aitken, eds. and trans. *Flavius Philostratus: Heroikos.* SBLWGRW 1. Atlanta: SBL, 2001.

Malherbe, *Exhortation*. Malherbe, Abraham J. *Moral Exhortation, a Greco-Roman Sourcebook.* LEC 4. Philadelphia: Westminster, 1986.

Malherbe and Ferguson, *Gregory of Nyssa*. Malherbe, Abraham J., and Everett Ferguson. *Gregory of Nyssa* The Life of Moses. New York: REFS, 1978.

Malina and Neyrey, *Portraits*. Malina, Bruce J., and Jerome H. Neyrey. *Portraits of Paul: An Archaeology of Ancient Personality.* Louisville: Westminster John Knox, 1996.

Marcus, *Mark*. Marcus, Joel. *Mark.* 2 vols. AB 27, 27A. New Haven: Yale University Press, 1999-2009.

Marguerat, *Histoire*. Marguerat, Daniel. *La première histoire du christianisme (les Actes des apôtres).* LD 180. Paris: Cerf, 1999.

Marincola, "Introduction." Marincola, John. "Introduction." Pages 1–9 in *A Companion to Greek and Roman Historiography.* Edited by John Marincola. 2 vols. Oxford: Blackwell, 2007.

Marincola, "Speeches." Marincola, John. "Speeches in Classical Historiography." Pages 118–32 in *A Companion to Greek and Roman Historiography.* Edited by John Marincola. 2 vols. Oxford: Blackwell, 2007.

Martin, *New Testament*. Martin, Ralph P. *New Testament Foundations.* 2 vols. Exeter: Paternoster, 1975-1978.

Martin, "Tacitus." Martin, Ronald H. "Tacitus." OCD^4 1426-28.

Martin, "Tacitus on Agricola." Martin, Ronald H. "Tacitus on Agricola: Truth and Stereotype." Pages 9-12 in *Form and Fabric: Studies in Rome's Material Past in Honour of B. R. Hartley.* Edited by Joanna Bird. Oxbow Monograph 80. Oxford: Oxbow, 1998.

Mason, *Josephus and New Testament*. Mason, Steve. *Josephus and the New Testament.* Peabody, Mass.: Hendrickson, 1992.

Mason, *Life*. Mason, Steve, ed. *Life of Josephus*, by Flavius Josephus. Vol. 9 of *Flavius Josephus: Translation and Commentary.* Edited by Steve Mason. Leiden: Die Deutsche Bibliothek: 2001.

Massey, "Disagreement." Massey, Preston T. "Disagreement in the Greco-Roman Literary Tradition and the Implications for Gospel Research." *BBR* 22.1 (2012): 51-80.

Mayer, "Abrahambildes." Mayer, Günter. "Aspekte des Abrahambildes in der hellenistisch-jüdischen Literatur." *EvT* 32 (2, 1972): 118–27.

McGill, "Seneca on Plagiarizing." McGill, Scott. "Seneca the Elder on Plagiarizing Cicero's *Verrines*." *Rhetorica* 23 (4, 2005): 337–46.

McGing, "Philo's Adaptation." McGing, Brian. "Philo's Adaptation of the Bible in His Life of Moses." Pages 117–40 in *The Limits of Ancient Biography.* Edited by Brian McGing and Judith Mossman. Swansea: The Classical Press of Wales, 2006.

McInerney, "Arrian and Romance." McInerney, Jeremy. "Arrian and the Greek Alexander Romance." *CW* 100 (4, 2007): 424–30.

McIver, "Eyewitnesses." McIver, Robert K. "Eyewitnesses as guarantors of the accuracy of the gospel traditions in the light of psychological research." *Journal of Biblical Literature* 131 (3, 2012): 529-46.

McKnight, "Lion Proselytes." McKnight, Scot. "*De Vita Mosis* 1.147: Lion Proselytes in Philo?" *Studia Philonica Annual* 1 (1989): 58-62.

McKnight, "Matthew." McKnight, Scot. "Matthew as 'Gospel.'" Pages 59-75 in *Jesus, Matthew's Gospel and Early Christianity: Studies in Memory of Graham N. Stanton.* Edited by D. M. Gurtner, J. Willitts and R.A. Burridge. LNTS 435. London: T. & T. Clark, 2011.

McNamara, *Judaism.* McNamara, Martin. *Palestinian Judaism and the New Testament.* GNS 4; Wilmington, DE: Michael Glazier, 1983.

Meeks, *Moral World.* Meeks, Wayne A. *The Moral World of the First Christians.* LEC 6. Philadelphia: Westminster, 1986.

Meeks, *Prophet-King.* Meeks, Wayne A. *The Prophet-King: Moses Traditions and the Johannine Christology.* NovTSup 14. Leiden: Brill, 1967.

Meier, "Circle." Meier, John P. "The Circle of the Twelve: Did It Exist during Jesus' Public Ministry?" *JBL* 116 (3, 1997): 635–72.

Meiser, "Gattung." Meiser, Martin. "Gattung, Adressaten und Intention von Philos 'In Flaccum.'" *JSJ* 30 (4, 1999): 418–30.

Meister, "Herodotus." Meister, Klaus. "Herodotus." 6:265-271 in *Brill's New Pauly*. Leiden, Boston: Brill, 2005.

Meister, "Historiography: Greece." Meister, Klaus. "Historiography: Greece." *BrillPauly* 6:418–21.

Merkle, "True Story." Merkle, Stefan. "Telling the True Story of the Trojan War: The Eyewitness Account of Dictys of Crete." Pages 183–96 in *The Search for the Ancient Novel.* Edited by James Tatum. Baltimore: Johns Hopkins University Press, 1994.

Mellor, *Roman Historians.* Mellor, Ronald. *Roman Historians.* New York: Routledge, 1999.

Milikowsky, "Midrash." Milikowsky, Chaim. "Midrash as Fiction and Midrash as History: What Did the Rabbis Mean?" Pages 117–27 in *Ancient Fiction: The Matrix of Early Christian and Jewish Narrative.* Edited by Jo-Ann A. Brant, Charles W. Hedrick, and Chris Shea. SBLSymS 32. Atlanta: SBL, 2005.

Millard, "Literacy." Millard, Alan. "Literacy in the Time of Jesus." *BAR* 29 (4, 2003): 36-45.

Millard, *Reading.* Millard, Alan. *Reading and Writing in the Time of Jesus.* The Biblical Seminar 69. Sheffield: Sheffield Academic Press, 2000.

Milnor, "Literacy." Milnor, Kristina. "Literary Literacy in Roman Pompeii: The Case of Vergil's *Aeneid.*" Pages 288-319 in *Ancient Literacies: The Culture of Reading in Greece and Rome.* Edited by William A. Johnson and Holt N. Parker. New York: Oxford University Press, 2009.

Moessner, "Poetics." Moessner, David P. "The Appeal and Power of Poetics (Luke 1:1–4): Luke's Superior Credentials (παρηκολουθηκότι), Narrative Sequence (καθεξῆς), and Firmness of Understanding (ἡ ἀσφάλεια) for the Reader." Pages 84–123 in *Jesus and the Heritage of Israel: Luke's Narrative Claim upon Israel's Legacy*. Edited by David P. Moessner. Luke the Interpreter of Israel 1. Harrisburg, Pa.: Trinity Press International, 1999.

Moessner, "Prologues." Moessner, David P. "The Lukan Prologues in the Light of Ancient Narrative Hermeneutics: Παρηκολουθηκότι and the Credentialed Author." Pages 399–417 in *The Unity of Luke-Acts*. Edited by Joseph Verheyden. BETL 142. Leuven: Leuven University Press, 1999.

Moessner, "Voice." Moessner, David P. "The Living and Enduring Voice of Papias." Paper presented in the "Memory, Narrative, and Christology in the Synoptic Gospels" Seminar at the Annual Meeting of the Society for New Testament Studies. Montreal, Canada, 2016.

Momigliano, *Development.* Momigliano, Arnaldo. *Development of Greek Biography*. Cambridge, MA: Harvard University Press, 1972.

Momigliano, *Historiography.* Momigliano, Arnaldo. *Essays in Ancient and Modern Historiography*. Middletown, Conn.: Wesleyan University Press; Oxford: Blackwell, 1977.

Moniot, "Profile." Moniot, Henri. "Profile of a Historiography: Oral Tradition and Historical Research in Africa." Pages 50–58 in *African Historiographies: What History for Which Africa?* Edited by Bogumil Jewsiewicki and David Newbury. SSAMD 12. Beverly Hills, Calif.: Sage, 1986.

Montanari, "Hypomnema." Montanari, Franco. "Hypomnema." Pages 641–43 in vol. 6 of *Brill's New Pauly: Encyclopaedia of the Ancient World*. Ed. Hubert Cancik and Helmuth Schneider. Leiden, Boston: Brill, 2005.

Moore, "Introduction." Moore, Clifford H. "Introduction: Life and Works of Tacitus." Pages vii–xiii in vol. 1 of *Tacitus*. Translated by Clifford H. Moore and John Jackson. 4 vols. LCL. London: Heinemann; Cambridge, Mass.: Harvard University Press, 1931–37.

Morgan, "Fiction." Morgan, J. R. "Fiction and History: Historiography and the Novel." Pages 553–64 in *A Companion to Greek and Roman Historiography*. Edited by John Marincola. 2 vols. Oxford: Blackwell, 2007.

Mosley, "Reporting." Mosley, A. W. "Historical Reporting in the Ancient World." *NTS* 12 (1, 1965): 10–26.

Mossman, "Plutarch and Biography." Mossman, Judith. "Plutarch and English Biography." *Herm* 183 (2007): 75–100.

Moule, *Birth.* Moule, C. F. D. *The Birth of the New Testament.* BNTC. London: A. & C. Black, 1962.

Muntz, "Diodorus Siculus." Muntz, Charles E. "Diodorus Siculus and Megasthenes: A Reappraisal." *CP* 107 (1, 2012): 21–37.

Muntz, "Sources." Muntz, Charles E. "The Sources of Diodorus Siculus, Book 1." *CQ* 61 (2, 2011): 574–94.

Murphy, "Idolatry." Murphy, Frederick J. "Retelling the Bible: Idolatry in Pseudo-Philo." *JBL* 107 (2, 1988): 275–87.

Musnick, "Historical Commentary." Musnick, Larry Jason. "A Historical Commentary on Cornelius Nepos' *Life of Themistocles*." MA diss., University of Cape Town, 2008.

Nesselrath, "Lucianus." Nesselrath, Heinz-Günther. "Lucianus." 7:836-845 in *Brill's New Pauly*. Leiden, Boston: Brill, 2005.

Nesselrath, "Xenophon." Nesselrath, Heinz-Günther. "Xenophon." 15:824-33 in *Brill's New Pauly*. Leiden, Boston: Brill, 2005.

Neusner, "Cleanse." Neusner, Jacob. "'First Cleanse the Inside.'" *New Testament Studies* 22 (1976): 486-95.

Neusner, "Foreword." Neusner, Jacob. Foreword. Pages xxv–xlvi in *Memory and Manuscript: Oral Tradition and Written Transmission in Rabbinic Judaism and Early Christianity; Tradition and Transmission in Early Christianity*. By Birger Gerhardsson. Grand Rapids: Eerdmans, 1998.

Neusner, "Idea of History." Neusner, Jacob. "The Idea of History in Rabbinic Judaism. What Kinds of Questions Did the Ancient Rabbis Answer?" *NewBlackfr* 90 (1027, 2009): 277-94.

Neusner, *Legend*. Neusner, Jacob. *Development of a Legend: Studies on the Traditions Concerning Yohanan ben Zakkai*. Studia Post-Biblica vol. sextum decimum. Leiden: E. J. Brill, 1970.

Neusner, *Talmudic Biography*. Neusner, Jacob. *In Search of Talmudic Biography: The Problem of the Attributed Saying*. BJS 70. Chico, CA: Scholars Press, 1984.

Neusner, *The Incarnation of God*. Neusner, Jacob. *The Incarnation of God: The Character of Divinity in Formative Judaism*. Philadelphia: Fortress, 1988.

Neusner, *Why No Gospels*. Neusner, Jacob. *Why No Gospels in Talmudic Judaism?* BJS 135. Atlanta: Scholars, 1988.

Nicolai, "Place of History." Nicolai, Roberto. "The Place of History in the Ancient World." Pages 13–26 in *A Companion to Greek and Roman Historiography*. Edited by John Marincola. 2 vols. Oxford: Blackwell, 2007.

Niehoff, "Josephus' Narrative Technique." Niehoff, Maren R. "Two Examples of Josephus' Narrative Technique in His 'Rewritten Bible.'" *JSJ* 27 (1996): 31–45.

Niehoff, "Philo." Niehoff, Maren R. "Philo and Plutarch as Biographers: Parallel Responses to Roman Stoicism." *GRBS* 52 (3, 2012): 361-92.

Nisula, "Time Has Passed." Nisula, Timo. "'Time Has Passed since You Sent Your Letter': Letter Phraseology in 1 and 2 Maccabees." *JSP* 14 (2005): 201-22.

Noll and Nystrom, *Clouds*. Noll, Mark A., and Carolyn Nystrom. *Clouds of Witnesses: Christian Voices from Africa and Asia*. Downers Grove, Ill.: InterVarsity, 2011.

O'Brien, *Alexander*. O'Brien, John Maxwell. *Alexander the Great: The Invisible Enemy*. New York: Routledge, 1992.

Olbricht, "Delivery." Olbricht, Thomas H. "Delivery and Memory." Pages 159–67 in *Handbook of Classical Rhetoric in the Hellenistic Period, 330 B.C.–A.D. 400*. Edited by Stanley E. Porter. Leiden: Brill, 1997.

Oldfather, "Introduction." Oldfather, C. H. Introduction. Pages vii–xxvii in vol. 1 of *Diodorus Siculus*. Translated by C. H. Oldfather et al. 12 vols. LCL. London: Heinmann; Cambridge, Mass.: Harvard University Press, 1933–67.

Palmer, "Monograph." Palmer, Darryl W. "Acts and the Ancient Historical Monograph." Pages 1–29 in *The Book of Acts in Its Ancient Literary Setting*. Edited by Bruce W. Winter and Andrew D. Clarke. Vol. 1 of *The Book of Acts in Its First Century Setting*. Edited by Bruce W. Winter. Grand Rapids: Eerdmans; Carlisle, U.K.: Paternoster, 1993.

Parker, "Letters in II Maccabees." Parker, Victor. "The Letters in II Maccabees: Reflexions on the Book's Composition," *ZAW* 119 (2007): 386-402.

Parker, "Swiftly runs the word." Parker, Emily. " Swiftly runs the word : Philo's doctrine of mediation in De Vita Mosis." M.A. thesis, Dalhousie University 2010.

Parsenios, "Rhetoric." Parsenios, George. "How and in What Ways Does John's Rhetoric Reflect Jesus' Rhetoric?" Paper presented at the Princeton-Prague Symposium on the Historical Jesus, Princeton, N.J., March 18, 2016.

Payne, "Midrash." Payne, Philip Barton. "Midrash and History in the Gospels with Special Reference to R. H. Gundry's *Matthew*." 3:177-215 in *Gospel Perspectives*. 6 vols. Vol. 3: *Studies in Midrash and Historiography*. Edited by R. T. France and David Wenham. Sheffield: JSOT Press, 1983.

Pearson, *Lost Histories*. Pearson, Lionel. *The Lost Histories of Alexander the Great*. Chico, CA: Scholars Press, 1983.

Pearson and Porter, "Genres." Pearson, Brook W. R. and Stanley E. Porter. "The Genres of the New Testament." Pages 131-65 in *Handbook to Exegesis of the New Testament*. Edited by Stanley E. Porter. NTTS 25. Leiden: Brill, 1997.

Pelling, *Plutarch*. Pelling, Christopher B. R. *Plutarch and History*. Havertwon: The Classic Press of Wales, 2011.

Pelling, "Plutarch's Adaptation." Pelling, Christoper B. R. "Plutarch's Adaptation of His Source-Material." *JHS* 100 (1980): 127–40.

Pelling, "Plutarch's Method." Pelling, Christopher B. R. "Plutarch's Method of Work in the Roman Lives." *JHS* 99 (1979): 74–96.

Penner, "Discourse." Penner, Todd. "Civilizing Discourse: Acts, Declamation, and the Rhetoric of the *polis*." Pages 65–104 in *Contextualizing Acts: Lukan Narrative and Greco-Roman Discourse*. Edited by Todd Penner and Caroline Vander Stichele. SBLSymS 20. Atlanta: SBL, 2003.

Penner, *Praise*. Penner, Todd. *In Praise of Christian Origins: Stephen and the Hellenists in Lukan Apologetic Historiography*. Foreword by David L. Balch. New York and London: T&T Clark, 2004.

Pennington, *Reading the Gospels Wisely*. Pennington, Jonathan T. *Reading the Gospels Wisely: A Narrative and Theological Introduction.* Grand Rapids, MI: Baker Academic, 2012.

Perkins, "World." Perkins, Judith. "The Social World of the *Acts of Peter*." Pages 296–307 in *The Search for the Ancient Novel*. Edited by James Tatum. Baltimore: Johns Hopkins University Press, 1994.

Perrin, "Historical Criticism." Perrin, Norman. "Historical Criticism, Literary Criticism, and Hermeneutics: The Interpretation of the Parables of Jesus and the Gospel of Mark Today." *JR* 52 (1972): 361–75.

Perrin, "Overlooked Evidence." Perrin, Nicholas. "NHC II,2 and the Oxyrhynchus Fragments (P.Oxy 1, 654, 655): Overlooked Evidence for a Syriac *Gospel of Thomas*," *VC* 58 (2004): 138-51.

Perrin, *Thomas and Tatian*. Perrin, Nicholas. *Thomas and Tatian: The Relationship between the* Gospel of Thomas *and the* Diatessaron. SBL Academia Biblica 5. Atlanta: Society of Biblical Literature, 2002.

Pervo, *Acts*. Pervo, Richard I. *Acts: A Commentary*. Minneapolis: Fortress, 2009.

Petersen, "Can One Speak." Petersen, Norman R. "Can One Speak of a Gospel Genre?" *Neotestamentica* 28 (1994): 137-58.

Petit, "Traversée exemplaire." Petit, Madeleine. "À propos d'une traversée exemplaire du désert du Sinaï selon Philon (*Hypothetica* VI, 2–3.8): Texte biblique et apologétique concernant Moïse chez quelques écrivains juifs." *Sem* 26 (1976): 137–42.

Piccione, "Παιδεία." Piccione, Rosa Maria. "De vita Mosis 1.60-62: Philon und die griechische παιδεία." 345-57 in *Philo und das Neue Testament. Wechselseitige Wahrnehmungen. I. Internationales Symposium zum Corpus Judaeo-Hellenisticum (Eisenach/Jena, Mai 2003)*. Edited by Roland Deines and Karl-Wilhelm Niebuhr. WUNT 172. Tübingen: Mohr Siebeck, 2004.

Pilch, "Naming." Pilch, John J. "Naming the Nameless in the Bible." *BibT* 44 (5, 2006): 315–20.

Pitcher, "Characterization." Pitcher, L. V. "Characterization in Ancient Historiography." Pages 102–17 in *A Companion to Greek and Roman Historiography*. Edited by John Marincola. Malden, MA: Wiley-Blackwell, 2011.

Pitts, "Source Citation." Pitts, Andrew W. "Source Citation in Greek Historiography and in Luke(-Acts)." Pages 349–88 in *Christian Origins and Greco-Roman Culture: Social and Literary Contexts for the New Testament*. Edited by Stanley E. Porter and Andrew W. Pitts. Leiden: Brill, 2013.

Pizzuto-Pomaco, "Shame." Pizzuto-Pomaco, Julia. "From Shame to Honour: Mediterranean Women in Romans 16." PhD dissertation, University of St. Andrews, 2003.

Plümacher, "Fiktion und Wunder." Plümacher, Eckhard. "ΤΕΡΑΤΕΙΑ: Fiktion und Wunder in der hellenistisch-römischen Geschichtsschreibung und in der Apostelgeschichte." *ZNW* 89 (1–2, 1998): 66–90.

Plümacher, *Geschichte*. Plümacher, Eckhard. *Geschichte und Geschichten: Aufsätze zur Apostelgeschichte und zu den Johannesakten.* Edited by Jens Schröter and Ralph Brucker. WUNT 170. Tübingen: Mohr Siebeck, 2004.
Porciani, "Enigma." Porciani, Leone. "The Enigma of Discourse: A View of Thucydides." Pages 328–35 in *A Companion to Greek and Roman Historiography.* Edited by John Marincola. 2 vols. Oxford: Blackwell, 2007.
Porter, "Reconstructing." Porter, Stanley E. "What Do We Know and How Do We Know It? Reconstructing Early Christianity from its Manuscripts." Pages 41-70 in *Christian Origins and Greco-Roman Culture: Social and Literary Contexts for the New Testament.* Edited by Stanley Porter and Andrew W. Pitts. Vol. 1 of Early Christianity in its Hellenistic Context. Vol. 9 in Texts and Editions for New Testament Study. Leiden: Brill, 2013.
Porter and Holmén, *Handbook*. Porter, Stanley E., and Tom Holmén, editors. *Handbook for the Study of the Historical Jesus.* 4 vols. Leiden: Brill, 2011.
Porter, "We Passages." Porter, Stanley E. "Excursus: The 'We' Passages." Pages 545–74 in *The Book of Acts in Its Graeco-Roman Setting.* Edited by David W. J. Gill and Conrad Gempf. Vol. 2 of *The Book of Acts in Its First Century Setting.* Edited by Bruce W. Winter. Grand Rapids: Eerdmans; Carlisle, U.K.: Paternoster, 1994.
Powell, *Figure*. Powell, Mark Allan. *Jesus as a Figure in History: How Modern Historians View the Man from Galilee.* 2nd ed. Louisville: Westminster John Knox, 2013.
Powell, *Introducing*. Powell, Mark Allen. *Introducing the New Testament: A Historical, Literary, and Theological Survey.* Grand Rapids: Baker, 2009.
Pretzler, "Pausanias and Tradition." Pretzler, Maria. "Pausanias and Oral Tradition." *Classical Quarterly* 55 (1, 2005): 235–49.
Price, *Shrinking*. Price, Robert M. *The Incredible Shrinking Son of Man: How Reliable Is the Gospel Tradition?* Amherst, N.Y.: Prometheus, 2003.
Pryke, *Style*. Pryke, E. J. *Redactional Style in the Marcan Gospel: A Study of Syntax and Vocabulary as Guides to Redaction in Mark.* Cambridge: Cambridge University Press, 1978.
Pryzwansky, "Nepos." Pryzwansky, Molly M. "Cornelius Nepos: Key Issues and Critical Approaches. " *Classical Journal* 105 (2009): 97-108.
Rajak, *Josephus*. Rajak, Tessa. *Josephus: The Historian and His Society.* London: Duckworth, 1983.
Rajak, "Justus of Tiberias." Rajak, Tessa. "Josephus and Justus of Tiberias." Pages 81–94 in *Josephus, Judaism, and Christianity.* Edited by Louis H. Feldman and Gohei Hata. Detroit: Wayne State University Press, 1987.
Raphael, "Travail." Raphael, Freddy. "Le Travail de la memoire et les limites de l'histoire orale." *Annales* 35 (1, Jan. 1980): 127-45.
Rebenich, "Historical Prose." Rebenich, Stefan. "Historical Prose." Pages 265–337 in *Handbook of Classical Rhetoric in the Hellenistic Period, 330 B.C.–A.D. 400.* Edited by Stanley E. Porter. Leiden: Brill, 1997.

Redman, "Eyewitnesses." Redman, Judith C. S. "How Accurate Are Eyewitnesses? Bauckham and the Eyewitnesses in the Light of Psychological Research." *JBL* 129 (1, 2010): 177–97.

Reinmuth, "Zwischen Investitur und Testament." Reinmuth, Eckart. "Zwischen Investitur und Testament: Beobachtungen zur Rezeption des Josuabuches im Liber antiquitatum biblicarum." *JSP* 16 (1, 2002): 24–43.

Reiser, *Sprache*. Reiser, Marius. *Sprache und literarische Formen des Neuen Testaments: Eine Einführung.* UTB 2197. Paderborn: Schöningh, 2001.

Remus, *Healer*. Remus, Harold. *Jesus as Healer.* UJT. Cambridge: Cambridge University Press, 1997.

Remus, "Thaumaturges." Remus, Harold. "Moses and the Thaumaturges: Philo's De Vita Mosis as a Rescue Operation." *Laval Théologique et Philosophique* 52 (3, 1996): 665-80.

Renan, *Vie de Jésus*. Renan, Ernest. *Vie de Jésus.* Histoire des origines du christianisme 1. Paris: Michel Lévy, 1863.

Renan, *Life of Jesus*. Renan, Ernest. *The Life of Jesus.* Translated by Charles E. Wilbour. New York: Carleton, 1874.

Reuss, *Nouvelle*. Reuss, Édouard. "Flavius Joseph." *Nouvelle Revue de Theologie* 4 (1859) 253-319.

Reydams-Schils, "Authority." Reydams-Schils, G. "Authority and Agency in Stoicism." *Greek, Roman and Byzantine Studies* 51 (2, 2011): 296-322.

Rhodes, "Documents." Rhodes, P. J. "Documents and the Greek Historians." Pages 56–66 in *A Companion to Greek and Roman Historiography.* Edited by John Marincola. 2 vols. Oxford: Blackwell, 2007.

Riaud, "Réflexions." Riaud, J. "Quelques réflexions sur les Thérapeutes d'Alexandre à la lumière de *De vita Mosis* II, 67." Pages 184-91 in *Heirs of the Septuagint: Philo, Hellenistic Judaism and early Christianity. Festschrift for Earle Hilgert.* Edited by David T Runia, David M Hay, and David Winston. Brown Judaic Studies 230; Studia Philonica Annual, 3. Atlanta: Scholars Press, 1991.

Richardson, et al., "Vipsanius Agrippa, Marcus." Richardson, Geoffrey W., Theodore J. Cadoux and Barbara M. Levick. "Vipsanius Agrippa, Marcus." *OCD*[4] 1554-55.

Richardson and Gooch, "Logia." Richardson, Peter, and Peter Gooch. "Logia of Jesus in 1 Corinthians." Pages 39–62 in *The Jesus Tradition outside the Gospels.* Edited by David Wenham. Gospel Perspectives 5. Sheffield, U.K.: JSOT Press, 1984.

Riches, "Introduction." Riches, John. Introduction to *The Place of the Gospels in the General History of Literature*, by Karl Ludwig Schmidt. Translated by Byron R. McCane. Columbia: University of South Carolina Press, 2002.

Riesenfeld, *Tradition*. Riesenfeld, Harald. *The Gospel Tradition.* Philadelphia: Fortress, 1970.

Riesner, "Education élémentaire." Riesner, Rainer. "Education élémentaire juive et tradition évangélique." *Hokhma* 21 (1982): 51–64.

Riesner, *Lehrer.* Riesner, Rainer. *Jesus als Lehrer: Eine Untersuchung zum Ursprung der Evangelien-Überlieferung.* 2nd ed. WUNT 2. Reihe, 7. Tübingen: J. C. B. Mohr, 1984.

Riggsby, "Memoir." Riggsby, Andrew M. "Memoir and Autobiography in Republican Rome." Pages 266–74 in *A Companion to Greek and Roman Historiography.* Edited by John Marincola. 2 vols. Oxford: Blackwell, 2007.

Robbins, *Quotes.* Robbins, Vernon K. *Ancient Quotes and Anecdotes: From Crib to Crypt.* Sonoma, Fla.: Polebridge, 1989.

Robbins, *Study.* Robbins, William Joseph. "A study in Jewish and Hellenistic legend with special reference to Philo's *Life of Moses* ..." PhD dissertation, Brown University 1947.

Robbins, *Teacher.* Robbins, Vernon K. *Jesus the Teacher: A Socio-rhetorical Interpretation of Mark.* Minneapolis: Augsburg Fortress, 1992.

Robeck, *Mission.* Robeck, Cecil M., Jr. *The Azusa Street Mission and Revival: The Birth of the Global Pentecostal Movement.* Nashville: Thomas Nelson, 2006.

Roberts, "Xenophon." Roberts, John. "Xenophon." *ODCW* 827-30.

Robertson, "Account." Robertson, Stuart Dunbar. "The Account of the Ancient Israelite Tabernacle and First Priesthood in The 'Jewish Antiquities' of Flavius Josephus." PhD dissertation, Annenberg Research Institute, Philadelphia, 1991.

Rodgers, "Justice for Justus." Rodgers, Zuleika. "Justice for Justus: A Re-examination of Justus of Tiberias' Role." Pages 169-92 in *The Limits of Ancient Biography.* Edited by Brian McGing and Judith Mossman. Swansea: The Classical Press of Wales, 2006.

Rodriguez, *Memory.* Rodriguez, Rafael. *Structuring Early Christian Memory: Jesus in Tradition, Performance and Text.* Library of New Testament Studies 407. London: T&T Clark, 2010.

Rolfe, "Introduction." Rolfe, J. C. Introduction to *Cornelius Nepos.* Pages vii-xii in *Cornelius Nepos.* Translated by J. C. Rolfe. LCL. Cambridge: Harvard University Press, 1929.

Rolfe, "Introduction." Rolfe, J. C. Introduction to *The Lives of the Caesars.* Pages xvii–xxxi in vol. 1 of *Suetonius.* Translated by J. C. Rolfe. 2 vols. LCL. London: Heinemann; New York: Macmillan; Cambridge, Mass.: Harvard University Press, 1914.

Rolfe, *Nepos.* *Cornelius Nepos.* Translated by J. C. Rolfe. Loeb Classical Library. Cambridge, MA: Harvard University Press, 1929-1994.

Rolfe, et al. "Nepos." Rolfe, J. C., Gavin B. Townend, Antony Spawforth. "Cornelius Nepos." 380 in *The Oxford Classical Dictionary.*

Romm, *Alexander.* Romm, James S. *Alexander The Great: Selections From Arrian, Diodorus, Plutarch, and Quintus Curtius.* Indianapolis: Hackett Publishing, 2005.

Roncace, "Portraits." Roncace, Mark. "Josephus' (Real) Portraits of Deborah and Gideon: A Reading of *Antiquities* 5.198–232." *JSJ* 31 (3, 2000): 247–74.

Roncace, "Samson." Roncace, Mark. "Another Portrait of Josephus' Portrait of Samson." *JSJ* 35 (2, 2004): 185–207.

Rondholz, "Crossing." Rondholz, Anke. "Crossing the Rubicon. A Historiographical Study." *Mnemosyne* 62 (3, 2009): 432–50.

Rook, "Names." Rook, John T. "The Names of the Wives from Adam to Abraham in the Book of *Jubilees*." *JSP* 7 (1990): 105–17.

Rothschild, *Rhetoric of History*. Rothschild, Clare K. *Luke-Acts and the Rhetoric of History: An Investigation of Early Christian Historiography*. WUNT 2.175. Tübingen: Mohr Siebeck, 2004.

Rowe, "Style." Rowe, Galen O. "Style." Pages 121–57 in *Handbook of Classical Rhetoric in the Hellenistic Period, 330 B.C.–A.D. 400*. Edited by Stanley E. Porter. Leiden: Brill, 1997.

Rüpke, "Knowledge." Rüpke, Jörg. "Knowledge of Religion in Valerius Maximus' *Exempla*: Roman Historiography and Tiberian Memory Culture." Pages 89-111 in *Memory in Ancient Rome and Early Christianity*. Edited by Karl Galinsky. Oxford: Oxford University Press, 2016.

Russell, "Coriolanus." Russell, D. A. "Plutarch's Life of Coriolanus." *JRS* 53 (1963): 21–28.

Russell, "Plutarch." Russell, Donald A. F. M. "Plutarch." 1200-1 in *OCD*.

Russell, "Reading Plutarch's Lives." Russell, D. A. "On Reading Plutarch's Lives." *GR* 13 (1966): 139–54.

Safrai, "Education." Safrai, Shemuel. "Education and the Study of the Torah." Pages 945–70 in *The Jewish People in the First Century: Historical Geography, Political History, Social, Cultural and Religious Life and Institutions*. 2 vols. Edited by S. Safrai and M. Stern with D. Flusser and W. C. van Unnik. Section 1 of Compendia Rerum Iudaicarum ad Novum Testamentum. Vol. 1: Assen: Van Gorcum & Comp., B.V., 1974; Vol. 2: Philadelphia: Fortress Press, 1976.

Saïd, "Myth." Saïd, Suzanne. "Myth and Historiography." Pages 76–88 in *A Companion to Greek and Roman Historiography*. Edited by John Marincola. 2 vols. Oxford: Blackwell, 2007.

Salmon and Potter, "Bedriacum." Salmon, Edward T., and T. W. Potter. "Bedriacum (or Betriacum)." 237 in *OCD*.

Salvador, *Histoire*. Salvador, J. *Histoire de la Domination Romaine en Judée*. Paris, 1847.

Samuel, "Royal Journals." Samuel, Alan E. "Alexander's 'Royal Journals,'" *Historia* 14 (1965): 1-12.

Sanders, *Figure*. Sanders, E. P. *The Historical Figure of Jesus*. New York: Penguin, 1993.

Sanders, *Jesus and Judaism*. Sanders, E. P. *Jesus and Judaism*. Philadelphia: Fortress, 1985.

Sanders, *Paul*. Sanders, E. P. *Paul: The Apostle's Life, Letters, and Thought*. Minneapolis: Fortress, 2015.

Sanders, *Tendencies*. Sanders, E. P. *The Tendencies of the Synoptic Tradition*. SNTSMS 9. Cambridge: Cambridge University Press, 1969.

Satlow, "Philosophers." Satlow, Michael L. "Theophrastus's Jewish Philosophers." *Journal of Jewish Studies* 59 (1, 2008): 1-20.

Satterthwaite, "Background." Satterthwaite, Philip E. "Acts against the Background of Classical Rhetoric." Pages 337–79 in *The Book of Acts in Its Ancient Literary Setting*. Edited by Bruce W. Winter and Andrew D. Clark. Vol. 1 of *The Book of Acts in Its First Century Setting*. Edited by Bruce W. Winter. Grand Rapids: Eerdmans; Carlisle, U.K.: Paternoster, 1993.

Saulnier, "Josèphe." Saulnier, Christiane. "Flavius Josèphe et la propagande flavienne." *RB* 96 (4, 1989): 545–62.

Schacter, "Sins." Schacter, Daniel L. "The Seven Sins of Memory: Insights from Psychology and Cognitive Neuroscience." *American Psychologist* 54 (1999): 182-203.

Schacter and Addis, "Neuroscience." Schacter, Daniel L., and Donna Rose Addis. "The Cognitive Neuroscience of Constructive Memory: Remembering the Past and Imagining the Future." *Philosophical Transactions of the Royal Society* B362 (2007): 773-86.

Schacter, Norman and Koutstaal, "Neuroscience." Schacter, Daniel L., Kenneth A. Norman and Wilma Koutstaal. "The Cognitive Neuroscience of Constructive Memory." *Annual Review of Psychology* 49 (1998): 289-318.

Schepens, "History." Schepens, Guido. "History and *Historia*: Inquiry in the Greek Historians." Pages 39–55 in *A Companion to Greek and Roman Historiography*. Edited by John Marincola. 2 vols. Oxford: Blackwell, 2007.

Schmeling, "Spectrum." Schmeling, Gareth. "The Spectrum of Narrative: Authority of the Author." Pages 19–29 in *Ancient Fiction and Early Christian Narrative*. Edited by Ronald F. Hock, J. Bradley Chance, and Judith Perkins. SBLSymS 6. Atlanta: SBL, 1998.

Schmeller, "Gegenwelten." Schmeller, Thomas. "Gegenwelten: Zum Vergleich zwischen paulinischen Gemeinden und nichtchristlichen Gruppen." *BZ* 47 (2, 2003): 167–85.

Schmidt, ***Der Rahmen.*** Schmidt, Karl Ludwig. *Der Rahmen Der Geschichte Jesu : Literarkritische Untersuchungen Zur ältesten Jesusüberlieferung*. Berlin: Trowitzsch & Sohn, 1919.

Schmidt, "Die Stellung der Evangelien." Schmidt, Karl Ludwig. "Die Stellung der Evangelien in der allgemeinen Literaturgeschichte." Pages 50-134 in *ΕΥΧΑΡΙΣΤΗΡΙΟΝ: Studien zur Religion und Literatur des Alten und Neuen Testaments. 2. Teil: Zur Religion und Literatur des Neuen Testaments*. Edited by H. Schmidt. FS H. Gunkel; Göttingen: Vandenhoeck & Ruprecht, 1923.

Schmidt, ***The Place of the Gospels.*** Schmidt, Karl Ludwig. *The Place of the Gospels in the General History of Literature*. Translated by Byron R. McCane. Columbia, SC: University of South Carolina Press, 2002.

Schmitz, "Auferstehung und Epiphanie." Schmitz, Barbara. "Auferstehung und Epiphanie: Jenseits- und Körperkonzepte im Zweiten Makkabäerbuch." Pages 105-42 in *The Human Body in Death and Resurrection.* Edited by Tobias Nicklas, Friedrich V. Reiterer, and Joseph Verheyden. Berlin: de Gruyter, 2009.

Schorch, "Libraries in 2 Macc." Schorch, Stefan. "The Libraries in 2 Macc 2:13-15, and the Torah as a Public Document in Second Century BC Judaism." Pages 169-80 in *The Books of the Maccabees: History, Theology, Ideology.* Edited by Géza G. Xeravits and József Zsengellér. JSJsup 118. Leiden: Brill, 2007.

Schürer, *Geschichte.* Schürer, Emil. *Geschichte des Jüdischen Volkes im Zeitalter Jesu Christi.* Leipzig: Hinrich, 1898-1901.

Schwartz, *2 Maccabees.* Schwartz, Daniel R. *2 Maccabees.* CEJL. Berlin: de Gruyter, 2008.

Scott, "Divine Man." Scott, Ian W. "Is Philo's Moses a Divine Man?" *Studia Philonica Annual* 14 (2002): 87-111.

Sedley, "Debate." David Sedley, "The Stoic-Platonist Debate on *kathêkonta*," 128-52 in *Topics in Stoic Philosophy.* Edited by Katerina Ierodiakonou. Oxford, New York: Oxford University Press, 1999.

Shanks, "Inscription." Shanks, Hershel. "Inscription Reveals Roots of Maccabean Revolt." *BAR* 34 (6, 2008): 56–59.

Sheeley, *Asides.* Sheeley, Steven M. *Narrative Asides in Luke-Acts.* JSNTSup 72. Sheffield, U.K.: Sheffield Academic, 1992.

Shuler, *Genre.* Shuler, Philip L. *A Genre for the Gospels: The Biographical Character of Matthew.* Philadelphia: Fortress, 1982.

Shuler, "Moses." Shuler, Philip L. "Philo's Moses and Matthew's Jesus: A Comparative Study in Ancient Literature." *Studia Philonica Annual* 2 (1990): 86-103.

Shutt, *Studies.* Shutt, R. J. H. *Studies in Josephus.* London: SPCK, 1961.

Simkovich, "Greek Influence." Simkovich, Malka Zeiger. "Greek Influence on the Composition of 2 Maccabees," *JSJ* 42 (2011): 293-310.

Simpson, *Literature.* Simpson, William Kelly, ed. *The Literature of Ancient Egypt: An Anthology of Stories, Instructions, Stelae, Autobiographies, and Poetry.* 3rd ed. New Haven: Yale University Press, 2003.

Sloan, "Similitudes." Sloan, David B. "The τίς ἐξ ὑμῶν Similitudes and the Extent of Q." *JSNT* 38 (3, 2016): 339-55.

Small, "Artificial Memory." Small, Jocelyn Penny. "Artificial Memory and the Writing Habits of the Literate." *Helios* 22 (2, 1995): 159–66.

Small, "Memory." Small, Jocelyn Penny. "Memory and the Roman Orator." Pages 195–206 in *A Companion to Roman Rhetoric.* Edited by William Dominik and Jon Hall. Oxford: Blackwell, 2007.

Small, *Wax Tablets.* Small, Jocelyn Penny. *Wax Tablets of the Mind: Cognitive Studies of Memory and Literacy in Classical Antiquity.* London: Routledge, 1997.

Smith, "A Divine Tragedy." Smith, Stephen H. "A Divine Tragedy: Some Observations on the Dramatic Structure of Mark's Gospel." *NovT* 37 (1995): 209–31.
Smith, "Comparison." Smith, Morton. "A Comparison of Early Christian and Early Rabbinic Tradition." *JBL* 82 (2, 1963): 169–76.
Smith, "Gospels." Smith, D. Moody. "When Did the Gospels Become Scripture?" *JBL* 119 (1, 2000): 3–20.
Smith, *Parallels.* Smith, Morton. *Tannaitic Parallels to the Gospels.* Philadelphia: Society of Biblical Literature, 1951.
Smith, "Prolegomena." Smith, Morton. "Prolegomena to a Discussion of Aretalogies, Divine Men, the Gospels and Jesus." *JBL* 90 (1971): 174–99.
Smith and Cornell, "L. Cornelius Balbus." Smith, C. J. and T. J. Cornell. "L. Cornelius Balbus." Pages 383-84 in *The Fragments of the Roman Historians: Introduction.* Edited by T. J. Cornell. Vol. 1 of *The Fragments of the Roman Historians.* Edited by T. J. Cornell. Oxford: Oxford University Press, 2013.
Soares Prabhu, *Quotations.* Soares Prabhu, George M. *The Formula Quotations in the Infancy Narrative of Matthew: An Enquiry into the Tradition History of Mt 1–2.* Rome: Biblical Institute Press, 1976.
Sorabji, *Emotion.* Sorabji, Richard. *Emotion and Peace of Mind: From Stoic Agitation to Christian Temptation.* The Gifford Lectures. New York: Oxford University Press, 2000.
Sorek, *Ancient Historians.* Sorek, Susan. *Ancient Historians: A Student Handbook.* New York: Continuum, 2012.
Squires, "Plan." Squires, John T. "The Plan of God." Pages 19–39 in *Witness to the Gospel: The Theology of Acts.* Edited by I. Howard Marshall and David Peterson. Grand Rapids: Eerdmans, 1998.
Stadter, "Biography and History." Stadter, Philip A. "Biography and History." Pages 528–40 in *A Companion to Greek and Roman Historiography.* Edited by John Marincola. Malden, MA: Wiley-Blackwell, 2011.
Stadter, "Compositional Technique." Stadter, Philip A. "Plutarch's Compositional Technique: The Anecdote Collections and the Parallel Lives." *GRBS* 54 (2014): 665–86.
Stadter, "Introduction." Stadter, Philip A. Introduction to *Roman Lives: A Selection of Eight Roman Lives,* by Plutarch. Translated by Robin Waterfield. Oxford: Oxford University Press, 1999.
Stadter, "Narrative." Stadter, Philip A. "Fictional Narrative in the Cyropaideia." *American Journal of Philology* 112 (1991): 461-91.
Stamps, "Children." Stamps, D. L. "Children in Late Antiquity." Pages 197–201 in *Dictionary of New Testament Background.* Edited by Craig A. Evans and Stanley E. Porter. Downers Grove, IL: InterVarsity Press, 2000.
Stanton, "Foreword." Stanton, Graham. Foreword to *What are the Gospels? A Comparison with Graeco-Roman Biography,* by Richard A. Burridge. 2nd ed. Grand Rapids: Eerdmans, 2004.

Stanton, *Gospels.* Stanton, Graham N. *The Gospels and Jesus.* Oxford Bible Series. Oxford: Oxford University Press, 1989.
Stanton, *Jesus.* Stanton, Graham N. *Jesus of Nazareth in New Testament Preaching.* SNTSMS 27. Cambridge: Cambridge University Press, 1974.
Stanton, *New People.* Stanton, Graham N. *A Gospel for a New People: Studies in Matthew.* Edinburgh: T & T Clark, 1990.
Stanton, *Preaching.* Stanton, Graham N. *Jesus of Nazareth in New Testament Preaching.* Cambridge: Cambridge University Press, 1974.
Stanton, *Truth?* Stanton, Graham N. *Gospel Truth? New Light on Jesus and the Gospels.* London: HarperCollins, 1995.
Stein, "'Criteria.'" Stein, Robert H. "The 'Criteria' for Authenticity." Pages 225–63 in vol. 1 of *Studies of History and Tradition in the Four Gospels.* Edited by R. T. France and David Wenham. 2 vols. Gospel Perspectives 1–2. Sheffield, U.K.: JSOT Press, 1980–81.
Stein, *Difficult Passages.* Stein, Robert H. *Difficult Passages in the Gospels.* Grand Rapids: Baker Academic, 1984.
Stein, *Mark.* Stein, Robert H. *Mark.* BECNT. Grand Rapids: Baker Academic, 2008.
Stein, *Synoptic Gospels.* Stein, Robert H. *Studying Synoptic Gospels: Origin and Interpretation.* Grand Rapids: Baker Academic, 2001.
Stem, "Lessons." Stem, Rex. "The Exemplary Lessons of Livy's Romulus." *TAPA* 137 (2007): 435–71.
Stem, *Political Biographies.* Stem, Stephen Rex. *The Political Biographies of Cornelius Nepos.* Ann Arbor: University of Michigan Press, 2012.
Sterling, "Appropriation." Sterling, Gregory E. "The Jewish Appropriation of Hellenistic Historiography." Pages 231–43 in *A Companion to Greek and Roman Historiography.* Edited by John Marincola. 2 vols. Oxford: Blackwell, 2007.
Sterling, *Historiography.* Sterling, Gregory E. *Historiography and Self-Definition: Josephos, Luke-Acts, and Apologetic Historiography.* NovTSup 64. Leiden: Brill, 1992.
Sterling, *Sisters.* Sterling, Dorothy, ed. *We Are Your Sisters: Black Women in the Nineteenth Century.* New York: W. W. Norton, 1984.
Stern, *Authors.* Stern, Menahem, ed. *Greek and Latin Authors on Jews and Judaism.* 3 vols. Jerusalem: Israel Academy of Sciences and Humanities, 1974–84.
Stern, "Life of Josephus." Stern, Pnina. "Life of Josephus: The Autobiography of Flavius Josephus." *Journal for the Study of Judaism* 41 (1, 2010): 63-93.
Steyn, "Elemente." Steyn, Gert J. "Elements of the universe in Philo's *De Vita Mosis:* Cosmological theology or theological cosmology?" *In die Skriflig* 47 (n.2, Jul. 2013): 9 pages, online.
Stock, Gajsar, and Güntürkün, " Neuroscience of Memory." Stock, Ann-Kathrin, Hannah Gajsar, and Onur Güntürkün. "The Neuroscience of Memory." Pages 369-91 in *Memory in Ancient Rome and Early Christianity.* Edited by Karl Galinsky. Oxford: Oxford University Press, 2016.

Stowers, "Resemble Philosophy?" Stowers, Stanley K. "Does Pauline Christianity Resemble a Hellenistic Philosophy?" Pages 81–102 in *Paul beyond the Judaism/Hellenism Divide*. Edited by Troels Engberg-Pedersen. Louisville: Westminster John Knox, 2001.
Stuart, *Epochs*. Stuart, Duane Reed. *Epochs of Greek and Roman Biography*. Berkeley: University of California Press, 1928.
Stuhlmacher, "The Genre(s) of the Gospels." Stuhlmacher, Peter. "The Genre(s) of the Gospels: Response to P. L. Shuler." Pages 484–94 in *The Interrelations of the Gospels: A Symposium Led by M. -É Boismard, W. R. Farmer, F. Neirynck, Jerusalem 1984*. Edited by David L. Dungan. BETL 95. Leuven: Leuven University Press, 1990.
Talbert, *Mediterranean Milieu*. Talbert, Charles H. *Reading Luke-Acts in Its Mediterranean Milieu*. NovTSup 107. Leiden: Brill, 2003.
Talbert, "Response." Talbert, Charles H. "Oral and Independent or Literary and Interdependent? A Response to Albert B. Lord." Pages 93-102 in *The Relationships Among the Gospels: An Interdisciplinary Dialogue*. Ed. William O. Walker, Jr. San Antonio: Trinity University Press, 1978.
Talbert, "Review." Talbert, Charles H. Review of Richard A. Burridge, *What Are the Gospels? JBL* 112 (4, 1993): 714–15.
Talbert, *What is a Gospel?* Talbert, Charles H. *What is a Gospel? The Genre of the Canonical Gospels*. London: SPCK, 1977.
Tarn, *Alexander*. Tarn, W. W. *Alexander the Great*, Vol. 1. Cambridge: Cambridge University Press, 1948.
Taylor, "Quest." Taylor, Nicholas H. "Paul and the Historical Jesus Quest." *Neotestamentica* 37 (1, 2003): 105-26.
Termini, "Part." Termini, Cristina. "The Historical Part of the Pentateuch According to Philo of Alexandria: Biography, Genealogy, and the Philosophical Meaning of the Patriarchal Lives." Pages 265-95 in *History and Identity: How Israel's Later Authors Viewed Its Earlier History*. Edited by Núria Calduch-Benages and Jan Liesen. Deuterocanonical and cognate literature yearbook, 2006. Berlin; New York: Walter de Gruyter, 2006.
Theissen, *Gospels*. Theissen, Gerd. *The Gospels in Context: Social and Political History in the Synoptic Tradition*. Translated by Linda M. Maloney. Minneapolis: Fortress, 1991.
Theissen and Merz, *Historical Jesus*. Theissen, Gerd and Annette Merz. *The Historical Jesus: A Comprehensive Guide*. Minneapolis: Fortress Press, 1998.
Thomas, "Psychoanalytic." Thomas, K. R. "A Psychoanalytic study of Alexander the Great." *Psychoanalysis Review* 82 (1995): 859-901.
Thomas, "Writing." Thomas, Rosalind. "Writing, Reading, Public and Private "Literacies": Functional Literacy and Democratic Literacy in Greece." Pages 13-45 in *Ancient Literacies: The Culture of Reading in Greece and Rome*. Edited by William A. Johnson and Holt N. Parker. New York: Oxford University Press, 2009.
Thorburn, "Tiberius." Thorburn, John E. "Suetonius' Tiberius: A Proxemic Approach." *Classical Philology* 103 (4, 2008): 435-48.

Tilling, *Christology*. Tilling, Chris. *Paul's Divine Christology*. Tübingen: Mohr Siebeck, 2012. Repr., Grand Rapids: Eerdmans, 2015

Titchener, "Cornelius Nepos." Titchener, Frances. "Cornelius Nepos and the Biographical Tradition." *GR* 50 (2003): 85–99.

Tolbert, *Sowing the Gospel*. Tolbert, Mary Ann. *Sowing the Gospel: Mark's World in Literary-Historical Perspective*. Minneapolis: Fortress, 1989.

Tomkins, *Wilberforce*. Tomkins, Stephen. *William Wilberforce: A Biography*. Grand Rapids and Cambridge: Eerdmans, 2007.

Touati, *Literacy*. Touati, Samia. *Literacy, Information, and Development in Morocco during the 1990s*. Lanham, MD: University Press of America, 2012.

Townend, "Date of Composition." Townend, Gavin B. "The Date of Composition of Suetonius' *Caesares*." *ClQ* 9.2 (1959): 285-293.

Townend and Spawforth, "Cornelius Nepos." Townend, Gavin B. and Antony J. S. Spawforth. "Cornelius Nepos." *OCD⁴* 380.

Tucker, *Knowledge*. Tucker, Aviezer. *Our Knowledge of the Past: A Philosophy of Historiography*. Cambridge: Cambridge University Press, 2004.

Tuckett, "Gospel of Thomas." Tuckett, Christopher M. "The Gospel of Thomas: Evidence for Jesus?" *Nederlands Theologisch Tijdschrift* 52 (1, 1998): 17-32.

Tuckett, *Nag Hammadi*. Tuckett, Christopher M. *Nag Hammadi and the Gospel Tradition: Synoptic Tradition in the Nag Hammadi Library*. Ed. John Riches. Edinburgh: T. & T. Clark, 1986.

Tuckett, "Review." Tuckett, C. M. Review of *What Are the Gospels? A Comparison with Graeco-Roman Biography* (1992), by Richard A. Burridge. *Theology* 96 (1993): 74-75.

Tuckett, "Sources." Tuckett, Christopher M. "Sources and Methods." Pages 121–37 in *The Cambridge Companion to Jesus*. Edited by Markus Bockmuehl. Cambridge: Cambridge University Press, 2001.

Tuckett, "Thomas." Tuckett, Christopher M. "Thomas and the Synoptics." *NovT* 30 (2, 1988): 132-57.

Turner, *Matthew*. Turner, David L. *Matthew*. BECNT. Grand Rapids: Baker Academic, 2008.

Van der Kooij, "Death of Josiah." Van der Kooij, Arie. "The Death of Josiah according to 1 Esdras." *Textus* 19 (1998): 97–109.

Van Seters, *Historiography*. Van Seters, John. *In Search of History: Historiography in the Ancient World and the Origins of Biblical History*. Winona Lake, IN: Eisenbrauns, 1997.

Vansina, "Afterthoughts." Vansina, Jan. "Afterthoughts on the Historiography of Oral Tradition." Pages 105–10 in *African Historiographies: What History for Which Africa?* Edited by Bogumil Jewsiewicki and David Newbury. SSAMD 12. Beverly Hills, Calif.: Sage, 1986.

Van Veldhuizen, "Moses." Van Veldhuizen, Milo. "Moses: A Model of Hellenistic Philanthropia." *RefR* 38 (3, 1985): 215–24.

Vermes, *Jesus the Jew*. Vermes, Geza. *Jesus the Jew: A Historian's Reading of the Gospels*. Philadelphia: Fortress, 1973.
Vermes, *World*. Vermes, Geza. *Jesus and the World of Judaism*. London: SCM, 1983. Philadelphia: Fortress, 1984.
Votaw, "Contemporary Biographies." Votaw, Clyde Weber. "The Gospels and Contemporary Biographies." *AmJT* 19 (1915): 45–73.
Wade-Gery, "Thucydides." Wade-Gery, Henry Theodore. "Thucydides." *OCD*^{3} 1516–19.
Wagner, *Literacy*. Wagner, Daniel A. *Literacy, Culture and Development: Becoming Literate in Morocco*. Cambridge: Cambridge University Press, 1993.
Wagner and Lotfi, "Learning." Wagner, Daniel A., and Abdelhamid Lotfi. "Learning to Read by 'Rote.'" *International Journal of the Sociology of Language* 42 (1983): 111–21.
Walbank, "Fortune." Walbank, Frank W. "Fortune (*tychē*) in Polybius." Pages 349–55 in *A Companion to Greek and Roman Historiography*. Edited by John Marincola. 2 vols. Oxford: Blackwell, 2007.
Walde, "Mnemonics." Walde, Christine. "Mnemonics." Pages 96-97 in vol. 9 of *Brill's New Pauly: Encyclopaedia of the Ancient World*. Ed. Hubert Cancik and Helmuth Schneider. Leiden, Boston: Brill, 2006.
Walde, "Mnemosyne." Walde, Christine. "Mnemosyne." *BrillPauly* 9:97-98.
Wallace, *Christianity*. Wallace, J. Warner. *Cold-Case Christianity: A Homicide Detective Investigates the Claims of the Gospels*. Foreword by Lee Strobel. Colorado Springs: David C. Cook, 2013.
Walton, "Impact." Walton, Steve. "What Are the Gospels? Richard Burridge's Impact on Scholarly Understanding of the Genre of the Gospels." *Currents in Biblical Research* 14 (1, 2015): 81-93.
Walton, "Rhetorical Criticism." Walton, Steve. "Rhetorical Criticism: An Introduction." *Themelios* 21 (1996): 4-9.
Wandrey, "Literature: Jewish-Hellenistic." Wandrey, Irina. "Literature: Jewish-Hellenistic." *BrillPauly* 7:694–99.
Wardman, "Plutarch's Methods." Wardman, Alan E. "Plutarch's Methods in the Lives." *ClQ* 21 (1971): 254–61.
Watson, "Education." Watson, Duane F. "Education: Jewish and Greco-Roman." Pages 308–13 in *Dictionary of New Testament Background*. Edited by Craig A. Evans and Stanley E. Porter. Downers Grove, IL: InterVarsity Press, 2000.
Weeden, "Theory." Weeden, Theodore J. "Kenneth Bailey's Theory of Oral Tradition: A Theory Contested by Its Evidence." *JSHJ* 7 (1, 2009): 3-43.
Wellek and Warren, *Theory of Literature*. Wellek, René, and Austin Warren. *Theory of Literature*. New York: Harcourt, 1949.
Wenham, *Rediscovery*. Wenham, David. *The Rediscovery of Jesus' Eschatological Discourse*. Gospel Perspectives 4. Sheffield, U.K.: JSOT Press, 1984.

Wenham, "Story." Wenham, David. "The Story of Jesus Known to Paul." Pages 297–311 in *Jesus of Nazareth, Lord and Christ: Essays on the Historical Jesus and New Testament Christology*. Edited by Joel B. Green and Max Turner. Grand Rapids: Eerdmans; Carlisle, U.K.: Paternoster, 1994.

Werner, "Studies." Werner, Shirley. "Literacy Studies in Classics: The Last Twenty Years," Pages 333-82 in *Ancient Literacies: The Culture of Reading in Greece and Rome*. Edited by William A. Johnson and Holt N. Parker. New York: Oxford University Press, 2009.

West, Martin Litchfield. "Rhapsodes." West, Martin Litchfield. "Rhapsodes." *OCD³* 1311–12.

Wheaton, "The Festival." Wheaton, Gerry. "The Festival of Hanukkah in 2 Maccabees: Its Meaning and Function," *CBQ* 74 (2012): 247-62.

Whitmarsh, "Lucian of Samosata." Whitmarsh, Tim. "Lucian of Samosata." *OEAGR* 4:288-291.

Whittaker, "Introduction." Whittaker, C. R. Introduction. Pages ix–lxxxvii in vol. 1 of Herodian, *History*. Translated by C. R. Whittaker. 2 vols. LCL. Cambridge, Mass.: Harvard University Press, 1969.

Wiersma, "Novel." Wiersma, S. "The Ancient Greek Novel and Its Heroines: A Female Paradox." *Mnemosyne* 43 (1–2, 1990): 109–23.

Wigger, *Saint*. Wigger, John. *American Saint: Francis Asbury and the Methodists*. Oxford: Oxford University Press, 2009.

Wilken, "Christians." Wilken, Robert L. "The Christians as the Romans (and Greeks) Saw Them." Pages 100–125 in *The Shaping of Christianity in the Second and Third Centuries*. Vol. 1 of *Jewish and Christian Self-Definition*. Edited by E. P. Sanders. Philadelphia: Fortress, 1980.

Wilken, "Collegia." Wilken, Robert. "Collegia, Philosophical Schools, and Theology." Pages 268–91 in *The Catacombs and the Colosseum: The Roman Empire as the Setting of Primitive Christianity*. Edited by Stephen Benko and John J. O'Rourke. Valley Forge, Pa.: Judson, 1971.

Wilken, "Interpretation." Wilken, Robert. "Toward a Social Interpretation of Early Christian Apologetics." *CH* 39 (4, 1970): 437–58.

Wilkins, *Discipleship*. Wilkins, Michael J. *Discipleship in the Ancient World and Matthew's Gospel*. 2nd ed. Grand Rapids: Baker, 1995. First ed.: Leiden: Brill, 1988.

Williams, "1 Maccabees." Williams, David S. "Recent Research in 1 Maccabees," *CR:BS* 9 (2001): 169-84.

Williams, "2 Maccabees." Williams, David S. "Recent Research In 2 Maccabees," *CBR* 2 (2003): 69-83.

Williams, "Germanicus." Williams, Kathryn F. "Tacitus' Germanicus and the Principate." *Latomus* 68 (1, 2009): 117–30.

Williamson, *Chronicles*. Williamson, H. G. M. *1 and 2 Chronicles*. NCBC. Grand Rapids: Eerdmans; London: Marshall, Morgan & Scott, 1982.

Wills, "Aesop Tradition." Wills, Lawrence M. "The Aesop Tradition." Pages 222–37 in *The Historical Jesus in Context*. Edited by Amy-Jill Levine, Dale C. Allison Jr., and John Dominic Crossan. PrRR. Princeton: Princeton University Press, 2006.

Winter, "Burden of Proof." Winter, Dagmar. "The Burden of Proof in Jesus Research." Pages 1:843-51 in *Handbook for the Study of the Historical Jesus*. 4 vols. Edited by Tom Holmén and Stanley E. Porter. Leiden: Brill, 2011.

Winterbottom, "*Recitatio*." Winterbottom, Michael. "*Recitatio*." *OCD³* 1295–96.

Wintermute, "Introduction." Wintermute, Orval S. Introduction to "Jubilees." *OTP* 2:35–50.

Wise, "Introduction to 4Q158." Wise, Michael O. Introduction to 4Q158. *DSSNT* 199–200.

Witherington, *Acts*. Witherington, Ben, III. *The Acts of the Apostles: A Socio-rhetorical Commentary*. Grand Rapids: Eerdmans, 1998.

Witherington, *Christology*. Witherington, Ben, III. *The Christology of Jesus*. Minneapolis: Augsburg Fortress, 1990.

Witherington, *Gospel of Mark*. Witherington, Ben, III. *The Gospel of Mark: A Socio-Rhetorical Commentary*. Grand Rapids, MI: Eerdsman, 2001.

Witherington, *Sage*. Witherington, Ben, III. *Jesus the Sage: The Pilgrimage of Wisdom*. Minneapolis: Fortress, 1994.

Wojciechowski, "Tradition." Wojciechowski, Michael. "Aesopic Tradition in the New Testament." *JGRCJ* 5 (2008): 99-109.

Woodman, *Rhetoric*. Woodman, A. J. *Rhetoric in Classical Historiography: Four Studies*. London: Croom Helm, 1988.

Woodman, "Tacitus." Woodman, A. J. "Tacitus." *OEAGR* 6:419-23.

Woolf, "Literacy." Woolf, Greg. "Literacy or Literacies in Rome?" Pages 46-68 in *Ancient Literacies: The Culture of Reading in Greece and Rome*. Edited by William A. Johnson and Holt N. Parker. New York: Oxford University Press, 2009.

Worthington, *Alexander*. Worthington, Ian. *Alexander the Great: A Reader*. New York: Routledge, 2012.

Worthington, "How 'Great'?" Worthington, Ian. "How 'Great' Was Alexander?" *Ancient History Bulletin* 13 (1999): 39-55.

Wright, *Faithfulness*. Wright, N. T. *Paul and the Faithfulness of God*. Vol. 4 of Christian Origins and the Question of God. Book 2 (parts 3 and 4). Minneapolis: Fortress, 2013.

Wright, *How God*. Wright, N.T. *How God Became King: Getting to the Heart of the Gospels*. London: SPCK, 2012.

Wright, "Midrash." Wright, Addison G. "The Literary Genre Midrash." *CBQ* 28 (2, 1966): 105–38; (4, 1966): 417–57.

Wright, *People*. Wright, N. T. *The New Testament and the People of God*. Vol. 1 of Christian Origins and the Question of God. Minneapolis: Fortress; London: SPCK, 1992.

Xenophontos, "Comedy." Xenophontos, Sophia A. "Comedy in Plutarch's Parallel Lives." *GRBS* 52 (4, 2012): 603-31.

Yamamori and Chan, *Witnesses.* Yamamori, Tetsunao, and Kim-kwong Chan. *Witnesses to Power: Stories of God's Quiet Work in a Changing China.* Waynesboro, Ga., and Carlisle, U.K.: Paternoster, 2000.

Yamauchi, "Historic Homer." Yamauchi, Edwin M. "Historic Homer: Did It Happen?" *BAR* 33 (2, 2007): 28–37, 76.

Ytterbrink, *Biography.* Ytterbrink, Maria. *The Third Gospel for the First Time: Luke within the Context of Ancient Biography.* Lund, Swed.: Lund University—Centrum för teologi och religionsvetenskap, 2004.

Ytterbrink, *The Third Gospel.* Ytterbrink, Maria. *The Third Gospel for the First Time: Luke within the Context of Ancient Biography.* Lund: Lund University—Centrum för teologi och religionsvetenskap, 2004.

Zadorojnyi, "Ethico-Politics." Zadorojnyi, Alexei V. "The Ethico-Politics of Writing in Plutarch's Life of Dion." *Journal of Hellenic Studies* 131 (2011): 147-63.

Zambrini, "Historians." Zambrini, Andrea. "The Historians of Alexander the Great." Pages 210–20 in *A Companion to Greek and Roman Historiography.* Edited by John Marincola. 2 vols. Oxford: Blackwell, 2007.

Zlotnick, "Memory." Zlotnick, Dov. "Memory and the Integrity of the Oral Tradition." *JANESCU* 16-17 (1984-1985): 229-41.

Zsengellér, "Temple Propaganda." Zsengellér, József. "Maccabees and Temple Propaganda." Pages 181-95 in *The Books of the Maccabees: History, Theology, Ideology.* Edited by Géza G. Xeravits and József Zsengellér. JSJsup 118. Leiden: Brill, 2007.

Zubaida, *Law.* Zubaida, Sami. *Law and Power in the Islamic World.* New York: I. B. Tauris, 2005.

Zuntz, "Heide." Zuntz, Günther. "Eine Heide las da Markusevangelium." Pages 205-22 in *Markus-Philologie.* Edited by Hubert Cancik. WUNT 33. Tübingen: Mohr, 1984.

Zwiep, "Orality." Zwiep, Arie. "Orality and Memory in the Story of Jairus and the Haemorrhaging Woman (Mark 5:21-43 parr.): an Attempt (Not) to Go beyond What is Written." Paper presented in the "Memory, Narrative, and Christology in the Synoptic Gospels" Seminar at the Annual Meeting of the Society for New Testament Studies. Montreal, Canada, 4 August 2016.

Index of Modern Authors

Abel, F. M., 312n33
Abrahams, I., 352n189
Abramowski, Luise, 334n36
Achtemeier, Paul J., 34n251
Adams, Sean A., 66n51
Addis, Donna Rose, 332n16
Aguilar, Mario I., 315n40
Aitken, Ellen Bradshaw, 41n290
Alexander, Loveday C. A., 26n187, 56n50, 338n54, 339n61, 340n71, 340nn73-74, 340n82, 342n97, 342n99
Alexander, Philip S., 70nn69-70
Alfred, Chris, 37, 77
Allison, Dale C., 6n29, 7n33, 15n83, 35n259, 333n24, 333n26, 333n28, 334, 334nn30-32, 334n35, 348n156, 350n168
Anderson, R. Dean, Jr., 11n58, 338n56
Argyle, A. W., 256n87
Arndt, W. F., 339n63
Aron-Schnapper, Dominique, 344n123
Ash, Rhiannon, 29n215, 36n266, 165n56
Assman, Jan, 3n7
Atkinson, J. E., 207n41
Attridge, Harold W., 32n233
Aune, David E., 3n10, 13n75, 13n76, 16, 16n91, 19n121, 20n129, 20n132, 21n134, 22n151, 26n187, 29n211, 30n222, 31n227, 32n234, 35n259, 42n299, 47n2, 60n11, 61n13,
62n19, 66n51, 68n59, 71n73, 145n12, 148n22, 170, 170n78, 202n7, 301n4, 332n19, 336n41, 338n55, 342n98, 344n117, 349n158
Badian, Ernst, 169nn72-73, 201n2, 247n50, 248n51
Bailey, Kenneth Ewing, 339n61, 347n145, 349n158
Balch, David L., 5, 60n5
Baldwin, Barry, 95n56
Balsdon, John P.V.D., 252n75
Bar-Kochva, Bezalel, 303n11, 309n23
Barr, David L., 5n23
Bauckham, Richard, 5n18, 27n193, 33n241, 35n259, 41n295, 53, 53nn30-31, 54n32, 65, 65nn41-42, 66n43, 222n18, 261n1, 317n47, 332n14, 332n16, 333, 333n24, 333nn26-28, 334, 334nn29-30, 334n30, 334n32, 348n153, 350n168
Bauer, David R., 59n1
Bauer, Walter, 339n63
Bauernfeind, Otto, 28n202
Baum, Armin D., 31n228
Baynham, E. J., 17n107, 26n180, 203n9
Bazin, Jean, 345n131
Beard, Mary, 347n143
Beavis, Mary Ann, 173nn2-3
Becking, Bob, 317, 317n48
Begg, Christopher T., 32n231, 32n232, 39n279, 40n281, 40n284

Bellemore, Jane, 84, 84nn24-26
Beneker, Jeffrey, 9n50, 42n304, 44n315, 62n16, 162n44
Benoit, Pierre, 331n8
Ben Zeev, Miriam Pucci, 20n133
Berchmann, R. M., 39n275
Bergren, Theodore A., 11n59
Berlin, Andrea M., 267nn44-45
Bernal, Martin, 41n296
Bernheim, Ernst, 61, 61n15
Berthelot, Katell, 43n312, 303n12
Bilde, Per, 266, 266n38, 266nn40-42, 267n52, 268n53, 271, 271nn71-72
Bilezikian, Gilbert G., 60n8
Black, C. Clifton, 11n58
Black, Matthew, 334n36
Blass, F., 334n36
Bloch, René, 40n280
Blomberg, Craig L., 42n301, 60n11, 68n55
Bloomer, W. Martin, 338n49
Blyth, Dougal, 341n83
Bock, Darrell L., 42n301
Borgen, Peder, 11n59
Bosch-Veciana, A., 342n105
Bosworth, A. B., 26n180, 34n254, 202n5, 203nn14-15, 204n22, 205n27, 206n35, 206n37, 207n38, 213, 213n56
Bovon, François, 56, 56n48
Bowersock, G. W., 28n205, 79n6, 218
Bowie, Ewen Lyall, 34n248

Index of Modern Authors

Bowman, John, 39n277
Boyd, Gregory A., 60n11, 64n36, 68n55, 164n53, 263, 263nn10-11, 332n11, 343n113, 344n122, 345n132, 346nn133-134, 350n168, 351n181, 353n197
Boyd-Taylor, Cameron, 36n265
Bradley, Keith R., 146n18
Bravo, Benedetto, 5n18, 145n11
Briscoe, John, 244n35, 244nn38-40, 245n45, 249n60
Brown, Truesdell S., 14n80, 17n107, 23n155, 25n167, 26n187
Brown, Raymond E., 202n6, 263, 263n14
Brownson, Carleton L., 17n107, 240n26
Bruce, F. F., 334n36
Brunt, P. A., 206n36, 210n50
Bryan, Christopher, 173n5
Bultmann, Rudolf, 48, 48nn4-8, 55, 60n10, 62n18, 63-65
Bünker, Michael, 28n202
Burgersdijk, D.W.P., 190, 191n18, 193n28
Burnette-Bletsch, Rhonda, 41n292
Burr, Kevin, 238n18
Burridge, Richard A., 3n10, 4, 4n12, 5n20, 5n23, 5n24, 9n47, 9n50, 12n67, 13n75, 15n90, 22n151, 32n238, 36, 36n266, 47-57 passim, 59, 59nn2-3, 60n3, 61n13, 62n21, 65, 65nn37-40, 66, 66n44, 66n46, 66n49, 67, 67n52, 67n54, 68nn56-57, 70, 70nn67-69, 70n71, 103, 103n1, 103n2, 104n4, 145n11, 170n78, 202n7, 218n8, 226n24, 235, 235nn1-3, 236, 236n6,

244n41, 245n47, 261, 261n1, 263, 263nn12-13, 301n4, 319n2, 323n2, 350n173
Buszard, Bradley, 37n269, 167n65
Byrskog, Samuel, 5n18, 8nn40-41, 15n86, 19n117, 24n159, 27n189, 27n191, 68n61, 332n11, 336n41, 337nn47-48, 344n117, 344n119, 344n122, 345n132, 346n138
Cadoux, Theodore J., 247n50, 248n51, 248n54
Caird, G. B., 8n43, 9n43
Cancik, Hubert, 5n18
Canevet, Mariette, 32n236, 40n281
Carey, Holly J., 2n4, 41, 43, 319, 321n13
Carr, David M., 338n54
Carroll, Robert P., 302n10
Cartledge, Paul Anthony, 240n27
Cary, Earnest, 72, 252n74
Casey, Maurice, 51
Champion, Craige B., 11n63
Chan, Kim-kwong, 346n139
Chaplin, Jane D., 9n51
Charlesworth, James H., 35n259, 347n145, 352n193
Cheon, Samuel, 43n308
Chilver, Guy E. F., 248n53
Chiu, Angeline, 33n243
Chrétien, Jean-Pierre, 344n124
Christian, Timothy, 37, 103
Clark, T., 342n104
Clifford, Hywel, 39n276
Cohen, Shaye J. D., 28n202, 32n233, 42n301, 164n52, 264nn22-24, 265nn25-29, 266, 266n32, 266nn34-37, 268n56, 269, 269n58, 269n61, 271n70, 272n76, 273n80

Collins, Adela Yarbro, 55, 55n45, 60n5, 66, 66n50, 173n4
Conybeare, F. C., 34n249
Conzelmann, Hans, 49, 49n11
Cook, Brad L., 21n142
Copeland, Rita, 30n219
Cornell, T. J., 244n39, 245nn45-46, 248n55
Cotter, Wendy J., 352n191
Croke, Brian, 18n113
Cross, Anthony R., 3n10
Crossan, John Dominic, 3n10, 12n64, 143n6
Culpepper, R. Alan, 3n7, 340nn71-72, 340n83, 344n116
Cunningham, Scott, 42n301
Curchin, Leonard A., 347n143
Damgaard, Finn, 39n275
Damon, Cynthia, 9n43, 22n149
Dancy, J. C., 312n34, 316n41
Danker, Frederick W., 339n63
Darko, Daniel K., 12n64
Davies, W. D., 331n8, 349n161
Debrunner, A., 334n36
DeConick, April D., 35n259, 333n20, 333n25, 349n160
Demoen, Kristoffel, 34n248
Derrenbacker, Robert A., 72n74
DeSilva, David A., 237nn10-11
Dewald, Carolyn, 11n58, 145n14
De Wet, Chris L., 310n26, 312n30
Dewey, Joanna, 347n143
Dibelius, Martin, 23n158, 341n93
Dihle, Albrecht, 9n47, 31n227
Dillon, John M., 3n9
Dobbeler, Stephanie von, 11n59

Dorey, T. A., 104
Downing, F. Gerald, 22n151, 66n48, 67, 67nn53-54, 71n73, 72n79
Draper, Jonathan, 350n169
Droge, A. J., 36n261
Droysen, G., 201n2
Drummond, Andrew, 244n35, 244nn38-40, 245n45, 249n60
Drury, John, 29n209, 30n220, 166n62
Duff, Timothy E., 30n216, 62n21
Dungan, David L., 351n181
Dunn, James D. G., 8, 9n44, 60n3, 71n72, 302, 302n5, 318n53, 345n132, 346n138, 348nn151-52, 349nn157-58, 349n160
Eddy, Paul Rhodes, 60n11, 64n36, 68n55, 164n53, 263, 263nn10-11, 332n11, 343n113, 344n122, 345n132, 346nn133-134, 350n168, 351n181, 353n197
Edwards, Catherine, 191, 191n20
Edwards, James R., 55, 55n42
Egelhaaf-Gaiser, Ulrike, 29n208
Ehrensperger, Kathy, 338n54
Ehrman, Bart D., 4n16, 53, 53nn27-28, 348n150
Eickelman, Dale F., 345n127
Eisman, M. M., 32n233
Elliott, Matthew, 334n30
Endres, John C., 33n240
Engels, Donald W., 256n87
England, Frank Ernest, 60n8
Epp, Eldon Jay, 60n11
Eshleman, Kendra, 12n64
Evans, Craig A., 35n259, 258n96, 337n44, 347n143
Évrard, Étienne, 21n137, 37n268
Fantuzzi, Marco, 33n243

Farrell, Joseph, 337n47
Farrington, Scott T., 33n242
Feldman, Louis H., 30n217, 32n232, 32n239, 39nn275-78, 40nn281-82, 40n285, 43n308, 43nn310-12, 214n59, 277, 277nn1-2, 277n4, 281n10, 281n12, 287n41, 289n47, 291n51
Ferguson, Everett, 39n275
Filson, Floyd V., 334n36
Finkelberg, Margalit, 346n141
Fischer, David Hackett, 237n8
Fisk, Bruce N., 31n227, 43n311
Fitzgerald, John, 60n3
Flaig, Egon, 250n65, 250n67, 250n70
Fornara, C. W., 10nn54-55, 11n63, 13n75, 13n78, 16n94, 19n121, 19n122, 21n134, 21n135, 27n195, 29nn211-12, 29n214, 165n54, 165n56, 165n60
Forsythe, Gary, 23n153, 165n60
Fox, Robin Lane, 213, 213n56
France, R. T., 54, 54n35, 55, 55n40
Fredricksmeyer, E. A., 201n2
Frenkel, Diana, 303n13
Freyne, Sean, 4n15, 346n137
Frickenschmidt, Dirk, 3n10, 60n3, 202n7
Frye, Roland Mushat, 350n171
Funk, Robert W., 334n36
Gafni, Isaiah M., 164n52
Gager, John G., 342n105
Gaines, Robert N., 337n48
Gajsar, Hannah, 331n9, 332n14, 333n28, 334n29, 348n155
Galinsky, Karl, 3n7, 9n51, 16n92, 18n114, 332n12,

333n27, 334n28, 337n48, 346n135
Gamble, Harry, 344n117
Gathercole, Simon J., 353n195
Geiger, Joseph, 105, 105n9, 138n20
Geljon, Albert C., 39n275
Gempf, Conrad, 165n60, 343n107, 343n109
Georgiadou, Aristoula, 62n16
Gera, Dov, 40n288
Gerhardsson, Birger, 341nn93-95, 343n112, 349n162
Gingrich, F. W., 339n63
Goh, Benson, 38, 173
Goldhill, Simon, 344n117
Goldingay, John, 47
Gondola, Charles Didier, 351n178
Gooch, Peter, 351n181
Goodacre, Mark, 331n5
Goodenough, Erwin R., 39n275
Goodman, Martin, 341n91
Goody, Jack, 344n121
Görgemanns, Herwig, 61n13, 162n45
Goshen-Gottstein, Alon, 70n69
Gossage, A. J., 78n1, 87, 87n33, 88, 88n36, 92n49
Goulder, M. D., 42n301, 60n7, 349n162
Gowing, Alain M., 9n51
Grabbe, Lester L., 301n2, 302n7, 316n44
Graham, William Albert, 345n127
Granata, Giovanna, 39n275
Grant, Michael, 261n2
Graves, Robert, 274n83
Gray, Richard, 351n176
Gray, Vivenne, 239n20, 239n22, 240n29
Gregory, Andrew, 71n73
Griffin, Miriam T., 192n26, 196, 197, 197n46
Gulick, Anna, 344-45n126

Gundry, Robert H., 23n158, 27n197, 42n301
Güntürkün, Onur, 331n9, 332n14, 333n28, 334n29, 348n155
Gyselinck, Wannes, 34n248
Habinek, Thomas, 344n117
Hacham, Noah, 40n286
Hack, R. K., 62n16
Hadas, Moses, 10n56, 11n61, 16n92, 29n215, 60n4, 143n5, 147n21, 164n51
Hägg, Tomas, 2n5, 3n5, 3n8, 3n10, 5n21, 6n28, 9n47, 11n62, 14n79, 14n80, 15n82, 15n86, 15n88, 17nn103-105, 29n214, 30n218, 31n228, 33n244, 34nn245-48, 34nn254-55, 35nn256-57, 37, 37n270, 38nn271-73, 44n313, 143n9, 148n23, 162n44, 165n59, 167n65, 169nn72-73, 335n37, 350n173
Hagner, Donald A., 334n36, 342n100
Hamilton, J. R., 207n39, 213, 213n56
Hammond, N. G. L., 206n34, 207n38, 207n41, 212n52, 213, 213n57
Hanet, Daniele, 344n123
Hanson, William S., 17n104
Harmon, A. M., 214n61, 253nn76-77
Harms, Robert, 346n133
Harrington, Daniel J., 31n227
Hartman, Lars, 31n228
Harvey, John D., 336n42, 345n130, 346n140
Hays, Richard B., 353n195
Hazel, John, 226n29, 231n31
Head, Peter M., 347n143
Heath, Malcolm, 338n54
Hellholm, David, 64n36
Helms, Randel, 60n6

Hemer, Colin J., 23n153, 30n222, 238n18
Henderson, John Jordan, 38, 146n16, 261
Hendricks, William N., III, 203n11, 203n13, 208, 208n45
Hengel, Martin, 1, 1n2, 27n195, 60n3
Henige, David, 346n133
Hershbell, Jackson, 3n9
Heyer, C. J. den, 35n259
Hezser, Catherine, 347n143
Hicks, R. D., 240
Hidalgo, Esteban, 40, 40n285, 277
Hilbert, Benjamin D. H., 40n287, 315n39
Hill, David, 334n36, 351n180
Hock, Ronald F., 7n32, 254n80
Hoeree, Joris, 344n123
Höffken, Peter, 32n232
Hofmann, Heinz, 35n259
Holladay, Carl, 32n239
Hollander, William den, 12n64
Holmén, Tom, 352n193
Holmes, Michael, 7n31, 30n223, 331n10, 334n36, 348n153, 350n174
Hoogbergen, Wim, 344n123
Hooker, Morna D., 173n2
Horton, Robin, 344n124
Hose, Martin, 5n21, 14n80, 145n11
Houston, George W., 21n134
Howell, Martha, 238, 238n14, 238n17, 239n19, 247n48, 253
Hübenthal, Sandra, 330n3, 346n135
Huizinga, Johan, 301n1
Hunt, Rosalie Hall, 13n75
Hurtado, Larry W., 50, 50n18, 343n113, 353n195
Hutton, Maurice, 251n72
Iglesias, Esther, 346n133
Iverson, Kelly R., 332n11

Jackson, Bill, 27n192
Jackson, John, 214n60
Jacoby, Felix, 201n4, 204n20, 207n41
Janin, Hunt, 345n127
Jeffers, James S., 338n55
Jenkinson, Edna, 104, 104n6, 105
Jeremias, Joachim, 23n155, 334n36
Jervell, Jacob, 26n188
Johnson, Dennis, 345n127
Johnson, Luke Timothy, 36n265
Johnson, Sara, 40n286
Jones, C. P., 34n248, 40n288, 194, 194nn36-38, 254n79, 255, 255nn81-82, 255n84, 256nn85-87, 256nn90-91, 256nn90-91, 257n92
Jones, Horace Leonard, 206n33
Jost, I. M., 264-65
Judge, Edwin M., 9, 9n46, 10n52, 342n98
Kaesser, Christian, 5n24
Keane, Catherine, 5n24
Kee, Howard Clark, 3n10
Keener, Craig S., 1, 3n10, 5n19, 8n37, 15n84, 16n100, 18n109, 19n120, 21n136, 21n140, 22n151, 23n155, 24n163, 25n178, 26n184, 27n195, 29nn206-7, 30n218, 31n225, 31n227, 31n229, 32n232, 33n240, 34n250, 34n253, 38, 39n279, 42n301, 43n311, 44, 44n316, 54, 54n33, 54n36, 54n38, 55, 55n39, 59n1, 60n3, 60n11, 61n13, 67n54, 68, 68n58, 68n60, 69, 69nn62-64, 70n66, 72n75, 73n85, 106n15, 143, 143nn1-3, 147, 164n53, 168n66, 173-74, 173n1, 173n5, 174nn6-10, 190n17, 191, 191n19, 191n23, 192n24,

193, 193n27, 193nn29-32, 194nn33-34, 195, 195nn40-41, 196, 196nn42-45, 198, 198nn49-51, 199, 199nn53-54, 200nn55-56, 201n1, 202n7, 204nn17-18, 208n47, 215n63, 217, 217n1, 230, 262, 262nn6-8, 272n77, 301n4, 308n21, 317n49, 327, 329, 329n1, 330n3, 331n10, 332n18, 334n32, 335n38, 336n39, 338n59, 341n84, 343n111, 347nn147-148, 348n153, 348n156, 349n159, 351n179, 351n181, 352n183, 352n192, 353nn194-96, 353n198
Keener, Médine Moussounga, 164n53, 335n38, 344, 344n125, 347n148
Keith, Chris, 344n118
Kelber, Werner H., 341-42n95
Kelhoffer, James A., 10n51
Kennedy, George A., 3n9, 3n10, 5, 5n19, 5n23, 18n113, 28n204, 61n13, 68n59, 143n4, 143n8, 145nn10-11, 147n21, 169n74, 202n7, 334n36, 335n37, 337n46, 337n48, 340n75, 343nn109-10, 345n129, 349n160
Keyes, Clinton Walker, 205n31
Keylock, Leslie R., 35n259
Kierspel, Lars, 258n95
Kilburn, K., 18n115, 26n183
Kirk, Alan, 332n15, 347n143, 348n155
Klauck, Hans-Josef, 34n248, 34n251, 44n316
Kloppenborg, John S., 332n15-17, 333n20, 333nn25-26, 336n40, 344nn120-121, 348n155, 349n158, 349n160

Koester, Helmut, 161n43
Koskenniemi, Erkki, 342n104
Koutstaal, Wilma, 332n16
Kraft, Robert, 42n298
Krasser, Helmut, 13n75, 35n259
Krentz, Edgar, 237n11
Kümmel, Werner George, 22n151
Kurz, William S., 9n49
Kwon, Youngju, 37, 59
Ladouceur, David J., 28n202
Laistner, M. L. W., 2n5, 3n5, 3n9, 8n42, 9n44, 10n56, 11n58, 11n63, 14n81, 17n107, 21n139, 23n153, 23n155, 24n162, 143n5, 156n35, 335n37
Lalleman, Pieter J., 35n259
Lamour, Denis, 42n304
Lanfranchi, Pierluigi, 40n283
Lang, Manfred, 10n54
Laqueur, Richard, 265, 266n32
Lavery, Gerald B., 16n96
Lee, Soo-Kwang, 38, 201
Levene, D. S., 198n52
Levick, Barbara M., 252n75
Levine, Amy-Jill, 35n258
Lewis, Bernard, 345n129
Lewis, Naphtali, 347n143
Lichtenberger, Hermann, 302n6, 308n21, 317n50
Licona, Michael R., 2n4, 8n43, 43-44, 59n1, 71n72, 75nn93-94, 236, 237, 237n7, 243, 323, 323n1, 323n4
Liefeld, Walter Lewis, 341n87
Lincoln, Andrew T., 54, 54n34, 54n37
Lindemann, Andreas, 49, 49n11
Long, V. Phillips, 42n304
Lord, Albert B., 27n198, 345n129
Lotfi, Abdelhamid, 345n127
Lutz, Cora E., 343n109

Luz, Menahem, 28n202
Luz, Ulrich, 42n301, 55, 56n47
Lyons, George, 12n67
Mack, Burton L., 340n71
Maclean, Jennifer K. Berenson, 41n290
MacRae, George W., 60n11
Malherbe, Abraham J., 23n157, 39n275
Malina, Bruce J., 15n85
Manson, T. W., 334n36
Marchant, E. C., 79n6, 239n26, 240n26
Marcus, Joel, 55, 55nn43-44, 173n5, 202n6
Marguerat, Daniel, 10n54, 21n140
Marincola, John, 12n65, 18n113, 27n193, 29n215, 139, 139n21, 165n60
Martin, Ralph P., 49, 49n10
Martin, Ronald H., 17n104, 21n138, 146n18, 168n68, 250n70, 251n72
Mason, Steve, 12n64, 262nn4-5, 264n19, 265, 265nn30-31, 266, 266nn33-34, 267n43, 268, 268n56, 270n62, 271, 271nn73-75
Massey, Preston T., 7n34, 199n54
Mayer, Günter, 342n105
McGill, Scott, 148n22
McGing, Brian, 72n75, 73n84
McInerney, Jeremy, 9n51
McIver, Robert K., 333n24, 334nn32-34
McKnight, Scot, 39n275, 56, 56nn52-53, 57, 57nn54-55
McNamara, Martin, 352n185
Meeks, Wayne A., 39n276, 40n281, 342n98
Meier, John P., 35n258, 348n154
Meiser, Martin, 12n68

Meister, Klaus, 12n65, 13n72, 20n132, 26n181, 163n48, 336n41
Mellor, Ronald, 174n8, 197, 197n47, 226n25
Merkle, Stefan, 33n244
Merz, Annette, 258n96, 352n190
Michel, Otto, 28n202
Milikowsky, Chaim, 40n279
Millard, Alan, 347n143
Milnor, Kristina, 343n113
Moessner, David P., 7n31, 24n161, 30n223, 333n19, 350n174
Momigliano, Arnaldo, 11n63, 89n42
Mommsen, Theodor, 244n38
Moniot, Henri, 344n122, 344n124
Montanari, Franco, 342n106
Moore, Clifford H., 10n56, 250
Morgan, J. R., 36n262
Mosley, A. W., 28n203, 143n5
Mossman, Judith, 29n215, 30n219, 36n266, 165n56
Moule, C. F. D., 48, 49n9
Moussounga, Emmanuel, 164n53
Muntz, Charles E., 21n138, 37n269
Murphy, Frederick J., 41n297
Murphy, Roland E., 340n71
Musnick, Larry Jason, 105, 105n14, 115n18, 138n20
Musser, Joe, 345n127
Nesselrath, Heinz-Günther, 239n20, 239nn23-24, 240n28, 253n76
Neusner, Jacob, 31n226, 70nn69-70, 341n95, 352n185
Neyrey, Jerome H., 15n85
Nicolai, Roberto, 15n86
Niehoff, Maren R., 32n236, 43n308, 71n73
Nisula, Timo, 311n29

Noll, Mark A., 345n128, 345n130
Norlin, George, 79n6
Norman, Kenneth A., 332n16
Nystrom, Carolyn, 345n128, 345n130
O'Brien, John Maxwell, 201n2
Olbricht, Thomas H., 337n48, 338n52
Oldfather, C. H., 19n123, 208n46
O'Neil, E. N., 254n80
Overman, J. Andrew, 267nn44-45
Palmer, Darryl W., 13n75
Parker, Emily, 39n275
Parker, Victor, 303n14
Parsenios, George, 33n241
Payne, Philip Barton, 42n301
Pearson, Brook W. R., 53, 53nn25-26
Pearson, Lionel, 204-5n24, 205n26, 205nn28-29, 213, 213n56
Pelling, Christopher B. R., 15n82, 62, 62n17, 72n76, 72n78, 72n80, 73nn81-83, 74, 74n89, 74nn91-92, 75, 323, 323n4, 324n6
Penner, Todd, 11n62, 15n85, 16n91, 36n263, 40n286, 145n13
Pennington, Jonathan T., 4n15, 174n9
Perkins, Judith, 35n259
Perrin, Bernadotte, 78n3, 88n40, 89n43, 207n40, 210n51, 219, 241
Perrin, Nicholas, 35n259, 331n5
Perrin, Norman, 66n47
Pervo, Richard I., 143n8
Petersen, Norman R., 52, 52n22
Petit, Madeleine, 32n236
Piccione, Rosa Maria, 40n282
Pilch, John J., 41n295

Pitcher, L. V., 29n215, 62n21, 165n56
Pitts, Andrew W., 5, 5n22, 71n73, 145n11
Pizzuto-Pomaco, Julia, 345n126
Plümacher, Eckhard, 3n10, 13n75
Pokorny, Petr, 352n193
Porciani, Leone, 145n14
Porter, Stanley E., 35n259, 35n260, 53, 53nn25-26, 347n143, 352n193
Potter, T. W., 159n42
Powell, Mark Allan, 35n258, 263, 263n15
Pretzler, Maria, 20n127, 347n146
Prevenier, Walter, 238, 238n14, 238n17, 239n19, 247n48, 253
Price, Robert M., 351n175
Pryke, E. J., 329n2
Pryzwansky, Molly M., 2n5, 103n2, 104, 104nn5-6, 104n8, 105, 105nn10-12
Rackham, H., 23n156, 244n37
Rajak, Tessa, 32n233, 266, 266n39
Raphael, Freddy, 346n133
Rebenich, Stefan, 35n259, 36n265
Redman, Judith C. S., 331n9, 332nn12-13, 333n24, 333nn27-28, 334n30, 334n32, 345n129, 346n136, 348n149, 348n155
Reinmuth, Eckart, 11n59
Reiser, Marius, 31n228
Remus, Harold, 34n251, 39n277
Renan, Ernest, 48n3
Reuss, Édouard, 265, 265n28, 266
Reydams-Schils, G., 340n76
Reynolds, Adrian, 40, 301
Rhea, Brian, 352n193

Rhodes, P. J., 21n142, 24n159, 24n162, 25n168, 169n72
Riaud, J., 39n275
Richardson, Geoffrey W., 248n52
Richardson, Peter, 351n181
Riches, John, 61n12
Riesenfeld, Harald, 341n93
Riesner, Rainer, 342n101, 347n142
Riggsby, Andrew M., 12n67
Robbins, Vernon K., 3n10, 9n47, 334n36, 341n87, 350n173
Robbins, William Joseph, 39n275
Robeck, Cecil M., Jr., 26n185
Roberts, John, 239n20
Robertson, Stuart Dunbar, 40n284
Rodgers, Zuleika, 267n43, 273n79, 273n81
Rodriguez, Rafael, 344n121
Rolfe, J. C., 15n86, 27n196, 83, 83nn18-19, 83n21, 94n50, 100n77, 103n2, 104, 104nn3-4, 104n7, 131n19, 156n35, 207n42, 208n44, 212n54, 226, 226nn27-28, 241, 244n35, 244n36, 244n42, 245, 245nn43-44, 249, 252n75
Romm, James S., 203n15, 213, 213n58
Roncace, Mark, 32n232
Rondholz, Anke, 21n138, 162n44
Rook, John T., 41n296
Rothschild, Clare K., 15n86, 36n265, 145n14
Rowe, Galen O., 11n58
Rüpke, Jörg, 10, 10n53, 11n57, 30n222
Russell, Donald A. F. M., 62n19, 73, 73nn86-88, 74, 74nn90-91, 146n19, 205n32
Safrai, Shemuel, 343n112

Saïd, Suzanne, 18n109, 29n210
Salmon, Edward T., 159n42
Salvador, J., 265, 265n26
Samuel, Alan E., 213, 213n56
Sanders, E. P., 7n30, 30n222, 35n258, 333n21, 348n154, 350, 350n170
Satlow, Michael L., 342n105
Satterthwaite, Philip E., 338n52
Saulnier, Christiane, 12n64
Schacter, Daniel L., 332n16, 348n155
Schepens, Guido, 19nn121-122, 27n196
Schermann, Theodor, 41n295
Schleiermacher, Friedrich, 334n36
Schmeling, Gareth, 33n244
Schmeller, Thomas, 342n99
Schmidt, Karl Ludwig, 22n151, 48, 48n4, 55, 60, 60n9, 61-63
Schmitz, Barbara, 313n36
Schorch, Stefan, 316n46
Schürer, Emil, 265, 265n30, 266
Schwartz, Daniel R., 207n41, 302n6, 304n16, 311nn27-28, 316n46, 317n52
Schwemer, Anna Marie, 1n2
Scott, Ian W., 32n239
Seager, Robin J., 248nn53-54
Sedley, David, 340n74
Shackleton Bailey, D. R., 247, 247n49
Shanks, Hershel, 40n288
Sheeley, Steven M., 11n58
Sherwin-White, A. N., 244n38
Shuler, Philip L., 15n85, 32n238, 42n299, 44n316, 47, 47n1, 51, 59n3, 170n78, 202n7, 301n4, 350n166

Shutt, R. J. H., 267n47, 267n50
Simkovich, Malka Zeiger, 302n9, 312n32
Simpson, William Kelly, 3n5, 12n67
Sloan, David B., 331n5
Small, Jocelyn Penny, 72nn76-77, 337, 337n46, 337nn48-49, 350n167
Smith, C. J., 248n55
Smith, D. Moody, 31n230
Smith, Morton, 60n4, 341n94, 342n96, 352n186
Smith, Stephen H., 60n8
Soares Prabhu, George M., 42n301
Solages, B. de, 334n36
Sorabji, Richard, 337n49
Sorek, Susan, 239n20, 239n25
Spawforth, Antony J. S., 244n37, 244n39
Squires, John T., 13n73
Stadter, Philip A., 5, 5n20, 12n67, 34n246, 61n13, 66n51, 71n73, 73n85, 75-76n95, 145n11, 191, 191nn21-22
Stamps, D. L., 338n59
Stanton, Graham, 3n10, 4, 4n11, 4n13, 30n222, 31n227, 50, 50nn12-15, 52, 52n23, 53, 53n24, 59n3, 60n3, 61n13, 62nn20-21, 162n45, 263n9, 332n19, 334n36, 334n36, 352n190
Stein, Robert H., 30n222, 54, 54n35, 55, 55n41, 204n16, 209n49, 317n51, 318n55, 327, 327n14
Stem, Stephen Rex, 10n54, 221n15
Sterling, Dorothy, 13n75
Sterling, Gregory E., 8n39, 12n68
Stern, Menahem, 342n105
Stern, Pnina, 8n39
Steyn, G. J., 39n275

Stock, Ann-Kathrin, 331n9, 332n14, 333n28, 334n29, 348n155
Stowers, Stanley K., 342n98
Stuart, Duane Reed, 78, 78n5, 79n6, 81n12, 88, 88n41
Stuhlmacher, Peter, 60n10
Talbert, Charles H., 3n10, 4n13, 13n74, 47, 47n1, 51, 59n3, 68n59, 69-70, 69n65, 147n21, 165n58, 202n7, 301n4, 344n117
Tarn, W. W., 201n2, 206n34, 207n41
Taylor, Nicholas H., 351n181
Termini, Cristina, 32n238
Thackeray, H. St. J., 43n310
Theissen, Gerd, 35n258, 258n96, 331n4, 341n86, 351n182, 352n190
Thiselton, Anthony, 47
Thomas, K. R., 201n2
Thomas, Rosalind, 343n113
Thorburn, John E., 30n221
Tilling, Chris, 353n195
Titchener, Frances B., 29n215, 36n266, 74n91, 83, 83n18, 105, 105n13, 165n56
Tolbert, Mary Ann, 60n6, 173n3
Tomkins, Stephen, 9n45
Touati, Samia, 345n127
Townend, Gavin B., 194, 194n35, 194n39, 244n37, 244n39
Trapp, M. B., 11
Tucker, Aviezer, 145n14
Tuckett, Christopher M., 35n259, 52, 52n22
Turner, David L., 56, 56n49
Van der Kooij, Arie, 11n59
Van Seters, John, 301n1, 301n3, 302, 302n8, 302n10
Vansina, Jan, 345n129
Van Veldhuizen, Milo, 3n7, 32n232

Vermes, Geza, 338n57, 352n188
Votaw, Clyde Weber, 61n13
Waarden, J.A. van, 190, 191n18, 193n28
Wade-Gery, Henry Theodore, 12n66, 25n167
Wagner, Daniel A., 345n127
Walbank, Frank W., 11n61
Walde, Christine, 337nn47-48
Wallace, J. Warner, 8n38, 345n131
Walton, Steve, 2n4, 36, 47, 52n21
Wandrey, Irina, 12n68
Wardman, Alan E., 62n16
Warren, Austin, 66, 66n45
Waterfield, Robin, 191
Watson, Duane F., 338nn53-54, 338n59
Watt, I., 344n121
Weeden, Theodore J., 349n158
Wellek, René, 66, 66n45
Welles, C. Bradford, 208n43, 212n53
Wenham, David, 351n181
Wentling, Judith L., 5n23
Werner, Shirley, 332n11
West, Martin Litchfield, 346n140
Wheaton, Gerry, 304n15
Whiston, William, 262n4
Whitmarsh, Tim, 253n76, 254n78
Whittaker, C. R., 17n106, 17n108, 18n112
Wiersma, S., 36n261
Wigger, John, 9n44, 26n187
Wilken, Robert L., 342nn98-99
Wilkins, Michael J., 339n60
Williams, David S., 308n20, 309n24, 313n37
Williams, Kathryn F., 10n56
Williamson, H. G. M., 43n309
Wills, Lawrence M., 143n7
Winter, Dagmar, 6n26

Winterbottom, Michael, 163n46
Wintermute, Orval S., 42n299
Wise, Michael O., 30n224
Wiseman, T. P., 9n43
Witherington, Ben, III, 13n74, 23n158, 29n213, 165n55, 170n78, 173n5, 341n86
Wojciechowski, Michael, 35n257
Woldemariam, Fasil, 38, 217
Woodman, A. J., 9n43, 143n5, 250nn65-66, 250nn69-71, 334n30
Woolf, Greg, 343n113
Worthington, Ian, 201nn2-3
Wright, Addison G., 41n289
Wright, Edward T., 38, 235
Wright, N. T., 57, 57n56, 334, 335n37, 352n190
Wright, Wilmer Cave, 254
Xenophontos, Sophia A., 16n95
Yamamori, Tetsunao, 346n139
Yamauchi, Edwin M., 345n129
Yardley, J. C., 212n55
Yonge, C. D., 278n5
Ytterbrink, Maria, 3n10, 60n3, 202n7
Zadorojnyi, Alexei V., 336n43
Zambrini, Andrea, 22n148, 34n255, 143n8
Zlotnick, Dov, 341n91
Zsengellér, József, 310n25
Zubaida, Sami, 345n127
Zuntz, Günther, 3n10
Zwiep, Arie, 329n2

Subject Index

Accuracy, expectations of, 18-21
Africa, 1n1, 344n125, 347
Agesilaus biographies, 217-34
Alexander biographies, 201-15
Apocryphal acts, 35n259
Apocryphal gospels, 33, 34, 35
Aramaic, 267, 333n21, 341
Aretalogy, 60
Arrian, 38; see esp. ancient references index
Asbury, Francis, 9n44
Asia, 1n1
Atticus (historical source), 82
Bias, 15-18, 77-102
Biographies, ancient, passim
Burridge, Richard, 47-57
Characterization, 29, 36, 61-63, 80, 165n56, 193n32, 198n49, 210, 321
Churchill, Winston, 9, 335
Communal memory, 347-48
Cornelius Nepos, 103-42
Ctesias, 208n46
Cultural memory, 11, 13n71, 43, 154, 252n75, 253, 254, 274, 318n53, 329-30n3
Damis, 34
Dinon, 82, 83, 105, 207n39
Disciples, 3, 9n47, 16, 331, 334, 339-43, 347-48, 351-54
Duris, 90, 91, 207n39, 219, 231
Ephorus, 27n196, 90, 91, 105, 107, 138, 139

Epideictic, 6, 16n91, 17n104
Ethiopia, 1n1
Euripides the Tragedian, 86
Europe, 1n1
Eyewitnesses, 8n38, 19nn121-22, 20n126, 23, 26-27, 28n202, 33, 38, 85, 93, 94n52, 95, 97n63, 98, 99, 100, 144-45, 164n53, 167, 169, 170, 192, 193n31, 197, 205, 217-19, 222, 224, 230, 232, 238, 251, 253, 303n11, 317n47, 330-37, 344n122, 345n131, 348-50
Fabius Pictor, 86
Fabius Rusticus, 85, 168
Flexibility, 6-8
Folk traditions, 41n289, 48, 60-63, 173, 330, 331; see also *Kleinliteratur*
Galba biographies, 173-200
Genre criticism, 51
Gist, 27n193, 72n76, 132, 139, 333, 334n32, 339n61, 343-45, 350, 353
Hadith, 345
Haggadah, 31n227, 39, 41
Hermogenes, 80, 82, 99
Hochliteratur, 48, 60
Honor, 12n67, 15n87, 16, 79, 87n34, 209, 221n17, 226, 228, 241, 252, 257, 320, 326
Josephus's *Life* (autobiography), 261-76
Kimbangu, Simon, 351
Kleinliteratur, 48, 60
Latin America, 1n1
Lewis, C. S., 335

Living memory, 28, 33, 35, 145, 169, 193n31, 330n3, 331, 336, 346, 349
Maccabean literature, 301-18
Memory, 6n27, 27n193, 44, 50, 52, 71, 331-48, 353; lapses or limitations of, 27, 37, 72, 116, 120, 126, 132, 135, 139, 140, 153n32, 162, 199, 200, 236, 272, 330, 332n11, 333, 335, 345, 350; see also *cultural memory*; *living memory*
Midrash, 22n150, 31, 40n279, 41, 42n301, 60
Mirror reading, 51
Mixed genres, 2n3
Moral lessons, 9-11
Mythography, 31n227, 41n290, 44
Myths, mythology, 18n109, 19, 26, 28n204, 29, 64, 78, 87, 88, 91n45, 202
Nepos, Cornelius, 2n5, 3n5, 37; see further ancient sources index
Nicolaus (Nicolas) of Damascus, 3n5, 22n150, 33n244, 78n4
North America, 1n1
Note-taking, 342-43
Novels, ancient, 4, 5, 6, 13, 33, 35, 36, 44n314, 104, 144, 167, 169, 173; see also particular novels in the ancient sources index
Omens, 197
Oral tradition, 6, 20, 21, 23, 27, 35, 44, 48, 169,

411

412   Subject Index

192n24, 214, 217, 220, 231, 232, 233, 278, 280, 329-33, 336, 341-42, 344-49, 353
Otho biographies, 143-71
Peripatetics, 2n5, 3n9
Perspectives, varied, 8-13
Pleasure, 13
Political agendas, 11-12
Polycrates, 80, 82
Postmodern historiography, 8n43
Puerto Rico, 1n1
Q source, 35, 35n259, 168n67, 170, 331, 331n5, 334n32, 334n36, 347, 349n160
Qur'an, 345, 346
Ramabai, Pandita, 345
Redaction criticism, 23, 51, 53, 70, 220, 226, 230, 277-78, 286-87, 315, 325, 329n2
Royal Ephemerides (of Alexander), 206, 207, 210, 211, 213
Sabbatai Sevi, 351
Salvation history, 31n230
Shame, 220, 321; see also *honor*
Singapore, 1n1
Sitz im Leben, 51
South Korea, 1n1
Spithridates, 79
Sui generis, 48, 52, 60, 63, 64, 66, 263
Sulpicius Blitho, 82, 105, 141
Tendenz, 6, 11
Thatcher, Margaret, 9
Theological agendas, 12-13
Theopompus, 25n168, 82, 83, 90, 91, 219, 233
Timaeus, 20, 24, 27n196, 82, 105, 141
United Kingdom, 1n1
Valerius Maximus, 30n222; see esp. ancient references index
Variations, 7, 8, 72, 146n16, 148, 162, 164, 199, 200, 213, 214, 229, 261, 262, 271, 275, 309, 315, 331, 345-46
Verbatim transmission rare, 40, 71-72, 134, 148, 291, 300, 333, 337, 338, 341, 344, 345, 353
Wilberforce, William, 9n45
Xenophon, 2n5, 33, 38; see further ancient sources index
Zimbabwe, 1n1

Scripture Index

OLD TESTAMENT

Genesis
11:6	43n311
12:1-3	288n44
12:2-3	283
12:7	43n311
18:22-33	43n308
22	43n308
35:28-29	281
38:25	42n300
38:25-6	42n300
47:28	281
49:15	42n300
49:28	42n300
50:26	41n294

Exodus
1:1a	281
1:1-17:15	286
1:8-10	281
1:11	281
1:14	281
1:15-21	281n11
1:22	281
2:1-2	281
2:2b	278
2:2-3	281
2:3	281n11
2:4-10	281
2:5a	279
2:10a	281
2:11a	281
2:11b-15a	281
2:12-14	288n43
2:13-14	281n13
2:15b	281, 289n48
2:16-17	282, 282n14, 287n42
2:17a	297
2:18-21	282
2:23a	282
3:1	282n15
3:1-2a	282
3:3-6	282n17
3:3-4:16	288n43
3:7	282
3:8	282n17
3:9-10a	282
3:11-12	282n17
3:13-14	282
3:15-16a	282
3:18	282
4:1-4	282
4:5	282n17
4:6-7	292
4:6-16	282
4:10	292
4:18a	282
4:19	282
4:20	282
4:24-25	282n18
4:27-31	282
5:1-21	282
6:14-27	281
7:1	280n7, 283
7:1-2	282
7:8-13	282
7:11b	297

7:19	282n19	12:35-36	283
7:19-21	282	12:37-38	283
7:24-25	282	12:43-45	283
8:5	282n19	12:51	283
8:5-6	283, 290	13:17-18	284
8:8	283, 292	13:19	41n294
8:11	283	13:21-22	279, 284
8:13b-14	283	14:3-7	284
8:15	283	14:5	292
8:16	282n19	14:6-8	290
8:16-17	283	14:9-10a	284
8:19b	283	14:10b-12	284
8:21	282n19, 283	14:11-12	294
8:22-23a	283	14:13-14	284, 295
8:24	283	14:15-16	284
9:3	283	14:19-20	284
9:4	283	14:20b-22	284
9:5	282n19	14:24-25	284
9:5-6a	283	14:27-29	284
9:6b	283	14:31-15:1	284
9:8	282n19	15:1	284
9:8-11	283	15:20-21a	284
9:18	283	15:22-24	284
9:22	282n19	15:25	284
9:22-25	283	15:26-27	284n26
9:25-26	283	15:27	284, 288n45
9:34	283	16:1-3	284
10:7	293	16:3	284
10:12	282n19	16:3-4	284
10:12-15	283	16:12	284
10:16-20	283	16:12b	284
10:21	282n19	16:13a	284
10:21-23a	283	16:13b-20	284
10:22-23a	279	16:22-30	284
10:22-23	283	16:23	284
11:4-6	283	16:31	284
11:5a	283	16:35	284
11:7	283	17:1b-2a	284
12	326	17:1-7	73
12:12	283	17:3b	284
12:29	282n19	17:5-6	284
12:29-30	283	17:6	280n6
12:30b	279	17:8-11	284

Scripture Index

17:11	288n45
17:13	284
17:15	284
19:5b-6a	283, 288n44
20:21	280n7, 284
32:1	283
33:11a	283n24

Numbers
12:3	281
13	286
13:2-3a	285
13:3b	285
13:18	295
13:18-21	285
13:19-21a	296
13:21b	296
13:22-25	285
13:26-34	285
20-25	286
20:14-21	285
20:21	298
21:1-3	285
21:14	21n141
21:16-18	285
21:21-25	285
22:2-5	285, 289n48
22:7-8	285
22:8	293
22:13	285, 293
22:15-19	285
22:21	285
22:22-35	285
22:36-41	285
23:1	293
23:1-10	285, 293
23:13-24	285
23:25	294
23:25-30	285
24:1-9	285
24:10-14	285
24:13-14	289n46
24:14	289n46
25:1-3	286, 289n46, 299
25:1-13	286
25:16-18	286
31	40
31-32	286
31:1-7	286
31:2	289n46
31:3	286n38
31:7-24	286
31:25-54	286
32:1-15	286
32:16-24	286
32:33-38	286

Deuteronomy
1:20-25	285
4:6-8	281
4:44	281
33:5	284

Joshua
10:13	21n141

Judges
11:16-18	285

1 Samuel
9:2	42n306
18:17	41n293
18:21-25	41n293
18:27	41n292

2 Samuel
passim	42n304
1:18	21n141
11:1-27	43
12:9-10	43

1 Kings
14:19	21n141, 167n63
14:29	21n141, 167n63
15:5	43

15:7	21n141, 167n63
15:23	21n141, 167n63
15:31	21n141, 167n63

2 Kings
9:27	31n229

1 Chronicles
27:24	21n141
29:29	21n141

2 Chronicles
16:11	21n141
20:34	21n141
22:9	31n229
24:27	21n141

Ezra
passim	22n150

Nehemiah
passim	22n150

Proverbs
3:1	342n103
3:11-12	282

NEW TESTAMENT

Matthew
passim	7, 27n197, 30-32, 35, 40, 42n301, 54-57, 61, 168n67, 170, 171n78, 174, 192, 197, 208, 227, 235, 258, 275, 321, 325, 331n6, 334n36, 350
1:2-16	331
6:9-10	352
7:2	352
7:13-14	350
8:11	350
9:18-26	324n7
11:16	352
15:2	339n70
19:3	352
20:20-21	75
20:20-28	325n11
21:18-22	324n8
26:17-20	326n13
27:5	331n10
27:46	321n9

Mark
passim	3n10, 7, 27n197, 30, 30n220, 30n223, 32, 35, 35n259, 43, 48-50, 52, 54-56, 61, 64, 66, 67, 146, 147, 167, 170, 173, 174, 192, 202n6, 208, 227, 235, 258, 262n5, 321, 325, 327, 331, 331n6, 334n36, 339, 347, 350, 350n174, 351n178
2:14	343, 347n143
2:15-17	320n7
5:21-43	324n7
7:3	339n70
7:5	339n70
7:14	352
7:24-30	321n8
7:27	352
8:34	321n11
10:2	352
10:25	352

10:35-37	75	**John**	
10:35-45	325n11	passim	3n9, 4, 30n220,
11:11-14	324n8		31, 35, 40, 54,
11:19-21	324n8		55, 72n79, 75,
13:1-2	202n6		235, 258, 261n3,
13:14	202n6		324, 326, 327
14:12-18	326n13	13:1-2	327
15:25	327n15	13:23	348n153
15:33	258	18:28	327
15:34	321n9	19:14	327n15
15:38	321n13	19:26-27	348n153
15:39	7	19:35	348n153
16:1-8	321n10	20:30	337
		21:23	337
Luke		21:24	348n153
passim	2, 3n10, 7, 30,	21:25	147
	35, 36n261, 40,		
	56, 143n2,	**Acts**	
	168n67, 170,	passim	36n261, 56,
	192, 197, 208,		143n2, 348n147
	235, 258, 324,	1:3	325
	325, 330n3	1:18	331n10
1:1	3n6, 14, 23, 24,	1:21-22	348
	168n70, 169,	8:30	52
	170, 331, 331n6,	20:35	337
	331n10, 350	21:8	353
1:1-2	203, 330, 353	21:17-18	353
1:1-4	204n16	25:14-22	164n51
1:2	170, 339n68		
1:2-3	353	**Romans**	
1:3-4	353	5:6	258
3:24-38	331	5:8	258
6:27-42	334n32	5:10	258
6:38	352	8:3	327n16
7:31	352	8:34	258
8:40-56	324n7	16:3	215n63
11:2	352	16:5	215n63
13:24	350	16:21-33	215n63
13:29	350		
22:7-15	326n13	**1 Corinthians**	
23:47	7	1:17-18	258
		1:23	258

2:2	258
2:8	258
5:7	327n16
7:10	351
7:10-12	351
7:12	351
7:25	351
9:14	351
11:23	339n68, 351
15	56, 321n13
15:3	339n68, 351
15:3-4	258
15:5-7	336, 339
15:6-7	348
16:10	215n63
16:12	215n63
16:17	215n63
16:19	215n63

2 Corinthians
11:8-33	12n67
13:4	258

Galatians
1	271
1:11-24	12n67
1:14	339n70
1:17-19	339
1:18-19	336
2:1-2	339
2:7-10	339
2:9	336
3:1	258
3:13	258
6:12	258
6:14	258

Ephesians
2:20	43
5:2	327n16

Philippians
2:8	258
2:30	215n63
4:18	215n63
4:22	215n63

Colossians
1:19-20	258
4:10-15	215n63

1 Thessalonians
2:14-16	258
4:15	351

2 Thessalonians
2:15	339n69

1 Timothy
6:13	258

Hebrews
10:10	327n16
10:14	327n16
11:24-26	283n23
13:11-12	327n16

1 John
passim	348n153

Revelation
passim	336n43
2:14	289n46
21:14	43

Extrabiblical Ancient Sources Index

OLD TESTAMENT APOCRYPHA

1 Esdras
passim 22n150

Judith/Jdt
1:1 36n262
1:7 36n262

1 Maccabees
passim 10n51, 40n286, 164n52, 301-18
1:1—7:50 303
1:1-64 303
2:1-70 303
3:1-26 303
3:1—6:16 302
3:27-39 314
3:27-60 303
3:27—6:16 303
3:35-59 304
4:1-61 303
4:35-36 305
4:35-59 304-7
4:41-44 305
4:42 310
4:45-46 305, 310
4:47-51 306
4:52-54 306, 311
4:55-56 306
4:57-58 307
4:59 307
5:1—6:16 303
6:17—7:50 303
8 267n45

2 Maccabees
passim 10n51, 40, 40n286, 301-18
1:1—2:18 304
2:1-8 41n292
2:19-32 304
2:23 303n14
2:24-25 13, 21n141, 30n222, 310
2:25 342
3:1—4:50 304
3:25-26 12n70
5:1—7:42 304
6:12-16 312
6:18-31 321n12
7 30n221, 310n26
8:1—10:9 302, 303, 304
8:8-11 314
9:28-29 305
9:28—10:9 304-7
10:1 305, 310
10:1-8 304
10:2 305, 310
10:3 306
10:4-5 306, 311
10:6 306
10:7 307
10:8 307
10:9 303, 307, 308

10:10—15:37   304
15:38-39   304

3 Maccabees
passim   40n286

4 Maccabees
4:15   26n185
5—7   321n12
12:7   30n221

Sirach
28:7   342n103

Tobit
1:2-4   36n262

OLD TESTAMENT PSEUDEPIGRAPHA

Demetrius the Chronographer
Frg. 5   41n291

Ezekiel *Exagôgê*
passim   40n283

Joseph and Asenath
passim   41n293
23   42n300

Jubilees
4:1   41n291
4:9   41n291
11:14-15   41nn294-95
12:14   41n291
13:11   41n291
13:17-18   42n299
13:18   41n294
13:22   41n294
14:21—16:22   42n299
17:4-14   42n299
19.15-16   42n300
27:1   41n291
27:4-5   41n291
27:6-7   42n300
28:6-7   42n300
29:13   42n299
29:14-20   41n292
30:2-17   42n300
41   42n300

L.A.B. (Pseudo-Philo)
passim   41n295, 41n297
12:1-10   43n311
12:2-3   42n298
12:3   43n311
12:4   43n311
31   41n292
40:1   41n295

Let. Aris.
154   342n103

Lives of the Prophets
19 (Joad), §30   41n295

Testament of Issachar
3:1   42n300

Testament of Job
9—15   41n292
39:12-13/9-10 42n298
40:3/4   42n298

Testament of Joseph
3:1   41n292

Testament of Judah
8—12   42n300

Testament of Zebulon
1:5-7   42n299

DEAD SEA SCROLLS

1QapGen^{ar}
20.10-11   42n300

4Q158   30n224

4Q160
fr. 3-5   41n294
fr. 7   41n294

11QT
56.18   42n300

CD (Damascus Document)
4.20—5.3   42n300

JOSEPHUS

Ag. Ap./Against Apion
1.12   331n7
1.15   28n205, 145n10
1.18   25n167
1.24-25   28n205, 145n10
1.26   146n15
1.45   28
1.45-49   27n190, 336n41
1.46   28
1.47   28
1.49   28
1.56   27n190, 28,
                 336n41
1.58   28n205, 145n10
1.60   342n103,
                 346n137
1.60-66   17n107
2.178   346n137
2.204   342n103,
                 346n137

Antiquities
passim   168n69
1.6-7   267n52
1.17   43n310
1.46   164n52
1.94   167n63
1.159   167n63
2.266   39n279
2.232-37   40n282
3.79-99   17n107, 43
3.95-99   43
4.25-34   164n52
4.129-30   289n46
4.134-38   164n52
4.211   342n103,
                 346n137
6.203   41n292
12.358-59   12n70
13.297   339n70, 342n102
13.408   339n70, 342n102
17.350-52   13
17.353   13
18.12-15   312n31
18.15   313n35
18.16-17   312n34
18.18-22   312n31
18.63-64   214, 214n59, 258
18.252   8n35
18.259   32n235
19.68   25
19.78-83   164n51
19.106-7   25
19.134   169n77
20.154   3n6, 14n81, 24,
                 168
20.164-66   264n21
20.266   27, 268n54

J. W./Jewish War
passim   28n201, 261-75
1.2-3   27n190, 336n41
1.3   267n51
2.119-66   312n31

2.164-65	312n34	75	270
2.166	313n35	79	269
2.183	8n35	85	269
2.481	268, 270	87-88	265
2.513-58	270n65	126	270
2.566-68	270n66	126-48	269
2.570-71	269	127	269
2.572	270n67	131	268
2.572-75	269	137	270
2.574	268	145	269
2.592	270	147	270
2.595	269, 270	187-88	268
2.595-613	269	187-89	269
2.597	268	190-335	269
2.600-1	270	197	268
2.610	269	200-1	269
2.612	270	336-67	12n67, 265
2.624	269	339	17n107
2.624-25	269	357	27n190, 28, 336n41
2.625	269		
2.626-31	269	359	39n274
2.628	268, 269	359-60	27
3.399-408	267n49	361-66	28
4.3	43n310	362	39n274
4.323	264n21	364-67	39n274
6.93-176	273n82	365-67	17n108
		368-72	269
		370	269
		371-72	269

Life

passim	28n201, 39, 146, 261-75
1-16	166n62
10	338n59
11	341n89
13-16	267n46
17	267n48
28-29	270n68
30-31	270n69
36-42	265
41	265
45	270
46-61	269
48	268
49-53	268n57

Philo

Special Laws

4.107	342n103

Vit. Mos./Life of Moses

passim	32, 39-41, 236, 320
1	277-300
1.1-4	281
1.4	278
1.5-7	281
1.8-11	281

1.9	279	1.135	279
1.12-17	281	1.137	291n51
1.13-14	279	1.140-42	283, 288n43
1.18-24	281	1.143	291n52
1.20-23	40n282	1.143-46	283
1.24	279	1.146	289n47
1.25-31	281	1.147-54	283
1.32-39	281	1.148	286, 288n44
1.40-45	281	1.150-54	287n42
1.43	320n5	1.155-62	283
1.44	320n6	1.158	280n7
1.44-45	288n43	1.163	289
1.46-50	281	1.163-66	284
1.47	289n48	1.165-66	280
1.51	282n14	1.167	292
1.51-57	282, 287n42	1.167-69	284
1.54	298	1.168	290
1.58-62	282	1.170-75	284
1.63-65	282n15	1.171-72	295
1.63-67	282	1.173-75	295
1.65-66	39n279	1.176-80	284
1.67	288n45	1.181-86	284
1.68-70	282, 288n45	1.187-90	284, 288n45
1.71-84	282, 288n43	1.188	289n48
1.79	292	1.191-95	284
1.83	292	1.192	289n48
1.85-91	282	1.196-205	284
1.88	281n9	1.206-9	284
1.91-96	282	1.210-13	284, 320n3
1.92	297	1.211	280n6, 291n52
1.96-101	282	1.212-13	288n44
1.96-139	287n41	1.214-19	284
1.102-5	282	1.217-18	288n45
1.103-4	291	1.220-26	285
1.104	290	1.222-26	297
1.105	292	1.227-31	285
1.106-12	283	1.232-36	285
1.113-19	283	1.237-43	285
1.120-25	283	1.244-46	299
1.122	293	1.244-49	285
1.126-29	283	1.250-54	285
1.130-33	283	1.255-57	285
1.134-39	283	1.258-62	285

1.263-64	289n48	**Babylonian Talmud Nedarim**	
1.263-68	285	50a	343n114
1.263-99	39n277		
1.264-65	280, 280n8	**Babylonian Talmud Pesahim**	
1.266	293	49b	343n114
1.269-74	285		
1.275-79	285	**Babylonian Talmud Sanhedrin**	
1.277	293		
1.278-79	294	43a	258
1.280-84	285	106a	288-9n46
1.285	294		
1.285-91	285	**Ecclesiastes Rabbah**	
1.292-94	285	2:15, §2	39n277
1.294	289n46		
1.294-300	288n46	**Exodus Rabbah**	
1.295	289n46	10:4	41n293
1.295-99	286, 299-300	32:3	39n277
1.300	289n46		
1.300-4	286	**Genesis Rabbah**	
1.305-8	286	43:3	41n293
1.309-14	286		
1.315-18	286	**Leviticus Rabbah**	
1.319-27	286	6:6	23n157
1.328-34	286	15:2	23n157
1.334	277		
2	277, 286	**Mekilta Pisha (Lauterbach)**	
2.25-44	277	1.135-36	341n92
2.65	277	1.150-53	342n103
2.161-73	43n311		
2.165	43n311	**Mishna Abod. Zar.**	
2.169	43n311	3:6	349n163

RABBINIC WORKS

Mishna Eduyoth
1:3   341n84

Abot R. Nathan, Rec. A
1   340n76
25   340n76

Mishna Gittin
9:10   352n184

Babylonian Talmud Baba Batra
15b   39n277

Mishna Shabbat
9:1   349n163

Mishna Sukkot
2:10 352n187

Numbers Rabbah
14:20 39n277

Pesiqta Rabbati
49:5 41n293

Pesiqta Rab Kahana
4:3 41n293

Pirke Aboth
passim 338n57
3:17 352n187
5:21 342n103

Sipra Shemini Mekhilta deMiluim
99.5.6 340n76

Sipre Deuteronomy
48.1.1-4 341n91
48.2.6 341, 341n92
221.1.1 341n90
269.1.1 352n184
357.18.1-2 39n277

Tg. Neof. 1
Gen 38:25 42n300

Tg. Ps.-Jon.
Gen 38:25-26 42n300
Gen 49:28 42n300
Gen 50:26 41n294
Exod 13:19 41n294

Tosefta Berakot
1:11 352n187
6:18 352n187

Tosefta Piska
2:15-16 341n90

Tosefta Sanhedrin
1:2 352n187
8:9 352n187

Tosefta Yebamoth
3:1 341n92

Yerushalmi Ketuvot
12:4, §8 41n291

Yerushalmi Sota
9:13, §2 22n143, 25n170

PATRISTIC AND OTHER EARLY CHRISTIAN SOURCES

Augustine
Harmony of the Gospels
21.51 30n223, 333n19

1 Clement
7.2 339n69

Didache
passim 350

Epistle to Diognetus
11.1 339n68
11.6 339n69

Eusebius
H.E.
3.10.8-11 268n55
3.19-20 274n86
3.39 30n223
3.39.1 334n36
4.3.1-2 337n44

P.E.
9.27.7   41n293
9.29.16   41n291

Georgius Syncellus
Chronology
passim   258

Hier.
Chron.
159   245n45

C. Ioh.
12   244n39

Hippolytus *Refutation of All Heresies*
1.15   343n109

Julius Africanus *Chronology*
Frg. 18   258

Justin *1 Apology*
66   334n36
67   334n36

Justin *Dial.*
103.8   334n36
106.3   334n36

Martyrdom of Polycarp
6.2   331n10
9—19   321n12

Origen *Comm. Jo.*
10.2   15n83
10.4   15n83

Origen *Princ.*
4.3.4   15n83

Papias (Holmes)
3.1   334n36, 348n153
3.3   336n43
3.4   336, 336n43
3.4-5   348n153
3.5-6   336n43, 348n153
3.7   339n69
3.8   339n69
3.11   339n69
3.14   339nn68-69
3.14-16   334n36
3.15   7n31, 30n223,
                     43, 333n19,
                     334n36, 350n174
3.16   334n36, 347n143
3.17   348n153
5.1   334n36, 348n153
6.3   334n36
7.3   348n153
7.3-4   350n174
14.1   336n43
18.1-7   331n10
20.1   339n68
21.1   7n31, 339n68

Protevangelium of James
passim   35n258

OTHER GREEK AND LATIN WORKS AND AUTHORS

Aeschines
Embassy
48   338
112   338

Alciphron *Farmers*
11 (Sitalces to Oenopion), 3.14
                     343n114

38 (Euthydicus to Philiscus), 3.40
                                343n114

Aphthonius *Progymn.*
3.23S, 4R   349n165
4.9-10   349n165

Apollodorus *Bib.*
1.3.1   346n140
1.4.3   22n143
1.5.2   22n143
1.9.15   22n143
1.9.19   22n143
2.3.1   22n143
2.5.11   22n143

Appian
Hist. rom.
pref. 12   19
3.12.1-2   12n70
11.9.56   22n143, 167n64,
                 204n17
12.1.1   22n143, 167n64

Aristotle *Poet.*
9.2, 1451b   18n114
9.2-3, 1451b   145n15
9.3, 1451b   18n114
15.4-5, 1454a   25n176

Arius Didymus
Epitome of Stoic Ethics
2.7.7b, p. 44.26   337n47
2.7.11k, pp. 80.36—82.1
                    343n109

Arrian *Alex./Anab.*
passim   201-15
1, pref. 1   206
1, pref. 1-2   22n144, 167n64
1, pref. 2   206n36
1, pref. 2-3   26n187, 336n41

2.16.6   29n210
2.18.1   163n49
3.3.6   22n145
3.21-23   8n36
4.7.4   16n95, 16n100,
                 42n303
4.8.1-4.9.6   16n95, 16n100,
                 42n303
4.9.2-3   22n143, 167n64
4.10.8   11n58
4.14.1-4   22n143, 167n64
4.28.1-2   29
5.1.2   28n205
5.3.1   22n143, 167n64
5.5.1   206
5.5.1—5.6.8   206
5.6.2   206
5.14.3-6   206, 206n37
5.14.4   22n143, 167n64
6.2.3   205n25
6.2.4   21n142, 167n63
6.11.8   26n187, 336n41
6.28.2   26n180
7.14.2   22n143, 167n64,
                 167n64
7.14.4-6   25n176
7.25   210
7.25.1—7.26.3   210
7.26   207, 211
7.27   211
7.27.1-3   22n143, 167n64
7.28.2   209

Indica
5.3   206
7.1   18
15.7   26n180
17.6   206
18—42   203n12, 205, 207
18.9   205n25
20   205n25
43.14   203n12

Athenaeus *Deipnosophists*
5.215-16	25n176
5.219	25n176
12.523ab	12n70

Aulus Gellius *Attic Nights*
Pref. 2	343n108
Pref. 22	343n108
6.1.2-4	44n316
7.10.1	340n71
7.17.1-2	21n134
7.17.3	21n134
8.3	339
10.12.8-10	29n209
11.17	21n134
13.20.1	21n134
15.28.1	245n45

Babrius
78	12n70

Caesar (Julius)
Commentarii
Passim	271

Callimachus *Hymn*
6.63	352n191

Cicero
Att.
1.1.3—1.1.4	249n64
1.5.4	248n55
2.1	335n37
2.17.1	74
7.2.2	247
7.13.3	248n55
10.17.2	247
10.18.3	248n56
14.10.3	248n55
15.13.3	248n55

Balb. 248

Brutus
93.324	338n51

De or.
2.52	16n92
2.351	337n48

Fam.
2.1—2.5	249n59
2A	249n59
5.12.4	13n78
5.12.5	13n75
15.16.1	244n38

Fin.
3.3.10	343n108
5.5.12	343n108

Leg.
1.2	205, 205n31
1.2.5	18n114

Nat. d.
3.16.42	23n156

Part. or.
22	42n299

Quint. fratr.
1.1.8.23	11n61, 34n245

Verr.
2.5.72.184-89	12n70

Cornelius Nepos
Fragments, passim	105, 244n42
1 (Miltiades), passim	105
2 (Themistocles), passim	103-41
2 (Themistocles), 1	138, 139
2 (Themistocles), 1.1	82, 106
2 (Themistocles), 1.1-4	106

Ancient Sources Index   429

2 (Themistocles), 1.2	107
2 (Themistocles), 1.3	107
2 (Themistocles), 1.4	105, 108, 138, 139
2 (Themistocles), 2—6	139
2 (Themistocles), 2.1	108
2 (Themistocles), 2.1-6	106
2 (Themistocles), 2.2-4	109, 112
2 (Themistocles), 2.3	109
2 (Themistocles), 2.4	110
2 (Themistocles), 2.5	110, 139
2 (Themistocles), 2.6	110, 111
2 (Themistocles), 2.6—3.1	106
2 (Themistocles), 2.7	111
2 (Themistocles), 2.7-8	111
2 (Themistocles), 2.8	109, 112
2 (Themistocles), 3.1	112, 113
2 (Themistocles), 3.2	113, 114, 139, 140
2 (Themistocles), 3.2-4	106
2 (Themistocles), 3.3	114
2 (Themistocles), 3.4	114
2 (Themistocles), 4.1—5.1	106
2 (Themistocles), 4.2-3	116
2 (Themistocles), 4.3-4	116
2 (Themistocles), 4.5	117, 118
2 (Themistocles), 5.1	118
2 (Themistocles), 5.1-2	119
2 (Themistocles), 5.1-3	106
2 (Themistocles), 5.2	120, 121, 139
2 (Themistocles), 5.3	121
2 (Themistocles), 6.1	122
2 (Themistocles), 6.1—7.6	106
2 (Themistocles), 6.2	123, 124
2 (Themistocles), 6.3	124
2 (Themistocles), 6.3-4	124
2 (Themistocles), 6.4	124
2 (Themistocles), 6.4-5	124
2 (Themistocles), 6.5	125
2 (Themistocles), 7—10	139
2 (Themistocles), 7.1	126
2 (Themistocles), 7.2	126, 127, 130, 139, 140
2 (Themistocles), 7.3	127, 128
2 (Themistocles), 7.4-5	128
2 (Themistocles), 7.6	129
2 (Themistocles), 8.1	130
2 (Themistocles), 8.1-7	106
2 (Themistocles), 8.2	130
2 (Themistocles), 8.2-3	130
2 (Themistocles), 8.3	131, 139, 140
2 (Themistocles), 8.4	131, 132, 139
2 (Themistocles), 8.5	132, 133
2 (Themistocles), 8.6	133
2 (Themistocles), 8.7	133, 134
2 (Themistocles), 9.1	82, 83n19, 105, 134, 138, 139
2 (Themistocles), 9.1-2	105
2 (Themistocles), 9.1—10.3	106
2 (Themistocles), 9.2-4	134, 135
2 (Themistocles), 10.1	135, 136
2 (Themistocles), 10.2	136
2 (Themistocles), 10.3	136, 137
2 (Themistocles), 10.3-5	106
2 (Themistocles), 10.4	82, 83n20, 105, 137
2 (Themistocles), 10.4-5	105, 138, 139
2 (Themistocles), 10.5	137
3 (Aristides), passim	105
4 (Pausanias), 1.1	30n217
4 (Pausanias), 2.2	105
5 (Cimon), passim	105
6 (Lysander), 1.1	226

430 Ancient Sources Index

6 (Lysander), 2.1	105	16 (Pelopidas), 1	226n27
6 (Lysander), 4.1-3	82	16 (Pelopidas), 1.1	9n48, 30n217, 105, 245
7 (Alcibiades), 1	141		
7 (Alcibiades), 1.1	82, 105, 140	16 (Pelopidas), 3.1	11n58
7 (Alcibiades), 2	141	17 (Agesilaus), 1	221, 222, 223, 224
7 (Alcibiades), 2.2	82, 105, 140		
7 (Alcibiades), 2.3	105	17 (Agesilaus), 1.1	105, 141, 218n5, 226
7 (Alcibiades), 4.6	105		
7 (Alcibiades), 7.3	83		
7 (Alcibiades), 10.4	83		
7 (Alcibiades), 11.1	22n143, 82, 105, 167n64	17 (Agesilaus), 2	223
		17 (Agesilaus), 2.1	228, 229
		17 (Agesilaus), 3	222, 223, 225
7 (Alcibiades), 11.1-2			
7 (Alcibiades), 11.1-6	105	17 (Agesilaus), 4	222, 223, 225, 226, 226n26
8 (Thrasybulus), passim	105		
8 (Thrasybulus), 1.1-5	83n22, 99		
9 (Conon), 5.4	22n143, 82, 83, 83n21, 105, 167n64	17 (Agesilaus), 4.8	12n70
		17 (Agesilaus), 5	222, 223, 225, 226n26
10 (Dion), passim	105		
11 (Iphicrates), passim	105	17 (Agesilaus), 6	222, 223, 226, 226n26
11 (Iphicrates), 3.2	16n96, 16n100, 42n303, 82, 83		
		17 (Agesilaus), 7	223, 226, 226n26
12 (Chabrias), passim	105		
13 (Timotheus), passim	105		
13 (Timotheus), 4.5-6	83n22, 100n77	17 (Agesilaus), 8	223, 241
		18 (Eumenes), passim	105
14 (Datames), 2.2	105	19 (Phocion), passim	105
		20 (Timoleon), passim	105
		21 (On Kings), passim	105
14 (Datames), 6.8	83n22, 100n77	22 (Hamilcar), passim	105
		23 (Hannibal), 8.2	82, 83, 105, 141
15 (Epaminondas), 4.6	105		
15 (Epaminondas), 10.1-4	83n22, 100n77	23 (Hannibal), 11.1	82, 83
		23 (Hannibal), 13.1	105, 141

23 (Hannibal), 13.2   105, 141
23 (Hannibal), 13.3   26n187, 105, 336n41
24 (Cato), 3.3   105
24 (Cato), 3.5   245n42
25 (Atticus), passim   105, 236, 244-49, 257n94
25 (Atticus), 4.5   244n40
25 (Atticus), 5.1—5.2   249n63
25 (Atticus), 13—18   37n270
25 (Atticus), 13.6-7   246
25 (Atticus), 13.7   26n187, 336n41
25 (Atticus), 17.1   26n187, 100, 336n41
25 (Atticus), 19.1   244n36
25 (Atticus), 19.4   247
25 (Atticus), 21.1   244n35
25 (Atticus), 21.1—22.4   246
25 (Atticus), 22.3   244n35

Chronica
passim   244n42

Exempla
passim   244n42

Life of Cato
passim   244n42

Life of Cicero
passim   244n42

Love Poems
passim   244n42

Corpus inscriptionum graecarum (CIG)
2.2077   346n141

Dio Cassius *Roman History*
Frg.   13n71
1.1.1-2   13n75, 15n86, 17n107, 21, 168n70
1.5.4   11n58
5.50.1   249n62
62.11.3-4   25n176, 29n211
63.27.3—63.29.2   162n44
66.20.1   252nn73-74
66.20.3   252

Dio Chrysostom *Or.*
18.10   25n167, 339n67
18.19   338
36.9   346n141
61   165n56

Diodorus Siculus *Bibliotheca historica*
passim   202n8
1.1.3   13n73
1.4.1   20n129
1.4.4-5   19n123
1.6.2   28n204, 28n205, 145n10
1.9.2   28n205, 145n10
2.7.3   208, 208n46
4.1.1   28n205, 145n10
4.4.1-5   22n149
4.8.3-5   28n205, 145n10
9.5.21   208n44
10.5.1   340n79
14.63.1   12n70
14.69.4   12n70
14.76.3   12n70
15.1.1   11n60
16.58.6   12n70

17.1—18.6	208	1.6.3	23n155
17.4.8	208	1.6.3-5	11n60
17.65.5	208	1.12.3	28n205, 145n10
17.73	8n36	1.39.1	29n210
17.73.4	208	1.41.1	29n210
17.85.2	208	1.84.4	29n210
17.92.1	208	1.87.4	22n143, 167n64
17.102.5-7	208, 208n43	Bk. 3	12n65
17.110.7	208	3.35.1-4	22n143, 167n64
17.115.5	208	4.6.1	26n179
17.117.3-4	212	4.59.2	13n71
7.117.3—17.118.2		4.61.2	13n71
	212	7.65.2	11n58
17.118.1	208	8.56.1	13
20.1.2	147n21	8.79.1	22n143, 167n64
20.2.1	147n21	9.22.1-5	25n172
27.4.3	12n70	9.39.1-6	12n65
31.10.2	11n58		
37.4.1	11n60	*Comp.*	
		6	72

Diogenes Laertius *Lives of Eminent Philosophers*

passim	350n173	*Demosth.*	
1.23	25n170	41	147n21
1.48	23n156	47	13n75
2.6.48	239n21	57	25n165
2.6.51	240		
6.1.5	336	*Din.*	
6.1.13	25n170	11	25n165
6.2.31	338n54		
8.2.67-72	25n170	*Lysias*	
9.12.113	331n7	1	5n25
10.1.12	340n72	8	15n90
		11	25n165

Dionysius of Halicarnassus
Ant. rom.

		Pomp.	
passim	73	3	12n66, 30n221
1.1.1	21n140, 167n63	*Thuc.*	
1.1.2-4	18n110, 145n15	1	16n98
1.2.1	10	5	28n205, 145n10
1.4.2	18n110, 145n15	5-7	29n206
1.6.1	21n142, 23n155, 167n63, 204n17	6	29n210

7	26n187, 336n41	137F 18-19	205n30
8	18n111, 145n15	137F 21	205n30
9	30n221	138	202n4
13	17n106	139	201n4
19	25n166	618-828	204n20
34	25n167		
55	19n118		

Ennius *Annales*
Passim   18n114

Epictetus
Diatr.
1.preface   341n85, 343n111
2.19.29   340n76

Enchir.
passim   30n222

Eunapius *Lives*
453   27n198, 336
454   254
458   341
459   16n98
459-61   15n89
460   27n196
461   15n89, 16n98
481   338n54
494   338
502   338n50

FGrH
72F 15-17   204n21
72F 29   204n21
117   206
119-23   206
124   201n4, 204
125   201n4
126   206
133   201n4
134   202n4
137   201n4, 205

Fronto
Ad Verum Imp.
2.3   340n76

Eloq.
3.5   7n32

Ep. M. Caes.
4.5   21n134

Gorgias *Helen*
9   13n78

Hermogenes
Inv.
2.7.120   349n165

Issues
33   163n49

Method in Forceful Speaking
24.440   7n32, 349n164

Progymn.
3.6-7   350n172
3.7   349n165
4.8-10   338n56
7.15   44n316

Herodian/Hdn *History of the Empire*
1.1.1-2   18
1.1.3   18, 20
7.9.4   22n143, 167n64
7.9.9   22n143, 167n64

Herodotus/Hdt *History*

1.1	19
1.4.1	19
1.22.2	19
1.34	11n58
2.4	12n65
2.32	12n65
2.50	12n65
2.52	19n121, 20n129
2.58	12n65
2.77	12n65
2.82	12n65
2.99	26n187
2.123.3	11n58
4.205	11n58
5.26	19
7.138	110
7.138-39	111
7.140	111
7.140-41	111
7.142	111
7.143	106, 107, 112
7.144	109, 110, 112
7.152	26n181
7.173	106, 108
7.175	112
7.184-86	110, 139
7.213-34	113
7.222-34	113
8.1-2	113
8.2	114
8.4-6	114
8.6	114
8.15-17	114
8.18-21	114
8.22	115
8.40-41	112
8.48	113
8.51	112, 120
8.52-53	115
8.56	115
8.57	115
8.57-63	116
8.74	116
8.75-76	116, 117
8.76	117
8.78-82	117
8.80	117
8.83	117
8.83-98	117
8.85	117
8.86	118
8.91	118
8.92	118
8.97	120
8.97-107	118
8.98	121
8.108	118, 119
8.108-110	119
8.109	119
8.110	106, 121
8.111	121
8.112	121
8.113	120
8.115	120
8.124	122, 126
8.125	122
9.85	24
9.120	11n58

Hesiod
W.D.

158-60	28n205
165	28n205

Homer
Il.

passim	25n177, 42n302, 346, 346n141
2.557	23n156
8.527	352n191
9.373	352n191
11.362	352n191
20.449	352n191
21.394	352n191
21.421	352n191

22.345	352n191		
		Maxim	
Od.		1.2-5	7n32, 349n164
passim	346	2.3	7n32, 349n164
11.424	352n191	3.2	7n32, 349n164
11.600ff	23n156		
17.248	352n191	*Life of Aesop*	
18.338	352n191	passim	29n209, 30n220, 35nn256-57, 143n7, 166n62
19.91	352n191		
22.35	352n191		
		1	43n307
Iamblichus			
Vit. pyth.		Livy	
passim	16, 17	Pref. 9-10	10n51
20.94	340n78	1—10	28n204
28.148	339n64	1.pref.10	11
28.149	339n65	1.1.1	29n208
29.164	340n77	3.8.10	29n209
29.165	340n79	4.29.5-6	26n182
31.188	340n80	6.1.2-3	28n205, 145n10
35.256	340n77	7.6.6	26n186, 28n205, 145n10
		9.44.6	22n143, 167n64, 204n17
Isocrates			
Evagoras		21.1.3	12n65
passim	78, 79n6	23.19.17	22n143, 167n64, 204n17
8	79n6		
		23.47.8	26n182
Justin (Marcus Junianus Justinus) *Epitome of the Philippic History of Pompeius Trogus*		25.11.20	26n186, 145n10
		25.17.1-6	22n143, 167n64
		34.54.4-8	22n149
		42.11.1	22n150
9.8.14-15	210	42.28.12	12n70
9.8.17	210		
12.14-15	212	Longinus *Subl.*	
12.15	212	11.1	349n165
		Lucan *C.W.*	
Libanius		passim	33n243
Anecdote			
1.4	7n32, 349n164	Lucian	
2.3	7n32, 349n164	*Alex.*	
3.2	339n62	61	339nn63-64
4.1	339n62		

Demonax

passim	236, 253-57
1	254, 254n79
4	255
5	255n83
11	255
18	255
27	256n91
45	256n91
57	256n88
63	254n79, 256n91
65-67	255
66	255
67	254, 255, 257

Hermotimus

1	340n81
2	343n109

History

passim	18
4-6	17n106
7	18, 29n213, 165n55
7-13	350n166
8	18n114
8-9	15n86
12	18, 145n15
24-25	18, 145n15
27	17n106
39-40	15n86
40	18
47	26n187
59	10
60	26nn182-83

Nigrinus

12-14	256n87

Peregrinus

3	338
11	214n61, 259

Runaways

12	343n115
14	343n115

Zeus Rants/Z. Rants

24	12n70
32	12n70

Lysias *Or.*

20.22, §160	27n194
23.2-8, §§166-67	20n126

Maximus of Tyre/Max. Tyre *Or.*

1.9	43n307
22.5	11, 13

Menander Rhetor

1.1.333.31-1.1.334.5	19n119
2.1-2, 371.5-6	44n316
2.3, 379.2-4	349n165

Mus. Ruf./Musonius Rufus (Lutz)

1, p. 36.6-7	16n99, 340n76
51, p. 144.3-7	338n54

Nicolaus of Damascus
Life of Augustus

passim	78n4, 84-85, 100n78, 101n80, 146
30	84
36	84
59	84
66	84
74	84
96	84

Ovid *Fasti*
6.1-2	22n143
6.97-100	22n143

P. Egerton	23n155

Pausanias
1.23.2	20n127, 347
2.5.5	22n143
2.26.3-7	22n143
3.23.5	12n70
9.31.7	26n179, 28n205, 145n10
9.33.6	12n70
9.39.12	12n70

Phaedrus
2, prol. 8	7n32
4.11.1-13	12n70

Philostratus
Hrk./Heroikos
10.1-4	42n306
10.3	42n306
26.4	42n306
26.13	42n306
29.2	42n306
31.5	42n304
33.39-40	42n306
34.5	43n307
48.1	42n306
49.3	42n306

Vit. Apoll.
passim	33-34, 143n7, 263
1.4-5	44n316
1.14	340n77
1.19	340n77
2.30	340n77
3.16	340n77
4.22	256n89
5.21	341n87
5.38	340n76
7.22	340n76

Vit. soph.
passim	14n80
1.11.495	337
1.21.516	24n164, 25n170
1.22.523	348n156
1.22.524	341, 347
1.24.529	348
2.1.554	29n210
2.1.562-63	25n175
2.4.570	22n143, 23n154, 167n64
2.5.576	20n124, 20n128, 22n146, 25n170, 167n64
2.8.578	339
2.21.602	15n89
2.21.602-3	16n97, 42n303
2.21.603	15n89
2.23.606	20, 20n128
2.29.621	16n97, 349
2.33.628	16n97

Photius *Bibl.*
33	264n18, 264n20
47	264nn16-17

Plato
Phaedo
passim	3n10

Rep.
passim	281n12

Pliny the Elder *Hist. nat.*
Pref. 17	24, 204n19
Pref. 18	24
Pref. 22	204n19
1	245n45

2	245n46	6	221n17, 222, 223, 224n22, 225, 228, 229
3.127	244n38, 245n46		
4	245n46		
7.24.88	337n45	7	221n17, 222, 223, 224n22, 225
9.137	244n37		
33.24.83	12n70	8	219, 220, 223, 224n22, 225, 226, 232

Pliny the Younger *Ep.*

1.1.1	162n45	9	221n17, 222, 223, 224n22, 225
2.3.3	338		
3.3.5	17	10	222, 223, 225, 227, 233
3.7.11	146n17		
5.5.3	19	11	222, 223, 225
5.8.1-2	15n87	12	222
5.8.5	19	13	223, 232
5.8.8	338n59	14	223, 233
5.8.9-11	15n86	15	222, 223, 225, 226, 231
5.8.12	21n134		
5.8.12-13	14n80	16	222, 223, 225, 233
5.12.1-2	163n46		
6.27.1-2	17	17	223, 225
7.17.3	19, 145n15	18	223, 225, 234
7.33	146n15	19	222, 223, 225, 231, 232, 234
8.4.1	19, 145n15		
9.1.3-4	27n199	20	222, 223, 231, 232
9.19.5	19, 27n196		
9.33.1	18n114, 24, 145n15, 169n76	21	225
		22	222, 223, 225, 226

Plutarch
Ages.

		23	223, 225, 226
1	221n17, 222, 223, 224n22	24	222, 223, 225, 226
2	221n17, 222, 223, 224n22	25	222
		26	222, 223, 225, 233
3	222, 223, 224n22, 225, 231	27	223, 225, 226
		28	223, 225, 226
4	221, 221n17, 222, 223, 224, 224n22, 233	29	223, 226
		30	223
		31	222, 223, 225
5	221n17, 222, 223, 224n22, 232	32	222, 223, 225, 233

33	222, 223, 225, 233	39.4	90, 91n45
34	222, 223, 225, 226, 232	39.5	90, 91n45

Alc. and Cor.

2.2	90
2.3	91n47
3.2	91n47

35	223
36	223, 225
36-37	241n32
37	223
38	223, 223
39	223
40	222, 225, 226, 241

Alex.

passim	201-15, 327
1	207, 207n40
1.1	14, 51
1.1-2	29n213, 165n55
1.1-3	30, 198n49, 327n17
1.3	14n79
3.3	207n39
3.6	207n39
4.4	207n39
4.5	207n39
8.2	207n39
15.2	207n39
16.15	207n39
18.4	207n39
20.4-5	24, 41n295
20.9	207n39
21.9	207n39
23.4	207n39
24.3	163n49
24.14	207n39
26.3	207n39
27.4	207n39
30.7	21n142, 167n63
31.2-3	21n142, 167n63
31.3	22n143, 167n64
31.5	207n39
33.1	207n39
33.10	207n39
36.4	207n39
37.4	30n221
38.4	21n142, 22n143, 167n63, 167n64
41.3-4	163n49

Alc.

passim	89, 91, 91n47
1.1	90
1.2	90
1.4	90
3.1	90, 91n46
5.5-6	209
6.2	90
10.1	90
10.3	90
11.1	90, 91
12.2	90
13.2	90
13.3	90
13.5	90
16.2	90
17.1.3	209
17.4	90, 91n45
20.4	90, 90n44
21.1	90, 91n45
22.3	90
23.3	90
23.4	90
26.5	199
26.6	90
29.2	90
32.2-3	90, 91
32.5	90
33.1	90
39.2	90

43.2	8n36	30.6	75
46.1	207n39	31.3	75
46.1-2	22, 167n64	42.1	163nn49-50
46.2	25n175, 207n39, 207n39	60.6	326n12
		63.5	163n50
49.3	163n49	64.3	163n50
54.1	207n39	68.2	163n50
54.4	207n39	69.5	163n50
55.9	207n39		
56.1	30n221	*Cam.*	
60.6	42n306, 207n39	31.4	13n71
61.1	207n39		
61.3	207n39	*Cato Minor*	
65.2	207n39	passim	236, 323n3, 325
66	205n25	30.9-10	74
70.2	207n39	31.6	74
70.3	8, 350n166	43.1-6	325n9
75.6	207n39, 212	51	73
76	210		
76.1	207n39	*Cic.*	
76.1—77.3	210	passim	44, 72n78, 324
77	211	19.1-4	72, 324n5
77.3	212	20.4—21.5	72, 324n5
		44.2	163n50
Antony			
passim	72n78, 323n3, 326	*Cim.*	
		2.4-5	16n96, 16n100, 42n303
5.10	75		
Arist.		*Cleomenes*	
19.5-6	24	passim	320
		1.4	320n4
Brutus		6.4	320n4
passim	72n78, 323n3	8.2	320n4
Caes.		*Coriolanus*	
passim	72n78, 323n3, 324, 326	passim	91, 91n47
		1.2	91n47
1.1-4	30n220, 166n62	2.2	73
7.3—8.1	324n6	3.4	90
7.7	72	8.3	91n47
14.7	74	9.9	74
30.4	75		

10.7-8	74	7.1	189
11.2-5	91n47	7.1-3	177
13.6	74	7.2	92
14.4	90	7.3	181
15.4	91n47	8.1	92
20.4	90	8.2	196
24.1	90	8.4	196
24.1—25.3	92n48	10.4	196
26.2	90	11.2	180
32.4-6	91n47	12.3	180
37.3	90	13.1	154
38.1	90	14.3	178
38.4	91n47	14.4	92
		15.2	178, 180, 181
Crass.		15.3-4	179
passim	323n3, 324, 325	16.1	179
13.3	72, 324n5	16.2-3	181
15.5	325n10	16.4	180
		17.1	180
Demosth.		17.1-2	154
2.1-2	20n131	17.2-5	182
5.5	22n143, 25n175,	17.4-5	155n34
	167n64, 335n37	18.1-2	182
11.1	26n187, 336n41	18.1-3	196
29.4—30.4	22n143, 167n64	19.2	149
		19.3	149
Educ.		19.4	92, 149
13, *Mor.* 9E	338n54	19.4-5	92, 150
		19.5	92, 150
Galba		20.1	96n59, 150
passim	78n4, 92, 173-	20.2	150, 182
	200	20.3	154
2.2	178, 178n13	20.3-4	150
2.3	182	20.4	154
3	198	21.1	183
3.1	92, 151, 175, 176	21.1-2	151, 154
3.1—4.4	193	21.2	150, 151, 183
3.2	92, 176, 196, 198	22.4-5	165n57
3.3	92, 176	22.5-6	155
4.2	92, 177, 196	22.6	158
4.2-3	177, 196	22.7—23.1	155
4.4	92, 154	23.1	151, 183
5.1-2	177	23.1-2	183

23.2	151, 165n61, 183, 184, 196, 198	*Mal. Hdt.*	
		20, *Mor.* 859B	26n186
23.3	184	*M. Cato*	
23.4	150, 151, 162	5.1	16n98
24.1	150, 151, 152n28, 153, 185	5.5	16n98
		12.4	16n98
24.2	151, 185	*Nicias*	
24.3	185	passim	327
24.3-4	152	1.5	327n17
24.4	152, 185		
25.1	92, 152	*Otho*	
25.2	152	passim	78n4, 92
25.3	92, 152, 185, 186	1.1	154
25.4	151, 154	2.1-3	155
25.5	186	2.3	155
26.1	154, 185	3	156n35
26.1—27.6	153	3.1	154
26.1-2	186	3.2	92, 93, 154
26.3-4	186	3.3	156
26.4	153	3.4	156
26.5	153, 163, 186	3.6	156
27.1	153, 153n31, 186	3.6-7	156
27.2	187	3.8	157, 165n61
27.2-4	92	4.1	155
27.3	188	4.2	155
27.4	153, 154, 166, 188	4.3	155
		5.1	155, 158
27.5	154n33, 189	5.2	156, 157, 163
27.6	189	5.3	155, 157, 158, 162
28.1	154		
28.2	188	6—7	157
28.3	188	6.1—7.1	157
29.1	151	6.3	158
29.1-4	189	6.4	158
29.4	154	6.5	93, 158
Isis		7.1	158
8, *Mor.* 353F	26n179	7.3-5	158
Lyc.		7.4	157, 158
1	219	7.5	158
1.1	25n170	8.1	157, 158, 159, 162

8.2-3	158	2.1	87
8.4	158	2.2	87
8.4—9.3	158	2.3	87
9.1	93, 159	2.6	86
9.3	92, 93	3.1	86
10.1	157, 162	4.2	87
10.2	158	4.3	87
10.2-3	159	5.3	87
10.3	158, 159	5.4	87
11.4	158	8.7	86
13.1	158, 158n40	9.3	87
13.3	157	9.5	86, 87n34
13.4-5	158	10.1	87n34
13.5	159	12.1	87, 88n38
13.5-6	158	12.3-4	86
14.1	26n187, 92, 93, 168	13.2	87
		13.3	87, 88n38
14.2	168n72	14.1	86
15	165n58	14.1-2	87, 89
15.3-6	165n57	14.4	87
15.3—17.2	160, 165n61	14.6	86, 87
16.1-2	160	14.7	87
16.2	160	15.2	86
16.3	160	15.3	87
17.1	160, 161	15.5	87
17.2	160	16.8	86, 88n38
17.3	161	17.5	87, 89
17.3-4	161	20.2	88n38
17.4	161	20.4	87
18.1	93, 168n72	20.6	87
18.2	161	21.2	87, 87n34
		21.6	87, 89n43
Pompey		21.7	87
passim	323n3, 325, 327	22.1	87, 87n34
8.7	327n17	22.4	87
47.10	74	23.3	87
52.3	325n9	26.8	87
58.6	75	27.5	87
		27.5-6	87n34
Romulus		27.6	87
passim	78n4, 86-89	28.1	87
1.1	87	29.3	87
1.2	87	29.6-7	87

29.7 87

Sulla
9.4   163n49
28.6 163n49
37.2 163n50

Themistocles
11.2   350n172
25.1-2 22n143, 24, 167n64
27.1   22n143, 25n174, 167n64
32.3-4 22n143, 167n64

Theseus
passim 77, 78n4, 86-89
1.3   29n206, 29n210
3.2   86
5.3   86, 100n79
10.1   87
10.2-3 87
11.2   87
12.2   87
15.1   87, 88
15.2   86
16.1   86
16.2   86
16.3   87
17.3   86
17.5   86
18.2   87
19.1   86, 87, 88
19.2   86
20.1   87
20.2   86, 87
20.3-4 86
20.5   87
21.1   219n11
21.2   86, 87
22.1   87
22.3   87
23.1   87
23.2   87
23.3   86, 87
25.2   86
25.3   87
25.4   87, 87n34
25.5   86
26.1   86, 87, 88n35
26.2   86
26.2-3 86
27.2   86, 88n36
27.3   78n3
27.3-4 86
27.4   87
27.5   88n38
27.6   87
28.1   86, 89
28.2   86
29.1   87, 88n40
29.2   87
29.4   86, 87, 88n35
29.4-5 86, 88n35
29.5   86
30.4   86
30.5   87
31.1   87
32.1   87
32.2   87
32.3   219n11
32.4   86
32.5   86, 87
33.2   87
34.1   86, 87, 87n34
34.2   86, 87, 88, 89
35.2   86
36.1   87
36.3   86, 87

Polybius *Histories*
1.1.1   10, 204n18
1.4.11   13n75
1.35.1-10 9n51, 11n58
2.16.13-15 18n109
2.56.1-2   23

2.56.3	23	12.28.1-5	26n187
2.56.13	12n69	15.36.10	17n108
3.4.1	15n86	20.12.8	26n187
3.4.13	26n187	28.4.8	19n121
3.6.1-3.7.3	12n69, 25n173	31.9.1-4	12n70
3.6.10	25n173	32.15.14	12n70
3.20.1-5	25n173	34.2.4	18n109
3.31.11-13	12n69	34,2.9-11	18n109
3.31.13	13n75	34.4.2	18
3.32.2	12n69	36.9.1-17	11
3.32.4	25n171	38.4.8	19n121
3.32.5	25n173		
3.33.17-18	20n130		
3.33.18	25n175		

Proclus *Poetics*
Essay 5
K58.6-14   9n49

3.48.12	19n121, 20n129
4.2.2	19n121
4.38.11	19n121, 20n129
4.40.2	18n109
4.43.6	18n109

Ps.-Callisthenes *Alexander*
passim	5n23, 13n75, 33-35, 143nn7-8
1.35	163n49

6.11.4-6	17n108
6.11.7-8	17n108
8.8.3-6	15n86
9.2.1	18n109
9.2.5	25n173

Quintilian
Decl.
323 intro   12n70

10.4.5—10.5.5	163n49
10.11.4	19n121, 20n129
10.21.8	15n86, 16n93
10.26.9	15n87

Inst.
1.pref. 7-8	343n111
1.3.1	338n54
2.4.15	338n55
2.4.18-19	28n204
3.8	67
4.2.113	7n32
9.3.23	11n58
10.1.74-75	205, 205n32
11.2.1-51	338n50
11.2.2	343n109
11.2.25	343n109
11.2.27	337
11.2.33	337
11.2.34-35	337

12.4c.3	20
12.4c.1-5	20n125
12.4c.4-5	20
12.4d.1-2	20n126
12.7.1	15n86
12.9.2	20
12.17.1—12.22.7	204n24
12.24.5	18n109
12.25d.1	24, 168n70
12.25e.1	3n9, 20, 24n160, 335n37
12.25e.7	20
12.25g.1	26n187
12.25i.2	20, 24n160
12.27.1-6	26n187

Quintus Curtius Rufus

passim	201-15
1.45	203n10
2.1	203n10
3.12.18-20	210
4.2.17	163n49
5	203n10
5.13	8n36
5.28	8n36
6	203n10
9	203n10
9.5.21	208
9.8.15	207, 207n42
10	203n10
10.5.1-6	212
10.5.2-6	212
10.14-17	212

Rhet. Her.

3.16.28	337
3.22	333n28
3.22.35	337n48

Satyrus *Euripides*

passim	236

Seneca the Elder
Controv.

passim	337
1.pref. 2	337, 346n140
1.pref.4	30n221, 333n23
1.pref.18	338
1.pref.19	148n22, 337, 346n140

Historical Fragments

1	12n69

Suas.

2.19	148n22
3.2	343
3.7	148n22

Seneca the Younger
Ep. Lucil.

94.27-28	350
108.4	341n88
108.6	343n109
108.9-10	349n156
108.17	16n99, 340n76
108.20	16n99, 340n76
108.22	16n99, 340n76
110.14	16n99, 340n76
110.20	16n99, 340n76
117.6	16n98

Serapion, Mara bar

259

Silius Italicus

3.168-71	163n49

Socrates *Ep.*

20	340n71

Strabo *Geog.*

2.5.10	27n195
11.5.4	205, 206n33
11.11.4	204n23
13.1.13	204n23
13.1.27	204n23
13.4.6-8	204n23
14.1.7	204n23
14.3.9	204n23
14.4.1	204n23
15.1.8	205n26
15.1.13	205n26
17.1.43	204nn23-24

Suetonius
Augustus

passim	236
3.2	93
4.2	94
7.1	94, 99

7.2	94	4.1-4	93
10.4	94	4.5	93
11.1	94	4.6	93
35.2	94, 98	15.3	94
63.2	94	21.2	94
69.2	94	32.1	95
70.2	94, 99	33.4	94
70.4	94	44.2	94, 95, 96n58
71.1	99	44.3	95, 96n58
72.1	94		
74.1	94	*Domitian*	
77.1	94	1.1	95
79.2	94, 97	1.2	157, 163
80.1	94	2	274n83, 274n84
87—88	97n67	3.2	16n96
90.1	94	10	274n88
91	163n47	11	274n85
94.3	94	11.3	94
94.4	44n316	12	274n87
94.4-8	94	14.2	95
94.8	94	18.2	94
		19.1	94, 97n65
Caligula		22.1	95
1.2	95	23	252n75
2.1	95	23.2	95
3.1	94		
4.1	95	*Galba*	
5.1	95	passim	78n4, 98, 173-200
8.1	94, 99n74	2	198
8.1-4	96n57	2.1—3.4	175, 193
8.3	94, 99	2.1	175, 196
12.2	95	3.1	95, 96n58, 194
19.3	94, 95, 96, 97n65	3.2	95
23.2	94	3.3	194
25.1	95	4.1	94, 175, 193n30
32.1	95	4.1-3	193
36.1	94	4.2	194
49.3	94, 97n65	4.2-3	175
50.2	95	4.3	194
51.1	96n62, 100	4.4	176
		5	198
Claudius		5.1	193
1.4	94, 95, 96n58		

5.2	175, 176, 195	*Julius*	
5.2—6.1	193	1.3	94
6.1	175	9.2	93, 95
6.2	176	9.2-4	96n60
6.3	176	9.3	21, 93, 169, 195n41
7.1	176		
7.2	176	9.4	93
8.1	176, 177	10.1	93
8.2	177	29.1	94
9.1	177	30.2	93
9.1-2	193	30.3	94, 96n57
9.2	177, 195	30.4	93
10.1-3	177	30.5	93
10.4	177	33.1	94, 96n61
10.5	195	42.3	93
11.1	178, 195	45.1	42n305
12.1	178	45.3	94, 96
12.2	155, 179	46.1	94, 96
12.3	179, 195	47.1	94, 96
14.1	179	48.1	94, 96
14.2	154, 180, 181	49.1	93, 94, 96, 99n75
14.3	181	49.1-4	96n60
15.1	95, 181	49.2	93, 96
15.1-2	195	49.3-4	93
15.2	181, 182	49.4	94
16.1	182	52	16n101
16.2	182	52.2	93, 96n63
17.1	183, 184, 196, 198	52.3	93, 95n55
		53.1	93
18.1-3	184, 195	55.1	93
18.2	163	55.2	94
18.3	95, 151, 165n61, 183	55.4	93, 97n65
		56	21n135
19—20	166	56.1	94
19.1	151n27, 185, 195	56.2	93
19.2	186	56.3	93
20.1	94, 95, 186, 187, 199	56.4	93
		56.6	97n65
20.2	187, 188	71.2	93
21.1—23.1	189	71.3	93
22	154	71.4	93
22.1	95, 195	73-75	16n101
23.1	189, 195	74.1	93

76.1	17n101, 93	6.2	95, 151, 152, 162, 185
76.2	93	6.3	152, 153, 165, 165n61
77.1	93		
78.1	94, 96n58	7.1	153, 154
81	163n50	7.2	95, 155, 163
81.2	93	8.1	155
83.1	93, 94	8.1-2	156
86.1	94	8.2	156
86.2	93, 94	8.2-3	162
86.3	93	8.3—9.1	162
86.4	93	9.1	157, 158, 166
21.4-6	93	9.1-2	162
		9.2	157, 159
Nero		9.3	159
1.1	95	10.1	26n187, 94, 159, 169
1.2	95		
2.2	94	10.2	160, 165, 165n61
7.1	95	10.2—11.1	159
13.2	95	11.1	160
18.2	94	11.2	160, 161
19.1	94	12.1	95, 159
19.3	17n102	12.2	161
21.3	95	15.1-3	159
23.3	95	15.3-6	159
37.2	95, 98		
49.4	154	*Tiberius*	
51	42n305	5.1	94
53.1	95	21.2	94
54.1	95	52.3	94
		61.1	94
Otho		61.6	94, 96n62, 100
passim	78n4, 98, 143-71	61.7	95n54
1.1-3	149	67.2	94
2.1	95, 149	67.3-4	95n54
2.2	149	68.1-2	42n305
3.1-2	150	78.2	94, 96n58
3.1	149, 149n24		
3.2	95, 149n24, 150	*Titus*	
4.1	150, 162. 182	2.1	95
4.2	150	3.2	94, 97n65
5.1	151	8.1	94
5.2	150, 151	9.2	95, 98
6.1	150, 151		

Vergil
33	163n46

Vespasian
passim	16
1.1	94
1.2	95, 96n58
1.3	157, 163
1.4	26n187, 95, 169, 195n41
2	267n49
4.3	95
5.5	163n47
16.2	94, 95
16.3	95, 96, 96n57
21—23	98
25.1	94, 95

Vitellius
1.1	95, 96n61
1.2-3	94
1.2—2.1	96n58
2.1	95
7.1	95, 96n57, 154
10.1	159
14.5	95
15.2	159
15.2-3	157, 163

Tacitus
Agricola
passim	16n97, 17, 23n152, 30n218, 78n4, 80n9, 85-86, 101, 146, 236, 250-53, 257n94
1	10
4	85
9	169n77
9.6	251n72
10	85
10.5	252n73
22	85
29	85
37	85
40	85
43	85
43.1—44.1	252
44	42n305
45.4	251
45.5	251
46.3-4	10n51

Annals
passim	250
1	22n149
1—4	250n68
1.1	238n15
2.14	163
2.67	25n170
2.71-72	165
2.73	23n153
2.76	165
2.77	165
2.82-83	169n77
2.88	23n153
3.1	164n51
3.16	25n170
3.18	11n61, 25n170
3.65	10, 17n108
4.7	165
4.10	25n170, 168n71
4.11	18, 145n15, 168n71
4.24	169n77
4.32-33	13n77
4.33	10, 14n80
4.34	168
4.35	168
4.43	25n169
4.52	165
4.53	168
4.54	29n215, 165
4.57	23n153, 168
4.62-63	164n51

4.68-69	165	*Dial.*	
5	250n68	passim	250
5.1-2	10n56	16	25n174
5.9	164n51, 168	38	338n51
6	250n68		
6.48	165	*Germania*	
6.51	29n215	passim	250
11	250n68		
11.7	165	*Histories*	
12—15	250n68	passim	250
12.2	166	1	192
12.48	165	1—4	250n68
12.52	157n37	1.1	18, 250
12.65	164n51, 165	1.4	192
13.12	149	1.5	178, 182, 192
13.20	23n153	1.6	154, 177, 179, 180, 181
13.20.2	168		
13.21	165	1.7	178, 179, 180
13.45	149	1.10	180
13.46	149, 150	1.11	180
14	22n149	1.12	180
14.2	168	1.13	149, 149n25, 150, 151, 180, 181, 182, 183
14.31-39	158		
14.39	10n56		
14.51	25n170	1.14	151, 154, 183, 198
14.53-54	166		
14.55-56	166	1.14-15	151
14.58	169n77	1.15-16	151, 165, 165n61, 183, 198
14.58-59	25n170		
15.38	25n170	1.17	183, 184
15.44	214, 214n60, 258	1.18	151, 176, 183, 184, 196, 198
15.51	166		
15.53	26n179	1.19	184
15.54	25n170	1.20	181
15.61	168	1.21	151
15.63	24, 162	1.22	150, 162
15.73	26n185	1.23	150, 176
16	250n68	1.24-25	150, 166
16.3	25n170	1.24-26	166
16.6	25n170, 26n179	1.25	185
16.15	11n58	1.26	154
16.22	165	1.27	151, 152, 152n29, 185
16.30-32	164n51		

1.27-28	152	2.11-12	157
1.28	152, 185	2.11-33	162
1.29	151	2.11-45	166
1.29-30	153, 165, 165n61, 186	2.14	157
		2.15	157
1.31	187	2.17-23	157
1.31-49	153	2.21-27	158
1.32-34	185	2.23	157
1.33	185	2.24	157, 158
1.33-35	186	2.25-26	158
1.36	153	2.25-28	157
1.37	153	2.27-31	158
1.37-38	153, 165, 165n61, 186	2.32	158, 158n41
		2.32-33	158
1.40	186, 187	2.33	157, 157n39, 158, 163
1.41	153, 153n31, 187		
1.42	154	2.34	158
1.43	153, 163, 166, 186, 188, 199	2.35	159
		2.36	157n38, 158
1.44	155, 163, 189	2.37	158
1.45	153-54, 189	2.39	157
1.46	153, 154, 157, 163	2.39-40	157n37
		2.42	159, 169n77
1.47	154, 188	2.42-45	159
1.48	154	2.44-45	159
1.49	175, 176, 188, 189, 193	2.45	159
		2.46	159
1.50-70	155	2.47	159, 165n58
1.51	169n77	2.47-48	160, 165, 165n61
1.71	154, 155, 158	2.48	160
1.72	155, 182	2.49	160, 161
1.74	155, 158	2.50	149, 159
1.75	157n37	2.51	157n38
1.77	157n37, 157n38	2.55	157, 158
1.78	154	2.57	159
1.80	156, 156n35	2.60	158
1.81	156	2.63	157
1.82	152n30, 156, 157	2.78	163
1.83-84	156, 165, 165n61	2.79	267n49
1.87	155, 157, 158	2.99	157n38
1.88	155, 156	3.59	157n38
1.90	157, 158, 163	3.64	157
2.1-7	166	3.65	157n38

Ancient Sources Index 453

3.69-70	157n38	1.22.1-2	19n122
3.73-75	157n38	1.22.2-3	19n122, 336
4.12	169n77	1.22.3	27n193, 336
4.23	169n77	1.23.1-2	25n166
4.34	169n77	1.23.3	28n205
4.38	169n77	1.73.5	120
4.46	169n77	1.74.1	113, 117, 126
4.54	169n77	1.85.1	339n66
4.83	163	1.89.3	112, 123
5	250n68	1.90.1	124
		1.90.1-2	124

Theon *Progymn.* (Butts)

		1.90.3	124, 125
passim	199n54, 254n80	1.90.3-4	125
1.46-52	25n176	1.90.5	126
1.93-171	7n32, 333n22,	1.91.1	126, 127, 140
	349n164	1.91.2	127
2.5-8	338	1.91.3	127, 128
2.79-81	25n176	1.91.4	128
2.115-23	349n165	1.91.5	128
3.224-40	30n222, 349n165	1.91.6	128
3.241-76	26n179	1.91.7	129
4.37-42	30n222	1.92.1	129
4.73-79	37n267, 332n18,	1.93.1-2	125
	338n58, 350	1.93.3	122
4.80-82	30n222, 349n165	1.93.5-6	123
4.112-16	26n179	1.93.4	109
4.126-34	26n179	1.93.7	123
5.388-441	37n267, 332n18,	1.93.8	130
	338n58, 350	1.135.2	130
5.487-501	26n179	1.135.3	130, 131
8.2-3	25n176	1.136.1	131
		1.136.1-2	131

Thucydides *History of the Peloponnesian War*

		1.136.3	132
		1.136.4	132
1.1.1-2	25n166	1.137.1	132, 133
1.3.2-3	25, 25n174	1.137.2	133
1.3.3	25n168	1.137.3	134
1.10.1-2	25, 25n177	1.137.4	119, 134, 138
1.14.3	109	1.138.1	135, 136
1.21.1	28n205, 29n207,	1.138.2	136
	145n10	1.138.3	108, 131, 138
1.21.1-2	29n210	1.138.4	137
1.21.2	25n166, 29n207	1.138.4-6	138

1.138.5	136, 137	2.72.1-2	11n58
1.138.6	137, 138	2.75.2	11n58
3.54.4	113	2.91.2-3	11n58
4.1	115	2.92.5	14n80
4.2	115	2.94.2-3	143n5
4.36.3	113	2.94.3	143n5
		2.98.2-3	11n58
		2.126.1	14n80
		2.129.1—2.130.5	143n5

Valerius Maximus

1.1.ext. 3	12n70
1.1.ext. 5	12n70
1.1.18-21	12n70
1.7.ext. 1	163n49
1.7.ext. 1-10	163n50
1.7.1	163n49
1.7.1-8	163n50
1.7.2	163n50
1.7.3	163n49
2.pref.	11
5.7.ext. 1	22n149, 23n153, 167n64
6.8.3	22n149, 23n153, 167n64
8.7.ext. 16	337n45
8.15.ext. 1	340n76

Velleius Paterculus *History of Rome*

1.3.2-3	25n168
1.14.1	30n221
2.4.6	25n170
2.18.1	12n65
2.18.5	29n215
2.25.3	29n215
2.27.5	25n170
2.28.2	29n215
2.38.1-2.40.1	30n221
2.41.1-2	11n58
2.48.4	25n170
2.48.5	23, 168n70
2.57.2	163n50
2.59.1	30n221
2.66.3-5	11n58
2.70.1	163n50

Xenophon
Agesilaus

passim	78-80, 239-43, 257n94
1.5	222
1.6	223, 228
1.6-7	228
1.7	223, 225, 229
1.8	225
1.10	225
1.12	223
1.13	223, 225
1.14	225
1.16	225
1.18	221n16
1.20	222
1.21	221n16
1.23	223, 225
1.25	222, 225
1.27	239n26
1.28	223
1.29	222, 225
1.31	223
1.32	223
1.33	223, 225
1.34	223
1.35	223, 226
1.36	223, 227, 227n30
1.37	221n16
1.38	225
2.1	225
2.2	222, 225
2.5	225

Ancient Sources Index   455

2.6	222, 223	5.1	79n7, 221n16
2.7	79nn6-7, 223	5.2	221n16
2.7-8	227n30	5.3	221n16
2.9	223, 225, 240n28	5.3-4	227n30
2.10	223	5.4	223
2.11	223	5.5	223
2.12	223, 240n28	5.6	79, 222, 223, 227
2.13	223	5.7	218, 227n30
2.14	240n28	6.1	79n7, 218, 221n16, 222
2.16	223, 225		
2.17	225	6.5	222
2.18	222, 225	6.8	222
2.19	225	7.1	79n7
2.20	222, 226	7.2	221n16
2.21	79n7, 225, 226, 227	7.5	223, 225
		7.6	223
2.22	223, 226	7.7	223
2.23	226	8.1	79n7
2.24	222, 225, 226, 227n30	8.3	223
		8.4	227n30
2.26	222, 226	8.6-7	227n30
2.27	226	8.7	222
2.27-28	227n30	8.8	221n16
2.28	241n31	9.1	79n7, 221n16
2.28-31	241n31	9.2	221n16
2.29	225, 226	9.3	221n16
2.31	222, 241	9.6	222
2.37	227n30	10.2	221n16, 222, 227
3.1	26n187, 79n7, 218, 221, 227n30, 336n41	11.1	79n7, 221n16, 223, 227n30
		11.2	221n16, 223
3.2	222, 223	11.3	221n16
3.2-3	79	11.5	221n16
3.3	222, 223	11.9	79
3.4	223	11.10	222
3.5	221n16, 223	11.13	221n16, 223
3.25	223	11.16	241
3.31	226		
4.1	79n7	*Anab.*	
4.2	221n16	5.2.24	12
4.4	227	5.3.6	240n26
4.5	79, 222		
4.7	79n6		

Apol.
1   341n85
2   26n187, 336n41

Cyr.
passim   11n61, 33-34,
               143n7
1.2.1   347n144
2.2.5   81n12
3.1.17   11n61

Hell.
3   219
3.1.2   27n197

Mem.
passim   78, 80-82
1.1.1   80
1.1.10   80
1.2.3   341n88
1.2.9   80
1.2.30   80
1.2.31   80, 99n76
1.2.49   80
1.2.51   80
1.2.53   80, 99n76
1.2.55   80
1.2.56   80
1.2.58   80, 81
1.2.64   80
1.3.1   80n10, 81
1.3.1-4   81
1.3.5   81
1.3.5-15   81
1.4.1   80, 81
1.4.1-18   81n13
1.4.1-19   81
1.4.2   80, 81, 99n76
1.4.19   80, 81, 99n76
1.5   81n14
1.5.1   81
1.5.1—1.6.15   81
1.5.6   81n12, 81n14

1.6.14   81n12
1.7.1   81
1.7.1-5   81
1.7.5   80, 81, 99n76
2.1.1   80, 81, 99n76
2.1.1-34   81
2.4.1   80, 99n76
2.5.1   80, 99n76
2.6.1   80, 81, 99n76
2.6.1-39   81
2.7.1   81
2.7.1—2.10.6   81
2.9.1   80, 81, 99n76
2.10.1   80, 81, 99n76
3   82
3.1.1   81
3.1.1—3.7.9   81
3.10.1   81
3.10.1—3.11.18 81
4.1.1   81
4.1.1-5   81
4.2.1   81
4.2.1-40   81
4.3.1   81
4.3.1-17   81
4.3.2   80, 81, 99n76
4.3.2-17   81n15
4.4.1   81
4.4.1-25   81
4.4.5   99n76
4.5.1   81
4.5.1-12   81
4.5.2   80, 81, 99n76
4.5.11   81n16
4.6.1   81
4.6.1-14   81
4.7.1   80, 81
4.7.1-10   81
4.8.1   82, 82n17
4.8.1-10   82
4.8.4   80, 82
4.8.4-10   99
4.8.11   16, 80

Symp.
3.5-6 346n140

Zonaras
7.11 13n71

www.ingramcontent.com/pod-product-compliance
Ingram Content Group UK Ltd.
Pitfield, Milton Keynes, MK11 3LW, UK
UKHW021315180426
11947UKWH00015B/1239